Japanese and German Enterprises

Toshio Yamazaki

Japanese and German Enterprises

Comparison of Industrial Concentration System and Business Management

Springer

Toshio Yamazaki
College of Business Administration
Ritsumeikan University
Ibaraki, Osaka, Japan

ISBN 978-981-97-4882-2 ISBN 978-981-97-4880-8 (eBook)
https://doi.org/10.1007/978-981-97-4880-8

This Springer imprint is published by the registered company Springer Nature Singapore Pte Ltd.
The registered company address is: 152 Beach Road, #21-01/04 Gateway East, Singapore 189721, Singapore

For my wife, Naomi and son, Tomotaka

Preface

This book aims to provide original knowledge about the development of business management after the Second World War in Japan and Germany. It also examines the movements toward global regionalization in Japan and Germany and the determinants of these movements from various international perspectives.

In the postwar era, both Japan and Germany were brought under the US global strategy, and they achieved corporate and economic progress by deploying American technology and management methods and building unique systems of industrial concentration. However, the current economic and business situations in both countries are vastly different. Japan has historically relied heavily on the United States for trade purposes and lacks complementary relationships between product areas and industries in the US market. It is noteworthy that Asia as a whole has yet to establish a common market. In comparison, Germany gained independence from the United States and moved toward European integration. This integrative development into the European region was another type of Europeanization.

This book examines and explains the characteristics and structures of management in postwar Japan and Germany, assuming that commonalities and differences in the postwar development of both nations were determined by business management. It examines a wide range of business management topics, including enterprise concentration, management systems, production systems, management education, marketing, organizational structure, business strategy, and corporate governance. Consequently, the approach taken is broad and systematic, encompassing not only the specific field of business management but also the domain of American management. The origins of the system formed between the 1950s and 1960s that regulated the postwar characteristics of Japanese and German capitalism are explored at the business management level by comparing and contrasting business management processes in Japan and Germany.

This study attempts to explain how Japanese-style and German-style management and their distinct characteristics emerged, while conforming to exogenous factors and constraints in each country. It also illustrates how they evolved as a result of endogenous determinants. The changes in business management, the resulting mechanisms of corporate development, and their social and economic significance are illustrated through such analysis. This book examines the total structure of business management in Japan and Germany, with a particular focus on the influence of international and regional economic integration on market structures in Europe, the United States, and Asia, as well as industrial and trade structures and the characteristics of Japanese and German capitalism.

This book introduces four distinct perspectives on the development of postwar capitalism and business management in Japan and Germany.

The first perspective examines the overall structures of postwar Japanese and German management styles in relation to capitalism in those countries. There is a branch of management research in Japan that combines perspectives from political economy, industrial economics, and business economics. The author employs this school of thought to address salient economic and industrial factors, including the system of industrial concentration and its relationship to competition structure, as well as factors inherent at the enterprise level.

Second, this book examines the transformation of business management in postwar Japan and Germany as a result of the implementation of American management methods. It considers how the deployment of US technology and management methods affected business management in Japan and Germany and identifies any unique developments that emerged, apart from similarities with the United States. From the perspective of structural analysis, this book elucidates the comprehensive alterations to business management that resulted from the implementation of American management methods.

Third, this book offers a multifactorial analysis of business management through the use of the "total system of business management" and "reframing." The former refers to a structural framework for conditions that define the established methods of business management within the characteristics of capitalism as they are practiced in a specific country. The book analyzes business management in relation to the structures of Japanese and German capitalism, as well as the cooperative interdependent structures that arose from industry coordination. Furthermore, the implementation of American-style management is considered using the author's reframing framework. Reframing is the process by which business management methods and systems defined by structural characteristics of a country's capitalism are transformed into a different style through adaptation, modification, and adjustment to make them compatible with the structural characteristics of capitalism in another country. The application of the author's two original frameworks to this analysis enables the development of a unique understanding of business management and capitalism in Japan and Germany.

Fourth, the author compares Japanese and German business management in terms of regional conditions, including market structure, competition structure in Japan and Europe, and accumulation structures of Japanese capitalism within Asia and German capitalism within Europe. The transformation of business management in both countries during the 1950s and 1960s is highlighted, with particular attention paid to the regional economic characteristics of both countries and their relationships with the United States. The contrast between the Japanese and American market structures that regulate the competition system and the German and European market structures that regulate the competition system is demonstrated to be a significant differentiating factor. The author then examines why Japan was unable to establish an accumulation structure in Asia as Germany did in Europe, instead relying on American influence.

This book is structured in a specific manner. Chapter 1 introduces the book's purpose and significance by explaining the various issues covered, such as current economic and business conditions in Germany and Japan. It also identifies research topics, reviews prior research, and introduces the two novel analytical frameworks.

Part I considers the overall system of business management and the characteristics of business management in postwar Japan and Germany. The second chapter defines the overall system of business management as a structural framework for defining the established methods of business management within the context of capitalism in a specific country. Chapter 3 compares the characteristics of Japanese-style management and German-style management with those in the United States.

In Part II, the development of a new system of industrial concentration, post-WWII, is considered to be inextricably linked to postwar Japanese and German business management. As the cornerstones of capitalism's accumulation structures in both countries, large corporate groups and industrial systems based on industry–bank relationships were important phenomena for postwar corporate development. Chapter 4 considers the restructuring of the system for large corporate groups in relation to the dissolution of monopolies under the occupation policy, and their reconcentration after the war. Chapter 5 examines the development of a new system of oligopolistic industrial concentration based on industry–bank relationships. This is an important issue related to cooperative inter-firm relationships, the system of corporate governance, corporate development, and capitalisms accumulation structures in Japan and Germany.

In Part III, Chaps. 6–12, the changes in business management and the significance of the deployment and transfer of US management methods are considered. The implementation of American-style management systems in Japan and Germany is explored, including the resultant changes in corporate management in both countries. Chapter 6 discusses the deployment of American management education in relation to universities' role in management education, eligibility criteria for executive management, and the manager promotion system in Japanese and German enterprises. Chapters 7–9 examine the deployment of American-style management and production systems in relation to environmental factors in Japan and Germany. These factors include labor relations, the worker participation system (codetermination), management values and traditions, and market structures. The major issues regarding the deployment of American-style management and production systems are human relations, industrial engineering (IE), and the Ford system. Chapter 7 analyzes the deployment of human relations, with a particular focus on the transformation of labor relations and those in the management system. Chapter 8 discusses the implementation of IE, an advanced form of scientific management originating in the United States. Chapter 9 explores the deployment of the Ford system, the rollout of the mass production system, and Japanese and German manufacturing. Chapter 10 examines the implementation of American methods for adapting to mass-markets in relation to various factors, including the characteristics of US and European markets, domestic markets, production- and technology-oriented management values, the composition of executive management, and changes in the structure of competition. Chapter 11 examines the deployment of divisional structures through the analysis of case studies of typical corporations from major industries in relation to changes in business strategy, management systems and practices, and managers' traditional attitudes. Based on the preceding discussions, Chap. 12 presents an analysis of the changes in business management in Japan and Germany during the postwar period through the early 1970s, applying the author's original framework, "The Reframing of Americanization," as described in Chap. 1.

Building upon the preceding chapters' discussions, Part IV turns its attention to pivotal issues that have emerged over the past five decades. Chapter 13 delves into the reforms and developments of mass production systems from the 1970s to the 1980s, which were pursued as a countermeasure to the limitations of the American mass production system, epitomized by the Ford system. Chapter 14 examines the transformation toward shareholder value-oriented management and corporate governance after the 1990s, representing a resurgence of Americanized business management.

Based on the preceding discussions, Chap. 15 explains the pursuit of economic rationality in each country that is deeply concerned with the characteristics of business management through a comparison of the United States, Japan, and Germany. Furthermore, it elucidates the import of a comparative analysis of business management in Japan and Germany by examining the factors influencing corporate expansion, including postwar reforms, economic democratization, industrial development, industrial structure development, inter-firm relationships, and regional conditions.

I am indebted to those who have provided me with guidance and assistance throughout the writing of this book. Professor Masaki Nakata, emeritus professor at Ritsumeikan University in Japan, advised me to undertake this study. He also provided me with invaluable instructions that were instrumental in enabling me to complete this book. I would like to thank Professor Christian Kleinschmidt of the University of Marburg for giving me the opportunity to study at his university as a visiting scholar. I am also grateful to my family, in particular my wife, Naomi, who encouraged me and supported my research, and my son, Tomotaka, who gave me the strength to complete my research. I am indebted to their support and understanding, without which this book would not have been possible. I dedicate this book to my wife and son.

Ibaraki, Osaka, Japan
May 2024

Toshio Yamazaki

Contents

About the Author

Toshio Yamazaki Dr. in Business Administration, Ritsumeikan University, is Professor at the College of Business Administration, Ritsumeikan University. He previously held the positions of Assistant Professor, Lecturer, and Associate Professor at the Faculty of Humanities and Economics, Kochi University; Associate Professor at the College of Business Administration, Ritsumeikan University; and Visiting Scholar at the Free University of Berlin, University of Cologne, University of Marburg, Goethe University Frankfurt, and Humboldt University of Berlin.

Professor Yamazaki's areas of expertise include management studies and comparative business history. His main research field is the history of business management and inter-firm relationships. He served as director of the Japan Association for the Comparative Studies of Management of Japan from 2011 to 2017. He is the editor of the *Journal of Business Management* (edited by the Japan Association of Business Management, language: Japanese).

Professor Yamazaki has published numerous monographs and articles, including the book *German Business Management: A Japanese Perspective on Regional Development Factors* (Springer, 2013), which was awarded the Japan Association for the Comparative Studies of Management Academic Prize.

List of Figures

List of Tables

Chapter 1
Introduction: Research Topics and Analytical Framework

Abstract This chapter clarifies the purpose and significance of this book. It first compares contemporary economic and business conditions in Japan and Germany, which were not only defeated nations of WWII but also major trading countries after the war. Next, research topics are described by considering major issues in postwar Japanese and German capitalism and management, focusing on the postwar boom years, in particular through the early 1970s, and the subsequent period. In addition, the findings of previous research on related topics are examined. Furthermore, two original frameworks developed by the author will be introduced—"total system of business management" and "reframing"—which provide the foundations for a multi-factorial analysis of business management. These frameworks underpin this book's unique explanation of business management and capitalism in Japan and Germany.

Keywords Americanization · German business management · Industrial concentration · Japanese business management · Productivity movement · Reframing · Total system of business management

1.1 Awareness of the Issues of This Book

How are capitalism and business management in Japan to be understood from the perspective of Germany as a European nation? How are capitalism and business management in Germany to be understood from the perspective of Japan as an Asian country? The purpose of this book is to explore these phenomena in both countries from an international comparative perspective.

There are some important commonalities between Japan and Germany. Both Japan and Germany as defeated nations in World War II received significant American leadership and support after the war. Both countries developed their enterprises, industries, and economies by deploying and adapting technology and management methods from the United States while establishing their own systems of industrial concentration. By these means, both nations became major trading countries.

T. Yamazaki, *Japanese and German Enterprises*,
https://doi.org/10.1007/978-981-97-4880-8_1

However, contemporary economic and business conditions differ greatly between Japan and Germany. In trade, American influence on Japanese business is still strong. Japan could not and cannot establish a complementary relationship with American industrial sectors and their products in the American market. Furthermore, a common market structure like the European Union does not exist in Asia. In contrast to Japan, Germany has developed independently of American influence and become part of a well-integrated regional economy.

Japanese enterprises first pursued advances in US markets after the war and thereafter made inroads into European markets, Asian markets, and specifically, the Chinese market. However, Japanese companies could not avoid trade frictions with the United States. Historically, such trends can be seen in the textile industry, the iron and steel industry, the automobile industry, and the electric and electronics industries. In particular, after the 1980s, Japanese companies attempted to transfer production bases overseas, including to the United States and East Asia in response to trade frictions and fluctuations in yen versus dollar exchange. They sought to establish the most suitable global composition and structure of productive forces after the 1990s, which made Asian countries an appealing choice. Indeed, such globalization and regionalization emphasized the Asian area to a greater extent than companies in other countries did (Yamazaki 2005, Chap. 8). However, even today, a common market structure, such as that of the EU, does not exist in Asia.

In contrast, Germany pursued "Europeanization" in a twofold meaning after the war. German enterprises moved toward regionalization based on the European area by establishing total structures and styles of business management that were compatible with the conditions of European markets. On the other hand, Germany also pursued the expansion of European integration as a basis for accumulation, which made European countries an important criterion. Indeed, this trend became stronger after the 1990s. Although Americanization re-emerged while globalization progressed, in Europe, market integration and the unification of some European currencies in the form of the EU increased and deepened with Europeanization through eastward expansion. Germany assumed a central role in Europeanization as the largest industrial nation in postwar Europe.

What were the driving forces that created those differences between Japan and Germany? This book explores this question from an international comparative perspective, based on the understanding that the origins of the distinct characteristics of Japanese and German business management after World War II were developed in the postwar period till the end of the 1960s. How did development of the system of industrial concentration as the basis of big business and business management determine the current conditions of enterprise and capitalism in both countries? How did changes of business management after the 1970s to the present in Japan and Germany determine corporate expansion in both countries? It is important to clarify commonalities and differences in business management between both nations and how the development of business management, including the Americanization of business management, determined the direction and characteristics of regionalization as an important result of corporate expansion. However, the question remains as to these significant research topics. This book analyzes them paying attention to some momentous conditions surrounding enterprises such as economic relationships with the United States and the deployment of American management methods, industrial concentration system, regional situations, and characteristics of Japanese capitalism and German capitalism.

1.2 Research Topics

This section identifies research topics by examining major issues in capitalism and business management in Japan and Germany after the war.

Prior to World War II, market problems were the most significant bottleneck in business management, stifling the development of productive forces in both Japan and Germany; however, these circumstances significantly changed postwar. Domestic market conditions radically changed in the interest of protecting worker rights. These trends were observed in leading European nations, laying the groundwork for European export markets. International market conditions were not only supported by the US-led world economic system, that is, the free trade system and international monetary system, but also were complemented by the formation of a common market in Western Europe. Tremendous changes can be observed in postwar historical conditions, specifically regarding broader and deeper global market connections (Yamazaki 1997, 2001a, b, 2009, 2013, 2015).

However, in the period immediately following the end of the war, productive forces and economic might greatly differed between the United States and European countries as well as between the United States and Japan. Thus, "catching up" became one of the most imminent issues in each nation. The deployment of US technology and management methods significantly aided in dealing with this problem; the necessary conditions for achieving this goal were created with US guidance and assistance. Furthermore, the productivity movement led by the United States, as part of this country's global strategy, played a critical role in the international expansion of organizational endeavors. Under the Marshall Plan, "technical assistance" created a large-scale framework for supporting learning and introduction of US technology and management methods in each country. This new framework enabled the deployment of US technology and management methods in European nations including Germany, tremendously changing business management. A similar level of US assistance was seen in Japan.

As a result, the productivity movement resulted in each nation's industrial development and economic restructuring based on US-style productive forces. These changes transformed the prewar industrial structure, such that it no longer adjusted the focus of producer goods but on the consumer goods sector, thus emphasizing a shift to mass production. Japan's and West Germany's high rates of economic growth from the 1950s through the 1960s secured an economic structure characterized by US-style mass production, mass distribution, and mass consumption, which was appropriate to mass consumer societies. These changes indicated a trend toward the Americanization of the economy; Americanization of technology and business management was a key component of these changes (Kudo 1999, p. 453).

This type of Americanization aided corporate expansion and economic growth in Japan and Germany. In particular, the American mass production system, represented by the Ford system, was modified in accordance with country-specific conditions during periods of the postwar high economic growth, which had big roles in corporate expansion. In the period after the 1970s, however, limitations of this mass production system became prominent under the structural changes of capitalism and the shift toward low economic growth, and reforms of the production system consequently became an important management problem. In both Japan and Germany, reforms of mass production system were performed with a view to reinforcing their international competitiveness. However, there were differences (as well as some commonalities) in the development of the production system between both countries. For example, the Japanese production system achieved high economic performance from the 1970s to the late 1980s and its introduction was attempted in other countries, as seen in the phenomenon known as "Japanization." In contrast, in Germany, the reforms of the production system in the same period had certain limitations, which created difficulties for the country in its attempt to catch up to the Japanese system. Therefore, clarifying the characteristics and significance of the developments of the production systems during this period is an important research topic.

After the 1990s, the "Americanization" of business management typified by the transformation toward shareholder value-oriented management model and capital market-oriented corporate governance system emerged again under the US-led "financialization," the globalization of finance, and the increasing pressure of the capital market and strongly influenced enterprises and their management in many countries. However, such a transformation toward the American management model greatly differs among nations with no tendency of convergence. Along with commonalities with the United States, what types of unique developments emerged? How was the US management model reformed to accommodate Japanese or German conditions? What was the significance of these developments? The implementation of the American-style management model in both nations and its effects on corporate management are worth clarifying.

This book analyzes the transformation of business management in Japan and Germany after the war and explains the characteristics and structures of management in both countries from the perspectives of international comparison as well as comparison between industries and enterprises. Business management will be analyzed in relation to the system of industrial concentration and the characteristics and accumulation structure of Japanese and German capitalism. This book explores changes in business management during the postwar period through the early 1970s focusing on the industrial concentration system and the deployment of American management methods. It also considers important issues in the period from the 1970s to the late 1980s such as the reforms of mass production systems that were deeply concerned with the difference of international competitive power between Japan and Germany as well as between Japan and the United States. Moreover, the transformation toward shareholder value-oriented management and corporate governance system after the 1990s, representing a resurgence of Americanized business management, is considered. By comparing the changes in Japan's and Germany's business management, this book attempts to gauge answers to the question as to which characteristics and significances of business management in Japan and Germany have and what created differences in the movement toward global regionalization between both nations, from an international comparative perspective.

First, this book attempts to clarify the characteristics and significance of the postwar system of industrial concentration as the big business system in Japan and Germany. It analyzes two main issues, that is, large corporate groups and industry–bank relationships. Both have played an important role in the postwar development of corporations and capitalism's accumulation structures in Japan and Germany. Industrial concentration exhibited new postwar developments in both countries. Monopolies that had been dissolved by the postwar occupation policy were reconcentrated. In addition, the system of large corporate groups began to re-emerge and reconcentrate, and with it came new developments in the system of large corporate groups. The system, as the cornerstone of industrial concentration, played a crucial role in the formation of the accumulation structure of Japanese and German capitalism. Therefore, this book considers the restructuring of a system for large corporate groups in relation to the dissolution of monopolies under the occupation policy and their reconcentration after the war. Industry–bank relationships are also important issues related to cooperative inter-firm relationships, the system of corporate governance, and corporate development. In Japan, industry–bank relationships were restructured through the dissolution of the *zaibatsu* and the formation of large corporate groups that included a wide array of industries. In Germany, industry–bank relationships developed through various mechanisms such as banks' credit and securities businesses, the shareholdings and deposited stock system, the assignment of directors from banks to corporations, and the advisory board system. Therefore, herein, industry–bank relationships are considered in relation to characteristics of large corporate groups and competition structures in Japan and Germany.

Second, this book examines how business management in Japan and Germany changed with the deployment of US technology and management methods. Beyond commonalities with the United States, what types of unique developments emerged? From a structural analysis perspective, this research reveals the overall picture of changes in business management that accompanied the deployment of American management methods. These changes included the adaptation of systems to local conditions based on the overall structure of, and relationship with, Japanese capitalism or German capitalism in business management. That being said, it is important to consider the implications on various economic and social conditions vis-à-vis US intentions and postwar Japanese and German corporations' strategic intentions, business management traditions, management values, common labor practices, labor relations, and market structures. American management methods are often based on the principles of efficiency and productivity improvements and others that were related to business policy conditions or environmental factors (e.g., systems and practices, management values, and management culture). Therefore, it is important to consider the relationships between the principle of economic rationality emphasized in business and management methods and understand them in relation to the deployment of American management methods.

Third, in this book, the overall nature and status of business management will be examined through a comprehensive understanding of these changes, and Japan's and Germany's responses to these changes. How were US management methods reformed to accommodate Japanese conditions? And how were Japanese or German management styles and characteristics created? What was the significance of these developments? This book will explore these questions. It considers many fields concerning business management, such as concentration of enterprise, management systems, production systems, management education, marketing, organizational structure, business strategy, and corporate governance; this is executed generally and systematically without limitation to specific fields or themes in business management.

Fourth, this book examines regional conditions and relationships with the United States by looking at how the growth of Japanese and German corporations during the boom years of the 1950s and 1960s created the situations that emerged in subsequent periods. In other words, through Germany's interpretation of the Americanization of business management, how were economic relations (in terms of the division of labor and foreign trade patterns) in the European region built on the basis of different industrial structures and the strengthening of competitiveness in Europe? How were these related to the developments independent of the US and the Europeanization movement that resulted in today's EU? To answer these questions, it is necessary to clarify these points and comprehend the origins of the European integration movement. This book examines the European market structures and the resultant competition. Also, it considers external environmental factors such as the characteristics and relevance of the German and European industrial structure. Furthermore, the origin of Germany's movement toward European integration is to be explored from the perspective of internal structural changes in business management and the external environmental factors.

From the standpoint of Japan, the direction of European integration and the progress of an expansion based on an integrated Europe was an important German characteristic. Since the beginning of the postwar era, there were no advanced economies in the Asian region that could be considered strong export destinations for Japan, particularly because many East Asian countries had previously been colonies with low levels of economic development. Thus, because Japan was left with no option but to rely on exports to the United States, its most lucrative market, this book compares Japan's situation with that of Germany.

1.3 Prior Research and Issues Thereafter

This section considers the findings of previous research on related topics in relation to the aforementioned research topics.

In terms of their relevance to the central research topic of this book, there are numerous important studies that consider changes in business management such as the deployment of American management methods in Japan and Germany from the postwar boom years to the early 1970s. However, to the best of our knowledge, regarding Japan or Germany, no studies have hitherto provided an overall structural analysis that fully focuses on the economic and industrial factors (regarding the system of industrial concentration) without being subject to limitations imposed by factors inherent to the level of enterprises. Studies into business management do not address the relevance of business management issues to the structural characteristics of Japanese or German capitalism. Moreover, few studies sufficiently relate economic and industrial factors of business management to reproduction (accumulation) structures in Japanese capitalism or German capitalism. It is only through such overall structural analysis that we can sufficiently explain changes in business management, the resulting mechanisms of corporate development, and their social and economic significance.

Studies on corporate-level issues also seem to have omitted several factors. Drawing on these studies, the topics undertaken in this text are important aspects of the deployment and transfer of American management methods. The primary characteristics of US management methods deployed in the 1950s and 1960s were (1) management and production systems (human relations, industrial engineering, statical quality control, and the Ford system); (2) management education methods; (3) responses to markets coinciding with advancements in mass production (marketing, public relations, and operations research); and (4) the divisional structure (Yamazaki 2013; Kleinschmidt 2002). Regarding the deployment of American management methods in Germany, Kleinschmidt (2002) and Hilger (2004) provide detailed research results of each method. However, existing studies often limit their analyses to specific management methods or areas and provide only a rudimentary analysis of this book's overall subject. Few studies provide an overall analysis of these primary management methods.

Some studies clarify the selective adaptation in the deployment of American technology and management (Kleinschmidt 2002; Zeitlin 2000, pp.11, 15–20; Hilger 2004, p.278; Schröter 2005, p.59; Kipping and Bjanar 1998, pp.14, 383). Zeitlin emphasizes the significance of creative modifications of American methods and the hybridizations of American management with Japanese or German management (Zeitlin 2000, pp.11, 15–20). However, studies that consider the deployment of American management methods and changes of business management with such movement do not always identify which elements of American and Japanese or German management methods were combined, how they were hybridized, and which factors determined the hybridization. Indeed, several studies that provide outstanding analyses of issues on Americanization in Japanese corporations or German corporations do not sufficiently explain the details of hybridization or the process of modifying US management methods. They also do not individually or comprehensively explain the factors that caused hybridization and modifications. Further, we found no comprehensive structural analyses that explain business management through the deployment of US methods (Kudo et al. 2004; Zeitlin and Herrigel 2000;

Kleinschmidt 2002; Feldenkirchen 2004; Kudo et al. 2004; Schröter 2005; Kipping and Bjanar 1998; Hilger 2004; Djelic 1998; Gourvish and Tiratsoo 1998; Engwall and Zamagni 1998; Barjot 2002; Berghahn 1985; McCreary 1964; Hasegawa 1960; Nihon keieihsa dantai renmei 1965; Natori 1965; Sakamoto 1964; Zennihon noritsu renmei ningen noryoku kaihatu senta 1981; Sangyo kunren hakusho henshu iinkai 1971; Nishizawa 1996; Nihon seisansei honbu 1964; Noguchi 1968; Fujimoto 1997; Shimokawa 1997; Obara 1994; Kondo and Wakabayashi 1999; Nihon seisansei honbu soshiki kenkyukai 1975; Yoshihara et al. 1981; Harasawa 1997; Imanishi 1988; Nakahashi 1981; Ono 1979). Similar research limitations can be found in topics such as the transition to a shareholder value-oriented management model and corporate governance system in the Americanization process after the 1990s (Höpner 2003; Streeck and Höpner 2003; Vitols 2000; Zugehör 2003; Alff 2007; Beck et al. 2005; Siegwart and Mahari 2002; Küke 2002; Mäntysaari 2005; Storz and Lageman 2005; Windolf 2005; Schlie and Warner 2000; Völcker 2009; Huffschmid et al. 2009). Mauro F. Guillén explores historical patterns related to the adoption of the three major models or paradigms of scientific management, human relations, and structural analysis by conducting an international comparison of two liberal-democratic countries (the United States and the United Kingdom) and two corporatist countries (Germany and Spain). Guillén's book focuses on analyzing "configurations of factors producing different or similar outcomes of adoption"; however, it does not consider all major factors in the Americanization of business management after World War II (Guillén 1994).

Furthermore, considering studies regarding the reforms of mass production system after the 1970s, though there are many prominent research results, how the prevail of the module production system after the 1990s in Europe including Germany was determined by the significance and limitations of reforms in the 1970s and the 1980s while being high performance of Japanese production system is not clarified. However, it is imperative for grasping the differences in mass production system between Japan and Germany after the 1990s and their significance to clarify the origin of the transformation toward the module production system in European nations including Germany (Kern and Schumann 1990; Schumann et al. 1994; Malsch and Seltz 1988; Freyssenet et al. 1998; Jürgens et al. 1993; Boyer et al. 1998; Haipeter 2000; Heidemann et al. 1992; Lung et al. 1999; Hudson and Schamp 1995; Meißner et al. 1994; Zwickel 1996; Jürgens 1990; Roth 1996a, b; Altmann et al. 1992; Volkswagen AG 1980). In this book, this important research topic is examined through comparison of production system reforms in Japan and Germany.

Studies that examine management characteristics in major countries such as the United States, Germany, Japan, the United Kingdom, and France or countries in the European region attempt to clarify essential features observed in each nation and common traits between some countries from a comparative perspective. However, the majority of them do not always clarify a specific country's own management style in relation to various management methods and the deployment process of American management methods that greatly influenced management transformations after the war. This is also true for a comparison with Japan and Germany (McCann 2014; Edfelt 2010; Hampden-Turner and Trompenaars 1993; Klarfeld 2004; Lane 1989;

Lane 1992; Turcq 1994; Calori and Woot 1994; Calori and Laweence 1991; Calori 1991; Calori 1994; Calori and Dofour 1995; Calori and Seidel 1994; Cassis 1997; Barsoux and Lawrence 1991; Atamer and Johnson 1991; Mayer and Whittington 1999; Kudo et al 2004; Ohashi et al 1995, 1999).

There are also very few examples in the literature which analyze the development of business management in both Japan and Germany from the end of World War II to the present, especially from the perspective of international comparison. The studies that do exist in this respect generally only consider specific themes of business management. It is important to compare and contrast the unique Japanese and German factors, as well as demonstrate the changes in business management methods in both countries from a unified perspective. Importantly, from a uniform perspective, it is insufficient for various authors to present their findings in individual chapters, which are then edited by one or more individuals (Kudo et al. 2004; Maekawa 1997; Ohashi et al. 1995, 1999).

1.4 Analytical Framework

Next, this section explains an analytical framework. In Japan, a school of thought analyzes and understands the dynamics of business management paying attention to mutual relationships between political, industrial, and business economics, which comprise the structure of economics (Maekawa 1970, 1993, 1997; Kanbayashi 1976; Hayashi 1972; Yamazaki 2005). Among these mutual relationships, this school of thought considers the causes of various problems and the unique styles and characteristics of business management, particularly those in developed countries. It also examines the societal significance of objective changes, as well as the relationship between change and development. In this book, the economic and industrial factors of business management and corporate activities that create reproduction and accumulation structures beyond specific corporate-level factors, given a country's capitalistic nature, are thoroughly examined.

Using this type of analytical approach, this book seeks to comprehend Japanese and German capitalisms by examining business management and its relationship to the problem of industrial concentration. Thus, this book by nature is a study of business management as an element of economics.

While this book applies the above-mentioned research methods, it also examines various aspects and situations using a unique analytical framework for a total system of business management, wherein we analyze overall business management. Further, this book establishes the concept of "reframing," using it to analyze the various problems in deploying American management methods that created conducive conditions for business management changes in the postwar era.

1.4.1 Total System of Business Management as a Framework for Structural Analysis

First, a total system of business management is a structural framework comprising conditions that define the established methods of business management within the confines of capitalism in a specific country. This conceptual framework helps understand the overall relationships and structure of business management in the country. The concept of the total system of business management comprises two parts: first, the external factors in business management, including external environmental factors such as the structure of a country's capitalist system, industrial systems, and labor relations; and second, the internal factors related to corporate structures, including structural factors of management such as the system of industrial relations, management, and organization in corporations and executive management systems such as single- and two-layered structures. The relationship between these two phenomena is influenced by the state of business management and external factors of capitalism, which define the development of business management in a country. This state of management is affected by corporate-level institutional characteristics and mechanisms. Further, internal factors in corporate structures influence external environmental factors, such as the double-layered structure of executive management, thereby defining corporate networks through the supervisory board function. Thus, these two phenomena are interconnected.

When considering overall ties with business management, the "global structure of capitalism" reveals mutual relationships within the capitalist bloc. However, the leadership and aid of developed nations signify a problem in these relationships, particularly in international markets and capital, as the framework for the global structure of capitalism is centered on the postwar United States. Although this global structure of capitalism lies outside the total system of business management, it defines, or at least influences, this system. Under the global structure of capitalism, the total system of business management determines a given country's established methods of business management.

The eight elements comprising these external environmental factors within the total system of business management are the following: (1) state–enterprise relationships, (2) labor relations, (3) industrial systems based on inter-firm relationships, (4) financial systems, (5) the structure of productive forces, (6) industrial structures, (7) market structures, and (8) enterprise–market relationships. These eight elements are explained below.

State–enterprise relationships comprise state regulative policies, particularly anti-monopoly, trade, and industrial policies. For example, in Germany, issues with the economic principles of social market economy and anti-monopoly regulations were related to regulative policy. One important goal of trade policy was the integration of West Germany into capitalistic markets and the establishment of a common market through European integration. The issues of investment promotion measures and the state's intervention in the productivity movement were critical components of industrial policy. Regarding industrial policy, it is important to compare measurements in Germany with special protection measures known as the "convey" system that was taken for financial sector that emphasized the continuance and profit of financial institutions including small and weak institutions through regulations restricting competition by discretion rather than the rule in Japan (Nishimura 2003, pp. 387–388).

The labor relations framework revolved around collective agreements, worker participation in management, and labor unions. In corporate structures, these were external environmental factors and the specific state of industrial relations within corporations was an internal structural factor. In Germany, industries were confronted with codetermination issues at the corporate management level, in addition to the dual system of regional collective agreements and labor relations through codetermination at the plant level. The system of codetermination is of great significance for labor–management relationships, German production and marketing strategies, and the production structure and system that supported these strategies. It is critical to investigate the impact of labor relationships on business management via the codetermination system, as well as the role of social redistribution in the postwar economic order known as the social market economy. When assessing the influence of industrial relations on business management in Japan and Germany, differences in not only the regulating powers of trade unions but also the promotional functions of management must be considered.

In Germany, inter-corporate ownership and control structures, inter-corporate relationships, industrial systems based on industry–bank relationships, and large corporate group systems are examples of industrial systems based on inter-firm relationships or industry-level systems based on collaborative inter-firm relationships. In Germany, these industrial systems not merely demonstrate cooperative capitalism with regulative functions and a new approach toward monopolies and industrial concentration, which supported the system of large corporate groups, but also built mechanisms for governance. In contrast, in Japan, big banks played an important role as main banks in the industrial groups that were formed after the war. These points are closely connected with the collaborative industrial (regulatory) system based on industry–bank relationships.

Financial systems had issues with corporate financing and the widespread expansion of international ties in financial markets based on what is now known as information technology networks. There are differences in financial system among nations. The development of an interconnected financial system consolidated the universal banking system, which existed in prewar Germany, the house banks, the role of the big banks within the universal banking system, and the credit and security businesses. In contrast, in Japan, the separate system of credit businesses and securities businesses, the separation between commercial banks and trust banks, and between long-term financial institutions and short-term financial institutions was adopted (Nishimura 2003, pp. 32–33, 213; Shikano 2013a, pp. 47–51). Such differences became an important factor influencing business management.

Changes in the structure of productive forces were influenced by the historical development of productive forces, the system of vocational education and specialized skills, and labor utilization reflected in production. In addition to the prewar tradition of "flexible quality production," which differed from the US mass production system, Germany had a history of developing mass production systems with production flexibility and scale merit with lower production volume (von Freyberg 1989; Siegel and Freyberg 1991; Stahlmann 1993). The foundation of a production structure relied on skilled workers who were supported by a system of vocational education and specialized skills, such as the Meister system. Although based on the deployment of US technology and management methods, these factors strongly influenced postwar changes in the structure of productive forces.

Concerning the structure of productive forces, an important element related to characteristics of Japanese capitalism, Japanese enterprises established a flexible mass production system that was compatible with the narrow and diverse domestic market (Fujimoto 1997, pp. 57, 59, 74, 100, 102; Hashimoto 2001, pp. 241–242) under the cooperative labor relations system and the internal labor market by realizing the flexible formation of work organization and the synchronization between production processes.

Regarding industrial structures, particularly those defined by the expansion process of capitalism in each country, the nature of these structures, the composition of internationally competitive industrial sectors, and the characteristics of these industries were important issues. The issues included the following: the composition of key industrial sectors; industrial characteristics (technological, market, and product characteristics); each company's position within the national economy, demonstrated by their interconnectedness within industrial sectors and within international competition; and their relationship with (i.e., relative degree of reliance upon) the state. Among these issues, changes in German business management were associated with their level of transformation, such as the transition from an industrial structure based on producer goods to one focused on the durable consumer goods sector. In contrast to Germany, in Japan, the development of heavy industries was stunted before World War II but, along with chemical industries and durable consumer goods industries, they expanded rapidly after the war.

Commodity, labor, and financial markets are all parts of market structures. For Germany's commodity markets, the nature of its target markets, the composition of the regions and export market products, trade policy in export destination countries, and competition structures were all closely related to corporate management behavior. Along with the characteristics of German market, the nature and meaning of the European market played a significant role, and such conditions for a common market were important issues that affected the development of business management. Comparing German market conditions with those of the United States, in which standardization was very advanced, differences in market conditions such as a consumer emphasis on quality or functionality are to be noted. These market conditions were inextricably linked to corporate product strategy, marketing activities, and labor utilization. In European markets, complementary relationships in industrial and product areas were based on German industrial structures, with the heavy and chemical industries and processing and assembly industries at their core. In addition, there were strong differences in industrial structures among European nations compared with those of other regions. This situation may be related to the state of German business management, which has adapted to European market conditions. In contrast, Japanese enterprises tended to rely on the domestic market and the US market that have characteristics of emphasizing quality, measured by relatively few defects, and pursued establishing a business management system that was compatible with such market conditions. Therefore, it is imperative to consider business management and corporate expansion in relation to the characteristics of market paying attention to the regional composition of the export markets.

In enterprise–market relationships, the influence of Japanese or German marketization on business management and industrial concentration became a problem. As expressed by the term "coordinated market economy" (Hall and Soskice 2001, 2007, pp. iii–xx), there existed characteristics of marketization in postwar Japan and Germany and a market economy system that integrated measures to deal with the "limits of marketization." The system's characteristics can be seen in social redistribution functions based on social market economic principles, a framework for industrial relations based on the codetermination system and its effects on the labor market, and a system for regulating interests in an industrial system based on the universal banking system and industry–bank relationships. Such characteristics of marketization are deeply integrated with the development of business management.

What were the types of business management changes in the overall structures and relevancies mentioned above and the interconnected factors in our eight elements? This book clarifies this very crucial question.

1.4.2 *The Process of Reframing as an Analytical Framework Regarding International Transfer of Management Methods*

Reframing, that is, the framework for exploring various problems with the deployment of US management methods is described below. Reframing in this text refers to business management methods and systems that are defined by structural characteristics of a country's capitalism and how these are adapted, modified, and made compatible with the structural characteristics of capitalism in a nation to which it is transferred. Among these, structural characteristics of this capitalism are concerned with the state of existence of the following items: a structure of productive forces, industrial structures, and market structures. These three Japanese and Germany characteristics are inextricably linked to reframing. In addition, management values, business management traditions, cultural factors, and definability from an institutional perspective are also closely concerned with reframing.

The structure of productive forces, industrial structures, and market structures are factors included in the total system of business management. In particular, regarding the structure of commodity markets, a nation's domestic market and export market characteristics, along with its regional and product compositions, are matters of market structure. These issues are closely concerned with price and quality competition and other competitive structures in a market. Thus, management methods must be developed in accordance with differences in market structure. Labor markets are linked to a country's regulatory mechanisms, the state of labor relations, and the worker participation in management. Financial markets are linked to market participation in the credit business and security market, as well as their composition and the financial institution system. In industrial structures, characteristics of industrial development and international competition are important issues, as are the structure of productive forces, adapted to market and industrial structures, and the characteristics of the structure of productive forces, reflected in the development process. To some extent, the characteristics of the structure of productive forces are concerned with systems of specialized skills and vocational education, and they have a significant impact on the deployment of foreign elements of productive forces and the state of labor utilization.

These various elements that comprise a nation's capitalism's structural characteristics are inextricably linked to management values and business management traditions, culture, and systems. As some studies point out (Hofstede 1980; Schröter 2005; Berghahn 1985, p.333; Hilger 2004, p.287), the influence of culture on business management and the deployment of American management methods is great. Business management traditions and culture are interrelated with business management standards and values. Even concerning capitalism, wherein the pursuit of profit is the greatest goal, a country's corporate standards and values are not necessarily suitable for other countries. For example, the United States has traditionally emphasized pragmatist standards and values, and both the United States and the United Kingdom have placed a high value on obtaining financial profit through interest-bearing capital; in contrast, continental Europe and Japan do not necessarily regard these as top priorities. Decisions on where to place value, that is, production, technology, quality, or marketing policies, which are more directly tied to profit, specifically short-term profit, greatly affect corporate behavior. Management values and business management culture, on the other hand are not simply matters of general culture but are inextricably linked with the structural characteristics of target markets identified by corporations. For example, if the commodity market in a certain nation or region prioritizes product quality or functionality, enterprises emphasize values and differentiation in technology or production because management values conform to market characteristics. As a result, market characteristics are closely related to management standards and values identified as important by businesses.

Institutional factors include legal systems that cover all types of regulations, industrial relations, specialized skill systems, and educational systems. Labor relations define business management characteristics, such as investment in labor education based on labor conditions and employment security systems, corporate product and market strategies based on these investments, and production and management systems adapted to these strategies. The development of managers and executives, as well as skilled workers, is inextricably linked to a country's educational system. Furthermore, production systems have an impact on management standards and values. A nation's production regime is closely concerned with institutional factors, labor market regulations, the complementarity of education and training systems, financial systems, inter-firm relationships, and corporate governance from the standpoint of market competition and technology transfer in discussions about varieties of capitalism (Hall and Soskice 2001). As a result, when a country's production systems and management methods that supported these systems are deployed in other nations, these institutional factors often influence the reframing of management methods.

The postwar reform was also an important institutional factor influencing the Japanese-style or German-style adaptation of Americanization. For instance, such cases can be observed in the measurements such as the purge of top business leaders and their effects. In contrast to Germany, in Japan, the business world experienced a shift between generations due to the removal of the top business leaders from older generations initiated by the US occupation policy. There were a lot of cases in which many new managers of postwar "zaibatsu"-type companies who were promoted from the ranks of middle management had not received sufficient training as top management at the time of their promotion (Miyajima 1991, pp. 139–140; Miyajima 1992, pp. 212–213; Miyazaki 1966, p. 224), which became an important factor determining the necessity to deploy American education methods for executives. Therefore, it is important to compare the Americanization process of business management and the consequent changes in Japan and Germany in connection with the influences of the postwar reforms.

This concept of reframing addresses the conditionality of structural characteristics tied to reproduction mechanisms of capitalism, particularly in the nation in which management methods and systems are created and that to which they are transferred and deployed. The management methods and systems of the originating country are adapted and modified to the capitalist structure of the country to which they are transferred. In addition, as these methods and systems begin to function, their circumstances define the structure and characteristics of capitalism and the aspects of reproduction structure in that nation. Reframing, in this text, focuses on problems that occur when the social system in an organization, specifically a corporation, is transferred to another country. Thus, the receiving country's capitalistic characteristics are modified or revised to an adaptable form when the originating nation's management methods, created for its own capitalistic structural characteristics, are introduced and spread throughout a foreign country using that country's methods.

Accordingly, reframing is the process of structural adaptation in response to different environmental conditions and a method of structural analysis, whereby the overall structure of business management is foundational. Abo (1994) provides a comprehensive analysis of "hybridization" and the transfer of Japanese production systems outside of Japan to grasp the issues of international management method transfer. This research focuses on exporting Japanese systems, or system "application" (transfer) and "adaptation" (modifications adaptive to local conditions). In other words, it considers the problem of how two systems from different nations function when combined using certain proportions (Abo 1994, 2007b). Study by Abo et al. in 2007 uses "the 'application-adaptation (hybrid) evaluation model' and the 'five-point grading system' as an analytical framework for research" (Abo 2007a, pp.10–13).

Such a viewpoint differs from the analytical framework of this book, which emphasizes clarifying factors of modification of business management. The same can be said of the previously mentioned study on "hybridization" in the deployment of US technology and management methods (Zeitlin and Herrigel 2000; Kleinschmidt 2002; Hilger 2004; Kudo et al. 2004; Schröter 2005; Feldenkirchen 2004).

The analytical framework used in this book differs from that used in previous research. In examining the issues of transferring business management systems to foreign countries, Liker et al. (1999) defines "recontextualization," as "a reconstruction of the context of environmental and system elements for the modification and deployment of systems, such that they are compatible with specific market and societal conditions of the country in question." According to Liker et al., recontextualization is "the transformation of the meaning of firm offerings (e.g., technologies, work practices, or products) as they are uprooted from one cultural environment and transplanted to another." The process of recontextualizing focuses on how company deliverables are initially understood and how values evolve in new environments (Liker et al. 1999, p. 118). In contrast, the concept of reframing used in this book attempts to explain factors governing the restructuring of management methods within overall structural relationships.

Based on the unique structural analysis framework for the "total system of business management" and "reframing," this book attempts to present an overall structural analysis of business management. Furthermore, it offers an analysis of capitalism based on a structural analysis of business management. Ideas based on these analytical frameworks attempt to consider the phenomena of amendments, modifications, and improvements to management methods as seen in the structural characteristics of capitalism in the countries in question, as well as the various factors affecting business management as seen in the overall system of business management. Two analytical frameworks used in this book allows for a unified view of international comparison when considering business management and corporate expansion in multiple nations. This book explores the overall structural changes to business management in Japan and Germany, the issue of what defines a nation's unique state of business management, and how that is significant, using this analytical framework.

Drawing on the premises clarified in this chapter, in Part I, the overview of the total system of business management in postwar Japan and Germany as a structural framework for conditions that define the established methods of business management within the characteristics of capitalism in a certain country (Chap. 2) and fundamental characteristics of Japanese-style management and German-style management are considered compared with those in the United States (Chap. 3). Analyses in this part clarify the postwar frameworks of Japanese and German business management. Part II will consider the development of a new system of industrial concentration. In this part, new developments in the system of large corporate groups (Chap. 4) and industrial systems based on industry–bank relationships (Chap. 5) as an issue of industrial concentration closely tied to the characteristics of Japanese capitalism and German capitalism will be examined. Chapters 6–12 in Part III explore the changes in business management and the significance of the deployment and transfer of US management methods in the postwar period through the early 1970s. In Part IV, as major management issues, reforms to mass production systems from the 1970s to the late 1980s will be analyzed (Chap. 13) and transformations toward the American management model, represented by shareholder value-oriented management and capital market-oriented corporate governance system (Chap. 14) will be examined. In Chap. 15, conclusion of this book will be clarified.

The ideas herein are based on the following studies and reports, which are related to the book's theme and various original historical documents: annual reports of major corporations in Japan and Germany, historical documents located in the archives of major industrial corporations, the German Federal Archives, The National Archives in Washington D.C., and the Rhenish-Westphalian Economic Archives in Cologne.

References

Abo T (ed) (1994) Hybrid factory. The Japanese production system in the United States. Oxford University Press, New York

Abo T (2007a) Comparison of Japanese hybrid factories in the world: Generalities and pecularities of patterns in the international transfer of the Japanese management and production systems. In: Abo T (ed) Japanese hybrid factories. A comparison of global production strategies. Palgrave Macmillan, Basingstoke, pp 1–35

Abo T (ed) (2007b) Japanese hybrid factories. A comparison of global production strategies. Palgrave Macmillan, Basingstoke

Alff M (2007) Automobilkonzern unter Druck. Beschäftigungsentwicklung bei Opel, Volkswagen und der Shareholder Value. VDM Verlag Dr. Müller, Saarbrücken

Altmann N, Köhler C, Meil P (eds) (1992) Technology and work in German industry. Routledge

Atamer T, Johnson G (1991) Conclusions. In: Calori R, Lawrence P (eds) The business of Europe. Managing change. SAGE, London, pp 218–229

Barjot D (ed) (2002) Catching up with America. Productivity missions and the diffusion of American economic and technological influence after the Second World War. Presse de Luniversite de Paris-Sorbonne, Paris

Barsoux J-L, Lawrence P (1991) Countries, cultures and constraints. In: Calori R, Lawrence P (eds) The business of Europe. Managing change. SAGE, London, pp 198–217

Beck S, Klobes F, Scherrer C (eds) (2005) Surviving globalization? Perspectives for the German economic model. Springer, Dordrecht

Berghahn V (1985) Unternehmer und Politik in der Bundesrepublik. Suhrkamp, Frankfurt am Main

Boyer R, Charron E, Jürgens U, Tolliday S (eds) (1998) Between imitation and innovation. The transfer and hybridization of productive models in the international automobile industry. Oxford University Press, Oxford

Calori R (1991) Markets and managers. In: Calori R, Lawrence P (eds) The business of Europe. Managing change. SAGE, London, pp 167–217

Calori R (1994) The diversity of management systems. In: Calori R, Woot P de (eds) A European management model. Beyond diversity. Prentice Hall, New York, Tokyo, pp 11–30

Calori R, Dofour B (1995) Management European style. In: Acad Manag Exec 9(3):61–73

Calori R, Lawrence P (eds) (1991) The business of Europe. Managing change. SAGE, London

Calori R, Seidel F (1994) The dynamics of management systems in Europe. In: Calori R, Woot P de (eds) A European management model. Beyond diversity. Prentice Hall, New York, Tokyo, pp 55–78

Calori R, Woot P de (eds) (1994) A European management model. Beyond diversity. Prentice Hall, New York, Tokyo

Cassis YF (1997) Big business. The European experience in the twentieth century. Oxford University Press, New York
Djelic M-L (1998) Exporting the American model. The Postwar transformation of European business. Oxford University Press, Oxford
Edfelt RB (2010) Global comparative management. A functional approach. SAGE, Thousand Oaks
Engwall L, Zamagni V (eds) (1998) Management education in historical perspective. Manchester University Press, Manchester
Feldenkirchen W (2004) The Americanization of the German electrical industry after 1945. Siemens as a case study. In: Kudo A, Kipping M, Schröter HG (eds) German and Japanese business in the boom years. Transforming American management and technology models. Routledge, London, pp 116–137
Freyssenet M, Mair A, Shimizu K, Volpato G (eds) (1998) One best way? Trajectories and industrial models of the world's automobile producers. Oxford University Press, Oxford
Fujimoto T (1997) *Seisan Sisutemu no Sinka Ron* (*Evolution of production system*). Yuhikaku, Tokyo
Gourvish TR, Tiratsoo N (eds) (1998) Missionaries and managers: American influences on European management education, 1945–60. Manchester University Press, Manchester, New York
Guillén NF (1994) Models of management. Works, authority, and organization in a comparative perspective. The University of Chicago Press, Chicago, London
Haipeter T (2000) Mitbestimmung bei VW. Neue Chancen für die betriebliche Interessenvertretung, 1st edn. Westfälisches Dampfboot, München
Hall PA, Soskice D (eds) (2001) Varieties of capitalism: the institutional foundations of comparative advantage. Oxford University Press, Oxford
Hall PA, Soskice D (2007) Nihongoban eno jyobun. Shihonsyugi no tayousei to Nihon (Preface for Japanese edition. Varieties of caitalism and Japan). In: Hall PA, Soskice D (eds) Shihonsyugi no tayousei (Varieties of capitalism). Nakanishiyashuppan, Kyoto, pp ii–xix
Hampden-Turner C, Trompenaars A (1993) The seven cultures of capitalism: value systems for creating wealth in the United States, Japan, Germany, France, Britain, Sweden, and the Netherlands. Currency and Doubleday, New York
Harasawa Y (1997) Nihonteki jigyobusei no seiritsu katei (Emergence of Japanese divisional structure). In: Keizaigaku (Economics) 48(6):17–33
Hasegawa H (1960) Nihon no hyuman rireshonzu (Human relations in Japan). Otsuki shoten, Tokyo
Hashimoto J (2001) Sengo Nihon keizai no seicho kozo (Growth structure of postwar Japan). Yuhikaku, Tokyo
Hayashi A (1972) Gendai Doitsu kigyoron (Modern German enterprise). Mineruva shobo, Kyoto
Heidemann W, Kohlhoff AP, Zeuner C (eds) (1992) Qualifizierung in der Autoproduktion. Europäische Automobilkonzern reagieren auf die japanische lean production. Schüren, Marburg
Hilger S (2004) „Amerikanisierung" deutscher Unternehmen. Wettbewerbsstrategien und Unternehmenspolitik bei Henkel, Siemens und Daimler-Benz (1945/49-1975). Franz Steiner Verlag, Stuttgart
Höpner M (2003) Wer beherrscht die Unternehmen? Shareholder Value, Managerschaft und Mitbestimmung in Deutschland. Campus, Frankfurt am Main
Hofstede G (1980) Cultures consequences: International differences in work-related value. Sage, Beverly Hills, Calif
Hudson R, Schamp EW (eds) (1995) Towards a new map of automobile manufacturing in Europe? New production concepts and spatial restructuring. Springer, Berlin
Huffschmid J, Köppen M, Rhode W (eds) (2009) Finanzinvestoren: Retter oder Raubritte? Neue Herausforderungen durch die internationalen Kapitalmärkte. Kapitalmärkte. VSA-Verlag, Hamburg
Imanishi S (1988) Jigyobusei no kaimei (Elucidation of divisional structure). Manejimentosha, Tokyo
Jürgens U (1990) Produkutionskonzepte und Standortstrategien in der Weltautomobilindustrie. In: WSI Mitteilungen 43(9):596–602

Jürgens U, Malsch T, Dohse K (1993) Breaking from Taylorism. Changing forms of work in the automobili industry. Cambridge University Press, Cambridge

Kanbayashi T (1976) Keieikeizaigaku kigyo riron (Business economics—theory of enterprise). Tokoro shoten, Tokyo

Kern H, Schumann M (1990) Das Ende der Arbeitsteilung? Rationalisierung in der industriellen Produktion, 2nd edn. C. H. Beck, München

Kipping M, Bjarnar O (eds) (1998) The Americanization of European business. The Marshall plan and the transfer of US management models. Routledge, London

Klarfeld A, Mabey C (2004) Management development in Europe: Do national models persist? In: Eur Manag J 22(6):649–657

Kleinschmidt C (2002) Der produktive Blick. Wahrnehmung amerikanischer und japanischer Management- und Produktionsmethoden durch deutsche Unternehmer 1950–1985. Akademie Verlag, Berlin

Kondo F, Wakabayashi Y (eds) (1999) Nihonkigyo no masu maketingushi (History of mass marketing of Japanese enterprises). Dobunkan, Tokyo

Kudo A (1999) 20 Seiki Doitsu shihonshugi (20th-century German capitalism). Tokyo Daigaku Shuppankai, Tokyo

Kudo A, Kipping M, Schröteret HG (eds) (2004) German and Japanese business in the boom years. Transforming American management and technology models. Routledge, London

Küke J (2002) Corporate governance in Germany. An empirical investigation. Physica-Verlag, Heidelberg

Lane C (1989) Management and labour in Europe. The industrial enterprise in Germany, Britain and France. Eduard Elgar, Aldeshot

Lane C (1992) European business systems: Britain and Germany compared. In: Whitley R (ed) European business systems. Firms and markets in their national contexts. SAGE, London, pp 64–97

Liker JK, Fruin WM, Adler PS (eds) (1999) Remade in America. Transporting and transforming Japanese management systems. Oxford University Press, New York

Lung Y, Chanaron J-J, Fujimoto T, Raff D (eds) (1999) Coping with variety in the auto industry. Ashgate, Hampshire

Maekawa K (1970) Doitsu dokusen kigyo no hatten katei (Developoment of German monopolistic enterprises). Mineruva shobo

Maekawa K (1993) Gendai kigyo kenkyu no kiso (Foundation of study of contemporary enterprise). Moriyama shoten, Tokyo

Maekawa K (1997) Nichidoku hikaku kigyoron eno michi (Comparative study of Japanese and German enterprise). Moriyama shoten, Tokyo

Mäntysaari P (2005) Comparative corporate Governance. Shareholders as a rulemaker, Springer, Heidelberg

Malsch T, Seltz R (eds) (1988) Die neuen Produktionskonzepte auf dem Prüfstand. Beiträge zur Entwicklung der Industriearbeit, 2nd ed. Edition Sigma, Berlin

Mayer M, Whittington R (1999) Euro-elites: top Britisch, French and German managers in the 1980s and 1990s. In: Eur Manag J 17(4):403–408

McCann L (2014) International and comparative foundations of political economies. SAGE, London

McCreary EA (1964) The Americanization of Europe. The impact of Americans and American business on the uncommon market. Doubleday & Co., New York

Meiβner H-R, Kisker KP, Bochum U, Aβmann J (1994) Die Teile und Die Herrschaft. Die Reorganisation der Automobilproduktion und der Zulieferbeziehungen. Edition Sigma, Berlin

Miyajima H (1991) "Zaikai Tsuiho" to Shin Keieisha no Tojyo (Purge of managers from the economic world and emergence of new top managers). In: Will 10(7):136–144

Miyajima H (1992) Zaibatsu Kaitai (Dissolution of Zaibatsu). In: Hosei Daigaku Sangyo Jyoho Senta, Hashimoto J, Takeda H (eds) Nihon Keizai no Hatten to Kigyou Shudan (Development of Japanese economy and corporate groups). Tokyo Daigaku Shuppankai, Tokyo, pp 203–254

Miyazaki G (1966) *Sengo Nihon no Keizaikiko* (*Japanese economic system after World War II*). Shin Hyoron, Tokyo

Nakahashi K (1981) Jigyobusei kigyo ni okeru soshiki sekkei (Organizational design in enterprise with divisional structure). In: Shogaku tokyu (Commercial Study) 31(3–4):41–79

Natori J (1965) Zoho keiei no HR (Human relations), enlarged edn. Waseda daigaku shuppankai, Tokyo

Nihon keieihsa dantai renmei (ed) (1965) Wagakuni romu kanri no gensei. Dai nikai romu kanri shoseido chosa (Present conditions of labor management. Second investigation of labor management systems). Nihon keieisha dantai renmei kohobu, Tokyo

Nihon seisansei honbu (ed) (1964) Indasutoriaru enjiniaringu. Indasutoriaru manejimento senmon shisatsudan hokokusho (Industrial engineering. Report of special inspection team of industrial management). Nihon seisansei honbu, Tokyo

Nihon seisansei honbu soshiki kenkyukai (ed) (1975) Kigyo senryaku to keiei soshiki (Business strategy and management organization). Nihon seisansei honbu, Tokyo

Nishimura Y (2003) Nihon no kinyu seido kaikaku (Reform of financial system in Japan). Toyo keizai shinposha, Tokyo

Nishizawa T (1996) Business studies and management education in Japan's economic development. An institutional perspective. In: Amdam RP (ed) Management, education and competitiveness. Europe, Japan and the United States. Routledge, London, New York, pp 96–110

Noguchi T (1968) Seisan kanri no keieigaku (Business administration of production management). Zeimu keiri kyokai, Tokyo

Obara H (1994) Nihon maketingushi—Gendai ryutsu no shiteki kozu—(History of marketing in Japan—Historical structure of modern distribution—). Chuo keizasha, Tokyo

Ohashi S, Oda A, Schanz G (eds) (1995) Nihonteki keiei to doitsuteki keiei (Japanese management and German management). Chikura shobo, Tokyo

Ohashi S, Miyama A, Kaido N (eds) (1999) Nihon to Doitsu no keiei (Business management in Japan and Germany). Zeimu keiri kyokai, Tokyo

Ono T (1979) Nihon kigyo no soshiki senryaku (Organizational strategy of Japanese enterprises). Manejimentosha, Tokyo

Roth S (1996a) Automobilhersteller und ihre Zuliefer in Deutschland und Japan. In: Zwickel K (ed) Vorbild Japan? Stärken und schwächen der Industrieorte Deutschland und Japan. Bund-Verlag, Köln, pp 175–205

Roth S (1996b) Produktionskonzepte in Japan und Deutschland: Eine gewerkschaftliche Vergleichsstudie in der Automobilindustrie. In: Zwickel K (ed) Vorbild Japan? Stärken und schwächen der Industrieorte Deutschland und Japan. Bund-Verlag, Köln, pp 102–174

Sakamoto F (1964) Nihon keiei kyoikushi jyosetsu (An introduction to management education in Japan). Daiyamondosha, Tokyo

Sangyo kunren hakusho henshu iinkai (ed) (1971) Sangyo kunren hyakunenshi (100 years history of industrial training), Nihon sangyo kunren kyokai, Tokyo

Shikano Y (2013) Nihon no kinyu seido (Financial system in Japan), 3rd edn. Toyo keizai shinposha, Tokyo

Schlie EH, Warner M (2000) The 'Americanization' of German management. In: J Gen Manag 25(3):33–49

Schröter HG (2005) Americanization of the European economy. A compact survey of American economic influence in Europe since the 1880s. Springer, Dordrecht

Schumann M, Kinsky VB, Kuhlmann M, Kort C, Neumann U (1994) Trendreport Rationalisierung. Automobilindustrie, Werkzeugmaschinenbau, Chemische Industrie, 2nd edn. Edition Sigma, Berlin

Shimokawa K (1997) Maketingu. Rekishi to kokusai hikaku (Marketing. History and international comparison), 2nd ed. Bunshindo, Tokyo

Siegel T, Freyberg TV (1991) Industrielle Rationalisierung unter dem Nationalsozialismus. Campus, Frankfurt am Main

Siegwart H, Mahari J (2002), Ruffner M (Gasthrsg) Corporate Governance, Shareholder Value & Finanz. Helbing & Lichtenhahn, Basel
Stahlmann M (1993) Die Erste Revolution in der Autoindustrie. Management und Arbeitspolitik von 1900–1940. Campus, Frankfurt am Main
Storz C, Lageman B (eds) (2005) Konvergenz oder Divergenz? Der Wandel der Unternehemensstrukturen in Japan und Deutschland. Metropolis-Verlag, Marburg
Streeck W, Höpner M (eds) (2003) Alle Macht dem Markt? Fallstudien zur Abwicklung der Deutchland AG. Campus, Berlin, New York
Turcq D (1994) Is there a US company management style in Europe? In: Calori R, Woot P de (eds), A European management model. Beyond diversity. Prentice Hall, New York, Tokyo, pp 82–110
Vitols S (2000) The reconstruction of German corporate governance: Reassessing the role of capital market pressures. Wissenschaftszentrum Berlin für Sozialforschung
Völcker M (2009) 'Das Wars mit der Deutschland AG'—Der Schareholder-Value-Kapitalismus und dessen (soziale) Folgen, 1st edn. GRIN Verlag, München
Volkswagen AG (1980) Gruppenarbeit in der Motorenmontage. Ein Vergleich von Arbeitsstrukturen. Campus, Frankfurt am Main
von Freyberg T (1989) Industrielle Rationalisierung in der Weimarer Republik: Untersucht an Beispielen aus dem Maschinenbau und der Elektroindustrie. Campus, Frankfurt am Main
Windolf P (ed) (2005) Finazmarkt-Kapitalismus. Analysen zum Wandel von Produktionsregimen. VS Verlag für Sozialwissenschaften, Wiesbaden
Yamazaki T (1997) Doitsu kigyo kanrishi kenkyu (History of business management in Germany). Moriyama syoten, Tokyo
Yamazaki T (2001a) Vaimaruki Doitsu gorika undo no tenkai (Rationalization movement in Germany during the Weimar era). Moriyama shoten, Tokyo
Yamazaki T (2001b) Natisuki Doitsu gorika undo no tenkai (Rationalization movement in Germany during the Nazi era). Moriyama shoten, Tokyo
Yamazaki T (2005) Gendai Keieigaku no Saikoutiku (A study of the reconstruction of business management study). Moriyama Shoten, Tokyo
Yamazaki T (2009) Sengo Doitsu shihonsyugi to kigyo keiei (German capitalism and business management after World War II). Moriyama shoten, Tokyo
Yamazaki T (2013) Gendai no Doitsu kigyo—Sono gurobaru chiikika to keiei tokushitsu —(Contemporary German enterprises—their global-regionalization and characteristics of business management—). Moriyama shoten, Tokyo
Yamazaki T (2015) Doitsu senzenki keieishi kenkyu (German business history until the end of World War II). Moriyama shoten, Tokyo
Yoshihara H, Sakuma A, Itamai H et al (1981) Nihon kigyo no takakuka senryaku (Diversification strategy in Japanese enterprise). Nihon keizai shinbunsha, Tokyo
Zeitlin J, Herrigel G (eds) (2000) Americanization and its limits. Reworking US technology and management in post-war Europe and Japan. Oxford University Press, Oxford
Zennihon noritsu renmei ningen noryoku kaihatu senta (ed) (1981) Sengo kigyonai kyoiku hensenshi (Changes in in-company training after Word War II). Zennihon noritsu renmei ningen noryoku kaihatu senta, Tokyo
Zugehör R (2003) Die Zukunft des rheinischen Kapitalismus: Unternehmen zwischen Kapitalmarkt und Mitbestimmung. Leske+Budrich, Opladen
Zwickel K (ed) (1996) Vorbild Japan? Stärken und schwächen der Industrieorte Deutschland und Japan. Bund-Verlag, Köln

Part I
Total System of Business Management and Characteristics of Management in Japan and Germany

Chapter 2
Overview of the Total System of Business Management in Postwar Japan and Germany

Abstract Following discussions in Chap. 1, this chapter examines the total system of business management in postwar Japan and Germany as the structural framework defining a country's management style applying the author's original framework. It considers various aspects and situations, wherein we analyze overall business management. The total system of business management is an analytical method for explaining the overall relationships and structure of business management. Of two parts that comprised the concept of the total system of business management, that is, the external and internal factors in business management, eight factors regarding the former in Japan and Germany are clarified.

Keywords Enterprise-market relationships · Financial system · Industrial system based on inter-firm relationships · Industrial structure · Labor relations · Market structure · Productive structure · State–enterprise relationships · Total system of business management

In Part I, the overall total system of business management in Japan and Germany as a structural framework for conditions that define the established methods of business management within the characteristics of capitalism as implemented in a certain country is examined using the author's analytical framework. The fundamental characteristics of Japanese-style management and German-style management after WWII are compared to those in the United States. This section's analyses clarify the postwar frameworks of Japanese and German business management.

This chapter explores the total system of business management.[1] The total system of business management denotes a structural framework for conditions that define the established methods of business management within the characteristics of capitalism as implemented in a certain country. It is an analytical method for explaining the overall relationships and structure of business management. Of the external environmental factors and internal factors in business management as two parts that

[1] The first content analysis related to Germany in this chapter is Chap. 10 of the author's book "*German Business Management: A Japanese Perspective on Regional Development Factors,*" which was published by Springer in 2013.

T. Yamazaki, *Japanese and German Enterprises*,
https://doi.org/10.1007/978-981-97-4880-8_2

comprise the concept of the total system of business management, the external factors relating to corporate structures are examined. The eight elements comprising these external environmental factors within the total system of business management are the following: (1) state–enterprise relationships, (2) labor relations, (3) industrial systems based on inter-firm relationships, (4) financial systems, (5) the structure of productive forces, (6) industrial structures, (7) market structures, and (8) enterprise–market relationships. The total system of business management is composed of eight factors: These factors define the development of business management.

In terms of the analysis framework for the total system of business management, this chapter provides an overview of the environmental factors of business management based on mutual relations. Sections 2.1 and 2.2 will discuss the overall relevance of the total system of business management in postwar Japan and Germany, respectively.

2.1 Overview of the Total System of Business Management in Japan After World War II

First, observing conditions in Japan, in terms of state–enterprise relations, pure holding companies, treasury stock acquisitions, ownership, and cartels were all prohibited by anti-monopoly regulations under US occupation policies. However, industrial groups that included a wide array of industries were formed under the relaxation of regulations of the Anti-Monopoly Act (Kosei torihiki iinkai jimukyoku 1997; Okurasho zaiseishi shitsu 1982). In trade policy, despite the trend toward the liberalization of trade and capital, the concentration of foreign currencies into the state and management and employment of foreign currencies by the state occurred under the auspices of the Foreign Exchange and Foreign Trade Act. This law also regulated the import of products and quantities through the allocation of foreign currencies. In addition, the introduction of foreign capital was regulated by the Foreign Investment Act. While this law promoted the introduction of foreign capital with a view to introducing foreign technologies, a policy of selective introduction of foreign capital with fixed limitations was adopted (Imura 2000, pp. 109–115).

Regarding industrial policy, initiatives for fostering and protecting industry and policies for promoting priority strategic industries were adopted. Special protective measurements for finance that emphasized the continuance and profit of financial institutions including small and weak institutions were also instituted through regulations restricting competition by discretion rather than rule. Such measures are known as the "convey" system (Nishimura 2003, pp. 387–388; Okazaki and Okuno 1993, pp. 11–13; Paku 2013, pp. 93, 97, 109). In addition, investment aid measures, such as various special depreciation systems, represented by extraordinary depreciation, favorable tax treatment for corporations, and the re-evaluation of corporate assets were adopted during the period until the realization of high economic growth (Imura

2000, pp. 116–117; Ito et al. 1988, pp. 19–20). Furthermore, measures for industrial structure adjustment were pursued in the period of structural depression, and industrial reorganization and rationalization were promoted by state intervention (Ito et al. 1988, pp. 26–27; Nakatani 1983, Chap. 5). Such industrial policies promoted the rapid development and expansion of the heavy and chemical industries in the postwar boom years. In this way, state–enterprise relations in Japan were strongly characterized by the protection of domestic industry to a greater extent than in other countries.

The system of labor relations had three basic pillars in Japan: lifetime employment, seniority wage systems, and enterprise trade unions, which revolved around regular employees (OECD 1977). The legal system for protecting workers' rights was developed through three major labor laws, that is the Labor Standard Law, the Trade Union Law, and the Labor Relation Adjustment Law. Lifetime employment is, as the name suggests, employment throughout one's entire life, and on the basis of this system, workers in large Japanese corporations were given opportunities to earn higher wages (i.e., increments) and designations (i.e., promotions), in return for their loyalty to the company. With such rigidity in the labor market, the seniority order system, one of the principles of the order of personnel and their wages, was formed through lifetime employment relations. Japanese-style enterprise trade unions were formed only from labor relations built on lifetime employment. Labor unions' basic units of activity were formed according to individual corporations; thus, labor conditions were negotiated and agreed upon according to individual corporate conditions, and would generally not go beyond those bounds. In this sense, Japanese labor unions were not horizontally organized by industry, but divided by and bounded within each corporation. Therefore, a unified labor movement, as in Europe and the United States, was difficult to develop. Also, the power of collective bargaining was hampered and cooperative labor relations integrated into corporations was the norm. Agreements through collective bargaining or collective agreements were mostly at the corporate level (Okouchi 1980, pp. 10–13, 105–106; Mori 1981, pp. 367, 371–372; Takahashi 1970, p. 9). On this note, the collective agreement system was vastly different from Germany's industry-wide system. The system of worker participation in management did not wait for new laws or other forms of governmental intervention. Rather, participation voluntarily occurred in small group activities with QC circles or joint labor-management consultation systems, which negotiated and discussed labor-management issues on the premise of creating trustworthy relationships between labor and management.

However, a legal codetermination system, such as that in Germany, did not exist at the plant level and certainly not at the top management level. Joint labor-management consultation systems proliferated with the collaboration of labor and management as per the productivity movement of 1955, and gradually took shape through discussions on productivity improvement issues (Urabe and Omura 1983, pp. 101–102; Hirano 1976, pp. 205–206, 210; Roshikankei Chosakai 1963, pp. 17–18). In Japan, joint labor-management consultation systems differed from collective bargaining and were established on the foundation of horizontal corporate labor relations through enterprise trade unions. Taken from systemic and functional perspectives, collective bargaining and joint labor-management consultation systems, which were essentially heterogeneous, became tightly woven together in Japan (Urabe and Omura 1983, pp. 105, 108–110, 112–113; Roshikankei Chosakai 1963, p. 55). In other words, official collective bargaining as defined by collective agreements was carried out formally and tended to be extremely rare; indeed, collective bargaining became a mere facade (Hirano 1976, pp. 209–210). Further, matters of labor conditions were the focus of not only collective bargaining but also the joint labor-management consultation system, which occupied a greater position (Urabe and Omura 1983, pp. 117–118, 123–124). In Japan, as the floor managers in shops became union members and leaders, they took on the function of labor management. This type of industrial partnership between labor and management was not common to large corporations in Europe or the United States (Maekawa 1997, pp. 247, 310, 313; Aoyama 1981, pp. 94–96). Based on the above framework for labor relations, Japan's labor protection did not face hindrances as did Germany's codetermination system. This led to circumstances enabling easier dismissals and reassignments (Maekawa 1997, p. 87). Moreover, the wage gap between large corporations and small and medium enterprises, and that between medium and small enterprises became greater in Japan than in Germany (Maekawa 1997, pp. 119–120, 126; Sugaya 1977, p. 105).

Industrial systems based on inter-firm relationships in Japan can be seen in the large corporate group system, industry–bank relationships, and the inter-firm relationships based on continuous long-term and exclusive trade relations between large corporations and small and medium enterprises and between medium and small enterprises under the multilayered hierarchical subcontracting system. The system of large corporate groups that spanned several industries, with industrial corporations, banks, and trading companies as its core, and the industrial system based on industry–bank relationships in which large banks were aligned with each industrial group indicates Japanese characteristics of the industrial concentration system. Such systems were deeply related to the corporate governance system that was concerned with management autonomy against capital market pressures and monitoring of management by stockholders. Inter-firm relationships based on long-term continuous and exclusive trade relations under the subcontracting system peculiar to Japan were an important foundation for the development of the Japanese mass production system in the process and assembly industries, such as the automobile and electrical industries.

Next, examining the financial system that had deep connections with the industrial system based on industry–bank relationships, characteristics of the Japanese system can be seen in the leading role of the Bank of Japan as a central bank to financial institutions and the system based on the principle of division of labor, such as the separate system of credit businesses and securities businesses, the separation between commercial banks and trust banks, and between long-term financial institutions and short-term financial institutions (Nishimura 2003, pp. 32–33, 213; Shikano 2013, pp. 47–51). In Japan, through powers of supervision and monitoring, the financial administration authorities had played roles in the function of corporate governance in financial institutions as well as in the primary functions, such as the maintenance of credit and prevention of chains of financial panic. Therefore, the financial system in Japan was deeply related to the corporate governance system (Sheard 1997, pp. 20,

153, 225–226). The Bank of Japan adopted measures to change the amount of funds that was available for financial institutions and companies in non-financial sectors by window guidance which restricted the loan amounts of commercial banks (Cargill et al. 1997, pp. 30–31, 52–54), while developing measures for regulating the amount of funds by using the official discount rate operation (Tanaka 1985, Chap. 7). In addition, the system of loans to affiliated companies under the main banking system and the system of joint financing by financial institutions in the competitive relationship were important foundations of corporate finance.

Concerning the structure of productive forces, an important element related to characteristics of Japanese capitalism, Japanese enterprises established a flexible mass production system that was compatible with the narrow and diverse domestic market (Fujimoto 1997, pp. 57, 59, 74, 100, 102; Hashimoto 2001, pp. 241–242) under the cooperative labor relations system and the internal labor market by realizing the flexible formation of work organization and the synchronization between production processes. Such movement had built foundations for the further evolution of the mass production system and the development of management emphasizing policies of market segmentation and product differentiation during the period from the 1970s to the 1980s, which greatly contributed to establishing international competitiveness.

When considering industrial structure, the heavy and chemical industries in Japan developed at a much slower rate than those in the United States and Germany before the war. Industrial structures rapidly developed in the postwar era in the durable consumer goods industries as well as the heavy and chemical industries. The deployment of technology and management methods from the US and industrial policies emphasizing the development of the heavy and chemical industries as the key industries played significant roles in industrial structure dynamics. However, the international competitiveness of Japanese corporations in the process and assembly industries resulted in trade friction with foreign countries, as seen in the trade friction between Japan and the United States, which forced Japanese enterprises to further develop their productive forces for maintaining and reinforcing international competitive advantage in the context of appreciation of the yen against the dollar.

Further, in terms of market structure, the labor market based on the lifetime employment system was an important characteristic and promoted workers' loyalty to companies and cooperative relationships between management and labor. In the financial market, the large roles of banks' credit businesses, the delay in the development of the securities market compared with that in the United States and the United Kingdom, and the closed and exclusive market, represented by loans to affiliated companies under the main banking system can be regarded as prominent characteristics. Such features were not only strongly related to the industrial system based on inter-firm relationships and the financial system but were also an important factor that determined the Japanese system of industrial concentration.

The commodity market, which accounts for the majority of Japan's exports, greatly influenced business management in Japan. In both Japan and the United States, the emphasis was clearly placed on product quality vis-à-vis few defective products and low defective rate of parts in these markets. This characteristic of the commodity market in Japan and the United States was an important foundation for the high competitiveness of Japanese enterprises in the US market, Japanese companies' heavy dependence on the American market in exports, and the movement to establish productive forces by thorough rationalization for reinforcing international competitive power.

Building upon the previous analysis, in looking at enterprise–market relationships, which are related to the state of marketization, Hall and Soskice point out that Japan can be regarded as a "coordinated market economy," similar to Germany in this respect. However, while Germany is a "coordinated market economy on the industry base," Japan is a "coordinated market economy on the group base." Regarding labor relations, it was possible for Japanese enterprises to coordinate employment flexibly by making their workers move to lower-wage companies within the vertical corporate group under the internal labor market and enterprise trade union (Hall and Soskice 2007, pp. iii–xx).

In Japan, negotiations over wages tended to reach an agreement at a standard approximately common across plural industrial sectors while the negotiation was carried out at the level of a specific industrial sector, as seen in the so-called "Shunto." In examining enterprise–market relationships vis-à-vis the financial and industrial systems, in the industrial groups, large city banks as the core of the group furnished loans to affiliated companies for member enterprises within the group. Such loans were also supplemented by the joint financing system. By such systems, the stable provision and collection of funds were secured, thus testifying to the coordinating functions in the financial market. The multilateral trade relationships between banks and industrial enterprises, between trading companies and industrial companies, and between industrial enterprises in each industrial group also exhibited adjusting functions between demand and supply. Furthermore, trade relations based on the multi-layered hierarchical subcontracting system peculiar to Japan provided similar coordinating functions. The Japanese system of "coordinated market economy on the group base" played a significant role in the response to marketization limits in a different way from the systems in Germany.

Figure 2.1 is a graphical overview of the total system of business management in postwar Japan based on our discussions.

2.2 Overview of the Total System of Business Management in Germany After World War II

Following that, in an examination of state–enterprise relations in Germany, regulatory mechanisms under the Restrictive Trade Practices Act, which dealt with regulatory and anti-monopoly policies, were linked to an industrial system based on inter-firm relations. They influenced business development based on trust, which replaced cartels, and a complementary division of labor in the product fields within large corporate groups. Within industrial policy, investment aid policy, as well as currency

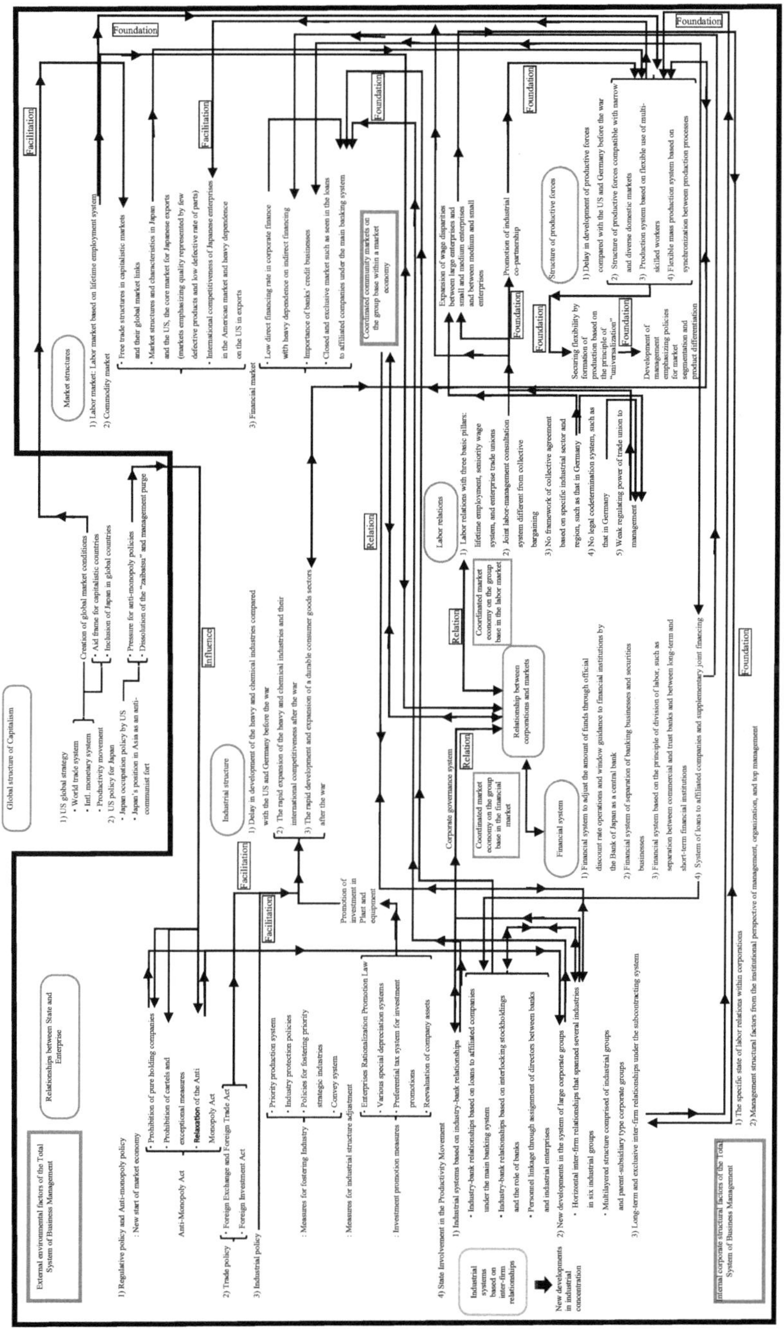

Fig. 2.1 Overview of postwar Japan's total system of business management.
Source This figure was compiled by the author, based on discussions in this chapter

reform and re-evaluation of company assets, had a significant impact on the financial market by encouraging corporate self-financing and lowering the rate of direct financing through the issuance of securities. The overall industrial structure was also influenced by industrial policy. It supported international competitive power in the capital goods market structure, which was the foundation for the industrial structure and heavily weighted toward goods-producing industries. Furthermore, trade policy efforts to form a common market structure, such as that in Western Europe, were underway; however, the government's response to the policy had a significant impact on the structure of commodities markets. The establishment of a common market contributed to the further strengthening and supplementation of the European region's global market connectivity. It also promoted the building of a foreign trade pattern based on German international competitive power, which was biased toward exportation in markets of that region and a "complementary division of labor in industrial and product fields." Economic integration efforts aimed at establishing blocks of a market control system for German enterprises on a Western European scale, against the backdrop of gaps in productive forces and competitiveness gaps with Germany's neighboring countries.

For labor relations, the basic characteristics of the new framework for labor relations in postwar Germany can be observed in a dual system (a) the ability to negotiate agreements governing sales conditions for trade unions and the general framework for labor unions and employer associations; (b) works constitutions, which are agreements that specifically govern labor conditions between work councils and management based on collective agreements (Jentsch 1995, p. 218). Collective agreements were applied to corporations within a region's particular industry, and as a result, regardless of corporate size, wages tended to be applied horizontally (Allen 2006, pp. 81–82). A system of industry-specific collective agreements in each region was an important source of regulatory power for labor unions. Such a system contributed to the reduction of intra-corporate wage disparities in industries, which, together with codetermination at the plant level, strengthened the foundation for employment and wage security, as well as social redistribution in a social market economy. By creating and reinforcing domestic markets, these safety nets coordinated labor markets and expanded commodity markets. The framework for systematic coordination to solve labor-management conflicts also contributed to stable and harmonious coordination (Thelen 1991, pp. 2, 13).

Furthermore, the codetermination system at the top levels of management secured autonomy in response to capital market pressures on business management caused by worker participation in supervisory boards. This independence was bolstered further by ties between an industrial system based on industry–bank relations. Even investment in vocational education for the company's workforce was encouraged by the systems. Investments in education and training laid the groundwork for diverse quality production that relied on skilled workers, as well as the development of production and marketing strategies in Germany (regarding diversified quality production, see Abelshauser 2003; Streeck 1992, 1997). As a result, the system promoted German corporate competitiveness and contributed to the building and maintenance of a foreign trade pattern that complemented industrial and product fields in European markets.

Industrial systems based on inter-firm and industry–bank relationships secured autonomy through coordination among banks and between industries and banks, and the involvement of bank representatives on corporate supervisory boards. The universal banking system, a specific banking sector, is an important component of the German model of capitalism. Companies can design long-term strategies that are compatible with job security, skill acquisition, and high wages through close relationships between the company and the bank (Amable 2003, pp. 12–13). Furthermore, industrial systems based on industry–bank relationships brought about a German-style system of corporate governance. The codetermination system established by the Codetermination Act of 1976 was based on a structure with an equal number of labor and capital market members on the supervisory board. This type of system weakened the influence of shareholders in capital markets. Moreover, because the system of corporate governance was based on industry–bank coordination, it reinforced autonomy of management against shareholders in collaboration with the codetermination system. This system of industrial concentration hastened the building of complementary relationships in product fields on the basis of product quality in the market, which further repressed price competition among enterprises. The system assisted German corporations in avoiding fierce price competition and served as an important foundation for the development of management methods that adopted a management style that focused on competing with quality. In response to global and domestic competition, such reforms aided in the development of large-scale businesses that incorporated cooperative relationships.

Next, considering the financial system which had deep connections with the industrial system based on industry–bank relationships, financial systems had issues related to corporate financing. Mutual ties based on the universal banking system between credit businesses and securities businesses, as well as the role of the house bank among large-scale banks, served as an organizational foundation for the development of the collaborative industrial system based on industry–bank relations. The mutual ties also regulated the financial market structure, where credit and securities businesses were combined; this type of market structure is an important factor that determines the system of corporate governance in Germany.

In addition, one of the most important characteristics of the "structure of productive forces," an element of German capitalism, was a production system based on vocational education and specialist qualifications, such as those provided under the Meister system. This encouraged the development of experience and skill, as well as investment in vocational education for company employees. Germany had a history of developing production systems based on prewar concepts of flexible production emphasizing quality and development of production systems aimed at achieving improved scale merit through lower production volume and flexibility in response to changes in product demand (von Freyberg 1989; Siegel and Freyberg 1991; Stahlmann 1993). These built the foundation for the development of diversified quality production that relied on skilled workers. Thus, despite popular perceptions of "Americanization" following World War II, the historical development of productive forces, the system of vocational education and specialized skills, and labor utilization reflected in production all influenced changes in the structure of productive forces.

In the postwar era, industrial structures quickly developed in the durable consumer goods industries, as well as in the heavily represented producer goods industries and the heavy and chemical industries, which had international competitive power even before the war. The characteristics of the industrial structures contained (1) formation of German-style production systems, (2) international competitiveness in and skewed exporting toward European markets, and (3) a foreign trade pattern that complemented these industrial and product fields. In terms of the composition of industries with international competitiveness and their characteristics (technological, market, and product characteristics), an obvious nature can be observed in the predominance of sectors where product quality emphasizing functionality based on technological superiority was an important point determining competitive strength in the markets. Germany has built an industrial structure based on such industrial sectors after the war.

Moreover, looking at market structures, they contain commodity, finance, and labor markets. For commodity markets, a country's domestic and export market characteristics, the composition of regions and export market products, trade policy in export destination countries, and competition structures were all deeply concerned with not only price and quality competition and other competitive structures in a market but also company management behavior. Characteristics of German and European markets, which emphasized product quality and functionality, were important in the development of postwar business management and the Americanization of technology and management and were different from those in the United States, where standardization was advanced. These market conditions were inextricably linked to corporate product strategy, marketing activities, and labor utilization. These market structures fostered diverse quality production centered on niche market segments and laid the groundwork for a labor division system that supplemented production fields in large corporate groups. Under such market conditions, German competitive strength in European markets, along with the bias toward exporting to these regions, built a pattern of foreign trade with a division of labor in a form complementary to their industrial and production fields. Since before the war, German heavy and chemical industries had a competitive advantage in the European market, and the complementary relationship of industrial and production fields was plain from the rapid development of processing and assembly industries postwar; this type of complementary relationship was stronger in Europe than in other regions. The common market in Europe had great meaning for the capitalistic accumulation of German enterprises. Given European markets that were regulated by such a structure of productive forces, the characteristics of the German industrial structure and the mutually complementary relationship were strong in comparison with other regions. This highlights the importance of Germany's diverse quality production. In addition, credit and securities businesses were combined in financial markets, which became the basis of a system that jointly formed the cornerstone of the universal banking system.

Building on the previous analysis, one can see the characteristics of a coordinated market economy in the labor market and its link with labor relations in enterprise–market relationships that are related to the state of marketization. In the industrial system, based on the financial system and industry–bank relations, there are characteristics of a coordinated market economy in the financial market. Furthermore, in terms of market structure, it has a relationship with a coordinated market economy in the commodities market, as it avoids price competition by focusing on quality competition through product specialization. The strength of competition is the most fundamental dimension that distinguishes various types of capitalism in product markets. Models of capitalism indicate different characteristics according to the pattern of dominant competition in the product's market (Amable 2003, p. 113). In nations characterized as free-market economies such as the United States and the United Kingdom, regulation of products markets is excessively low (Amable 2003, p. 16), competition tends to be intense, and coordination is generally done through price channels. In product markets of nations of continental Europe including Germany, competition is less keen than in the United States and the United Kingdom (Amable 2003, p. 121).

It is worth noting that the market economy, which was coordinated at the highest levels of management through the codetermination system, and the industrial system, which was based on industry–bank relations, were both issues that were closely related to enterprise–market relationships. These issues were facilitated by the development of a German-style system of corporate governance that differed from the market-oriented corporate governance with emphasis on financial markets. To address the "limitations of marketization," measures such as social redistribution functions based on the principles of a social market economy, a framework of industrial relations based on the codetermination system, and an interest coordination system in an industrial system based on the universal banking system and industry–bank relations were implemented. Such characteristics of marketization are deeply integrated with the development of German-style business management emphasizing the significance of enterprise as a "social institution" or "social community."

Figure 2.2 is a graphical overview of the total system of business management in postwar Germany based on our discussions.

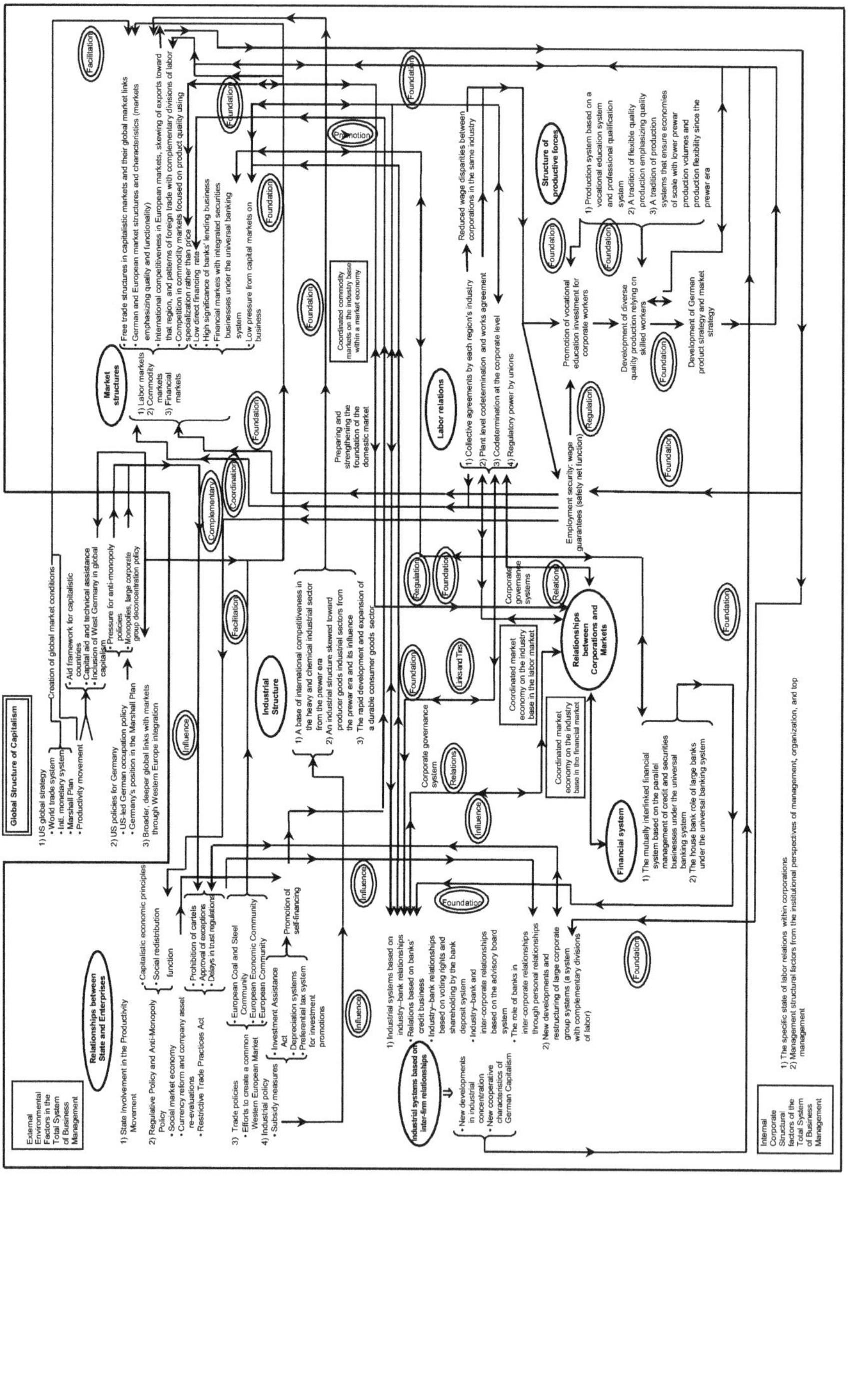

Fig. 2.2 Overview of postwar Germany's total system of business management.
Source This figure was compiled by the author, based on discussions in this chapter

References

Abelshauser W (2003) Kulturkamp. Der deutsche Weg in die neue Wirtschaft und die amerikanische Herausforderung. Kulturverlag Kadmos, Berlin

Allen MMC (2006) The varieties of capitalism paradigm. Explaining Germany's comparative advantage? Palgrave Macmillan, Basingstoke

Amable B (2003) The diversity of modern capitalism. Oxford University Press, Oxford

Aoyama S (1981) Gendai "nihonteki roshikankei" no tokushitsu to saihen (Characteristics and reorganization of "modern Japanese labor relations"). In: Hasegawa H (ed) Gendai nihon kigyo to roshikankei (Modern Japanese enterprises and labor relations). Rodo jyunposha, Tokyo, pp 53–112

Cargill TF, Hutchison MM, Ito T (1997) The political economy of Japanese monetary policy. The MIT Press, Cambridge, Massachusetts

Fujimoto T (1997) Seisan Sisutemu no Sinka Ron (Evolution of production system). Yuhikaku, Tokyo

Hall PA, Soskice D (2007) Nihongoban eno jyobun. Shihonshugi no tayosei to Nihon (Preface for Japanese edition. Varieties of capitalism and Japan). In: Hall PA, Soskice D (eds) Shihonshugi no tayosei (Varieties of capitalism). Nakanishiya shuppan, Kyoto, pp ii–xix

Hashimoto J (2001) Sengo nihon Keizai no seicho kozo (Growth structure of Japanese economy after World War II). Yuhikaku, Tokyo

Hirano K (1976) Sengo nihon ni okeru roshikankei no tenkai (Development of industrial relations in Japan after World War II). In: Kimoto S (ed) Roshikankei ron (Industrial relations). Nihon hyoronsha, Tokyo, pp 193–216

Imura K (2000) Gendai nihon keizairon (Modern Japanese Economy), New edition. Yuhikaku, Tokyo

Ito M, Kiyono K, Okuno M et al (1988) Sangyo seisaku no keizai bunseki (Economic analysis of industrial policy). Tokyo daigaku shuppankai, Tokyo

Jentsch WM (1995) Doitsu kigyo ni okeru roshikankei (Industrial relations in German Enterprise). In: Ohashi S, Oda A, Schanz G (eds) Nihonteki keiei to doitsuteki keiei (Japanese business management and German business management). Chikura shobo, Tokyo, pp 217–234

Kosei torihiki iinkai jimukyoku (ed) (1997) Dokusen kinshi seisaku sanjyunenshi (30-year history of anti-monopoly policy). Okurasho insatukyoku, Tokyo

Maekawa K (1997) Nichidoku hikaku kigyoron heno michi (Comparative study of Japanese and German enterprise). Moriyama shoten, Tokyo

Mori G (1981) Nihonteki roshikankei sisutemu no tokusitu to kongo no tenbo (Characteristics and future of Japanese labor relations system). In: Mori G (ed) Nihon no roshikankei sisutemu (Labor relations sytem in Japan). Nihon rodo kyokai, Tokyo, pp 359–185

Nakatani M (1983) Gendai kigyo kozo to kanri kinou (Structure of modern enterprises and management function). Chuo keizaisha, Tokyo

Nishimura Y (2003) Nihon no kinyu seido kaikaku (Reform of financial system in Japan). Toyo keizai shinposha, Tokyo

OECD (1977) The development of industrial relations system. Some implications of Japanese experience, I, II. OECD, Paris

Okazaki T, Okuno M (1993) Gendai nihon no Keizai sisutemu to sono rekishiteki genryu (Economic system in Japan and its historical origin). In: Okazaki T, Okumura M (eds) Gendai nihon no Keizai sisutemu to sono rekisiteki genryu (Economic system in Japan and its historical origin). Nihon Keizai shinbunsha, Tokyo, pp 1–34

Okouchi (1980) Roshikankei ron (Labor relations). Rodo junposha, Tokyo

Okurasho zaiseishi shitsu (ed) (1982) Showa zaisehishi. Shusen kara kowa made (History of public finance in the Showa period from the end of World War II to reconciliation), vol 2, Toyo Keizai shinposha, Tokyo

Paku S (2013) Nihon no kinyu gyosei no henka no seijikeizaigaku (Political ecoomy of changes in financial administration). In: Akiba M (ed) Grobaraizeishon no naka no Ajia. Atarashi bunsekikadai no teiji (Asia in the globalization. New reserch topics). Hirosaki daigaku shuppankai, Hirosaki

Roshikankei chosaka (1963) Roshikankei to ningen kankei (2) (Labor relations and human relations, 2) Chuo koron jigyo shuppan, Tokyo

Sheard P (1997) Mein bank sihonshugi no kiki. Toyo Keizai shinposha, Tokyo

Shikano Y (2013) Nihon no kinyu seido (Financial system in Japan), 3rd edn. Toyo Keizai shinposha, Tokyo

Siegel T, Freyberg TV (1991) Industrielle Rationalisierung unter dem Nationalsozialisumus. Campus, Frankfurt am Main

Stahlmann M (1993) Die Erste Revolution in der Autoindustrie. Management und Arbeitspolitik von 1900–1940. Campus, Frankfurt am Main

Streeck W (1992) Social institutions and economic performance: studies of industrial relations in advanced capitalist economies. Sage, London

Streeck W (1997) German capitalism: do it exist? Can it survive? In: Crouch C, Streeck W (eds) Political economy of modern capitalism. Mapping convergence and diversity. Sage, London, pp 33–54

Sugaya A (1977) Roshikankei ron no kihon mondai (Fundamental problems of labor relations). Horitsu bunkasha, Kyoto

Takahashi K (1970) Nihonteki roshikankei no kenkyu (Study of Japanese labor relations), enlarged edn. Miraisha, Tokyo

Tanaka I (1985) Nihon ginko kinyu seisakushi (History of banking policy in Japan), enlarged edn. Yuhikaku, Tokyo

Thelen KA (1991) Union of parts. Labor politics in postwar Germany. Cornell University Press, Ithaca

Urabe K, Omura K (1983) Nihonteki roshikankei no tankyu (Exploration of Japanese labor relations). Chuo keizaisha, Tokyo

von Freyberg T (1989) Industrielle Rationalisierung in der Weimarer Republik: Untersucht an Beispielen aus dem Maschinenbau und der Elektroindustrie. Campus, Frankfurt am Main

Chapter 3
Business Management Characteristics in Japan and Germany

Abstract Chapter 2 looked at the overall system of business management as a structural framework for conditions that define the established methods of business management within the characteristics of capitalism as they are implemented in a specific country. Following the topics of the preceding chapter, this chapter examines fundamental characteristics of Japanese-style management and German-style management after the war, paying special attention to some important indicators such as long-term orientation or short-term orientation, profit orientation or growth orientation, emphasis on the rate of return of investment (ROI) or market share, production orientation or marketing orientation, production and technique orientation or financial earnings orientation, individualism or collectivism, emphasis on competition or cooperation, and shareholder or stakeholder orientation. It attempts to clarify key features of business management in each country by comparing them with those of the United States, the most influential management model postwar, and other European countries.

Keywords Collectivism · Individualism · Long-term orientation · Market share orientation · Marketing orientation · Production orientation · Professionalism · Profit orientation · Shareholder orientation · Short-term orientation · Stakeholder orientation

Based on the previous discussions in Chap. 2, this chapter compares the fundamental characteristics of management in Japan and Germany after World War II with those in the United States and other major European countries. In general, differences and characteristics of business management can be observed between countries, as well as commonalities. Following the war, various American management methods and systems were deployed in many countries as part of the productivity movement led by the United States and therefore, resulting in commonality of business management among many nations. However, Japanese or German business management styles and their specific characteristics, for example, were adapted to Japanese conditions or German and European conditions while retaining a country-specific management style.

T. Yamazaki, *Japanese and German Enterprises*,
https://doi.org/10.1007/978-981-97-4880-8_3

When comparing business management on a global scale, it is useful to employ a few key indicators. This chapter investigates essential features in Japan and Germany by employing some key indicators and grasping characteristics indicated in representative indicators from other countries. In this chapter's analysis, various indicators such as production orientation or marketing and market orientation, production and technique orientation or financial earnings orientation, profit orientation or growth orientation, emphasis on the rate of return of investment (ROI) or market share, long-term-oriented management or short-term-oriented management, shareholder orientation or stakeholder orientation, individualism or collectivism, generalism or specialism, existence or absence of professionalism, and emphasis on competition or cooperation. This chapter attempts to grasp fundamental characteristics of business management in Japan and Germany as indicated by these key indicators in comparison with those of other major countries.

First, in Sect. 3.1, commonalities in business management are considered among major countries such as Japan, Germany, the United States, and other European nations, as well as those between Japan and Germany. Based on the analysis in Sect. 3.1, in Sects. 3.2 and 3.3, fundamental characteristics of business management in Japan and Germany are compared with those in the United States. These discussions will clarify the general characteristics of business management in each country after the war.

3.1 Commonalities of Business Management Among Major Countries

This section compares postwar characteristics of Japanese-style management and German-style management with those of American-style management and other European countries.

As Dominique Turcq points out, among the various indicators useful for understanding the similarities and differences in business management in each country, "shareholders and managers' perspectives are often drastically different for US and European companies, resulting in differing practical implications of how they manage change in Europe." These differences between US and European firms can be attributed to "differing *stakeholder* interests." The fact that European companies are forced to consider factors such as stakeholder or constituent interests, which determines commonality indicated by stakeholder orientation, long-term orientation, and emphasis on growth and market share among European nations as opposed to shareholder orientation, short-term orientation, and emphasis on profit in the United States (Turcq 1994, p. 98; Calori 1994, p. 22). However, this is generally true for continental Europe rather than the United Kingdom. Whereas continental European CEOs frequently have technical backgrounds and pursue careers in production and engineering, "senior British managers are more likely to have accounting and finance backgrounds" (Edfelt 2010, p. 95). Such similarities among continental European nations, as well as the differences between these countries and the United Kingdom, are deeply concerned with managers' time orientation and goals.

Meanwhile, some similarities can be found in business management in the United States and the United Kingdom (Turcq 1994, p. 83; Calori 1994, p. 20). Floris Maljers who was chairman of Unilever's management board, emphasized that "the British in many respects have management habits which are more related to the American than those on the continent." According to Baron Daniel Janssen, who was chairman of Solvay's executive committee, "the British, like the Americans, are more oriented towards short-term and quick financial profits than the Germans, or even the other nationalities on the continent" (Calori and Dofour 1995, p. 61). In both the United States and the United Kingdom, enterprises tend to orient toward short-term profit, shareholder interests, and financial results as a result of the trend to rely on direct financing through the issuance of stocks (Cassis 1997, p. 177) and the strong pressure of capital market development not seen in other countries. Manager turnover is high due to the external labor market for executives and remuneration for top management is much higher than in other countries such as Germany and Japan, which promotes and forces the short-term management (Calori and Dofour 1995, pp. 44, 61–62, 65, 67, 69; Calori 1994, pp. 13–15, 22; Edfelt 2010, pp. 44, 61, 65; Turcq 1994, p. 98; Barsoux and Lawrence 1991, p. 199).

Individualism is also an important characteristic of management in the United States and the United Kingdom. American and British managers place a strong emphasis on individual's well-being as the foundation of their value sense (Hampden-Turner and Trompenaars 1993, p. 13), which is deeply concerned with specialization and thorough individual responsibility for job and performance. An individual who strives for excellence is oriented and required in both countries (Hampden-Turner and Trompenaars 1993, p. 355).

Management in Japan and Germany share similar paradigms such as organized competition, long-term orientation, stakeholder orientation, high investment, stable capital structures, a sense of community, and employee loyalty to the firm (Calori 1994, pp. 15, 27). For a long time after the war, the strong trend toward indirect financing based on bank credit served as an important foundation for stakeholder-oriented management because of the slow development of capital markets. Collectivism is also a distinguishing feature of Japanese and German management. For Japanese, German, and French managers, their value senses are first built on the basis of group well-being, and attention can be paid to an individual after satisfying the group's necessity (Hampden-Turner and Trompenaars 1993, p. 13). However, there are some significant differences between the two countries.

Among the above-mentioned characteristics observed between some countries in determining characteristics of business management, whether management in a specific country is shareholder or stakeholder oriented is an important issue closely related to the corporate governance system. This is also deeply concerned with the problem of the value concept, which is heavily emphasized in management.

3.2 Characteristics of Japanese Business Management

One of the characteristics of Japanese management is the emphasis on long-term growth, quality, integration, and consensus, whereas in the United States, management is oriented toward competition, profit orientation, professionalism, and individualism (Calori and Seidel 1994, p. 73). While tough competition and shareholders who control top management in the United States force companies to focus on short-term profits, Japanese companies focus on long-term growth, sometimes at the expense of short-term profitability (Calori and Dofour 1995, p. 69). Management philosophies and practices in the United States and Japan are frequently characterized as two extremes on several dimensions, such as the United States' short-term profit orientation versus the Japanese long-term growth orientation (Calori and Dofour 1995, p. 67). Whereas managerial professionalism in the United States is reflected in high managerial mobility between employers (Edfelt 2010, p. 44) and short-term orientation in US companies is attributable in part to high managerial mobility (Edfelt 2010, p. 61), internal promotion system in Japanese enterprises is inextricably linked with management's long-term orientation and corporate expansion emphasizing market share. One of the peculiar advantages of Japanese enterprises is that they design long-term strategies and consistently aim for growth rather than profit. Japanese firms strive to gain market share until other firms, as competitors, cease competing and withdraw from the market of competitors (Hampden-Turner and Trompenaars 1993, p. 135). Such efforts are supported by industrial groups comprised of large enterprises from a variety of industrial sectors. Each group's member companies worked hard to increase market share rather than maximize profit in each business unit (Hampden-Turner and Trompenaars 1993, p. 191). In contrast, US businesses place a premium on profit, profit per share, and return on investment (ROI) (Hampden-Turner and Trompenaars 1993, p. 182). In the United States, ROI is regarded as criterion for judging the value of businesses, and allocating investment to business that will generate the greatest profit using ROI is pursued (Sloan 1990, p. 50). In Japan and Europe, enterprises were able to implement longer-term strategies supported by patient capital financing based on long-term relationships between bank and company, which explains why manufacturing industries in Japan outperformed their counterparts in the United States (Amable 2003, p. 20).

For a US firm, shareholder value is the sole criterion for success; as a result, corporate decisions are centered on maximizing earnings, returns, or some other measure of value (Turcq 1994, p. 98). Indeed, since the 1990s, there has been increasing pressure on the shareholder value-oriented American management model and corporate governance system. Convergence into such American system, however, is not always seen in Japan.

Collectivism is another important feature of Japanese management. Clearly, the Japanese have a strong collective orientation (Calori and Dofour 1995, p. 69). Whereas in the United States, functionalism is emphasized, in Japan, social relationships are emphasized (Hampden-Turner and Trompenaars 1993, p. 110). The Japanese ensure quality by creating the whole from individual parts, and quality is a non-negotiable factor in all production processes under such thinking (Hampden-Turner and Trompenaars 1993, p. 120). Workers are encouraged to develop a variety of skills, allowing the team to take on significant responsibility and solve problems of their own. Cooperative collectivism served as an important foundation for the elastic personnel arrangement and the flexible formation of work organization under the labor relation system based on lifetime employment, the seniority-focused wage system, and the company union. It also promoted management methods that emphasized roles and autonomy on the production site, which were closely related to Japanese-style small group activities like the QC circle and the suggestion system. In contrast, in US businesses, the results to be achieved by each individual are predetermined and specified in the job description (Hampden-Turner and Trompenaars 1993, p. 126). The strongest individualism of US managers implies that an individual is regarded as a fundamental unit and the source of all company's successes, and this value concept is embedded in the American way of creating wealth (Hampden-Turner and Trompenaars 1993, p. 48). On the other hand, "European companies tend to balance individualism and collectivism" (Calori and Dofour 1995, p. 69).

In terms of competition, the Japanese are said to struggle with "controlled competition." It is a collaborative competition (Hampden-Turner and Trompenaars 1993, p. 129). While Japanese firms learn how to differentiate, improve, and evaluate products and manufacturing processes through competition, they grasp and introduce what is considered best and how to promote its application through competition (Hampden-Turner and Trompenaars 1993, p. 130).

3.3 Characteristics of German Business Management

German enterprises' production orientation is one of the most prominent characteristics of business management and it is instilled "by education and training at all hierarchical levels and thus is diffused right through the enterprise" (Lane 1989, p. 98). "The production-oriented German style has an inbuilt integrating focus which provides a common basis for relationships and encourages cooperative attitudes" (Lane 1989, p. 103). The cooperative works culture is fostered not only by the training system, but also by the industrial relations system, particularly by the works council. The autonomy and responsibility fostered by work organization are paralleled and enhanced by a participative industrial relations style based on a codetermination system (Lane 1989, p. 298). "A production-orientation also implies a concern for, and pride in, a high-quality product with which the firm becomes identified" (Lane 1989, p. 99; Smyser 1992, p. 68). Values, according to the Germans, should be deeply embedded in products with high true worth (Hampden-Turner and Trompenaars 1993, p. 213). A production-oriented economy implies an emphasis on the manufacturing industry, and this sector is further emphasized by the fact that Germany specializes in capital goods, particularly machinery for the production process (Hampden-Turner and Trompenaars 1993, p. 209).

German managers are "specialists" in a specific field (Lane 1989, p. 92), whereas Japanese managers are "generalists" who are developed through "internal job rotation" and British top managers consider themselves to be "generalists" (Calori 1994, pp. 15, 28). German managers are typically specialized and technically oriented (Calori and Seidel 1994, p. 63). Germans are technically savvy, with "technical understanding widespread among German managers" (Barsoux and Lawrence 1991, p. 203). The dynamics of professional management were not emphasized for the Germans, implying not generalism but specialism, particularly technical specialism (Lawrence 1994, p. 147). In comparison with other countries, Germany's "tendency to place engineers in top management positions" created "different values and attitudes that have been shaped over a long period of history" and which executives with technical backgrounds acquired through specialization and education. "The educational process, in particular, is critical in reproducing not only technical skills but also fundamental value orientations" (Lane 1989, pp. 100–101).

Leo McCann observed in 2014 that "top management in Germany has traditionally been dominated by doctorates in engineering, quite a contrast to the finance, legal and marketing-dominated MBAs that run US companies, meaning that German corporations are not market-focused enough" (McCann 2014, p. 176). German CEOs are more likely than their American counterparts to have engineering and technical backgrounds (Edfelt, 2010, p. 100). The ratio of managers with technical backgrounds in fields such as manufacturing, design, or service to all managers in Germany is high (Smyser 1992, p. 70).

All other countries were dominated by technical backgrounds in 1993 and top managers remained loyal to their technical traditions (Mayer and Whittington 1999, pp. 406–407). Despite significant internal and external pressures from the 1980s to the end of the 1990s, top management profiles in Germany changed very little, and German executives remained strongly focused on engineering (Mayer and Whittington 1999, p. 403). German executives are more likely to believe that well-made products will be purchased confidently and eagerly, and they place a premium on customer satisfaction (Smyser 1992, p. 68; Lawrence 1980, p. 94; Lawrence 1994, p. 148).

Production and related functions are the organizational hub of establishments in Germany, where there is a much greater emphasis on the utilization of shopfloor expertise than in other countries such as the United Kingdom (Lane 1992, p. 85). The functional approach to human development is used in Germany (Klarfeld 2004, p. 651). Management education influences not only the levels and nature of technical competence, but also managerial identity and value orientations (Lane 1992, p. 71). Long-term, internal development of managers within the firm, aided by technically specific qualifications, is prioritized in the German model (Klarfeld 2004, p. 655). Promotion in the German enterprise follows a functionally specialized path and "cross-functional retraining is relatively rare" (Lane 1989, p. 92). The prestige of vocational education and training is high, as is the homogeneity of competence and orientation within the firm (Lane 1992, p. 75). An important component of the German management system is a focus on vocational training (Dickson 2015, p. 15). Due to social harmony and low rate of employee turnover in the Rheinland

and Japanese models of capitalism, the contribution of investment in education and training to company profit is ensured (Hampden-Turner and Trompenaars 1993, p. 367).

"Made in Germany" is "an important component of both German firms' competitive advantage and German national identity" (see Head 1992, a book cover). The competitiveness of German manufacturing enterprises can be seen to be derived from two core institutional complexes: "the system of vocational education and training" and "the system of industrial relations." This type of education and training system not only produced "high levels of technical skill throughout the industrial enterprise," but also "a homogeneity of skills at all levels of the hierarchy" (Lane 1989, p. 298). Employers' investments in training have yielded significant returns in terms of worker productivity and commitment to quality production. Greater commitment had been secured by increased job security negotiated by German workers (Lane 1989, p. 299). Labor relations in postwar Germany, on the other hand, differ from those in the Anglo-Saxon countries in that they are more strictly regulated. Employee involvement in management is an important feature of labor relations (Lawrence 1994, p. 140). "Historically, European managers were forced to negotiate due to the strength of the labor unions in order to avoid or manage labor conflicts, which consume a significant amount of management time" (Calori and Dofour 1995, p. 64). "Rather than being a method of sharing power, Codetermination generates intense communication flows" (Calori 1994, p. 26). In Germany, the codetermination system stimulated communication and dialogue (Calori and Dofour 1995, p. 64).

German firms generally competed on quality rather than price, pursuing incremental product and process improvements to maintain market share in high-value domestic and export markets (McCann 2014, p. 169). Price competition is something they dislike. In Germany, businesses compete in niche markets for market share rather than market control. German managers at all levels of management focus their efforts on two goals: product quality and product service. Customer satisfaction is prioritized by managers (Smyser 1992, p. 68; Lawrence 1994, p. 148). Germany became well-known for its export-led, high-quality manufacturing industries, with the products of its cutting-edge multinationals, "recognized the world over for dependability, safety, attractive design and build quality" (McCann 2014, pp. 145, 165). Export products became well-known for their durability, high build quality, and dependability. "German companies had been successful in differentiating their products" (Calori 1991, p. 193). In contrast to Germany, Japanese businesses place a premium on product quality, as evidenced by the low defective rate of parts and product breakdown. These are not the same as product functionality and durability factors that German companies tend to emphasize. There are several strong competitors differentiated in the higher segment of the German automobile industry. German car manufacturing had been at the top of the industry for a long time (Calori 1991, pp. 191–192). In Europe, two historical trends have emerged: (1) the homogenization of purchasing behavior and (2) customers' specific thinking and emphasis on product quality (Atamer and Johnson 1991, p. 225). German enterprises' differentiation strategy is appropriate for the market characteristics of European markets.

Whereas American and British firms are more focused on short-term and immediate financial profits than German firms (Calori and Dofour 1995, pp. 61, 68; Calori 1994, pp. 14–15), the long-term orientation of German firms can be seen in "the priority of industrial goals over short-term financial objectives" (Calori 1994, p. 26). Unlike Americans, Germans reject the notion that profit is the "only true goal of a company" (Hampden-Turner and Trompenaars 1993, p. 212). Long-term, trusted relationships with banks and insurers that provide "patient" capital have traditionally been maintained by German firms (McCann 2014, p. 145). Patient capital enables "the institutionalization of processes of continuous improvement, long-term careers, training and skill certification, as well as the promotion of a productivist culture in which staff and managers at all levels of the firm shape deep knowledge of the company's products and services" in addition to Germany-specific production concept known as "diversified quality production" (McCann 2014, p. 168. As to diversified quality production, see Abelshauser 2003; Streeck 1992, 1997). This trend has encouraged German businesses to be more long-term oriented. European firms are often forced to consider a slew of other factors in addition to stakeholder or constituent interests, which can stymie profit maximization, at least in the short run (Turcq 1994, p. 98). This is also true for Germany.

"Long-term cooperative relationships between employers and employees, producers and customers, and, most importantly, between different firms within the same industry" characterize the German production regime. The dominance of craft-based flexible production with skilled labor, the high share of engineers in management, strong vertical integration and regional clusters, the instrumental role of banks in investment planning and financing, and the high service content of industrial quality products were the building blocks of this architecture (Vonyó 2018, p. 141). The German production regime is an important component that supports "diversified quality production" and has contributed to German manufacturers' competitive advantage. Germany's strength can be seen in the capital goods industry, where tightly structured interrelationships between suppliers, industries, labor unions, and customers are built (Hampden-Turner and Trompenaars 1993, pp. 98–99).

In this chapter, the fundamental characteristics of postwar business management in Japan and Germany are clarified through comparison with the United States and other European countries. However, given the evolution of business management and corporate expansion, how each nation's unique management characteristics have emerged and how they are reflected in basic management characteristics clarified in this chapter in processes such as the deployment of American management methods and the establishment of an industrial concentration system are important research topics. As a result, in the Americanization process of business management, in addition to essential features grasped by various important indicators analyzed in this chapter, it is critical to elucidate how Japanese or German business management styles and their particular characteristics were created under Japanese conditions or German and European conditions while still retaining a country-specific management style. Part III and Chap. 14 of this book will go over such research topics in depth. These analyses seek to answer the following questions: "What are the issues arising from Japanese and German methods of conforming to American methods?"

and "How did traditional and cultural factors in business management, as well as institutional factors, influence the development of American management methods, and how do they relate to the structural characteristics of Japanese capitalism or German capitalism?".

Furthermore, as evidenced by the shift toward American shareholder-value management model and a capital market-oriented corporate governance system, tremendous changes in enterprise circumstances have occurred since the 1990s as a result of the globalization and the Americanization of business management processes. Such movements have resulted in a shift in the characteristics of business management in each country. As a result, understanding current conditions and significance of changes is critical. This research topic will be discussed further in Chap. 14.

References

Abelshauser W (2003) Kulturkamp. Der deutsche Weg in die neue Wirtschaft und die amerikanische Herausforderung. Kulturverlag Kadmos, Berlin

Amable B (2003) The diversity of modern capitalism. Oxford University Press, Oxford

Atamer T, Johnson G (1991) Conclusions. In: Roland C, Lawrence P (eds) The business of Europe. Managing change. SAGE, London, pp 218–229

Barsoux J-L, Lawrence P (1991) Countries, cultures and constraints. In: Calori R, Lawrence P (eds) The business of Europe. Managing change. SAGE, London, pp 198–217

Calori R (1991) Markets and managers. In: Calori R, Lawrence P (eds) The business of Europe. Managing change. SAGE, London, pp 167–217

Calori R (1994) The diversity of management systems. In: Calori R, Woot P de (eds) A European management model. Beyond diversity. Prentice Hall, New York, Tokyo, pp 11–30

Calori R, Dofour B (1995) Management European style. In: Acad Manag Exec 9(3):61–73

Calori R, Seidel F (1994) The dynamics of management systems in Europe. In: Calori R, Woot P de (eds) A European management model. Beyond diversity. Prentice Hall, New York, Tokyo, pp 55–78

Cassis YF (1997) Big business. The European experience in the twentieth century. Oxford University Press, New York

Dickson T (2015) A model of co-operation: management European business: as the 'European way' comes under pressure from shareholder value economics. In: Financial Times, 13 April 2000, p 15

Edfelt RB (2010) Global comparative management. A functional approach. SAGE, Thousand Oaks

Hampden-Turner C, Trompenaars A (1993) The seven cultures of capitalism: value systems for creating wealth in the United States, Japan, Germany, France, Britain, Sweden, and the Netherlands. Currency and Doubleday, New York

Head D (1992) Made in Germany. The corporate identity of a nation. Hodder & Stoughton, London

Klarfeld A (2004) Christopher Mabey, management development in Europe: do national models persist? In: Eur Manag J 22(6):649–657

Lane C (1989) Management and labour in Europe. The industrial enterprise in Germany, Britain and France. Eduard Elgar, Aldeshot

Lane C (1992) European business systems: Britain and Germany compared. In: Whittley R (ed) European business systems. Firms and markets in their national contexts. SAGE, London, pp 64–97

Lawrence P (1980) Managers and management in West Germany. Croom Helm, London

Lawrence P (1994) German management: at the interface between Eastern and Western Europe. In: Calori R, Woot P de (eds) A European management model. Beyond diversity, Prentice Hall, New York, pp 133–163
McCann L (2014) International and comparative foundations of political economics. SAGE, London
Mayer M, Whittington R (1999) Euro-elites: top Britisch, French and German managers in the 1980s and 1990s. In: Eur Manag J 17(4):403–408
Sloan Jr AP (1990) My years with general motors, (ed) McDonald J, Stevens C. Currency, Doubleday, New York
Smyser WR (1992) The economy of United Germany: colossus at crossroads. St. Martin's Press, New York
Streeck W (1992) Social institutions and economic performance: studies of industrial relations in advanced capitalist economies. Sage, London
Streeck W (1997) German capitalism: do it exist? Can it survive? In: Crouch C, Streeck W (eds) Political economy of modern capitalism. Mapping convergence and diversity. Sage, London, pp 33–54
Turcq D (1994) Is there a US company management style in Europe? In: Roland C, Woot P de (eds) A European management model. Beyond diversity, Prentice Hall, New York, Tokyo, pp 82–110
Vonyó T (2018) The Economic consequences of the war. West Germany's growth miracle after 1945. Cambridge University Press, Cambridge

Part II
System of Postwar Industrial Concentration

Chapter 4
Structures and Functions of Large Corporate Groups

Abstract Part II considers the development of a new system of industrial concentration after World War II. In this part, new developments in the system of large corporate groups and industrial systems based on industry–bank relationships as an issue of industrial concentration closely tied to the characteristics of Japanese capitalism and German capitalism will be examined. This chapter discusses the development of a new system of industrial concentration post WWII in relation to large corporate group systems. Post WWII, large corporate group systems evolved during the dissolution and reconcentration of monopolies in Japan and Germany. They have played an important role in postwar development of corporation and Japanese and German capitalism's accumulation structures. Therefore, this chapter considers the restructuring of a system for large corporate groups in relation to the dissolution of monopolies under the occupation policy and their reconcentration after the war. First, it examines the dissolution of monopolies by victorious nations such as the United States and its influence. Next, it analyzes the reconcentration of monopolies beginning in the 1950s and new developments in the system of large corporate groups that accompanied reconcentration. Drawing on this discussion, this chapter explains the manner in which large business operations were restructured through reconcentration or concentration, and the characteristics and significance of the system of large corporate groups.

Keywords Deconcentration policy · Industrial concentration · Inter-firm relationship · Large corporate groups · Reconcentaration of monopolies

Both Germany and Japan as defeated nations in the World War II developed their enterprises, industries, and economy by establishing their own systems of industrial concentration while deploying and adapting technology and management methods from the USA. By these means, both nations became major trading countries. Industrial concentration exhibited new postwar developments.

In Part II, inter-firm relationships are considered as problems that were deeply connected with those of postwar Japanese and German business management. When examining industrial concentration, the cooperative mechanisms for corporations

T. Yamazaki, *Japanese and German Enterprises*,
https://doi.org/10.1007/978-981-97-4880-8_4

are the most characteristic manifestation of corporate group systems, particularly in relation to ties between industries and banks. As the cornerstones of Japanese and German capitalism's accumulation structures, they were important processes for postwar corporate development in both nations. Industry–bank relationships were found before the war and emerged in the postwar era as a new development in the industrial system; they served as a cooperative system between industries and banks as well as among corporations themselves. The reconcentration of monopolies, which were dissolved as part of the postwar occupation policy, and the corporate group systems progressed apace. Therefore, Part II examines this new development in the system of corporate groups and the industrial systems based on industry–bank relationships and clarifies the structures, characteristics, and significance of the system of industrial concentration in Japan and Germany after World War II.

The restructuring of corporate group systems will be discussed in this chapter, as will the characteristics and significance of the new industrial concentration system in postwar Japan and Germany.[1] For corporate group systems, the postwar occupation policy dissolved the concentration of monopolies and catalyzed new developments in large corporate groups through the reorganization of business structures that were adaptive to oligopolistic competition; it was not simply a return of the prewar structure. Thus, this chapter examines the internal restructuring of corporate group systems that formed the cornerstone of new developments in postwar industrial concentration.

Section 4.1 examines the deconcentration of monopolies by victorious nations, such as the United States, and their influence in Japan and Germany. Sections 4.2 and 4.3 consider the reconcentration of monopolies and new developments in the system of large corporate groups that accompanied reconcentration in Japan and Germany, respectively. The characteristics and significance of these new developments are clarified in Sect. 4.4 on the basis of these discussions.

4.1 Influence of the US Deconcentration Policy on Monopolies in Japan and Germany

4.1.1 Influence of the US Deconcentration Policy on Monopolies in Japan

First, the influence of the US deconcentration policy on monopolies is considered. As E M. Hadley pointed out, "the United States position, which became the Allied position, called for the removal of the *zaibatsu* families from their position of business power and severing the tie—ownership, personnel, credit, contracts—which bound the component corporations into combine structure" (Hadley 1970, p. 10). In prewar

[1] The first content analysis related to Germany in this chapter is Chap. 5 of the author's book "*German Business Management: A Japanese Perspective on Regional Development Factors*," which was published by Springer in 2013.

Japan, major corporations in each business sector, including banks, were part of the *zaibatsu* families and *zaibatsu* parent (holding) companies. Although corporate stocks were publicly traded, the percentage of shares held by *Zaibatsu* families was high. As a result, dissolution was focused on *zaibatsu* parent companies and certain major corporations and *zaibatsu* stocks were released to the market; however, banks were not included in these dissolutions. The prohibition of holding companies and regulation of treasury stock acquisitions and ownership formed six industrial groups (Maekawa 1997, pp. 23, 58–59, 247, 263–264; Miyamoto et al. 2007, pp. 246–249; Okumura 1976, pp. 21; Miyazaki 1966, pp. 221–222, 227–228).

The release of stocks almost completely dismantled not only the stockholding structure but also the rule of affiliated companies based on the stockholdings of large independent enterprises. For the direct-descendant company of the *zaibatsu*, such a measure brought about the liberalization of personnel rights in the affiliated companies under the direct control of the main office headquarters, the loss of stable shareholders, the disappearance of the means for interest adjustment, and the exchange of information among the affiliated companies due to the dissolution of the head office (Miyajima 1992, pp. 206–210; Miyamoto et al. 2007, pp. 250–251).

However, banks were not the object of the dissolution; that is, financing relations between banks and industrial enterprises of the *zaibatzu* were not cut off by the dismantling of the *zaibatsu*. Instead, such relations served as a basis for establishing large corporate groups in the postwar period. The continuation of trade relations primarily based on the financing relations of banks was one reason why the interlocking shareholdings between companies that belonged to the same *zaibatsu* group occurred and the overall framework of the large corporate groups was maintained through versatile ties, including trade relationships and the human connection between companies (Kudo 1982, pp. 212–213, 223).

The continuation of such a framework also had an important meaning for reconcentration in the form of industrial groups. The greater emphasis placed on financial institutions' stockholdings, compared with that on industrial enterprises' stockholdings, and the increase in the dependency of industrial enterprises on financial institutions of the same group demonstrated the important position and role of financial institutions in the reorganization process of postwar corporate groups (Giga 1958, p. 366). Meanwhile, most of the operating departments, which were managed by the constituent company under the influence of the *zaibatsu*, were maintained, rather than dissolved. Thus, the affiliated companies that were free from the rule of the financial combine family (*zaibatsu* family) were reorganized through horizontal and equal combination. The situation in which banks were retained without being dismantled had a significant role in such reorganization (Okumura 1976, pp. 39–43).

Finally, an important characteristic of the United States' policy toward Japan was that it aimed to maintain monopolistic industrial enterprises and banks, despite the discontinuation of the Japanese form of capital combination, such as the ownership and retention of control structures by the holding company as a parent company in the *zaibatsu* group (Suzuki 1993, p. 49). An important reason for the adoption of such a policy was the fact that the US policy in Asia aimed at resurrecting Japanese enterprises. Therefore, the major companies and large banks that were under the influence of the *zaibatsu* but were nevertheless retained became the leading figures in the postwar big business system. In addition, the condition that both entities were to be directly combined was established (Suzuki 2008, p. 27).

4.1.2 Influence of the US Deconcentration Policy on Monopolies in Germany

4.1.2.1 Expansion of Monopoly Deconcentration Policy

Following that, the dissolution of monopolies by victorious nations and its impact on Germany are investigated. In terms of monopoly deconcentration policy, the United States believes that excessive German economic and political power should be curtailed through monopoly dissolution and decartelization (Schlieper 1986, p. 156). The basic policy goal was to transform Germany into an oligopolistic market based on the competition principle, very similar to that of the United States (Berghahn 1985, p. 280; Djelic 1998, p. 167).

The dissolution of the coal and the iron and steel industries had a significant impact on these industries (Berghahn 1986, pp. 95, 110). The eight large corporate groups in the heavy industries were eventually divided into 23 steel companies. The steel division of Vereinigte Stahlwerke AG was divided into 13 separate enterprises, three of which were allocated to the coal sector, one to processing, and one to trading (Fiereder 1989, p. 237; Uebbing 1991, p. 55). Krupp's main plant, the Friedrich–Alfred–Hutte iron works, was split up and dissolved into two separate companies, Hüttenwerk Rheinhausen AG and Essener Kruppzechen [*Historisches Archiv Krupp*, WA70/1, Headquarters Military Government L/K MOERS (15.10.1945), p. 1; Der Volkswirt 1954b, p. 24]. Previously, Krupp had been able to globally produce superior products in both quality and price through its effective cooperation and complementary functioning with materials industries and processing plants. However, its ties to these stages of production were severed, and the company underwent significant change because of the destruction of such ties (Der Volkswirt 1954a, p. 49; Der Volkswirt 1956c, pp. 28, 30). Among other large enterprises, this type of dissolution also occurred at Mannesmann, Hoesch, and Gutehoffnung, (Der Volkswirt 1952a, pp. 24–25; Der Volkswirt 1953b, p. 23; Der Volkswirt 1952b, pp. 23–24; Der Volkswirt 1954c, p. 24; Der Volkswirt 1953a, p. 21). However, West Germany strongly opposed the occupation forces' plan to completely separate the coal industry from the iron and steel industries, and the parallel management of both iron and steel and coal companies was permitted with a maximum limit of 75% coke consumption (Tohara 1974, p. 141).

The chemical firm IG Farben was also dissolved, resulting in a restructured oligopoly of three main companies: BASF, Bayer, and Hoechst (Vgl. Kleinkamp 1977; Gross 1950). Major changes in capital relationships also occurred. The banking sector was divided into 30 small-scale regional banks, with specific bank operations restricted to a single state region (Pohl 1986, pp. 102–104; Djelic 1998; Stolper et al. 1964, pp. 227–228). Despite these dissolutions and restructurings, the universal banking system was preserved, which has a critical factor in the new development of the industrial system based on industry–bank relationships.

4.1.2.2 Significance of Monopoly Dissolution and Restructuring

The dissolution of large enterprises was a huge setback to the corporations; nevertheless, it was also an opportunity for monopolistic companies to undergo a rationalized process of restructuring. For instance, in the case of Vereinigte Stahlwerke, dissolution provided an opportunity to restructure as a large enterprise with a scope appropriate for management, with a functional monopoly or oligopolistic system. In addition, IG Farben was able to liquidate an immovable, excessive group in order to create a functional, large corporate group with a more rational structure that responded to postwar technological reforms while allowing them to pioneer new areas and expand their base (Tohara 1974, pp. 145–147). The US proposal for organizational restructuring of the coal and iron and steel industries, which accompanied the dissolution of monopolies, attempted to rationalize these industries, thus cutting down costs and improving efficiency while increasing production (Berghahn 1986, pp. 90, 95, 108–109; Djelic 1998, p. 166). US postwar reforms primarily focused on market restructuring by terminating monopolies and cartels and the achievement of economies of scale (Herrigel 2000, p. 361).

For example, during the monopoly dissolution process in the iron and steel industry, a significant amount of production capacity was allocated to other steel production units. As a result, components of the industry's rolling mill capacity spread throughout the entire industry rather than within a single corporation. This type of production capacity allocation created oligopolistic conditions, which not only increased the cost of diversification but also created potential incentives for corporate growth by increasing in the scale of corporate rolling mills (Herrigel 2000, p. 364). Through a policy of dissolution, the prewar structure of domestic markets was replaced by an oligopolistic structure, and previously existing monopolies and specialization were displaced by mass production (Herrigel 2000, pp. 352–353, 368). Significantly, the dissolution and restructuring of the heavy industries resulted in greater control of the machine department. Krupp, Gutehoffnung, Klöckner, and other large corporations demonstrated and laid the groundwork for the rapid development of the heavy machinery sector (Sasaki 1975, p. 65). Such industrial restructuring laid the groundwork for the expansion of corporate activities suitable for oligopolistic competition, which differed from the prewar German iron and steel industry structure, industrial organization, and market structure assumptions.

IG Farben's dissolution in the chemical industry revived inter-firm relationships in the same form taken before the company was created. However, in response to the shift from coal to petroleum chemistry, a unique, multifaceted industrial complex was created to produce synthetic rubber, synthetic resins, synthetic fibers, and other petroleum-based products, resulting in the industry's three giants. This was not simply a return to prewar conditions, but rather a rational restructuring that resulted in a more competitive inter-corporate structure (Kudo 1999, p. 378). The resolutions resulted in two achievements: (1) the chemical market was restructured along competitive lines and (2) new and sufficiently large-scale units were established to serve as an engine useful for the rebuilding and growth of Western Europe, as well as survival in the multilateral liberal capitalistic world trade system dominated by the United States (Berghahn 1986, p. 95).

Thus, the restructuring of corporate organizations to their prewar form was not the primary objective; rather, it was to create resilient trust structures (Maekawa 1970, pp. 147–148). The latter half of the 1950s was the reconcentration of monopolies, and next topic to be discussed is new developments in the system of large corporate groups.

4.2 New Developments in the System of Large Corporate Groups in Japan

These foregoing discussions lead to new developments in the system of large corporate groups in Japan. After World War II, while six large industrial groups, comprising companies in numerous industries, banks, and general trading companies, were formed, the grouping of the company in the affiliate of the same capital by enterprises belonging to each industrial group or the independent company also occurred. Accordingly, a multilayered structure of grouping existed during the period. This implies that large corporate groups in Japan adopted the multilayered structure wherein big businesses having a vertical affiliate combine enjoyed equal relations (Kobayashi 1977b, p. 134). Therefore, these two types of combination of enterprise are examined.

4.2.1 Formation of the Six Industrial Groups and Their Industrial Concentrations

4.2.1.1 Characteristics of the Postwar Industrial Groups

First, the six industrial groups are analyzed. Dissolution of *Zaibatsu* parent companies and certain major corporations, the prohibition of holding companies, and regulation of treasury stock acquisitions and ownership were important methods of the formation of six industrial groups. In these industrial groups, enterprises were concentrated by interlocking stockholding and forming large corporations, which were horizontally rather than vertically joined within capital groups and had substantial holdings of other companies' stocks. The large corporate groups formed in postwar Japan spanned several industries, with industrial corporations, banks, and trading companies at its core. The industrial groups comprised a full set of industries and conducted financing, interlocking stockholding, mutual business transactions, and joint investments internally. Banks and trading companies played a significant role in this scheme. These groups coordinated among themselves through an organization, the Network of Presidents, with decisions primarily made be by those in a certain position, such as presidents of group companies (Maekawa 1997, pp. 23, 58–59, 247, 263–264; Miyamoto et al. 2007, pp. 246–249, 252–253; Okumura 1976, pp. 12, 21–23; Miyazaki 1966, pp. 221–222, 224–225, 227–228; Kikkawa 1992a, pp. 62–63, 69, 73, 77).

Industrial groups are organizations in which banks, general trading companies, and enterprises from different industries are combined according to their stockholding relationships. Each industrial group contained not only the corporation that was a member of presidents' clubs as core enterprises of the group but also other member enterprises (Okumura 1975a, pp. 164–165). The fact that banks and general trading companies are the core parts of industrial groups means that such groups could not function without them (Okumura 1975b, p. 324). In the industrial groups of the three old *zaibatsu* groups (the Mitsubishi Group, the Mitsui Group, and the Sumitomo Group), banks played an important role as the organizer of the regrouping process (Koyama and Dolles 1994, p. 424). In addition, the capital power of financial institutions was an important factor in determining the strengths and weaknesses of each group combination. Regarding this point, the Mitsui Group, for example, was at a disadvantage compared with the Mitsubishi Group or the Sumitomo Group (Nakamura 1968a, pp. 193, 196–197; Nakamura 1968b, pp. 173–174; Noguchi 1968, p. 18). Conversely, the non-*zaibatsu* groups, such as the Fuyo Group, the Sanwa Group, and the Daiichi Ginko Group, formed industrial groups through the cooperation between those banks and trading companies that were competing with the industrial group of the prewar old financial combine (Zaibatsu) (Suzuta 1976, pp. 13–14, 201). Regarding the role of banks, as seen in the example of Mitsubishi Bank, financial institutions (city banks in particular) became the core of the industrial groups, assuming two forms of control: (1) control as one of the largest shareholders; and (2) financial control (Сутягина 1973, p. 149).

In these industrial groups, corporations were able to use supplementary functions to bridge the gaps in organizational capabilities and corporate planning for entering new industries such as oil and nuclear power (Kikkawa 1991, p. 142; Kikkawa 1996, pp. 192–200; Mikami 1976, pp. 245, 253–255). Moreover, as seen in the coal mining and shipping industries, the industrial groups promoted the arrangement of the depressed industry by supporting entry into other industries and re-employing the surplus personnel from other companies of the same group in order to smoothen out the transformation of the industrial structure to a greater degree (Kikkawa 1996, pp. 200–206; Kikkawa 1992b, pp. 288–293).

Such industrial groupings effectively supported trade between industrial enterprises and financial institutions as well as that between financial institutions and trading companies. Furthermore, such groupings were used as a strategy for securing certain markets. Such merits of industrial groupings were reciprocal since each industrial group included many different industries (Shimada 2010, pp. 120–123). In Japan, the industrial groups were advantageous when dealing with non-member companies through insider trading between main member enterprises of the same group and the promotion of accumulation of capital (Sakamoto 1993, pp. 6–7). The industrial groups also performed additional functions such as reducing transaction costs, promoting the exchange of information, supporting risk sharing, and highlighting the merits of mutual trade (kikkawa 1996, pp. 22, 134, 148, 231). Among these types of industrial groups, interlocking shareholding stabilized shareholders (Kikkawa 1992a, p. 69). In corporate governance, Japanese banks and corporate groups functioned as a defense against external pressures by interlocking stockholdings within the groups. The following section examines the main methods of combining in industrial groups.

4.2.1.2 Interlocking Stockholdings and Their Significance

First, interlocking stockholdings are examined. New managers who were liberated from the control by the *zaibatsu* parent companies after the dissolution of the *zaibatsu* faced the possibility of being monitored by the stock market. This also promoted interlocking shareholdings in response to the risk of the stocks being cornered by large shareholders, which actually occurred because of the need for and purpose of stockholder stabilization. Moreover, financial institutions became the center of the cross-shareholdings in each group, whereas presidents' clubs (a network of presidents) helped with the adjustments in such defensive measures (Miyajima 1992, pp. 209–210, 245). Since financial holding companies were prohibited by the Anti-Monopoly Act in 1947, companies could only select the method of cross-stockholding as a means of combining ownership relations (Narusaka 1974, p. 74; Futatsuki 1976, pp. 51–57).

The fundamental function of industrial groups at the moment of their formation was the stabilization of stockholders (Kikkawa 1996, pp. 22, 142–143, 152, 229, 231). However, the method for establishing a stable shareholder structure through interlocking stockholdings was not necessarily limited to the cross-holdings between companies of the same group or between enterprises and banks of the same group. In addition, industrial groups were not always necessarily a form of mutual stockholdings between members of the industrial groups. Instead, they were created on the basis of the combination formed in order to secure the conditions of accumulation, which included loans to affiliated companies (Suzuki 1998, pp. 36–37). The interlocking shareholdings themselves were not stockholding structures peculiar to the industrial groups, but they were universal in the postwar big business system. The main reason why the stable shareholder structure was created in the form of industrial groups was because of reciprocal trading relations, which served as the basis for the cross-holdings of stocks. Annulus ring or matrix-type cross-holdings of stocks were formed among companies that were members of presidents' clubs. Moreover, general trading companies and large city banks acted as two main pillars in interlocking shareholdings. These points illustrate the distinctiveness of the interlocking stockholdings in the industrial groups after World War II (Suzuki 1998, pp. 104, 106–109, 112; Suzuki 2008, pp. 213–214; Okumura 1976, pp. 21, 108).

There were also differences in the time of formation of the industrial group between the old *zaibatzu* groups and the groups affiliated with the banks. This was because of the conditions surrounding the stockholdings of affiliated companies at the end of the war and the powerful effects of the dissolution of the *zaibatsu*. In the old *zaibatsu* groups, wherein most of the stock ownership was closed and the influence of the dissolution of the *zaibatsu* was larger, the formation of the industrial group occurred early (Kikkawa 1996, p. 147).

In the interlocking stockholdings within the industrial groups, additional funds were not necessary (at least for a certain part of the cross-shareholdings) since the purchase amount of stocks became the financial source for each partner company. Therefore, the purpose of stock ownership within the industrial groups did not rely on corporate financing function of stocks. In addition, the ratio of the stockholdings, in the form of cross-shareholdings that did not require funds, began to substantially increase after the 1960s (Futatsuki 1975, pp. 24–27). In general, the Japanese characteristics and the significance of interlocking stockholdings for the stabilization of shareholders relied on this point.

Participation in industrial groups enabled its member companies to avoid pressure from the stock market and secure management autonomy (Hashimoto 1992, pp. 12–13). The function of stabilizing shareholders in the industrial groups also made it easy for the salaried managers of member companies to choose the growth-oriented type of corporate strategy with a long-term view, thereby promoting such management (Kikkawa 1996, p. 133; Kikkawa 1995, p. 263). Although the ratio of the cross-holdings of stocks generally decreased after the mid-1950s, interlocking stockholdings were further strengthened in response to the liberalization of capital and the measure of stockholder stabilization that occurred after the mid-1960s (Kobayashi 1980, pp. 132–133; Kobayashi 1977a, pp. 85–86; Nakatani 1983, pp. 81–82; Nakatani 1984, p. 18; Sakamoto 1996, p. 207). Moreover, the liberalization of capital and the collapse of the stock market, as seen in the securities recession after 1965, promoted interlocking stockholdings and the formation of presidents' clubs in the industrial groups affiliated with banks. This formation was based on two points: the cohesion of the industrial groups and the release of stocks that were closed (Kyuno 1995, p. 42; Yoshida and Uchiyama 1970, p. 186).

In addition, financial institutions and trading companies included a high ratio of shareholdings in the industrial groups at the point of structure of the cross-shareholding, which reflected versatile linkages in regard to trade in the group. The concentration of stockholdings in the powerful companies in the group reflected the technological and industrial linkages among these companies (Kudo 1982, p. 235). In addition, there were many cases in which linkages in the trade between companies became an important premise of the cross-stockholdings. Such stockholdings reflected the degree of perfection required in the industrial linkages, which formed the foundations of certain interest groups, such as industrial groups (Suzuki 1993, p. 99). The fact that companies combined by the cross-shareholdings of stocks could compete for the purchase of raw materials had a significant meaning. The significance of the one-set principle of industrial groups also relied on this point (Futatsuki 1976, pp. 32–33, 60). Furthermore, the number of brands and stocks that the trading companies held overwhelmed those of the industrial companies. Even among the member firms of the industrial groups, banks and trading companies played significant roles in interlocking shareholdings. Such shareholdings in the industrial group were formed through the cross-shareholdings between banks and industrial enterprises and those between banks and trading companies (Suzuki 1993, p. 118).

For the Mitsubishi Group, the ratio of cross-stockholdings to all issued stocks in 1960, 1965, 1970, 1975, and 1980 (for 1960 and 1965, the numerical values are for the first half of each year; for 1970 and 1975, the numerical values are for September; and for 1980, the numerical value is for March) were 21.28%, 17.20%, 20.71%, 26.41%, and 26.15%, respectively. The relevant numerical values for the same years in the Mitsui Group were 11.59%, 10.04%, 14.14%, 17.23%, and 18.35%, respectively, and those for the Sumitomo Group were 22.17%, 18.79%, 21.83%, 24.71%, and 26.19%, respectively. Similarly, the relevant numerical figures for the same years in the Fuyo Group were 12.47%, 10.85%, 15.26%, 19.23%, and 19.06%, respectively, and those for Sanwa Group were 7.89%, 9.02%, 11.18%, 13.15%, and 11.74%, respectively. The numerical values for the same years in the Daiichi Kangyo Bank Group (for 1960, 1965, and 1970, the Daiichi Bank Group) were 13.37%, 10.26%, 17.19%, 16.76%, and 15.52%, respectively. The average ratios regarding the cross-shareholdings of the six industrial groups (i.e., Mitsubishi Group, Mitsui Group, Sumitomo Group, Fuyo Group, Sanwa Group, and Daiichi Kangyo Bank Group) were 14.79%, 12.69%, 16.72%, 19.58%, and 19.50%, respectively. Finally, the relevant numerical values regarding the averages of the three old *zaibatsu* groups in the same five years were 18.35%, 15.34%, 18.89%, 22.78%, and 23.56%, respectively, and those for the three non-*zaibatsu* groups were 11.24%, 10.04%, 14.54%, 16.38%, and 15.44%, respectively (Shadan hojin keizai chosa kyokai 1962, p. 96; Shadan hojin keizai chosa kyokai 1968, p. 12; Shadan hojin keizai chosa kyokai 1978, p. 9; Shadan hojin keizai chosa kyokai 1983, the general condision, p. 11).

4.2.1.3 Presidents' Clubs and Their Functions

Next, presidents' clubs are considered as the network of presidents in the industrial group. An arrangement was established before World War II whereby decision-making for the combined *zaibatsu* network overwhelmingly focused on the top holding company (Hadley 1970, p. 211). The dissolution of the *zaibatsu* parent (holding) companies represented the end of the communication between affiliated companies (Miyajima 1992, p. 210; Nakamura 1968a, p. 187; Nakamura 1968b, pp. 158–159). In addition, the exclusion of the *zaibatsu* enterprises' management and the purge of business leaders from their companies as a means of initiating an economic purge brought about a complete transformation of management activities. The Japanese business world also experienced a generational shift in management because of the removal of top business leaders of older generations. In this regard, many new managers of the postwar *zibatsu*-type companies were promoted from the ranks of middle management, such as factory manager and department head.

However, there were numerous cases in which new managers had not received sufficient training at the time of their promotions to top management. They also faced difficulties, such as issues related to the Excessive Economic Power Deconcentration Law, serious labor dispute, liquidity crisis, and crisis of management autonomy, after which they made efforts to create informal, mutual communication organizations in order to deal with these issues. Consequently, the presidents' clubs were formed to promote such communication between companies. In addition, fostering the abilities of managers promoted to top management was also deemed a critical task (Miyajima 1991, pp.139–140; Miyajima 1992, pp. 210–214). Furthermore, the establishment of the presidents' clubs was aimed at overcoming the lack of the leadership of new managers in industrial groups (Sakamoto 1991, p. 156).

In this regard, presidents' clubs were established as organizations that could coordinate autonomous cooperation between various companies (Hirai 2013, pp. 34–35). In the industrial groups, the exchange of information and coordination between member companies were performed through such coordinating organizations. In three old *zaibatsu* groups (i.e., Mitsubishi, Sumitomo, and Mitsui), presidents' clubs were formed on the basis of cross-shareholdings (Nakatani 1984, p. 18). In addition, financial institutions assumed important roles in the formation and functioning of these clubs. However, banks did not always an absolute advantage, even though financial institutions formed the core of the Network of Presidents (Miyazaki 1966, p. 225). Moreover, although industrial groups comprising full sets of industries were broadening, from the standpoint of inter-firm information sharing, the Network did not always adopt mechanisms that supported banks–industry relationships, as was the case in Germany.

Presidents' clubs were arbitrary organizations that did not intervene in decision-making processes of the affiliated direct-descendant companies of the *zaibatsu* parent company (Hashimoto 1992, pp. 1–2; Hashimoto 1991, pp. 160–161). Instead, presidents' clubs played various roles, such as establishing new businesses, securing the cooperation of the group in order to aid enterprises within the group that may be floundering in depressed industries, and ensuring harmony between all companies of the group (Morikawa 1993, p. 72). Moreover, presidents' clubs promoted economical rationality through information exchange as well as the adjustment of interests between member companies taking the existing uncertainty into consideration, with such rationality being secured by the interlocking stockholding as a system. These clubs eventually took charge of coordinating the logic between the individual companies and the industrial groups (Kudo 1982, p. 244) and fostering mutual confidence among the member companies (Sakuma 1995, p. 26). However, since each club was a representative of the enterprise and each member of the club enjoyed autonomy and equality, there was no hierarchical relationship. Thus, the possibility in which the decision-making processes of the industrial groups as a whole could transcend the interests of each company was low (Narusaka 1974, pp. 75–76).

The member firms of presidents' clubs played an important role as a "linking pin" that connected presidents' clubs as a core system of the industrial group (Nakamura 1994, p. 103). The determination of the functions of presidents' clubs invited much debate. Some perspectives claimed that these clubs were responsible for information gathering and exchange between member companies, whereas others held that they oversaw the adjustment of interests. Some opinions even considered their function was to lead unified decision-making processes (Miyazaki 1966, pp. 222, 225; Miyazaki 1976, pp. 63, 249–250; Okumura 1983, pp. 99, 102–103; Сутягина 1973, pp. 162–163; Kikuchi 2005, p. 3; Mikami 1976, p. 247; Sumiya 1982, pp. 123–124; Fukuda 1985, pp. 128–129). Since the minutes of presidents' club meetings were not published, it is difficult to clearly understand the functions of such organizations. However, presidents' clubs could not carry out the coordination of interests that extended beyond the scope of the industrial group.

4.2.1.4 Loan to Affiliated Companies in the Industrial Groups

Next, loans to affiliated companies in the industrial group are examined. Since problems of such financing systems as an important means of securing industry–bank relationships under the main banking system will be analyzed in Chap. 3, this subsection analyzes the characteristics and significance of such a financing system as a measure of forming industrial groups and combining member companies within the groups. Industrial groups were led by large city banks, which also controlled financing businesses that supported the combining of enterprises. In this regard, the loans to the affiliated companies of industrial groups played important roles in forming certain relationships of the combination between companies (Kudo 1982, p. 230). The relationships between large city banks and industrial enterprises strengthened because of the loans to affiliated companies, and the system of the predominance of the banks progressed rapidly. Meanwhile, the relationships between the interlocking stockholdings and the personnel connections were also strengthened by such a financing system, and the unity of the company in industrial groups was reinforced (Uno 1972, p. 7). Thus, the banks eventually assumed pivotal positions among industrial groups of the old *zaibatsu* companies. The continuation of loans to affiliated companies of the same group reinforced not only the cross-shareholding relationships between the member companies of such groups but also the personnel connections through the dispatch of directors and presidents' clubs in the old *zaibatsu* industrial groups. Such a financing system also spread into the enterprises of non-*zaibatsu* groups as the changes regarding the industrial structure of heavy and chemical industries advanced. As a result, large banks of non-*zaibatsu* groups such as Fuji Bank, Sanwa Bank, and Daiichi Bank also promoted the formation of industrial groups through loans to affiliated companies (Uno 1972, pp. 7, 9).

Securing trade networks and ensuring the effective use of loans to member companies from the large banks of the same industrial groups highlighted the concentration of financing of the same old *zaibatsu* enterprises as well as the lending competition between such banks (Kudo 1994, p. 31). Compared with other banks, six large city banks of the industrial groups stood out in the loans provided to various companies, especially in regard to listed companies, the number of affiliated companies, and the number of dispatched directors. However, besides the central role of the city banks within the industrial groups, the trust banks and the life insurance companies also played important roles in the reinforcement of city banks' financial power to enterprises in the groups (Sumiya 1982, pp. 114–115; Okumura 1976, pp. 120–121; Hadley 1970, p. 232; Nakatani 1984, p. 18). The system of loans to affiliated companies by city banks was supplemented by their affiliation with all financial institutions, including regional banks, mutual banks, Shinkin Bank, trust banks, and life insurance companies (Sakamoto 1981, p. 53). As Hadley (1970, p. 278) pointed out, in many cases, the primary position assumed by city banks was not through their own undertakings but a combination of activities by city banks; trust banks; and marine, fire, and life insurance companies.

Competition among city banks for the affiliation to enterprises focused on securing a system of monetary flow in the group by using inter-industrial relationships and raising financing efficiency (Sakamoto 1980a, p. 52). In addition, the loans to affiliated companies in the group allowed the industrial groups to accumulate interest and obtain certain discounts as financial costs that main companies paid for substantial profits in the industrial group (Sakamoto 1980a, pp. 58–59). Meanwhile, the banks that maintained dominant positions in the banking sector were those that could build a system wherein payments and settlements were completed at the bank. One condition that supported them was the exclusive trading relationships between banks and large enterprises, exhibiting one set-like industrial setting. Competition between banks that aimed at expanding market shares and financing affiliations while maintaining a system of joint financing between banks eventually forced city banks to form trading relationships with large businesses in every industry. The combination of the industrial groups embodying the general industrial linkages that did not arise as the industrial company's motive was based on such interests, at least from the banks' perspectives (Suzuki 1993, p. 151). Moreover, in the industrial groups, the drafting of investment plans was performed under the premise that a large number of companies were to be bound together by the complicated industrial linkages that mutually guaranteed demand. This was one reason why the influential large banks devoted themselves to the formation of industrial groups, which were characterized as the one-set system (Kigyo Shudan Kenkyuukai 1964, p. 88). Organizing the main customers as a group of large enterprises that embodied the one-set type of industrial linkage was a common financial strategy for large banks (Suzuki 2008, pp. 57–59).

From the viewpoint of major city banks in industrial groups, the process whereby these banks competed for securing lucrative large enterprises in the growth industries as the main customer included arranging and organizing the large companies of the main client so that the industrial groups could embody all of the industrial linkages (Suzuki 2008, pp. 57–59). As a result of "the one-set principle of new industries of each group" (the investment behavior that attempted to rule these industries according to the financing affiliation of each bank), rival companies came to overlap various industries, which became an important factor that intensified market competition in these industries (Miyazaki 1966, pp. 52–53, 55; Miyazaki 1990, pp. 30–31). However, there were differences between the old *zaibatsu* groups and the non-*zaibatsu* financial groups. For example, in the former, few powerful companies were arranged in each industrial department, whereas in the latter, there were cases in which many firms existed in the same industry (Uetake 1993, p. 149).

Loans to affiliated companies functioned as "the pipe of the fund" for growth industries in which banks were the first to examine the situations as well as "the last creditors" in the transformation of the declining industry (Okazaki 1992, pp. 324–326; Hashimoto 1992, pp. 12–13). In periods of high economic growth, loans to affiliated companies functioned as a system for saving costs. In addition, they helped enterprises adapt to the industrial structure and the growth of the company as well as reduced the pressure from the capital market by interlocking shareholdings. However, from the 1970s to the 1980s, the scale of both cross-stockholdings and loans to affiliated companies reduced and the functions of these measures, which were visible during periods of high economic growth, disappeared (Okazaki 1992, pp. 327–330). All of the various conditions that brought about the incentives of this financing system, such as rapid economic growth, development of heavy and chemical industries, expansion of equipment, and enormous capital requirement, also disappeared with the shift to low economic growth and the eventual downsizing of business activities. As a result, loans to affiliated companies no longer had the same positive effects as those during periods of high economic growth (Sakamoto 1980b, p. 31).

It is important to consider the significance of the loans to affiliated companies in relation to the system of joint financing. Although companies under this system received financing from main banks, they also borrowed money from other financial institutions. Conversely, the banks provided credit to those companies for which they did not act as the main bank. Thus, loans to affiliated companies were jointly financed and a complementary relationship existed in which the system of joint financing was based on the system of loans to affiliated companies. Banks of the industrial groups also mobilized and used other financial institutions as long as they could maintain their positions as the main banks. The affiliation of other financial institutions by large banks was also simultaneously promoted during this process (Okumura 1976, pp. 119–122). The structure of funds supply in the company involved the financing of the industrial groups through the loans to affiliated companies based on joint financed loans. Given the immaturity of the capital market, this structure made up for and adjusted capital needs by forming the group (Masaki 1985, p. 113). The development of the provision of loans to affiliated companies and the system of joint financing between banks were mainly based on the condition that the vigor of the manufacturing companies exceeded the growth rate of the funds supply power of the leading financial institutions (Miyazaki 1966, p. 244). However, such joint financing also reflected the competition over securing excellent lending partnerships between city banks, despite existing cooperation between them that aimed at limiting competition (Suzuki 1998, p. 232). Such cooperation was an attempt to achieve mutual entries in the industrial groups under the actual situation of competition among groups and to further expand and strengthen the financial functions of the loans to the affiliated companies. Accordingly, further progress of the cooperative system between industrial groups was promoted (Okumura 1976, p. 164; Sakamoto 1980a, p. 65).

4.2.1.5 Role of Trading Companies and the Significance of Reciprocal Trade in Industrial Groups

This subsection analyzes reciprocal trade relations and the role of trading companies in the industrial group. Trading companies not only represented the distribution sector but also combined with industrial groups through methods such as stockholding, corporate financing, dispatching of directors, gathering domestic and foreign information, and organizing activities, all of which extended into many industrial sectors (Sumiya 1982, p. 115). Trading companies also played an objective role of organizing the cooperation between companies and embodying the general industrial linkage by mediating mutual trading relations (Suzuki 1993, p. 104). Overall, the roles of the trading companies in the industrial groups included the following functions: (1) dealing, (2) financial, (3) information gathering, (4) organizer, and (5) development. In some instances, trading companies even served as mediators in information gathering, organizing, and development (Fukuda 1985, pp. 144–146). Moreover, there were close cooperative relationships between trading companies and large city banks of the same industrial groups in order to perform these various functions (Okumura 1976, p. 23).

In Japan, there were numerous cases wherein trading within the industrial groups was mutual business, since there were many cases wherein general trading companies mediated business activities between member companies of the group. In this regard, compared with firms outside of the industrial groups, member firms of the industrial groups could enjoy more advantageous positions. This advantageous position was a result of major general trading companies' efforts to increase the sales of companies in the group through preferential treatment. Trading enterprises of the group could help realize this advantageous standpoint even for those enterprises outside of the group. Trading enterprises of the group recognized this advantageous standpoint for those enterprises outside of the group. In this way, the merits of mutual trade emerged from the situation wherein trading companies also had dealings with the companies outside of the groups. General trading firms eventually assumed the core position in the industrial groups through trade with many companies (both in and outside of the groups). For the member firms of the industrial groups, such advantages enabled them to expand sales on a constant basis (Okumura 1976, pp. 132–135, 138–139; Okumura 1975a, pp. 173–174; Okumura 1975b, pp. 329–330). The advantages of mutual dealings by trading firms relied on the expansion of trade through mutual business activities in the group (Isoda 1976, p. 14).

The predominance that a trading company as a core enterprise of the industrial group could expect to have over other trading companies depended on the scale merit arising from the use of the trading firm inside the group by enterprises in wide-ranging industries (Shimada 2010, p. 259). However, such mutual trade was based on interlocking stockholdings, through which the relationships based on the unified interests between the companies of the groups and the trading companies were formed (Okumura 1975b, p. 330). By the interposition of the trading companies, it was possible to frequently use the strong sales and information networks that manufacturing firm previously did not have access to. Thus, trading firms were jointly used by enterprises in the industrial groups, which can be seen in the high holding ratios of the companies within the same groups to the issued stocks of the trading companies (Shimada 2010, p. 260).

In addition, regarding their financial functions, general trading companies offered a significant amount of inter-business credit in the form of commercial credit with a promissory note to industrial enterprises through the borrowed funds from the banks in the group. These companies also developed trading firm finance as a means of complementing the loan from the bank during periods of high economic growth (Yamazaki 1995, pp. 57, 63–64). Unlike bank financing, trading firm financing was based on concrete trading, which reflected the actual trading situations in the groups (Tanaka 2004, p. 91). Since the dealing networks that trading companies organized were also credit networks, the trading companies played a role in facilitating trade between the companies of each industrial group and the member companies in the group through the network of transactions within the group (Suzuki 1993, pp. 114, 117–118). More specifically, the loans from large city banks enabled enormous trading companies to perform financing, especially in the form of loans to affiliated companies in the industrial groups (Okumura 1976, p. 140). Meanwhile, large banks expanded the financing domain and made fund management more efficient by combining the wide network of physical distribution with the network of financing (Kudo 1994, p. 33). However, the financing structure of the leading banks began to regress after 1965. While the financial accommodations to the member companies in the groups were made by the general trading companies, the transformation of general trading firms into holding companies through stockholding advanced. As a result, unity in the industrial groups was further strengthened with two core entities, i.e., banks and trading companies (Masaki 1985, p. 114).

In 1975, in the three industrial old *zaibatsu* groups, the ratio of sales for member companies of the presidents' clubs in the same industrial group to the total sales of the trading companies in 1975 was approximately 5–6% and the ratio of purchases from member firms of the presidents' club in the same group to the total purchases of trading firms was a little less than 2%. However, the ratio of the sales for the core trading companies to the total sales of the member companies of the presidents' club and the ratio of purchases from the core trading companies to the total purchases of the member companies of the presidents' club were both approximately 30%. When considering certain products, such as automobiles and home appliances, that were sold without dealing with trading companies, these numerical values are considerably high (Kosei torihiki iinkai 1975, p. 56). Furthermore, taking an average of six industrial groups, sales-dependent rates in the group companies (excluding the financial sectors) and in the manufacturing companies within the group in fiscal year 1981 were 10.8% and 20.4%, respectively. The relevant average numerical values for the group companies and the manufacturing companies within the group in the three old *zaibatsu* groups were 13.4% and 29.0%, respectively. The similar average values for these two types of companies in the other three industrial groups were 8.6% and 14.9%, respectively. On the other hand, the respective average purchase-dependent rates for these two types of companies were 11.7% and 12.4% in the six groups,

14.8% and 18.6% in the three *zaibatsu* groups, and 9.1% and 8.2% in the other three groups (Kosei torihiki iinkai 1983, p. 24).

4.2.1.6 Assignment of Directors

Next, the assignment of directors among member companies in the industrial group is analyzed. The assignment of directors from banks held an important meaning even though it was primarily observed between banks and industrial enterprises, trading companies and industrial companies, and banks and trading companies. Large increases in the personnel connections between banks and manufacturing firms after the war meant that banks (to some extent) controlled certain duties within the industrial groups in place of the dissolved *zaibatsu* parent company (Сутягина 1973, p. 153). The personnel connections between banks and trading companies also held a significant meaning. According to Hadley (1970, p. 248), in the Mitsubishi Group, there is evidence of persuasion in the context of common trade names and trademarks among the core companies.

The corporate groups of the independent, large enterprises that did not belong to the industrial groups were organized on the basis of the relationship between the parent company and the subsidiary company. In fact, there were many cases in which the directors were dispatched from top-ranking big businesses to subsidiary companies or associated companies. In contrast, there were many cases in which financial institutions and trading firms sent directors to member corporations in the industrial groups (Kobayashi 1980, p. 145). Many assignments of directors from banks to corporations in the groups depended on the condition that the banks were large shareholders among the enterprises and could easily provide loans to the affiliated companies (Okumura 1978, p. 101). In addition to corporate financing, another important function of the main banking system was corporate governance and monitoring (Aoki and Patrick 1994, p. xxii). However, assignments of directors from banks were not intended to influence the actions of companies. Instead, they basically aimed at monitoring the preservation of credit as well as the accumulation of information on borrowers (Miyajima 1992, pp. 233–234). Although Japanese banks executed financial functions within the industrial groups, they had weak control over the industries.

Therefore, the conditions under which the assignment of directors occurred inside industrial groups are evaluated. The ratios of the companies that were assigned a director from a member company to all companies of the same group in fiscal years 1977, 1981, and 1987 were 65.64%, 72.53%, and 67.69%, respectively, on average in six industrial groups; 71.22%, 77.42%, and 64.13%, respectively, on average in three old *zaibatsu* groups; and 60.07%, 67.63%, and 71.25%, respectively, on average in three other bank groups. In addition, the ratios of the firms that received directors from banks in these years were 55.51%, 58.97%, and 57.59%, respectively, on average in six industrial groups; 62.05%, 59.92%, and 55.96%, respectively, on average in the old *zaibatsu* groups; and 48.96%, 58.02%, and 59.61%, respectively, on average in the bank-type groups.

Conversely, the ratios of enterprises that received directors from trading companies in fiscal years 1977, 1981, and 1987 were 13.39%, 11.43%, and 9.99%, respectively, on average in six industrial groups; 23.26%, 21.29%, and 18.52%, respectively, on average in the old *zaibatsu* groups; and 3.52%, 1.57%, and 1.46%, respectively, on average in the bank-type groups. In addition, the ratios of the number of assigned directors from member companies to the total number of directors in the same industrial groups in fiscal years 1977, 1981, and 1987 were 8.29%, 8.69%, and 7.13%, respectively, on average in six industrial groups; 10.54%, 11.39%, and 8.65%, respectively, on average in three old *zaibats*u groups; and 6.04%, 5.98%, and 5.61%, respectively, on average in three bank-type groups. Furthermore, the ratios of the number of assigned directors from banks for the same years were 3.56%, 3.55%, and 3.92%, respectively, on average in six industrial groups; 3.95%, 3.60%, and 4.18%, respectively, on average in three old *zaibatsu* groups; and 3.17%, 3.50%, and 3.65%, respectively, on average in three bank-type groups. Finally, the ratios of the number of assigned directors from trading companies for the same three years were 0.85%, 0.54%, and 0.44%, respectively, on average in six industrial groups; 1.39%, 0.94%, and 0.82%, respectively, on average in old *zaibatsu* groups; and 0.30%, 0.13%, and 0.06%, respectively, on average in bank-type groups (Ueno 1989, pp. 49–50).

4.2.1.7 Establishment of Joint Companies and the Development of Joint Investments

Next, the establishment of joint companies and joint investment in the industrial group are discussed. The development of joint investments aimed at organizing new business (both in and outside of companies) in order to create profits as the industrial group and creating profits of the combination in such business. In this regard, the core trading company, which belonged to the individual industrial group, was at the center of such actions (Isoda 1976, pp. 16–17). Examples of joint investments by member companies of the industrial groups entering into new fields and growing business areas as a collective can be seen in the construction of petrochemical plants and their entry into the nuclear power industry in the 1950s; urban development, housing development, marine development, and development of information industry in the 1960s; the development of leisure and marine resources in the 1970s; and the development of advanced technology in the 1980s. Many joint investment companies were specifically established for such purposes (Sumiya 1982, pp. 130–131). Joint investment companies, many of which were founded in the first half of the 1970s, were unprecedented in their scale and the fact that they were simultaneously established by six industrial groups. Joint investment companies in the industrial group exhibited characteristics such as unilateral and closed ownerships by plural corporations and cooperative stance within the group. Thus, joint investment companies functioned as a means of concentration in the industrial group that was different from the interlocking stockholdings (Okumura 1976, pp. 142, 145–146).

4.2.2 Corporate Groups in the Same Capital of Big Business

In this section, corporate groups of the pyramid type in the same capital of big businesses are analyzed.

Increase in the number of associated companies arising from the establishment of subsidiaries by a parent company played an important role; the parent company tended to expand its control through shareholdings for the purpose of realizing advantages arising from the inter-firm relationships in the production technology (Futatsuki 1976, p. 22). For example, Hitachi Ltd. started increasing the number of affiliated enterprises on the basis of the need to establish higher diversified management as the Japanese economy was rebuilt, management performance improved, and the management scale of the company expanded. As a result, the number of affiliated enterprises in the Hitachi group significantly increased after 1955 (Kabushikigeisha Hitachi Seisakusyo rinji gojyushunen jigyobu shashi hensanbu 1960, p. 180). Large Japanese enterprises had promoted grouping in order to expand power by increasing the number of new spin-off subsidiary companies on the one hand and by acquiring more companies on the other hand. The grouping of the pyramid type of enterprise in the same capital rapidly progressed after the 1970s with the establishment of new spin-off subsidiary companies from the core fields of big businesses. Such a movement aimed at realizing the various degrees of deconcentration in management organization by separating certain business departments into subsidiary companies and creating a more flexible organization that exceeded the typical divisional structure found in many companies (Sakamoto 1987a, pp. 2, 6, 22–24). Moreover, the creation of an inside subsidiary aimed at introducing the principle of competition between the parent company and the subsidiary company or between subsidiaries by the conscious adoption of the form of the other company, such as a subsidiary company either created by spin-off of the department of the parent company or newly established by the parent company (Enomoto 1994, p. 169).

According to a survey in 1982 by the institute of Business Research, College of Economics, Nihon University, Japanese enterprises aimed at further segmenting the functions and realizing the merits arising from the use of various organizational forms by establishing affiliated enterprise. More than half of the companies that responded stated that the independence of the production or sales department and the desire to enter into a different field were the main reasons why the affiliated companies were established. In addition, approximately one-third of the companies indicated that the development, production, and sales of new products was their main reason for establishing affiliated companies (Nihon Daigaku keizai gakubu sangyo keiei kenkyusho 1982, pp. 3, 12). Currently, restructuring is carried out by including group companies as well as the parent company, especially when the need to develop an effective business strategy as a group increases. The reorganization of the division of labor in the group and the establishment of an overall strategy of the entire group are also important objectives under such circumstances (Teramoto 1996, p. 2; Teramoto 1994a, p. 3; Teramoto 1994b, p. 2; Takai 1996, pp. 16, 28).

In Japan, the division of companies into wholly owned, non-autonomous subsidiaries in charge of only one function of the main enterprise considerably increased. Such movements aimed at flexibly responding to changes of circumstance by leaning down the operation of the parent company itself or raising the total management efficiency through the separation of non-autonomous units in order to make them function as profit centers (Shimotani 1993, p. 45). In Japanese enterprises, there have been many cases wherein the process in which activities of companies were decided upon by distributing functions of production and sales to other firms, such as subsidiaries and affiliated firms, after which they were entirely responsible for the outcomes (Tanimoto 1994, p. 3).

For instance, in the Nippon Electric Group, affiliated companies were classified into two categories: (1) a company that was established by its affiliation with an existing enterprise and (2) a new spin-off subsidiary. In regard to the latter, numerous subsidiaries were created as spin-offs from the parent company, and such a movement became dominant after the 1970s (Enomoto 1994, pp. 143, 162). In this regard, all of the business groups in Nippon Electric had some production footholds in its subsidiaries as well as in the parent company itself, and they formed the system of production in a unified form (Sakamoto 1987b, pp. 31, 33, 39, 45–47). In particular, the grouping of companies by the establishment of subsidiaries was crucial in the concentration of functions of technological development and sales in the parent company (division) by founding local production subsidiaries devoted to mass production (Enomoto 1994, p. 160).

At Matsushita Electric, such spin-offs were actively carried out for the purpose of improving management efficiency (Shimotani 1998, pp. 158, 160–161). In the 1960s, active overseas expansions and rampant establishment of overseas subsidiaries were increasingly supported grouping. In fact, many overseas subsidiaries were successively founded to exploit new markets. The number of overseas subsidiaries increased by splitting off, reorganizing, and integrating (Shimotani 1998, pp. 146–147, 150). The affiliated companies were strongly connected with the parent company by vertical relevance in the business of manufacturing and sales and played important roles according to each relation of the division of labor and each rank in the group. Units of organization that composed the corporate group became an indispensable factor for the industrial headquarters through the close linkage with the managerial planning of industrial headquarters (Shimotani 1998, pp. 99, 108–110).

The iron and steel industry operated under different conditions from those in the electrical industry from the 1950s to the 1980s. For example, the Nippon Steel Corporation formed eight groups according to the field: (1) plain steel; (2) special steel; (3) steel material processing; (4) chemistry, energy, non-ferrous metal, and ceramic industry; (5) engineering; (6) distribution and transportation; (7) urban development, housing, and leisure; and (8) general service. Although the number of companies in the group later increased, many were deeply connected with the iron business. However, in the 1980s, with the transformation of business structures focusing on the iron and steel industry, the business development of new businesses required a considerable leap in advancement. Therefore, the reorganization of groups was carried out by the establishment of new group companies, the reinforcement of cooperation within the group, and rearrangement and selection of group companies. As a result, in the 1980s, a growing number of group enterprises became the subject of "multiple management" system that managed various business fields. Thus, in the iron and steel industry, large enterprises entered into new businesses by setting up many group companies as an effective means of diversification (Okamoto 1987, pp. 120, 123, 125–127, 129, 134, 136).

4.3 New Developments in the System of Large Corporate Groups in Germany

Based on the preceding examination, this section considers new development in the system of large corporate groups in Germany. It examines the restructuring of the system of large corporate groups within the reconcentration of monopolies that were previously dissolved under the victorious nations' occupation policy, as well as the later concentration of enterprises. Furthermore, corporate groups, such as industrial enterprises and banking firms, are taken into account.

4.3.1 Development of the Reconcentration of Monopolies

4.3.1.1 Background of the Reconcentration of Monopolies

Since the end of the Second World War, and especially during the crises of 1957 and 1958, Germany has witnessed a wave of enterprise amalgamations with large corporate group structures, laying the groundwork for mergers and acquisitions of subsidiaries. Enterprise concentration in the same capital groups was also central to this movement (Hahn and Tammer 1970, p. 24) and played an important part in the reconcentration of dissolved corporations.

From the latter half of the 1950s to the end of the decade, three factors influenced this reconcentration and new concentration: (1) the benefits of economies of scale, (2) the legal benefit of scale, and (3) psychological factors. First, these advancements realized economies of scale. Second, tax benefits were applied to vertically integrated corporations. Third, cartels and concentration, rather than competition, were always the *lingua franca* of Europe's economic system and were known to the market players [*National Archives*, RG59, 862A.33, Reconcentration in Iron, Steel and Coal Industries of the Federal Republic (5.10.1959), pp. 3–4].

National growth policies played a significant role in legal benefits, and four laws enacted by the government addressed this issue. The 1956 Transformation Law and 1957 Tax Law allowed large corporate groups to concentrate power on an unprecedented scale while excluding small shareholders. Revisions to corporate law allowed businesses to benefit from tax breaks by eliminating or reducing taxes on a portion of their profits and converting it into equity capital. Furthermore, in 1958 and 1959, the Restrictive Trade Practices Act publicly acknowledged approximately 250 cartels (D.W.I.-Berichte 1961, p. 5).

In conjunction with the European Coal and Steel Community (ECSC), the reconcentration of previously dissolved or split large corporate groups continued apace. Article 66 of the ECSC Convention, approved in May 1954, permitted the concentration of companies that did not obstruct market competition and granted relatively broad freedom for merging corporations in the coal, iron, and steel industries; these new rules accelerated reconcentration (Sieber 1958, p. 48; Wirtschke 2009). With reconcentration granted for vertically integrated enterprises affiliated with coal, iron, and steel plants, several previously dissolved coal, iron, and steel corporations, such as Mannesmann, Klöckner, and Rheinstahl-Phöenix, restructured their companies on the basis of the prewar foundation, that is, coal and steel consolidation [*National Archives*, RG59, 862A.054, Status of Decartelized and Deconcentrated German Coal and Steel Companies (23.6.1955), p. 1]. Among the 34 instances of enterprise concentration admitted by the ECSC in West Germany in 1962, 14 were concerned with the reconcentration of corporations that were forced to dissolve postwar (Abelshauser 2004, p. 245).

The result of intense competition was a powerful concentration of production in a relatively small number of large companies (D.W.I.-Berichte 1961, p. 5), and it increased in the latter half of the 1950s in response to the competitive conditions in the market. For example, according to Thyssen's 1957/1958 annual report, the Thyssen group of enterprises had four goals: (1) reinforcing already existing cooperative connections, (2) reinforcing resistance to market changes through horizontal integration of specialized production domains, (3) pursuit of new possibilities for rationalization and lower costs, and (4) greater competitive power (August Thyssen Hütte 1958, p. 11). The growing need for stronger group ties in order to adapt to the market's business environment and increase competitive strength necessitated reconcentration. The EEC member countries were clearly not complementary partners in their industrial production structure, but rather competitors; this competitive environment aided the concentration and consolidation process significantly (D.W.I.-Berichte 1962, p. 20).

The repeal and cancelation of allied nation regulations provided a significant opportunity for bank reconcentration. Following US admission in 1952, banks were zoned into three operational districts: northern, western, and southern districts, and consolidated into nine large banks through mergers. Deutsche Bank, Dresdner Bank, and Commerzbank, each inherited three financial institutions [*National Archives*, RG59, 862A.14, Reconcentration of German Commercial Banks (10.1.1957), p. 1; Djelic 1998, p. 165; Pohl 1986, pp. 102–104; Horstmann 1991]. The December 1956 law repealed the prohibition of mutual capital participation by banks, personal connections between executives from inherited banks, and limited issuance to registered stock only (Aizawa 1994, p. 49). The top three banks were allowed to reestablish themselves, with the exception of subsidiary financial institutions in Berlin, and return to their prewar institutions [*National Archives*, RG59, 862A.14, Reconcentration of

German Commercial Banks (10.1.1957), p. 1; Pohl 1986, p. 105; Wandel 1998, pp. 40–41]. The reconcentration occurred in 1957. The primary reasons given by Deutsche Bank were to improve their international standing and the new group's position in handling large accounts, secure greater flexibility in maintaining unified credit policies, and realize the economic potential of their business operations [*National Archives*, RG59, 862A.14, Present and Forthcoming Bank Merger in West Germany (3.5.1957)].

The top three banks strongly lobbied the government while demonstrating their initiative in their reconcentration efforts (Gall et al. 1995, pp. 526–544). At the time, the government had no objection to mergers, and even the majority of Social Democratic Party (SPD) leaders agreed to return to bank concentration [*National Archives*, RG59, 862A.14, US Policy regarding Reconcentration of German Banks (15.12.1955), p. 1]. With a new order in Europe emerging in the 1950s and with new cooperation models in the larger economic sphere, early postwar regulations on large German banks were no longer deemed appropriate but were rather considered unreasonable, an opinion that continued to gain momentum (Deutsche Bank 1970, p. 35).

Banks were critical in the concentration of monopolies and the introduction of new developments in the system of large corporate groups. Klöckner's reconcentration is an example of concentration via bank intermediaries, through which they obtained majority stakes in coal companies that split from a larger corporate group (Huffschmid 1954, p. 26; Der Volkswirt 1955a, p. 25).

4.3.1.2 Reconcentration of Monopolies and Development of Divisions of Labor in Business Domains

Building on the preceding developments, the next critical issue to be examined is how large business operations were restructured in the midst of reconcentration or concentration, and how the system of large corporate groups was restructured as a result. The coal, iron, and steel industries were the most visible examples of operations restructuring in conjunction with monopoly reconcentration.

As a result, this section focuses on these industries. Beginning in the 1950s, the iron and steel industry, experienced a two-stage process of enterprise concentration. The first stage was the return of a temporarily deconcentrated company to its previous state; this stage ended in 1958 and 1959 as reorganizations ended. In the second stage, many large corporate groups worked closely together on production and investment (D.W.I.-Berichte 1962, p. 1).

As previously discussed, the postwar era's monopoly dissolution was concerned with the "integrated economy" that underpinned productive forces in Germany's heavy industry. As a result, the reconcentration movement advanced with the goal of expanding production units and product types while reinforcing the vertical combination of the coal, iron, and steel industries (D.W.I.-Berichte 1955, p. 9; Yajima 1959 p. 53). These goals also included integrating production capacity in the iron and steel industry and utilizing advanced technologies (Herrigel 2000, p. 381).

In terms of Vereinigte Stahlwerke AG's successor companies, the Phoenix and Rheinrohr corporations merged due to the former's relationship with the latter as a supplier of semi-finished steels [*National Archives*, RG59, 862A.331, Merger of Rheinische Roehrenwerke AG and the Huettenwerke Phoenix AG with Approval of High Authority (11.2.1955); *thyssenkrupp Corporate Archive* (below *tkA*), NST/82, Zusatzprotokoll zur Niederschrift über die 38. Aufsichtsratssitzung der Hüttenwerke Phoenix AG am 2.07.1954 zur geplanten Fusion, S.7]. For Thyssen, the initial target of reconcentration was entirely related to the Duisburg region. They signed an Agreement of Community of Interests in September 1955 prior to merging capital. The following year, August Thyssen and Niederrheinische Hütte AG merged their companies through stock exchanges [*tkA*, A/33073, Die Schrit über die Entscheidung über die Genehmigung des Abschlusses eines Interessengemeinschaftsvertrages zwischen der August Tyssen-Hütte Aktiengesellschaft und der Niederrheinische Hütte Aktiengesellschaft durch die Hohe Behörde (23.5.1956), S. 1, S. 3; *tkA*, A/ 33073, Rückgängigmachung von Entflechtungsmaβnahmen im Bereich der August Thyssen-Hütte und der Niederrehinischen Hütte (16.1.1956), S. 3; Uebbing 1991, S. 60]. The effective complementary relationship between these two companies disappeared as a result of the dismantling of Thyssen's production equipment as part of the occupation policy. In addition, for Niederreinische Hütte, it became impossible to produce thick and medium plates because of the dismantlement of the production equipment. Consequently, the reconcentration of Thyssen and Niederrheinische Hütte, in response to these difficult conditions, aimed at filling the supply gap that could not be filled through a supply agreement [*tkA* A/30819, Abschluss eines Interessengemeinschaftsvertrages zwischen der August Thyssen-Hütte AG. und der Niederrheinische Hütte AG., Duisburg (15.9.1955), S. 7–9].

While Thyssen provided Niederrheinische Hütte semi-finished products, Niederrheinische Hütte supplied the wire plants of Westfälische Union with the necessary primary materials. Thus, this merger had not only organizational but also particularly integrated economic grounds [*tkA*, A/32196, MEMORANDUM über Steuerfragen bei dem Zusammenschluβ der August Thyssen-Hütte AG und der Phoenix-Rheinrohr AG]. Another objective of this merger was to secure the possibility of mutually coordinating the investments of August Thyssen and Niederrheinische Hütte for rationalization and cost reduction [*tkA*, A/32196, Zusammenschluβ im Sinne der Artikel 66 MUV zwischen der August Thyssen-Hütte AG (ATH) und der Phoenix-Rheinrohr AG vereinigte Hütten- und Röhrenwerke (PHOENIX) (29.10.1958)].

The second target of Thyssen's reconcentration was Deutsche Edelstahlwerke AG, with which they merged in 1957. Because August Thyssen did not have his own electric steel production plant in Duisburg, the possibility of cooperation in production technology, particularly for crude steel, was emphasized [*tkA*, A/30778, Pressenotiz zur Übernahme eines Mehrheitpakets der Deutsche Edelstahlwerke AG durch August Thyssen-Hütte AG (20.12.1956); Uebbing 1991, pp. 60, 330]. The merger of Thyssen with these two companies provided the impetus for the subsequent divisions of labor.

Thyssen valued the production of flat bars, semi-finished steels, and large profile iron. In response, Niederrheinische Hutte AG focused on rod wire and bar steel, whereas Deutsche Edelstahlwerke AG focused on the production of high-grade steel and other value-added steels [*tkA*, A/30819, Abschluss eines Interessengemeinschaftsvertrages zwischen der August Thyssen-Hütte AG. und der Niederrheinische Hütte AG., Duisburg (15.9.1955), S. 8–10; *tkA*, A/30819, Interessengemeinschaftsvertrag zwischen der Niederrheinische Hütte Aktiengesellschaft, Duisburg-Hochfeld, und der August Thyssen-Hütte Aktiengesellschaft, Duisburg-Hamborn (15.9.1955), Treue and Uebbing 1969, p. 219]. Thyssen gained band iron sales channels in 1957 and 1958/1961 by purchasing shares in Huttenwerke Siegerland AG and Rasselstein-Andernach's steel rolling company, respectively. These purchases also benefited from the product-by-product division of labor [*tkA*, A/31870, Unser Antrag auf Genehmigung des Zusammenschlusses unseres Unternehemens mit der Phoenix-Rheinrohr AG (27.4.1960), S. 3; *tkA*, A/31870, Die Schrift an den Herrn Bundesklanzler von Dr. Pferdmenges; *tkA*, A/31870, Der Brief an Herrn Dr. Robert Pferdmenges (3.9.1960); Treue and Uebbing 1969, pp. 215, 218; Kobayashi 1983, pp. 156–162]. In the postwar period, the new Thyssen group was the only capital group in West Germany with a steel production plant in which the most modern manufacturing equipment at the time was arranged. This plant was characterized by ultra-large-scale blast furnaces, LD converters, continuous rolling to automatic rolling mills, and a steel production system on a large scale. Post-dissolution and reconcentration restructuring was also important for such economies of scale (Kobayashi 1983, pp. 1, 179).

Reconcentration in the 1950s resulted in only four surviving enterprises by the early 1960s among the 13 successor companies resulting from Vereinigte Stahlwerke AG's postwar deconcentration: August Thyssen, Phoenix-Rheinrohr, Rhein Steel, and the Dortmund-Hörde Hütten Union. Within the majority of these, company mergers and expansions did not result in direct competition with the other corporations; instead, each company chose to expand and integrate production capacity in separate domains, pursuing profit through division of labor. That is, most of Vereinigte Stahlwerke AG's steel production capacity was once again folded into the operations of either Thyssen or Phoenix-Rheinrohr. This specialization of product supply in the rolled product markets for the most part did not overlap, and they enabled a product-based division of labor between the two companies. Whereas Phonix-Rheinrohr specialized in steel pipe, heavy plates, semi-finished steels, and raw iron, Thyssen specialized in lighter plate, semi-finished and finished rolled sheets, coils, rod wire, and specialty steel. As a result of Vereinigte Stahlwerke AG's dissolution, Rheinische Stahlwerke AG took over all of Vereinigte's interests, except those related to steel production. The Dormund-Hörde Hütten Union grew to be a significant crude steel producer; however, unlike the other large enterprises, it did not diversify into the iron and steel industry. By the early 1960s, the Union intended to focus on two areas: heavy plate and both bar and structural steel. Other large corporate groups such as Hoesch, Klöckner, Mannesmann, Hüttenwerk Oberhausen AG, and Krupp, largely followed the Dormund-Hörde Hütten Union's specialization strategy. Each company tried to organize the production of steel and rolled products in such a way that they could achieve a strong position in the limited number of markets [Herrigel 2000, pp. 381–383; *tkA*, A/31927B, Zusammenschluβ im Sinn des

Artikel 66 des Montanunionvetrages (MUV) zwischen der August Thyssen-Hütte AG (ATH) und der Phoenix-Rheinrohr AG Vereingte Hütte- und Röhrenwerke (Phoenix) (22.5.1962), S. 1; Huffschmid 1965, pp. 110–115, 149; Sieber 1958].

Further, corporations other than Vereinigte Stahlwerke AG are analyzed. A few years after the restructuring that followed dissolution, Flick, Gutehoffnung, Klöckner, Otto Wolff, and Hoesch re-emerged as integrated organizations with larger investments and production scales than the previous Vereinigte Stahlwerke AG (Petzina 1992, p. 532). By the mid-1950s, Mannesmann's disassociation from the coal company as a result of the postwar dissolution had been restored, and the restoration of an integrated organization had begun (Der Volkswirt 1955b, p. 27; Der Volkswirt 1956b, p. 27). Thereafter, in the fall of 1958, their six most important subsidiaries merged with the parent company (Vgl. Der Volkswirt 1959, p. 1439). Similarly, at Hoesch, two of the three successor companies that split due to dissolution were returned to the parent company. Vertical integration of coal and steel industries was required by the plan because it was a requirement for survival among Ruhr's coal and steel corporations (Der Volkswirt 1956a, pp. 36–37; Der Volkswirt 1957, p. 1163). In the late 1950s, Hoesch restructured as a large corporate group comprised of four core corporations, with many subsidiaries established thereafter (Vgl. Der Volkswirt 1960a, p. 1092; Der Volkswirt 1960b). Even at Krupp, Huttenwerk Rheinhausen AG assumed control over Bochmer Verein, a successor to Vereinigte Stahlwerke AG, primarily to benefit from the division of labor. Hüttenwerk Rheinhausen AG predominantly produced mass products through Thomas steel; in contrast, Bochmer Verein produced high-grade steel using LD processes and electric furnaces. This consolidation promoted the expansion of production programs and division of labor. In the processing sector, Krupp formed a lucrative consolidation for material supply with its supplier, Bochmer Verein (Yajima 1959, pp. 98–100). Dissolution measures at Gutehoffnung ended vertical ties, and the reconcentration movement influenced the reconsolidation of the steel and coal sectors in 1957. Hüttenwerk Oberhausen AG and Bergbau AG Neue Hoffnung expanded their energy-related concentration through ties with Ruhrchemie AG, where Bergbau AG Neue Hoffnung had capital investments (Yajima 1959, pp. 124–125). Thus, reconcentration in the coal and steel industries created more favorable conditions than those before dissolution.

In the late 1950s, the reconcentration of monopolistic enterprises was temporarily halted, but with the growth of fierce competition and pressure from the 1958 crisis, the process of accumulation and concentration proceeded in the second stage. The new economic advances that emerged in 1959 and 1960 were already forgotten as the economy stagnated again in 1961. In addition, in response to the powerful expansion, the Thyssen group began establishing close collaborative relationships with the Dortmund-Hörde and Hoesch groups in the early 1960s. Hoesch has begun the construction of a large steel pipe factory in collaboration with Mannesmann, and the cooperation of these three groups has been partially demonstrated in joint capital procurements and joint use of rolling facilities. Thyssen, Mannesmann, and Hoesch formed production and investment collaboration agreements in 1962 (D.W.I.-Berichte 1962, p. 2). As a result of increased competition at the end of the 1950s and the beginning of the 1960s, one form of concentration was the various agreements between large corporate groups for joint research and development activities and the allocation of production equipment for joint use (D.W.I.-Berichte 1961, pp. 5–6).

4.3.2 Significance of New Developments in Large Corporate Group Systems

Based on the preceding discussions, this subsection examines the significance of new developments in large corporate group systems that occurred as a result of monopoly dissolution and later reconcentration. To simplify management, large companies formed appropriate management scales during this period, which were founded through liquidation of large corporate groups; this was seen through the process of concentration and reconcentration of monopolies. This procedure established critical preconditions for thorough rationalization (D.W.I.-Berichte 1960, pp. 11, 13).

This type of concentration helped create a system that exhibited economies of scale through the benefits of specialization and division of labor. This approach aimed to reform systems that enabled large corporate groups to develop more effective operations in response to technological reform opportunities provided by US implementation under the transition to an oligopolistic competition system. In other words, this type of development strengthened the systems of inter-firm relationships; these relationships were formed for the expansion of corporate activities that addressed market segments adapted to oligopolistic competition in the form of "labor division complementary to each product." This type of measure for the iron and steel industry meant leveraging "integrated economy" benefits between the coal and steel industries to transform the system on the basis of cooperative inter-firm relationships in pursuit of scale merit through "division of labor with complementary products" between large corporate groups.

This systemic transition aggregated production, sales, and management as the foundation of an industrial system; in terms of maintaining economic consistency, it strengthened large corporate groups in Germany (Shimotani 2008, pp. 3–4, 8) functioning on the lines of organic parent–subsidiary corporate groups based on product-based division of labor. It improved the environment for business rationalization, facilitated the pursuit of economies of scale, and strengthened the foundation for collaboration-based market control. This postwar business structure was distinct from industrial concentration systems based on market control with a high level of concentration via giant trusts and broad-ranging cartels, which contained industrial sectors observed prior to World War II, particularly those in the 1920s (Yamazaki 2015, Chap. 4); instead, it more carefully pursued functional benefits.

Relationships with such "complementary product-based divisions of labor" proceeded between large corporate groups as well. Examples of such relationships can be found in the iron and steel and chemical industries. Concerning the chemical industry, Dyas and Thanheiser highlighted that "after deconcentration by the Allies, BASF emerged as the major German manufacture of basic chemicals. In contrast, Bayer and Hoechst were reconcentrated with a narrower raw materials base, but strong forward integration into plastics, fibers and pharmaceuticals" (Dyas and Thanheiser 1976, p. 92).

These relationships were significant as a systemic transformation to the monopolistic market control based on the economic benefits of the division of labor, as opposed to the prewar period's economic concentration through cartels. The system of large corporate groups developed as an important process in the progress of German corporations while exhibiting new characteristics of cooperation in German capitalism. This was a large-scale business system suitable for large corporate groups; however, it differed from Japan's industrial groups and the full-set industrial structure found in the postwar period. These were reforms to the system of large-scale business that incorporated collaborative relationships in response to global and domestic competition. The system assisted German corporations in avoiding intense price competition and served as an important foundation for the development of management methods that adopted a management style that focused on competing with quality.

4.3.3 Industrial Groups as Corporate Groups Formed by Banks

In Germany, large corporate groups, including industrial enterprises, were formed by large banks such as Deutsche Bank, Dresdner Bank, and Commerzbank. Although there were cross-shareholdings between the companies in the insurance sector (Inukai 1968, pp. 48–49), possession of the industrial companies' stocks by financial institutions was a frequent occurrence (Suzuki 1981, pp. 108, 114; Suzuki 1983, pp. 274, 277; Sakuma 1996b, p. 90).

Compared with Japanese banks, banks in Germany broadly associated with large corporate groups rather than with a specific corporate group (Maekawa 1997, p. 58). These ties were significant for the mechanisms and functions of information sharing and coordination, particularly in the interest of industrial system-based relationships between industries and banks. In contrast to Japan, large corporate groups in postwar Germany were not full-set types that encompassed a broad range of industries, but were essentially corporate groups based on a single-industry structure. Unlike Japan, where there were specific banks in each of the six industrial groups, in Germany, the banks generally combined large industrial companies (especially those with numerous subsidiaries and affiliated companies) in order to resolve any contradictions (Suzuki 1981, p. 114; Suzuki 1983, p. 227).

Regarding the corporate groups that were formed by banks, it is important to understand the structure of the groups built in each industry and the manner in which they were concentrated at an upper level. For example, Deutsche Bank played a leading role in the successful reorganization of the domestic and financial industries beyond the border in the process of formation of the financial group including industrial companies in which this bank was core (Ushiyama 1989, p. 73). In fact, in the first half of the 1980s, all 75 high-ranking companies in Germany belonged to either one or more groups of the three large banks—Deutsche Bank, Dresdner Bank, and Commerzbank—in capital relations and personnel connection (Pfeiffer 1989, pp.23–35; Pfeiffer 1993, 8; Ushiyama 1989, p. 81).

Industrial enterprises in Germany can be classified into groups where these three banks form the core on the basis of the combination relations between industrial companies and banks. Although the ratio of industrial enterprises' stockholdings held by banks tended to be extremely low compared with that held by the industrial groups in Japan, the deposited stocks to the bank played an important role. Moreover, whereas there were rarely relations regarding the shareholdings between industrial companies in the group, relations of such combination existed with industrial companies outside of the groups. This is an important characteristic of the stockholding relations in Germany in comparison with Japan (Sakuma 1996b, pp. 82–83, 90–91, 95).

When examining the assignments of supervisory board members in the industrial groups led by the three banks, the banks broadly conducted such assignments of supervisory board members to the company outside of the group as well as those in the group. In the assignment of supervisory board members in industrial enterprises of the same industrial group, its frequency tended to be lower than that of firms and member companies in other industrial groups. A rather close personnel connection also existed with companies outside of the group. Although there were rarely close combination relations such as those seen in Japanese enterprises in the industrial groups wherein the banks served as the core, there were broad combination relations with companies in other industrial groups, as evidenced by the assignment of supervisory board members by large banks. Moreover, in the industrial enterprises that belonged to specific banks, there were relationships such as the possession of voting rights through deposited stocks and the assignment of supervisory board members by the two other large banks. Furthermore, cooperative relationships also existed among the three large banks.

In this way, inter-firm relationships within the industrial groups in Germany were "radial relations led by banks" (Sakuma 1996b, p. 93), and such relations were not matrix types such as those seen in Japanese industrial groups. Neither direct investment relations nor the relations of personnel connections through the assignment of supervisory board members existed among the three large banks. However, there were indirect close combination relationships among the three large banks through major insurance companies such as Allianz AG and Münchener Rurückversicherung AG. Such relations had a significant impact since they could help bridge the gap between the large banks that did not have direct capital and personnel relations (Sakuma 1996b, pp. 90, 92–97, 103–104; Sakuma 1996a, p. 69). In addition, these relationships between banks and industrial enterprises and those between industrial companies that belong to different industrial groups led by banks showed an important characteristic of the cooperative system among German corporate groups. Conversely, in Japan, the relationships were more exclusive; that is, combination relationships with companies outside of the industrial group were rare, except for exceptional cases such as the repeated participation of a member enterprise in the presidents' clubs of different industrial groups (Suzuki 2002; Sogawa and Suzuki 1970, pp. 132, 137) and joint financing that exceeded the industrial group. Therefore, the conditions regarding such combination relations in Germany greatly differed from those in Japan.

4.4 Japanese and German Characteristics Regarding the System of Large Corporate Groups

At this point, the new developments of the system of large corporate groups in Japan and Germany have been discussed, especially in relation to the dissolution of monopolies (under the occupation policy of the victorious nations) and the reconcentration of monopolies afterward. These discussions form the basis of the following discussion on the Japanese and German characteristics of the postwar system of large corporate groups.

In postwar Japan, major corporations in each business sector as part of the *zaibatsu* and parent (holding) companies were dissolved. However, banks were not included in these dissolutions. The prohibition of holding companies and regulation of treasury stock acquisitions and ownership formed six industrial groups. In these industrial groups, enterprises were concentrated by interlocking stockholding and forming large corporations, which were horizontally rather than vertically joined within capital groups and had substantial holdings of other companies' stocks. Meanwhile, various companies pursued defensive actions because of the pressure from the capital market and thereby secured autonomy of management and the system of corporate governance unique to Japanese corporations.

The large corporate groups formed in postwar Japan spanned several industries, with industrial corporations, banks, and trading companies at its core. The industrial groups comprised a full set of industries and conducted financing, interlocking stockholding, mutual business transactions, and joint investments internally. Six industrial groups coordinated among themselves through an organization, the Network of Presidents, with decisions primarily made by those in a certain position, such as presidents of group companies. Japanese industrial groups created more advantageous conditions of accumulation and maintained constant relationships by forming a system of stable shareholders through interlocking stockholdings (Suzuki 1998, p. 238).

Furthermore, Japanese industrial groups were the corporate groups that extended into many industries through the formation of groups that embodied the full-set-type of industrial linkage, which differed from the large American corporate groups wherein the foothold of power or the field of main industry was relatively clear (Kobayashi 1979, p. 49). Industrial groups in Japan also differed from German corporate groups that were based on an industrial system.

The existence of the six industrial groups built the foundation of the Japanese management style that prioritized profits by securing management autonomy from the threats and pressures of the stock market, developing management from a long-term perspective, and promoting distribution policies that prioritized the employees. Industrial groups in Japan also functioned as a system of mutual insurance concerning corporate performance wherein banks helped industrial enterprises in case of emergency as well as poorly performing companies. In contrast, industrial enterprises emphasized the trading relations with banks even in normal situations. Thus, the system of mutual insurance became the mechanism that supported the stable growth of member companies in the groups (Nakatani 1983, pp. 80–84). In addition, the adjustment of interests between enterprises and the unified command under the combination relations in the industrial groups in Japan differed from those in Germany. Even though financial institutions formed the core of the Network of Presidents, banks were not always an absolute advantage. Moreover, although industrial groups comprising full sets of industries were broadening, from the standpoint of inter-firm information sharing, the Network did not always adopt mechanisms that supported banks–industry relationships, as was the case in Germany.

It is unclear whether the presidents' clubs carried out the functions of unified management and conduct of industrial groups. However, it can be stated that such functions of unified management, such as that seen in the parent company of large corporate groups of the pyramid-type structure in the same capital group, were not very effective. Hadley's (1970, pp. 268–269) findings indicate that the functions were insufficient to compel unity of behavior, particularly given the conglomerate quality of the groupings and the corporate decisions that are generally influenced by the member companies. The main difference between the large corporate groups in Japan and Germany was whether they effectively unified command. In Germany, large corporate groups had secured a certain level of competitiveness by strategically utilizing their collective strength through unified conduct, acting as a single enterprise (Takahashi 2000, p. 24). However, the indication that there had been no unified command in Japan holds true not for the organic parent-subsidiary corporate groups but for the industrial groups in their horizontal relations. There were also important organizations for exchanging information and coordinating interests, as seen in the aforementioned presidents' clubs in industrial groups, despite the fact that there were no such means to adjust interests between industrial groups. This became an important factor that brought about intense competition between large enterprises in many industries.

Japanese industrial groups exhibited a remarkable characteristic: industrial companies that composed industrial groups were arranged so that they could embody the industrial linkage as the whole, as if through "self-conclusion" (Suzuki 2008, p. 54). However, it is noteworthy that the formation of these industrial groups enforced every industrial sector to directly compete with other large corporations, and each industrial group had relatively large and competitive or evenly matched corporations (Maekawa 1997, p. 59).

In addition, when comparing the industrial group of the old *zaibatsu* type with the bank-type groups, except the *zaibatsu* type, in three groups of the latter group—the Fuyo (Fuji Bank) Group, the Sanwa Group, and the Daiich Kangyo Ginko (Daiichi Ginko) Group—independent individual enterprises formed each industrial group with the objective of creating opponents for the old *zaibatsu* groups, especially under the postwar competitive condition. This became an important factor that decreased the holdings ratios among the groups and delayed the formation of presidents' clubs. Such a historical process also brought about differences in the uniformity in the business or the placement of industry between the old *zaibatsu* groups and the bank-type groups. In the former groups, competition was avoided by building a system in which a division of labor was established on the basis of the principle that only one member company existed in a certain industry. As a result, trade between the fields of related business was relatively easy. Conversely, there were cases in which the companies that belonged to the same industrial groups in the bank-type groups were competing with one another (Kudo 1982, p. 23). Thus, these groups faced certain limitations due to the elimination of competition between the companies in the group. This was also an important factor that determined the postwar structure of intense competition in Japan.

The logic adopted in the combination of industrial groups was different from that of the *zaibatsu* groups in prewar Japan. This logic was that of the large industrial companies and banks that were forced to create more advantageous conditions in order to prevail over other companies successfully under the intensive competition (Kudo 1994, pp. 31–32). However, even in the Mitsubishi Group, wherein combination was especially strong among the six industrial groups, there were two behavioral principles: (1) "independence as a centripetal force toward original actions of each company instead of joint actions" and (2) "dependence as a centripetal force toward unity of the group rather than individual actions of the company" (Hirai 2013, pp. 415–416). These principles reveal an important characteristic of the combination of industrial groups in Japan. More specifically, since it was necessary that large enterprises combined with one another in the heavy and chemical industries, wherein detour production was the principle, and since combining banks and larger companies was necessary for pursuing the economy of scale based on the principles of mass production and selling and realization of large-scale equipment investment, Japanese industrial groups showed their economic merits in periods of high economic growth (Okumura 1995, p. 61). Moreover, since the movement toward expanding such industries advanced more rapidly in Germany than in Japan, both the necessity and inevitability of forming the structure of the corporate groups crossing various industries (as seen in Japan) were low.

In Japan, the necessity to fulfill the high capital demand induced by the expansion of the heavy and chemical industry and secure product demand compatible with the structure of productive forces in the postwar boom years determined the development of corporate groups in a wide range of industrial sectors. An important characteristic of Japanese capitalism after World War II was evident in the predominance of primary material industries in the economy (Murakami 2013, p. 58). Therefore, interrelationships between producer and consumer goods industries and between various producer goods sectors in terms of markets and demands had great significance for such a reproduction structure. The existence of several industrial enterprises as well as banks in the prewar *zaibatsu* was an important basis for developing corporate groups, including various industries that enabled their member companies to mutually complement the accumulation structure.

Furthermore, large corporate groups of the pyramid type in the same capital group formed by big businesses that composed the industrial group in the main industries and independent large enterprises in Japan correspond to the large corporate groups of an industrial base in Germany. In addition, the advantages of the function side, such as cost reduction, were not necessarily pursued using the various merits of decentralization through the formation of subsidiary companies. Instead, the advantages were secured through the division of labor according to the products and specializations of companies; consequently, this approach had important implications.

In contrast to Japan, large corporate groups in postwar Germany were not full-set types that encompassed a broad range of industries, but were essentially corporate groups based on a single-industry structure. The restructuring of large corporate groups formed industry-specific groups that were adaptive to postwar oligopolistic competition. This type of concentration helped create a system that exhibited economies of scale through the benefits of specialization and division of labor. The emphasis on functional aspects based on the division of labor among corporations was critical. This type of development strengthened the systems of inter-firm relationships; these relationships formed for the expansion of corporate activities that emphasized market segments adapted to oligopolistic competition in the form of "division of labor complementary to each product." The relationships between large corporate groups with such "complementary product-based divisions of labor" held important implications for the restriction of competition among firms in same industry.

In Germany, large industrial groups were not established by combining industrial enterprises and financial institutions, unlike the formation of the *zaibatsu* in prewar Japan (Takahashi 1997, p. 55). In addition, no large industrial group covered wide industrial fields, even after World War II (Koyama et al. 1998, p. 19). Meanwhile, the system of concentration was incorporated in the banks' sphere of influence through the formation of large corporate groups in each industry. However, unlike the developments in Japan, the continuous trading relationships between group companies in Germany did not have significance, except for such relations with the main large bank (Koyama et al. 1998, p. 20).

The postwar reforms regarding the system of large corporate groups included changes to the big business system, which incorporated cooperative relationships between enterprises in order to correspond to the oligopolistic competition in the domestic and global markets for both Japan and Germany. However, the German system established an important basis for companies to develop management by emphasizing on avoiding intense price competitions and specializing in high-quality competition, both of which greatly differed from those in Japan. The system of large corporate groups in Germany promoted the formation of complementary relationships in product fields on the basis of product quality in the market, which further restricted price competition among corporations. Since the German and European markets emphasized product quality and functionality, German competitiveness in

European markets, along with the bias toward exporting to these regions, created a pattern of foreign trade with a division of labor that was complementary to their industrial and production fields. These market structures developed a foundation that supported a labor division system that complemented production fields in large corporate groups.

Discussions in this chapter have examined new development in the postwar system of large corporate groups. However, an important problem that changed industrial concentration was the industrial system based on industry–bank relationships. Industrial systems based on industry–bank relationships were extremely important for the expansion of Japanese and German corporations. Therefore, this issue will be considered in Chap. 5.

References

Abelshauser W (2004) Deutsche Wirtschaftsgeschichte seit 1945. C. H. Beck, München

Aizawa K (1994) Oshu saikyo no kinyu teikoku (The strongest financial empire in Europe). Nihon keizai shinbunsha, Tokyo

Aoki M, Patrick H (1994) Introduction. In: Aoki M, Patrick H (eds) The Japanese main bank system. Its relevance for developing and transforming economies. Oxford University Press, Oxford, pp xxi–xxxii

Berghahn V (1985) Unternehmer und Politik in der Bundesrepublik. Suhrkamp, Frankfurt am Main

Berghahn VR (1986) The Americanization of German industry 1945–1973. Berg, Leamington Spa

Сутягина МВ (1973) Мицубиси. Наука, Москва

Der Volkswirt (1952a) Beendeter Mannesmann-Umbau. In: Der Volkswirt 6(16):24–25

Der Volkswirt (1952b) Die Neuordning bei Hoesch. In: Der Volkswirt 6(31):23–24

Der Volkswirt (1953a) Gutehoffnungshütte neu geordnet. In: Der Volkswirt 7(31):21–23

Der Volkswirt (1953b) Mannesmann für neue Aufgaben gerüstet. In: Der Volkswirt 7(25):23–25

Der Volkswirt (1954a) Fried. Krupp. Nur noch Verarbeitungsgesellschaft ohne Kohle und Stahl. In: Der Volkswirt, 8.Jg, Beilage zu Nr.44 vom 30. Oktober 1954, Das veranderte Gesicht der Montan-Industrie. Zum Eisenhuttentag, p 49

Der Volkswirt (1954b) Kruppbetriebe Im Existenzkampf. In: Der Volkswirt 8(1):24–25

Der Volkswirt (1954c) Liquidation der Hoesch AG. Die Nachfolgegesellschaften entwickeln sich günstig. In: Der Volkswirt 8(19):24–26

Der Volkswirt (1955a) Klöckner-Neuordnung abgeschlossen. In: Der Volkswirt 9(14):25–27

Der Volkswirt (1955b) Rückgliederung abgeschlossen. Die Mannesmann AG berichtet. In: Der Volkswirt 9(24):26–28

Der Volkswirt (1956a) Bald 2 Mill. t Stahl bei der Hoesch Werke AG. In: Der Volkswirt 10(20):36–39

Der Volkswirt (1956b) Der neue Mannesmann-Konzern. In: Der Volkswirt 10(27):27–29

Der Volkswirt (1956c) Weitere Konsolidierung bei Krupp. In: Der Volkswirt 10(14):28–30

Der Volkswirt (1957) Hoesch Werke AG geht auf 8 vH. In: Der Volkswirt 11(23):1163–1166

Der Volkswirt (1959) Mannesmann AG: Erfolgreiche Verarbeitung. Schulden konsolidiert—Zum dritt Mal 10 vH Dividende. In: Der Volkswirt 13(28):1439–1443

Der Volkswirt (1960a) Hoesch AG in solidem Fortschritt. Dividende von 8 auf 10 vH erhoht—Abrundendes Investitionsprogramm. In: Der Volkswirt 14(23):1092–1094

Der Volkswirt (1960b) Hoesch Aktiengesellschaft. In: Der Volkswirt 14(26):1282

Deutsche Bank AG (1970) 100 Jahre Deutsche Bank 1870–1970. Deutsche Bank AG, Frankfurt am Main

Djelic M-L (1998) Exporting the American model. The postwar transformation of European business. Oxford University Press, Oxford
D.W.I.-Berichte (1955) Der westdeutsche Steinkohlenbergbau. In: D.W.I.-Berichte 6(6):2–30
D.W.I.-Berichte (1960) Die neue Konzentrationswelle in der westdeutschen Industrie. In: D.W.I.-Berichte 11:10–15
D.W.I.-Berichte (1961) Der Stand der Konzentration der Produktion von Produktionsmitteln in Westdeutschland. In: D.W.I.-Berichte 12(2):5–13
D.W.I.-Berichte (1962) Die mächtigsten Konzern der EWG und Groβbritanniens in wichtigen Zweigen der Produktionsmittelindustrie. In: D.W.I.-Berichte 13(23):1–21
Dyas GP, Thanheiser HT (1976) The emerging European enterpreise. Strategy and structure in French and German industry. The Macmillan Press, London
Enomoto S (1994) Kyodai kigyo no gurupu senryaku (Group strategy of huge enterprises). In: Gendai kigyo kenkyukai (ed) Nihon no kigyokan kankei (Japanese inter-firm relationships). Chuo keizaisha, Tokyo, pp 141–174
Fiereder H (1989) Demontagen in Deutschland nach 1945 unter besonderer Berücksichtigung der Montanindustrie. In: Zeitschrift für Unternehmensgeschichte 34:209–239
Fukuda Y (1985) Kigyo shudan keisei to kodo keizai seicho (Formation of corporate groups and high economic growth). In: Shakai kagaku ronshu (j Soc Sci) 49:103–159
Futatsuki Y (1975) Kigyo shudan no nakano kinyu kikan (Financial institution in corporate group). In: Keizai hyoron (Econ Rev) 24(3):20–33
Futastuki Y (1976) Gendai nihon no kigyo shudan (Corporate groups in Japan). Toyo keizai shinposha, Tokyo
Gall L, Feldmann GD, James H et al (1995) Die Deutsche Bank 1870–1995. C. H. Beck, München
Giga S (1958) Kontsuerun to kontororu—Sengo nihon no "zaibatsu kaitai" to keiei seido—(Large corporate groups and control—"Dissolution of zaibatsu" and business system in Japan after World War II—). In: Nihon keiei gakkai (ed) Gijutsu kakushin to keieigaku (Technological innovation and business administration). Dobunkan, Tokyo, pp 360–377
Gross H (1950) Material zur Aufteilung der I.G. Farbenindustrie Aktiengesellschaft. Institut für Weltwirtschaft, Kiel
Hahn W, Tammer H (1970) Kapitalkonzentration in Westdeutschland an der Wende zum neuen Jahrzehnt. In: DWI-Berichte 21(8):21–29
Hadley EM (1970) Antitrust in Japan. Princeton University Press, Princeton, New Jersey
Hashimoto J (1991) Nihon keizai ron. 20 seiki shisutemu to nihon keizai (Japanese economy. The 20th century system and Japanese economy). Mineruva shobo, Kyoto
Hashimoto J (1992) Kadai to bunseki. Jyojutsu no shikaku (Research topics and analysis. Description and analytical viewpoint). In: Hosei daigaku jyoho senta, Hashimoto J, Takeda H (eds) Nihon keizai no hatten to kigyo shudan (Development of Japanese economy and corporate group). Tokyo daigaku shuppankai, Tokyo, pp 1–14
Herrigel G (2000) American occupation, market order, and democracy: reconfiguring the steel industry in Japan and German after the Second World War. In: Zeitlin J, Herrigel G (eds) Americanization and its limits. Reworking US technology and management in post-war Europe and Japan. Oxford University Press, Oxford, pp 340–399
Hirai K (2013) Sengogata kigyo shudan no keieishi—Sekyu kagaku sekyu kara mita Mitsubishi no sengo—(Business history of postwar corporate groups—Mitsubishi group viewed from the perspective of petrochemistry and petroleum—). Nihon keizai hyoronsha, Tokyo
Horstmann T (1991) Die Alliierten und die deutschen Groβbanken. Bankenpolitik nach dem Zweiten Welkrieg in Westdeutschland. Bouvier, Bonn
Huffschmid B (1954) In Zukunft wieder Klöckner-Werke AG. Rückkehr der Kohle zur Obergesellschaft. In: Der Volkswirt 8(45):26–28
Huffschmid B (1965) Das Stahlzeitalter beginnt erst. Verlag Modeme Industrie, München
Inukai T (1968) Nishi doitsu ni okeru sangyo shuchu (2) (Industrial concentration in West Germany, 2). In: Shoken keizai (JSIR J Financ Secur Markets) 101:22–60

Isoda K (1976) Kigyo shudan to sogo shosha (1)—Nihongata takokuseki kigyo no mosaku—(Corporate groups and general trading company—Exploring Japanese multinational enterprises—). In: Kobe gakuin daigaku keizaigaku ronshu (Kobe Gakuin University Econ Rev) 8(2):1–23

Kabushiki gaisha Hitachi seisakusho rinji gojushunen jigyobu shashi hensanbu (ed) (1960) Hitachi seisakushoshi 2 (History of Hitachi Ltd. 2). Kabushiki gaisha Hitachi seisakusho, Tokyo

Kigyo shudan kenkyukai (1964) Bunki ni tatsu nihon no kigyo shudan (Corporate groups in Japan at the turning point). In: Keizai hyoron (Econ Rev) 13(11):79–93

Kikkawa T (1991) Kigyo shudan no seiritsu to sono kino—Kigyo shudan wa menba kigyo no kodo ni donna eikyo wo oyobosuka—(Formation and functions of corporate groups—What influence do corporate groups exert on the behavior of member companies?—). In: Will, September 1991, pp 136–143

Kikkawa T (1992a) Kigyo shudan no seiritsu to sono kino (Formation and functions of corporate group. In: Morikawa M (ed) Bijinesuman no tameno sengo keieishi nyumon (Introduction to business history after World War II for businessmen). Nihon keizai shinbunsha, Tokyo, pp 62–85

Kikkawa T (1992b) Sengogata kigyou shudan no keisei (Formation of the postwar type of corporate groups). In: Hosei daigaku jyoho senta, Hashimoto J, Takeda H (eds) Nihon keizai no hatten to kigyo shudan (Development of Japanese economy and corporate group). Tokyo daigaku shuppankai, Tokyo, pp 255–304

Kikkawa T (1995) Chukan soshiki no henyo to kyosoteki kasen kozo no Keisei (Change in intermediary organizations and competing oligopolistic structures). In: Yamazaki H, Kikkawa T (eds) "Nihonteki" keiei no renzoku to danzetsu (Continuity and discontinuity of "Japanese" management). Iwanami shoten, Tokyo, pp 233–273

Kikkawa T (1996) Nihon no Kigyo Shudan (Japanese large corporate groups). Yuhikaku, Tokyo

Kikuchi H (2005) Kigyo shudan no keisei to kaitai: Shachokai no kenkyu (Formation and dismantlement of corporate groups: Study of the President club). Nihon Keizai hyoronsha, Tokyo

Kleinkamp H-D (1977) Die Entflechtung der I.G. Farbenindustrie A.G. und die Grundung der Nachfolgegesellschaft. In: Vierteljahrhefte fur Zeitgescichte 25(2):220–251

Kobayashi M (1983) Nishi Doitsu tekkogyo. Sengo dankai=Sengo gorika (The iron and steel industry in West Germany. The postwar stage—Rationalization after World War II). Yuhikaku, Tokyo

Kobayashi Y (1977a) Kigyo shudan no bunseki 8 (Analysis of corporate group 8). In: Keizai hyoron (Econ Rev) 26(11):85–103

Kobayashi Y (1977b) Kigyo shudan to sangyo soshiki—Sairon—(Corporate groups and industrial organization—A reexamination—). In: Keizaigaku kenkyu (Econ Study) 27(1):85–136

Kobayashi Y (1979) Hikaku kigyo shudan ron—Nihon to Amerika—(Comparison of corporate groups—Japan and the United States—). In: Keizai Semina (econ Seminar) 289:44–51

Kobayashi Y (1980) Kigyo shudan no bunseki (Analysis of corporate groups). Hokkaido daigaku tosho kankokai, Sapporo

Kosei torihiki iinkai (1975) Sogo shosha ni kansuru dai nikai chosa hokoku—Dokusen kinshi seisaku kara mita shosha mondai ni tsuite—(The second investigation regarding general trading company—Problems of trading companies viewed from anti-monopoly policy perspective—). In: Shukan kinyu zaisei jijyo (Monet Fiscal Cond Wkly) 26(5):54–59

Kosei torihiki iinkai jimukyoku keizaibu kigyoka (1983) Kigyo shudan no jittai ni tsuite (Conditions of corporate groups). In: Kosei torihiki (fair Trade) 394:20–26

Koyama A, Dolles H (1994) Nichidoku kigyo no hikaku bunseki no tameni (2) (Comparative analysis of enterprises in Japan and Germany). In: Gakushuin daigaku keizia ronshu (J Dep Econ Gakushuin University) 30(4):423–438

Koyama A, Tezuka K, Ueda Y et al (1998) Nihon to doitsu ni okeru kigyo gurupu no hikaku bunseki: Jyoronteki kosatsu (Comparative analysis of corporate groups in Japan and Germany). In: Gakushuin daigaku keizai keiei kenkyusho nenpo (Yearbook of Gakushuin Univ Res Inst Econ Manag) 11:17–37

Kudo A (1999) Gendai Doitsu kagaku kigyoushi—IG Farben no seiritsu tenkai kaitai—(Modern German chemical enterprises—Birth, development, and dismantlement of IG Farben—). Mineruva shobo
Kudo M (1982) Sengo kigyo shudan bunseki ni yosete (Analysis of postwar corporate group). In: Shogaku ronsan (Commer Rev) 24(1):201–245
Kudo M (1994) Kigyokan kankei no keizai riron (Economic theory of inter-firm relationships). In: Gendai kigyo kenkyukai (ed) Nihon no kigyokan kankei (Japanese inter-firm relationships). Chuo keizaisha, Tokyo, pp 13–39
Kyuno M (1995) Gurupu nai no ginko pawa ga yuraideiru (The bank's power within corporate group sways). In: Ekonomisuto (Economist) 73(23):42–45
Maekawa K (1970) Doitsu dokusen kigyo no hatten katei (Developoment of German monopolistic enterprises). Mineruva shobo
Maekawa K (1997) Nichidoku hikaku kigyoron heno michi (Comparative study of Japanese and German enterprise). Moriyama shoten, Tokyo
Masaki H (1985) Wagakuni no kigyo shudan kinyu no tenkai—Rokudai kigyo shudan no bunseki wo chushin ni—(Development of financing of corporate groups in Japan—Focusing on six large corporate groups—). In: Doshisha shogaku (Doshisya Bus Rev) 37(1):82–115
Mikami A (1976) Sumitomo gurupu to shachokai (Sumitomo goup and the President club). In: Kobayashi M, Shimokawa K, Sugiyama K et al (eds) Nihon keieishi wo manabu 3. Sengo keieishi (Learning Japanese business history 3. The postwar business history), vol 3, Yuhikaku, Tokyo, pp 244–256
Miyajima H (1991) "Zaikai Tsuiho" to Shin Keieisha no Tojyo (Purge of managers from the economic world and emergence of new top managers). In: Will 10(7):136–144
Miyajima H (1992) Zaibatsu kaitai. In: Hosei daigaku jyoho senta, Hashimoto J, Takeda H (eds) Nihon keizai no hatten to kigyo shudan. Tokyo daigaku shuppankai, Tokyo, pp 203–254
Miyamoto M, Abe T, Udagawa M et al (2007) Nihon keieishi (Japanese business history), Yuhikaku, Tokyo
Miyazaki G (1966) Sengo Nihon no Keizai kiko (Japanese economic system after World War II). Shin Hyoron, Tokyo
Miyazaki G (1976) Sengo nihon no kigyo shudan (The postwar corporate groups in Japan). Nihon keizai shinbunsha, Tokyo
Miyazaki G (1990) Kigyo shudan heno apurochi (Approach to corporate groups). In: Keizai hyoron (Econ Rev) 39(6):24–34
Morikawa H (1993) Zaibatsu kigyo shudan to sengo kigyo shudan (The zaibatsu corporate group and the postwar corporate group). In: Keieishigaku (Jpn Bus Hist Rev) 28(2):57–74
Murakami K (2013) Gendai Nihon saiseisan kozo bunseki (Analysis of reproduction structure of Japanese capitalism). Nihon Keizai hyoronsha, Tokyo
Nakamura M (1968a) Mitsui kontsuerun no hukkatsu katei (Revival process of the Mitsui corporate group). In: Noguchi T (ed) Mitsui kontsuerun (Mitsui corporate group). Shin hyoron, Tokyo, pp 177–199
Nakamura M (1968b) Sumitiomo kontsuerun no hukkatsu katei (Revival process of the Sumitomo corporate group). In: Noguchi T (ed) Sumitomo kontsuerun (Sumitomo corporate group). Shin hyoron, Tokyo, pp 149–174
Nakamura M (1994) Kigyo shudan no kozo—Kosei torihiki iinkai chosa ni miru—(Structure of corporate group—An analysis based on investigation of the Fair Trade Commission—). In: Meidai shogaku ronso (Meiji Univ Commer Rev) 76(2):85–103
Nakatani I (1983) Nihon keizai no "himitsu" wo toku kagi. Kigyo shudan to keiei (The key to clarify "secret" of Japanese economy. Corporate groups and management). In: Ekonomisuto (economist) 2500:78–85
Nakatani I (1984) Kigyo gurupu no keizai kino (Economic function of corporate groups). In: Kikan gendai keizai (contemp Econ) 58:14–24
Narusaka O (1974) Kigyo shudan ni kansuru ichi kosatsu (A study of corporate group). In: Chiba shodai ronso (Chiba Commer Univ Rev) 11(4-B), Shokei hen: 66–82

Nihon daigaku keizai gakubu sangyo keiei kenkyusho (ed) (1982) Kigyo shudan no keiei to kaikei ni kansuru jittai chosa (Investigation on actual conditions of management and accounting of corporate groups). Nihon daigaku keizai gakubu sangyo keiei kenkyusho, Tokyo

Noguchi T (1968) Mitsui kontsuerun no kiko to yakuwari (Institution and role of the Mitsui corporate group). In: Noguhi T (ed) Mitsui kontuerun (Mitsui corporate group). Shin hyoron, Tokyo, pp 16–26

Okamoto H (1987) Jigyo kozo no henkaku to kigyo gurupu (Change in business structure and corporate groups). In: Sakamoto K, Shimotani M (eds) Gendai nihon no kigyo gurupu (Corporate groups in Japan). Mineruva shobo, Kyoto, pp 113–138

Okazaki T (1992) Shihon jiyuka igo no kigyo shudan (Corporate groups after capital liberalization). In: Hosei daigaku jyoho senta, Hashimoto J, Takeda H (eds) Nihon keizai no hatten to kigyo shudan (Development of Japanese economy and corporate group). Tokyo daigaku shuppankai, Tokyo, pp 305–335

Okumura H (1975a) Hojin shihonshugi no kozo (Structure of corporate capitalism). Nihon hyoronsha, Tokyo

Okumura H (1975b) Nihon no kigyo shudan (Japanese corporate groups). In: Kikan chuo koron (Chuo Koron Quarterly) 51:314–336

Okumura H (1976) Nihon no rokudai kigyo shudan (Six large corporate groups in Japan). Daiyamondosha, Tokyo

Okumura H (1978) Kigyo shudan jidai no keieisha. Kabushiki gaisha wa dokohe iku (Managers in the age of corporate groups. Where will corporations go?). Nihon keizai shinbunsha, Tokyo

Okumura H (1983) Sin nihon no rokudai kigyo shudan (Six new corporate groups in Japan). Daiyamondosha, Tokyo

Okumura H (1995) Shachokai kaisan no susume (Recommendation of dissolution of the President club). In: Ekonomisuto (Economist) 72(23):60–61

Petzina D (1992) Zwischen Neuordnung und Krise. In: Dascher O, Kleinschmidt C (eds) Die Eisen- und Stahalindustrie im Dortmunder Raum. Wirtschaftliche Entwicklung, soziale Strukturen und technologischer Wandel im 19. und 20. Jahrhundert. Gesellschaft für Westfalische Wirtschaftsgeschichte E.V., Dortmund, pp 525–544

Pfeiffer H (1989) Die Macht am Main. Einfluß und Politik der Deutschen Großbanken. Paul-Rugenstein, Köln

Pfeiffer H (1993) Die Macht der Banken. Die personellen Verflechtungen der Commerzbank, der Deutschen Bank und der Dresdner Bank mit Unternehemen. Campus, Frankfurt am Main

Pohl M (1986) Entstehung und Entwicklung des Universalbanksystems: Konzentration und Krise als wichtige Faktoren. Fritz Knapp Verlag, Frankfurt am Main

Sakamoto K (1987a) Kigyo gurupu ron no kadai to shikaku (Research topics and analytical viewpoint in corporate group study). In: Sakamoto K, Shimotani M (eds) Gendai nihon no kigyo gurupu (Modern Japanese corporate groups). Mineruva shobo, Kyoto, pp 1–26

Sakamoto K (1987b) Seisan kogaisha no tenkai—Nippon denki no kesu—(Development of a production subsidiary—Case of the Nippon Electric Company—). In: Sakamoto K, Shimotani M (eds) Gendai nihon no kigyo gurupu (Modern Japanese corporate groups). Mineruva shobo, Kyoto, pp 27–49

Sakamoto T (1980a) Kigyo shudan zaimuron (1) (Finance of corporate groups 1). In: Dai ichi keidai ronshu (Dai Ichi Econ Univ Rev) 10(1):45–67

Sakamoto T (1980b) Kigyo shudan zaimuron (2) (Finance of corporate group 2). In: Dai ichi keidai ronshu (Dai Ichi Econ Univ Rev) 10(2):31–56

Sakamoto T (1981) Kigyo shudan zaimuron (4) (Finance of corporate group 4). In: Dai ichi keidai ronshu (Econ Rev Daiichi Keizai College) 10(4):41–62

Sakamoto T (1991) Kigyo shudan keie no shiteki bunseki (Historical analysis of the management of corporate groups). In: Soka keiei ronshu (Rev Bus Admin) 15(2):143–158

Sakamoto T (1993) Kigyo shudan keieiron (Management of corporate groups). Dobunkan shuppan, Tokyo

Sakamoto T (1996) Daikigyo no zaimu kanri to kigyo shudan (Financial management of large enterprises and corporate groups). In: Sakamoto T, Sakuma N (eds) Kigyo shudan kenkyu no hoho (Methodology of corporate group study). Bunshindo, Tokyo, pp 193–212
Sakuma N (1995) Kigyo shudan ni okeru shachokai no kino (Function of the President club in corporate groups). In: Soka keiei ronshu (Rev Bus Admin) 19(3):13–27
Sakuma N (1996a) Doitsu ni okeru daiginko to daikigyo (Large banks and large enterprises in Germany). In: Soka Keiei ronshu (rev Bus Admin) 21(2):63–78
Sakuma N (1996b) Doitsu no "kigyo shudan" (Corporate groups in Germany). In: Sakamoto T, Sakuma N (eds) Kigyo shudan kenkyu no hoho (Methodology of corporate group study). Bunshindo, Tokyo, pp 79–105
Sasaki K (1975) Gendai Yoroppa shihonshugi ron (Contemporary European capitalism). Yuhikaku, Tokyo
Schlieper A (1986) 150 Jahre Ruhrgebiet. Ein Kapitel deutscher Wirtschaftsgeschichte. Schwann, Dusseldorf
Shadan hojin keizai chosa kyokai (1962) Nenpo keiretsu no kenkyu (Yearbook of affiliation study)—Dai ichibu jyojyo kigyohen (Companies listed in the first section of the Tokyo Stock Exchange)—, 1962 nen ban (1962 edition). Shadan hojin keizai chosa kyokai, Tokyo
Shadan hojin keizai chosa kyokai (1968) Nenpo keiretsu no kenkyu (Yearbook of affiliation study)—Dai ichibu jyojyo kigyohen (Companies listed in the first section of the Tokyo Stock Exchange)—, 1968 nen ban (1968 edition). Shadan hojin keizai chosa kyokai, Tokyo
Shadan hojin keizai chosa kyokai (1978) Nenpo keiretsu no kenkyu (Yearbook of affiliation study)—Dai ichibu jyojyo kigyohen (Companies listed in the first section of the Tokyo Stock Exchange)—, 1978 nen ban (1978 edition). Shadan hojin keizai chosa kyokai, Tokyo
Shadan hojin keizai chosa kyokai (1983) Nenpo keiretsu no kenkyu (Yearbook of affiliation study)—Dai ichibu jyojyo kigyohen (Companies listed in the first section of the Tokyo Stock Exchange)—, 1983 nen ban (1983 edition). Shadan hojin keizai chosa kyokai, Tokyo
Shimada K (2010) Kigyokan kankei no kozo—Kigyo shudan keiretsu shosha—(Structure of inter-firm relationship—Corporate group, affiliation, and trading company—). Ryutsu keizai daigaku shuppankai, Ryugasaki
Shimotani M (1993) Nihon no keiretsu to kigyo gurupu (Japanese affiliation and corporate groups). Yuhikaku, Tokyo
Shimotani M (1998) Matsushita gurupu no rekishi to kozo (History and structure of the Matsushita corporate group). Yuhikaku, Tokyo
Shimotani M (2008) Shinko kontsuerun to zaibatsu. Riron to rekishi (Emerging corporate groups and Zaibatsu. Theory and history). Nihon keizai hyoronsha, Tokyo
Sieber G (1958) Die Rekonzentration der eisenschaffenden Industrie in Westdeutschland. In: WWI-Mitteilungen 11 (3): 46–55
Sogawa H, Suzuki S (1970) Sanwa kontsuerun (Sanwa corporate group). In: Noguchi T (ed) Fuji Sanwa Dai ichi (Furukawa Kawasaki) kontuerun [Coroporate groups of Fuji, Sanwa, and Dai ichi (Furukawa and Kawasaki)]. Asahi shuppansha, Tokyo, pp 88–139
Stolper G, Hauser K, Borchardt K (1964) Deutsche Wirtschaft seit 1870. J. C. B. Mohr, Tübingen
Sumiya T (1982) Nihon keizai to rokudai kigyo shudan (Japanese economy and six large corporate groups). Shin hyoron, Tokyo
Suzuki K (1993) Nihon no kigyo shudan—Sengo nihon no kigyo to ginko—(Japanese corporate groups—Enterprise and bank in postwar Japan—). Otsuki shoten, Tokyo
Suzuki K (1998) Mein banku to kigyo shudan—Sengo nihon no kigyokan shisutemu—(Main bank and corporate group—Inter-firm system in postwar Japan—). Mineruva shobo, Kyoto
Suzuki K (2002) Fukusu no kigyo shudan ni kamei suru kigyo no ginko torihiki kankei (Transaction relations of enterprises joining multiple corporate groups with banks). In: Momoyama gakuin daigaku sogo kenkyusho kiyo (St. Andrew's University Bull Res Inst) 28(1):59–91
Suzuki K (2008) Rokudai kigyo shudan no hokai (Collapse of six large corporate groups). Shinnihon shuppansha, Tokyo

Suzuki S (1981) Nishi Doitsu ni okeru kigyo shuchu ni tsuite (Enterprise concentration in West Germany). In: Mita shogaku kenkyu (Mita Bus Rev) 24(5):95–115

Suzuki S (1983) Nishi Doitsu ni okeru kigyo shuchu ni kansuru ichi kosatsu (A study of enterprise concentration in West Germany). In: Nihon keiie gakkai (ed) Sangyo gijutsu no shintenkai to keiei kanri no kadai (New development of industrial technology and tasks of business management). Chikura shobo, Tokyo, pp 272–280

Suzuta A (1976) Dai-Iichi kangin gurupu no subete (The whole of Dai-Ichi Kangyo Bank corporate group). Nihon jitsugaku shuppansha, Tokyo

Takahashi H (2000) Kontsuerun no toitsuteki shiki to jinteki ketsugo (United direction and personnel connection in corporate groups). In: Sogo seisaku kenkyu (j Policy Cult) 5:23–40

Takahashi I (1997) Doitsu kyoso seigen kinshiho no seiritsu to kozo (Birth and structute of the Restrictive Trade Practices Act). Sanseido, Tokyo

Takai T (1996) Toshiba gurupu keiei (Management of Thoshiba group). In: Teramoto Y (ed) Nihongata gurupu keiei no senryaku to shuho [2] <Seizogyo hen> (Strategy and method of Japanese-type management of corporate groups) [2] <Manufacturing industry edition>. Chuo keizaisha, Tokyo, pp 1–42

Tanaka A (2004) Kigyo shudan to sogo shosha no shin kyokumen (New phase of corporate groups and general trading company). In: Kagaku keizai (Chem Ind Econ), June 2004:86–94

Tanimoto K (1994) <Kigyokan kankei> to iu shiten (Viewpoint as "inter-firm relationship"). In: Gendai kigyo kenkyukai (ed) Nihon no kigyokan kankei (Inter-firm relationship in Japan). Chuo keizaisha, Tokyo, pp 1–9

Teramoto Y (1994a) Gendai no gurupu keiei no igi to kadai (Significance and problem of modern corporate group management). In: Teramoto Y (ed) Nihongata gurupu keiei no senryaku to shuho [I] <<Jyoho sabisu hen>> (Strategy and method of Japanese type management of corporate group [I], Information and service edition). Chuo keiziasha, Tokyo, pp 1–7

Teramoto Y (1994b) Maegaki (Preface). In: Teramoto Y (ed) Nihongata gurupu keiei no senryaku to shuho [I] <<Jyoho sabisu hen>> (Strategy and method of Japanese type management of corporate group [I], Information and service edition). Chuo keiziasha, Tokyo, pp 1–2

Teramoto Y (1996) Seizogyo no gurupu keiei no henkaku kadai (Reform problem of group management in the manufacturing industry). In: Teramoto Y (ed) Nihongata gurupu keiei no senryaku to shuho [2] <Seizogyo hen> (Strategy and method of Japanese type management of corporate group [2]), Manufacturing industry edition. Chuo keizaisha, Tokyo, pp 1–4

Tohara T (1974) Nishi Doitsu ni okeru sengo kaikaku (Postwar reform in West Germany). In: Tokyo daigaku shakai kagaku kenkyusho (ed) Sengo kaikaku 2: Kokusai kankyo (Postwar reform: International environment), vol 2. Tokyo daigaku shuppankai, Tokyo, pp 91–151

Treue W, Uebbing H (1969) Die Feuer verlöschen nie: August Thyssen-Hütte 1926–1966. Econ Verlag, Dusseldorf, Wien

Uebbing H (1991) Wege und Wegmarken. 100 Jahre Thyssen, 1891–1991. Siedler, Berlin

Ueno T (1989) Rokudai kigyo shudan no jittai ni tsuite (Actual conditions of six large corporate groups). In: Kosei torihiki (fair Trade) 464:46–56

Uetake A (1993) Kigyo shudan ron no genjyo to kadai (Present conditions and problems in corporate group study). In: Gendai keieigaku kenkyukai (ed) Gendai keieigaku no kihon kadai (Fundamental problems in modern management study). Bunshindo, Tokyo, pp 130–155

Uno H (1972) Sengo no kigyo shudan to sono mondaiten (Corporate groups after World War II and their challenges). In: Gakushuin daigaku keizai ronshu (J Dep Econ Gakushuin Univ) 8(3):3–30

Ushiyama M (1989) Doitsu ginko no kigyo shudanka seisaku (Corporate group policy of Deutsche Bank). In: Keizaigaku kenkyu (J Polit Econ) 55(4–5):71–105

Wandel E (1998) Banken und Versicherungen im 19. und 20. Jahrhundert. R. Oldenbourg, München

Wirtschke T (2009) Gefahr für den Wettbewerb? Die Fusionkontrolle der Europäischen Gemeinschaft für Kohle und Stahl und die 》Rekonzentration《 der Ruhrindustrie 1950–1963. Akademie Verlag, Berlin

Yajima C (1959) Ruru kontsuerun no hukkatsu (Resurrection of corporate groups in the Ruhr district). Keizai dantai rengokai, Tokyo

Yamazaki H (1995) Gaisetsu 1937–55 (General statement 1937–1955). In: Yamazaki H, Kikkawa T (eds) "Nihonteki" keiei no renzoku to danzetsu (Continuity and discontinuity of "Japanese" management). Iwanami shoten, Tokyo, pp 1–73

Yamazaki T (2015) Doitsu senzenki keieishi kenkyu (German business history until the end of World War II). Moriyama shoten, Tokyo

Yoshida M, Uchiyama T (1970) (Furukawa Kawasaki) kontsuerun [(Furukawa and Kawasaki) corporate groups]. In: Noguchi T (ed) Fuji Sanwa Dai-Ichi (Furukawa Kawasaki) kontsuerun [Fuji, Sanwa, and Dai-Ichi (Furukawa and Kawasaki) Corporate groups]. Asahi shuppansha, Tokyo, pp 142–187

Chapter 5
New Developments of the Industrial System Based on Industry–Bank Relationships

Abstract This chapter explores the development of a new system of oligopolistic industrial concentration based on industry–bank relationships after World War II. Industry–bank relationships are important issues in collaborative inter-firm relationships, corporate governance, enterprise development, and the accumulation structures of Japanese and German capitalism. In Japan, industry–bank relationships were restructured through the deconcentration of the *zaibatsu* and the formation of large corporate groups that spanned a wide array of industrial sectors. Industry–bank relationships developed in Germany through a variety of mechanisms, including banks' credit and securities businesses, the shareholdings and deposited stock system, the assignment of directors from banks to corporations, and the advisory board system. First, this chapter examines Japan's postwar industrial system based on industry–bank relationships. Second, it examines new developments in Germany's industrial systems based on industry–bank relationships. Drawing on these discussions, the Japanese and German characteristics and the significance of their industrial systems based on industry–bank relationships are clarified.

Keywords Corporate governance · Industrial concentration · Industry–bank relationship · Inter-firm relationship · Large corporate system · Universal banking system

Based on the analysis in Chap. 4, this chapter elucidates industry–bank relationships as a problem that was deeply concerned with that of postwar Japanese and German systems of industrial concentration and business management. Industrial concentration is closely related to business management and economic concentration because it is based on inter-firm relationships. The most distinctive manifestation of large business systems is the cooperative mechanisms for enterprises, particularly in relation to connections between banks and industries. Such an industrial concentration system has been the cornerstone of the capitalistic accumulation structure of each country. However, while there were general trends between the major nations, original developments in each country were also distinct. This holds good for both Japan and Germany.

T. Yamazaki, *Japanese and German Enterprises*,
https://doi.org/10.1007/978-981-97-4880-8_5

Large business systems, particularly in relation to ties between banks and industries were the cornerstone of Japanese and German capitalism's accumulation structure and were important processes in postwar German corporate expansion. In both Japan and Germany, industry–bank relationships were already found before World War II and emerged in the postwar era as a new development in the industrial system; they functioned as a collaborative system between industries and banks as well as among companies themselves. Industrial systems based on industry–bank relationships ensured autonomy through coordination between banks and between industries and banks, as well as the participation of bank representatives on corporate supervisory boards or boards of directors. This type of industrial system produced corporate governance systems in the Japanese and German styles.

In Japan, under the industrial groups that were formed after the dissolution of the *zaibatsu*, close combinations between industrial enterprises and banks were built and reinforced, with the core banks serving as the main banks of each group. Moreover, the banks established a close relationship with industrial enterprises within the industrial groups by utilizing financial business, coordinating interlocking stockholdings, establishing presidents' clubs, and assigning directors.

In contrast, industry–bank relationships developed in Germany through a variety of mechanisms, including banks' credit and securities businesses, the shareholdings and deposited stock system, the dispatch of directors not only from banks to corporations but also from industrial enterprises to banks, and the advisory council system. German characteristics of industrial concentration, which were based on prewar industry–bank relationships, included new developments in the industrial system that coordinated interests as well as conflicts and shared information between industry and banks and between corporations. Such systems that were based on cooperative inter-firm relationships not only demonstrated collaborative capitalism with regulative functions and a new approach toward industrial concentration and monopolies, which supported the system of large corporate groups, but also built mechanisms for corporate governance.

Therefore, this chapter analyzes the new developments in industrial systems and clarifies the characteristics and significance of the new industrial concentration system in postwar Japan and Germany.[1] "Industry" here refers not only to the manufacturing industry but, in a broader sense, also to the non-financial industries, including distribution and service industries. The industrial system based on industry–bank relationships was fundamental to the development of financial capital interests, which was based on a market control system for big businesses.

In Sect. 5.1 and Sect. 5.2, the issues of inter-firm relationships between industries and banks in an "organic" industrial system in Japan and Germany are explored. Given these discussions, Japanese and German characteristics of postwar industrial systems based on industry–bank relationships are elucidated in Sect. 5.3.

---

[1] The first content analysis related to Germany in this chapter is Chap. 5 of the author's book "*German Business Management: A Japanese Perspective on Regional Development Factors,*" which was published by Springer in 2013.

5.1 New Development of the Industrial System Based on Industry–Bank Relationships in Japan

First, the new development of an industrial system in Japan based on industry–bank relationships is considered. As analyzed in Chap. 4, some industrial groups were established after the deconcentration of the *zaibatsu*, the prohibition of holding companies, and the regulation of treasury stock acquisitions. When such corporate groups were viewed as a whole, both loans to affiliated companies and interlocking shareholdings were implemented in the same industrial groups in the convergent form. In many cases, these were reserved for other groups, which aided in maintaining the corporate groups' identity (Sakaguchi 1968, p. 82). In both loans to the affiliated companies and cross-stockholdings, the banks in the industrial groups held significant positions. Despite the dissolution of the *zaibatsu*, the banks could escape such dismantling. The relationships between industrial enterprises and banks in the *zaibatsu* continued as a result of the financial institutions' resources being preserved. This laid the groundwork for the formation of postwar industrial groups. Although the *zaibatsu* group's characteristics were lost, the overall framework of the groups was maintained through various connections such as trade between enterprises and personnel connections. As a result, the relationships between banks and corporations became closer, and the former played a leading role in re-establishing industrial groups (Kudo 1982, pp. 212–213, 223; Miyazaki 1966, pp. 48–49; Nakatani 1984, p. 18; Okumura 1976, pp. 41, 44; Sakaguchi 1966, p. 129; Сутягинар 1973, p. 142; Fukuda 1985, pp. 131, 133). Furthermore, the financing activities conducted by city banks facilitated the combining of companies during the zaibatsu's dissolution (Suzuki 1993, p. 57). The banks also aided in the control of certain business activities within the group by deploying directors to member companies.

Thus, this section examines the problems of industry–bank relationships in relation to the main banking system, the loans to affiliated enterprises, the interlocking stockholdings between banks and industrial enterprises, and the assignment of directors from banks to industrial companies. Because Japanese inter-firm relationships have already been discussed in Chap. 4 as a means of combining enterprises in the industrial groups, the importance of banks in such relationships (as seen in industry–bank relationships) is considered in this section.

5.1.1 Industry–Bank Relationships in Regard to the Main Banking System and the Loans to Affiliated Companies

This section discusses industry–bank relationships with respect to the main banking system and loans to affiliated companies. An important point in distinguishing the *zaibatsu* and the postwar industrial groups can be seen in the change in the roles of financial institutions led by banks. In each *zaibatsu* group, member enterprises generally carried out self-financing (Uno 1972, pp. 6–7; Miyazaki 1966, p. 235).

Although industrial enterprises under the influence of the *zaibatsu* deposited funds in the banks, loans made by the banks were avoided as much as possible. As a matter of fact, banks rarely provided funds to industrial firms and holding companies in the *zaibatsu*. On the contrary, among the postwar industrial groups, borrowing from banks was ordinarily the form of loans to affiliated companies (Morikawa 1993, pp. 72–72; Shibagaki 1971, p. 21). Whereas short-term loans were the focus of prewar *zaibatsu* banks, long-term loans for equipment investment played a significant role in postwar city bank financing. Long-term and continuous relationships were also important in the industrial groups. Thus, loans to affiliated companies were developed along with deposits of enterprises (Sakamoto 1993, p. 28).

As banks were not considered to be the objects of deconcentration, the financial methods of the banks were kept up even after World War II. Alternatively, to facilitate bank loans, corporate financing adopted a structure based on indirect finance under the finance administration. Loans to affiliated companies strengthened relationships between industrial enterprise and banks, and the system of bank predominance in the relations between banks and corporations advanced rapidly with overborrowing by banks that relied on the Bank of Japan as a central bank for financing (Uno 1972, pp. 7, 9).

An important characteristic of Japanese companies' corporate finances after World War II was the indirect finance method. However, not all companies were able to receive financing from financial institutions on the same terms. Meanwhile, the big banks tended to provide funds as a main bank to enterprises that belonged to the same industrial group (Takamura 1977, p. 65). Although banks that formed the core of industrial groups developed loans to affiliated companies for not only firms within the group but also those outside of the group (Okumura 1976, p. 122), affiliated banks within the group in which city banks served as the core guaranteed a stable securing of funds through the preferential allotment of capital to enterprises within the group. The main banking system involved banks and companies becoming accustomed to the reciprocal trade of financing and deposits. The system of loans to affiliated companies was central to its operation. In such a system, the expansion of banks within the group prompted the expansion of corporations within the same group, and vice versa (Sakamoto 1996, pp. 199–200; Sakamoto 1981, pp. 55–56). In addition, the intensive lending competition between city banks was developed under a method of funding adopted by companies that greatly depended on the indirect finance method. The greater part of the loans made by city banks was allocated for financing to large companies, and the concentrated finance to the affiliated enterprises was performed in such a way that loans to the affiliated companies expanded at a remarkable rate (Miyazaki 1966, pp. 46–47).

City banks built the close positive relationships of main trading with a few specific corporate groups, whereas there were negative results when they only financed limited capital for many corporate groups that were the main customers of other banks (Washio 1968a, p. 113). The system of loans to affiliated companies limited or excluded the competition and fluid relation among city banks in dealing with big businesses as the borrower under such close and exclusive relationships between big banks and large corporations within the group (Washio 1964, p. 118). Furthermore, as many large corporations established large corporate groups in which they held subsidiary companies and affiliated enterprises at the top of the pyramid, the phenomenon in which city banks became the primary lenders to large corporations meant that they became the primary lenders to the entire pyramid of large corporate groups (Washio 1968b, pp. 101, 103).

Generally, interlocking shareholdings supported loans to affiliated companies. Mutual business trade was developed and strengthened by such cross-stockholdings. Meanwhile, the major banks reduced their lending to companies outside of the groups and refocused their efforts on providing credit to companies within the groups, which aided the latter greatly (Okumura 1975a, p. 172; Okumura 1975b, pp. 327–328; Okumura 1976, p. 123). The chief purpose of main banks was to "grasp exclusive financial ties between the major city banks and large firms" (Suzuki 2008, pp. 55–56). Overall, the main banks' ratio of stockholdings was high in the enterprises wherein the financing rate of the banks in the group was also high (Kobayash 1976, p. 107). In this way, the dependence of big businesses on banks did not exist as mutual relations between the large companies as a whole and the leading banks as a whole but under the special affiliation system that was typically found in industrial groups (Futatsuki 1975, p. 29). This reveals an important Japanese characteristic of industry–bank relationships.

The financing relations that big banks (particularly city banks) within industrial groups formed with the corporations in the same group were developed in various industries. This is another important Japanese characteristic of industry–bank relationships. Moreover, affiliated financing was not a system which merely gathered corporate groups that had a common main bank in a mechanical manner. The industrial organization of numerous firms in industrial groups mirrored city banks' financing strategies (Suzuki 1993, pp. 90–91). Competition among city banks for enterprise affiliation aimed at securing a system of financial circulation within groups and improving financing efficiency through industrial linkages (Sakamoto 1980, p. 52). The condition that supported the system in which payment settlements were included within banks was "exclusive trading relations between banks and large companies with one set-like industrial placement" (Suzuki 1993, p. 15). Affiliated financing, on the other hand, was an aspect that embodied such relationships (Suzuki 1998, p. 23). Banks also pursued enterprise-supporting strategies in which the banks became the primary banks of each group to adapt to any changes in the industrial structure, as seen in the increasing proportion of the heavy and chemical industries in the overall industry (Okazaki 1992, p. 317). Furthermore, as considered in Chap. 4, loans to affiliated firms were supported by the system of joint loans. Thus, a striking characteristic of the main banks' relationships in these two types of loans is obvious (Suzuki 1993, p. 134; Suzuki 2008, p. 56).

Overall, industrial groups were composed of big banks which were designated as the main banks for each group. These banks resiliently and flexibly supplied the payments and settlements required for credit creation. These banks adopted the *keiretsu* financing system and capital procurement methods as Japanese companies generally utilized indirect financing in the postwar period. These banks also advised big businesses regarding issues such as external financing (Suzuki 1993, p. 140).

Keiretsu financing was, from the perspective of the six industrial groups' main banks, a method of distributing risk and avoiding an extreme concentration of borrowers. In addition, it also enabled the expansion of lending while reducing banks' screening and monitoring costs (Miyajima 1992, p. 238).

Furthermore, the debt guarantees made by banks for the member enterprises in the same industrial groups were through the substantial loans to the affiliated firms. During periods of high economic growth, banks in the same industrial groups, particularly the city banks that belonged to presidents' clubs, supported the funding of group enterprises bearing their last credit risks in the form of debt guarantees (Okazaki 1999, preface, pp. ii, 234–235, 319–322).

Although the main banking system played a great role in periods of high economic growth, the proportion of the banks borrowing in enterprises decreased rapidly at the industrial-group level after the latter half of the 1970s. Meanwhile, the rate and role of financing through the capital market in corporate finance increased. As a result, not only did the dependence on main banks declined but the dependence of banks on the industrial groups decreased. As a result, corporations generally avoided banks, and banks commonly averted industrial groups (Suzuki 1985, pp. 86, 88–89, 102), which influenced the industry–bank financial relationships.

In the Mitsubishi Group, the independent rates of member firms of the industrial groups (listed enterprises in the first section of the stock exchange) in 1955, 1960, 1965, 1970, 1975, 1980, 1985, and 1990 (for 1965, the figure is for the first half; for 1970 and 1975, the figures are for September; for 1980, 1985, and 1990, the figures are for March) were 19.95%, 20.94%, 18.15%, 27.31%, 26.95, 24.0%, 23.44%, and 20.15%, respectively. For the same years, the relevant figures in the Sumitomo Group were 21.3%, 18.16%, 17.8%, 28.12%, 25.22%, 23.29%, 22.28%, and 14.11%, respectively, and those for Mitsui Group were 20.6%, 16.16%, 14.31%, 23.32%, 20.43%, 17.04%, 16.01%, and 15.63%, respectively. Similarly, for the same years, the relevant numerical values in the Fuji (Fuyo) Group were 25.7%, 22.34%, 20.57%, 27.03%, 25.99%, 22.18%, 19.73%, and 18.93%, respectively, and those for the Sanwa Group were 24.8%, 22.99%, 19.23%, 21.96%, 21.82%, 20.6%, 18.31%, and 18.39%, respectively. Again, for the same years, similar figures for the Daiichi Kangyo Ginko Group (for 1965 and 1970, the Daiichi Ginko Group) were 20.4%, 15.36%, 13.85%, 12.92%, 18.02%, 15.25%, 14.82%, and 15.83%, respectively; those for the six industrial groups in average were 22.05%, 19.33%, 17.32%, 23.44%, 23.07%, 20.39%, 19.1%, and 17.17%, respectively; those for the three old *zaibatsu* groups in average were 20.47%, 18.42%, 16.75%, 26.25%, 24.2%, 21.44%, 20.58%, and 16.63%, respectively; and those for the three non-*zaibatsu* groups were 23.63%, 20.23%, 17.88%, 20.64%, 21.94%, 19.34%, 17.62%, and 17.72%, respectively (Shadan hojin keizai chosa kyokai 1961, p. 24; Shadan hojin keizai chosa kyokai 1968, p. 3; Shadan hojin keizai chosa kyokai 1978, p. 10; Shadan hojin keizai chosa kyokai 1983, the general condition, p. 8; Shadan hojikeizai chosa kyokai 1990, the general condition, p. 2; Shadan hojin keizia chosa kyokai 1993, p. 3).

In terms of financing ratios provided by city banks in industrial groups to member companies of presidents' clubs, the Mitsubishi Group had 13.66%, 11.71%, and 9.93% in 1974, 1984, and 1994, respectively. For the same years, the relevant figures in the Sumitomo Group were 13.66%, 14.11%, and 11.4%, respectively; those for the Mitsui Group were 11.49%, 9.31%, and 9.33%, respectively; those for the Fuji (Fuyo) Group were 13.19%, 9.94%, and 8.43%, respectively; those for the Sanwa Group 13.65%, 11.7%, and 10.16%, respectively; and those for the Daiichi Kangyo Ginko Group were 11.42%, 10.09%, and 10.38%, respectively. Meanwhile, in the same years, the financing ratios of the financing to group firms (except members of the presidents' clubs) for the Mitsubishi Group were 24.27%, 22.9%, and 29.08%, respectively; those for the Sumitomo Group were 18.1%, 22.92%, and 24.98%, respectively; those for the Mitsui Group were 14.81%, 21.88%, and 23.51%, respectively; those for the Fuji group were 17.79%, 21.71%, and 22.77%, respectively; those for the Sanwa Group were 26.82%, 28.45%, and 21.56%, respectively; and those for the Daiichi Kangyo Ginko Group were 44.56%, 51.91%, and 44.45%, respectively.

Moreover, in the same years (i.e., 1974, 1984, and 1994), the financing rates of the financing provided by trust banks to member companies of the presidents' clubs for the Mitsubishi Group were 10.46%, 7.64%, and 6.2%, respectively; those for the Sumitomo Group were 12.61%, 9.8%, and 6.43%, respectively; those for the Mitsui Group were 7.17%, 6.61%, and 6.62%, respectively; those for the Fuji Group were 8.2%, 5.88%, and 4.91%, respectively; and those for the Sanwa Group were 6.51%, 5.43%, and 4.44%, respectively. For the same years, the financing ratios of the financing by trust banks to member firms (except for members of the presidents' clubs) for the Mitsubishi Group were 14.18%, 12.67%, and 7.78%, respectively; those for the Sumitomo Group were 15.6%, 14.54%, and 11.25%, respectively; those for the Mitsui Group were 16.42%, 12.52%, and 10.37%, respectively; those for the Fuji Group were 16.73%, 12.7%, and 12.01%, respectively; and those for the Sanwa Group were 12.1%, 6.68%, and 10.77%, respectively (Tokyo daigaku shakaikagaku kenkyusho 2000, pp. 90–91).

5.1.2 Industry–Bank Relationships Based on Interlocking Stockholdings

The close relationships between banks and industrial companies were built through interlocking shareholdings as well as financing relations. In these relationships, the shareholding relations in the industrial groups were particularly significant. In addition, interlocking stockholdings were seen conspicuously within industrial groups. In such groups, financial institutions in the same group became the main shareholders of the major industrial enterprises in the groups and other industrial firms of the group complemented such interlocking shareholdings. Cross-stockholdings were reinforced by strengthening mutual connections in a way that the industrial corporations and other financial institutions in the groups became the shareholders of the main financial institutions (Fujii 1979, p. 68; Futatsuki 1975, p. 27). Overall, the interlocking stockholdings that characterized inter-firm relations in Japan were those among companies. The cross-shareholdings between industrial enterprises and banks played a central role in the interlocking shareholdings. Moreover, there were also cross-stockholdings between financial institutions (Matsumura 1997, p. 69).

The relations where banks became the axis of interlocking shareholdings of enterprises in the same group were created after World War II. The stockholdings of member companies by industrial firms that had pushed ahead the rebuilding advanced afterward and a model of the cross-shareholding was completed in around 1955 (Suzuki 1993, p. 43). Interlocking shareholdings facilitated capital increase by payment of the enterprise in the group smoothly and played the role of finance to prompt more borrowing from the bank in the decade following 1955 (Masaki 1985, p. 92). The stockholdings by bank aimed to strengthen the loan to affiliated firms and the affiliation of company.

Therefore, it was heterogeneous with pure investment based on the judgment of the investment value (Sakano 1967, p. 227). There was a clear positive relation between financing and shareholding in each bank that belonged to the industrial group. The intention behind the increase in stockholdings by enterprises that advanced in the latter half of the 1960s was to secure the stable shareholder of the company that issued stocks as well as to maintain and expand the financial institution's trade relationship (Okazaki 1992, pp. 312, 320; Kobayashi 1976, p. 107). In this period, the shareholding rate by bank showed a tendency to increase while the financing ratio to member firms in the industrial group tended to fall. The interlocking stockholding between group companies had a more important significance than the preferential loan by bank as a means of reinforcing unity (Kobayashi 1977, pp. 123–124, 127).

The high proportion of shareholdings held by financial institutions in the industrial groups reflected the versatile linkages of trade in the groups (Kudo 1982, p. 235). The roles that city banks assumed as the core of industrial groups widely differed between the loans to affiliated firms and the interlocking stockholdings. Furthermore, the contributions of the banks were not always great in the cross-shareholdings (Kikkawa 1996, p. 187). However, the universality of the banking transactions was the foundation for the cross-stockholdings (Suzuki 1998, pp. 106, 108–109, 112). Interlocking shareholdings between enterprises in the groups made the financial power of the financial institutions the starting point (Futatsuki 1975, p. 29). Even in the interlocking shareholdings between industrial enterprises, the close financing relationships between the industrial companies and banks built the basis of the cross-stockholdings. Therefore, the roles that big banks played in the cross-shareholdings were significant. In addition, with respect to the ownership structure and the execution of voting rights, as Japanese banks are not universal banks, they were unable to execute voting rights by using the deposited stocks, as seen in Germany. However, combining the cross-shareholdings within industrial groups played an important role in securing management autonomy by creating stable stockholders.

In 1953, 1958, 1963, 1968, 1974, 1984, and 1994, the shareholding ratios provided to member firms of the presidents' clubs by city banks belonging to the same group for the Mitsubishi Group were 1.89%, 2.48%, 2.9%, 3.3%, 4.6%, 4.02%, and 3.78%, respectively; those for the Sumitomo Group were 1.82%, 3.7%, 5.22%, 4.69%, 4.81%, 3.69%, and 3.52%, respectively; those for the Mitsui Group were 0.88%,

1.31%, 2.49%, 2.48%, 3.25%, 3.56%, and 3.44%, respectively; those for the Fuji (Fuyo) Group were 1.13%, 2.56%, 3.99%, 4.19%, 4.57%, 3.99%, and 3.62%, respectively; those for the Sanwa Group were 1.08%, 2.48%, 2.55%, 4.29%, 4.15%, 3.93%, and 3.5%, respectively; and those for the Daiichi Kangyo Ginko Group (for 1953, 1958, 1963, and 1968, the Daiichi Ginko Group) were 0.33%, 2.1%, 2.19%, 3.93%, 4.19%, 4.09%, and 3.18%, respectively. In the same years, the shareholding ratios provided by city banks to enterprises within the groups (except for member firms of the presidents' clubs) for Mitsubishi Group were 0.58%, 1.43%, 2.25%, 3.35%, 5.29%, 5.2%, and 4.33%, respectively; those for the Sumitomo Group were 1.42%, 2.74%, 2.96%, 4.01%, 4.12%, 4.15%, and 4.03%, respectively; those for the Mitsui Group were 1.02%, 1.48%, 1.97%, 2.37%, 3.9%, 3.59%, and 3.84%, respectively; those for the Fuji Group were 0.98%, 2.5%, 2.98%, 4.3%, 5.6%, 4.99%, and 4.46%; those for the Sanwa Group were 1.77%, 2.71%, 4.16%, 4.61%, 6.9%, 6.52%, and 6.24%, respectively; and those for the Daiichi Kangyo Ginko Group (for 1953, 1958, 1963, and 1968, the Daiich Ginko Group) were 0.55%, 1.58%, 1.97%, 3.47%, 5%, 4.82%, and 4.02%, respectively.

In the same years (i.e., 1953, 1958, 1963, 1968, 1974, 1984, and 1994), the shareholding ratios provided by trust banks to member firms of the presidents' clubs in the same group for the Mitsubishi Group were 2.56%, 3.69%, 4.23%, 1.18%, 2.51%, 2.51%, and 4.27%, respectively; those for the Sumitomo Group were 3.59%, 3.09%, 5.64%, 2.79%, 2.76%, 3.36%, and 4.88%, respectively; those for the Mitsui Group were 0.55%, 0.81%, 1.26%, 1.43%, 2.36%, 2.09%, and 3.48%, respectively; those for the Fuji Group were 0.04%, 0.05%, 0.58%, 1.23%, 1.31%, 1.66%, and 2.76%; and those for the Sanwa Group were 0%, 0%, 2.63%, 0.97%, 0.74%, 1.19%, and 2.49%, respectively. However, for the Daiichi Kangyo Ginko Group (the Daiich Ginko Group), the numerical values were 0% in all the years. In the same years, the stockholding ratios provided by trust banks to companies in the same group (except for the member enterprises of the presidents' clubs) for the Mitsubishi Group were 3.4%, 3.05%, 3.59%, 1.01%, 2.72%, 3.28%, and 3.9%, respectively; those for the Sumitomo Group were 1.47%, 1.29%, 3.93%, 0.87%, 2.12%, 2.27%, and 3.51%, respectively; those for the Mitsui Group were 1.42%, 1.17%, 1.27%, 0.6%, 3.15%, 2.87%, and 3.23%, respectively; those for the Fuji Group were 0.03%, 0.02%, 0.14%, 0.68%, 2.82%, 3.47%, and 4.28%, respectively; and those for the Sanwa Group were 0%, 0%, 3.69%, 0.5%, 1.66%, 2.6%, and 4.3%, respectively. However, for the Daiichi Kangyo Ginko Group (the Daiich Ginko Group), all of the figures were 0%, except for 0.03% in 1958 (Tokyo daigaku shakaikagaku kenkyusho 1999, pp. 74–81).

5.1.3 Industry–Bank Relationships Based on the Assignment of Directors

Another measure of establishing relationships between banks and industrial corporations was the dispatch of directors. After World War II, as parent companies of the *zaibatsu* dissolved, such assignments to other firms held a great significance in industrial groups that were rebuilt after the implementation of the dissolution policy. As personnel from banks were dispatched to leading posts in each member firm, the personnel connections between industrial companies and banks rapidly developed. This also reveals that banks (to some extent) took control of the industrial-groups' duties (Сутягина 1973, p. 153).

The assignment of directors from financial institutions in the groups also increased through stock ownership. Meanwhile, the number of director assignments was determined by the strength of the industrial groups' relationships, as well as loans to affiliated firms and shareholdings. Unlike in the period preceding World War II, dispatched directors (in many cases) were full-time directors who assumed executive responsibilities (Uno 1972, pp. 7, 20; Miyazaki 1966, p. 233). The directors appointed by the banks were also salaried managers in charge of accounting in many cases. They had no say in the management of the group's other businesses. As a result, the situation in which the directors were dispatched differed greatly from that prior to World War II (Miyazaki 1966, p. 233).

The dispatch of directors was not implemented without trade relations and shareholdings. The root of the power for groups was based on the relevant relationships between banks and industrial enterprises (Futatsuki 1993, p. 124). Many directors were dispatched from big enterprises at the top of the pyramid to subsidiary firms and associated companies in the corporate groups of independent large corporations that did not belong to the industrial groups and were organized as organic parent–subsidiary groups. In contrast, in industrial groups, many of the assigned directors were dispatched from financial institutions and trading companies (Kobayashi 1980, p. 145). In particular, there were many examples of directors being assigned from banks to industrial companies within the group. This was because banks were not only large stockholders of many enterprises but also, as the main banks, had numerous customers through their loans to affiliated firms (Okumura 1978, p. 101). This tendency was inextricably linked with the main banking system, which aimed at monitoring customers for credit preservation as well as accumulating information on borrowers rather than influencing their activities (Miyajima 1992, pp. 233–234).

Moreover, the higher the financing rates and shareholding were the greater were the number of directors assigned from banks to corporations (Sumiya 1982, p. 135). On the other hand, the differences in the power of the banks that emerged in the capital interlockings through financing and stockholdings activities were reflected through personnel connections (Nakamura 1968, p. 198). However, as pointed out by Hadley, personnel ties between banks and core enterprises of groups did not necessarily have a high correlation with the most important firms of the groups, bank ownership in the corporations, or the scale of borrowing from banks.

In examining the problems of personnel connection resulting from the dispatch of directors in connection with the organization of top management, banks in Japan performed the assignment themselves through their one-tier management system. Trading enterprises were often tied to numerous companies through the interlocking directorate, whereas financial institutions assigned many directors (Nakata et al. 1997, pp. 143, 149, 151, 168).

Next, the situations of personnel connections through the dispatch of directors from banks are considered. In 1970, 1975, and 1980, the number of directors assigned from the core city banks to member firms in each industrial group (listed companies in the first section of the stock exchange) for the Mitsubishi Group were 69, 86, and 106, respectively; those for the Sumitomo Group were 41, 65, and 70, respectively; those for the Mitsui Group were 31, 38, and 47, respectively; those for the Fuji (Fuyo) Group were 56, 67, and 91, respectively; those for the Sanwa Group were 33, 45, and 52, respectively; and those for the Daiichi Kangyo Ginko Group (for 1970, the Daiichi Ginko Group) were 29, 82, and 122, respectively. Meanwhile, in the same years, the number of dispatched directors from trust banks to member firms in the same group for the Mitsubishi Group was 15, 21, and 25, respectively; those for the Sumitomo Group were 7, 14, and 19, respectively; those for the Mitsui Group were 8, 10, and 13, respectively; those for the Fuji Group were 1, 2, and 3, respectively; and those for the Sanwa Group were 0, 2, and 1, respectively. Thus, the number of assigned directors from trust banks was markedly few compared with that from city banks (Shadan hojin keizai chosa kyokai 1970, p. 8; Shadan hojin keizai chosa kyokai 1975, p. 11; Shadan hojin keizai chosa kyokai 1980, p. 11).

In fiscal years 1977, 1981, 1985, and 1987, the ratios of member firms that were assigned directors from banks within the industrial group to all member firms of the groups for the six industrial groups on average were 55.51%, 58.97%, 58.14%, and 57.79%, respectively; those for the three old *zaibatsu*-type groups on average were 62.05%, 59.92%, 55.96%, and 55.96%, respectively; and those for the three non-*zaibatsu* and bank-type groups on average were 48.96%, 58.02%, 60.32%, and 59.61%, respectively. In addition, in the same years, the ratios of the number of assigned directors from banks to member enterprises within the industrial group to the total number of directors in the member enterprises for the six industrial groups on average were 3.56%, 3.65%, 3.64%, and 3.92%, respectively; those for the three old *zaibatsu*-type groups on average were 3.95%, 3.6%, 3.97%, and 4.18%, respectively; and those for the three bank-type groups on average were 3.17%, 3.5%, 3.3%, and 3.65%, respectively (Ueno 1989, pp. 49–50).

Although the ratios of member companies receiving assigned directors from city banks and trust banks in the same industrial groups to all member companies in the group generally decreased after the fiscal year 1981, the numerical values in fiscal year 1992 remained 41.28%. Furthermore, the ratio of member enterprises that received assigned directors from city banks to all member enterprises was 37.95% in the same year. However, the ratios of member companies that received assigned directors from city banks and trust banks in the same industrial groups to all member companies in the groups declined to 17.08% in fiscal year 1996. In the Mitsubishi Group, the ratio of member firms that were assigned directors from banks of the same groups to all member firms was 39.29% for fiscal year 1996, which was the highest numerical value among the six industrial groups. Meanwhile, the same ratio for the Sumitomo group was 0%. In addition, the ratio of the number of assigned directors from banks in the groups to the total number of assigned directors for the six industrial groups on average significantly declined from 44% in fiscal year 1992 to 16.3% in fiscal year 1996. Even in the Fuji Group, which indicated the highest figures in this regard, the rate in the fiscal year 1996 was only nearly 30% (Kosei torihiki iinkai jimukyoku 1998, pp. 56–58; Funahashi 1994, pp. 30, 32).

Furthermore, when it comes to the role of banks in industrial group coordination, the Network of Presidents played an important role in maintaining close industry–bank relationships as well as assigning directors to member firms from the banks (Kosei torihiki iinkai jimukyoku 1994, p. 13; Ueda 1994, pp. 130–131, 133, 135). Six large industrial groups coordinated among themselves through the presidents' clubs. However, banks did not necessarily have an absolute advantage, even though financial institutions formed the core of the Network of Presidents (Miyazaki 1966, pp. 225).

Through mechanisms such as the presidents' clubs, big banks in Japan certainly took part in the exchange of information and the adjustment of interests in the industrial groups. Other banks, on the other hand, held core positions in various industrial groups, because banks belonging to specific industrial groups did not develop close relationships with many enterprises in other industrial or corporate groups. Therefore, it was difficult (and sometimes impossible) for banks in the industrial groups to adjust interests between the groups; this situation greatly differs from the situation in Germany.

5.1.4 Industry–Bank Relationships and Corporate Governance

Industry–bank relationships are deeply related to the system of corporate governance. Although the function of big banks, as the primary banks for industrial enterprises, emerged prominently in the same corporate groups, it also occurred in corporations outside of the groups. In addition to corporate financing, another important function of the main banking system was corporate governance and monitoring (Aoki and Patrick 1994, p. xxii). However, there was a strong tendency for large banks in Japan assuming financing roles in industrial groups. Furthermore, Japanese banks did not always participate in the corporate governance that exceeded the sphere of the group to link their combination relations with many corporate groups.

5.2 New Development of the Industrial System Based on Industry–Bank Relationships in Germany

Next, new development of industrial systems based on Industry–Bank relationships in Germany is explored. First, Sect. 5.2.1 examines industrial system mechanisms based on industry–bank relationships. Next, Sect. 5.2.2 considers them from the perspective of corporate governance. The significance of the postwar development of industry–bank relationships will be explained in Sect. 5.2.3. In addition to the primary focus of this book, which is the period from the 1950s to the 1970s, this section further analyzes the period that immediately follows as well as more current circumstances.

The supervisory board, which played a key role in the assignment of directors from banks to enterprises, appointed and dismissed directors, provided business management advice to the managing board, and went above and beyond deliberation by recognizing rights in a variety of critical matters. According to Herrhausen (1973), supervisory boards at the time were undergoing a transformation from supervisory to advisory bodies for boards of directors; they exerted necessary control on the decision-making process to proactively ward off erroneous measures or actions (Herrhausen 1973, p. 32). This observation was pointed out in the 1986 annual report of Deutsche Bank as well (Deutsche Bank 1986, p. 17). Supervisory boards could indirectly affect business management through the appointment and dismissal of directors (Bleicher et al. 1984, pp. 28–29). These boards were also involved in corporate policy decision-making via deliberation (Gutenberg 1970, pp. 3, 5–6). Corporate law regulations permitted the supervisory board to participate in business policy decision-making through the assent of rights by specific boards of directors via supervisory board decisions or by-laws. In these cases, the supervisory board served as a second decision-making body along with the managing board (Bleicher et al. 1989, p. 55; Gutenberg 1970, p. 6). For example, if the supervisory board carried out its advisory function and provided an opinion on the board of directors' decision-making, the chairman of the supervisory board played an important role because corporate policies were developed collaboratively (Böhm 1992, p. 206). Although explicit guidance by the supervisory board to the board of directors was prohibited by corporate law, it was regularly observed; in fact, some research stressed the significant gap between the law and actual practice (Bleicher et al. 1989, p. 55). Nevertheless, the relationship between the supervisory board and the board of directors assumed diverse forms depending on the nation.

5.2.1 Industrial System Mechanisms Based on Industry–Bank Relationships

5.2.1.1 Banks' Influence on Corporations Through Credit and Securities Businesses

This section examines bank credit and securities businesses and the influence of banks on companies based on these businesses. Jeidels (1905) emphasized that, in the bank and industrial alliances, the formation of regular business relationships which were generally financial was the most basic type of alliance, and personal connections through the dispatch of directors to supervisory boards was a method complementing these relationships (Jeidels 1905). In terms of creditor–debtor relationships, a 1979 report by the Gessler committee, an advisory council to the Ministry of Finance, stated that the majority of large enterprises were able to obtain capital other than through bank credit. Furthermore, the 30 largest credit recipients had a sufficient number of creditor–debtor relationships with financial institutions and credit organizations. Apart from cases of debtor firm crises, banks could not usually exert much influence on corporations through credit supply, and house-bank relationships did not exist in large firms (Vgl. Bundesministerium der Finanzen 1979, pp. 157–158, 160–162). However, Gerhardt (1982) stressed that creditor–debtor relationships between banks and their debtors were not sufficiently examined by the Committee (Gerhardt 1982, p. 192). He emphasized that credit-based financial relationships were strongly affecting corporate business policy (Gerhardt 1982, p. 107). Furthermore, while Eglau (1990) cited examples of banks appointing supervisory board members to family-owned private companies and German subsidiaries of large foreign corporate groups, the positions of supervisory board members were typically based on long-term house bank-like relationships with the companies (Eglau 1990, pp. 181, 261–263). It was likely that banks' exercising of management functions was facilitated by its character as a creditor and its supervisory post (Hopt 1979, p. 237). For instance, big banks and companies built close alliances through the creditor–debtor relationship, and proposals presented at general meetings were generally coordinated in advance (Aizawa 1994, p. 117).

Further, the Gessler Committee reported concentration of the securities business in only a few big banks and ties between large companies and banks, with securities businesses functioning as intermediaries. In the period from the 1950s to the 1970s, particularly 1966–1975, the top ten financial institutions accounted for 44.7% of financial institutions participating in the Consortium for Issuance of Securities; moreover, domestic issuers of stocks, optional bonds, and convertible bonds totaled 58.3% and foreign issuers totaled 70%. Of the 71 publicly listed companies, the three big banks, namely, Deutsche Bank, Dresdner Bank, and Commerzbank, accounted for more than 98.6% of issuances among all banks. These three banks also accounted for a high rate of consortium leaders and co-managers at 81.7% and 80%, respectively (Bundesministerium der Finanzen 1979, pp. 452, 457). According to Edwards and Fischer (1994), the leaders of securities issuance syndicates were typically corporate house banks of joint-stock companies, i.e., the three banks listed above (Edwards and Fischer 1994, pp. 215–221).

As the securities business increased in size, house bank functions in the creditor–debtor relationship and the security issue business became important pillars of the industry–bank relationship. For example, as a universal bank, Deutsche Bank wielded considerable power in both corporate finance and the overall economy because it provided payment of plentiful accounts, working capital, and fixed investment capital and enabled the underwriting of corporate capital increases and bond issues (Aizawa 1994, p. 4).

Concerning industry–bank relationships, banks exercised influence by exercising voting rights through bank-owned and deposited stocks, in addition to the functions of the house bank in the security issue business and the intelligence obtained by serving as intermediaries in the credit business; this laid the groundwork for close connections. Generally, the interrelation between the scale of capital participation and the personnel connection between enterprises can be observed (Albach 1993, p. VII). Thus, it is critical to comprehensively analyze the interplay between the credit and securities businesses.

5.2.1.2 Banks' Influence on Industry Through Shareholdings and the Deposited Stock System

Next, banks' influence on industrial enterprises with regard to bank stockholdings and the deposited stock system is considered. The Monopoly Committee's 1976/1977 report emphasized the provision of critical competitive information to companies by financial institutions that owned stocks in those companies, as well as voting rights through proprietary ownership stocks or deposited stocks that supplemented those stocks, allowing banks to exert direct and indirect influence on the business policies of enterprises other than banks (Monopolkommission 1978, p. 338, Tz. 604). Such stock deposits in banks and banks' proxies exercising the voting rights were long-standing practices in Germany (Vgl. Schaad 1972, pp. 14–16) and were legalized by the 1937 Corporations Law (Lindhardt 1958, pp. 169, 171; Gottschalk 1990, p. 11; Schaad 1972, p. 17).

However, before World War II, a portion of shares deposited in banks was not very exercised in general meetings and large private shareholders often exercised their stocks (Kuhlmann 1949, p. 489). The exercise of voting rights as an industrial system based on industry–bank was not as significant in the prewar period as it was after World War II, which was concerned with laying the groundwork for the assignment of directors from banks to industries.

In terms of the banks' influence on companies, the impact of banks exercising voting rights through the deposited stock system was more important than the banks' stockholding itself. Even in this case, however, the influence of deposited stock voting rights was more often dependent on the shareholder ownership structure of these enterprises, and this was most likely for publicly traded corporations with scattered holdings and no control over stockholders (Hein and Flöter 1975, p. 352; Köstler et al. 2006, p. 78).

In individual- or family-owned companies, stocks that were distributed among small individual shareholders were sold through banks, which had collaborative relationships with share-issuing companies; often, the voting rights associated with those shares were entrusted to the banks owing to their friendly relationships with the issuing companies. The cooperative relationships between the corporations and banks were based on the former's intention. Such reciprocal relationships could also be observed in corporations with widely distributed stocks. In contrast, in management-controlled companies with widely distributed shares, the board of directors had a commanding position over the supervisory board, particularly in top-level decision-making and the selection of supervisory board members from banks during the general meeting; there were examples of banks exercising voting rights collaboratively with the management (Sakuma 2003, pp. 69–70, 75).

Concerning the exercise of voting rights, the total value of deposited stocks, including bank-deposited stocks, increased from DM 28.9 billion at the end of 1970 to DM 36.5 billion by the end of 1975. At the end of 1970, 73.7% of those stocks were deposited in credit banks, and by the end of 1975, the number fell to 71.3%, which was nonetheless a high rate (Hansen 1977, pp. 161–162). According to a Monopoly Committee report, in terms of revenue, in 56 of the top 100 corporations banks had 5% or more of their voting rights in the mid-1970s. Of these, in 18 enterprises banks had more than 75% of their voting right, in 12 between 50 and 75%, in 11 between 25 and 50%, and in 15 between 5 and 25% (Monopolkommission 1978, p. 296). Furthermore, considering the proportion of banks' voting rights in AEG, Hoechst, BASF, Siemens, and Bayer as of 1975 was high at 89.29%, 88.62%, 87.15%, 81.02%, and 79.09%, respectively. August Thyssen held a relatively low rate at 45.28%. However, the proportion of owner-held stock voting rights held by banks in these companies was not greater than 1% (Vgl. Monopolkommission 1978, p. 560), whereas banks exercising voting rights through the deposited stocks system were significant.

A survey by Gottschalk on 32 of the 100 largest corporations with widespread stockholding or bank-owned stocks (at 50% or more) in terms of added value in 1984 revealed that the percentage of voting rights for all banks in 1986 (or for a portion of the corporations in 1987) was 82.67% on average. For 22 of these companies, banks held voting rights greater than the 75% minimum required to make decisions on critical issues such as amending by-laws. Among the 32 enterprises, the top three banks held 45.44% of the exercisable voting rights on average and over 50% in 15 enterprises (Vgl. Gottschalk 1988, pp. 297–299). A 1992 survey by Baums and Fraune, which investigated 24 of the largest 100 public corporations that had a majority of widespread shareholding in terms of added value, revealed that the proportion of voting rights held by banks at these companies' general meetings was 84.09% on average while that through the deposited stocks system was 60.95%. Further, there were 11 companies holding greater than 75% of the voting rights through deposited stocks alone, 18 companies with banks holding 75% of the voting rights, and 17 companies at more than 90% (Vgl. Baums and Fraune 1995, pp. 98, 103). According to a 1994 study by Edwards and Fischer, German banks, particularly the top three banks, had a great deal of control over voting rights in enterprises, and this control was primarily through proxy voting rights via the deposited stock system (Edwards and Fischer 1994, p. 226).

5.2.1.3 Assignment of Directors from Banks to Corporations

The impact of exercising voting rights based on the deposited stocks system and bank stockholding was further realized through the dispatch of directors from banks. Personal connections with corporations, the assignment of supervisory board members who served as information conduits, the selection of directors, and participation in business policies provided the most secure foundation for banks to exert influence. Thus, close ties between non-bank corporations and banks were the most important factor in generating the power held by banks (Volkmann and Kronenberg 1994, p. 481). The impact of two important factors, capital holding and voting rights through the deposited stocks system, which was carried out by supervisory board members, became felt, and these positions became a mechanism for the transfer of this power (Vgl. Böhm 1992, p. 222). Therefore, this point is an issue to be next examined.

5.2.1.3.1 Information Sharing System and Banks' Assignment of Directors

First, this subsection considers information sharing systems enabled by the assignment of directors from banks to corporations. By combining finance-based information with that obtained from dispatched supervisory board members, banks were able to fill advisory and leadership roles in these corporations while also obtaining information valuable to external borrowers. Banks could gather significant inside information on multiple corporations by obtaining information about borrowers, corporate sales, and the financial statuses of credit supplies; this enabled them to serve as information storehouses and information conduits (Uetake 1997, p. 104). Specialized financial information and experience and guidance necessary to help the managing board avoid mistakes were important factors in reinforcing the role and significance of supervisory board member positions (Vgl. Deutsche Bank 1986, p. 17). In the case of companies that were assigned supervisory board members from banks, the preferential status of easier access to good information sources aided in the development of closer relationships (Eglau 1990, p. 192).

From a company's internal functional perspective, banks' sharing information, particularly know-how, often had great meaning in performing corporate consultant. Meanwhile, for external functioning, this system of information sharing among enterprises, with bank representatives on the supervisory board acting as intermediaries, has spread further depending on the likelihood of contact between enterprises and the supervisory board, namely, primarily through bank-assigned supervisory board members (Hopt 1979, pp. 235–238).

The dispatch of supervisory board members could also play a significant role in coordination among various departments and be the most decisive point for the overall system (Hopt 1979, p. 238). Banks tended to be familiar with industry issues and provided corporate borrowers with guidance and advice for decision-making across a wide range of management fields. For enterprises receiving the directors, the dispatch of directors from banks had great significance for obtaining opinions on the overall management as well as for procuring capital (Busse 1962, p. 51). Although only a few banks were represented on the supervisory board, banks participated in overall coordination to the best of their abilities; however, this allowed control of big banks' positions through supervisory board representation (Edwards and Fischer 1994, p. 220).

The supervisory board chairman was able to approach and attain all kinds of important and internal information through the directors' reports regarding critical matters (Bundesministerium der Finanzen 1979, p. 116). If a bank representative was assigned to a company and later appointed chairman of the supervisory board, the representative could wield far more power over company decision-making than other supervisory board members.

5.2.1.3.2 Assignment of Directors and Collaborative Relations Among Banks

Next, the assignment of directors that was based on cooperative relationships among banks is considered. The largest three banks, for example, as the largest stockholders, could exercise voting rights through the deposited stocks system. Furthermore, these banks formed collaborative relationships with combined capital, which supplemented banks' voting rights (Uetake 1997, p. 106). This was evident in the banks' general meetings where banks exercised voting rights. Gottschalk's survey examined the total number of shares and deposited stocks owned by investment companies and their parent banks; results revealed that the rate of Deutsche Bank's voting rights in 1986 was 47.17% and that of the top three banks was 60.36% on average. Dresdner Bank's percentages of shares and deposited stocks in its own general meeting were 47.08 and 64.04%, respectively, whereas Commerzbank's percentages were 34.58 and 60.81%, respectively; these rates were considerably high (Gottschalk 1988, pp. 297–298). Furthermore, against the total rate of voting rights, a 1992 study by Baums and Fraune revealed that Deutsche Bank's rate of voting rights was 32.07% and that among the top three banks was 49.24%. At Dresdner Bank, these percentages were 44.19 and 53.66%, and at Commerzbank, they were 18.49 and 48.27%, respectively (Vgl. Baums and Fraune 1995, p. 106). As a result, the top three banks held a very high rate of shares with voting rights, enabling them to control their annual meetings collaboratively and effectively (Böhm 1992, p. 75). H. Pfeiffer stressed that the controller of large banks were the large banks themselves (Pfeiffer 1986, p. 475). These cooperative inter-bank relationships laid the groundwork for control over large banks, and such control affected and controlled a wide range of industrial enterprises.

Besides the collaborative relationships that could be found in joint funding between banks (Vgl. Monopolkommission 2003, p. 231), in the exercising of voting rights through the deposited stocks system, banks were able to transfer voting rights deposited by customers to third parties such as other trusted banks (Hautsch 1979, p. 173; Yamaguchi 1981, p. 113). Even the transfer of voting rights through the deposited stocks system from small to large banks reinforced the influence of these cooperative inter-bank relationships on companies (Busse 1962, p. 65; Bundesministerium der Finanzen 1979, p. 568).

Banks had similar cooperative financing systems, such as the largest three banks' consortium for issuing securities, where positions, rankings, and allocations were approved in a predetermined manner (Poullain 1979, p. 80). Edwards and Fischer (1994) research stressed that for a long period of time the structure of this bank syndicate was extremely stable (Edwards and Fischer 1994, p. 215). The top three banks acted collaboratively in the exercise of voting rights at annual meetings, and for the greater part, were immovable as supervisory positions in the enterprises with which they dealt (Vgl. Gottschalk 1988, pp. 299–300). Other banks also tended to coorperate with the three biggest banks (Gottschalk 1988, p. 300; Bundesministerium der Finanzen 1979, p. 173). In addition, voting rights and deposited stocks provided opportunities to repress and control industrial relationships and competition among banks for industry work (Busse 1962, pp. 64, 66).

Even in activities involving the assignment of members to the supervisory board, this played an important role.

In this regard, the establishment of a "strong stockholder" structure based on the universal banking system was critical for the election of supervisory board members who served as capital-side representatives at general meetings (Takahashi 1997, p. 51).

Dispatching of supervisory board members can be observed in financial Institutions as well (Vgl. Bundesministerium der Finanzen 1979, p. 591). The gathering and sharing of critical information on borrower enterprises or corporations to which supervisory board members had been assigned was crucial.

5.2.1.3.3 Assignment of Directors Between Banks and Industries

In the case of director assignments between banks and industries, a Monopoly committee report from 1976/1977 found 137 examples of supervisory board members being selected from financial institutions, and 57 instances of financial institution assignees being chairmen or vice-chairmen, out of 51 surveyed enterprises.

There were 76 board members and 35 chairmen or vice-chairmen from the three largest banks, accounting for more than 55.5% and 61.4% of the total assignees from financial institutions, respectively (Monopolkommission 1978, pp. 574–577). For these 51 companies, if financial institutions had more than 25% of the voting rights, they had without exception secured at least one supervisory position, and if the financial institutions had more than 25% stock holding, they obtained chairman or vice-chairman positions on the supervisory board. Among the largest 100 corporations, 31 had financial institution representatives acting as chairmen of the supervisory board, and 35 had representatives functioning as vice-chairmen. The largest three banks held 21 chairmen and 19 vice-chairmen in these enterprises (Monopolkommission 1978, pp. 303–304, 307–308). The Gessler Committee clarified that, in 74 publicly traded companies surveyed in 1974 and 1975, there were 182 supervisory board members assigned from financial institutions and 37 chairmen of the supervisory board from financial institutions. The numbers of supervisory board members and chairmen assigned from the top three banks were 101 and 25, and respectively, accounted for 55.5% and 67.6% of those dispatched from financial institutions. In many situations, the same banks held the chairmanship of the supervisory board, and in a large number of cases, two supervisory seats, among the 74 publicly listed enterprises in which a bank had at least 25% of the voting rights in a given enterprise (Vgl. Bundesministerium der Finanzen 1979, pp. 173–174, 436, 438–439, 443–445).

In subsequent periods as well, according to the Gottschalk survey, in 1986, bankers or former bankers had 69 (27%) of the 256 supervisory positions within 27 non-bank companies. Of these, 50 positions, or approximately three-fourths, were populated by representatives of the biggest three banks (Gottschalk 1988, p. 300). Furthermore, Ziegler (1984) reported that among larger manufacturers, two, if not all three, of the top three banks had representation serving on supervisory boards. One decisive factor in the banks having so many representatives was the economic importance of the enterprises accepting the representatives (Vgl. Ziegler 1984, p. 597). Pfeiffer in 1993 found that the largest three banks had assigned 1,053 directors to other companies' supervisory boards in the 1990s, with 170 of them serving as supervisory board (or other control organs) chairmen, and 92 as vice-chairmen (Vgl. Pfeiffer 1993, pp. 151, 172, 182–183). In the 261 publicly traded firms surveyed by Hansen in 1993, at least one bank representative served as a supervisory board member, and 372 supervisory board members were dispatched from financial institutions. 192 (51.6 percent) of these were from the top three banks, and 59 corporations had bank representatives serving as supervisory board chairmen. The DAX30 companies had 73 supervisory positions filled by bank representatives, with 13 companies having bank directors in the chairman position of the supervisory board. The top three banks held a total of 56 supervisory positions in the DAX30 corporations, or 76.7% of the total (Hansen 1994a, R. 78). During the same time period, foreigners owned approximately one-fourth of the total market value of German stocks, with private investors owning more than one-fifth. However, the proportion of DAX30 supervisory board positions held by these two groups of investors was no more than about 5% each (Hansen 1994b, R. 404).

The mutual assignment of directors from industries to banks was also common; Pfeiffer (1993) clarified that there were up to 1,053 such cases in the personnel relationships of the three largest German Banks with 130 large companies, including the assignment of (1) directors and supervisory board members from non-bank companies to the supervisory boards or boards of directors of the top three banks and (2) supervisory board members from the top three banks to the supervisory boards or boards of directors of non-bank corporations (Vgl. Pfeiffer 1993, pp.181–183). Furthermore, there have been reports of corporate representatives serving on bank committees and other organizations. For example, the chairman of the board of BASF, one of the world's three largest chemical companies, was a member of a Deutsche Bank committee, and BASF's supervisory board chairman was traditionally a member of a similar organization at Commerzbank (Pfeiffer 1989, p. 15). In this way, supervisory board assignments from the largest three banks to non-bank companies and vice versa accounted for many of the personal ties between industries and banks.

5.2.1.4 System of Corporate-Bank and Inter-Corporate Information Sharing Through the Advisory Council System

The banks' personnel exchange structure for the sharing and exchanging information had a significant role in complementing industry–bank relationships through the dispatch of directors from banks. The advisory council, established for each bank's head office and region, served as a hub for information exchange between banks and corporations, as well as among corporations themselves.

Major enterprises assigned members to a central advisory council, in which industry leaders regularly reported to each other regarding their markets' conditions. Since they performed their board roles, they received advice and guidance as to various business issues (Eglau 1990, pp. 192–193). Before 1966, Dresdner Bank had a central advisory board that served as a coordinating entity between banks and industrial firms. These advisory boards were typically established by banks to maintain the level of personal ties previously enjoyed in response to the 1965 Corporations Law, which limited the number of mandates on the supervisory board that one person could hold (Vgl. Pfeiffer 1993, p. 477; Stanzick 1968, p. 72). Region-specific advisory councils had existed in Deutsche and Dresdner Banks since before World War II. Management representatives from a wide range of companies in various industrial sectors that served large banking customers and their regional organizational units comprised the regional advisory council. Regional advisory councils were established to strengthen relationships among various enterprises across business sectors and in each region for matters of business policy (Büschgen 1983, pp. 242–243; Koubek 1971, p. 261). Pfeiffer's (1993) research reveals that, among many medium-sized firms, the supervisory board's functions of regulation, consultation, and guidance were undertaken by the advisory council (Pfeiffer 1993, p. 181; Commerzbank AG 1970, p. 142). Persons appointed by the largest three banks to the supervisory or advisory board were regarded as "friendly" (Gottschalk 1988, p. 301). For example, it was critical for Deutsche Bank's advisory council to develop close and strong relationships with the bank's customers through its business and to propose new operations through those connections (Vgl. Schwarz 2003, p. 32).

Furthermore, through the top three banks' supervisory board, central advisory council, or regional advisory council members, several hundred business associations played a significant role in sharing ties with banks (Vgl. Pfeiffer 1987, pp. 29–31). With these personal organizational ties, close relationships between banks and industries created information conduits. These conduits were based on direct relationships between the two groups and also complemented by intermediary relationships of economic associations such as industrial and business associations and industry–bank relationships (Vgl. Koubek 1971, pp. 262–266).

5.2.2 Corporate Governance and Industry–Bank Relationships

5.2.2.1 Coorperative System of Corporate Governance Based on Industry–Bank Relationships

The industrial system based on industry–bank relationships created a cooperative system of corporate governance that has German characteristics, a phenomenon considered in this section.

The German separation of authority into a two-tiered system of top management for supervisory boards and boards of directors encouraged debates between those outside the company who provided valuable advice and those who ran the business. The ability of these dynamics to broaden corporations' perspectives and clearly defined responsibility was significant (Winnacker 1972, p. 467). This German management system demonstrates its significance and effectiveness as an industrial system based on industry–bank relationships because bank representatives serving as supervisory board members provide guidance based on the banks' wealth of information and know-how. With such decision-making mechanisms, business functions centered on the managing board demonstrate functions to monitor and regulate.

The high rate of voting rights held by banks, including voting rights through deposited stocks, the dispatch of supervisory board members, and industry–bank relationships based on personal ties through representatives on advisory councils, enabled a defensive mechanism against capital market pressures. Here, German characteristics in the corporate governance systems are considered. With the advancement of financial globalization since the 1990s, there has been increased pressure on shareholder value-oriented management through investment funds, business strategy execution, and general meeting selection of supervisory board members. In comparison to other European countries, the United States, and Japan, the conditions in this environment show that the German industrial system enabled banks to secure management autonomy and stability not only in corporations in which they held stock but also with borrowers.

However, with greater capital market pressures in today's financial globalization, this stable system is sometimes rocked to its foundation. Beginning in the 1990s, large banks transitioned from their traditional lending business to investment banking, and the assignment of directors from banks to companies declined. Furthermore, banks began to accept fewer corporate representatives for positions such as chairman of the supervisory board (Vgl. Zugehör 2003, pp. 68–70, 92–93, 173). These changes by banks were another step toward globalized capitalism, and banks themselves were regulated by changes in the conditions for capital accumulations. From the perspective of inter-firm relationships, banks were forced to intensify their relationships based on "selection and concentration" to realize greater efficiency.

5.2.2.2 Codetermination and Coorperative Systems of Corporate Governance in Industry–Bank Relationships

The relationship between issues of corporate governance based on close ties between industries and banks and the codetermination system at the supervisory board level must be analyzed.

The authority of the supervisory board chairman was expanded under the 1976 Law on Codetermination. The law granted two votes to the chairman in cases of conflicts between stockholders and labor representatives on the supervisory board. Conditions that were in the interest of the investors were important for coordinating interests with the supervisory board chairman. Furthermore, the number of labor representatives on the supervisory board being equal to that of shareholder representatives necessitated the formation of groups. The supervisory board chairman held an authority that enabled governance of certain types of opinions within the groups as well (Vgl. Eglau 1990, pp. 178–179). Largely based on this, when bank representatives acted as supervisory board chairmen in companies, they found it easier to demonstrate the governing and coordinating functions of their role on the basis of abundant data.

With the deployment of the 1976 Law on Codetermination, the supervisory board would regulate its meetings that were occasionally conducted to eliminate controversial issues from discussion; however, some have pointed out that the supervisory board tended to lose its authoritative position in matters of corporate policy being discussed in a critical fashion. Rather than an expansive board, the supervisory board chairman often played an important part as a critical debater for the managing board (Eglau 1990, pp. 166–167). In these cases, when bank representatives assumed the position of supervisory board chairman, it became simple to coordinate group interests on the basis of both internal and external, critical corporate information obtained by the supervisory board chairman from banks, which served as information sources.

The codetermination system decreases the rate of members erected from the shareholder side in the supervisory board and provides opportunities for autonomous corporate management. As the Codetermination Act for the Coal, Iron, and Steel Industries and the 1976 Law on Codetermination mandated 50% of the supervisory board to be composed of labor representatives, the number of external members on the board dropped. From the latter half of the 1970s, the 1976 Law on Codetermination reduced the number of bank representatives on the supervisory boards of German enterprises (Cable 1985, p. 33). Corporations used this as an opportunity to reduce potential external influence and involvement.

However, the decrease in supervisory positions held by stockholders allowed for conditions of easier fulfillment of banks' interests, with banks and inter-bank alliances holding a superior position in exercising voting rights through deposited stocks. Furthermore, through collaboration between banks and the corporations to which they assigned directors, the latter gained greater decision-making authority, including authority over the remaining supervisory board members and the suppression of outside influences. For these reasons, collaboration with banks took on further significance for industrial enterprises.

As above-mentioned, the codetermination system created conditions for a stronger functioning industrial system based on industry–bank relationships, while suppressing the influence of external shareholders. For banks, this was a mechanism for regulating their interests and realizing bank interests in enterprises to which banks dispatched directors.

Under the codetermination system, opportunities for companies to cooperate with labor representatives on the supervisory board were fortified as a defense mechanism against external pressures, which were heavily oriented toward the pursuit of short-term interests and represented by investment funds in present-day terms. From the objects of labor, it secured security and soundness in employment and corporate management. This feature further reinforced collaboration between management and labor. There is an industrial system based on industry–bank relationships in the form of a cooperative network for broad personal connections for capital supervisory board members. Cooperation with a supervisory board comprised of members from the capital side, such as bank representatives, becomes much more intensive in this type of industrial system.

Thus, preconditions for effective, direct control through the dispatch of bank representatives to corporate supervisory boards are met within joint-stock and limited liability companies under the 1976 Law of Codetermination or the Codetermination Act for the Coal, Iron, and Steel Industries. The Act requires companies to have codetermination with equal labor representation. Supervisory positions held by banks as creditors were effective for surveillance and providing approvals required by management in enterprises where this type of codetermination is used (Wiendieck 1992, p. 172, p. 176).

As made clear from the preceding analysis, Germany developed a system that had functions similar to that of corporate defense, developed to confront external pressures, and contrasted that of interlocking shareholdings, which characterized postwar Japan. At the supervisory board level, this type of corporate system was supported by industrial and codetermination systems based on industry–bank relationships, establishing an important feature of German corporate governance.

5.2.3 Significance of New Developments in Industry–Bank Relationships

Based on the foregoing discussions, regarding new developments in postwar industry–bank relationships and the industrial system upon which they were based, the types and possible significance of future developments that were different from those in the prewar era will be examined.

First, there is evidence of the development of an industrial and corporate governance system based on banks exercising voting rights through the deposited stock system. The issuance business was exceptional in the securities business, which was based on the prewar universal banking system. However, with the expansion of general investments in securities in the postwar period, the position of the securities business in the secondary market grew significantly. As a result, a system of bank agents exercising voting rights through the deposited stocks system was fully established. This practice established the necessary capital and personal ties for the postwar development of industrial concentration and the formation of a uniquely German industrial system, promoting information sharing and exchange between banks and industries and regulating their interests.

Second, the full-scale development of a network for sharing and exchanging information between industries and banks and among corporations through the bank's advisory council system and a system for regulating interests through that network can be seen. Although there were prewar cases of regional advisory councils, in the postwar era, central advisory councils were created and became the cornerstone of the advisory board system. Through the combination of central and regional advisory councils, a national and regional system of information sharing and exchanging between banks and industries and among corporations themselves was established. These systems differed from those based on the appointment of directors in that they were used to regulate the interests of banks and investors, as well as those of companies.

Third, the weakening influences and pressures from external stockholders, which emerged on account of the codetermination system program proposing equal labor representation on the supervisory board, established and reinforced a corporate governance system based on industry–bank relationships; its roles differed from those featured during the prewar period. The strengthened industry–bank relationships and the industrial system on which they were based also revealed the system's importance.

The significance of new postwar developments in the industry–bank relationships and the collaborative characteristics of German capitalism (Chandler 1990) can be seen in the fact that banks' strong influence over industries was due to cooperative relationships between the two groups, rather than the banks' desire to control the industries. The framework for bank stockholdings, the assignment of supervisory board members according to the exercising of voting rights based on the deposited stocks system, and the advisory council system resulted in information sharing and a support system dependent upon advice from banks and cooperative relationships with industrial enterprises. Banks' involvement in the joint responsibility for industrial policy and several corporate business policies (Busse 1962, p. 61) was an important element supporting the collaborative system, through which banks regulated and coordinated inter-corporate interests. Directors of banks and insurance firms were often critical for establishing personal ties among competing corporations (Vgl. Pfannschmidt 1993, p. 274). Moreover, German-style corporate governance based on the codetermination system complemented the industry–bank relationships. Inter-corporate collaborations were also supported by the assignment of directors and interlocking of directorates between industrial enterprises (Vgl. Schönwitz and Weber 1982; Decher 1990; Pfannschmidt 1993). This postwar German-style industrial system based on industry–bank relationships combined these elements and functioned in a framework that deeply connected each element.

Although primary changes can be seen in the 1990s and beyond, this cooperative structure in the postwar period allowed corporate management to not only plan for long-term business expansion but also to repress the impact of external stockholders and capital market pressures. As the core of German exports, this structure represented significant German development within the Americanization of business management, as management pursued long-term business expansion in line with German and European market structures.

5.3 Japanese and German Characteristics of Industrial System Based on Industry–Bank Relationships

The previous sections explored new developments in the industrial system based on industry–bank relationships in Japan and Germany after World War II. Building on these discussions, this section clarifies the Japanese and German characteristics of such an industrial system, particularly in relation to the role of banks.

In Japan, six industrial groups were established as the system of postwar industrial concentration. These industrial groups were made up of large enterprises that were inextricably linked to one another, as well as companies that were concentrated through interlocking shareholdings in the groups. The large corporate groups formed in postwar Japan spanned several industrial sectors, and financing, interlocking stockholdings, mutual business trade, and joint investments were internally developed. Moreover, banks played significant roles in these activities and occupied core positions in the industrial groups that they belonged to. However, regardless of the banks' status concerning interlocking shareholdings, securing stable stockholders and ensuring management autonomy were somewhat dependent on the ownership structure of each firm within the group. In this regard, German banks exerted considerable influence on industrial companies by exercising their voting rights through stockholdings and deposited stocks and building more direct relationships, such as by participating in business policy development of industrial enterprises.

In terms of inter-corporate information sharing and conflict resolution, six large corporate groups collaborated through an organization termed as the Network of Presidents, with decisions made primarily by those in positions of authority, such as presidents of group enterprises in Japan. Even though financial institutions were at the core of the president clubs, banks did not always have an absolute advantage. Furthermore, although industrial groups comprising full sets of industries were broadening, from the standpoint of inter-firm information sharing and exchanging, the Network did not always adopt mechanisms that supported banks–industry relationships, as was the case in Germany. In contrast, in Germany, the advisory council, created for banks' head offices and for each region, and business and industrial associations functioned as a focal point of information exchange between banks and corporations as well as among corporations themselves. It played an important part in complementing industry–bank relationships through the assignment of directors from banks. In this point, the role of Japanese banks greatly differed from that of German banks.

In Japan, banks assumed the core positions in each industrial group and the major banks functioned as the main banks in the industrial groups to which they belonged. However, as an important organ comprised of industrial groups, big banks did not establish combination relations with many corporate groups, including other industrial groups. As a result, Japanese banks were unable to perform functions beyond the sphere of the industrial group to which they belonged, such as information exchanges and the adjustment of interests. Compared with Japanese banks, banks in Germany broadly associated with large corporate groups rather than with a specific corporate group (Maekawa 1997, p. 58). German banks have widely developed combination relations with numerous groups in the competitive market and the enterprises that belong to such groups. This was significant in the adjustment of competing enterprises' interests, which was critical for the avoidance or alleviation of competition. The collaborative characteristic of German capitalism, as seen in the restraint of competition through the complementary division of labor in the product fields between companies or large corporate groups, was supported by the system of industrial concentration based on industry–bank relationships. These ties were extremely important for the mechanisms and functions of information sharing and coordination, especially in the context of industrial system-based relationships between banks and industries. Such differences between Japan and Germany were deeply concerned with the competitive structure and the function of industrial concentration that avoided competition, particularly price competition.

Moreover, when considering the system of industrial concentration based on bank relationships in relation to corporate governance, the following points are of significance. First, in terms of bank monitoring of companies as an important function in the Japanese main banking system, the rule of industrial enterprises by banks has been relatively weak. Japanese banks are not universal banks and are therefore unable to exert voting rights through deposited stocks, as is seen in Germany. In Japan, besides the assignment of directors, interlocking stockholdings within the industrial groups played a significant role in the combination between enterprises. In contrast, German banks used voting rights (including those obtained through deposited stocks) to establish combination relationships across various corporate groups (not limited to a single corporate group) that competed with each other. Therefore, the system of industrial concentration and the roles of banks in Germany were much greater than those in Japan. Furthermore, the codetermination system established by the Codetermination Act in 1976, which was based on a structure with an equal number of labor and capital market members on the supervisory board, weakened shareholders' influence in capital markets. Furthermore, because the corporate governance system was founded on the industry–bank coordination, it was strengthened in collaboration with the codetermination system.

Concerning the organization of top management, in Germany, the directors assigned occupied significant positions under the two-tier system, which was composed of supervisory boards and boards of directors. This was about the fact that supervisory board members are elected by stockholders at general meetings. The Japanese system, on the other hand, is a one-tier system comprised of boards of directors. As a result, assignments to boards of directors are included in the dispatch of top management members. However, it is also important to note that, while financial institutions in particular took on such assignments, trading companies occupied key positions in the network of interlocking directorates. The latter condition was mainly because trading companies in Japan assumed significant roles in the industrial groups.

Building upon our previous discussions, the next issue to be discussed is how Japanese and German business management changed at the corporate level with the deployment of American management methods, and the developments that emerged in Japan and Germany thereafter. This issue will be examined in Chaps. 6–12.

References

Aizawa K (1994) Oshu saikyo no kinyu teikoku (The strongest financial empire in Europe). Nihon keizai shinbunsha, Tokyo

Albach H (1993) Gleitwort. In: Pfannschmidt A Personelle Verflechtugen über Aufsichtsräte, Mehrfachmandate in deutschen Unternehmen. Gabler, Wiesbaden, S. VII–VIII

Aoki M, Patrick H (1994) Introduction. In: Aoki M, Patrick H (eds) The Japanese main bank system. Its relevance for developing and transforming economies. Oxford University Press, Oxford, pp xxi–xxxii

Baums T, Fraune C (1995) Institutionelle Anlage und Publikumgesellschaft: Eine empirische Untersuchung. In: Die Aktiengesellschaft 40(3):97–112

Bleicher K, Bortel K-D, Kleinmann R et al (1984) Unternehmungsverfassung und Spitzenorganisation. In: Zeitschrift Führung+Organisation 53(1):21–29

Bleicher K, Diethard LK, Paul H (1989) Unternehmungsverfassung und Spitzenorganisation. Fuhrung und Uberwachung von Aktiengesellschaften im internationalen Vergleich. Gabler, Wiesbaden

Böhm J (1992) Der Einfluβ der Banken auf Groβunternehmen. Steuer- und Wirtschaftsverlag, Hamburg

Bundesministerium der Finanzen (ed) (1979) Bericht der Studienkommission. Grundsatzfragen der Kreditwirtschaft (Schriftenreihe des Bundesministeriums der Finanzen, Heft 28). Stollfuss, Frankfurt am Main

Büschgen HE (1983) Die Groβbanken. Fritz Knapp Verlag, Frankfurt am Main

Busse A (1962) Depotstimmrecht der Banken. T. Gabler, Wiesbaden

Cable JR (1985) The bank-industry relationship in West Germany: performance and policy aspects. In: Schwalbach J (ed) Industry structure and performance. Edition Sigma, Berlin, pp 17–40

Chandler AD Jr (1990) Scale and scope: the dynamics of industrial capitalism. Harvard University Press, Cambridge

Commerzbank AG (1970) 100 Jahre Commerzbank 1870–1970. Knapp, Düsseldorf

Сутягина МВ (1973) Мицубиси. Наука, Москва

Decher CE (1990) Personelle Verflechtungen im Aktienkonzern. Verlag Recht und Wirtschaft, Heidelberg

Deutsche Bank AG (1986) Geschäftsbericht für das Jahr 1986. Deutsche Bank AG, Frankfurt am Main

Edwards J, Fischer K (1994) Banks, finance and investment in Germany. Cambridge University Press, Cambridge

Eglau HO (1990) Wie Gott in Frankfurt: Die Deutsche Bank und die deutsche Industrie, 3rd edn. Econ Verlag, Dusseldorf

Fujii M (1979) "Zaibatsu kaitai" seisaku to sengo kontsuerun no saihen (Dissolution policy of "zaibatsu" and reorganization of postwar corporate groups). In: Noguchi T (ed) Nihon no rokudai kontsuerun—Mitsubishi · Mitsui · Sumitomo · Dai-ichi kangin · Fuji · Sanwa— (Japanese six corporate groups—Mitsubishi, Mitsui, Sumitomo, Dai-Ichi kangyo, fuji, and Sanwa—). Shin hyoron, Tokyo, pp 62–72

Fukuda Y (1985) Kigyo shudan keisei to kodo keizai seicho (Formation of corporate groups and high economic growth). In: Shakai kagaku ronshu (J Soc Sci) 49:103–159

Funahashi K (1994) Dai goji rokudai kigyo shudan no jittai chosa (Fifth investigation regarding actual conditions of six large corporate groups). In: Kosei (Justice) 1365:26–32

Futatsuki Y (1975) Kigyo shudan no nakano kinyu kikan (Financial institution in corporate group). In: Keizai hyoron (Econ Rev) 24(3):20–33
Futatsuki Y (1993) Kosei torihiki iinkai jimukyoku hen "Nihon no rokudai kigyo shudan—Sono soshiki to kodo—" (Fair Trade Commission (ed.) 'Six corporate groups in Japan'—Their organization and behavior—). In: Kokumin keizai zassi (J Econ Bus Adm) 167(5):121–124
Gerhardt M (1982) Industriebezihungen der westdeutschen Banken. Sendler, Frankfurt am Main
Gottschalk A (1988) Der Stimmrechtseinfluβ der Banken in den Aktionarversammlungen von Groβunternehmen. In: WSI Mitteilungen 41(5):294–304
Gottschalk A (1990) Depotstimmrecht und die Macht der Banken. In: Die Tageszeitung 3108:11
Gutenberg E (1970) Funktionswandel des Aufsichtsrats. In: Zeitschrift für Betriebswirtschaft 40, Erganzungsheft, pp 1–10
Hansen H (1977) Die Wertpapierdepots der Bankkunden. In: Die Aktiengesellschaft 22(6):161–163
Hansen H (1994a) Das Gewicht der Banken in den Aufsichträten deutscher Aktiengesellschaften. In: Die Aktiengesellschaft 39(3):R76–R79
Hansen H (1994b) Die Zusammensetzung von Aufsichtsräten der DAX-Gesellschaften und die Auswirkungen auf ihre Effizienz. In: Die Aktiengesellschaft 39(11):R403–R404
Hein M, Flöter H (1975) Macht der Banken—Folgerungen aus der bisherigen Diskussion. In: WSI Mitteilungen 28(7):342–361
Hautsch G (1979) Das Imperium AEG-Telefunken: Ein multinationaler Konzern. Verlag Marxistische Blätter, Frankfurt am Main
Herrhausen A (1973) Überwachen allein genugt nicht. In: Manag Mag 2(1973):32–35
Hopt KJ (1979) Zur Funktion des Aufsichtsrats im Verhältnis von Industrie und Bankensystem. In: Horn N, Kocka J (eds) Recht und Entwicklung der Groβunternehmen im 19. und frühen 20. Jahrhundert. Wirtschaft-, sozial- und rechtshistorische Untersuchungen zur Industrialisierung im Deutschland, Frankreich, England und den USA. Vandenhoeck & Ruprecht, Göttingen, pp 227–242
Jeidels O (1905) Das Verhaltnis der deutschen Groβbanken zur Industrie mit besonderer Berücksichtigung der Eisenindustrie. Dunker & Humblot, Leipzig
Kikkawa T (1996) Nihon no Kigyo Shudan (Japanese large corporate groups). Yuhikaku, Tokyo
Kobayashi Y (1976) Kigyo shudan to sangyo soshiki (2) (Large corporate group and industrial organization, 2). In: Keizaigaku kenkyu (Econ Study) 26(4):41–113
Kobayashi Y (1977) Kigyo shudan to sangyo soshiki—Sairon—(Corporate groups and industrial organization—A reexamination—). In: Keizaigaku kenkyu (Econ Study) 27(1):85–136
Kobayashi Y (1980) Kigyo shudan no bunseki (Analysis of corporate groups). Hokkaido daigaku tosho kankokai, Sapporo
Kosei torihiki iinkai jimukyoku (ed) (1994) Saishin rokudai kigyo shudan no jittai: Kosei torihiki iinkai dai gokai chosa hokokusho "Kigyo shudan no jittai ni tsuite" (Latest actual conditions of six large corporate groups: Report of the 5th investigation by the Fair Trade Commission "Actual conditions of large corporate groups"). Toyo keizai shinposha, Tokyo
Kosei torihiki iinkai jimukyoku (ed) (1998) Kigyo shudan no jittai ni tsuite (Actual conditions of corporate groups). Kosei torihiki iinkai jimukyoku, Tokyo
Koubek N (1971) Personelle und institutionelle Verbindung der Bereiche "Produktion" und "Kapital" in der Wirtschaftsgesellschaft der BRD. In: WWI-Mitteilungen 24(8/9):258–274
Köstler R, Zachert U, Müller M (2006) Aufsichtsratepraxis, vol 8. Bund Verlag, Frankfurt am Main
Kudo M (1982) Sengo kigyo shudan bunseki ni yosete (Analysis of postwar corporate group). In: Shogaku ronsan (Commer Rev) 24(1):201–245
Kuhlmann H (1949) Die Banken in der Hauptversammlung. In: Zeitschrift für das gesamte Kreditswesen 2(21):489–490
Lindhardt H (1958) Wider das Depotstimmrecht der Banken. In: Die Aktiengesellschaft 3(8):169–176
Maekawa K (1997) Nichidoku hikaku kigyoron heno michi (Comparative study of Japanese and German enterprise). Moriyama shoten, Tokyo

Masaki H (1985) Wagakuni no kigyo shudan kinyu no tenkai—Rokudai kigyo shudan no bunseki wo chushin ni—(Development of financing of corporate groups in Japan—Focusing on six large corporate groups—). In: Doshisha shogaku (Doshisya Bus Rev) 37(1):82–115
Matsumura K (1997) Nihonteki keiei zaimu to koporeto・gabanansu (Japanese corporate finance and corporate governance). Chuo keizaisha, Tokyo
Miyajima H (1992) Zaibatsu Kaitai (Dissolution of Zaibatsu). In: Hosei Daigaku Sangyo Jyoho Senta, Hashimoto J, Takeda H (eds) Nihon Keizai no Hatten to Kigyou Shudan (Development of Japanese economy and corporate groups). Tokyo Daigaku Shuppankai, Tokyo, pp 203–254
Miyazaki G (1966) Sengo Nihon no Keizai kiko (Japanese economic system after World War II). Shin Hyoron, Tokyo
Monopolkommission (1978) Hauptgutachten 1976/77 (Haupugutachten II). Nomos-Verlagsgesellschaft, Baden-Baden, Fortschreitenden Konzentration bei Groβunternehmen
Monopolkommission (2003) Hauptgutachten 2000/2001 (Hauptgutachten XIV). Nomos-Verlagsgesellschaft, Baden-Baden, Netzwettbewerb durch Regulierung
Morikawa H (1993) Zaibatsu kigyo shudan to sengo kigyo shudan (The zaibatsu corporate group and the postwar corporate group). In: Keieishigaku (Jpn Bus Hist Rev) 28(2):57–74
Nakamura M (1968) Mitsui kontsuerun no hukkatsu katei (Revival process of the Mitsui corporate group). In: Noguchi T (ed) Mitsui kontsuerun (Mitsui corporate group). Shin hyoron, Tokyo, pp 177–199
Nakata N, Hosoi K, Iwanami F (1997) Kigyokan no Jinteki nettowaku—Torishimariyaku kenninsei no nichibei hikaku—(Personnel networks between enterprises—Comparison of interlocking directorships in Japan and the United States—). Dobunkan, Tokyo
Nakatani I (1984) Kigyo gurupu no keizai kino (Economic function of corporate groups). In: Kikan gendai keizai (Contemp Econ) 58:14–24
Okazaki K (1999) Kigyo shudan to keiretsu yushi (Corporate groups and loans to affiliated companies). Bunshindo, Tokyo
Okazaki T (1992) Shihon jiyuka igo no kigyo shudan (Corporate groups after capital liberalization). In: Hosei daigaku jyoho senta, Hashimoto J, Takeda H (eds) Nihon keizai no hatten to kigyo shudan (Development of Japanese economy and corporate group). Tokyo daigaku shuppankai, Tokyo, pp 305–335
Okumura H (1975a) Hojin shihonshugi no kozo (Structure of corporate capitalism). Nihon hyoronsha, Tokyo
Okumura H (1975b) Nihon no kigyo shudan (Japanese corporate groups). In: Kikan chuo koron (Chuo Koron Q) 51:314–336
Okumura H (1976) Nihon no rokudai kigyo shudan (Six large corporate groups in Japan). Daiyamondosha, Tokyo
Okumura H (1978) Kigyo shudan jidai no keieisha. Kabushiki gaisha wa dokohe iku (Managers in the age of corporate groups. Where will corporations go?). Nihon keizai shinbunsha, Tokyo
Pfannschmidt A (1993) Personelle Verflechtungen über Aufsichtsrate. Mehrfachmandate in deutschen Unternehmen. Gabler, Wiesbaden
Pfeiffer H (1986) Groβbanken und Finanzgruppen. Ausgewählte Ergebnisse einer Untersuchung der personellen Verflechtungen von Deutscher, Dresdner und Commerzbank. In: WSI Mitteilungen 39(7):473–481
Pfeiffer H (1987) Das Imperium der Deutsche Bank. Campus, Frankfurt am Main
Pfeiffer H (1989) BASF und die Deutsche Bank. In: WSI Mitteilungen 42(1):9–16
Pfeiffer H (1993) Die Macht der Banken. Die personellen Verflechtungen der Commerzbank, der Deutschen Bank und der Dresdner Bank mit Unternehemen. Campus, Frankfurt am Main
Poullain L (1979) Tätigkeitsbericht. Seewald, Stuttgart-Degerloch
Sakaguchi A (1966) Mitsubishi (Mitusbishi). Chuo koronsha, Tokyo
Sakaguchi Y (1968) Kontsuerun no rekishi to shihai kozo no bunseki (History and corporate structure of large corporate groups). In: Noguchi T (ed) Mitsubishi kontsuerun. Keiei to zaimu no sogo bunseki (Mitsubishi corporate group. Total analysis of management and finance). Shin hyoron, Tokyo, pp 76–82

Sakamoto T (1980a) Kigyo shudan zaimuron (1) (Finance of corporate groups 1). In: Dai ichi keidai ronshu (Dai Ichi Econ Univ Rev) 10(1):45–67
Sakamoto T (1981) Kigyo shudan zaimuron (4) (Finance of corporate group 4). In: Dai ichi keidai ronshu (The Econ Rev Daiichi Keizai College) 10(4):41–62
Sakamoto T (1993) Kigyo shudan keieiron (Management of corporate groups). Dobunkan shuppan, Tokyo
Sakamoto T (1996) Daikigyo no zaimu kanri to kigyo shudan (Financial management of large enterprises and corporate groups). In: Sakamoto T, Sakuma N (eds) Kigyo shudan kenkyu no hoho (Methodology of corporate group study). Bunshindo, Tokyo, pp 193–212
Sakano M (1967) Kaisetsu kikan toshika no doko (Commentary on the trends of institutional investors). In: Baum DJ, Stiles NB (Trans. by Sakano M) Kikan toshika to kaisha shihai (Institutional investors and corporate control). Toyo keizia shinposha,Tokyo, pp 201–243
Sakuma N (2003) Doitsu no kigyo touchi (Corporate governance in Germany). In: Nakamura M (ed) Kigyo rinri to kigyo touch (Business ethics and corporate governance). Bunshindo, Tokyo, pp 65–83
Schaad H-P (1972) Das Depotstimmrecht der Banken nach schweizerischem und deutschem Recht. Schulthess Polygraphischer Verlag, Zurich
Schönwitz D, Weber HJ (1982) Unternehmenskonzentration, Personelle Verflechtungen und Wettbewerb. Eine Unterschung auf Basis der 100 gröβten Konzern der BRD. Nomos-Verlagsgesellschaft, Baden-Baden
Schwarz F (2003) Die Deutsche Bank. Reise auf tunerner Fuβen. Campus, Frankfurt am Main
Shadan hojin keizai chosa kyokai (1961) Nenpo keiretsu no kenkyu (Yearbook of affiliation study) — Dai ichibu jyojyo kigyohen (Companies listed in the first section of the Tokyo Stock Exchange) —, 1961 nen ban (1961 edition). Shadan hojin keizai chosa kyokai, Tokyo
Shadan hojin keizai chosa kyokai (1968) Nenpo keiretsu no kenkyu (Yearbook of affiliation study) — Dai ichibu jyojyo kigyohen (Companies listed in the first section of the Tokyo Stock Exchange) —, 1968 nen ban (1968 edition). Shadan hojin keizai chosa kyokai, Tokyo
Shadan hojin keizai chosa kyokai (1970) Nenpo keiretsu no kenkyu (Yearbook of affiliation study) — Dai ichibu jyojyo kigyohen (Companies listed in the first section of the Tokyo Stock Exchange) —, 1970 nen ban (1970 edition). Shadan hojin keizai chosa kyokai, Tokyo
Shadan hojin keizai chosa kyokai (1975) Nenpo keiretsu no kenkyu (Yearbook of affiliation study) — Dai ichibu jyojyo kigyohen (Companies listed in the first section of the Tokyo Stock Exchange) —, 1975 nen ban (1975 edition). Shadan hojin keizai chosa kyokai, Tokyo
Shadan hojin keizai chosa kyokai (1978) Nenpo keiretsu no kenkyu (Yearbook of affiliation study) — Dai ichibu jyojyo kigyohen (Companies listed in the first section of the Tokyo Stock Exchange) —, 1978 nen ban (1978 edition). Shadan hojin keizai chosa kyokai, Tokyo
Shadan hojin keizai chosa kyokai (1980) Nenpo keiretsu no kenkyu (Yearbook of affiliation study) — Dai ichibu jyojyo kigyohen (Companies listed in the first section of the Tokyo Stock Exchange) —, 1980 nen ban (1980 edition). Shadan hojin keizai chosa kyokai, Tokyo
Shadan hojin keizai chosa kyokai (1983) Nenpo keiretsu no kenkyu (Yearbook of affiliation study) — Dai ichibu jyojyo kigyohen (Companies listed in the first section of the Tokyo Stock Exchange) —, 1983 nen ban (1983 edition). Shadan hojin keizai chosa kyokai, Tokyo
Shadan hojin keizai chosa kyokai (1990) Nenpo keiretsu no kenkyu (Yearbook of affiliation study) — Dai ichibu jyojyo kigyohen (Companies listed in the first section of the Tokyo Stock Exchange) —, 1990 nen ban (1990 edition). Shadan hojin keizai chosa kyokai, Tokyo

Shadan hojin keizai chosa kyokai (1993) Nenpo keiretsu no kenkyu (Yearbook of affiliation study) — Dai ichibu jyojyo kigyohen (Companies listed in the first section of the Tokyo Stock Exchange) —, 1993 nen ban (1993 edition). Shadan hojin keizai chosa kyokai, Tokyo

Shibagaki K (1971) "Zaibatsu" kara "kigyo shudan" he (From "zaibatsu" to "corporate group"). In: Keizai hyoron (Econ Rev) 20(3):17–28

Stanzick K-H (1968) Der ökonomische Konzentrationsprozeβ. In: Schäfer G, Nedelmann C (eds) Der CDU-Staat. Analysen zur Verfassungswirklichkeit der Bundesrepublik. Bd. I. Suhrkamp, Frankfurt am Main, pp 48–79

Sumiya T (1982) Nihon keizai to rokudai kigyo shudan (Japanese economy and six large corporate groups). Shin hyoron, Tokyo

Suzuki K (1985) Sangyo · kinyu saihenka no kigyo shudan (II) (Corporate groups under restructuring of industry and finance, II). In: Momoyama gakuin daigaku keizai keiei ronshu (St. Andrew's Univ Econ Bus Rev) 27(3):81–105

Suzuki K (1993) Nihon no kigyo shudan—Sengo nihon no kigyo to ginko— (Japanese corporate groups—Enterprise and bank in postwar Japan—). Otsuki shoten, Tokyo

Suzuki K (1998) Mein banku to kigyo shudan—Sengo nihon no kigyokan shisutemu— (Main bank and corporate group—Corporate system in postwar Japan—). Mineruva shobo, Kyoto (Chapter 3)

Suzuki K (2008) Rokudai kigyo shudan no hokai (Collapse of six large corporate groups). Shinnihon shuppansha, Tokyo

Takahashi T (1997) Kigyo soshiki to kigyo touchi (Corporate organizations and corporate governance). In: Takahashi T, Onishi T (eds) Doitsu no kigyo (German enterprise). Waseda daigaku shuppanbu, Tokyo, pp 34–53

Takamura J (1977) Mitsui gurupu no subete (The entire structure of the Mitsui corporate group). Nihon jitsugyo shuppansha, Tokyo

Takamura J (1994) Mitsui gurupu no subete (The entire structure of the Mitsui corporate group). Nihon jitsugyo shuppansha, Tokyo

Tokyo daigaku shakai kagaku kenkyusho (ed) (1999) Rokudai kigyo shudan · yushi keiretsu no kabushiki mochiai (Six large corporate groups. Cross-stockholdings within financing affiliation). Tokyo daigaku shakaikagaku kenkyusho, Tokyo

Tokyo daigaku shakai kagaku kenkyusho (ed) (2000) Rokudai kigyo shudan · yushi keiretsu no keiretsu yushi (Six large corporate groups. Cross-stockholdings within financing affiliation). Tokyo daigaku shakaikagaku kenkyusho, Tokyo

Ueda Y (1994) Rokudai Kigyo shudan ni okeru shachokai no igi (Significance of the President club in six large corporate groups). In: Gendai kigyo kenkyukai (ed) Nihon no kigyokan kankei (Japanese inter-firm relationships). Chuo keizaisha, Tokyo, pp 115–140

Ueno T (1989) Rokudai kigyo shudan no jittai ni tsuite (Conditions of six corporate groups). Kosei torihiki (Fair Trade) 464:46–56

Uetake T (1997) Kinyu kikan to kigyo (Financial institution and enterprise). In: Takahashi T, Onishi T (eds) Doitsu no kigyo. Waseda daigaku shuppanbu, Tokyo, pp 93–112

Uno H (1972) Sengo no kigyo shudan to sono mondaiten (Corporate groups after World War II and their challenges). In: Gakushuin daigaku keizai ronshu (The journal of the Department of Economics of Gakushuin University) 8(3):3–30

Volkmann G, Kronenberg B (1994) Bankenmacht und Aufsichtsrat. In: WSI Mitteilungen 47(8):481–487

Washio T (1964) Keiretsu yushi (Loan to affiliated companies). In: Ginko Kenkyu (Banks Bank) 392:118–125

Washio T (1968a) Toshi ginko ni okeru keiretsu yushi[3] — Bigu bijinesu to ginko-(Loan to affiliated companies in city bank[3] — Big business and bank-). In: Ginko Kenkyu (Banks Bank) 443:110–114

Washio T (1968b) Toshi ginko ni okeru keiretsu yushi[7] — Bigu bijinesu to ginko—. In: Ginko Kenkyu (Banks Bank) 449:100–104

Wiendieck M (1992) Unternehmensfinanzierung und Kontrolle durch Banken, Deutschland–Japan–USA. Gabler, Wiesbaden

Winnacker K (1972) Nie den Mut verlieren Erinnerungen an Schicksalsjahr der deutschen Chemie. Econ Verlag, Dusseldorf

Yamaguchi H (1981) Nishi Doitsu ni okeru ginko to kigyo no kankei (Relationship between bank and enterprise in West Germany). In: Shoken Keizai (JSIR J Financ Secur Mark) 135:103–131

Ziegler R (1984) Das Netz der Personen- und Kapitalverflechtungen deutscher und österreichischer Wirtschaftsunternehmen. In: Kölner Zeitschrift für Soziologie und Sozialpsychlogie 36(3):585–618

Zugehör R (2003) Die Zukunft des rheinischen Kapitalismus. Unternehmen zwischen Kapitalismus und Mitbestimmung. Lesket + Budrich, Opladen

Part III
Americanization of Business Management and "Reframing" from the Postwar Period to the Early 1970s

Chapter 6
Deployment of American Management Education

Abstract Following World War II, the European and Japanese enterprises, industries, and their economies were developed by deploying and adapting US technology and management methods. In addition, American management methods were deployed and implemented under the United States-led productivity movement. The major American management methods implemented in Japan and Germany were for management education. However, in both nations, many factors influenced the introduction of American management education. Therefore, this chapter discusses the deployment of American management education in relation to universities' roles in such education, government agencies, eligibility criteria for executive management, and the managerial promotion system in enterprises. American initiatives in management education reform, universities' roles in management education, the deployment of Training within Industry (TWI), and other top management education methods are also considered. First, this chapter examines the deployment of American management education in Japan, followed by a discussion of such deployment in Germany. Based on these discussions, Japanese and German characteristics are clarified to identify various factors restricting the deployment of American-style methods in management education.

Keywords Business school · Management education · Manager promotion system · Productivity movement · Role of university · Training within industry (TWI)

In Part II, the postwar system of industrial concentration in Japan and Germany as seen in industrial systems based on industry-bank relationships and large corporate groups was analyzed. In Part III transformation of business management and corporate expansion in both countries will be examined in relation to the deployment of American management methods. This chapter through 11 will focus on management education, management and production systems, methods of adapting to the mass market, and management organization in the deployment of American management methods and systems after World War II through the early 1970s and subsequent transformations in business management.

T. Yamazaki, *Japanese and German Enterprises*,
https://doi.org/10.1007/978-981-97-4880-8_6

The deployment of American management methods and systems varies widely between a specific management system and method as well as between industries and corporations. Thus, in addition to analyzing the overall situation, it is important to examine the differences and various factors influencing each industry and corporation.

In general, an extremely broad scope for the transfer of American business culture exists in Germany, extending into all functional management areas. Specifically, elements of management philosophy and language, skills, technology, know-how, and specialized methods and processes are some of the adopted aspects. However, unlike science and technology, management, organizational know-how, and techniques generally require extensive adaptations to the conditions of the importing country (Dyas and Thanheiser 1976, pp. 112–113). For example, in a German subsidiary of a US company, despite the former's subordinate relationship with the latter, the deployment of American-style innovations encountered numerous difficulties and did not go smoothly (Hartmann 1963, p. 192). Thus, significant issues exist, such as German corporate attitudes, responses, and the actual deployments in response to American management methods and systems. Moreover, the deployment of management education yields changes in business management itself, and German business management characteristics affects specialized processes.

This chapter, first, considers the deployment of American management education. After World War II, the role of middle management in the management and top management functions increased. In such an environment, reforms in management education became critical issues. The United States viewed reforms in management education in Europe as particularly important for the American-led productivity movement (Kleinschmidt 2002, p. 173, McGlade 1998c, p. 33). Thus, the deployment of management education was critical during the 1950s and 1960s. However, many factors influenced the introduction of American management education in Japan and Germany. This chapter discusses the deployment of American management education in relation to the effects of America's assistance, involvement of state, universities' role in management education, eligibility criteria for executive management, the manager promotion system, and characteristics of labor market.[1]

First, the deployment of American management education in Japan is considered in Sect. 6.1. Next, the deployment of American management education in Germany is examined in Sect. 6.2. Furthermore, in Sect. 6.3, characteristics of the deployment of American management education and the reform of management education through comparison between Japan and Germany are explored. Based on these foregoing discussions, Sect. 6.4 clarifies "reframing" in the deployment of American management education in both nations.

[1] The first content analysis related to Germany in this chapter is Chap. 6 of the author's book "*German Business Management: A Japanese Perspective on Regional Development Factors,*" which was published by Springer in 2013.

6.1 Deployment of American Management Education in Japan

6.1.1 Socio-economic Background Regarding Management Education Reform and American Initiatives

First, this section examines the socio-economic background to the deployment of American management education in Japan as well as American initiatives in management education reform.

Japan's increasing corporate modernization efforts after the war, as the legal recognition of labor unions and the growing labor movement heightened the conflict between labor and management. This environment called for reforms in management methods based on the family system, feudal family relations, as well as the irrational familial and paternalistic human relations that labor management had previously relied upon. Under such conditions, comprehensive management education methods that exceeded conventional levels of personnel management were required, and the development of American management education methods became an important issue (Mitsubishi Jyukogyo Kabushikigaisya Somubucho Saito 1967, p. 315). Meanwhile, the perception in Japanese firms that the deployment of American management education was very effective for overcoming any defects in companies' management methods and styles became the background for such deployment (Sangyo kunren 1965, p. 82).

In addition, Japanese businesses experienced a generational shift due to the removal of the top business leaders belonging to older generations. Many new managers of postwar "zaibatsu"-type companies were promoted from the ranks of middle management. In many cases, they had not even received sufficient training to become top managers at the time of their promotion (Miyajima 1991, pp. 139–140, Miyajima 1992, pp. 212–213, Miyazaki 1966, p. 224), which was one of the factors that called for the active introduction of American management methods. Such circumstances surrounding the managers and the necessity to modernize management were important factors in determining the stronger intention to introduce American management education methods in Japan than in Germany.

The United States gave significant assistance to Japan, which differed from that given to European nations and took the initiative to transfer American management education methods. Management Training Program (MTP), originally a training system for American supervisors, was first adapted for Japanese supervisors working on American Air Force bases during the postwar occupation period. Thereafter, Japanese corporations began using MTP to train middle management, and after several iterations MTP was modified according to Japan's requirements (Sugiyama 1968, p. 2; Sakamoto 1964, p. 153; Sakamoto 1963a, pp. 61–62). Further, Civil Communication Section (CCS) courses were implemented as a top management education method under the directive of the occupying military. GHQ implemented these courses in Japan on the basis of the recognition of serious deficiencies in the management of Japan's telecommunications industry (Sakamoto 1964, p. 158; Kudo 1981, pp. 101–102). As seen in these education methods, American initiatives and their roles in the deployment of American management education and management education reforms in Japan were far greater and more direct than those in Europe.

6.1.2 Development of In-firm Education in Postwar Boom Years

This section considers the development of management education in the postwar boom years. In-firm education and training in Japanese companies began as training for skilled workers. Old-fashioned education emphasizing "mentalism" was denied (under the influence of American pragmatism), after which education methods that were immediately useful for skilled workers were employed. However, they were not systematically placed into operation, and they were only sporadically implemented. Thus, in this stage, there was no management education in the true sense of the term. However, around 1950, the age of fixed-form education through the deployment of American methods began, after which various management education methods, such as Training within Industry (TWI), Management Training Program (MTP), Jinjiin Supervisor Training (JST), and Civil Communication Section (CCS), were enforced (Salkamoto 1964, pp. 143, 145, 148–149; Sakamoto 1963a, pp. 60–61).

From 1945 to 1955, the institutionalization of management education as part of in-company education began. In addition, the influence of new management education courses, introduced by the American occupation authority, was extremely apparent and significant. They combined ideas of management functions, scientific management, and human relations (Okazak-Ward 1993, p. 27). In 1955, the Japan Productivity Center was established and the first top management seminar was organized. Hence, within the first decade after 1945, the new development of management education had emerged (Sakamoto 1964, p. 144). However, limitations of fixed-form education methods, such as TWI, MTP, and CCS, gradually appeared after 1955. Under such conditions, the institutionalization of in-firm management education proceeded after 1958.

Many leading companies established education policies and principles as well as implementation policies based on them. In some cases, sections for supervising education in companies were united. As a result, management education in Japan was realized around 1960. In this process, reorganization of the Japanese management climate deepened, and "Japanization" proceeded in the form of management education that was compatible with the actual circumstances of each enterprise. This movement became widespread among managers after 1960. Therefore, Japanese firms had to proceed toward individualization to overcome the limitations of fixed-form education methods. Meanwhile, individualization that was compatible with the requirements of each company in Japan was pursued. The most characteristic one was "spirit education," which was set against American practical education based on pragmatism. During this period, the development of management education in small and medium-sized enterprises also demonstrated the trend of Japanization (Sakamoto 1964, pp. 183–184, 188–190, 195–197, 203, 259, 264, 266–267; Sakamoto 1963b, Nissan Jidosha 1975, p. 324).

In this way, the Japanization of American management education proceeded through company-specific training. During the 1960s, in-house education and training were broadly diffused against the background of rapid economic growth. Many pioneering firms had their own educational policies or training programs to meet their own firm-specific needs, based on the condition of lifetime employment (Nishizawa 1996, p. 108). From the late 1950s to the late 1960s, education systems were improved and enhanced according to management hierarchies (Kinoshita 1971, p. 45).

6.1.3 Role of Government Offices in Deployment of American Management Education

In Japan, government agencies strongly encouraged expanding education for managers and supervisors and played an important role in management education reform. Implementation of TWI, a method for supervisors, was achieved with technical assistance from the Ministry of Labor through the Employment Security Act and its amendments. MTP, a method for training managers, was also implemented with the considerable involvement of the Ministry of International Trade and Industry. MTP was modified according to Japan's requirements. This form of MTP was developed primarily for office manager training given by the National Personnel Authority, a government bureau, and was broadly referred to under the acronym JST. It was used to train managers at banks, insurance firms, government institutions, and other public associations. Furthermore, CCS cources were implemented under participation of the Ministry of Telecommunication (Oyamada 1981, pp. 59–61; Furukawa 1981, pp. 73–74; Sugiyama 1968, p. 2; Sangyokunrenhakusyo Henshu Iinkai 1971, pp. 334–335, 338–339; Sakamoto 1964, pp. 154–159; Shokugyo kunren 1977, p. 12).

6.1.4 Deployment of American Education Methods for Middle and Lower Management

This section examines the deployment of American education methods for middle and lower management. TWI played an important role as a method for training supervisors at the shop-floor level, and it satisfied the latent training needs of supervisors. As a result, it was well received among them. Meanwhile, the rise of labor union organizations within the company made its members even more insecure. Managers and supervisors could no longer depend on old behavioral patterns when directing and guiding their subordinates. However, since they lacked training, they were unfamiliar with any new approaches (Okazawa-Ward 1993, p. 31). At the management level, under the conditions of a rising labor movement and the remarkable decline of trust in management after the war, it was extremely important to overcome any limitations of management methods based on pre-war feudal family labor relations.

From the early 1950s, TWI particularly prevailed in large enterprises, after which the Ministry of Labor expanded its introduction to small- and medium-sized firms (Sangyokunrenhakusyo henshu iinkai 1971, p. 340). In small and medium-sized enterprises, the number of managers at the shop-floor level, such as foremen with many years of experience, increased with the modernization of offices and the clarification of management positions. Therefore, the number of firms that introduced TWI significantly increased (Sangyokunren hakusho hensshu iinkai 1971, p. 587). However, the ratio of diffusion regarding TWI in small and medium-sized firms was lower than that in large businesses. According to a 1963 survey by the Japan Federation of Employers' Associations, the ratios of the introduction of TWI-JI, TWI-JM, and TWI-JR were 35.5%, 29%, and 31%, respectively. In firms that employed more than 3,000 workers, the ratios were 63.9%, 62.3%, and 63.7%, respectively. Conversely, such ratios in small- and medium-sized companies with less than 300 employees were 13.9%, 8.3%, and 9.6%, respectively (Nihon keieisha dantai renmei 1965, pp. 1, 19, 50–51). In this way, TWI, which was diffused nationwide as an alternative to prewar education methods for foremen and shop-floor management, gradually prevailed in small and medium-sized businesses (Sangyokunren hakusyo henshu iinkai 1971, p. 560).

In Japan, human relations management methods were successful in the workplace after 1955. In many large enterprises, elaborate training that exceeded the level of management techniques concerning human relations was put into effect for supervisors. Overall, there were two types of training. One was training that emphasized the membership of the firm or organization for the purpose of promoting a sense of "togetherness" within a company. The other was training that focused on human relations and leadership skills for supervisors at the shop-floor level. Various methods and techniques based on studies of small groups in the field of psychology or social psychology were also introduced in these trainings (Nakayama et al. 1966, pp. 153–156).

The education of middle management began with the introduction of MTP. Between the 1950s and the 1960s, a trend emphasized training related to aspects of human relations (Sangyokunren hakusho henshu iinkai 1971, p. 9). MTP was the prevalent management education method (Sangyokunren hakusho henshu iinkai 1971, p. 334), and in the decade after 1945, it contributed to the establishment of a new management system and management order (Sato 1977, p. 16). The contribution of MTP to the diffusion of postwar new management thought was significant (Fujiseitetsu kabushikigaisya Shashi hensan iinkai 1981, p. 733).

In some cases, the results of behavioral scientific studies in the United States were used in the deployment of MTP. For instance, at the Nissan Motor Corporation, training courses for newly appointed section chiefs, which mainly consisted of lectures based on MTP, were not always effective. As a result, the company developed and implemented Management Basic Training (MBT), which adopted a dynamic management approach based on behavioral science (Nissan jidosha kabushikigaisha shashi hensan iinkai 1975, p. 325). A similar case occurred at the Kawasaki Steel Corporation. Based on MTP, this company changed the conventional approach of managing subordinates and made efforts to improve the workplace through behavioral science (Kawasaki seitetsu kabushikigaisha Shashi henshyu iinkai 1976, p. 548).

Thus, the results of human relations studies were used to train managers and supervisors, which contributed to improved human relations. In addition, criticism of fixed-form methods, such as TWI and MTP, from the standpoint of emphasizing the individuality of a company was also a factor in promoting leadership education (Kinoshita 1970, p. 51).

Fixed-form education played an important role in complementing the general foremen system. In this system, general foremen were given definite authority in line organization as well as substantial duties and powers as the person in charge of production. Under the adoption of line and staff organization, demarcations between line functions and staff functions were clearly determined. Training for managers and supervisors emphasized the management of subordinates and "job relations" rather than focusing on manufacturing techniques and business knowledge (Mogi 1981, p. 177; Sangyokunren hakusho henshu iinkai 1971, pp. 369, 373). At the Yawata Iron and Steel Corporation, the education of staff functions, as well as line functions, was established by first educating general foremen, who were in charge of not only production control but also personnel management and cost control (Yawata seitetsu kabushikigaisha shashi hensan iinkai 1981, Chap. 3).

At manufacturing companies such as the Toyota Motor Corporation, TWI, and MTP were used as a means of standardization and to implement industrial engineering. TWI was deployed in not only large enterprises but also subcontracting firms as part of company-wide improvements (Toyota jidosha kogyo kabushikigaisha shashi henshu iinkai 1958, p. 417; Toyota jidosha kogyo kabushikigaisha 1987, p. 278; Wada 2009, pp. 521–524, 526, Fujimoto 1997, p. 69). Thus, American management education methods played an important role as a means of rationalizing production. Such a trend was also seen in the iron and steel industry. For example, the Yawata Iron and Steel Corporation completed standard work methods using TWI, while other firms substituted work depending on the scientific analysis for work on the basis of perception (Nihon tekko renmei sengo tekkoshi henshu iinkai 1959, p. 997). The deployment of TWI to educate first-line supervisors at the Fuji Electric Corporation became an effective means of developing industrial engineering (Fuji denki seizo kabushikigaisha 1974, p. 225).

In Japan, TWI was used for not only supervisors but also middle management. On the one hand, there were many cases in which enterprises applied MTP to train supervisors at the shop-floor level and to train the chiefs of departments, sections, or subsections (Kawasaki jyukogyo kabushikigaisha shashi hensansitsu Murotani 1959, p. 777; Romu kanri kokunai shisatsudan 1957, p. 54; Dainiji roshi kyoryoku taisei kokunai shisatsudan 1958, p. 122; Sangyo kunren kokunai shisatsudan kyushu timu 1957,

p. 42; Sangyo kunren seisansei sisatsudan 1957, p. 25; Nissan jidosha kabushikigaisha somubu chosaka 1965, p. 297). While TWI was used and mainly diffused to educate first-line supervisors, MTP was primarily used for chiefs of departments or sections in manufacturing enterprises (Nakayama 1969, p. 7). However, these training methods were used flexibly in many companies.

6.1.5 Deployment of American Methods for Top Management Education

This section considers the deployment of top management education methods. After 1950, the Japan Federation of Employers' Associations endeavored to spread CCS courses throughout the country. In 1955, after the Japan Industrial Training Association was established, CCS courses were successfully diffused nationwide. However, the contents of the CCS courses dramatically changed with the progress of innovation and the pervasion of management education. Initially, fixed-form courses using textbooks were dominant. However, lecture-style education and meeting-style training in small groups were subsequently used for top management (Sangyo kunren hakusho henshu iinkai 1971, p. 385; Sangyo kunren 1965, p. 82).

According to a 1963 investigation by the Japanese Federation of Employers' Associations, the ratio of firms that implemented education for top management was 55.3%; among these companies, the ratio of firms that used CCS courses was 18.6% (Nihon keieisha dantai renmei 1965, pp. 1, 5, 52–53). However, CCS courses disappeared after 1975. There are three reasons for their disappearance. First, while in the postwar boom years many firms only focused attention on rationalization within the management, in the early 1970s, managers were forced to adapt themselves to the environment. Second, the participants in the MTP courses went on to become top management. Third, the reflection of fixed-form education occurred (Kudo 1981, pp. 102–104). As a replacement for CCS, education for top management via external organizations saw tremendous growth. In addition to the executive management seminars sponsored by the Japan Productivity Center, there were education courses published by regional bank associations, Keio University, the Japan Management Development Association, business consultants, the Japan Federation of Employers' Associations, and the Nippon Omni-Management Association (Kudo 1981, pp. 104–109; Sugiyama 1968, p. 4; Sakamoto 1964, pp. 172–180).

Although the training courses based on American methods of top management education were implemented, such approaches were not diffused among higher education facilities such as business schools. In Japan, the establishment of business administration education in universities occurred later than in the United States and Germany. In fact, the management studies boom in Japan only occurred after 1955. Such management studies and labor market characteristics, such as those seen in various companies' internal promotion systems, were related to the small role of business schools.

6.1.6 Reflections Regarding Deployment of American Management Education Methods and Japanese Development

Fixed-form type of education methods represented by TWI, MTP, and CCS were distinctly American in nature, and drew criticism and concern because they were not characteristically compatible with Japan's management culture, specifically paternalism, the seniority order system, and lifetime employment. Moreover, because they were standardized methods, they were not only inappropriate for the corporations' specific issues and needs but also lacked situational awareness and opportunities for decision-making needed to solve day-to-day management issues. Therefore, Japanese corporations began to enact their own education policies and programs and disseminate new management education that applied a variety of education methods, introduced by newly established management education associations (Oyamada 1981, pp. 62–63; Furukawa 1981, pp. 77–78; Sugiyama 1968, pp. 2–4; Sakamoto 1964, pp. 165–166).

Issues such as those mentioned above, arising from the deployment of American-style management education, occurred because of the rigid character of fixed-form education, which standardized the American style, regardless of the systemic differences in hiring, personnel change, promotion, and other functions. In Japan, industries generally relied excessively on fixed-form training courses (Kamei and Shiraki 1971, p. 129, Hasegawa 1960, p. 173, Okuda 1961, pp. 120, 150–153; Sangyo kunren 1966, p.45). In addition, it was impossible to inject fundamental ideas of American rationalism and individualism into Japanese management training. Thus, American-style methods were adapted incorporating Japan's ideology of collectivism and efficiency, as well as skill-based education, which included industrial co-partnership, a sense of belonging within the company, and management education (Shimokawa 1976, p. 58).

After 1955, criticism of American labor management began to appear, and the movement toward removing fixed-form types of education emerged. By the 1960s, new results of studies in the field of management and organization theories were introduced. These factors led to the removal of fixed-form types of education (Kinoshita 1971, p. 46).

In addition, the actual circumstances in Japan and companies' peculiar conditions were not considered, especially regarding the implementation of American fixed-form education (Nakamura 1966, p. 12). One evaluation found that CCS and MTP courses were not suitable for management education in Japan due to their contents, which mainly focused on American management techniques and organizational theories dating back to the 1920s (Sangyo kunren hakusho henshu iinkai 1971, p. 1; Okamoto 1971, p. 28). The conditions of rationalization of management and the existence of a democratized workplace led to the creation of the contents of American fixed-form education methods (Nakayama 1971, p. 18). In Japanese companies, the positions and roles of supervisors at the shop-floor level differed from those in the United States. TWI was only a short-term training method that mainly focused on supervision techniques. Thus, it was difficult for supervisors to acquire professional skills through TWI. However, the personnel involved did not always sufficiently recognize such facts. As a result, under excessive expectations and overestimations, the uncritical introduction of American fixed-form education methods occurred (Nakayama et al. 1966, pp. 135–137; IE 1968, p. 11).

In this situation, many companies implemented TWI and MTP with the original contents and established education policies and principles. Management education associations also diffused new management education methods. In fact, the diversification of education methods and new movements toward the implementation of management education emerged in real management (Kudo 1981, pp. 104–105; Sugiyama 1968, pp. 4–5). After 1955 TWI courses suitable for actual circumstances in Japan have appeared (Kobayashi 1969, p. 40). Attempts to modify TWI through an investigation of the positions and roles of supervisors from a new viewpoint appeared. The reinforcement of supplementary instruction as a follow up to education and on-the-job training (OJT) were typical cases of such attempts (Nakayama et al. 1966, pp. 136–137). In TWI, there were many cases in which supplementary instruction was implemented as retraining. For instance, in the shipbuilding industry, such instruction concerning skills by TWI and training for safety improvement were put into effect (Rosei jiho 1960, p. 13). However, TWI was not always ideally implemented in enterprises. In fact, the introduction of basic courses that taught standardized techniques of TWI for supervisors and instruction methods using such techniques and applying them to practical business affairs at the shop-floor level were incomplete (Kondo 1968, p. 41).

Regarding MTP, in 1957, the Fuji Iron and Steel Corporation began re-examining the approach to create its own version, and it completed the original manual in 1958. MTP based on this manual formed the basis of manager education at the company (Fuji seitetsu kabushikigaisha shashi hensan iinkai 1981, p. 733). The Kawasak Steel Corporation also absorbed MTP into its original management courses for chief clerks after 1963 (Kawasaki seitetsu kabushikigaisha shashi henshu iinkai 1976, pp. 547–548). In contrast, the Mitsubishi Electric Corporation revised MTP to its own version in 1951, after which the first revised management course was implemented for its subsection managers in 1954 (Mitsubishi denki kabushikigaisha shashi hensansitsu 1982, p. 345). Thus, American education methods, represented by the aforementioned TWI and MTP cases, were adopted on the basis of company-specific conditions (Sangyo kunren seisansei kokunai shisatsudan 1957, p. 14).

From 1955 to 1965, criticism of American fixed-form education became stronger for three reasons. First, in the latter half of the 1950s, emphasis on the contents of supervisors' work moved from safety, education, and human relations to quality, cost performance, subordinates' evaluations, grievance disposition, and labor problems. Thus, the contents of each fixed-form education course were no longer suitable. Second, it became more important to develop education programs that satisfied specific workplace conditions. Third, such approaches hindered businesses due to their introduction during busy periods that focused on innovation (Nakayama et al. 1966, pp. 187, 189).

In the 1960s, the necessity of developing a company's education system that did not include fixed-form education methods increased (Romu kenkyu henshubu 1961, p. 11; Keieisha 1963, p. 46; Nakajima 1963; Furuya 1971, Aonuma 1977, p. 11). As a result, the number of enterprises that attempted to use management education methods flexibly, such as partially custom-made or custom-made methods, also increased (Kano 1966, p. 51). With regard to top management education, an investigation in 1963 by the Japan Federation of Employers' Associations pointed out that the ratio of companies that used CCS courses was only 8.4%. In contrast, the ratio of companies that implemented their own courses was 16.5%, and the ratio of large businesses with more than 5,000 employees that implemented their own cources was 36.2% (Nihon keieisha dantai renmei 1965, pp. 1, 19, 52–53). In addition, according to a 1969 survey, the ratio of enterprises that developed their own education courses was 40%, and the ratio of large firms was approximately 80%. However, in terms of educating managers and supervisors, revised fixed-form education methods, such as MTP and training programs for foremen according to company-specific needs, were dominant (Rosei jiho 1969, pp. 28–29, 31–32; kansai keieisha kyokai and Nihon sangyo kunren kyokai kansai shibu 1970, p. 7). In the mid-1960s, the movement to establish appropriate education and training systems (according to the environment of each enterprise) appeared to overcome the limitations of conventional fixed-form education methods. Thus, in-firm training in Japan reached a turning point (Nihon tekko renmei jimukyoku et al. 1964, p. 97).

During the 1960s, due to rapid changes in the external environment, organizational training that emphasized human relations was reconsidered. Many companies implemented training programs to enhance the abilities of managers, deepen their business knowledge, and educate managers on general topics, such as international politics and economics. In addition, self-development for overcoming the limitations of group training and improving management and professional abilities was strongly required (Sangyo kunren hakusho henshu iinkai 1971, p. 364). In the late 1960s, it became important to implement group training, daily instruction, and self-development in a well-balanced manner (Onitake 1969, p. 27).

Therefore, after 1965, various diversification methods were developed, and management education in Japan arrived at the stage of quantitative and qualitative reinforcement and expansion. However, the importance of group education according to hierarchies declined after peaking around 1965. Subsequently, emphasis was placed on OJT and self-development (Sangyo kunren hakusho henshu iinkai 1971, pp. 420, 422). Under the development of ability-based personnel management, the importance of self-development by motivation from within was stressed (Oyamada 1972, p. 41). During this period, such emphasis on self-development in management education was strongly related to the state of management that aimed at improving the self-esteem of individuals in the workplace through small-group education (Nikkeiren noryokushugi kanri kenkyukai 1968, pp. 20–21, 68–69).

In Japan, fixed-form management education methods deployed from the United States were used for a long time. By 1974, CCS seminars were attended by more than 1,000 top executives (Okazak-Ward 1993, p. 472). TWI also continued to be a core method of supervisor education, and its effective training method was the basis of many in-company training courses in the mid-1970s (Kaji 1976, p. 26). TWI and MTP were continually revised, and by 1988, more than 600,000 managers participated in MTP courses, while 20,000 TWI trainers had been produced (Okazak-Ward 1993, p. 472).

6.2 Deployment of American Management Education in Germany

Next, the German deployment of American-style management education will be considered. American initiatives in transforming management education and the role of German universities within the education are discussed in Sects. 6.2.1 and 6.2.2, respectively. In Sect. 6.2.3, the deployment of American-style management education methods is considered and in Sect. 6.2.4 the various factors that defined that state of affairs are examined.

6.2.1 Socio-economic Background Regarding Management Education Reform and American Initiatives

First, this section considers the socio-economic background of management education reforms and American initiatives. The process of transferring American-style methods in this field to Western Europe can be observed in the following three steps: (1) the creation of the US Technical Assistance and Productivity Program (USTA&P) as an important element of assistance of the Marshal Plan; (2) the combination of American universities and European management reforms; and (3) the internationalization of American-style management education. The USTA&P was prepared to directly send American technology specialists and management consultants for enterprises that were interested in implementing management and production reforms; the program also provided factory observation opportunities and retraining seminars. Furthermore, until business schools similar to those in the United States were founded in Western Europe, programs run by productivity centers in each country as well as the USTA&P played a significant role in providing education. To combine American universities and European management innovations, the USTA&P constantly cooperated with American colleges and universities, which were concerned about providing management education courses for visiting teams, in response to the increasing numbers of European managers. Universities in the United States played a crucial role in providing organization and support for TWI programs. The USTA&P's programs for management education remarkably multiplied contact between American and European scholars and students. Since 1958, these programs opened paths to continually propagate management knowledge through universities and companies. The dramatic growth of international students in the United States further internationalized American-style management education. Beginning in the 1960s, Europe became the center of academic exchange between the United States and foreign countries (McGlade 1998b, pp. 51–58, 62, 64).

At the time, the American perception of conditions was that European executives were resistant to constructive changes, unaware of their roles in forming long-term planning. In addition, they tended to be involved in many day-to-day activities of the corporation; thus, changing their attitudes was considered indispensable (OEEC 1954, pp. 5, 13–14). In such an environment, USTA&P's goal was to implement an American model of management research and managerial and executive education for European universities and professors (McGlade 1998c, p. 33). USTA&P was initiated to facilitate effectual communication between leading executives and industrialists in Europe and the United States in alliance with business associations, employer associations, and employer organizations, such as the National Management Council (NMC) and the National Association of Manufacturers in America, through seminars and workshops conducted in cooperation with several eminent US universities (McGlade 1998c, p. 18, McGlade 1998a, p. 27). For instance, in the early 1950s, appropriate management education programs were implemented within the USTA&P framework in collaboration with OEEC, the International Chamber of Commerce, the European Productivity Agency (EPA), and each nation's productivity center. Executives representing leading companies, such as P&G, DuPont, Eastman Kodak, Ford, GE, and those from NMC, various universities, and research organizations were involved in the program (Kleinschmidt 2002, S. 296). The transfer of the American model into Germany was considered for top-manager education and retraining projects, with the assistance of the Mutual Security Agency (MSA) and Foreign Operations Administration. The MSA had already planned to create a management education center by 1953 (Kleinschmidt 2002, SS. 75–77).

From Germany's standpoint, intensive research focusing on management education commenced between 1949 and 1950 in groups of delegations dispatched to the United States (Feldenkirchen 2004, p. 120). Moreover, several special delegations for technical assistance planning in the 1950s regarded education and training in this field as one reason for the American economy's superiority (Kipping 1998, p. 102). This perspective and understanding created the background for Germany's deployment of American-style methods.

Thus, although the initiative shown by the United States was crucial, American support for the EPA decreased after 1956; thereafter, the Ford Foundation increased its involvement (Boel 1998, pp. 38, 42). Since the early 1950s, this foundation had been involved in the financial and organizational aspects of management education in Europe. Furthermore, through the proliferation of intensive education and research programs, it had functioned as a cultural intermediary in endeavors to standardize management education and professional requirements. The principal goal of the Ford Foundation was to transfer the basics of America's "organizational synthesis" into Europe, rather than export educational programs and curricula (Gemelli 1996, pp. 42, 47, 55).

6.2.2 Role of German Universities in Management Education and Their Limitations

Section 6.2.1 clarified that America's initiatives in transforming postwar management education and management education reforms were significant. In the 1950s and 1960s, the transfer of American-style management education into Europe varied greatly by nation, and no country remained unaffected (Schröter 2005, pp. 104–105). The level of influence depended considerably on traditional management education within German universities.

From the historical perspective, three different models exist for management education systems: German, Latin, and American. Management education in the German model was practiced outside universities in one of two higher education institutions: the engineering college and the commercial college. In the Latin model used in France, Italy, and Spain, while overall education focused on law, economics, and organization management, micro aspects such as schools providing opportunities to systematically learn business management were neglected. However, the American model of management education was established from the beginning as an element of the overall system of higher education. The emphasis was placed on the actual decision-making in market conditions, and business schools played a significant role. The response to and absorption of American thinking into management education was principally dependent on that country's education system (Schröter 2005, pp. 97–99).

Regarding education systems, German universities focused on academic research rather than specialized education. The differences between the Germans, who emphasized science and theory, and the Americans, with their tendency toward pragmatism, obstructed the deployment of American-style methods in German universities. In the German system, a person's promotion and compensation were determined by the type of school from which they graduated. Also, Germany had two qualification categories: "capable of work" ("Berufsfähig"), which is gained from educational institutions, and "ready for work" ("Betriebsfertig"), acquired during OJT. Although top managers and executives believed in the core pragmatic values provided during OJT, they could apply only limited pressure to modernize curricula (Schröter 2005, pp. 103–104). Endeavors to change this style of education faced intense objection from within schools, which rejected replacing theory with practicality (Locke RR 1996, p. 76).

Moreover, German commercial colleges had not obtained the status of providers of basic, broadly shared education for executives, as American business schools had. This more narrowly focused the perceptions developed thereof because manufacturing executives recognized the education attained in German engineering colleges. Germany's commercial colleges, unlike American MBA programs, concentrated primarily on business economics rather than management. They were not regarded as a tool for nurturing executives due to the lack of pragmatic characteristics in terms of their study and education. In the American model, the purpose of education was management development, which differentiated between education for management functions and that for operational functions. Generally, it was highly unusual for engineers in the United States to fill important executive roles (Amdam 1996, pp. 4–6). Hence, the American-style method regarding the function of management was not conducive to the German environment, in which those with an engineering background were often enterprise leaders.

Furthermore, as observed in disputes concerning business administration methods, business economics needed to become a scholarly effort to be recognized as an academic field in universities. In addition, by choosing to either become pragmatically useful in management practice or maintain the traditional methods, elements of a scientific nature or standards of theoretical science inevitably took precedence. In such situations, the relationship between higher education and management practice had to be always tenuous. To complicate matters further, the system of the difficult postdoctoral thesis must be promoted to a research professor in a university, along with the long research program it entailed, thereby decreasing any possibility of long-term work experience before becoming a professor. As a result, academicians with a high level of scholarly ability, but no actual experience in management were promoted to a professorship (Locke 1996, pp. 74–75).

Against this background, the industrial world voiced its demands for reforms in the university system. However, the traditional German university system remained largely intact after 1945, and the academic persona was even strengthened. Consequently, the business world pursued alternative solutions, the most powerful option of which was the American model (Kipping 1998, pp. 99, 101).

6.2.3 *Deployment of American Management Education*

6.2.3.1 TWI Implementation

This section examines the deployment of American-style management education methods in greater detail. TWI education courses based on American education materials were useful intermediaries for facilitating stability in labor and industrial relations with management, improving relationships between superiors and subordinates, work methods and technological knowledge, and providing guidance for subordinates (Kleinschmidt 2002, p. 74).

Occupation authorities implemented TWI in Germany by organizing education and training courses for leaders of employee education in September 1948. Many enthusiastic individuals reinforced interest in the TWI program, which was diffused further with the support of a few enterprises such as Bosch. Note that these corporations attempted to promote harmonious relationships in the workplace, and courses were conducted for both management and employee representatives. By mid-1953, 160 sessions of trainer education courses had been implemented, and approximately 80,000 individuals had participated in nearly 8,000 education courses (Kipping 2004, p. 35).

As the American corporate involvement in the USTA&P management education project had ended, American universities began collaborating to pick up the slack (McGlade 1998c, p. 19). In 1951, American universities began organizing and implementing TWI programs. University participation played a crucial role in the USTA&P campaign to improve management education and support management retraining in postwar Europe (McGlade 1998c, pp. 24–25). Moreover, with the support of this program, thousands of European executives and scholars obtained unrivaled opportunities to observe and learn at American universities and enterprises. Upon their return, they brought these American management techniques with them (McGlade 1998c, p. 28).

The RKW (National Board for Economy and Efficiency) also contributed to management education and retraining by visiting America in response to American professionals' invite [*National Archives*, RG469, Mission to Germany, Productivity and Technical Assistance Division, Subject Files of the Chief, 1953–1956, Council for International Progress in Management (USA), Inc (11.12.1953), *National Archives*, RG469, Mission to Germany, Productivity and Technical Assistance Division, Subject Files of the Chief, 1953–1956, TA09-217, Program for the TA-B-Project 09-217 Top Management, *National Archives*, RG469, Mission to Germany, Productivity and Technical Assistance Division, Subject Files of the Chief, 1953–1956, Berlin Top Management Team (7.10.1953)] and conducting own TWI education courses [*National Archives*, RG469, Mission to Germany, Productivity and Technical Assistance Division, Subject Files of the Chief, 1953–1956, Durchführung des TA-B-Projectes 09-216—Management Training, *National Archives*, RG469, Mission to Germany, Productivity and Technical Assistance Division, Subject Files of the Chief, 1953–1956, Management Program for Berlin—Management Training Team (22.6.1953)]. REFA also rendered services to the implementation of TWI and incorporated TWI activities within its education and training programs in 1954 (Pechhold 1974, p. 155, *REFA-Nachrichten* 1954, p. 75). Having REFA personnel engaged in the TWI program indicates the scope of REFA's public involvement in education (REFA-Nachrichten 1955, p. 16). The long-term collaboration between REFA and TWI also exemplifies how highly TWI education material was rated in the development of REFA employees (Jaeckel 1961, p. 222).

In this historical viewpoint, examining TWI implementation in detail, we determine that three TWI courses were held by the chemical industrial firm, Henkel, during work hours: job instruction, labor relations, and job design (or job improvement). Among them, job design was the most intensive, and these courses were implemented for the first time in 1964 within the framework of in-company retraining [*Henkel Archiv*, K160, Betriebliche Ausbildungs- und Bildungsarbeit (5.7.1960), p. 2, *Henkel Archiv*, K160, Niederschrift über die Meisterbesprechung Nr.11 vom 17.11.64, p. 2]. Bayer had also conducted TWI courses in 1950. The TWI system aimed to quickly and simply train workers and make supervisors, particularly forepersons and gang bosses, proficient appropriately and humanely managing employees [*Bayer Archiv*, 210-001, TWI (Training within Industry)-System, p. 1, *Bayer Archiv*, 221/6, TWI (Training within Industry)-Kursus]. Bayer also addressed the importance of methods for creating and maintaining good relationships with those in the plant for the system's educational purposes [*Bayer Archiv*, 210-001, TWI (Training within Industry)-System, p. 2]. Thereafter, TWI was developed to cover human relations problems in depth. TWI participants agreed that leadership and involvement by those in personnel management were decisive for good management, and that TWI was an effective method to secure this leadership [*Bayer Archiv*, 221/6, TWI (Training within Industry)-Kursus].

Similar programs regarding issues of human relationships and in-company retraining of middle management were undertaken at Glanzstoff, Volkswagen, Bahlsen, Continental, and other enterprises. The American influence was clearly obvious in TWI courses and supervisor training courses, which were conducted during the 1950s. Beginning in the latter half of the 1950s, the supervisor training and retraining courses adopted by these companies were different in both content and form compared with their prewar equivalents (Kleinschmidt 2002, pp. 192–194).

The serious shortage of young managers in the 1950s brought about the idea of using American methods for the systematic training. R. Meine, the head of human resources at Siemens, sought to reinforce the continuous education program and job training based on the American model and concentrated all of Siemens' education activities. In 1956, Siemens began preparatory management training for young employees and managers. In 1959, they began week-long master classes to provide advanced instruction to lower and middle management (Feldenkirchen 2004, p. 128). The textile manufacturers Spinnerei und Weberei Offenburg AG had no formal training program until 1954, when they began investigating the use of the TWI program [*National Archives*, RG469, Productivity and Technical Assist Division Labor Advisor Subject Files 1952–54, TA-Work, Labor and Human Relations Survey Report for Spinnere und Webrei Offenburg A.G. (3.3.1954)].

6.2.3.2 Deployment of Top Management Education Methods

Next, in considering education and retraining for executives, German executives took a different path from that of Americans, given the value Germans placed on obtaining what they considered executive attributes. They focused their studies on law, business economics, and engineering, in particular, as they had done before entering the workforce. Their executive development education was principally short training courses, wherein they explored specialized topics instead of general management issues (Locke 1996, pp. 98, 100. For information on business school issues in Germany see Locke 1989, pp. 164–176).

Most of the content of American-style executive development programs was missing in German universities; only a few had begun offering short-term seminars for executives in 1966. The majority of these followed American instances of education for top management. These courses reflected the demands of the industrial world in their nontraditional content, education methods, and their pragmatic orientation and were implemented outside the university system. Their adherence to an outline dictated by industry was an important characteristic. Executive development programs supplemented university training as well as the in-house selection process of top management both within and outside of companies (Kipping 1998, pp. 104–108).

For instance, among the brief 3- to 5-day training courses conducted by various associations for incumbent executives, certain German university professors individually held retraining and reeducation lectures in specialized areas in their spare time. However, most lecturers were incumbent executives themselves, and this sort of retraining was different from the American model in that they gave lectures outside academia (Locke 1996, p. 78). Documentation for a 1956 technical assistance project mentioned that although top management education in the United States was predominant within universities, this type of education in Germany was implemented outside universities [*National Archives*, RG469, Mission to Germany, Productivity and Technical Assistance Division, Subject Files of the Chief, 1953–1956, Projekt 329/1–329/4: Ausbildung von deutschen Lehrkräften auf dem Gebiet der Betriebsführung in USA (24.11.1956)].

In this manner, private companies and business associations took the initiative in advancing management education. Endeavors by industrial associations contained two famous management debates held in Baden-Baden in 1951 and 1952, Baden-Baden seminars from 1955, and activities of the loosely aligned group known as the Wuppertal Circle (Kipping 1998, pp. 102–103, Jahresbericht des Bundesverbandes der Deutschen Industrie 1955, pp. 101–102, Jahresbericht des Bundesverbandes der Deutschen Industrie 1956, pp. 86, 88, Jahresbericht des Bundesverbandes der Deutschen Industrie 1959, p. 85). The Baden-Baden seminars included debates to discuss American-style management methods and facilitate their introduction at an industry level. Moreover, they provided a forum to exchange theories and ideas on retraining and re-educating executives. They supplemented commercial colleges' educational offerings by building at least a partial bridge between academic and practical experience (Kleinschmidt 1998, p. 184, Kleinschmidt 2002, p. 299, Jahresbericht des Bundesverbandes der Deutschen Industrie 1956, p. 88, Jahresbericht des Bundesverbandes der Deutschen Industrie 1959, p. 88). A working group built by the Federation of German Industries in 1953 reviewed various case studies from Harvard Business School and other international sources. However, this working group eventually selected not to imitate those case studies, deciding instead to transmit knowledge and develop methods unique to Germany through the exchange of ideas between two generations of top management (Kipping 2004, pp. 41–42).

Germany tended to launch formal programs for executive development in each industry. This approach was motivated by the training objective of instilling entrepreneurial spirit, attitudes, and values (Granick 1962, pp. 117–118, Hartmann 1959, p. 264). The aim of the training was essentially ideological, and universities were ill-suited for this task. D. Granick highlighted that top executives could be further integrated into the world of entrepreneurship through seminars such as the Baden-Baden seminar; such programs would allow these executives to learn with their peers and strengthen their ideological resolve (Granick 1962, pp. 117–118). In German industrial organizations, ultimate authority based on the recognition that managerial authority was predominantly vested in the Unternehmer (entrepreneur) himself held primacy over functional authority (Hartmann 1959, pp. 261, 277, Hartmann 1963, pp. 287–289). This seemed to be related to views of management education that were dominant in the business world.

RKW was also involved in the deployment of methods for top management education. For instance, in November 1953, 33 top executives from Berlin and their aides assembled in RKW's Berlin branch office to listen to and debate on American management consultants concerning "management development." Looking at this as an opportunity, the stakeholders implemented a seven-week seminar. This event was in response to the need for better education for managers and executives in many organizations (*National Archives*, RG469, Mission to Germany, Labor Advisor, Subject Files, 1952–1954, Field Statistics, Management Development in Berlin, pp. 1–2). Consulting and intermediary institutions also participated; for instance, Carl Duisberg-Gesellschaft, which was responsible for personnel development, created a German-American exchange program in cooperation with the Harvard Business School (*National Archives*, RG469, Mission to Germany, Productivity and Technical Assistance Division, Subject Files of the Chief, 1953–1956, Carl Duisberg-Gesellschaft für Nachwuchsförderung e.V, Halbjahresbericht der Geschäftsleitung für die Zeit vom 1. April bis 30. November 1955, *National Archives*, RG469, Mission to Germany, Productivity and Technical Assistance Division, Subject Files of the Chief, 1953–1956, A letter from Carl Duisberg-Gesellschaft für Nachwuchsförderung e.V.).

Along with these additional company efforts, in the 1950s, many German enterprises began institutionalizing their management education (Kipping 1998, p. 103). Internal company education rose to a new level and was primarily based on the American model. Apart from internal management seminars, in which the American case method was used in debates and discussions, Bayer implemented staff training, where board members shared their experiences within their area of expertise. However, it became clear in the mid-1960s that the business community's endeavors and private initiatives, focusing on the sharing of experiences and using materials lacking in scientific methods, were insufficient. Thus, renewed interest was generated in establishing business schools (Kleinschmidt 2002, pp. 300–301).

Germany's attempt to institute its first business school center, which followed the American model, failed due to its education system's decentralized structure (Kleinschmidt 2002, p. 78). Nevertheless, in the latter half of the 1960s, a German business school was finally established, and the Universitätsseminar der Wirtschaft's founding in 1968 also played a significant role. However, except for the College for Business Management at Koblenz, the age had no other institutions of this sort (Kleinschmidt 2002 p. 306, European School of Management and Technology 2009).

The use of American education materials in courses designed for top management education in universities and specialized courses began in the 1960s and expanded rapidly (Dyas and Thanheiser 1976, p. 112), however, business schools did not become a ubiquitous phenomenon at that time. In Germany, the topics studied by executives at universities were neither related to their promotion nor significant for their development. Executive selection remained traditionally grounded in actual experience and results, with most executives working at one company for long periods before being promoted to the top. These practices were an essential factor in determining the strength of resistance to the American model and in delaying the introduction of business schools (Engwall and Zamagni 1998, pp. 11, 15, Kipping 1998, p. 96).

6.2.4 Limitations in the Deployment of American-Style Management Education and Their Factors

Based on the preceding considerations, the various factors that restricted the deployment of American-style methods in management education are considered.

The TWI program was first observed in supervisor and foreperson education. It emphasized methods for better communication that could improve the labor climate through the development of more effective information policies. However, TWI was often met with a lukewarm reception (Kleinschmidt 2002, p. 185). It originated in America, and never took hold as firmly as it did in Germany. Although TWI was customized to the German environment, the number of TWI programs conducted under the USTA&P in Germany was fewer than in other European countries. West Germany held only 134 TWI courses from the fall of 1948 (in the western region) to the summer of 1952, whereas the Netherlands for instance held more than 6,000 courses and the UK more than 30,000 in the same period. The TWI courses had relatively few participants from German companies (Kleinschmidt 2002, p. 75), and institutions, such as business schools, which supported executive development effectively in the United States, did not become popular and were not Americanized. At the time, individual organizations implementing retraining and reeducation for German managers and executives remained separated and witnessed limited change. The elements that did change were the types of retraining and the content within enterprises. For instance, week-long or several-week seminars were held for specialists and operational personnel in middle and upper management to learn about and discuss the latest American-style management methods (Kleinschmidt 2002, p. 78).

The relationship with America from the European perspective is notable. For example, the EPA's improvements to management education were not an American product but an adaptation and fusion of European methods. B. Boel points out that "even in the 1950s, US-European relations in the field of management education were not a one-way affair" (Boel 1998, p. 46). A complex matrix of several factors determined the overall impact of the American drive for management education in Europe. Amidst this, progress was particularly dependent on each program's effectiveness and the amount of resistance from managers and educators (Gourvish and Tiratsoo 1998, p. 9).

The attempts to adapt and implement the American model of management education into Europe during the period of the Marshall Plan and the productivity movement had modest effects, with a few exceptions. The conversion of traditional forms and their replacement with modern management education methods required another decade, and the influence of this process was smallest in German-speaking countries (Schröter 2005, p. 121). The direct transfer of programs from the American model, such as top management education and TWI, was also unsuccessful in German companies owing to their traditional views on managerial social policies. Within the field of management education, American development aid also had relatively little effect (Kleinschmidt 2002, pp. 79, 83). Comparing American and Western European expansion, C. Kleinschmidt stressed that education and retraining for German executives and managers adhered to a "special path." This "German stubbornness" is the main cause of the poor acceptance of the American-style business school model and its low possibility of adoption. Moreover, it yields the total emphasis on theory rather than practical work in the commercial colleges' economics-focused education. Hence, the German's chosen path is proposed as a German model, an alternative to American-style management (Kleinschmidt 2002, pp. 398–399).

6.3 The Characteristics of Japanese and German Deployment of American Management Education

This chapter has considered the deployment of American management education methods in Japan and Germany after World War II. Based on the previous discussions, this section examines the characteristics and significance of management education reforms in both nations.

Indeed, German and Japanese universities did not play a substantial role in training executives and managers compared with American universities. Nevertheless, in contrast with Germany, with its extensive history of management studies, this period's management studies boom had a tremendous impact in Japan. Unlike those in Japan, corporations, executive management education, philosophies of and objectives for top management education, as well as the industry intentions they reflected, the internal promotion system and other factors had a greater impact in Germany. There is also a remarkable manifestation in the negligence of practical viewpoints in business administration education and the delay in the diffusion among business schools.

In regard to the deployment of American management education methods, Japan was more influenced by America than Germany; in fact, Japanese government agencies strongly encouraged expanding education for managers and supervisors. Unlike in Germany, American management education methods were revised in Japan to match the company's and/or country's specific conditions, as seen in MTP and CCS. In addition, compared with Germany, there was much more room for American systems to match its conditions to those of Japan. This was an important factor that allowed American methods to be employed in Japan for such a long time. Moreover, the effects of postwar reforms by the victorious nations in Japan were greater than those in Germany. As a result of the generational shift in management caused by the dissolution of the *zaibatsu* and the purge of management, American management education methods became extremely important for proprietors in the new generation to supplement their immaturity and shortage of experience as top management. Such a situation promoted the introduction of American methods, a delay in the development of business management, and the necessity of its modernization in Japanese firms. These are important factors that highlight the differences between these two countries.

The legal recognition of labor unions and the growing labor movement heightened the conflict between labor and management. This environment called for reforms in management methods based on the family system, feudal family relations, as well as the irrational familial and paternalistic human relations that labor management had previously relied upon. However, American management education methods were adapted to Japanese collectivism, principles of efficiency, industrial relations, and differences between the positions and roles of supervisors in Japan and the United States.

Despite post-WWII reforms, legislation regarding enterprises was maintained in West Germany. As a result, the supervisory board authority was as strong as it was before and the older generation of managers continued to be active, such that a comparison cannot even be made with the situation in Japan (Kudo et al. 2004, pp. 19–24, Schröter 2005, p. 219). As a result, influences from German management values and ideologies on the power and authority of top management continued to exist. Thus, the original methods of education, such as the exchange of ideas between two generations of top management for executive development, continued to play important roles in the training and retraining of top management.

Corporations, executive management education, philosophies of and objectives for top management education, as well as the industry intentions they reflected, the internal promotion system and other factors had a greater impact in Germany than in Japan. Indeed, the use of American methods for top management education became an important issue for the business world as an alternative to the lack of practical training in German universities. However, education systems and methods based on the transmission of knowledge and exchanges of ideas between two generations of top management (based on executive networks) were emphasized. In Germany, there was an ideological foundation that supported the ideas that occupation was given by God, the trusted power and authority of an executive should not be violated, and management values should emphasize technique, quality, and production. Therefore, American top management education methods based on these pragmatic ideas were more incompatible with conditions in Germany than with those in Japan. Furthermore, the tendency to emphasize managers' skills at the shop-floor level, based on the dual system of education that consisted of school and vocational education, also influenced the use of TWI. In reality, the rate of TWI adoption was slower than in the United States.

There is another important difference between Japan and Germany regarding the deployment of American management education methods in influencing the establishment of professionalism. In the United States, the power and authority of top management are based on "function," and their positions as top executives and the role of education is strongly related to the level of professionalism. In addition, professionalism represents the functional division of labor and the formation of management. In the United States, such professionalism has been established through the progress of subdivision and business specialization (Yamada 1981, pp. 50, 58, 61). Such a management environment has not only led to the appearance of fixed-form management education methods but also raised their importance and significance.

In contrast, management professionalism has not always been effectively established in Japan. The situation in Germany was similar to that in Japan. For example, management tends to be exclusive because its authority, which is considered superior, is based on "trust" rather than "function." Such management values and environments were important factors in the delay of establishing professionalism and the deconcentration of management (Yamazaki 2009; Yamazaki 2013; Hartmann 1963, p. 113; Hartmann 1968, pp. 271–272, 282–283, 286–289; Hartmann 1959, pp. 261, 271–272, 274–27; Dyas and Thanheiser 1976, pp. 104–105), which significantly affected the employment of American fixed-form education methods in Germany.

6.4 Reframing in the Deployment of American Management Education in Japan and Germany

Building upon the preceding discussions, we explored "reframing" in the deployment of American management education in Japan and Germany in this section. As explained in Chap. 1, reframing refers to business management methods and systems that are defined by structural characteristics of a country's capitalism and how these are adapted, modified, and made compatible with the structural characteristics of capitalism in the country to which these are transferred. Five factors are related to reframing: (1) structures of productive forces, (2) industrial structures, (3) market structures, (4) management values and cultural factors, and (5) institutional factors. Factors (3), (4), and (5) are structural characteristics of Japanese capitalism or German capitalism.

Considering the amalgamation of American and Japanese elements, we can observe hybridization in the development of a suggestion system combined with TWI and job improvement activities and a mixture of American method and Japanese concepts emphasizing production spots. In Japan, Job Methods (JM) in TWI, a course in continuous development, not only indoctrinated individuals into an "improvement" frame of mind but also taught them how to find opportunities for improvement, how to generate ideas to take advantage of these opportunities, and how to put such ideas into practice (Robinson and Schroeder 1993, p. 51). Hence, TWI contributed to creating opportunities for various Japanese-style development activities (Nemoto 1992, pp. 167–168). In fact, many Japanese firms introduced suggestion systems to follow up on-the-job modification movement begun by TWI (Japan Human Relations Association 1988, p. 202).

Some factors determine the "reframing" in the deployment of American management methods. Of these factors, management values and characteristics based on Japanese collectivism and management climate influenced the specific development of management education methods for middle and lower management. In particular, the management climate is for lifetime employment and seniority wage and concept emphasizing the workplace as the production spot. Although necessities to overcome management system-based family-ism and paternalism before the war promoted the introduction of American management education methods, the influence of radical changes in the management system might become factors that restricted drastic reforms. These were deeply concerned with the limitations of American fixed-form management education methods and became an important foundation for flexible labor formation under the teamwork system and small-group activities represented by the quality control (QC) circle and the suggestion system as an element of Japanese-style management.

Next, we examine the institutional factors impacting the Japanese style of adaptation in the process of Americanization. The progress of generational change in top managers brought about by postwar reforms promoted the deployment of American management education. The notable necessities of manager and supervisor training corresponding to the legal approval of workers' rights and labor movements also promoted such deployment. However, Japanese labor-management systems, such as employment, personnel changes, and promotion and characteristics of education systems in this country, were important factors for creating the conditions of American fixed-form education methods. These methods were not always compatible with Japan's management culture and companies' specific needs. Limits of Japanese universities' role in business management education due to the late arrival of the management boom also influenced the deployment of American methods.

Other factors affecting the reframing in the deployment of American management education are labor market characteristics. The labor market based on the lifetime employment system decreased necessity and significance of business school as an institute of top management education method. The executives in Japan have no external labor market, and internal promotion system was dominant, which was not appropriate for American top management education methods.

By contrast, in Germany, the American style of management education was not always appropriate, given extant education systems and traditions, such as the role that universities play within management education, education and characteristics sought in executives, corporate promotion systems, and executives' internal labor markets arising from them. Under such circumstances, hybridization can be seen in the combination of methods for intergenerational opinion and materials and methods from the United States.

Considering the amalgamation of American and German elements, we can observe hybridization in the methods for intergenerational opinion exchange and materials and methods from the United States while promoting knowledge dissemination based on executive networks in business associations.

Given the deployment of American management education concerning important factors determining the reframing, we determine that management values and traditions emphasizing technological values as well as skills and traditions of management social policy in German companies extensively influenced the implementation of American management methods. A high proportion of executives with a technical background restricted American top management education methods represented by the business school. Executives' and educators' resistance to the deployment of TWI based on their non-pragmatic value perspectives also affected manager education.

Next, examining the institutional factors impacting the German style of adaptation during the Americanization process, we determine the following factors that greatly influenced the implementation of American management education: the state of the German education system and its traditions; the characteristics of business management education, such as the negligence of practical viewpoints; and the limitations of German universities' role in business management education. In Germany, the older generation of executives remained active despite postwar reform, which restrained the broad introduction of American methods. The existence and substantial role of executive networks in the business world became an important alternative of American top management education methods.

Labor market characteristics were also factors determining the reframing in the deployment of American management education. Desired traits in executives and managers and the influence of corporate promotions and appraisal systems on the labor market for executives and managers acted as an important factor that restricted the broad use of methods developed in the United States. In Germany, people spend their career in the firm and are promoted within each company (Caroli 1994, p. 27), and top management is traditionally promoted through the ranks (McCann 2014, p. 145). Promotion in the German enterprise follows a functionally specialized route, and "retraining across functions is relatively rare" (Lane 1989, p. 92). Thus, in the German management system, "the loyalty of managers (and employees in general) who spend their career in a single firm" tended to give priority to in-house training (Caroli 1994, p. 26).

The American style of management education was therefore not always appropriate in Germany, given extant education systems and traditions, such as the role of universities within management education, the education and characteristics sought in executives, the corporate promotion systems, and the subsequent internal labor markets of executives.

In Germany, based on this point, management values and a management climate emphasizing technology and a relatively long-term perspective were already well rooted after the war. They functioned counter to a personnel policy, thoroughly grounded in a doctrine of efficiency that reflected management values and a management climate based on American pragmatism. Despite considerable American influence, the German system could not be transformed overnight. The most significant factor behind management education and executive management education changes was the nation's overall education system and the strength of its management education system, along with cultural factors such as management styles and traditions for learning that could transcend national borders (Amdam 1996, p. 11).

During the Americanization process, through the reproduction of management values and business culture based on the exchange of ideas between different generations of top management and the companies' internal promotion systems, the modified management education in Germany has built the foundation of business strategies and the mode of corporate behavior emphasizing technology and quality, which are compatible with the market structure in Europe. Thus, it has helped the overall success of Germany in the global economy, particularly in the European markets that emphasize technology, quality, and functionality. This role and function of management education could not be expected from the educational opportunities provided by universities or colleges in both the United States and Germany.

Regarding the conditions surrounding the introduction of American management education in Japan and Germany during the postwar boom years as well as "reframing" and the factors defining, Table 6.1 shows an inline comparison of the respective countries, based on the discussion so far in this chapter.

Thus, the deployment of American management education methods and the modification thereof after the war were strongly determined by the development path of enterprises in each country and became an important factor in creating characteristics of Japanese-style or German-style management.

"The Anglo-Saxon concept of management as a unified profession is still not accepted" at the end of the 1980s; "consequently, there exists no general management education in Germany" (Lane 1989, p. 92). This is concerned with the delay in business school diffusion as an important means of education for the US manager. In the 1990s, executive and manager development and education in American-style business schools have obtained unprecedented importance. The problem then arises that the global competition and market principles beginning in the 1990s, wrought dramatic changes to the conditions that supported German management values and management styles, causing a resurgence of Americanization. In Japan as well, influence of the United States became stronger, which has facilitated expansion of management education at business school.

Table 6.1 Comparison of conditions surrounding the introduction of American management education in Japan and Germany

Deployment and factors affecting them	Management methods			
	Management education			
	Japanese management methods		German management methods	
	Top management education	Manager education	Top management education	Manager education
Overall conditions in the deployment of American management methods	• Top management education through CCS courses based on American education methods • Top management education by outside institutions as alternatives to CCS courses • Delay in adoption of business school programs	• Significant role of TWI as education method of superintendent at production spots • MTP as one of the most diffused manager education methods • Manager education based on American research in psychology and behavioral sciences	• Top management education efforts using US education materials • Delay in adoption of business school programs	• TWI deployment in foreman education • Slow pace of TWI adoption compared to the US and other countries

(continued)

Table 6.1 (continued)

Deployment and factors affecting them	Management methods			
	Management education			
	Japanese management methods		German management methods	
	Top management education	Manager education	Top management education	Manager education
Deployment characteristics of American management methods	• Deployment of American management education for securing personnel available for scientific management and modernization of human relations • Deployment of American top manager education methods corresponding to the generational shift of executives due to the dissolution of the "*zaibatsu*" and manager purge • Big roles of government offices in the deployment of American management education • Supplementing the general foreman system by TWI • Roles of TWI and MTP vis-à-vis rationalization • Long-term deployment and implementation of American management education methods • Deployment of methods for the education of managers and supervisors without distinguishing between them		• Strong US initiative and support in technical assistance and productivity programs • Development of organizational planning through the EPA • RKW efforts and involvement • The pursuit of US methods of business management education as an alternative to the lack of practical training in German universities • Education through executive networks in business associations • US university cooperation and its roles • The deployment of TWI relating to human relations issues	

(continued)

Table 6.1 (continued)

Deployment and factors affecting them	Management methods			
	Management education			
	Japanese management methods		German management methods	
	Top management education	Manager education	Top management education	Manager education
Modifications in American management methods	• Limits of American fixed-form management education methods • Deployment of in-company education emphasizing OJT and self-development under ability-based personnel management • OJT as a TWI more compatible with Japanese conditions • Modifications of American management education methods with a view to making them more compatible with Japanese conditions (MTP and CCS)		• The development and distribution of German top management and manager education according to individual organizations (e.g., short-term seminars on the latest US management methods, etc.)	

(continued)

Table 6.1 (continued)

Deployment and factors affecting them	Management methods			
	Management education			
	Japanese management methods		German management methods	
	Top management education	Manager education	Top management education	Manager education
Amalgamation of American and Japanese elements	• Development of suggestion systems combined with TWI and job improvement activities • Mix of American methods and Japanese concepts emphasizing production spots (improvement activities and self-development)		• Knowledge dissemination based on executive networks in business associations and the amalgamation of methods for intergenerational opinion exchange and materials and methods from the US	

(continued)

Table 6.1 (continued)

Deployment and factors affecting them		Management methods			
		Management education			
		Japanese management methods		German management methods	
		Top management education	Manager education	Top management education	Manager education
Factors of modification of American management method	Influence of traditions, cultural factors, and management values	• Necessities to overcome limits of management based on family-ism and paternalism before the war • Management values and characteristics based on Japanese collectivism • Management climate of lifetime employment and seniority wage		• Management values and traditions emphasizing the value of technology and skills • Traditions of managerial social policy in German corporations	
				• High proportion of executives with a technical background	• Executives' educations' resistance to the development of TWI

(continued)

Table 6.1 (continued)

Deployment and factors affecting them		Management methods			
		Management education			
		Japanese management methods		German management methods	
		Top management education	Manager education	Top management education	Manager education
	Influence of institutional factors	• Influences of Japanese labor management systems, such as employment, personnel changes, and promotion • Characteristics of education systems in Japan • Limits of universities' role in business management education (late arrival of the management boom) • Progress of generational change of top managers due to postwar reforms • Strong necessities of manager and supervisor training corresponding to the legal approval of workers' rights and labor movements		• The state of the German education system and its traditions • Characteristics of business management education (negligence of practical viewpoints) • Limits of universities' role in business management education • The older generation of executives continuing on due to corporate legislation despite postwar reform • Education systems based on executive networks	

(continued)

Table 6.1 (continued)

Deployment and factors affecting them		Management methods			
		Management education			
		Japanese management methods		German management methods	
		Top management education	Manager education	Top management education	Manager education
	Influencing factors of the productive forces	–		–	
	Influence of industrial structure factors	–		–	
	Influence of market structure factors	• Influences of labor market based on lifetime employment system		• Desired traits in executives and managers and the influence of corporate promotions and appraisal systems on the labor market for executives and managers	

Source This table was compiled by the author, based on discussions in this chapter

References

Amdam RP (1996) Introduction. In: Amdam RP (ed) Management, education and competitiveness. Europe, Japan and the United States. Routledge, London, pp 1–16

Aonuma (1977) Kobetsuka, koseika jidai no kyoiku sutafu (Educational staff in the age of individualization and personalization). In: Sangyo kunren (Ind Train) 23(4):8–13

Boel B (1998) The European productivity agency and the development of management education in Western Europe in the 1950s. In: Gourvish T, Tiratsoo N (eds) Missionaries and managers: American influences on European management education, 1945–60. Manchester University Press, Manchester, pp 33–49

Calori R (1994) The diversity of management systems. In: Calori R, Woot P de (eds) A European management model. Beyond diversity. Printice Hall, pp 11–30

Dai niji roshi kyoryoku taisei kokunai shisatsudan (1958) Dai niji roshi kyoryoku taisei kokunai shisatsudan hokokusho (Second report of the domestic inspection team for coorporative system between labor and management). Zaidan hojin nihon seisansei honbu, shadan hojin nihon kagaku kogyokai, Tokyo

Dyas GR, Thanheiser HT (1976) The emerging European enterprise. Strategy and structure in French and German industry. Macmillan, London

Engwall L, Zamagni V (1998) Introduction. In: Engwall L, Zamagni V (eds) Management education in historical perspective. Manchester University Press, Manchester, pp 1–18

European School of Management and Technology (2009) USW Netwerk: 30 Jahre Managerfortbildung in Schloss Gracht. hhttp://www.esmt.org/deu/usw.-netwerk-30-jahre-Managerfortbildung-in-schloss-gracht/. Accessed 3 June 2009

Feldenkirchen W (2004) The Americanization of the German electrical industry after 1945. Siemens as a case study. In: Kudo A, Kipping M, Schröter HG (eds) German and Japanese business in the boom years. Transforming American management and technology models. Routledge, London, pp 116–137

Fuji denki seizo kabushiki gaisha (1974) Fuji denki shashi II (1957–1973) (History of Fuji Electric Co. Ltd. II 1957–1973). Fuji denki seizo kabushiki gaisha, Tokyo

Fuji seitetsu kabushiki geisha shashi hensan iinkai (ed) (1981) Hono to tomoni (With blaze). Shinnihon seitetsu kabushiki gaisha, Tokyo

Fujimoto T (1997) Seisan Sisutemu no Sinka Ron (Evolution of production system). Yuhikaku, Tokyo

Furukawa E (1981) Kanrisha kyoiku (Manager education). In: Zennihon noritsu renmei ningen noryoku kaihatu senta (ed) Sengo kigyonai kyoiku hensenshi (History of changes in in-company education). In: Zennihon noritsu renmei ningen noryoku kaihatu senta, Tokyo, pp 73–101

Furuya Y (1971) Kankyo henka ni taiou shita kunren wo (Training coresponding with circumstance changes). In: Keieisha (Executives) 25(6):16–19

Gemelli G (1996) American influence on European management education. The role of the ford foundation. In: Amdam RP (ed) Management, education and competitiveness. Europe, Japan and the United States. Routledge, London, pp 38–68

Gourvish T, Tiratsoo N (1998) Missionaries and managers: an introduction. In: Gourvish T, Tiratsoo N (eds) Missionaries and managers: American influences on European management education, 1945–60. Manchester University Press, Manchester, pp 1–12

Granick D (1962) The European executive. Weidenfeld & Nicolson, London

Hartmann H (1959) Authority and organization in German management. Princeton University Press, Princeton

Hartmann H (1963) Amerikanische Firmen in Deutschland: Beobachtungen über Kontakte und Kontraste zwischen Industriegesellschaften. Westdeutche Verlag, Koln

Hartmann H (1968) Der deutsche Unternehmer: Autorität und Organisation. Europäische Verlagsanstalt, Frankfurt am Main
Hasegawa H (1960) Nihon no hyuman rireshonzu (Human relations in Japan). Otsuki shoten, Tokyo
IE (1968) Foaman no nichi ou bei kakusa wo kataru (Comparison of foremen in Japan, Europe, and the US). In: IE 10(5):8–17
Jaeckel B (1961) 10 Jahre REFA-Bundesverband. In: REFA-Nachrichten 14(6):221–226
Jahresbericht des Bundesverbandes der Deutschen Industrie (1955) Förderung des Unternehmernachwuchses. In: Jahresbericht des Bundesverbandes der Deutschen Industrie 1. Mai 1954–30. April 1955, Köln: SS 99–103
Jahresbericht des Bundesverbandes der Deutschen Industrie (1956) Förderung des industriellen Führungsnachwuchses. In: Jahresbericht des Bundesverbandes der Deutschen Industrie 1. Mai 1955–30. April 1956, Köln, pp 86–88
Jahresbericht des Bundesverbandes der Deutschen Industrie (1959) Die Förderungdes industriellen Führungsnachwuchses.In: Jahresbericht des Bundesverbandes der Deutschen Industrie 1. Mai 1958–30. April 1959, Köln, pp 85–87
Japan Human Relations Association (1988) More about suggestion systems, In: Japan Human Relations Association(ed) The idea book: Improvement through TEI (Total employee involvement). Productivity Press, Cambridge, Massachusetts, pp 199–208
Kaji T (1976) Kantokusha no anzen kunren (Saftey education for superintendents). In: Sangyo kunren (Ind Train) 22(7):26–27
Kamei T, Shiraki T (1971) Keiei kyoiku ron (Management education). Maruzen, Tokyo
Kano M (1966) Teikei kunren no kangaekata to OLT no suishin (A line of thinking of fixed form of training and pursuit of OLT). In: Sangyo kunren (Ind Train) 12(10):49–56
Kansai keieisha kyokai, Nihon sangyo kunren kyokai kansai shibu (1970) Kigyonai kyoiku no doko (Trend of in-company education). In: Sangyo kunren (Ind Train) 16(3):2–23
Kawasaki jukogyo kabusiki gaisha shashi hensansitsu Tanimoto Akiji (ed) (1959) Kawsaki jukogyo kabusiki gaishya shashi (honshi) (History of Kawasaki Heavy Industries, Ltd., main history). Kawasaki jukogyo kabusiki gaisha, Kobe
Kawasaki seitetsu kabushiki gaisha shashi henshu iinkai (ed) (1976) Kawasaki seitetsu nijugonenshi (25-year history of Kawasaki Steel Corporation). Kawasaki seitetsu kabushiki gaisha, Kobe
Keieisha (1963) Tantosha ni kiku kigyonai kunren no mondaiten (Problems of in-company training based on an interview with the person in charge). In: Keieisha (Executive) 17(4):46–53
Kinoshita S (1970) Noryoku kaihatsu soshiki (3) (Organization for ability development). In: Sangyo kunren (Ind Train) 16(4):49–56
Kinoshita S (1971) Sangyo kunren giho no atarashii hoko (New trends of industrial training methods). In: Keieisha (Executive) 25(6):44–47
Kipping M (1998) The hidden business school: management training in Germany since 1945. In: Engwall L, Zamagni V (eds) Management education in historical perspective. Manchester University Press, Manchester, pp 95–110
Kipping M (2004) 'Importing' American ideas to West Germany, 1940s to 1970s. In: Kudo A, Kipping M, Schröter HG (eds) German and Japanese business in the boom years. Transforming American management and technology models. Routledge, London, pp 30–53
Kleinschmidt C (1998) An Americanized company in Germany. The Vereinigte Glanzstoff Fabriken AG in the, (1950). In: Kipping M, Bjarnar O (eds) The Americanization of European business. The Marshall plan and the transfer of US management models. Routledge, London, pp 171–189
Kleinschmidt C (2002) Der produktive Blick. Wahrnehmung amerikanischer und japanischer Management- und Produktionsmethoden durch deutsche Unternehmer 1950–1985. Akademie Verlag, Berlin
Kobayashi M (1969) TWI no ayumi (History of TWI). In: Sangyo kunren (Ind Train) 11(12):40–41

Kondo E (1968) TWI no tenkai to tsuishido (Development of TWI and supplementary instruction). In: Sangyo kunren (Ind Train) 14(5):39–45
Kudo H (1981) Keieisha kyoiku (Education for top managers). In: Zennihon noritsu renmei ningen noryoku kaihatsu senta (ed) Sengo kigyonai kyoiku hensenshi (History of changes in in-company education after World War II). Zennihon noritsu renmei ningen noryoku kaihatu senta, Tokyo, pp 101–114
Kudo A, Kipping M, Schröter HG (2004) Americanization. Historical and conceptual issues. In: Kudo A, Kipping M, Schröter HG (eds) German and Japanese business in the boom years. Transforming American management and technology models. Routledge, London, pp 1–29
Lane C (1989) Management and Labour in Europe. The Industrial Enterprise in Germany, Britain and France, Eduard Elgar, Aldeshot
Locke RR (1989) Management and higher education since 1940. The influences of America and Japan on West Germany, Great Britain, and France. Cambridge University Press, Cambridge
Locke RR (1996) The collapse of the American management Mystique. Oxford University Press, New York
McCann L (2014) International and comparative foundations of political economies. SAGE, London
McGlade J (1998a) From business reform program to production drive. The transformation of US technical assistance to West Europe. In: Kipping M, Bjarnar O (eds) The Americanization of European business. The Marshall plan and the transfer of US management models. Routledge, London, pp 18–34
McGlade J (1998b) The big push: the export of American business education to West Europe after the Second World War. In: Engwall L, Zamagni V (eds) Management education in historical perspective. Manchester University Press, Manchester, pp 50–65
McGlade J (1998c) The US technical assistance and productivity program and the education of Western European managers, 1948–58. In: Gourvish TR, Tiratsoo N (eds) Missionaries and managers: American influences on European management education, 1945–60. Manchester University Press, Manchester, pp 13–33
Mitsubishi denki kabushiki gaisha shashi hensansitsu (ed) (1982) Mitsubishi denki shashi: Soritsu rokujushunen (History of Mitsubishi Electric Corporation. Sixty years after foundation). Mitsubishi denki kabushiki gaisha, Tokyo
Mitsubishi jukogyo kabushiki gaisha somubucho Saito Okichi (ed) (1967) Mitsubishi zosen kabushiki gaishashi (History of Mitsubishi Shipbuilding Co. Ltd.). Mitsubishi jukogyo kabushiki gaisha, Tokyo
Miyajima H (1991) "Zaikai tsuiho" to shin keieisha no tojyo (Purge of managers from the economic world and emergence of new top managers). In: Will 10(7):136–144
Miyajima H (1992) Zaibatsu kaitai (Dissolution of Zaibatsu). In: Hosei daigaku sangyo jyoho senta, Hashimoto J, Takeda H (eds) Nihon keizai no hatten to Kigyou shudan (Development of Japanese economy and corporate groups). Tokyo daigaku shuppankai, Tokyo, pp 203–254
Miyazaki G (1966) Sengo Nihon no Keizaikiko (Japanese economic system after World War II). Shin Hyoron, Tokyo
Mogi K (1981) Kigyonai kunren no doko to tokushitsu (Trends of the characteristics of in-company training). In: Kimoto S (ed) Gendai nihon kigyo to jinji kanri (Modern Japanese enterprise and personnel managament). Rodo jyunposha, Tokyo
Nakajima K (1963) Kigyonai kunren no hansei to atarashii tenkai (Reflection and new development of in-company training). In: Keieisha (Executives) 17(4):14–17
Nakamura M (1966) Jikoshindan ni yoru kunren nizu no hakken (Finding training needs by self-diagnosis). In: Sangyo kunren (Ind Train) 12(6):2–17
Nakayama S (1969) Sengo "romu kanri seido" no hensen (Changes in the "labor management system" after World War II). In: Rosei jiho (labor Admin Rev) 2000:4–14

Nakayama S (1971) Amerikashiki romu kanri no kozai (Merits and Demerits of American-type labor management). In: Keieisha (Executives) 25(4):14–18
Nakayama S, Tsurumaki T, Okamoto H (1966) Korekara no kyoiku kunren (Education and training from now on). Nihon seisansei honbu, Tokyo
Nemoto M (1992) Toppu · bukacho no tameno TQC seiko no hiketsu sanju kajyo (30 key TQC articles of success for top management and heads of departments and sections). Nikkagiren, Tokyo
Nihon keieisha dantai renmei (ed) (1965) Wagakuni romu kanri no gensei (The present condition of labor management in Japan). Nihon keieisha dantai renmei kohobu, Tokyo
Nihon tekko renmei jimukyoku et al (1964) Showa sanjuhachinen no nihon tekkogyo kaiko (Retrospective study of the iron and steel industry in Japan in 1963). Tekkokai (Iron and Steel World) 14(5):24–106
Nihon tekko renmei sengo tekkoshi henshu iinkai (ed) (1959) Sengo Tekkoshi (History of the iron and steel industry after World War II). Nihon tekko renmei, Tokyo
Nikkeiren noryokushugi kanri kenkyukai (ed) (1968) Noryokushugi kanri (Management based on merit and ability). Nihon keieisha dantai renmei kohobu, Tokyo
Nishizawa T (1996) Business studies and management education in Japan's economic development. An institutional perspective. In: Amdam RP (ed), Management, education and competitiveness. Europe, Japan and the United States. Routledge, London, New York, 1996, pp 96–110
Nissan jidosha kabushiki gaisha somubu chosaka (ed) (1965) Nissan jidosha sanjunenshi (30-year history of Nissan Motor Corporation), Nissan jidosha kabushiki gaisha, Yokohama
Nissan jidosha kabushiki gaisha shashi hensan iinkai (ed) (1975) Nissan jidoshashi 1964–1973 (Nissan motor corporation 1964–1973). Nissan jidosha kabushiki gaisha, Tokyo
OEEC (1954) Problems of business management. American opinion, European opinion (Technical Assistance Mission, No. 129). OEEC, Paris
Okamoto H (1971) Shokugyo kunren no yokyu tuyomaru (Increasing requirement of vocational training). In: Keieisha (Executives) 6(25):26–29
Okazak-Ward L (1993) Management education and training in Japan. Grahm & Trotman, London
Okuda K (1961) Ningen kankei to kigyonai kyoiku kunren (Human relations and in-company education and training). In: Nihon rodo kyokai (ed) Romu kanri to chingin (Labor management and wage). Nihon rodo kyokai, Tokyo, pp 109–181
Onitake T (1969) Fuji seitestu ni okeru kanrisha kyoiku (Manager education in Fuji Iron and Steel Corporation). In: Sangyo kunren (Ind Train) 15(1):27–32
Oyamada E (1972) Ningenteki sokumen kara mita sengo sangyo kunren no hensen to tenbo (Changes and view of industrial training from the perspective of the human aspect). In: Sangyo kunren (Ind Train) 18(4):34–45
Oyamada E (1981) Kantokusha kunren (Superintendent training). In: Zennihon noritsu renmei ningen noryoku kaihatsu senta (ed) Sengo kigyonai kyoiku hensenshi (History of changes in in-company education after World War II). Zennihon noritsu renmei ningen noryoku kaihatsu senta, Tokyo, pp 59–72
Pechhold E (1974) 50 Jahre REFA. Beuth, Berlin/Köln/Frankfurt am Main
REFA-Nachrichten (1954) 30 Jahre REFA. Vortrag von Herrn Min.-Dir. I. R. Dr. Kurt Magnus auf der Mitglieder-Versammlung in Bad Dürkheim. In: REFA-Nachrichten 7(4):73–76
REFA-Nachrichten (1955) Zur Übenahme der deutschen TWI-Arbeit durch den REFA. In: REFA-Nachrichten 8(1):16
Robinson AG, Schroeder DM (1993) Training, Continuous Improvement, and Human Relations: The U.S. TWI Programs and the Japanese Management Style. In: California Manag Rev 35(2):35–57

Romu kanri kokunai sisatsudan (1957) Romu kanri kokunai shisatsudan hokokusho (Report of the domestic inspection team for labor management). Zaidan hojin nihon seisansei honbu, Seisansei sikoku chiho honbu, Takamatsu

Romu kenkyu henshubu (1961) Kigyo ni okeru gijutsusha kyoiku (In-company education of engineers). In: Romu kenkyu (Labor Manag Study) 14(5):10–14

Rosei jiho (1960) Yakuzukeko no kyouiku kunren wa ikani okonawarete iruka (Education and training of factory workers in positions of responsibility). In: Rosei jiho (labor Admin Rev) 1570:2–16

Rosei jiho (1969) Saikin ni okeru kigyonai kyoiku kunren no doko (The latest trends of in-company training). In: Rosei jiho (labor Admin Rev) 2016:28–42

Sakamoto F (1963a) Sengo keiei kyoiku no ayumi (jyo) (History of management education after World War II, 1). In: Bijinesu (Business) 7(5):60–64

Sakamoto F (1963b) Sengo keiei kyoiku no ayumi (History of management education after World War II). In: Bijinesu (Business) 7(7):142–147

Sakamoto F (1964) Nihon keiei kyoikushi jyosetsu (An introduction to the history of management education in Japan). Daiyamondosha, Tokyo

Sangyo kunren (1965) Kyokai junen no ayumi (Ten-year history of the Japan Industrial and Vocational Training Association). In: Sangyo kunren (Ind Train) 11(9):2–84

Sangyo kunren (1966) TWI seishin no hakken (Finding of TWI spirit). In: Sangyo kunren (Ind Train) 12(8):4–48

Sangyo kunren (1977) TWI ni tsuite (On TWI). In: Sangyo kunren (Ind Train) 19(2):11–18

Sangyo kunren hakusho henshu iinkai (ed) (1971) Sangyo kunren hyakunenshi (100-year history of industrial training). Nihon sangyo kunren kyokai, Tokyo

Sangyo kunren kokunai shisatsudan kyushu timu (1957) Sangyo kunren kokunai shisatsudan kyushu timu hokokusho (Report of kyushu team of the domestic inspection team for industrial training). Seisansei kyushu chiho honbu, Nihon sangyo kunren kyokai kyushu shibu, Fukuoka

Sangyo kunren seisansei kokunai shisatsudan (1957) Sangyo kunren seisansei kokunai shisatsudan hokokusho (Report of the domestic productivity inspection team for industrial training). Nihon seisansei honbu, Nihon sangyo kunren kyokai, Tokyo

Sato K (1977) MTP insutorakuta wa kaku kodo suru (MTP instructor acts in this manner). In: Sangyo kunren (Ind Train) 23(1):16–20

Schröter HG (2005) Americanization of the European economy. A compact survey of American economic influence in Europe since the 1880s. Springer, Dordrecht

Shimokawa K (1976) Sengo no keieisha to keieikanri (Managers and business management after World War II). In: Kobayashi M, Shimokawa K, Sugiyama K et al (eds) Nihon keieishi wo manabu (Leaning of Japanese business history after World War II), vol 3. Yuhikaku, Tokyo, pp 46–65

Sugiyama T (1968) Keiei kyoiku shu (Collection of management education). In: Nihon keiei seisaku gakkai (ed) Keiei shiryo shutaisei III (Compiled data of business administrations III). Nihon sogo shuppan kiko, Tokyo, pp 1–30

Toyota jidosha kabushiki gaisha (ed) (1987) Sozo kagirinaku (Unlimited creation). Toyota jidosha kabushiki gaisha, Toyota

Toyota jidosha kogyo kabushiki gaisha shashi henshu iinkai (ed) (1958) Toyota jidosha nijunenshi (20-year history of Toyota Motor Corporation), Toyota jidosha kogyo kabushiki gaisha, Tokyo

Wada K (2009) Monozukuri no guwa (A fable of manufacturing). Nagoya daigaku shuppankai, Nagoya

Yamada M (1981) Amerika no keiei fudo (American management climate). Daiyamondo sha, Tokyo

Yamazaki T (2009) Sengo Doitsu shihonsyugi to kigyo keiei (German capitalism and business management after World War II). Moriyama shoten, Tokyo

Yamazaki T (2013) Gendai no Doitsu kigyo—Sono gurobaru chiikika to keikei tokusitsu—(Contemporary German enteprisees—their global-regionalization and characteristics of business management—). Moriyama shoten, Tokyo

Yawata seitetsu kabushiki gaisha shashi hensan iinkai (ed) (1981) Hono to Tomoni (With a blaze). Shin nihon seitetsu kabushiki gaisha, Tokyo

Zennihon noritsu renmei ningen noryoku kaihatu senta (ed) (1981) Sengo kigyonai kyoiku hensenshi (History of changes in in-company education after World War II). Zennihon noritsu renmei ningen noryoku kaihatu senta, Tokyo

Chapter 7
Deployment of Human Relations

Abstract This chapter analyzes the deployment of human relations concerning the transformation of the management system and industrial relations. Socioeconomic backgrounds and actual situations of the deployment of human relations greatly differed between Japan and Germany. For instance, in Japan, human relations measures were deployed in response to the conflict between management and labor, which resulted from the regal recognition of labor unions, the growing labor movement, and the need to modernize and democratize management. In contrast, Germany did not need to modernize its management as strongly as Japan. Consequently, the United States facilitated the introduction of human relations aiming at labor relation reforms. However, in general, many factors affected the implementation of human relations measures. Therefore, this chapter considers the deployment of human relations, paying attention to environmental factors, such as management values and traditions, industrial relations, the worker participation system (the codetermination system), and market structure. It also examines the Japanese and German characteristics regarding the deployment of human relations. Based on these discussions, this chapter clarifies the progress of reframing in Japan and Germany's Americanization process.

Keywords Codetermination · Human relations · Labor relations · Management system · Rhenish capitalism

Chapter 6 considered the implementation of American management education but from this chapter and Chap. 9, we turn our attention to human relations, industrial engineering (IE), and the Ford system regarding the deployment of American-style management and production systems. In these chapters, how American-style management systems were implemented in Japan and Germany and the resulting changes in corporate management will be discussed. This chapter and Chap. 8 will examine human relations and industrial engineering, respectively. In Chap. 9, the deployment of the Ford system and the resulting production system reforms will be analyzed.

T. Yamazaki, *Japanese and German Enterprises*,
https://doi.org/10.1007/978-981-97-4880-8_7

This chapter considers the deployment of human relations.[1] Sections 7.1 and 7.2 examine human relation deployment in Japan and Germany, respectively. In Sect. 7.3, Japanese and German characteristics of human relations deployment are considered. Building upon discussions in these sections, in Sect. 7.4, "reframing" in the deployment of human relations in both countries will be clarified.

7.1 Deployment of Human Relations in Japan

7.1.1 Socio-economic Background Regarding the Deployment of Human Relations in Japan

First, the socio-economic background of human relations deployment in Japan is explored. In Japan, human relations played significant roles in increasing corporate modernization endeavors after the war, as the legal recognition of labor unions and the growing labor movement strengthened the conflict between management and labor. This circumstance required the transforming management methods based on the family system, feudal family relations, and the irrational familial and paternalistic human relations that labor management had previously relied upon. Human relations was deployed in response to this demand. In particular, small- and medium-sized companies demanded further reforms to labor-management methods and initiated deploying human relations under the direction of the Japan Productivity Center and business associations. Within larger enterprises, human relations were used particularly to improve corporate consciousness and as a labor union countermeasure with regard to the lifetime employment system (Hasegawa 1960a; Nakamura 1958, p. 221; Ewatari 1954, p. 20). Under the movement toward the democratization of management, transforming prewar, irrational human relations into those compatible with new management became the primary purpose of human relations management in industrial companies. This was one of the Japanese characteristics of the deployment of human relations (Ewatari 1954, p. 20; Odaka 1958, p. 18).

In addition, with the advancement of changes and innovations in the labor process, determining how each enterprise could improve the morale of its workers became all the more important (Hasegawa 1960a, pp. 76–77; Tsuchiya 1976, p. 294). For example, at the Nissan Motor Corporation, with the prompt development of new products and the modernization of equipment around 1954, attempts were made to improve the constitution of human relations (Nissan jidosha kabusikigaisha somubu chosaka 1965, p. 291).

---

[1] The first content analysis related to Germany in this chapter is Chap. 7 of the author's book "*German Business Management: A Japanese Perspective on Regional Development Factors*," which was published by Springer in 2013.

7.1.2 General Conditions of the Deployment of Human Relations

This section considers the general conditions of the deployment of human relations. Various measurements regarding communication within enterprises were adopted for the first time between 1951 and 1952 (Nakayama 1969, p. 8). First, a morale survey of employees was administered by Professor Kunio Odaka from the University of Tokyo in the Kawasaki Ironworks of the Nihon Steel Corporation (Odaka 1953, p. 5). At this point, the 1947–1951 period can be regarded as the years when ideas and theories of human relations were first presented, whereas the 1951–1955 period can be considered the time in which human relations measures were first implemented. In contrast, the period after 1955 can be viewed as the time when human relations were diffused and efforts to deploy such an American management method reached a turning point (Hasegawa 1960a, pp. 67, 74; Mizutani 1957, p. 146).

The various methods of the human relations morale survey were based on the premise of human relations management and the use of company newsletters as the fundamental means of communication. On the contrary, the use of suggestion systems was the foundation for participation in management (Odaka 1958, p. 21). However, in the early 1960s, individual measurements were only introduced dispersively, and equal human relations based on matured self-consciousness in the modern sense were not be observed. Under such situations, ample development of American human relations management methods based on modern human relations encountered certain limitations (Mori 1961, pp. 185, 189–190).

Based on several survey results, this section examines general conditions of human relations deployment. According to an investigation in July 1956 by the Japan Federation of Employers' Associations, of the total 87 enterprises that answered, 63 companies in manufacturing industries introduced human relations. Upon a closer examination of the companies that were conducting human relations measurements, six used company newsletters, five adopted the suggestion system, seven used morale surveys, three implemented workplace roundtable conferences, one simply facilitated the company handbook for employees, and two offered tours of the plant for employees' families. Including firms that were planning to introduce human relations methods, the relevant numerical values were 11, 9, 12, 4, 2, and 2, respectively. Interest was also high concerning democratic personnel management, promotion of ingenuity and contrivance based on employee autonomy, improvement of morale through the early detection of workers' discontent/dissatisfaction, and establishing a work environment based on such information. However, some enterprises did not introduce human relations measures at this stage despite their high interest. Therefore, at that time, the realization of human relations management had not yet become a general phenomenon (Nihon keieisha dantain renmei 1956, pp. 1, 13–14).

According to another survey implemented in December 1956 by the Japan Federation of the Employers' Association, all the participating firms were interested in human relations management, and many cognized its necessity. Above all, measures for communication were adopted in most of the enterprises. Moreover, the companies' rate that implemented morale or opinion surveys to employees ranged from 30% to nearly 40%. Conversely, the usage rate of grievance disposition systems or personnel counseling was relatively low. However, during this period, human relations management methods had been deployed in numerous firms. In addition, the implementation rate of various methods increased remarkably in four or five years until the end of 1956. Thus, a shift can be observed from the introduction and implementation stage to the spread of human relations management. In terms of the reason for such interest and necessity by the enterprises, the rate of "in-house human collaborative relationship" was 78.2%. The relevant numerical values of "productivity improvement by the rise of morale" and "sufficiently communicating the intention of the company" were 44.3% and 49.4%, respectively. Therefore, improvements within in-company communication and morale were particularly emphasized.

In terms of individual measurements of human relations, the usage rate of communication was 97.7% while the relevant numerical values of personnel counseling or grievance disposition and opinion surveys or morale surveys were 49.4% and 37.9%, respectively. As to the methods for communication, company newsletters were used in 69% of the enterprises while measures for communication between employees and managers were adopted in 90.8% of the enterprises. The adoption rate of workplace roundtable conferences was 48.4%. In contrast, the usage rate of personnel counseling was only 16.7%. Thus, personnel counseling was the least used. Although the adoption rate of grievance disposition was 45.2%, the challenge was in how to apply the method and use it in the context of Japanese companies. Furthermore, the usage rate of companies that utilized labor management, roundtable conferences, informed trade unions, and joint labor-management consulting committees was 78.2%. In contrast, the usage rate of firms which established production committees was only 31%. However, the usage rate of companies that held production committee meetings on a regular basis was approximately 92%. The diffusion rates regarding family communication through public relations activities, home visits, and plant tours were approximately 30%, 22%, and 26%, respectively. These numerical values were lower than those of other measurements of human relations management (Nihon keieisha dantai renme 1957, pp. 1–5, 8–14, 16–18, 20–22).

Moreover, according to the results of a survey in December 1963 by the Japan Federation of Employers' Association, the suggestion system was adopted the most as bottom-up communication from employees to the management (71.6%). Even in small and medium-sized enterprises, the relevant numerical value was more than 50%. Conversely, company newsletters were the most popular top-down communication method (84.9%). However, there were differences based on company size. The adoption rates of newsletters in enterprises with fewer than 100 employees and those with fewer than 300 but more than 100 were 20.6% and 49%, respectively. While the proportion of firms that established workplace roundtable conferences was 58.2%, the usage rates of handbooks for employees and morale surveys or opinion surveys were 13.9% and 28.6%, respectively. The usage rate of companies that adopted an employee interview system was 23.8%. An important characteristic of Japanese management can be seen in human relations management, including the entire family. The proportion of family recreation policy implementation was 31.9%, and these policies prevailed in terms of measures for such purposes. Meanwhile, the diffusion rates of plant tours, family communication, and home visits were approximately 20%, 20%, and 12.4%, respectively (Nihon keieisha dantairenmei 1965, pp. 5, 27–29, 66–67).

Whereas the diffusion of human relations advanced in big businesses, its introduction in small and medium-sized companies was delayed. There were even aspects of paternalistic and family-like labor management in small and medium-sized firms. However, in-firm communication and coordination between labor and management were not sufficient. The formation of modern human relations was an important issue in overcoming such limitations of personnel management. Therefore, the deployment of human relations gradually went ahead in small and medium-sized enterprises after 1957 (Hasegawa 1960a, pp. 179–180). Human relations were also used directly as a promotional means for corporate consciousness and countermeasures to labor unions connecting with systems such as lifetime employment in large companies. In contrast, in small and medium-sized companies, the primary goal of human relations management was the improvement of productivity and production growth. There are many cases where measurements of human relations were used to secure low-wage systems and agreements between enterprises. Furthermore, institutions such as the Japan Productivity Center and the Japan Federation of Employers' Associations guided the deployment of human relations in small- and medium-sized businesses and introduced new labor-management systems to improve the rationalization and constitution of subcontracting enterprises as well as small- and medium-sized firms (Hasegawa 1960a, pp. 181, 191–192; Hasegawa 1960b, pp. 49, 51–52).

7.1.3 Deployment of Various Methods of Human Relations

Section 7.1.2 has analyzed the general conditions of human relations deployment. Building on the preceding examinations, this section considers the deployment of various measurements of human relations in further detail.

Company Newsletters: In the iron and steel industry, company bulletins were introduced as a measure of in-house communication around 1948. In those days, bulletins and notices were published to offer information to labor unions and improve human relations. The issue of in-firm communication was emphasized in the 5th Iron and Steel Committee of the ILO in 1954 (Nihon tekko renmei sengo tekkoshi henshu iinkai 1959, p. 985).

At the Kawasaki Steel Corporation, the "Kawasaki Steel Newspaper" was published as a newsletter in addition to the "Newssheet" as a formal measure of public relations within the company. By 1957, business establishment "tip-offs," which included detailed information and news concerning certain colleagues, were published in every business (Kawasaki seitetus kabushikikgaisha shashi henshu iinkai 1976, p. 505). At the Hitachi Shipbuilding Company, human relations management held an important position in labor management from 1955 to 1965. In addition, company newsletters were published to raise the morale of workers and increase their collaboration in the workplace. More specifically, this company published the "Hitachi Shipbuilding Newsletter" beginning in September 1951 and the "Labor Special Future" beginning in September 1954. Furthermore, various businesses published "tip-offs," such factory reports, as a means of communication between general employees, managers and supervisors, and their families (Hitachi Zosen Kabushikigaisha 1958, p. 397).

According to a survey by the Japan Association of Corporate Executives in 1963, the rate of companies which published newsletters was 80%. The relevant numerical value in firms with total assets of more than 20 billion yen was 95.7%. The proportion of enterprises that emphasized "information on internal news" was 72.9%. In terms of relevant numerical values, "conveying the conditions of the company," "informing management policy widely," and "friendship and exchange among employees" were 56.1%, 58.7%, and 64.9%, respectively (Keizai Doyukai 1963, pp. 3–5).

Many corporations aimed at promoting cooperative consciousness to not only workers but also their families by using company newsletters. Therefore, the characteristic of human relations can be found in the "management by the whole family." The purpose of such a movement was to substitute the family for the preservation function of labor, which should have been initially preserved by the enterprise (Hasegawa 1960a, pp. 96, 105, 107).

Suggestion Systems: Although there were various aspects regarding job instructions of TWI, prewar commendation, and contrivance systems, the number of followers were few, and the effectiveness of mutual communication was small (Nihon tekko renmei sengo tekkoshi henshun iinkai 1959, p. 985). However, after 1955, when the productivity movement began in Japan, the number of firms that adopted suggestion systems rapidly increased. For instance, according to an investigation by the Japan Federation of Employers' Associations in October 1957, the rate of companies that used a suggestion system as an independent system was 82.4%. Furthermore, the proportion of enterprises that adopted it within four years was 70.4%. Thus, many enterprises began to implement such systems during the latter half of the 1950s (Nihon keieisha dantai renmei kanto keieisha kyokai 1958, pp. 1–2).

By the early 1960s, suggestion systems were introduced in most of the representative enterprises. As to other companies, one survey made clear that suggestion systems were adopted in more than half of the participating firms. There are various reasons for such usefulness and the significant role they played in human relations and the coordination of employee management (Shimizu 1961, p. 16).

According to a 1963 survey by the Japan Association of Corporate Executives, 75.2% of companies utilized suggestion systems. Regarding its adoption by period, the rate of firms that introduced it by 1958 was 49.4%. The relevant numerical value of enterprises which implemented it between 1959 and 1962 was 37.4%. Most of the contents of the systems focused on "the improvement of production technology," for which its rate was 70.9% while the proportion for "business procedures" was 15.9% and that for "product policies" was 8.2% (Keizai doyukai 1963, pp. 125–129).

Although suggestion systems were important methods for communication between management and employees, the deployment of human relations in Japan was based on supervisor training methods created in the United States and concerned with education for job improvement (Shimizu 1961, p. 17). In fact, many Japanese companies adopted suggestion systems to follow up on the job modification movement begun by TWI (Japan Human Relations Association 1988, p. 202). Meanwhile, in the United States, suggestion systems were implemented as a measure of consultative management for promoting employees' self-consciousness and grievance disposition. By contrast, suggestion systems in Japan were developed on the basis of the TWI job methods, not as measurements for mutual communication. A 1958 report by the productivity inspection team of industrial training in the Japan Productivity Center clarified that it was necessary to re-examine the suggestion system approach to establish it as part of communication programs (Nihon seisansei honbu 1958c, p. 15). For example, at the Kawasaki Steel Corporation, the introduction of a suggestion system for improvement dated back to the deployment of TWI in the early 1950s. This enterprise recognized the necessity of a suggestion system to improve the efficacy of TWI, after which it set up the education subsection at the central office in July 1954 and reconsidered a corporate-wide education system. Under such situations, the suggestion system for improvement, established in 1955, had become an effective measure to enhance employees' awareness of human relations management (Kawasaki seitetsu shashi henshu iinkai 1976, p. 416). In this way, the suggestion system was introduced as not only a means of communication but also a measurement for improving human relations within the enterprise.

Regarding the method of submitting suggestions, in Japan, suggestions were generally submitted through the manager, which is a characteristic of the suggestion system unique to this country (Shimizu 1961, p. 17). For instance, according to a survey by the Japan Federation of Employers' Associations in October 1957, the proportion of submitting a suggestion through the head of the section to which the employee belonged was 47.1%, which exceeded the ratio of the ballot box method (21.9%). The former method aimed to allow managers to immediately grasp the condition and involve them in making certain improvements (Nihon keieisha danntai renmei kanto keieisha kyokai 1958, pp. 4–5). For the attitude of employees toward the suggestion system, the same survey clarified that the rate of enterprises in which they were collaborative was 71.3% (Nihon keieisha danntai renmei kanto keieisha kyokai 1958, p. 18).

Suggestion systems were adopted to rationalize rather than serve as a measure of communication between employees and management. For example, at the Nissan Motor Corporation, a suggestion system was implemented in June 1955 to determine the effect of company-wide cost reductions made the year before. In this case, obtaining suggestions from the employees in each factory effectively achieved such effects (Nissan jidosha kabushikigaisha somubu chosaka 1965, p. 295).

Attitude Surveys: Morale surveys began to be implemented in the latter half of the 1950s. However, this movement only relied on standardized styles, especially because interviews were somewhat unreliable. During this period, in a few cases, survey results for business management were used (Nihon seisansei honbu 1958c, p. 15). Whereas attitude surveys by professional counselors were limited, those administered by upper management were many. This was connected with the general foreperson's role of consulting with subordinates, which was mainly implemented in the iron and steel industry (Hasegawa 1960a, p. 144). For instance, the Nihon Kokan Corporation conducted a morale survey in 1952 and utilized its results to improve the foreman system (Nihon tekko renmei sengoshi henshu iinkai 1959, p. 985).

According to a 1963 investigation by the Japan Association of Corporate Executives, the rate of firms that implemented attitude surveys in the previous three years or more than three years earlier were 27.5% or 7.4%, respectively (total value 34.9%). However, the proportion of companies which did not conduct a survey over the previous three years was 64%. Among the enterprises that did implement an attitude survey over the previous three years, the ratios of "discovering a communication bottleneck in the company," "grasping an employee's sense of belonging to the company," and "finding of dissatisfaction and groan of employee" were 12.8%, 27.8%, and 48.9%, respectively (Keizai doyukai 1963, pp. 133–136). Overall, attitude surveys gave a certain "scientific basis" to labor management, and they were useful as a measure of rationalizing labor management and implementing labor audits (Hasegawa 1960a, p. 138).

Personnel Counseling System: As mentioned in Sect. 7.1.2, this measure was not widely used in human relations. Such a situation did not change even in the 1960s. A 1963 survey by the Japan Association of Corporate Executives found that only 14% of companies utilized a personnel counseling system while 83.9% of enterprises did not use such a system. During the period when this system was adopted, 30.8% of firms introduced it by 1958. Thus, the adoption period of personnel counseling systems was later than that of the suggestion systems. For example, in companies which provided personnel counseling, most of the consultations (between 1960 and 1963) were issues that occurred because of job transfers and reshuffling personnel. The proportion of such counseling was 25% among enterprises that had a personnel counseling system. Consultations regarding issues of human relations at the workplace accounted for 23.5% (Keizai doyukai 1963, pp. 125, 127, 129, 131–133). According to these findings, the deployment of a personnel counseling system was not advanced compared to other methods of human relations.

Grievance Disposition Systems: Although such systems have been discussed in previous articles by employers, there were only a few cases where grievance disposition systems were really utilized in the early 1960s. In this system, training must be conducted to increase the abilities of managers and supervisors at the lowest levels so grievances could be effectively handled. Despite such a need, such training was limited. At this point, a considerable difference exists between Japan and the United States. In respect of the latter, responsibilities were given to foremen, and most of the complaints were settled at the workplace level (Kawada 1961, pp. 13–15; Whitehill et al. 1958, pp. 30, 33; Nihon seisansei honbu 1958a, p. 150). However, in Japan, complaints were not considered through collective bargaining but the use of grievance disposition systems (Hirano 1976, p. 210). For example, at the Nissan Motor Corporation, a written agreement concerning grievance dispositions was made between labor and management in December 1952 to improve productivity and democratize the workplace by improving in-firm human relations (Nissan idosha kabushikigaisha somubu chosaka 1965, p. 296).

Welfare Service Measure: This important measure focused on psychological and ideological effects rather than economic effects as part of human relations management after World War II (Hasegawa 1967, pp. 648–649). A report on company welfare programs in April 1968 by the Council for Industrial Structure took notice of a change in the emphasis of welfare service to human relation functions (Tsusho sangyo sho kigyokyoku 1968, pp. 74–75). Before the war, welfare measures were implemented on the basis of certain principles and paternalism. However, concerning company objectives, a welfare service system could help raise productivity by strengthening employees' sense of belonging to an enterprise (Hasegawa 1960a, pp. 151, 154–155).

According to an investigation in FY1953 by the Japan Federation of Employers' Associations, the rate of measures related to housing was 27.8%. The relevant numerical values regarding the mutual benefit system culture, livelihood assistance, and physical training and recreation were 9.1%, 17.4%, and 21.4%, respectively (Matsumoto 1955, pp. 1, 3). Another survey by the Japan Federation of Employers' Associations in October 1958 found that similar numerical values were 71.4% with respect to culture and physical training, 79.4% concerning recreation, and 82.7% regarding housing. These measures were used in many enterprises. The relevant numerical value concerning an in-house deposit system for employees was 38.2%, and this system indicated a certain rate of diffusion (Nihon keieisha dantai renmei 1959, pp. 1, 108–109). According to a 1963 survey by the Japan Association of Corporate Executives (overlap answer), the proportion of welfare services items emphasized by the enterprise were as follows: 52.3% for housing and assistance with housing expenses; 43% for medical, health, and sanitation facilities; 37.6% for assistance with cultural and physical activities; 25.8% for internal lending systems; 22.3% for dining and assistance in food expenses; and 21.7% for various types of recreational activities. The percentage of companies which intended to increase welfare expenses was 60.7%. Therefore, the improvement of morale was especially emphasized as the purpose of having a welfare program (Keizai doyukai 1963, pp. 146–148, 151–152).

7.2 Deployment of Human Relations in Germany

7.2.1 Socio-economic Background Regarding the Deployment of Human Relations in Germany

Based on these discussions, the following section analyzes the deployment of human relations in Germany.

First, Sect. 7.2.1 considers the socio-economic background of the human relations deployment. From the American viewpoint, the transfer of human relations to the European nations was deeply concerned with attempts to reform labor relations in these nations. According to the United States, a problem common to OEEC member countries was the necessity to remove restrictive practices by trade unions, thus reinforcing the development of free (independent) labor unions (Takagi 1962, p. 17). Through its assistance to West Germany, the United States expected to resolve union collective bargaining at the company level, not the national level (Takagi 1962, p. 40). The US technical assistance plan, which was aimed at improving productivity, was also regarded as being closely related to the development of industrial relations (Kleinschmidt 2002, p. 173). In Europe, US business and political leaders enforced the adoption of labor relations along the lines of the US model, which would be based on the "human relations" approach (Schröter 2005, pp. 197, 199).

Thus, from the American perspective, human relations were a crucial issue in responding to the apparent insufficiency and slow development of postwar Germany; it was thus an important type of "development assistance" (Kleinschmidt 2002, p. 173). Therefore, human relations were regarded as the most important pillar among the numerous projects the United States initiated as part of the USTA&P, and the United States intensely supported it. During this time, US employers' associations and the US government itself supported establishing industrial relations through human relations to ward off instability on the shop-floor level and conflicts with trade unions (Kleinschmidt 2004, p. 170). Deployment of human relations began early, as it was a priority for the United States, in Germany's endeavors to adopt US management models as part of the movement.

Similarly, from the German perspective, human relations methods were accepted to build harmonious relations with various groups within a company. America's superiority in productivity could not be explained only by better technology and a rationalized management organization; rather, one factor viewed as important in its productivity and high profitability was the stable industrial relations resulting from its human relations measures. The reports of nearly every study trip to the United States are firm on this point (Kleinschmidt 2002, p. 177). For instance, according to one official in the Federation of German Industries in 1954, there was a collegial environment existed between US management and labor that was not seen in German enterprises [*National Archives*, RG469, Mission to Germany, Labor Advisor, Subject Files, 1952–54, A letter about Human Relations Seminar to Mr. C. Mahhder (3.2.1954)]. A research group traveling in the United States observed the important role of labor relations, or human relations, in the country's economic life around the 1950s (Der

Arbeitgeber 1950, p. 12). In West German enterprises, American human relations concepts attracted attention as a measure of liberating Germany from its prewar ideological burden (Hilger 2004, p. 244). The Management Technology Council reports on the electrical manufacturer Siemens and Halske AG highlighted the significance of the human relations movement in their psychological climate between 1945 and 1958 (*Siemens Archiv Akten*, 64/Lt350, Betriebstechnische Tagung 1958, 10 Jahre Aufbau—Rückblick und Vorschau 1948–1958, pp. 15–19).

New methods of human relations did not immediately take hold in this type of climate. However, human relations had a tremendous influence, and the idea of the importance of workers as human beings was evident in the period's newly Germanized concept of human relations (Wiesen 2001, p. 191).

7.2.2 *Efforts Regarding the Deployment of Human Relations*

Next, this section considers the endeavors to deploy human relations. The primary route for learning about human relations and transferring that knowledge was international conferences and study trips to the United States and educational programs.

First, as to international conferences, the first talks between German and US management personnel were held in August 1951 at Baden-Baden. They discussed various issues related to human relations, and the improvement of human relations emerged as a major theme in modern research [*Bundesarchiv Koblenz*, B102/37023, Management Development and Human Relations. OEEC-EPZ-Projekte im Rahmen der Technischen Hilfeleistung (8.3.1955), pp. 1–2]. At the 1954 10th annual International Management Congress, the betterment of human relations as a management methodology was a major theme (*Bundesarchiv Koblenz*, B393/17, Xth International Management Congress. In *Management Methods of Improving Human Relations*, Sao Paulo, 1954), and efforts to deploy human relations grew internationally. In the European Productivity Agency's Project 312 of the mid-1950s, the Agency proposed the organization of a twofold project: a debate of industrial-social research on human relations in industry and an international seminar [*National Archives*, RG469, Off African and European Operations Regional Organizations Staff. European Productivity Agency (EPA) Project File, 1950–57, Productivity and Applied Research Committee. Human Relations in Industry. E.P.A. Project No. 312 (28.12.1954), p. 2; *National Archives*, RG469, Off African and European Operations Regional Organizations Staff. European Productivity Agency (EPA) Project File, 1950–57, Productivity and Applied Research Committee, Human Relations in Industry, E.P.A. Project No. 312 (26.10.1955), pp. 1–2].

Among the study trips to the United States, the RKW, German Productivity Center, for instance, discussed human relations in their *Productivity in the USA* report in one of their 1953 study trips (RKW 1953, pp. 44–45). Additionally, an RKW study trip in March–April 1954 included RKW representatives as well as members from the

German Federation of Trade Unions, REFA, the German Ministry of Labor, Braunschweig Engineering College's Institute for Industrial Psychology and Personnel management, and Max Planck Institute for Industrial Psychology, among others (Kleinschmidt 2002, pp. 72–73). A 1956 report noted that the US economy had seen strong results from its use of human relations, which was far more advanced than Germany's, and stressed the possibility of importing basic human relations concepts (Bramesfeld et al. 1956, p. 96). In human relations education programs, Germany's RKW, the REFA, Braunschweig Engineering College's Institute for Industrial Psychology and Personnel Management, and other institutions contributed to human relations, for which special programs were organized (Kleinschmidt 2002, p. 72).

Additionally, among human relations endeavors conducted by enterprises, the managers of human resources and welfare departments were the first to work on human relations issues. P. G. v. Beckerath, the head of Bayer's welfare department in 1951, included both the factory communities of 1920s' Germany and American human relations methods (Kleinschmidt 2002, p. 178). This fusion of American-oriented thinking regarding human resource policy and welfare policy combined with prewar ideas was also observed in Glanzstoff, in which human relations views merged with 1920s' labor research in "psychotechnology." This combination of human relations and human resource methodologies conforming to prewar traditions permeated Glanzstoff for a long term (Kleinschmidt 2002, pp. 181–182). Germany's tradition of industrial psychology that could be traced to the interwar period helped pave the way for increasing interest in ideas related to human relations and their adoption (Berghahn 1986, p. 250).

Siemens also took up human relations issues in the early 1950s, strongly stimulating healthy and harmonious relations between superiors and subordinates and among workers. According to a 1952 document, many observations stated in a publication regarding human relations based on American thinking offered opportunities for considering and examining unique methods [*Siemens Archiv Akten*, 12,799, "Human Relations" im Haus Siemens (22.1.1952), pp. 9, 11, *Siemens Archiv Akten*, 12,799, "Human Relations" (25.2.1952); *Siemens Archiv Akten*, 12,799, Human Relations (16.11.1953); *Siemens Archiv Akten*, 12,799, Bericht Nr.2 über die Besprechung zwischen WL ZEL Berlin und BR ZEL am 30.9.53 (27.10.1953)]. Another document from the same enterprise in the same year indicated particular interest in the results of US research in psychological business management [*Siemens Archiv Akten*, 12,799, Rationalisierung als betriebspsychologiche Aufgabe (Januar 1952), pp. 4, 6].

By the mid-1950s, human relations had become a fashionable topic in European conferences and debates [*National Archives*, RG469, Off African and European Operations Regional Organizations Staff. European Productivity Agency (EPA) Project File, 1950–57, Human Relations in Industry. E.P.A. Project No. 312, Stage A—Florence Discussions (21.3.1955), p. 2]. Scientific discussions on this theme, particularly arguments and publications in economics and sociology, arrived at their peak during the 10 years from the mid-1950s to the mid-1960s (Kleinschmidt 2002, p. 191). All corporate endeavors concerning human relations within management, labor climate improvement, and employee education and information were influenced from the 1950s onward by the human relations and TWI movements based on US models. German enterprises had previous experience in creating worker information, industrial relations, and internal corporate education, and these aspects increased the likelihood of human relations importation into Germany (Kleinschmidt 2002, pp. 195–196).

As publications focusing on workers began to appear in the early 1950s, new thinking regarding human and collaborative relations was diffused by various means. Of those, the internal corporate newsletter, originally initiated by numerous companies in the 1920s, was revived in the late 1940s and early 1950s as an important means through which the new consideration of industrial workers could be indicated. In 1951, approximately 200 such newsletters were published by West German firms, but within two years that number swelled to four hundred (Wiesen 2001, pp. 192–193). In a 1955 publication, T. Pilker and others surveying steel companies to which the Montan Codetermination Act (an act for the coal, iron, and steel industries) was applied, stated that, at the time of the survey, company newsletters and the like had not yet become an effective medium of disseminating remarkably significant information (Pirker et al. 1955, p. 427). By 1957, however, 441 different corporate newsletters were being published, with a total distribution of nearly five million copies. Particularly within the medium- and large-sized firms, these newsletters were a superior measure of communication for management, explaining management actions toward workers and promoting the exchange of ideas between labor and management (Bundesvereinigung der Deutschen Arbeitgeberverbände 1957, p. 255).

These company newsletters attempted to grasp all aspects of worker life in terms of human relations concepts. Many newsletters were titled to suggest to employees that the enterprise was attempting to embrace the technical concept of "human relations." "*The Factory and Me*" (Hoesch AG); "*Our Factory*" (Bayer AG); "*My Factory*" (Chemische Werke Kalk G.m.b.H.); "*Touch*" (Brown, Boveri and Cie AG); and other similar titles implied to workers an identity with no special interests (Kauders 1960, pp. 23–24). One of Opel's company newsletters published in 1949 raised the issue of encouraging employee trust in corporate management in non-decision-making contexts. From portraying the ideal worker to displaying photographs of employees considered to be role models by the corporate leadership (Neugebauer 1997, pp. 195, 197–199, 212), corporate newsletters were used as a medium to improve labor and human relations and facilitate competition among workers.

Even in this area, German enterprises, particularly in connection with ideas for work communities, depended on prewar experience and traditions in which the German Technical Training Institute (Dinta) hastened the spread of company newsletters. However, in the 1950s, most previously suspended wartime and postwar magazines had resumed publication, and German companies aligned themselves with US models. At this time, in addition to newsletters, labor discussions, and retraining seminars, the dissemination of internal management information became more sundry, and some firms used periodically published notices and informational pamphlets; some also used videos for this purpose (Kleinschmidt 2002, p. 195).

This approach applied human relations theory more broadly for a psychological and ideological effect. Unlike previous methods, its use was intended to influence workers, their families, and their surroundings in every aspect of life. Rationalization, new technology related to the productivity movement, increased labor intensity, threat of mass layoffs, and the resulting stronger pressure on wages were all veiled within human relations (Kauders 1960, pp. 15–16).

Of these efforts, at least a few elements of the American model were adopted by German enterprises. These elements influenced communication between lower-level supervisors, such as supervisors and foremen, and employees; they also had an effect on information structures and labor relations within companies. The knowledge and actions of those implementing the American model for industrial relations simultaneously led to the reproduction of a corporate structure in the context of German legal regulations, modifying the original model. Thus, the American model of human relations facilitated the development of labor relations within German firms (Kleinschmidt 2002, p. 203).

7.2.3 Limitations of the Deployment of Human Relations and Their Factors

The deployment of human relations, as considered above, had a large influence on the labor climate in German enterprises and in industrial relations. However, in production and technology, the American model tended to be strongly favored. Meanwhile, from the early 1950s onward, US know-how was widely into Germany, and the objection held true of human relations' introduction concerning the amount of emphasis placed on discussing and implementing human relations themes. In reality, only a minuscule fraction of the American human relations model was brought to an end being implemented in German companies. This is due to the attitudes of employees and their representatives, discussions on codetermination beginning at the end of the 1940s, and social and managerial traditions in German labor relations. C. Kleinschmidt attributed the utter failure of German firms in implementing American human relations and industrial relations strategies to the realities of German management in the 1950s (Kleinschmidt 2002, pp. 173–175). In a 1958 report based on an inspection of Europe, two Japanese persons found that the basic policy of activities contained in the theme of "human beings and labor" was expressed in a foreign language as "human relations" but noted that this was not always equal to the US method (Osikawa and Takagi 1959, pp. 67, 83). Peter Lawrence also pointed out that the term "human relations" was usually used in the original English word, but this use was infrequent. Although the words "communication" and "motivation" were used, they were not "key words in the German managers' vocabulary." German managers tended not to recognize the importance of communication (Lawrence 1980, pp. 101–102).

Numerous cases of strong resistance by companies and labor against the deployment of human relations can be observed. For instance, at Bayer, certain board members and personnel in the engineering department resisted undertaking foremen education courses as they found them unnecessary. Until the 1960s, most board members of large businesses in the German chemical industry, particularly chemists, neglected human relations. Technical departments were particularly skeptical about combining human resources and welfare departments owing to common disputes over authority, making it necessary to separate the technical departments from human relations; these attitudes were in resistance to human relations. Similar opposition could be observed in other enterprises, and there was resistance from employee representatives and trade unions. Codetermination was also a challenge in which United States and German traditions and influence played a role (Kleinschmidt 2002, pp. 185–186). The human relations approach appeared to be redundant at the time due to industrial peace (Guillén 1994, p. 272). As Mauro F. Guillén pointed out, in Germany, the practical rejection of human relations was the general condition in the 1950s and 1960s (Guillén 1994, p. 136). Human relations did not prevail as either an ideology or a set of techniques (Guillén 1994, p. 329; Kaste 1981, S. 39–40). However, in the 1950s, education initiatives for foremen were undertaken, which led to debates among the participants; these educational initiatives encompassed lectures, film screenings, and exchange of experiences and information. An important topic raised in these debates was personnel management issues regarding forepersons and subordinates [*Bayer Archiv*, 221/6, Meisterarbeitsgemeinschaft (25.6.1956), *BayerArchiv*, 221/6, Auswertung der Ergebnisse der Zweiten Meisterarbeitsgemeinschaft (20.7.1956), *Bayer Archiv*, 221/6, Meisterarbeitsgemeinschaft (5.9.1955), *Bayer Archiv*, 221/6, Meisterausbidung (9.7.1953), *Bayer Archiv*, 329/737, Die Schrift von Sozial- und Personal Abteilung an Zwiste am 1. Dezember 1954)].

Original management models, such as the Harzburg model, also had a great effect. In contrast to the authoritarian management style, this model proposed delegating not just labor but authority and responsibility of everything related to the work in an endeavor to highly lighten the burden of those in various management positions (Obst 1970, pp. 80, 82; Kaste 1981, S. 66). Many firms found this model attractive; after the 1950s and 1960s, it was widely adopted in Germany (Kleinschmidt 2002, pp. 198–199; Kaste 1981, S. 65; Berghahn 1986, pp. 256–257; Zepf 1972, pp. 154–158; Guillén 1994, pp. 148–149).

Additionally, as human relations methodologies were prompted with the US intent for reform of labor relations in mind, they met intense skepticism and objection in Germany. In the United States, various efforts to improve productivity through technical assistance were closely tied with industrial relations initiatives in facilitating human relations and TWI, and human relations plans within German enterprises were an important part of comprehensive political oppositions, or "missions" (Kleinschmidt 2004, p. 168). For those reasons, the Germans' skepticism and objection were naturally severe.

Great changes to the labor relations framework stemming from the Codetermination Act repressed the prevalence of human relations. Although German businesspersons were concerned about management models for direct communication between management and employees as a "management partnership," industrial relations were shaped by the great impact of legal regulations and state intervention. These cultural and political differences between Germany and the United States underpinned the extraordinary differences in industrial relations (Kleinschmidt 2002, p. 202).

For large German companies, the codetermination debate was particularly heated in the early 1950s, when US development was assumed to provide an attractive alternative to the German model for labor relations, which was based on the strength of trade unions. However, within the fields of "foreperson training" or "worker conferences" and TWI, the 1951 Montan Codetermination Act and the 1952 Works Council Act prevented a broader adoption of American-style human relations. These two laws are characteristic of the failed attempts to create industrial relations in German companies along with those in the United States. Instead, a German model for labor relations was created, based on legal regulations and rooted in the traditions of corporatism, with trade unions being an integral part and industrial relations embedded therein. This model approved much greater codetermination rights than the American model in labor safety, employee education, remuneration, and various other issues of managerial social policies (Betriebliche Sozialpolitik). Consequently, attempts to adopt Americanization in human relations steadily decreased in German enterprises from 1955 onward (Kleinschmidt 2004, pp. 169, 171; Kleinschmidt 2002, p. 190). This new framework for industrial relations in Germany, based on the restraint imposed by codetermination rights and labor union, became a significant alternative to the American model.

In this way, German companies' deployment of human relations did not bring about broad adoption even as an industrial relations model. In 1963, Hartmann noted that human relations, after being imported into Germany as a trendy strategy in the early 1950s, lost its luster and was considered simply as an almost unimportable product of US economic culture (Hartmann 1963, p. 173). By the end of the 1950s, the postwar craze for new values and a society modeled upon the US abated. Many efforts to deploy these reforms disappeared, human relations being a main instance (Hartmann 1959, p. 271).

Hence, human relations deployment in enterprises first concentrated on various issues that could not be automatically solved by legal regulations or formal codetermination regulations. Such niche operations appeared in the improvement of "human relations" and the "labor climate," and relations between forepersons and subordinates were the issues at hand (Kleinschmidt 2002, pp. 191–192). These attempts to apply human relations at the corporate level, in which discussions of codetermination and management collaboration were more crucial, were limited, and even for the German personnel system, the use of partial knowledge from human relations schools of thought was selective at most (Hilger 2004, pp. 244–245).

As the aforementioned examinations concerning the deployment of human relations reveal, these human relations management methodologies and the labor relations activities based on them were set against the background of the historically strong, pragmatic management culture of the United States, whether in the practical application of management principles like "efficiency improvement" or company activity mechanisms, or within the labor climate. Thus, management methodologies and practices, which place the highest value on the principle of "efficiency improvement" were not always appropriate for Germany. This is due to management philosophies on personnel composition issues, with managers generally coming from technical fields, German management traditions, and the resulting emphasis on technology and quality. Additionally, because of the US' powerful political motive of labor relations reform, the push for deployment and transfer of human relations were not at all aligned with Germany circumstances for acceptance. In postwar Germany, industrial relations derived not from management methodologies as in the United States, but rather from systems embedded in the law. This point is closely concerned with postwar German capitalism, as can be seen in the phrases "coordinated market economy" and "Rhineland model of capitalism" ("Rhenish capitalism") (Hall and Soskice, 2001; Albert 2001).

7.3 The Characteristics of Japanese and German Deployment of Human Relations

Building upon the foregoing analysis, this section examines Japanese and German characteristics in the deployment of human relations.

In Japan, human relations methods were deployed to respond to the necessity to replace management methods based on the internal paternalistic and familial relations with modern management styles and methods. The conflict between management and labor caused by the regal recognition of trade unions and growing labor movement required reforms in management methods, and human relations were deployed in response to this demand. Therefore, the broad deployment of various human relations measures typically contained corporate newsletters, suggestion systems, human resource consultation, employee attitude surveys, and employee welfare activities along with a focus on labor harmony within the deployment of human relations (Hasegawa 1960a; Nakamura 1958, p. 221; Ewatari 1954, p. 20). In addition, the fact that of various measures of human relations management, emphasis of deployment of them in Japanese enterprises was placed on publishing company newsletters to improve relations between management and labor and raise corporate consciousness was also due to the necessity to modernize and democratize management. However, Japan's management culture, with its peculiar paternalism, lifetime employment, and seniority order system, was not fully prepared to deploy and commit to the original American-style human relations model.

In the United States, some industrial labor unions were horizontally organized by the industry. In contrast, Japanese-style enterprise trade unions were established only from industrial relations based on lifetime employment. Labor unions' basic units of activity were built according to individual companies; thus, labor conditions were negotiated and reached an agreement according to individual corporate conditions, and would ordinarily not go beyond those bounds (Okouchi 1980, pp. 10–13,

105–106; Mori 1981, pp. 367, 371–372; Takahashi 1970, p. 9; Natori 1965, p. 513; Sugaya 1977, pp. 10–13, 105–106). Unlike the United States, in which rationalism was diffused and wage levels were high, in Japan, aspects of human relations were deployed while being combined with Japanese human relations that emphasized "-isms," such as "family-ism" (Nakamura 1958, p. 221). Trends toward paternalism and management philosophy based on "family-ism" were strong. When human relations were forcibly introduced, a mixture of management styles based on "family-ism" and human relations management could be easily created (Odaka 1958, pp. 20–21; Whitehill et al. 1958, pp. 30, 34). According to the aforementioned survey in 1963 by the Japan Association of Corporate Executives, whereas 75.6% of companies did not regard informal organization at the workplace as an important issue in business management, the rate of enterprises that did was only 20.6% (Keizai doyukai 1963, pp. 143–144). The difference between the United States and Japan regarding this point is an important characteristic.

Japanese firms emphasize human cooperative relationships and improvement in communication. This was related to the lack of dialogue between management and labor. Moreover, there were differences of conditional structures between the United States and Japan and between Japan and Germany, which determined the morale of workers (Ando 1961, p. 12). For example, foremen primarily function as the front line in the execution of human relations. Thus, they have the extensive authority to manage employee affairs and implement endeavors to improve human relations, as seen in the United States (Nihon seisansei honbu 1958b, p. 7). However, in Japan, there were many cases in which such authority was not delegated to the foremen in the workplace (Nihon seisansei honbu 1958a, pp. 19, 34). This exerted a great impact on the introduction and development of human relations.

The system of worker participation in management did not wait for new laws or other forms of governmental intervention. Rather, participation voluntarily occurred in small group activities with QC circles or joint labor-management consultation systems, which negotiated and discussed labor-management issues under the premise of creating trustworthy relationships between management and labor. However, a legal codetermination system, such as that in Germany, did not exist at the plant level and the top management level. Joint labor-management consultation systems proliferated with the cooperation of management and labor as per the productivity movement of 1955, and gradually took shape through discussions of productivity improvement issues (Urabe and Omura 1983, pp. 101–102; Hirano 1976, pp. 205–206, 210; Roshikankei Chosakai 1963, pp. 17–18).

In Japan, joint labor-management consultation systems differed from collective bargaining and were built on the foundation of horizontal corporate labor relations through enterprise trade unions. From systemic and functional perspectives, joint labor-management consultation systems and collective bargaining, essentially heterogeneous, became tightly woven together and were distinctive to Japan's systems (Urabe and Omura 1983, pp. 105, 108–110, 112–113; Roshikankei Chosakai 1963, p. 55). In other words, official collective bargaining as defined by collective agreements was done formally and tended to be extremely rare; collective bargaining became a mere façade (Hirano 1976, pp. 209–210). In addition, matters of labor conditions were the focus of collective bargaining and the joint labor-management consultation system, which occupied a larger position. Japanese-style industrial relations were oriented toward the labor-management consultation, and even in collective bargaining matters, where conflicts of interest occurred, issues tended to be settled harmoniously and uniquely by the joint labor-management consultation system (Urabe and Omura 1983, pp. 117–118, 123–124).

The structural characteristic determined by various conditions, such as Japanese industrial relations and the social consciousness of employees, must have had a great impact on the introduction and development of human relations (Nagashima 1954, p. 24). Characteristics seen in the backwardness of management in Japanese industrial firms and complications of labor relations were factors making the introduction of human relations as inefficient as in the United States (Awaji 1957, p. 7). In big businesses, the broad introduction of human relations methods and the establishment of collaborative relationships by them were facilitated while being determined by groupism under the labor market that focused on lifetime employment and seniority-focused wage systems (Tsuchiya 1976, pp. 294–295; Nakayama 1971, pp. 14–15; Takezawa 1961, pp. 9, 13). However, there were paternalistic relationships of mutual trust in Japanese companies. Therefore, several measurements developed in the United States based on cold, contract-like human relations were not appropriated in the Japanese context (Tsuchiya 1976, p. 295).

The fact that suggestion activities played great roles in enhancing the morale of workers and improving product quality in Japanese corporations was also closely related to collectivism. In this point, though the deployment of human relations and TWI affected the introduction of suggestion systems, the purpose of such systems was to improve efficiency and increase production rather than create good human relations in the workplace through two-way communication from workers to management and from management to labor force.

In contrast, Germany did not need to modernize its management as strongly as did Japan. Although reforms in human relations-driven labor were commenced at the behest of the United States rather than by Germany's own volition, the legal establishment of systems for employee participation in management, typified by codetermination, built a strong framework for industrial relations. The deep-rooted differences between Europe and the United States in terms of understanding and implementing workers' participation in the management process were an obstacle in the Americanization of European economic life (Schröter 2005, p. 193). The complementary labor agreement with codetermination at the plant and top management levels established the framework of labor relations in the post-World War II period. Thus, the politically motivated attempt by the United States to prompt the introduction of human relations to transform industrial relations was unsuccessful. As has been made clear from these instances, actual situations for the deployment of human relations greatly differed between Japan and Germany.

In Germany, industrial relations derived not from management methodologies as in the United States, but rather from systems embedded in the law. As a result, the deployment of human relations in enterprises was limited. The primary fields of the deployment of human relations can be seen in issues that could not be automatically solved by legal regulations such as codetermination system. Emphasis on implementing human relations measures can be seen in improving human relations and labor climate in workshops and relations between managers and subordinates. These were problems out of codetermination system. As Volker R. Berghahn showed, whether and to what extent the principles developed in the United States were applicable to Germany should be examined due to the different economic structures and psychological situations in the two countries (Berghahn 1986, p. 251).

The traditional German-style labor relations, emphasizing technology and skills, were also an important background in the quest to design a method suitable for the German adaptation of the American management system and style. This can be said to have had a strong impact on the management of enterprises besides the issues of management, in general, based on the "efficiency principle." American pragmatic management has established the background for the introduction of management methods such as those in human and labor relations. This method emphasizes the management principle of "increased efficiency" in corporate behavior mechanisms for management practices and the labor environment. Hence, certain aspects of the various types of American measures were remarkably incompatible with German traditions and management values, emphasizing technology, quality, and production. Moreover, the managerial philosophy related to personnel structure, populated by managers with technological backgrounds, was also incompatible. Managerial philosophy related to personnel structure and managers with technological backgrounds also affected ideas concerning whether American human relations concepts and methods were compatible with conditions in Germany.

7.4 Reframing in the Deployment of Human Relations in Japan and Germany

Finally, this section analyzes the "reframing" in the deployment of human relations in Japan and Germany.

Looking at the amalgamation of American and Japanese elements, we can view hybridization in two points: (1) mix of American human relations and relationships based on Japanese family-ism and (2) hybridization of American methods based on cold, contracting human relations and Japanese methods emphasizing behavioral patterns based on collectivism.

Although American human relations methods were broadly deployed in Japan while in Germany deployment was sparse, various factors influenced the implementation of such measures. Therefore, in examining the deployment of human relations in relation to some important factors that influenced the implementation of such American management methods, impacts of management values and management traditions and cultures, such as management values based on Japanese collectivism and mutual trust between members of enterprise can be seen in the following regards. Japanese norms vis-à-vis the deployment of human relations, such as seen in measures of human relations management including the entity family and fusion of human relations management and managerial family-ism were also instances of the impact of management values based on collectivism. The old-style family-ism represented by paternalistic human relations and feudal family relations in the period before World War II and management values based on "trust relationships" rather than "contract relationships" exerted influence on the deployment of human relations.

Next, considering the institutional factors affecting the Japanese style of adaptation during the Americanization process, the framework of collective agreement and its Japanese characteristics led to a trend to avoiding collective bargaining. In big businesses, human relations methods were deployed as countermeasures to labor unions and a mechanism for increasing corporate consciousness under labor relations with the three basic pillars of lifetime employment system, seniority wage system, and company trade unions. Such Japanese collaborative industrial relations facilitated the deployment of human relations as rationalization meausures such as job improvement and increase of work efficiency at workplaces based on close relationships between supervisors and subordinates. However, the supervisor system with insufficient delegation of authority to low-level managers at production spots exerted a negative impact on the deployment of the grievance disposition system. The deployment of various measurements for better communication within enterprises was emphasized due to the lack of legal institutions for communication between labor and management, such as work councils in Germany. In Japan, under the specific industrial relations and collectivism, the promotion of rationalization countermeasures for workers rather than the creation of good human relations in the workplace was greatly emphasized and pursued in the implementation of human relations.

Labor market characteristics were also factors determining the reframing in the deployment of human relations. The market structure factor seen in Japan's lifetime employment system influenced Japanese development focusing on collectivism in the deployment of such American management methods. In large firms, human relations measurements were adopted directly as a promotional method for company consciousness and countermeasures to trade unions and as an important means of establishing cooperative relations under the systems such as lifetime employment and seniority order system based on it.

Thus, reframing of the Americanization process promoted Japanese-style management based on collectivism and trust between the enterprise and the workforce. It also contributed to the reproduction of management values emphasizing active collaborative behavior in the workplace and the autonomous commitment of workers.

Meanwhile, as to the reframing in the deployment of human relations in Germany, the hybridization of American and German elements can be observed in the following points. First, the fusion of US orientation in corporate personnel policy and social policy with prewar works community concepts in Germany, second, amalgamation of human relations viewpoints and prewar German labor science research viewpoints, and third, the return of prewar company publications based on human relations perspectives.

Examining the deployment of human relations concerning some factors determining the reframing, though reforms in human relations-driven labor relations were initiated at the behest of the United States rather than by Germany's own intention, the legal establishment of systems for worker participation in management, represented by codetermination, formed a powerful framework for industrial relations. The complementary labor agreement with codetermination at the plant and top management levels built labor relations framework during the postwar period. Thus, the politically motivated attempt by the United States to prompt the introduction of human relations for transforming industrial relations ended in failure. As verified by these instances, institutional factors greatly influenced conditions for the deployment of human relations in Germany. T. Armbrüster observed in 2005 that the codetermination and the works council tended to be considered a better method in Germany to resolve labor relations than the human relations approach (Armbrüster 2005, p. 87). Thus, in Germany, industrial relations derived not from management methodologies as in the United States, but rather from systems embedded in the law. Consequently, the deployment of human relations in enterprises was limited.

Whereas the traditional German-style industrial relations, emphasizing technology and skills, was an important background factor in the quest to design a method suitable for the German adaptation of American management system and style, the structural characteristics determined by various conditions, such as labor relations and the social consciousness of employees greatly affected the deployment of American human relations measurements.

Impacts of management values and management traditions and cultures were great. Management values emphasizing technology, quality, and production in German corporations repressed the implementation of human relations methods such as observed in Japan. Such management values reflected not only the characteristics of European markets as a core of export but also the high proportion of executives and managers with technical backgrounds, which prompted the reproduction of values for management in German enterprises in the deployment of human relations. Uniquely German management models such as the Harzburg model also exerted influence on the implementation of American human relations measures.

In this way, among the five factors determining the reframing in the transfer of management methods and systems well established in a particular country to another country, in the deployment of human relations, two factors of "management values and cultural factors" and "institutional factors" greatly affected Japanese or German specific adaptation, correction, and adjustment to better fit into the environmental conditions of the country in which reframing was done. However, in comparing Japan and Germany, in Japan, as seen in labor market structure based on the lifetime employment system, the characteristic of market structure was one of the factors determining the reframing in the deployment of human relations through promoting company consciousness and collaborative relationships between labor and management.

Regarding the conditions surrounding the introduction of human relations in Japan and Germany in the period of the postwar boom years as well as "reframing" and the factors defining, Table 7.1 shows an inline comparison of the respective countries, based on analysis so far in this chapter.

Table 7.1 Comparison of conditions surrounding the introduction of human relations in Japan and Germany

Deployment and factors affecting them	Management methods	
	Human relations	
	Japanese management methods	German management methods
Overall conditions in the deployment of American management methods	• Deployment of human relations for the purposes of modernizing and democratizing management after the war • Broad deployment of human relations measures • Deployment of human relations determined by collective behavioral patterns in companies and corresponding promotion of cooperative relations in workplaces • Inactive deployment of personnel counseling compared with other human relations methods • Deployment of human relations with the purpose of rationalization such as job improvement and increasing work efficiency	• Sparse deployments in German corporations • Failed US attempt to transfer US labor relations on the basis of human relations deployment • Use of human relations focusing on issues that are not automatically solved by codetermination or legal regulations (e.g., relations between the foreman and subordinates, etc.)

(continued)

Table 7.1 (continued)

Deployment and factors affecting them	Management methods	
	Human relations	
	Japanese management methods	German management methods
Deployment characteristics of American management methods	• Emphasis on improvement of communication and workers' morale by deploying human relations • Deployment of human relations as a measure for increasing corporate consciousness and countermeasures to trade unions in large enterprises • Deployment of human relations in small and medium enterprises • Important role of human relations as the foundation of manufacturing in combination with Japanese improvement suggestion activities • Emphasis on cooperative relationships between management and labor in the deployment of human relations	• Strong US support and promotion of technical assistance and productivity programs as a priority • Involvement of institutions such as RKW and universities • Human relations deployment as a means of stabilizing labor relations to advance rationalization

(continued)

Table 7.1 (continued)

Deployment and factors affecting them	Management methods	
	Human relations	
	Japanese management methods	German management methods
Modifications in American management methods	• Japanese ways of deploying human relations, such as seen in methods of human relations management including the entity family • The submission of suggestions through managers with a view to making managers immediately grasp the situations of subordinates and involving them in the necessary improvements • Emphasis on improvement of workers' morale in welfare service measures • Avoidance of collective bargaining by using the claim disposition system • Use of attitude surveys as an important measure of labor audits	• Alternatives to improving psychological aspects of human relations by improving labor environment under the codetermination system

(continued)

Table 7.1 (continued)

Deployment and factors affecting them		Management methods	
		Human relations	
		Japanese management methods	German management methods
Amalgamation of American and Japanese elements		• Hybridization of American human relations and human relationships based on Japanese family-ism • Hybridization of American methods based on cold contracting human relations and Japanese methods emphasizing behavioral patterns based on collectivism	• US orientation in corporate personnel policy and social policy and its amalgamation with prewar works community concepts • Amalgamation of human relations viewpoints and prewar labor science research viewpoints • The return of prewar company publications based on human relations perspectives
Factors of modification of American management method	Influence of traditions, cultural factors, and management values	• Management values based on "trust relationships" rather than "contract relationships" • Influences of family-ism and paternalism before the war (necessities to transform them) • Management values based on behavioral style of collectivism	• Constraints in management values emphasizing technology, quality, and production • Management values reflecting the high proportion of executives and managers from technical fields • Influence of uniquely German management models such as the Harzburg model

(continued)

Table 7.1 (continued)

Deployment and factors affecting them		Management methods	
		Human relations	
		Japanese management methods	German management methods
	Influence of institutional factors	• Undeveloped labor relations before the war (necessities to overcome it) • Labor democratization and enhancement of labor movements • Weak regulating powers of trade unions to management • Lack of legal institutions for communication between management and labor, such as work councils in Germany • Supervisor system with insufficient delegation of authority to low-level managers at production spots	• Conflict between the US's intention to reform labor relations through human relations deployment and Germany's traditional labor relations • Traditional labor relations and constraints from labor resistance and opposition • Codetermination system's inhibitory influence
	Influencing factors of the productive forces	–	–
	Influence of industrial structure factors	–	–
	Influence of market structure factors	• Influences of labor market based on the lifetime employment system	–

Source This table was compiled by the author, based on discussions in this chapter

References

Albert M (2001) Capitalisme contre Capitalisme. du Seuil, Paris

Ando M (1961) Ningen kankei kanri ni ningen ni taisuru aijyo wo (Importance of affection for humans in human relations management). In: Romu kenkyu (Labor Manag Study) 14(12):9–10

Armbrüster T (2005) Management and organization in Germany. Adlerhot, Ashgate

Awaji E (1957) Ningen kankei ron no mondaiten (Problems of human relations). In: Romu kenkyu (Labor Manag Study) 10(5):2–9

Berghahn V (1986) The Americanization of West German industry 1945–1973. Cambridge University Press, Cambridge

Bramesfeld E, Herwig B, Honnacker A et al (1956) Human relations in industrie. Die menschlichen Beziehungen in der Industrie. Beobachtungen einer deutschen Studiengruppe in USA (RKW-Auslandsdienst, Heft 41). C. Hanser, München

Bundesvereinigung der Deutschen Arbeitgeberverbande (1957) Jahresbericht. BDA, Koln

Der Arbeitgeber (1950) "Human relations" in der deutschen Wirtschaft. In: Der Arbeitgeber 10:12–13

Ewatari S (1954) Romu kanri no kindaika ni tsuite (Modernization of personnel management). In: Noda N, Mori G (eds) Romu kanri kindaika no jitsurei (Cases of modernization of personnel management). Daiyamondosha, Tokyo, pp 15–27

Guillén NF (1994) Models of management. Works, authority, and organization in a comparative perspective. The University of Chicago Press, Chicago, London

Hall PA, Soskice D (eds) (2001) Varieties of capitalism: the institutional foundations of comparative advantage. Oxford University Press, Oxford

Hartmann H (1959) Authority and organization in German management. Princeton University Press, Princeton

Hartmann H (1963) Amerikanische Firmen in Deutschland. Westdeutscher Verlag, Köln

Hasegawa H (1960a) Nihon no hyuman rireshonzu (Human relations in Japan). Otsuki shoten, Tokyo

Hasegawa H (1960b) Wagakuni ni okeru hyuman rireshonzu no ichi sokumen (An aspect of human relations in Japan). In: Nihon keiei gakkai (ed) Nihon no keiei (Japanese management). Moriyama shoten, Tokyo, pp 45–52

Hasegawa H (1967) Fukurikosei oyobi koyo no antei (Welfare services and stabilization of employment). In Mori A (ed) Keieigaku jiten (Management dictionary). Toyokeizai shinposha, Tokyo, pp 648–649

Hilger S (2004) „Amerikanisierung" deutscher Unternehmen. Wettbewerbsstrategien und Unternehmenspolitik bei Henkel, Siemens und Daimler-Benz (1945/49–1975). Franz Steiner Verlag, Stuttagart

Hirano K (1976) Sengo nihon ni okeru roshi kankei no tenkai (Development of labor relations in postwar Japan). In: Kimoto S (ed) Roshi kankei ron (Labor relations). Nihon hyoronsha, Tokyo, pp 193–216

Hitachi zosen kabushikigaisha (1958) Hitachi zosen hyakunenshi (100-year history of Hitachi Zosen Corporation). Hitachi zosen kabushikigaisha, Osaka

Japan Human Relations Association (1988) More about suggestion systems. In: Japan Human Relations Association (ed) The idea book: Improvement through TEI (Total employee involvement). Productivity Press, Cambridge, Massachusetts, pp 199–208

Kaste H (1981) Arbeitgeber und Humanisierung der Arbeit. Eine Exemplarische Analyse. Leske Verlag+Budrich GmbH, Opladen

Kauders M (1960) Westdeutsche Werkzeitungen und ihre Rolle als Instrument zur Verarbeitung der "Human Relations" in den Monopolbetrieben nach 1945. In: Jahrbuch fur Wirtschaftsgeschichte 1960, II, pp 9–46

Kawasaki seitetsu kabushikigaisha shashi henshu iinkai (ed) (1976) Kawasaki seitetsu nijugonenshi (25-year history of Kawasaki Steel Corporation). Kawasaki seitetsu kabushikigaisha, Kobe
Kawada H (1961) Kujyo shori seido no katsuyo ni tsuite (Practical use of grievance disposition system). In: Romu kenkyu (Labor Manag Study) 14(2):12–15
Keizai doyukai (1963) Rodo shijyo no henka to kigyou katsudo (Changes in labor market and corporate behavior). Keizai doyukai, Tokyo
Kleinschmidt C (2002) Der produktive Blick. Wahrnehmung amerikanischer und japanischer Management- und Produktionsmethoden durch deutsche Unternehmer 1950–1985. Akademie Verlag, Berlin
Kleinschmidt C (2004) America and the resurgence of the German chemical and rubber industry after the Second World War. Hüls, Glanzstoff and Continental. In: Kudo A, Kipping M, Schröter HG (eds) German and Japanese business in the boom years. Transforming American management and technology models. Routledge, London, pp 161–174
Lawrence P (1980) Managers and management in West Germany. Croom Helm, London
Matsumoto R (ed) (1955) Roshi kankei ni okeru hukuri kosei kankei no genjyo (The present conditions of welfare service management in labor relations). Nihon keieisha dantai renmei, Kanto keieisha kyokai, Tokyo
Mizutani M (1957) Wagakuni ningen kankein kanri no genjyo to mondaiten (Actual conditions and problems of human relations management in Japan). In: Nihon keieisha dantai renmei (ed) Human riresyonzu (Human relations). Nihon keieisha dantai renmei kohobu, Tokyo, pp 110–181
Mori G (1961) Sengo nihon no romu kanri (Labor management in postwar Japan). Daiyamondosha, Tokyo
Mori G (1981) Nihonteki roshi kankei shisutemu no tokushitsu to kongo no tenbo (Characteristics and future of the Japanese labor relations system). In: Mori G (ed) Nihon no roshi kankei shisutemu (Labor relations system in Japan). Nihon rodo kyokai, Tokyo, pp 359–385
Nagashima R (1954) Nihon ni okeru ningen kankei kanri (Human relations management in Japan). In: Romu kenkyu (Labor Manag Study) 7(1):24–31
Nakamura S (1958) Nihon seisansei kojyo undoshi (History of productivity movements). Keiso shobo, Tokyo
Nakayama S (1969) Sengo "romu kanri seido" no hensen (Changes in the labor management system after World War II). In: Rosei jiho (labor Adm Rev) 2000:4–14
Nakayama S (1971) Amerikashiki romu kanri no kozai (Merits and demerits of American-type labor management). In: Keieisha (Executives) 25(4):14–18
Natori J (1965) Zoho keiei no HR (Human relations), enlarged edn. Waseda daigaku shuppankai, Tokyo
Neugebauer A (1997) Etablierung der Sachzwange. Werkzeitschrift und soziale Wirklichkeit nach dem Zweiten Weltkrieg. In: Heyl B, Neugebauer A (eds) »... ohne Rücksicht auf die Verhältniss«. Opel zwischen Weltwirtschaftkrise und Wiederaufbau. Brandes & Aspel, Frankfurt am Main, pp 195–216
Nihon keieisha dantai renmei (ed) (1956) Saikin ni okeru romu kanri syoseido heno kanshin keiko (Recent trend of interest in labor relations system). Nihon keieisha dantai renmei, Kanto keieisha kyokai, Tokyo
Nihon keieisha dantai renmei (ed) (1957) Wagakuni ningen kankei kanri no genjyo (The present condition of human relations management in Japan). Nihon keieisha dantai renmei, Kanto keieisha kyokai, Tokyo
Nihon keieisha dantai renmei (ed) (1959) Romu kanri tokei soran (Statistics of personnel management). Nihon keieisha dantai renmei kohobu, Tokyo
Nihon keieisha dantai renmei (ed) (1965) Wagakuni romu kanri no gensei (The present situation of labor management in Japan). Nihon keieisha dantai renmei kohobu, Tokyo

Nihon keieisha dantai renmei, Kanto keieisha kyokai (eds) (1958) Wagakuni ni okeru teian seido no genjyo (The present condition of suggestion system in Japan). Nihon keieisha dantai renmei, Kanto keieisha kyokai, Tokyo
Nihon seisansei hombu (ed) (1958a) Foaman seido (Foreman system). Nihon seisansei honbu, Tokyo
Nihon seisansei honbu (ed) (1958b) Hyuman rireshon (Human relations). Nihon seisansei honbu, Tokyo
Nihon seisansei hombu (ed) (1958c) Sangyo kunren (Industrial training). Nihon seisansei honbu, Tokyo
Nihon tekko renmei sengo tekkoshi henshu iinkai (ed) (1959) Sengo Tekkoshi (History of the iron and steel industry after World War II). Nihon tekko renmei, Tokyo
Nissan jidosha kabushikigaisha somubu chosaka (ed) (1965) Nissan jidosha sanjunenshi (30 years history of Nissan Motor Corporation). Nissan jidosha kabushikigaisha, Yokohama
Obst P (1970) Das „Harzburger Modell" in organisatorischer Sicht. In: Zeitschrift für Organisation 39(2):80–82
Odaka K (1953) Jugyoin taido chosa no hoho ni tsuite (Method of attitude survey of employees). In: Shukan nichiroken shiryo (Nichroken Material Weekly) 6(21):3–17
Odaka (1958) Ningen kankei to roshi kankei (Human relations and industrial relations). In: Keieisha (Executives) 12(6):17–22
Okouchi K (1980) Roshi kankei ron (Labor relations). Rodo jyunposha, Tokyo
Osikawa I, Takagi K (1959) Yoroppa seisansei tsushin (Eurpopean productivity report). Nihon seisansei honbu, Tokyo
Pirker T, Braun S, Lutz B et al (1955) Arbeiter Management Mitbestimmung. Ein industriesoziologische Untersuchung der Struktur, der Organisation und des Verhaltens der Arbeiterbelegschaften in Werken der deutschen Eisen- und Stahlindustrie, fur das Mitbestimmungsgesetz gilt. Ring-Verlag, Stuttgart
RKW (1953) Produktivität in USA. Eine Eindrücke einer deutschen Studiengruppe von einer Reise durch USA (RKW-Auslandsdienst, Heft 20). C. Hanser, Munchen
Roshikankei chosakai (1963) Roshikankei to ningenkankei (2) (Industrial relations and human relations, 2). Chuokoron jigyo shuppan, Tokyo
Schröter HG (2005) Americanization of the European economy. A compact survey of American economic influence in Europe since the 1880s. Springer, Dordrecht
Shimizu H (1961) Teian seido no are kore (Suggestion sytem is from now). In: Romu kenkyu (Labor Manag Study) 14(2):16–19
Sugaya A (1977) Roshi kankei ron no kihon mondai (Fundamental problem of labor management theory). Horitsu bunkasha, Kyoto
Takagi K (1962) Nishiyoroppa ni okeru seisansei undo (The productivity movement in Western Europe). Nihon seisansei honbu, Tokyo
Takahashi K (1970) Nihonteki roshi kankei no kenkyu (Study of Japanese labor relations), enlarged edn. Miraisha, Tokyo
Takezawa S (1961) Nihon no keiei to ningen kankei (Management and human relations in Japan). In: Rodo hogaku kenkyu kaiho (Bull Labor Law Study) 2(13):1–35
Tsuchiya M (1976) Kigyo keiei no kindaika (Modernization of business management). In: Kobayashi M, Shimokawa K, Sugiyama K et al (eds) Nihon keieishi wo manabu 3. Sengo keieishi (Learning Japanese business history 3. The postwar business history), vol 3. Yuhikaku, Tokyo, pp 282–300
Tsusho sangyosho kigyokyoku (ed) (1968) Kigyou hukuri kosei (Corporate welfare services). Tsusho sangyosho kigyokyoku, Tokyo
Urabe K, Omura K (1983) Nihonteki roshi kankei no tankyu (Exploration of Japanese labor relations). Chuo keizaisha, Tokyo

Whitehill Jr AM, Tanaka S, Yoshino K et al (1958) Kanri to ningen kankei no shoten to amerika no soiten ni tsuite. In: Keieisha (Executives) 12(6):28–35

Wiesen SJ (2001) West German industry and the challenge of Nazi past, 1945–1955. The University of North Carolina Press, Chapel Hill

Zepf G (1972) Kooperativer Führungsstil und Organisation. Betriebswirtschaftlicher Verlag Dr. Th. Gabler, Wiesbaden

Chapter 8
Deployment of Industrial Engineering

Abstract Regarding the deployment of American-style management, this chapter discusses that the implementation of industrial engineering (IE), an advanced form of scientific management originating in the United States, played an important role in production management and rationalization in Japan and Germany after World War II. The primary issue was the implementation of the work-factor (WF) method and Methods Time Measurement (MTM) for the deployment of IE. Thus, this chapter examines the deployment of IE in relation to the problems of work measurement and method engineering, the role of industrial engineers, and the influence of institutions on the implementation and promotion of IE, such as the Verband für Arbeitsstudien (REFA) and the German MTM Association in Germany and the Japan Iron and Steel Federation in Japan. Through these discussions, this chapter clarifies the Japanese and German characteristics regarding the deployment of IE and their significance.

Keywords Industrial engineering (IE) · Management system · Methods time measurement (MTM) · REFA · Work factor

In Chap. 7, we considered the deployment of human relations but in this chapter, we turn our attention to industrial engineering (IE) regarding the deployment of American-style management systems. IE is an advanced form of scientific management that originated in America and gained broad acceptance after World War II. IE can be considered as the next level of development (Kirchner 1970, p. 440), and the United States had a decisively leading role in the IE field. A Siemens US study trip report in 1963, the end of the productivity movement, noted that the predetermined time method then being implemented in the world of capitalism was without exception developed and tested in the United States prior to being made public. For example, WF (work factor) was developed in the United States in the mid-1930s (*Siemens Archiv Akten*, 16020, Aus Theorie und Praxis des Industrial Engineering in den USA. Berichtüber eine Studienreise September/Oktober 1963, p. 123), implemented after 1938, and then used internationally from 1952. In the International Management Conference held in September 1963, there was a discussion on issues of WF time standards and WF use *Bundesarchiv Koblenz*, B393/27, International

T. Yamazaki, *Japanese and German Enterprises*,
https://doi.org/10.1007/978-981-97-4880-8_8

Conference on Work-Factor Time Standards (26–27.9.1963). MTM (methods time measurement) was developed by H. B. Maynard, G. J. Stegemerten, and J. L. Schwab in the 1940s at Westinghouse (Maynard et al 1948; *Siemens Archiv Akten*, 16,020, Aus Theorie und Praxis des Industrial Engineering in den USA, p. 33), and spread in many countries after the war. However, many factors influenced the introduction of IE in Japan and Germany. Therefore, in this chapter, we examine the deployment of IE in both countries.[1]

Sections 8.1 and 8.2 analyze the deployment of industrial engineering in Japan and Germany, respectively. In Sect. 8.3, characteristics of deployment of industrial engineering methods through comparison between Japan and Germany will be considered. Based on these discussions, in Sect. 8.4, "reframing" in the deployment of IE in both nations is clarified.

8.1 Deployment of Industrial Engineering in Japan

8.1.1 Socio-economic Background Regarding the Deployment of Industrial Engineering in Japan

This section examines the socio-economic background related to the deployment of IE in Japan in the second half of the twentieth century. In 1956, an iron and steel productivity inspection team produced a report claiming that the disparity in productivity between the United States and Japan owed itself to the lack of IE in the latter and recommended its urgent introduction (Nihon seisansei honbu 1956, pp. 1, 4–5, 21–23, 98–99). In 1957, a study group, led by E L. Fuse, an American IE expert, was established by eight companies forming part of the Japan Iron and Steel Federation. Two years later, the group formed a committee to promote the deployment of IE (Nihon tekko renmei tekko jyunenshi henshu iinkai 1969, pp. 595–597, Yawata seitetsu shashi hensan jikko iinkai 1980, p. 32). IE contributed significantly to American industry by indicating certain standards (Nihon tekko renmei IE shiryo kenkyukai 1958, p. 35). However, in Japan, when implementing IE for measurement and management, standards were still lacking even in the latter half of the 1950s (Tekkokai 1957, pp. 34–35). As a result, work measurement became increasingly important. For instance, at the Mitsubishi Electric Corporation, the head of work measurement played a major role in IE at the end of the 1950s (Hachimaki 1958, p. 30). Work factor was therefore an important consideration and, consequently, a contract was signed between the Japan Management Association and the American Work-Factor Company in 1958, which laid the foundation for introducing WF to the business world in Japan (Konno 1982, p. 227).

---

[1] The first content analysis related to Germany in this chapter is Chap. 7 of the author's book "*German Business Management: A Japanese Perspective on Regional Development Factors*," which was published by Springer in 2013.

The competitive environment in which Japanese companies were operating also encouraged the deployment of IE. Several large businesses with similar capacities, all of which belonged to six major industrial groups, were in competition, and over-investment in plants and equipment, and newly formed business alliances promoted the implememtation of IE (Noguchi et al. 1965, p. 229). Moreover, in 1962, IE introduction and systematization became necessary in response to intensifying international competition and trade liberalization. For this reason, the number of companies that introduced IE dramatically increased in the 1960s (Noguchi 1968, p. 195, Nihon tekko remei jimukyoku et al. 1962, p. 71). In the Japanese iron and steel industry, a substantial reduction in the number of workers would be a critical concern for the management as an anti-recession measure, leading to the expansion of the established standard time (Yasui 1986, p. 201). The number of indirect personnel (e.g., research and design, logistics, administration) in the iron and steel industry in Japan exceeded that in the American industry despite having superior equipment and machinery compared with those in the United States (Miyajima 1963, p. 239). IE therefore became essential to minimize costs.

Furthermore, the introduction of a flow production system and the development of innovation also increased the importance of deploying IE. In addition, as production increased with automation, adjustments in the time standard of each process became important for ensuring cost-effectiveness.

In the 1970s, in the context of low economic growth brought on by the oil crisis, IE was deployed with a particular focus on saving on labor, reducing costs, and restructuring personnel in several industries, including the iron and steel industry (IE mondai kenkyukai 1975a, pp. 77–78). In the electrical industry, while standardization and guarantee of quality were effective, cost reduction was indispensable considering the mass mobilization of young women in the workforce, the deepening division of labor in the factory, and the thoroughness of the mass production system (through the use of conveyors) (IE mondai kenkyukai 1975b, p. 99; IE mondai kenkyukai 1975c, p. 139).

8.1.2 General Conditions of the Deployment of Industrial Engineering

This section examines the general conditions influencing the deployment of IE in Japan. The WF method was introduced in 1950 while MTM was first implemented in 1957 (Indasutoriaru enjiniaringu 1959, p. 81; Miharada 1965, p. 28; Tsusho sangyosho gorika shingikai 1967, p. 62). In the latter half of the 1950s, IE introduction and adaptation in industrial enterprises advanced due to the 1955 productivity movement. However, IE was still not implemented systematically, with its development focused on operational management. During this stage, the emphasis was primarily on human, systems, and method engineering (Noguchi 1968, pp. 170, 196, 207–208; Nihon tekko renmei jimukyoku et al. 1962, p. 71). By the end of the 1950s, the WF method gained momentum (Ono 1959, p. 60), playing an important role in method engineering (Ikenaga 1962, p. 786).

However, even in this period, unlike in the US, the organization of IE in Japan was not well developed; there was an urgent need to establish work and time standards and train industrial engineers (Nihon seisansei honbu 1960, pp. 22, 39–40, 58, 133–135; Ozaki 1959, pp. 362, 366). This reflected the fact that, whereas in the United States IE was a recognized profession, industrial engineers were still considered non-professionals in Japan (Omura 1962, pp. 915, 926).

For this reason, the systematization of IE became necessary. Nevertheless, rather than adjusting IE content, Japanese companies placed greater emphasis on reshuffling the management based on work standardization (time–motion studies). Thus, the systemization of IE was delayed. In addition, Japanese companies instituted various methodologies for work rationalization (e.g., production management, cost control, etc.). However, even in the late 1950s, the concept of *function* as the focus of IE in a company was insufficiently established (Noguchi 1968, pp. 171, 196–197; Noguchi et al. 1965, pp. 224–225, 228; Indasutoriaru enjiniaringu kokunai shisatudan 1958, p. 232).

IE was eventually established and systematized in the 1960s by integrating scientific management techniques. Cases attesting to this change could be observed in key industrial sectors such as iron and steel, electrical, and petrochemical (Inoue 1976, p. 28). For instance, in the iron and steel industry, while IE activities had initially been limited to work improvement, the focus on standard setting eventually increased (Nihon tekko renmei jimukyoku et al. 1962, p. 71). Predetermined time standard systems (PTSs) used in Japan included the WF method and MTM. By the mid-1960s, the use of the WF method became rather widespread, exceeding that of MTM (Quick and Ikenaga 1965, pp. 1100–1101; Bijinesu 1960, pp. 69, 73; Konno 1982, p. 227). In contrast, in the US, the most widely used method was MTM (Nihon seisansei honbu 1960, p. 102; Nihon seisansei honbu 1964, p. 42; Konno 1982, p. 227).

Therefore, IE deployment differed greatly between the two countries. As late as the 1970s, integration of IE activities in various fields was lacking across Japanese industry (Ono 1970, pp. 26, 31). Companies still performed work measurement and improvement, standardization, quality control, process control, and cost control independently. A shift from individual applications to general and systematic adaptations of IE could be observed around 1970 (Hibi 1975, p. 30).

In Japan, the education of industrial engineers had already become important in the early 1960s (Furukawa et al. 1961, p. 103). However, as indicated by a 1967 survey, industrial engineers were not considered professionals, and they mainly focused on methods. In many cases, industrial engineers in Japan were of inferior quality to those in the United States, for example, their time studies still primarily used stopwatches as opposed to the Work-Factor method or MTM (Taniguchi 1967, pp. 1197–1200). In addition, the role of factory engineers greatly differed in Japan and the United States. For example, in the US, as several examinations related to production aspects were performed before shifting to production, factory engineers were not always necessary. Conversely, in Japan, investigations regarding production technology were not performed adequately. Therefore, technical issues frequently occurred after the start of production, and several factory engineers were required to solve these problems (Ueda 1967, pp. 135, 137). By the mid-1960s, system improvements were mainly being performed in the American iron and steel industry, and the standard and system for wage setting had become the focus of IE in Japan. This focus took the form of design and improvement of total systems, comprising personnel, machinery, and materials. However, the process of setting standards concerning personnel remained incomplete at this stage (Uchiyama 1966, p. 34).

One cause for this incompleteness in IE in Japan was the low skill levels of industrial engineers (Takeda 1967, p. 580). As a result, around the end of the 1960s, greater emphasis was placed on method study and improvement as opposed to work measurement. In addition, standard time was generally employed as the standard for measuring efficiency, planning production, calculating personnel, and estimating cost (Omura 1969, p. 16; Shida 1968, p. 11). IE focused on other aspects of business management, such as standardizing work or establishing standard values for management purposes (Jyuji 1968, p. 6).

Furthermore, the deployment of IE differed significantly between industries. For example, IE advanced the most in the iron and steel and processing and assembly industries, particularly in the automobile and electrical industries. Finally, there were also significant differences between individual companies in the same industries. For instance, in the mid-1970s, the use of modern IE methods was rare among small and medium-sized firms (Hibi 1975, p. 31). The following section examines the introduction of IE in the main industries and their representative companies.

8.1.3 Deployment of Industrial Engineering in Major Industrial Sectors

8.1.3.1 Iron and Steel Industry

In the iron and steel industry, IE achieved results in method engineering. Improving work methods and performing standard setting were two pillars of IE (Nihon tekko renmei junenshi henshu iinkai 1969, pp. 606–607). Iron and steel enterprises introduced IE for quality improvement and cost reduction in the first rationalization plans from 1951 to 1955 and fully utilized an IE system in the second rationalization plans from 1956 to 1960. During this period, standardization for realizing consistency in production using automation technology was promoted. Moreover, IE was synthesized, systematized, and introduced in earnest for planning work duties, setting standard work times, and monitoring (Inoue 1976, p. 30). Furthermore, personnel assessments were implemented at the company level, and improvements in management functions, such as investigations regarding equipment capacity, process control, transportation management, and inventory control, became important (Nihon tekko renmei jimukyoku et al. 1963, p. 81).

Standard time was applied to labor management most commonly around 1962, when personnel rationalization was necessary due to recession (Nihon tekko renmei junenshi henu iinkai 1969, pp. 607–608; Goji et al. 1969, p. 896). Thus, reducing the number of workers based on the setting of standard time was prioritized in IE (Yasui 1986, p. 207). During the 1960s, the importance of rationalization of personnel, contract management, and approaches to management issues increased. Consequently, IE became increasingly important for top management (Nihon tekko renmei jimukyoku 1966, p. 100; Nihon tekko renmei jimukyoku 1967, p. 95). By the end of the decade, IE was being used in the design of management systems, analysis of management issues, productivity improvement, and cost reduction. IE was also applied to personnel rationalization in indirect departments (Nihon tekko renmei junenshi henshu iinkai 1969, pp. 605, 608). There were five overall goals: (1) improving work and equipment, (2) setting standard time for workers, (3) designing management systems, (4) providing consultations, and (5) other business-related activities. Furthermore, deciding the number of regular personnel was one of the most important parts of many IE projects, followed by improvements in production and clerical efficiency, management of equipment, standard setting, and process control (Ono 1968, pp. 665–670). In many iron and steel companies, standard time was applied to the new system of efficiency wages, and conventional personnel assessments were implemented in the latter half of the 1960s (Nihon tekko renmei jimukyoku 1968, p. 103). From the late 1960s to the early 1970s, self-management activities were critical in method engineering and for improving morale. Thus, IE became increasingly important for promoting self-management (Nihon tekko renmei jimukyoku 1972, p. 80).

Cost reduction was also an important part of IE activities after 1973, particularly during the oil crisis (Nihon tekko renmei jimukyoku 1974, p. 80; Nihon tekko renmei jimukyoku 1975, pp. 100–101; Nihon tekko renmei jimukyoku 1976, pp. 65–66; Nihon tekko renmei jimukyoku 1978, p. 66). Subsequently, the role of IE was crucial in the implementation of fixed-cost reduction measures during the 1980s. To promote production efficiency in the upstream and downstream processes of the organization, IE continued to focus on improvements from all perspectives (Tekko no ai ii 1984, pp. 14–15).

8.1.3.2 Automobile Industry

The introduction of WF as a new method of standard setting was effective, especially with regard to the ratio of labor costs to production costs, which was very high in the assembly industry (Kikuchi 1968, p. 608; Sakano 1963, pp. 220, 223–225). For example, at the Nissan Motor Corporation, due to new product releases, constantly changing automobile models, and new factory openings, various problems became common, especially those related to factory layout and material handling. In addition, there were issues related to cost reduction and equipment investment (Takai et al. 1968, p. 8; Omura 1959c, p. 450; Sakano 1963, p. 225). Under such conditions, the training of IE staff became essential. By the end of the 1950s, top management, such as those at the Toyo Kogyo Corporation, began to recognize the necessity of having industrial engineers on their staff (Omura 1959c, p. 450).

In 1955, at the Nissan Motor Corporation, imbalances in setting standard time using the stopwatch method and the adoption of a group premium wage system yielded constant complaints from workers (Tsusho sangyosho gorika shingikai 1967, p. 73; Kyushu indasutoriaru enjiniaringu kokunai shisatsudan 1959, p. 18). In response, the company created a master table of all work-related activities and a standard time was set for every section. Nissan instituted company-wide application of standard time via the WF method and established a management system. In this case, work improvement and efficiency control were the main fields of IE. In addition, the company pursued cost reductions for parts purchased from other companies. These reductions were based on work measurement and improvement methods for parts-manufacturing companies, decisions regarding various costs according to value analysis (VA), and the establishment of specialized lines (Nissan jidosha kabushikigaisha somubu chosaka 1965, p. 294; Kyushu indasutoriaru enjiniaringu kokunai shisatsudan 1959, p. 18; Tsusho sangyosho gourika shingikai 1967, pp. 62–63, 79; Omura 1959b, pp. 101, 103–104; Sakano 1963, pp. 202, 206). Management of the number of work hours (mainly based on standard time) was also implemented. While the WF method was primarily adopted for manual work, machining time was based on technological considerations and statistical methods (Tsusho sangyosho gorika shingikai 1967, pp. 65–66).

Nissan eventually established IE departments at central-office levels. Such departments played a role in top management and engaged in IE activities at the factory level (Tsusho sangyosho gourika shingikai 1967, p. 64). For example, at the Toyo Kogyo Corporation, a master table regarding the standardization of work was created in 1949, after which the WF method was adopted in 1955. In 1958, the company introduced work sampling and standard time was established. Moreover, precision in measurements of the operating rate was improved (Toyokogyo kabushikigaisha gojunenshi 1972, pp. 301–302).

8.1.3.3 Electrical Industry

In the electrical industry the stopwatch method was used for time studies until the mid-1950s after which the conversion to the WF method was completed by the end of the 1950s. However, in this particular industry, MTM remained in its infancy; consequently, it was not adopted. At that time, representative companies in IE continued to emphasize the following aspects: work standards and standard time, cost reductions, plant layout, standardization, and suggestion systems. Moreover, quality standards were established; technical alliances with foreign firms had a substantial influence on these standards. This was a typical characteristic of the electrical industry (Sato 1959, pp. 266–267).

However, there were differences between the sections of the industry focusing on mass-produced products and those focusing on individual-order production. For example, for home appliances, a domain in which mass production via conveyors was dominant, setting a standard time was achieved using the WF method, and in many cases, standard time was used for both process and personnel planning (Tsusho sangyosho kigyoukyoku 1969, p. 105). In contrast, as large-sized individual orders started being produced, the Kawasaki factory of the Fuji Electric Corporation employed the stopwatch method in time studies. It was only in the early 1960s that the WF method and MTM were adopted (Omura 1961, p. 194).

Regarding individual enterprises, in 1950, the Mitsubishi Electric Corporation introduced the WF method to improve the estimation techniques of elementary motion. In 1951, the company introduced a training program for work-factor engineers, and by 1954, the WF value was adopted as the standard time value. Company-wide standard time was established for mass and individual production (Mitsubishi-denki kabushikigaisha shashi hensansitsu 1982, pp. 106, 275). In the Itami factory of the Fuji Electric Corporation, the core IE activities from the late 1950s to the early 1960s included the creation of a work-study subsection, which was responsible for measuring work performance and making method improvements (Omura 1960, pp. 170–172). In the mid-1960s, the Matsushita Electric Corporation in particular emphasized traditional rather than modern IE. This company also made an effort to improve material handling, realize premeditated production, shorten production schedules, and reduce the overall production period by introducing method engineering and conveyor systems (Daisanji aiii kokunai shisatsudan 1965, p. 18).

8.2 Deployment of Industrial Engineering in Germany

8.2.1 Social-economic Background Regarding the Deployment of Industrial Engineering in Germany

In this section the deployment of IE in Germany is examined. Already by 1948 in Germany manufacturers had begun to place great significance on work study (Kothe 1948, p. 10). For example, electrical manufacturer AEG noted that from the 1950s to the 1960s, the rationalization of work and time studies influenced productivity improvement [*Historisches Archiv des Deutschen Technikmuseums*, GS2052, Programm für durchzuführende Arbeits- u. Zeitstudienim Geschäftsjahr 1959/60 (12.10.1959), *Historisches Archiv des Deutschen Technikmuseums*, GS2052, Programm für durchzuführende Rationalisierungsmaβnahmen im Geschäftsjahr 1960/61 (2.12.1960), *Historisches Archiv des Deutschen Technikmuseums*, GS2052, Programm für durchzuführende Rationalisierungsmaβnahmen im Geschäftsjahr 1961/62 (5.12.1961), *Historisches Archiv des Deutschen Technikmuseums*, GS2052, Programm für Rationalisierung im Geschäftsjahr 1964 (8.6.1964), *Historisches Archiv des Deutschen Technikmuseums*, GS2052, Programm für durchzuführende Rationalisierungsmaβnahmen im Geschäftsjahr 1966 (21.1.1966), *Historisches Archiv des Deutschen Technikmuseums*, GS2052, Geschäftsbericht 1959/60 an Dir. Mempel (2.12.1960), *Historisches Archiv des Deutschen Technikmuseums*, GS2052, Geschäftsbericht 1960/61 an Dir. Mempel (5.12.1961), *Historisches Archiv des Deutschen Technikmuseums*, GS2052, Geschäftsbericht1962/63 an Dir. Mempel (2.6.1964), *Historisches Archiv des Deutschen Technikmuseums*, GS2052, Durchzuführte Rationalisierungsvorhaben im Geschäftsjahr 1963, *Historisches Archiv des Deutschen Technikmuseums*, GS2052, Durchzuführte Rationalisierungsvorhaben im Geschäftsjahr 1966 (5.4.1967)]. By the mid-1950s, the activities and wage payment methods of German organization REFA were becoming prominent (Free 1955, p. 67, Pavel 1957, p. 22). For example, in a March 1956 survey of 2,655 corporations conducted by Ifo, REFA systems accounted for nearly 80% of the work study methods used by manufacturers (REFA-Nachrichten 1956, pp. 91–94; Pechhold 1956, p. 147).

However, the situation changed by the latter half of the 1950s. The increasing importance of work and time studies based on the US predetermined time method became particularly apparent. Even in West Germany, the use of such methods expanded greatly by the end of the 1950s (Schmiede and Schudlich 1981, p. 359), and REFA was instrumental in its deployment. In the early 1960s, REFA was at the IE expansion stage and had translated a US handbook into German (Billhardt 1962, p. 249). Upon the publication of this translated *IE Handbook*, the first education course in this field was conducted using improved teaching methods (REFA-Nachrichten 1964, p. 186). By approximately 1960, the original industrial engineering training had been around for quite some time in Anglo-Saxon countries; in West Germany, in contrast, opportunities to receive training in the IE field were largely nonexistent apart from the efforts of several organizations like REFA (Bramesfeld 1960, pp. 1259–1260).

IE training began to significantly increase in Germany in the 1960s. The structure of training events fundamentally changed in 1969, with IE courses comprising 24.7% of all education courses conducted by REFA (REFA-Nachrichten 1970, p. 77). In addition, the number of work-study personnel trained in WF and MTM had grown to 2,491 by 1966 (Schmiede and Schudlich 1981, p. 360). There were a total of 52 IE seminars by the mid-1973, and about half of the candidates who completed the course worked in IE positions, with the remainder becoming managers responsible for production control or business management, heads of human resources departments, or their assistants (Pechhold 1974, pp. 219–220). Regarding IE materials and books, a companion volume to the *IE Handbook* was published in 1967, thereby completing the REFA standard works for engineer training. Furthermore, REFA's third report was published in the form of a magazine for work studies and IE managers (Pechhold 1974, p. 195), and from 1971 onward, they published the bi-monthly *Industrial Engineering Magazine* (Pechhold 1974, p. 233).

In the mid-1950s, when Germany was at full employment, wages and cost pressures made improvement of work efficiency more important, which affected the diffusion of IE. Because of this situation, the predetermined time method was implemented primarily for labor efficiency (in job design). However, the overall diffusion of the predetermined time method was first considered successful during the downturn of 1966/67 and the subsequent easing of labor market restrictions (Schmiede and Schudlich 1981, p. 369). In the following section, the deployment of WF and MTM is examined in detail.

8.2.2 Deployment of the Work-Factor Method

WF was deployed with the cooperation of US corporations and through licensing the methods. REFA assisted in the deployment and spread of predetermined time methods such as WF (Schmiede and Schudlich 1981, pp. 400–401). On February 1, 1958, REFA and the Work-Factor Company signed an agreement regarding implementing WF training courses in West Berlin and West Germany (*Siemens Archiv Akten*, 7882, Beurteilung und Einsatzmöglichkeit des Work-Factor-Verfahrens. Das Work-Factor-Verfahren als Hilfsmittel der Arbeitsgestaltug und der arbeitstechnischen Vorplanung, p. 9, Jaeckel 1961, p. 223). The Work-Factor Company was a technical consulting firm that provided global IE services to economic and industrial institutions (*Siemens Archiv Akten*, 16020, Aus Theorie und Praxis des Industrial Engineering in den USA, p. 91). Following extensive research into number systems (MTM, WF, BMT, DMT, etc.), the REFA Institute for Labor Science became a licensee of the Work-Factor Company (*Siemens Archiv Akten*, 16020, Aus Theorie und Praxis des Industrial Engineering in den USA, p. 20, Jaeckel 1961, p. 223).

REFA also acquired the rights to translate the Work-Factor Handbook and the rights to use the German translation produced from the Dutch version held by Philips. The second WF training course organized in September 1958 was conducted by two individuals from Philips under contract from the Work-Factor Company (*Siemens Archiv Akten*, 7882, Beurteilung und Einsatzmöglichkeit des Work-Factor-Verfahrens, p. 10). However, the situation changed enormously in the 1960s: by 1964, REFA instructors were using their own German training materials (Pechhold 1974, p. 193). Corporations, such as AEG, Bosch, Siemens, and Olympia, acquired WF licenses and deployed the American system (Schmiede and Schudlich 1981, p. 360).

At the beginning of the 1960s, as the productivity movement that started with leadership and assistance of the United States in the late 1940s was drawing to a close, job design was becoming more important than standard time settings because of the rapid onset of mechanization (Deininger 1962, p. 146). REFA regarded WF as an appropriate tool for job design (*Siemens Archiv Akten*, 7882, Beurteilung und Einsatzmöglichkeit des Work-Factor-Verfahrens, S. 10), and the focus of its activities increasingly shifted away from predetermined time methods toward job design after the second half of the 1950s. In this way, the significance of motion study and WF deployment increased (Votsch H 1962, S. 62).

8.2.3 Deployment of MTM

Study trips under the US Technical Assistance Plan was important in the study and deployment of MTM methods, to which REFA also contributed greatly [Vgl. *Bundesarchiv koblenz*, B102/37261, Technische Akademie Bergische Land e.V.: TA-Studienreise nach USA auf dem Gebiet des MTM-Verfahrens (Methods Time Measurement) (13.10.1952)]. Many of REFA's regional branches provided information on US time study systems (Pechhold 1974, p. 125).

MTM was mostly used in the United States but its use was also spreading in Germany (Witte 1963, p. 104), and was primarily being taught and spread by foreign consulting engineers. In comparison with WF, MTM took effect in a gradual and more long-term manner. However, in 1963, companies that had executed it formed the German MTM Association (*Siemens Archiv Akten*, 16020, Aus Theorie und Praxis des Industrial Engineering in den USA, p. 20). The greatest impediment to European worker productivity, in addition to the delay in mass and large-scale lot production, was supposedly job design and work flow, which were far weaker here than in the US. The German MTM Association accepted the US predetermined time method in 1964/65, adapted it to the German context, and disseminated it throughout the country (Birn 1968, pp. 234, 236).

The German MTM Association's membership grew 2.6 times, from 115 corporations in 1966 to approximately 300 in 1973. The employees of these member companies more than quadrupled, from nearly 500,000 to 2,000,000. More than half of these member companies were in the precision equipment (30% in 1974) and metal processing (23% in 1974) industries; other industries included clothing (14%), steel (4%), chemical (4%), and service and banking (5%) (Vgl. Deutsche MTM Vereinigung e.V. 2002, p. 31; Mergner et al. 1974, pp. 175–176). In several cases, activities sponsored by organizations such as the German MTM Association were made possible with the cooperation of corporations and similar organizations in the US. The new US motion and time study methods were often implemented in Germany through private US companies (Schmiede and Schudlich 1981, p. 359).

8.2.4 Deployment of the Work-Factor Method and MTM in Major Industrial Sectors

IE methodologies were first deployed in various areas within mass production management, but the focus was on the electrical and automotive industries. At Bosch, a transition to WF methods began in the mid-1950s; in 1960, MTM deployment was started and work councils and company management signed a shop agreement. MTM deployment had special priority in the production department and was expanded for the first time, although on a smaller scale, to the maintenance and control departments (Rau 1968, pp. 169–170). Daimler-Benz also used MTM from the 1960s onward. Although, in retrospect, there were only a few cases of MTM being implemented at

Daimler-Benz and in the German automobile industry more generally, MTM proved to be the best tool for job design and time economics in various sectors within the electrical industry (Arlt 1978, p. 143).

A 1965 IG Metall report states that WF, MTM, and other predetermined time methods were gaining popularity in the metals industry. For instance, corporations in the steel industry were systematically streamlining maintenance and repair departments using predetermined time methods based on the deployment of wage incentive systems. The shipbuilding industry also increased its use of predetermined time methods (IG Metall 1965, pp. 127–128). The deployment of predetermined time methods in maintenance tasks could also be seen in the chemical and mining industries (Erdmann 1969, pp. 310–311). A 1969 report noted that the use of IE methods was not limited to the machinery or transportation equipment industries; it had spread to steel and metals, clothing, construction, chemicals, and even service industries (Schlaich 1969b, p. 6). For example, MTM was being used in the garment industry by the 1950s (Hopf 1979, p. 67), and all sorts of MTM-based data systems could be used to locate time data in the clothing and machinery industries (Hopf 1979, p. 72). For German industries, IE was important for creating satisfactory management results and competitive advantage (Schlaich 1969b, p. 7). The deployment of WF and MTM in the electrical industry and the chemical industry is considered below.

8.2.4.1 Electrical Industry

In the electrical industry, WF garnered attention at the end of the 1950s at Siemens as an aid to job design planners and production equipment designers, and both WF and MTM were the most popular work-study methods (*Siemens Archiv Akten*, 7882, Beurteilung und Einsatzmöglichkeit des Work-Factor-Verfahrens, pp. 1, 3, 9). Siemens implemented approximately 15 WF information education courses by 1962, and, in addition to sponsoring numerous seminars for supervisors and specialists, had roughly 100 WF-trained workers in their factories. The largest portion of these trained personnel worked in production preparation and work planning departments for large-lot and mass production. The Siemens Work-Factor Group, comprising nine members from three Siemens companies, was formed; the results of their work were tested and handed over to the REFA Institute, after which they could be adopted by any company that had WF-trained personnel (REFA-Nachrichten 1962, p. 257).

A study group with the theme "IE Theory and Practice in the US," participated in a US IE Institute international conference and a WF international conference, and visited Westinghouse, Bell and Howell, Teletype, and the Work-Factor Company. Siemens' WF instructors were instrumental in providing guidance for preparing Germany's public WF manual. By April 1964, a total of 615 people had participated in 35 WF training courses organized in West Germany. Twelve of these courses were taught internally for Siemens' organizations, which had approximately 150 trained WF personnel. In two particular teacher training courses, there were 31 REFA instructors qualified to teach, of which eight were Siemens' employees. At the time,

27 major corporations, such as Siemens, AEG, Olympia, and Zeiss, were formally using WF. It was becoming clear that WF would have to be adapted to the overall situation in Germany as well as to the specific environment within Siemens. To this end, Siemens formed a team of WF specialists. This study group applied Siemens' scientific human engineering research to psychological effects and specific operations in order to modify WF. This same group published a companion volume to the internal Siemens manual to enable the uniform use of WF across Siemens organizations (*Siemens Archiv Akten*, 16020, Aus Theorie und Praxis des Industrial Engineering in den USA, pp. 20, 22), and a document explaining WF was created in 1970 [*Siemens Archiv Akten*, 8679, Daten für die Gestaltung von Arbeitsplätzen (April 1970), Work-Factor-System (WF), Einführung].

8.2.4.2 Chemical Industry

Within the chemical industry, Glanzstoff decided to deploy WF in the REFA Institute training courses, and four-week basic and one-week information training courses were organized [*Rheinisch-Westfälisches Wirtschaftsarchiv zu Köln*, Abt 195, F5-5, Betriebsgebundene Work-Factor-Lehrgänge (15.5.1961)]. WF specialists from US consulting firms conducted practical and research work as part of the WF deployment. After a detailed examination of both WF and MTM methods, Glanzstoff pressed ahead in using the WF method [*Rheinisch-Westfälisches Wirtschaftsarchiv zu Köln*, Abt 195, F5-5, Anwendung des Work-Factor-Verfahrens bei Glanzstoff (12.12.1961), pp. 1–5].

A 1962 document by Glanzstoff's rationalization department showed that predetermined time methods such as WF and MTM were effective in making systematic improvements (*Rheinisch-Westfälisches Wirtschaftsarchiv zu Köln*, Abt 195, F5-5, Die Schrift der Rationalisierungsabteilung von 27.9.1962, p. 2). Time units of less than 1/1000 (0.06 s) became the elements of work analysis through film and predetermined time methods (WF and MTM). This was one reason BASF compared results from various time measurement devices using test film and high-speed camera photography and compared predetermined lengths of time as well (Lorenz 1962, p. 283). Deployment, however, varied by company. For example, Henkel used methods like IE to a very limited extent even in the second half of the 1960s (Hilger 2004, pp. 181–182).

With new methods such as IE, predetermined time methods were not negotiated between workers and those in charge of time measurements, as was the practice with the REFA methods. Instead, the use and modifications of performance measurements were negotiated between management and work councils that represented workers or between management and labor unions (Schmiede and Schudlich 1981, pp. 371–372). Despite tremendous opposition to certain aspects of the predetermined time method, labor unions did not oppose them in principle, which facilitated their implementation (Schmiede and Schudlich 1981, p. 362).

8.3 The Characteristics of Japanese and German Deployment of Industrial Engineering

8.3.1 *Japanese Deployment of Industrial Engineering*

Based on the foregoing discussions, this section will clarify Japanese and German characteristics in the deployment of industrial engineering. In terms of Japanese case first, the following elements can be isolated as the main characteristics of IE deployment.

(1) **Systematic efforts based on the cooperation of business associations**: In Japan, IE was promoted and developed by the sectors themselves, as in the case of the IE study committee in the iron and steel industry. There were no such efforts in other countries (Nihon tekko renmei junenshi henshu iinkai 1962, p. 612). This reflected a situation in which the results of process studies by institutions, such as REFA in Germany, did not exist in Japan.

(2) **Influence of function and role of supervisors at the workplace**: In Japan, first-line supervisors, who are comparable to foremen in the United States or meisters in Germany, did not exist. This shows that traditional IE was not utilized in factories and that the deployment of IE was still haphazard (Jyuji 1968, pp. 7–8). In addition, foremen in the United States had considerable authority compared with those in Japan (Kasahara and Tezuka 1963, p. 16; IE 1968, p. 11). Starting in the Yawata Iron and Steel Corporation in 1958, before being applied in many other companies, IE was systematically implemented in the workplace with the establishment of a line and staff organization with a general foreman system. Substantial power over subordinates was given to general foremen, and the function of IE was mainly absorbed into the staff organization. This process, in which the line manager (led by the general foreman) assumed the central role, became the primary function of IE (Yawata seitetsu kabushikigaisha shashi hensan iinkai 1981, pp. 706–707; Katsui 1968; Noguchi 1968, p. 177; Komatsu 1968, Sumitomo kinzoku kogyo kabushikigaisha shashi henshu iinkai 1967, pp. 169–170; Dai niji indasutoriaru enjiniaringu kokunai shisatsudan 1959, pp. 301–306). The general foreman thus became a principal figure in the implementation of IE sometimes being given responsibility for cost control, cost reductions, and overall labor management.

(3) **Development of small group activities at the workplace through IE**: In the field of IE in Japan, work measurement was a core concern in the 1950s and he 1960s (Ono 1968, p. 70). However, the work measurement that was so popular in the United States and Germany was not thought to be suitable for Japan, and many corporations focused entirely on continuous method engineering (Jyuji 1969, p. 2). Unlike in the US, where standard time was set in relation to wages and working hours, in Japan, it was also important to consider the number of work hours in the standard for making improvements and evaluating

results (Jyuji 1973a, p. 9; Jyuji 1973b, p. 47). Meanwhile, IE was implemented for quality control activities. For example, at the Kobe Steel Corporation, IE activities were developed as a part of its total quality control (TQC) effort to improve the company's constitution (Tekkokai 1964, p. 21).

(4) **The work standard in Japan versus the US**: In American-style work management, work standard and work time were regarded as work volume to be achieved by the worker as specified by the contract between management and worker. Conversely, in Japanese-style work management, the term only referred to the content of the work to be performed. Thus, it was more effective to use standard time not as a standard for evaluating the worker but as the "time criterion based on the established work standard." In the United States, in job design, the organization defines the nature of the job, after which it is assigned to an individual. In this case, job design forms the terms of the contract. However, Japanese-style job design presents the overall objective of the job and allows individuals a certain amount of flexibility (Jyuji 1973c, pp. 100–102).

(5) **Difference of emphasis in the use of predetermined time standard system between Japan and the US**: Regarding the use of a predetermined time standard system (PTS), for example, work improvement, cost accounting, and cost estimate were actively applied in the 1950s in both Japan and the United States. However, the application of IE in setting work methods (before shifting to production) was less pronounced in Japan than in the United States. In contrast, work planning of this kind and decisions regarding personnel were more pronounced in Japan than in the United States. In this case, emphasis on IE use differed greatly between the two countries (Indasutoriaru enjiniaringu 1959, p. 85).

(6) **IE as labor management**: In addition, IE was rolled out in connection with labor management functions. For example, different employment practices among Japanese corporations, such as the seniority wage system and lifetime employment, engendered inconsistent labor targets for IE (Ueda et al. 1967, p. 539). Furthermore, upon implementation of the work-factor method, most major Japanese manufacturers reformed wage systems, particularly wage rates along with job analysis (Inoue 1976, p. 29). IE was originally developed for work measurement and method improvement. However, it was eventually applied to a wider field in Japan (Wada and Jyuji 1967, p. 519; Nakayama et al. 1960, pp. 121–122).

(7) **The role of education of managers and supervisors**: There have been several cases in which American-style manager education and supervisor training, such as TWI (Training within Industry) and MTP (Management Training Program), were used to implement IE in Japan. For instance, at the Toyota Motor Corporation, TWI and MTP were used for full-scale standardization, and they were also introduced in subcontracting enterprises to make company-wide improvements (Toyota jidosha kogyo kabushikigaisha shashi henshu iinkai 1958, p. 417; Toyota jidosha kabushikigaisha 1987, p. 227; Wada 2009,

pp. 521–524; Fujimoto 1997, pp. 69, 117). The Yawata Iron and Steel Corporation also established a standard work method (Nihon tekko renmei sengo tekkoshi henshu iinkai 1959, p. 997). At the Fuji Electric Corporation, the introduction of TWI for training first-line supervisors enabled the effective development of IE (Fujidenkiseizo kabushikigaisha 1974, p. 225).

(8) **IE for top, middle, and lower management**: IE in Japan tends to be divided into three levels: (1) a central-office IE department that offers services for top management and general managers; (2) an IE department that provides services to the heads of production and plant managers; and (3) an IE section that offers services for individual workplaces (Daisanji Ai ii kokunai shisatsudan 1965, p. 153). In the mid-1960s in Japan, most IE development took place at the third level, with work improvements, setting a standard time, work sampling, work measurements, cost estimations, and design and management of inspection instruments as the core functions. At the second level, system engineering was carried out to some extent though not to the same extent as in the third level (Ueda 1966, pp. 1277–1278). However, IE was not effectively diffused from the top to the bottom levels of management (Block 1964, p. 515).

(9) **Insufficient recognition and operation by IE line managers**: Although the use of IE methods increased, there were still many problems in terms of the recognition of IE by line managers and operations by industrial engineers. IE efforts were thus, naturally, obstructed (Daisanji Ai ii kokunai shisatudan 1965, preface). The following five problems prevailed the field of IE: (1) activities regarding operation systems and control systems; (2) activities related to troubleshooting and improving existing systems; (3) rate of IE activities performed depending on the demands of line managers; (4) cases of high numbers of personnel in the IE section; and (5) inadequate or no company-wide IE deployment (Daisanji Ai ii kokunai shisatsudan 1965, pp. 177–178). Furthermore, in Japan, although the number of universities with IE sections in engineering departments had increased, IE education was advanced considerably late compared with that in the United States (Daisanji Ai ii kokunai shisatsudan 1965, pp. 146–147).

(10) **Development of IE including suppliers under Japanese subcontracting system**: In Japan, the large-scale presence of parts companies and cooperating firms, such as subcontracting firms, supported the production system of large enterprises. In these enterprises as well, detailed rationalization and improvement activities were promoted through the introduction of IE (Tsusho sangyosho gorika shingikai 1967, p. 79; Miyajima 1967, p. 331). Guidance and instruction in setting standards by large enterprises were a significant reason for building close inter-firm relationships and establishing production networks under Japanese subcontracting firms.

(11) **Influence of nationality and climate**: In the introduction of IE, differences in the material traits and climates of Japan and the United States were significant. Among the many management techniques introduced from the United States, management methods directly related to aspects such as quality control (QC) and value analysis (VA) were taking root by the latter half of the 1960s.

However, in the implementation of IE, different conditions can be observed between Japan and the United States due to a gap in the delegation of authority and accountability to the production site. In American companies, work began after responsibilities were prescribed and the authority of each member was predetermined. In contrast, vague organizational systems were in place and responsibilities were discussed after the work had begun in several cases in Japanese enterprises (Dai sanji Ai ii kokunai shisatsudan 1965, p. 150; Tshusho sangyosho kigyokyoku 1969, pp. 105–106, 133). Even at the end of the 1960s, in Japanese industry, the recognition of management, including IE, was insufficient as the responsibilities of front-line supervisors remained uncertain. Thus, it was necessary to establish management standards for front-line supervisors and clarify certain responsibilities (Tsusho sangyosho kigyokyoku 1969, p. 112). In the US, companies pragmatically searched for solutions by focusing on methods without establishing particular theorems and systems. In other words, once a new method was developed, it was widely used as the "standard." In contrast, such a spirit of pragmatism did not exist in Japan (Kuroita 1959, pp. 317–319).

8.3.2 German Deployment of Industrial Engineering

Next, characteristics of the German IE deployment are examined. The following items can be pointed out as the main characteristics of IE deployment.

(1) **Emphasis on the production management function**: Compared to Japan, Germany placed greater emphasis on the production management function. Moreover, Germany had the benefit of organizations such as the REFA, which were engaged in process studies and were an important factor in the IE rollout and in terms of the harmonization of German and American elements.
(2) **Characteristics of IE organization**: In Germany, even as late as the mid-1970s, it was rare that IE functions were exclusively performed by IE departments (Simon 1976, p. 116). While in the United States, industrial engineers were assigned to the staff departments, in Germany, they were assigned to the production lines (Fortschrittliche Betriebsführung und Industrial Engineering 1977, p. 354).
(3) **Educational background of IE engineers**: Even at the end of the 1960s only 13% of German staff in departments of work study, time study, and process planning were university graduate engineers as opposed to 46% in the United States (Schlaich 1969b, p. 5). Furthermore, institutions that trained IE personnel, such as REFA in Germany, were concerned about the low percentage of IE engineers graduating from their programs among the total number of engineers.
(4) **Involvement and influence of REFA**: American methods such as WF and MTM were strongly promoted by REFA, along with the cooperation of the Work-Factor Company, the German MTM Association, consultants, and others. Between the late 1950s and the first half of the 1960s, the considerable US

supremacy in terms of IE had greatly lessened compared with similar standard methods used in other progressive industrial countries (Hartmann 1963, p. 125). However, REFA had traditionally played an important role in Germany since the rationalization movement of the 1920s. Schlaich (1969a, p. 234) notes that, from an operational perspective, it is only natural that the spread of IE can mainly be attributed to REFA. A 1960 report by Hämmerling (1960, p. 127) noted that there were certainly efforts to reduce production times through a partial adoption of new methods such as MTM and WF, based on US practice, but these methods would not have succeeded without their incorporation into REFA's methods. A 1975 report by Schwartzman (Schwartmann 1975, p. 205) noted that German industry had built work studies based on REFA practices over the last several decades.

The dissemination of IE was related to REFA activities and was also greatly affected by US-based IE. REFA had long examined various predetermined time methods, including MTM and WF; based on the results, it had decided to support WF, obtaining a license to use and disseminate this method (Jaeckel 1961, p. 223; Pilz 1961, p. 124). However, REFA did not, for the most part, deprioritize its own systems in promoting WF. In relation to the aspect of hybridization, the following mix of American and German factors in management and production systems can be observed. Industrial engineering methods such as the Work-Factor Method and Methods-Time Measurement were incorporated into the traditional German REFA system. As a result, these US methods were not widely adopted in German industry, unlike in countries such as Sweden, where the creators of MTM, H. B. Maynard and his consulting firm, were highly successful in selling the method to corporations (Kipping 2004, p. 36). Thus, regarding the broad spread of American IE methods, a delay can be seen compared to Japan. In addition, the differences in the selection of the WF method or MTM among industries and enterprises were considerable.

In general, small and medium-sized firms in Germany enjoyed predominance over American competitors in the field of IE based on the existence of REFA and its unified theory and education practices. REFA also greatly improved productivity in the German economy by helping establish and maintain a relatively high level of IE in the country. Meanwhile, an organization with a unified theory and educational program, such as the Federation of Industrial Engineering in Germany, was not created in the United States (Fortschrittliche Betriebsführung und Industrial Engineering 1976, p. 342).

Therefore, procuring training and deployment routes for IE methodologies, such as the agreement with Work-Factor Company or the use of consulting firms, provided greater opportunities for the use of American-style methods compared with other management methods. Additionally, German organizations played a major part, as evident in the efforts and roles of REFA and the German MTM Association. However, the deployment and dissemination of American-style methods continued with the assistance of REFA's leadership in work studies and their activities in the 1920s, along with the attempts to apply these methods to German settings under REFA's strong influence.

In the postwar boom years, emphasis was placed on REFA activities in job design, work measurement, and work evaluation; by the 1970s, management organization issues had become the focus (Schelm 2004, pp. 14–16, 18). However, in Germany, even in the mid-1960s, techniques and methods in the field of business management, especially IE, did not always progress (Tokimura 1965, p. 730). Under such conditions, the deployment of IE continued to be based on work measurement rather than on the application of IE methods in various fields. Furthermore, the generalization and systematization of IE did not progress as it did in Japan.

8.4 Reframing in the Deployment of Industrial Engineering in Japan and Germany

Building upon the preceding analyses, this section explores the "reframing" in the deployment of IE in Japan and Germany.

A certain level of hybridization between American and Japanese elements can be observed in the introduction of the job-based wages under the rubric of the work-factor method. Use of standard work time was combined with job improvement and contributed to the development of improvement efficiency.

When examining the deployment of IE in Japan, with regard to important factors that affected the implementation of American management methods it is important to take into account influences of management values, traditions, and cultures. Particularly significant are Japanese collectivism and the mutual trust between members of a company, relationships between management and labor influenced by weak contracting. Work standards tended to be used not as the terms of workers' contracts but a loose standard. Standard work time was used as a benchmark in establishing goals evaluating the results of job improvement by general foremen. Management values emphasizing the role of production spots and relationships between management and labor based on weak contracting (organization and its operation in which relations of authorities and responsibilities were unclear) influenced the implementation of IE in Japan.

In reality, there were many cases in which the Japanese method of management was pursued, while mechanisms and principles for improving efficiency were introduced. In particular, owing to the influence of Japanese corporate traditions and management values, many Japanese companies opted for Japanese-style adaptation. Management values emphasizing the role of production spots, relationships between management and labor based on weak contracting, management systems such as the general foreman system, and the development of mass production based on flow production system and automation were prominent.

Evaluating the results, various systemic factors within companies, between enterprises, and in terms of industrial relations also influenced the Americanization of management methods. Special systems, such as subcontracting, influenced the deployment of American management methods. Such cases can be observed in the deployment and modifications of IE in subcontracting firms and affiliated companies under the leadership of large enterprises that were at the top of the pyramid of the subcontracting system. Other cases can be seen in the role of business associations in promoting the deployment of IE and influencing management systems such as the general foreman system.

Prior to WWII, there had been a significant delay in the development of productive forces in the heavy industries and the process and assembly industries in Japan. The heavy and chemical industries, as well as the durable consumer goods industry, rapidly expanded after the war. Introduction of the flow production system and innovations including automation promoted the deployment of IE methods. In Japan, IE was implemented in the form of various rationalization measures, such as production control, cost control for production modernization, and to decrease costs by means of rapid development of productive forces.

Regarding the influence of industrial structure, in Japan, rapid development and expansion of the heavy and chemical industries and the durable consumer goods industries after the war made the deployment of IE important for the improvement of efficiency and thorough rationalization.

Meanwhile, in Germany, considering the harmonization of American and German elements, IE methods were integrated into the German REFA. Such hybridization can be observed in the development of work studies based on REFA practices despite the strong influence of IE.

In Germany, in contrast to Japan, the Americanization process had been extensively reframed to suit Germany. The Taylor system, created in the US, had been modified to fit with the REFA system already in the 1920s (Pechhold 1974, p. 56) and this management tradition and experience enabled German enterprises to adapt elements of the American model for the local environment. This tradition of hybridization and adaptation greatly influenced the successful deployment of IE in the German case.

Insofar as the institutional factors influencing the German-style adaptations of American methods are concerned, the issues of various materials and the establishment of ideas related to the definition, classification, and subdivision of standard time by REFA contributed to improvements at the industry level. In contrast, such a technically authoritative national organization did not exist in Japan (Hamabe 1961, p. 46), and management centers and IE centers were only established during the research boom (the management boom and IE boom that took place in the latter half of the 1950s) (Omura 1959a, p. 33). Such differences had a significant effect on the introduction and development of IE in both countries, especially in the embodiment of the IE methods in REFA. In general, small and medium-sized firms in Germany enjoyed predominance over American competitors in the field of IE on the basis of the existence of REFA and its unified theory and education. REFA also greatly improved productivity in the German economy by helping establish and maintain a relatively high level of IE in the country. Meanwhile, an organization with a unified theory and educational program, such as the Federation of Industrial Engineering in Germany, was not created in the United States (Fortschrittliche Betriebsführung und Industrial Engineering 1976, p. 342). Thus, in Germany, path dependency appeared more prominently than in Japan.

Industrial structure also played an important part in contrast to Japan, in Germany, the metal industry, and the process and assembly industries were already developed from the prewar era and further developed and expanded after the war. Such situations promoted the deployment of IE and the involvement of elements of methods like these into the REFA system.

As discussed above, the deployment of American-style management methods relied on innovative learning and attempts to adapt American models to the local environment. Thus, there are significant issues such as Japanese and German corporate attitudes, responses, and the nature of the actual deployments in response to American management methods and systems; changes in business management itself with the deployment of management education; and the effect of Japanese or German business management characteristics on specialized processes.

Regarding the conditions surrounding the introduction of IE in Japan and Germany during the postwar boom years as well as "reframing" and the factors defining, Table 8.1 shows an inline comparison of the respective countries, based on the discussion so far in this chapter.

Table 8.1 Comparison of conditions surrounding the introduction of Industrial Engineering in Japan and Germany

Deployment and factors affecting them	Management methods	
	Industrial engineering	
	Japanese management methods	German management methods
Overall conditions in the deployment of American management methods	• Use of IE with two pillars of work measurement and method engineering • Broad deployment of IE mainly in the industrial sectors, such as the iron and steel industry, the electrical industry, and the automobile industry • Wider diffusion of WF than MTM • Delay in fixation of IE due to low ability and role of industrial engineers and diffusion of principles emphasizing production spots • Delay in fixation of classic IE and deployment of primary IE activities due to lack of first-line supervisors, such as foremen in the US and the Meister in Germany • Deployment of IE in subcontracting firms and affiliated companies as well as large corporations	• Deployments focused on WF and MTM • Deployments focused on processing and assembly, steel and metal, chemical, shipbuilding, and clothing industries • The delay in the spread of IE relative to other countries • Inter-industry and inter-corporate differences in the selection of WF and MTM

(continued)

Table 8.1 (continued)

Deployment and factors affecting them	Management methods	
	Industrial engineering	
	Japanese management methods	German management methods
Deployment characteristics of American management methods	• Important role of IE in method engineering • Deployment of IE with the introduction of flow production system and innovations (in particular automation) • Deployment of IE based on business contracts with the Work-Factor Company • Attempts to synthesize and systematize IE and delay in their progress • Promotion of IE by strong cooperation of the entire business world • Deployment of IE as various rationalization measures, such as production control and cost control • Deployment of IE combined with functions of labor management • Training of IE staff using American methods of manager and supervisor education, such as TWI and MTP • Absorption of IE functions into staff departments under the general foreman system	• Strong involvement and leadership of the REFA (e.g., IE introduction, launch of education courses, etc.) • REFA's prioritization of their own system • Deployments based on REFA's license agreement with the Work-Factor Company • The establishment of the German MTM Association and its effort
Modifications in American management methods	• Use of work standard not as the terms of workers' contracts but a loose standard • Use of standard work time as a standard in establishing goals of job improvement by general foremen and evaluating the results	• Creation and development of work study based on REFA thinking despite the influence of IE • Case of the application of human engineering research (Siemens)
Amalgamation of American and Japanese elements	• Introduction of the job-based wage under the deployment of WF	• Integration of IE methods into the REFA system

(continued)

Table 8.1 (continued)

Deployment and factors affecting them		Management methods	
		Industrial engineering	
		Japanese management methods	German management methods
Factors of modification of American management method	Influence of traditions, cultural factors, and management values	• Management values emphasizing the role of production spots • Relationships between management and labor based on weak contracting view (organization and its operation in which relations of authorities and responsibilities were unclear)	• Traditional German adaptations through modifications of the Taylor system to REFA in the 1920s
	Influence of institutional factors	• Role of business associations in promoting deployment of IE • Influences of management systems such as the general foreman system • Expansion of deployment of IE into small and medium enterprises under the subcontracting system	• Systematic foundation of REFA efforts in time and work studies • Promotion of implementation and execution based on acceptable views by unions • Case of implementation and execution through work agreements with work councils
	Influencing factors of the productive forces	—	—
	Influence of industrial structure factors	• Rapid development and expansion of the heavy and chemical industries and the durable consumer goods industries after World War II	• Development of the metals industry and the processing and assembly industries since the prewar era • Postwar development and expansion in the processing and assembly industries
	Influence of market structure factors	—	—

Source This table was compiled by the author, based on discussions in this chapter

References

Arlt J (1978) Erfahrungen und Tendenzen bei der MTM-Anwendung. Ein Bericht aus der Automobilindustrie. In: REFA-Nachrichten 31(3):143–147

Billhardt H (1962) Der Arbeitsablauf als Ansatzpunkte zur Rationalisierung. In: REFA-Nachrichten 15(6):249–254

Birn SA (1968) Ein Amerikaner sieht Europas Wirtschaft. Wichtigstes Problem: Mangel an Rationalisierungsfachleuten. In: Der Arbeitgeber 20(9):234–236

Bijinesu (1960) Kindai keiei no hanagata (Leading model of modern management). In: Bijinesu (business) 4(5):67–79

Block SM (1964) "Dentoteki IE" to "gendaiteki IE" no baransu wo kataru (Balance of "traditional" IE and "modern" IE). In: Indasutoriaru enjiniaringu (Ind Eng) 6(6):514–520

Bramesfeld E (1960) Arbeitswissenschaft und Betrieb. In: Stahl und Eisen 80(19):1257–1261

Dai niji indasutoriaru enjiniaringu kokunai shisatsudan (1959) Dai niji indasutoriaru enjiniaringu kokunai shisatsudan hokokusyo (Report of second industrial engineering domestic inspection team). Nihon seisansei honbu, Nihon indasutoriaru enjiniaringu kyokai, Tokyo

Dai sanji IE kokunai shisatsudan (1965) Nihon ni okeru IE no doko (Trend of IE in Japan). Nihon indasutoriarugu enjiniaringu kyokai, Kanto indasutoriaru enjiniaringu kyokai, Tokyo

Deininger (1962) Arbeitsstudium als Rationalisierungshilfe. In: Rationalisierung 13(6):146–147

Deutsche MTM Vereinigung e.V. (ed) (2002) MTM—Von Anfang an richtig. Deutsche MTM Vereinigung, Hamburug

Erdmann W (1969) Möglichkeiten und Grenzen der Zeitvorgabe bei Instandhaltungsarbeiten. Bericht uber Ergebnisse eines RKW-Unterschungsprojektes. In: REFA-Nachrichten 22(5):309–318

Fortschrittliche Betriebsführung und Industrial Engineering (1976) IE-Gespräch. In: Fortschrittliche Betriebsführung und Ind Eng 25(6):338–342

Fortschrittliche Betriebsführung und Industrial Engineering (1977) IE-Gespräch. In: Fortschrittliche Betriebsführung und Ind Eng 26(6):354–360

Free J (1955) Maschinenbau und Rationalisierung. In: Brandt L, Frenz G (eds) Industrielle Rationalisierung 1955. Verkehrs- und Wirtschaft-Verlag, Dortmund, pp 67–70

Fuji denki seizo kabushikigaisha (1974) Fuji denki shashi II (1957–1973) (History of Fuji Electric Co. Ltd. II 1957–1973). Fuji denki seizo kabushikigaisha, Tokyo

Fujimoto T (1997) Seisan Sisutemu no Sinka Ron (Evolution of production system). Yuhikaku, Tokyo

Furukawa H, Maeda S, Wada E et al (1961) Obei to wagakuni ni okeru IE kyoiku no genjyo (The present condition of IE education in Europe, the US, and Japan). In: IE Rev 9:103–122

Goji K et al (supvr), Noda K (ed) (1969) Gendai keieishi (Modern business history). Nihon seisansei honbu, Tokyo

Hachimaki N (1958) Denki kikai kogyo to indasutoriaru enjiniaringu (Electric engineering industry and industrial engineering). In: PR 9(2):27–32

Hamabe K (1961) Kokkateki na kiban wo motsu Doistu no ukeoi seido (Contracting system with a national foundation in Germay). In: Indasutoriaru enjiniaringu (Ind Eng) 3(6):457–462

Hämmerling F (1960) Die Mechanisierung von Montagen in der Elektroindustrie. In: Brandt L, Gardellini R, King A et al (eds) Industrielle Rationalisierung 1960. Verkehrs- und Wirtschafts-Verlag, Dortmund

Hartmann H (1963) Amerikanische Firmen in Deutschland: Beobachtungen über Kontakte und Kontraste zwischen Industriegesellschaften. Westdeutecher Verlag, Köln, Opladen

Hibi S (1975) Seisan kanri ron (Production management). Dobunkan shuppan, Tokyo

Hilger S (2004) „Amerikanisierung" deutscher Unternehmen. Wettbewerbsstrategien und Unternehmenspolitik bei Henkel, Siemens und Daimler-Benz (1945/49–1975). Franz Steiner Verlag, Stuttagart

Hopf H (1979) Die Anwendung von MTM-Analysiersystemen in der Bekleidungs- und Maschinenindustrie. In: REFA-Nachrichten 32(2):67–73

IE (1968) Foaman no niche ou bei kakusa wo kataru (Differences in foremen in Japan, Europe, and the US). In: IE 10(5):8–17
IE mondai kenkyukai (1975a) Gendai IEr no isiki to sono jittai. Tekko hen (Conciousness of modern IEr and his actual conditions: the iron and steel industry edition). In: IE Rev 16(3):77–79
IE mondai kenkyukai (1975b) Gendai IEr no isiki to sono jittai. Denki sangyo hen (Conciousness of modern IEr and his actual conditions. the electric industry edition). In: IE Rev 16(4):99–101
IE mondai kenkyukai (1975c) Gendai IEr no isiki to sono jittai—Tekkogyo to denki sangyo ni okeru IE to ningen mondai—(Conciousness of modern IEr and his actual conditions—IE and human problems in the iron and steel industry and electric industry—). In: IE Rev 16(5):138–140
Metall IG (1965) Geschaftsbericht 1962, 1963 und 1964 des Vorstandes der Industriegewerkschaft Metall für die Bundesrepublik Deutschland. IG Metall, Frankfurt am Main
Ikenaga K (1962) Seisan wo takameru kihonteki IE katsudo (Fundamental IE activities for increasing production). In: Indasutoriaru enjiniaringu (Ind Eng) 4(8):785–790
Indasutoriaru enjiniaringu (1959) PTS (kitei jikan hyojun) wa do katsuyo sarete iruka [How is PTS (predetermined time standard) used?]. In: Indasutoriaru enjiniaringu (Ind Eng) 1(2):81–90
Indasutoriaru enjiniaringu kokunai shisatsudan (1958) Indasutoriaru enjiniaringu kokunai shisatsudan hokokusho (Report of inspection team of industrial engineering). Nihon seisansei honbu, Tokyo
Inoue H (1976) Nihon ni okeru IE no tenkai to mujun (Development and contradiction of IE in Japan). In: Gijutsu to ningen (technol Human Being) 6:26–34
Jaeckel B (1961) 10 Jahre REFA-Bundesverband. In: REFA-Nachrichten 14(6):221–226
Jyuji S (1968) Rain kanbu no IE jissen ron (Practice of IE by line managers). In: Indasutoriaru enjiniaringu (Ind Eng) 10(2):4–9
Jyuji S (1969) Futatsu no sinro wo toru korekarano IE (The two future pathways for IE). In: IE 11(3):2–5
Jyuji S (1973a) Koten IE wa foaman no mono (Traditional foremen's IE). In: IE 15(5):3–10
Jyuji S (1973b) "Nihonryu" wo tsukuridasu tameni (To create "Japanese style IE"). In: IE 15(11):47–53
Jyuji S (1973c) Hito wo ikasu tameni wa mazu soshiki kaihatsu wo (Organizational development is important for making the best use of a person). In: IE 15(12):97–104
Kasahara S, Tezuka N (1963) Amerika no IE no genjyo (The present condition of American IE). In: IE Rev 20:5–29
Katsui H (1968) Atarashii sagyocho wa kono yoni sodatsu (New general foreman grows in this way). In: IE 10(5):18–24
Kikuchi T (1968) Kakusha ni okeru IE no jissi rei (Cases of implementing IE in each company). In: Nihon indasutoriaru enjiniaringu kyokai (ed) IE giho hando bukku (Handbook of IE technique). Maruzen, Tokyo, pp 559–603
Kipping K (2004) 'Importing' American ideas to West Germany, 1940s to 1970s. From associations to private consultancies. In: Kudo A, Kipping M, Schröter HG (eds) German and Japanese business in the boom years. Transforming American management and technology models. Routledge, London, pp 30–53
Kirchner J-H (1970) Förderung der Produktivität in Mittel- und Kleinbetrieben durch das Arbeitsstudium. In: REFA-Nachrichten 23(6):440
Komatsu H (1968) Sagyocho seido (General forman system). Rodo horei kyokai, Tokyo
Konno T (1982) WF (Work Factor) ho oyobi MTM no donyu (Deployment of WF (Work Factor) method and MTM). In: Nihon noritsu kyokai (ed) Keiei to tomoni. Nihon noritsu kyokai konsarutingu gijyutsu yonjunen (With management. 40-year history of consulting technique of Japan Management Association). Nihon noritsu kyokai, Tokyo, pp 226–228
Kothe E (1948) Sind Arbeitsstudien noch zeitgemaβ? In: Werkstatt und Betrieb 81:10–11
Kuroita S (1959) IE to kokuminsei (IE and nationality). In: Sakamoto F, Noda K, Matsuda T et al (supvr) Indasutoriaru enjiniaringu (Industrial engineering), Chuo koronsha, Tokyo, pp 317–322

Kyushu indasutoriaru enjiniaringu kokunain shisatsudan (1959) Kyushu indasutoriaru enjiniaringu kokunain shisatsudan hokokusho (Report of the Kyushu industrial engineering inspection team). Nihon seisansei honbu, Seisansei kyushu chiho honbu, Fukuoka

Lorenz FR (1962) Zur Frage der Erfassung kurzer Zeiten bei Arbeits- und Zeitstudien. In: Werkstatt und Betrieb 95(5):283–287

Maynard HB, Stegemerten GJ, Schwab JL (1948) Methods-time-measurement. McGrow-Hill, NewYork

Mergner U, Osterland M, Pelte K (1974) Die Entwicklung ausgewählter Arbeitsbedingungen in der BRD. Soziologisches Forschungsinstitut Gottingen, Gottingen

Miharada S (1965) IE heno kaigan to sono tenkai (Exploring IE and its development). In: Bijinesu (Business) 9(4):28–29

Mitsubishi denk kabushikigaisha shashi hensansitsu (ed) (1982) Mitsubishi denki shashi (Company history of Mitsubishi Electric Corporation). Soritsu rokujushunen. Mitsubishi denki kabushikigaisha, Tokyo

Miyajima S (1963) Tosha no IE katsudo: Kakudai sareta yakuwari wo motta IE bu no sechi to sono kino (IE activities of this firm: Establishment of IE department with enlarged role and function). In: IE Rev 23:229–240

Miyajima S (1967) IE wo seiko sasu niwa (To achieve success in IE). In: IE Rev 8(6):325–334

Nakayama T, Niizaki K, Suzuki T et al (1960) IE katsudo no genjyo to mondaiten. Zoku (The present condition of IE activities and problems, 2). In: Indasutoriaru enjiniaringu (Ind Eng) 2(2):121–128

Nihon seisansei honbu (ed) (1956) Tekko. Tekko seisansei shisatsudan hokokusho (The iron and steel industry. Report of the inspection team for the iron and steel industry). Nihon seisansei honbu, Tokyo

Nihon seisansei honbu (ed) (1960) Amerika no indasutoriaru enjiniaringu (American industrial engineering). Nihon seisansei honbu, Tokyo

Nihon seisansei honbu (ed) (1964) Indasutoriaru enjiniaringu. Indasutoriaru manejimento senmon shisatsudan hokokusho (Industrial engineering. Report of the special inspection team for industrial management). Nihon seisansei honbu, Tokyo

Nihon tekko renmei IE shiryo kenkyukai (1958) Indasutoriaru enjiniaringu no kenkyu to donyu ni tsuite (Study and deployment of industrial engineering). In: PR 9(2):33–40

Nihon tekko renmei jimukyoku et al (1962) Showa sanjurokunen no nihon tekkogyo kaiko (Retrospect of iron and steel industry in Japan in 1961). In: Tekkokai (Iron and Steel World) 12(5):6–78

Nihon tekko renmei jimukyoku et al (1963) Showa sanjunananen no nihon tekkogyo kaiko (Retrospect of iron and steel industry in Japan in 1962). In: Tekkokai (Iron and Steel World) 13(5):12–89

Nihon tekko renmei jimukyoku et al (1966) Showa yonjunen no nihon tekkogyo kaiko (Retrospect of iron and steel industry in Japan in 1965). In: Tekkokai (Iron and Steel World) 16(5):22–107

Nihon tekko renmei jimukyoku et al (1967) Showa yonjuichnen no nihon tekkogyo kaiko (Retrospect of iron and steel industry in Japan in 1966). In: Tekkokai (Iron and Steel World) 17(5):12–103

Nihon tekko renmei jimukyoku et al (1968) Showa yonjuninen no nihon tekkogyo kaiko (Retrospect of iron and steel industry in Japan in 1967). In: Tekkokai (Iron and Steel World) 18(5):12–107

Nihon tekko renmei jimukyoku et al (1972) Showa yonjurokunen no nihon tekkogyo kaiko (Retrospect of iron and steel industry in Japan in 1971). In: Tekkokai (Iron and Steel World) 22(5):12–110

Nihon tekko renmei jimukyoku et al (1974) Showa yonjuhachinen no nihon tekkogyo kaiko (Retrospect of iron and steel industry in Japan in 1973). In: Tekkokai (Iron and Steel World) 124(5):16–110

Nihon tekko renmei jimukyoku et al (1975) Showa yonjukyunen no nihon tekkogyo kaiko (Retrospect of iron and steel industry in Japan in 1974). In: Tekkokai (Iron and Steel World) 25(5):16–119

Nihon tekko renmei jimukyoku et al (1976) Showa gojunen no nihon tekkogyo kaiko (Retrospect of iron and steel industry in Japan in 1975). In: Tekkokai (Iron and Steel World) 26(5):6–93
Nihon tekko renmei jimukyoku et al (1978) Showa gojuninen no nihon tekkogyo kaiko. (Retrospect of iron and steel industry in Japan in 1977). In: Tekkokai (Iron and Steel World) 28(5):2–97
Nihon tekko renmei sengo tekkoshi henshu iinkai (ed) (1959) Sengo tekkoshi (History of Iron and steel industry after World War II). Nihon tekko renmei, Tokyo
Nihon tekko renmei tekko junenshi henshu iinkai (ed) (1969) Tekkko junenshi—Showa sanjusannen-yonjuninen (Ten-year history of the iron and steel industry from 1958 to 1967). Nihon tekkko renmei, Tokyo
Nissan jidosha kabushikigaisha somubu chosaka (ed) (1965) Nissan jidosha sanjunenshi (30-year history of Nissan Motor Corporation), Nissan jidosha kabushikigaisha, Yokohama
Noguchi T (1968) Seisan kanri no keieigaku (Business administration of production management). Zeimu keiri kyokai, Tokyo
Noguchi T, Ishizaka I, Sekiguchi M et al (1965) Keiei kanri soron (General remarks on business management). Chuo keizaisha, Tokyo
Omura M (1959a) Gijutsu senta wo chusin ni IE katsudo wo tenkai. Fuji tsushinki kawasaki kojyo (Development of IE activities with a focus on technical centers. Fuji Communication Equipment Company, Kawasaki factory). In: Indasutoriaru enjiniaringu (Ind Eng) 1(1):32–39
Omura M (1959b) Gijutsubu wo chushin ni haba no hiroi IE katsudo wo tenkai. Nissan jidosha honsha kojyo (Development of broad IE activities with a focus on the technical department. Nissan Motor Corporation, head office factory). In: Indasutoriaru enjiniaringu (Ind Eng) 1(2):97–104
Omura M (1959c) Sujimichi no toutta kanri shisutemu wo mezasu—Toyo kogyo kabusikigaisha—(Aiming for a cost-effective management system—Toyo Kogyo Industry Co. Ltd.—). In: Indasutoriaru enjiniaringu (Ind Eng) 1(7):445–454
Omura M (1960) Soshikika sareta zenshoteki IE katsudo wo tenkai—. Mitsubishi denki itami seisakusho—(Development of organized IE activities in the whole factory—Mitsubishi Electric Corporation Itami factory—). In: Indasutoriaru enjiniaringu (Ind Eng) 2(3):165–177
Omura M (1961) Zosan taisei ni michakku sita IE katsudo. Fuji denki seizo kabusiki gaisha Kawasaki kojyo (IE activities appropriate for increasing production. Fuji Electric Co. Ltd., Kawasaki factory). In: Indasutoriaru enjiniaringu (Ind Eng) 3(3):189–198
Omura M (1962) Nichibei no IE hikaku (Comparison of IE in Japanese and the US). In: Indasutoriaru enjiniaringu (Ind Eng) 4(10):914–926
Omura M (1969) Jittai kara mita nanajunendai no IE katsudo no hoko (Trend of IE activities in the 1970s from the viewpoint of actual conditions). In: IE 11(7):11–17
Ono S (1959) WF ho ni yoru hyojyun jikan settei rei (Cases of determinating time using the WF method). In: Indasutoriaru enjiniaringu (Ind Eng) 1(1):60–67
Ono S (1968) Kakusya ni okeru IE no jisshi rei. Tekko kogyo ni okeru jissirei (Cases of implementing IE in each company. The iron and steel industry). In: Nihon indasutoriaru enjiniaringu kyokai (ed) IE giho hando bukku (Handbook of IE technique). Maruzen, Tokyo, pp 659–680
Ono S (1970) Sogoteki IE katsudo no tenkai wo (Necessity for developing total IE activities). In: IE 12(10):26–31
Ozaki T (1959) Amerika no IE katsudo to nihon no genjyo (IE activities in the United States and the present condition in Japan). In: Indasutoriaru enjiniaringu (Ind Eng) (6):362–366
Pavel K-H (1957) Formen und Methoden der Rationalisierung. Verlag die Wirtschaft, Berlin
Pechhold E (1956) Weitere Ergebnisse der IfO-Erhebung über die Verbreitung des Arbeitsstudiums. In: REFA-Nachrichten 9(4):147
Pechhold E (1974) 50 Jahre REFA. Beuth, Berlin, Köln, Frankfut am Main
Pilz HE (1961) Die Einführung des Work-Factor-System in Deutschland. In: REFA-Nachrichten 14(4):124–125
Quick JH, Ikenaga K (1965) WF to sagyo sokutei (WF and work measurement). In: Indasutoriaru enjiniaring (Ind Eng) 7(12):1100–1106

Rau R (1968) Die Anwendung von MTM in einem Unternehmen der deutschen Kraftfahrzeug-Zubehör-Industrie. In: Pornschlegel H (ed) Verfahren vorbestimmter Zeiten. Bund-Verlag, Koln, pp 168–176
REFA-Nachrichten (1956) Die Verbreitung des Arbeitsstudiums und die Bedeutung der REFA-Arbeit in Zahlen. In: REFA-Nachrichten 9(3):91–94
REFA-Nachrichten (1962) Rationalisierung durch vorbestimmte Zeit. Bericht über die REFA-Tagung am 20 Juni 1962 in Darmstadt. In: REFA-Nachrichten 15(6):254–258
REFA-Nachrichten (1964) 40 Jahre REFA. Festvortrag von Dipl.-Ing. Antoni, Vorsitzer des REFA-Bundesverbandes, auf der Abschlußveranstaltung am 23. Mai 1964 in Hannover. In: REFA-Nachrichten 17(4):184–186
REFA-Nachrichten (1970) Geschaftsbericht des Verbandes fur Arbeitsstudien—REFA—e.v. für die Zeit vom 1. Januar bis 31. Dezember 1969. In: REFA-Nachrichten 23(3):177
Sakano T (1963) Tosha no kosuto daun hosaku to IE (Cost reduction measurements in this company and IE). In: IE Rev 23:219–228
Sato R (1959) Denki kogo (Electrical industry). In: Sakamoto F, Noda K, Matsuda T et al (supvr) Indasutoriaru enjiniaringu (Industrial engineering), Chuo koronsha, Tokyo, pp 263–270
Schelm B (2004) 80 Jahre REFA. In: REFA-Nachrichten 57 (3): 8–34
Schlaich K (1969a) Die Anpassung der Aufgaben und Methoden des Arbeitsstudiums an die wirtschaftliche und technische Entwicklung. In: REFA-Nachrichten 22(4):229–234
Schlaich K (1969b) Inhalt und Chancen des Industrial Engineering in der deutschen Wirtschaft. In: REFA-Nachrichten 22(1):1–7
Schmiede R, Schudlich E (1981) Die Entwicklung der Leistungsentlohnung in Deutschland. Ein historisch-theoretische Untersuchung zum Verhaltnis von Lohn und Leistung unter kapitalistischen Produktionsbedingungen, 4th edn. Campus, Frankfurt am Main
Schwartmann J (1975) Praktische Arbeitsgestaltung in der Automobilindustrie. In: REFA-Nachrichten 28(4):205–207
Shida M (1968) Nihon no IE koristsu wa naze hikui (Why is IE efficiency low in Japan?). In: IE 10(3):10–16
Simon W (1976) Aufgaben des Industrial Engineering und Eingliederung in die Unternehmensstruktur. In: Fortschrittliche Betriebsführung und Ind Eng 25(2):116–118
Sumitomo kinzoku kogyo kabushikigaisha shashi henshu iinkai (ed) (1967) Sumitomo kinzoku kogyo saikin junenshi (History of the last ten years of Sumitomo Metall Industry Industries Ltd.). Sumitomo kinzoku kogyo kabushikigaisha, Osaka
Takai K, Tanaka T, Akiniwa M et al (1968) IE no kibo wo kataru (I) [Expectations for IE (I)]. In: IE Rev 9(1):6–13
Takeda T (1967) Kihonteki IE katsudo no jissen wo teisho suru (Proposal of fundamental IE activities). In: Indasutoriaru enjiniaringu (Ind Eng) 9(6):579–584
Taniguchi K (1967) Jittai chosa yori mita kigyonai IE katsudo no nichibei hikaku (Comparion of IE activities in Japan and the United States based on an investigation of actual conditions). In: Indasutoriaru enjiniaringu (Ind Eng) 9(12):1196–1205
Tekkokai (1957) Indasutoriaru enjiniaringu to nihon no tekkogyo (Industrial engineering and the Japanese iron and steel industry). In: Tekkokai (Iron and Steel World) 7(11):34–43
Tekkokai (1964) Wagasha ni okeru IE katsudo no genkyo. Kabushikigaisha Kobe seikosho no maki (The present conditions of IE activities in this company. Kobe Steel Ltd.). In: Tekkokai (Iron and Steel World) 14(6):21–23
Tekko no IE (1984) Showa gojuhachinen tekko kakusha no IE katsudo (IE activity in each iron and steel company in 1983). In: Tekko no IE (Ind Eng Iron Steel Ind) 22(2):12–17
Tokimura K (1965) Yoroppa no IE jijyo (IE conditions in Europe). In: Indasutoriaru enjiniaringu (Ind Eng) 7(8):718–730
Toyo kogyo kabushikigaisha gojunenshi hensan iinkai (ed) (1972) 1920–1970 Toyo kogyo gojunenshi—Enkaku hen—(1920–1970 50-year history of Toyo Kogyo Industry Co. Ltd—History edition—). Toyo kogyo kabushikigaisha, huchu

Toyota jidosha kabushikigaisha (ed) (1987) Sozo kagirinaku (Unlimited crearion) Toyota jidosha kabushikigaisha, Toyota

Toyota jidosha kogyo kabushikigaisha shashi henshu iinkai (ed) (1958) Toyota jidosha nijunenshi (20 years history of Toyota Motor Corporation). Toyota jidosha kogyo kabushikigaisha, Tokyo

Tsusho sangyosho gorika shingikai (ed) (1967) IE no susumekata (Implelementaion of IE). Nihon noritsu kyokai, Tokyo

Tsusho sangyosho kigyokyoku (ed) (1969) Kokusaika jidai ni okeru wagakuni kigyo keiei no kodoka ni tsuite (Advancement of business administration in Japan in the age of internationalization). Tsusho sangyosho kigyokyoku, Tokyo

Uchiyama T (1966) Manejimento no kaizen (Management and improvement). In: Tekkokai (Iron and Steel World) 16(2):28–35

Ueda S (1966) IE maindo (IE mind). In: Nihon kikai koggakaishi (J Soc Mech Eng) 69(573):1276–1280

Ueda S (1967) IE no donyu to tenkai ni tsuite (Deployment and development of IE). In: IE Rev 8(3):135–143

Ueda S, Tsumura T, Omura M et al (1967) IE tenkai no tameno kiso ron (Basic theory for IE development). In: Indasutoriaru enjiniaringu (Ind Eng) 9(6):538–545

Votsch H (1962) Rationelle Auswertung Von Zeitstudien. In: REFA-Nachrichten 15(2):61–65

Wada E, Jyuji S (1967) IEr no yakuwari to kongo no kadai (Role and task of IEr). In: Indasutoriaru enjiniaringu (Ind Eng) 9(6):518–526

Wada K (2009) Monozukuri no guwa (A fable of manufacturing). Nagoya daigaku shuppankai, Nagoya

Witte IM (1963) Von den Grundlagen der Rationalisierung. Zum 85. Geburtstag von Lillian Gilbreth am 24. Mai 1963. In: Rationalisierung 14(5):103–104

Yasui T (1986) Gendai daikogyo no rodo to kanri (Labor and management of modern large industries). Mineruva shobo, Kyoto

Yawata seitetsusho shoshi hensan jikko iinkai (1980) Yawata seitetsusho hachijunenshi. Bumonshi gekan (80-year history of Yawata Iron & Steel Co. Ltd.: Branch history, 2). Shinnihon seitetsu yawata seitetsusho,Yawata seitetsu, Kitakyushu

Yawata seitetsu kabushikigaisha shashi hensan iinkai (ed) (1981) Hono to tomoni (With a blaze). Shin Nihon seitetsu kabushikigaisha, Tokyo

Chapter 9
Deployment of the Ford System

Abstract This chapter discusses the deployment of the Ford system, the rollout of the mass production system, and Japanese and German manufacturing. The Ford system, an American-style production system, played an important role in the realization of mass production as well as in the development of the Japanese and German economies after World War II. This chapter first analyzes Japan's deployment of the Ford system in relation to the characteristics of its domestic market, the synchronization of manufacturing processes, the features of work organization, and small group activities in the workplace. Then, the chapter examines the deployment of the Ford system in Germany in connection with the European market structure, characteristics of workers' skill, and industrial relations. Furthermore, on the basis of Japanese or German and European market characteristics and the role of skilled workers, it examines the manufacturing, as well as the characteristics of the rollout of the mass production system, in both countries. The overall purpose of this chapter is to clarify the Japanese and German characteristics regarding the deployment of the Ford system and the significances of the Japanese-style and German-style manufacturing.

Keywords Flow production · German manufacturing · Japanese manufacturing · Production system · Skilled worker · The Ford system

After World War II, management and production systems that were introduced from the United States played an extremely important role in the development of productive forces and the improvement of productivity in both Europe and Japan. In particular, the Ford system greatly contributed to the development of these economies, in addition to other American management methods such as human relations, industrial engineering (IE), and statistical quality control (SQC). Thus, this chapter describes how the Ford system, as an American-style production system, was deployed in Japan and Germany[1] and discusses the resulting changes in corporate management.

---

[1] The first content analysis related to Germany in this chapter is Chap. 7 of the author's book "*German Business Management: A Japanese Perspective on Regional Development Factors,*" which was published by Springer in 2013.

T. Yamazaki, *Japanese and German Enterprises*,
https://doi.org/10.1007/978-981-97-4880-8_9

The Ford system was implemented in Japan and Germany even before the war. However, the American-style mass production system did not prevail, owing to limitations in the market and delays in the expansion of the durable consumer goods market in both countries (For Germany, see Yamazaki 2001a, b, 2015; von Freyberg 1989; Siegel and von Freyberg 1991; Bönig 1993; Homburg 1991; Stahlmann 1993. For Japan, see Fujimoto and Tidd 1993b, pp. 34–37; Fujimoto 1997, pp. 106–110, Wada und Shiba 1995, pp. 138, 141; Yamamoto 1994, p. 278; Watanabe and Hirao 1972, p. 433). In the German automobile industry, which was the most pivotal, until the 1940s, the types of production organizations were definitively regulated by the markets it supplied. It has been noted that as long as that was the case, Americanism would only spread on a selective basis (Vgl. Braun 1995, pp. 67–68). In contrast, postwar market changes brought mass motorization, which enabled full-scale deployment of the Ford system. The US form of mass production was new to Europe in the 1950s (Schröter 2005, p. 71). The Ford system became commonplace afterward.

However, unique conditions existed in both Japan and Germany. There were common tendencies in the deployment of the Ford system and the development of mass production based on this system. Therefore, this chapter examines the issues of production system innovation through the deployment of the Ford system and the development of a mass production system in relation to the unique characteristics of the Japanese- and German-style manufacturing.

This chapter is structured as follows. Sections 9.1 and 9.2 consider the deployment of the Ford system in Japan and Germany, respectively. In Sect. 9.3, "reframing" in the deployment of the Ford system in both nations is clarified. On the basis of these foregoing discussions, Sect. 9.4 examines the manufacturing as well as the characteristics regarding the rollout of the mass production system in both countries.

9.1 Deployment of the Ford System in Japan

In the Japanese automobile industry, the Ford system was introduced in response to the domestic market, which, albeit quantitatively limited, had diverse needs (Fujimoto 1997; Liker 2004, pp. 7–8, 21). An important characteristic of this reform of the production system was the hybridization of the Ford production method and the conventional craft-like production system. According to Fujimoto (1997), at Toyota Motor Co., Ltd., (hereafter referred to as "Toyota"), the Ford production method and other techniques of production control and labor management (which were created in the United States) had been absorbed into the Toyota Production System as individual elements. However, the organizational capability unique to this enterprise in integrating all of these aspects into one system eventually played a significant role in the modification of the Ford system (Fujimoto 1997, pp. 68–69, 100–101, 120, 124). Shioji (1994) also pointed out that the Ford system was not completely introduced at Toyota; rather, it was restrictively and selectively integrated into the system. The situations of the deployment of American production and management systems differed in terms of individual elements. More specifically, time and motion studies were introduced in their entirety or imitated; there were numerous cases of such extensive introduction, such as the introduction of the suggestion box system as the system for capitalizing on the inventiveness and innovations of the workers themselves. The conveyor system was deployed partially and step-by-step. Conversely, line and staff organization was introduced restrictively, after which it was incrementally modified.

Additional changes included a change from large-lot production to small lot production, and the employment of flow-line production using the pull method (based on downstream processing) instead of the push method (based on upstream processing). Furthermore, there was a shift from the make-to-stock production strategy to the make-to-order method, which also required a transformation of the company's principles (Shioji 1994, pp. 52–53).

9.1.1 Japanese Development of a Mass Production System Under Restrictive Market Conditions

"Automation of production" became a slogan of the age in the postwar boom years, and in the automobile industry, the first transfer machines were introduced at Toyota and Nissan Motor Co., Ltd., (hereafter referred to as "Nissan") in 1956. However, it was the establishment of flow production, rather than automation of production, that was initially important for automobile enterprises at the time (Yamamoto 1994, p. 281). For example, at Toyota, the synchronized production system was not fully integrated into its shops. In fact, it was only imperfectly introduced in the assembly and machining departments before 1951, when the promotion of the "Five-Year Plan for the Modernization of the Production Facility" was initiated (Toyota jidosha kabushikigaisha 2013, p. 130). However, belt conveyors were fully integrated into the final assembly line and the parts supply line, which included engines, transmissions, and rear axles (Watanabe and Hirao 1972, p. 434).

After 1956, the acceleration of the flow of each process and their integration into the final assembly line was realized because of the modernization of the mass production system and the dramatic increase in compact car production. At that time, Toyota shifted from the partial flow production method, which included machining and assembly, to the complete flow production system. The introduction of the latter was implemented during the installation of new equipment with high-production efficiency in the latter half of the 1950s (Kohira 1968, pp. 294–295; Nihon choki shinyo ginko chosabu dai ikka 1963, p. 14). Thus, in the automobile industry, the full-scale introduction of the flow production method, the improvement and reinforcement of the production control system, and the delivery of parts for assembly at fixed days and times were promoted between 1953 to 1960 (Kohira 1968, p. 323).

From 1956 to 1959, the automation and specialization of general-purpose machines had advanced rapidly, corresponding with the rapid expansion of the compact and passenger car sectors. However, during the same period, flow production had not yet been introduced and the automation and specialization of machines were not realized because of the restrictions of the market (Iwagoshi 1963, pp. 83–84).

At Toyota, the automation of machines and equipment for flow production did progress over time (Kohira 1968, pp. 309, 314). In the machining process, the company first introduced high performance, special-purpose machine units and cemented-carbide bits, and then unitized special machines. Thereafter, it utilized transfer machines in the mid-1960s (Toyota jidosha kogyo kabushikigaisha shashi henshu iinkai 1967, p. 404). The most progressive example of improvements of this kind in the machining processes could be seen at the Kamigo Plant, which was established in 1965 (Toyota jidosha kogyo kabushikigaisha 1978, pp. 248–249).

At this automobile enterprise, the mass introduction of transfer machines in the machining process occurred in 1965 (Toyota jidosha kabushikigaisha 1987a, p. 114). These machines were finally adopted in most production processes in Japan, approximately one decade after they were introduced at Toyota and Nissan in 1956 (Nissan jidosha kabushikigaisha shashi hensan iinkai 1975, p. 57; Nissan jidosha kabuskigaisha somubu chosaka 1965, p. 329). Moreover, in its attempt to improve its transfer machines, Toyota introduced the principle of the Toyota Production System into transportation control process which brought in a couple of significant efficiency improvements. The first improvement was the development and application of full-work control, which enabled stopping upstream processes when work object processing capacity in the downstream processes reached a predetermined level. This prevented excessive wastage. The second improvement was in the development of the pull-over control, which stopped the supply of work objects from the upstream processes if work objects on the stock conveyor reached a fixed quantity (Toyota jidosha kabushikigaisha 2013, p. 136).

Furthermore, the number of processes decreased after the introduction of transfer machines, and the significance of skills related to machining declined with the transformation of machinery from general-purpose machines to specialized machines. As a result, the number of workers per machine assumed decreased. In addition, as work manuals and instruction cards made operating machines easier, it became possible to employ temporary workers (Tsuda and Sumiya 1963, p. 52).

In the press and body processes, there were cases in which the number of press machines (which mainly consisted of large, double-action equipment) increased and automation of the insertion and removal of iron plates was implemented. In some cases, the mechanization of press machines, the automation of the movement of work objects between press machines, and flow production in the press process by the conveyor were also implemented. In addition, the introduction of the transfer press was also attempted. Furthermore, in the process of cutting materials, not only were wait times for transportation removed by the use of a turntable and roller conveyor but the automation of the handling of scraps created through stamp blanking and the rationalization of transportation processes were performed (Toyota jidosha kogyo kabushikigaisha shashi henshu iinkai 1958, pp. 484–485; Toyota jidosha kogyo kabushikigaisha shashi henshu iinkai 1967, pp. 410, 414; Toyota jidosha kogyo kabushikigaisha 1978, p. 207; Nihon choki sinyo ginko chosabu 1963, p. 15; Nissan jidosha kabushikigaisha shashi hensan iinkai 1975, p. 54). Similar mechanization and automation also occurred in the casting and forging processes. For example, in the casting process, mold conveyors and molding machines were introduced (Toyota jidosha kabushikigaisha 1987a, pp. 255, 333; Toyota jidosha kogyo kabushikigaisha shashi henshu iinkai 1958, pp. 480–481; Tsuda and Sumiya 1963, pp. 51–51; Isuzu jidosha kabushikigaishashi henshu iinkai 1988, p. 200). In the forging process, flat-die forging using hammers was transformed into stamp forging that mainly used forging presses and upsetters (Toyota jidosha kabushikigaisha 1987a, p. 333; Toyota jidosha kogyo kabushikgaisha shashi henshu iinkai 1958, p. 482; Toyota jidosha kogyo kabushikigaisha 1978, p. 205; Tsuda and Sumiya 1963, p. 52).

However, in the pursuit of productivity, one characteristic of the deployment of the Ford system can be seen in the attempts to avoid dependence on equipment. Through selective deployment and modifications of structural elements of the Ford system, such as moving assembly lines or transfer machines, corporations could reintegrate these elements to respond to Japan's domestic market, which was varied and prone to change (Fujimoto 1997, pp. 116, 119, 121). Although transfer machines were specialized machines, Nissan attempted to increase generalization by enabling the machines to process two types of engines (Nissan jidosha kabushikigaisha somubu chosak 1965, p. 330). In this case, seeing as the conditions were different from those in the United States, where mass market and large production volume could be secured, selective introduction of technology was attempted.

In Japan, the growth of companies in the automobile industry—one of the pioneering industries in the introduction of the Ford system—was based on the concept of increasing demand by progressively introducing a variety of models. Although the rapid increase of production volumes was realized in the period of the postwar boom years, the number of base models also increased. Thus, flexibility in the production system was necessary, especially under the circumstance that large-lot production switched to small lot production. As a result, the introduction of certain machines was restricted to some extent and special-purpose machines and equipment were reconstructed to secure flexibility. Moreover, multi-skilled workers were pursued instead of single-skilled workers, and a flexible standard work system was adopted. This system was based on multi-skilled workers who participated in the revision of the work standard—which was changed frequently, unlike at a workplace run according to the Taylor principle in the United States—and a manager who promoted improvement at the workplace (Fujimoto 1997, pp. 57–59; 61–62; Fujimoto and Tidd 1993a, p. 39).

Finally, at Toyota, the Ford system was introduced by the end of the 1950s, and personnel who could revise standard worksheets were fully trained and integrated into the workplace. Many talented people who could revise standard worksheets began to be employed as the right of revising them was delegated to the workers (Wada 2009, pp. 543, 546).

9.1.2 Pursuit of the Synchronization of Production Processes and the Development of Just-In-Time Production

The following subsection considers the development of just-in-time production for the synchronization of production processes. Although Japanese companies introduced the Ford system after World War II, an important aspect of the development of its original production system was the pursuit of synchronization of production processes, as seen in the just-in-time production process. Just-in-time method is "a set of principles, tools, and techniques that allows a company to produce and deliver products in small quantities, with short lead times, to meet specific customer needs" (Liker 2004, p. 23).

Japan did not have the huge demand the United States had, so a structure was developed in which necessary parts were delivered in smaller lots, as needed, to perfectly match production trends. This was done in order to respond to a highly diverse product lineup in the context of limited demand, as can be observed in Toyota. That is, the goal was to synchronize parts supply with the workflow of each process using the "just-in-time" method (Shimokawa 2004, pp. 174, 183). The narrowness of domestic demand in Japan, insufficient planning on account of the impossibility of demand forecasts, and the lack of funds to hold the finished vehicles in stock were important background factors for understanding the withdrawal from downstream processes in favor of just-in-time processes (Shioji 1994, pp. 54–55).

Once systematic flow production was realized in the machining process, the improvement of the material handling of parts from the machining process to the assembly process became necessary. In response to this shift, the supermarket method was introduced (Toyota jidosha kabusikigaisha 2013, p. 135). This method was adopted at Toyota in 1954, after which the flow production of all processes based on the downstream process was pursued. As a result, intermediate stocks and warehouses were abolished, and it was possible to manage the entire production process as one unit. In this case, harmonization, as seen in the adjustment and synchronization of the entire automobile assembly process had been achieved (Toyota jidosha kogyo kabushikigaisha shashi hensan iinkai 1967, pp. 421, 423, 425).

At Toyota, the machining and assembly lines were synchronized in 1950 and the supermarket method was fully introduced into the machining factory by 1954. In addition, the assembly and body factories were synchronized in 1955. By 1960, the synchronization of all plants was carried out (Toyota jidosha kabushikigaisha 1987a, p. 130; Ono 1978, pp. 51, 53, 62). In 1953, the "kanban" system, a scheduling system for lean manufacturing and just-in-time manufacturing, was introduced, which played an important role in various aspects of Toyota's overall production. For example, it was adopted in the machining process, body-welding factory, parts manufacturing, body-molding, and lot production processes. Furthermore, the kanban system was also adopted in the assembly process of the new Motomachi Plant in 1954 and was expanded in the early 1960s to the processes in which it was most difficult to realize small lot production, such as the casting, forging, and heat-treating processes.

By 1962, the "kanban" system was implemented in the entire company (Ono 1978, p. 62; Toyota jidosha kabushikigaisha 1987a, p. 130; Fujimoto and Tidd 1993b, p. 39; Satake 1998, pp. 6–19). As a result, management was expanded to individual parts processing and preforms processing. Moreover, all processes from the production of formed and fabricated materials, such as casting and forging, to the final assembly were synchronized, which greatly contributed to the leveling of the quantity of work in each particular process and the reduction of stock volume (Toyota jidosha kogyo kabushikigaisha shashi hensan iinkai 1967, pp. 425–426).

Furthermore, synchronization between the automobile company and the parts manufacturing company was also attempted. For instance, Toyota started managing operation times between the company and its important suppliers on the basis of the delivery times according to the timetable as well as by establishing a minute trading relationship (Wada 2009, pp. 443–444). The timetable for practice deliveries at specific times of the day was later discontinued and the "just-in-time" method, in which the completion of each part coincided with the arrival of the delivery vehicle, was implemented. The "kanban" system as a tool for information regarding the withdrawal of parts or the ordering of production played an important role in the synchronization between the various production processes (Wada 2009, pp. 503, 528).

However, there were some differences, depending on whether such synchronization was performed between the production processes of the automobile company and those of the parts company. For example, while the pull method, which involves the withdrawal of parts by the downstream process, was adopted within Toyota's factories, the push method, which involves the delivery of parts was utilized by both Toyota and the parts manufacturers (Wada 2009, p. 538). In addition, Toyota began adopting the kanban method for subcontracted parts in 1965 (Toyota jidosha kabushikigaisha 1987, p. 130).

Finally, the "just-in-time" method required a smooth flow across all production processes, including the production processes of the parts companies (Wada and Shiba 1995, pp. 126–127; Wada 2009, p. 544). The push toward uniform flow in the entire production process was in response to the fact that the highly precise, interchangeable parts and abundant capital for the installation of the many conveyors needed were unavailable (Wada 2009, p. 544). Moreover, as the amount of one receipt by the downstream process influenced the processing lot in the upstream process (Satake 1998, p. 64), and once the kanban method spread throughout all of the factories, production leveling became a necessary condition in each process (Toyota jidosha kabushikigaisha 1987a, p. 374). For example, Toyota introduced a production process of this kind in 1953 (Toyota jidosha kabushikigaisha 1987a, p. 130). Furthermore, the realization of production leveling was deeply related to the expansion and promotion of multi-process handling, which enabled workers to cope with the changes in the layout, the amount of production, the type of products that were produced, and the work procedures (Shimokawa 2004, p. 185). Therefore, the formation of work organization became increasingly important.

9.1.3 Japanese Development of Formation of Work Organization

Although multi-machine handling by workers began at Toyota in 1947, multi-process handling was performed for the first time only in 1963 (Toyota jidousha kabushiki-gaisha 1987b, p. 131). This almost coincided with the full-scale adoption of the kanban system at Toyota in 1962. While the automatic feed and shut-off functions became the conditions for multi-machine handling by one worker (Satake 1998, p. 53), adjustments in the workload (man-hours) between processes were required for multi-process handling by a single worker. More specifically, methods indispensable for realizing multi-process handling by one worker, such as "the ability list according to products and processes" and "the standard work combination vote" were developed at Toyota after 1951 (Satake 1998, pp. 53, 57). The result of realizing such multi-process handling was significant in the machining process. In addition, the machine shop and machining factory shifted from the conventional lot production to the flow production system (Toyota jidosha kabushikigaisha 1987a, p. 256).

At Toyota, the extreme horizontal and vertical division of labor, such as the subdivision of work allotments and the rigid distinction of workers and managers that the Ford system foresaw, was not implemented. As a result, Japanese characteristics were also included in the formation of the work organization. Artisan production-type work organization was replaced by work standardization and direct control of the workplace. However, this reshuffling of standardized tasks created a multifunction work organization responsible for a sequence of processes rather than a single process. Moreover, a vertical structure between managers and single-skilled workers was avoided by means of the transfer of decision-making power and work-related responsibilities to supervisors and workers at the shop-floor level. While the conventional organization had disappeared, the production method that formerly relied on craftsmen was revised to another form by this original work organization and the delegation of decision-making power. The breakaway from a production method depending on craftsmen by means of work standardization and the training of the multi-process workers advanced simultaneously, and both were implemented in close connection. Toyota had already attempted to mix elements of the Ford production system with the conventional production system before the 1960s when it became possible to fully enjoy economies of scale (Fujimoto 1997, pp. 113, 116, 119, 121; Fujimoto and Tidd 1993a, p. 38; Fujimoto and Tidd 1993b, pp. 40–41, 47, 50).

In this way, it became important to create a work organization enabling flexible organizational operations and support a concise structure mainly based on multi-skilled workers (Shimokawa 2004, p. 174). Furthermore, in Japan, a multifunction work organization responsible for a sequence of processes rather than a single process also led to the transfer of decision-making power and responsibility for work improvements through employee suggestions and total quality control (TQC) to the shop-floor level (Fujimoto 1997, pp. 119, 121). This contributed to the systematic improvement of the workplace, which, in turn, enhanced the overall quality of production.

9.1.4 *Significance of the Japanese Development of the Ford System*

Based on the foregoing discussion, this section explores the significance of Japanese-style deployment and development of the Ford system. The essence of the Toyota Production System, which formed after the introduction of the Ford system, lies in "manufacturing technology" that emphasizes three elements: processing objects (work), standard work, and machinery. Manufacturing technology is distinguished from "production technology." The main issues relating to the latter include planning, arranging, and revising mechanical equipment as well as obtaining workers necessary for each production process (Satake 1998, pp. 73, 147–148). The development of the production system in Japan, as seen in the Toyota Production System, included original contents as well as the systematization of "manufacturing technology." In its reform of European and American styles, an important aspect was the mechanization even under the flow production. In contrast, the rationalization of work had been emphasized in the Japanese-style reform.

The ability of engineers to analyze work is inadequate in Europe and the United States as compared to Japan meaning that when casework improvement is attempted, attention is generally focused on the improvement of equipment before analyzing the work itself. Conversely, the existence of engineers who belong to the original category, such as the manufacturing engineer, and the knowledge of supervisors at the workplace created the conditions for improved efficiency in Japan (Nohara 2006, pp. 147–148). In 1970, when the Toyota Production System was fully implemented, the production investigation office was established as a staff organ in charge of introducing this production system and directing such activities in each factory and supplier (Toyota jidosha kabushikigaisha 1987a, p. 586). Thus, an effective production system at Toyota had been promoted at a level that exceeded the company's initial goal.

Toyota, as a representative case of the Japanese deployment and development of the Ford system, established a system capable of benefitting from the growth of the Japanese market (which exhibited high growth based on increasing demand), even before the rapid growth of the economy in the 1960s. Historically, there were three processes of the production method, listed as follows: (1) the craft production method, which included low productivity along with high diversity and flexibility because no standard existed; (2) the Ford system, based on high specialization; and (3) the flexible mass production method, which included both diversity and flexibility based on the standardization of product and process designs. Among Japanese automobile companies, Toyota concurrently pursued the second and third processes, since flexibility was required. Meanwhile, some Japanese companies, including Toyota, shifted to the flexible mass production system while passing through the second stage, as seen in the shift to the pure Ford system with limited flexibility. This can be understood as a "compressed life cycle" (Fujimoto and Tidd 1993b, pp. 50–52; Fujimoto 1997, pp. 60–61, 122–124; Fujimoto 1999, pp. 51–53). Toyota needed to adapt Ford's manufacturing process in order to achieve simultaneously "high quality, low cost, short lead times, and flexibility" (Liker 2004, pp. 8, 21).

Finally, the catchup process in the Japanese automobile industry, which started around 1950, reached a tentative conclusion around 1960. An example can be seen in the domestic prices of Japanese cars which were below the import prices of foreign cars in the same class (Takeda 1995, pp. 235–236). One important factor behind this trend was that it was based on Japanese-style development of the Ford system, as seen in the early shift to the flexible mass production system. In addition, under the shift of the competition pattern from price competition to model change competition in the automobile industry after 1965 (Watanabe and Hirao 1972, pp. 465–467), the development of a mass production system in Japan had a huge significance on the ability to cope with such changes in the competition structure.

9.2 Deployment of the Ford System in Germany

The following section examines issues related to production system innovation in the deployment of the Ford system and German-style manufacturing.

9.2.1 General Conditions in the Postwar Deployment of the Ford System

In Germany, the deployment of the Ford system occurred in the processing and assembly industries such as the automobile and electrical sectors, particularly in the final assembly of primary product lines such as radios, televisions, vacuum cleaners, washing machines, dishwashers, and electric ranges (Wittke 1996, p. 153). In 1953, there were few production fields that could viably use production lines based on American-style methods due to modifications in product and component design and structure as well as fluctuations in production volumes (Steeger 1953, p. 197). A 1956 report stated that flow production was still in its initial stages (Mennecke 1956, p. 45), but this situation changed drastically in the latter half of the 1950s. For example, a 1958 study noted that the principles of flow production had become much more widespread, completely eliminating the principle of organization by machine type (Lauke 1956, p. 41; Lauke 1958, p. 79). In 1963, Springer (1963, p. 769) also stated that the need for rationalization increasingly led to production via workflow in manufacturing industries.

The automobile industry was the sector most closely associated with the deployment of American-style methods, and the end of the 1950s witnessed a continuous transition away from smaller cars toward mid-sized vehicles in Germany (Der Volkswirt 1959, p. 2133). The deployment of the Ford system was a response to this trend, with the industry-wide adoption of Fordism accelerating during the last third of the

1950s (Wellhöner 1996, p. 16). The automobile industry's effort to rationalize in the 1950s and 1960s focused on large-scale production revolution using conveyor belt technology in body production, unit assembly, and final assembly departments (Vgl. Kern and Schumann 1984, p. 40). For example, according to a 1963 report, manual work dominated assembly in several cases despite the high standards already being achieved by using machines and automation in cutting and machining of processed parts (Goos 1963, p. 152). Thus, the rollout of the flow production system and its synchronization of overall assembly processes were particularly significant.

9.2.2 Deployment of the Ford System in the Automobile Industry

In the following section, case studies of corporations in the automobile industry are reviewed. These corporations are prime examples in which Ford system deployment was most dominant.

9.2.2.1 Volkswagen

Volkswagen was the trendsetter in adopting Ford production methods and in the formation of corresponding labor relations (Vgl. Wellhöner 1996; Kapitel 3; Klenke 1996, p. 219; Abelshauser 2005, pp. 98–102). In 1946, immediately after the war ended, numerous assembly and final assembly conveyors were already in operation for transmissions, axles, and engines, producing approximately 1,000–1,200 automobiles per month (Automobiltechnische Zeitschrift 1946, p. 45). Thereafter, efforts to modernize production by introducing the conveyor system were made in the latter half of the 1940s and the first half of the 1950s [*Volkswagen Archiv*, Z174/Nr.2037, Jahresbericht der Produktion für das Jahr 1950 (15.1.1951), S.2–3, *Volkswagen Archiv*, Z174/Nr.2037, Jahresbericht der Produktion für das Jahr 1951 (15.1.1952), S.3, *Volkswagen Archiv*, Z174/Nr.2037, Jahresbericht der Produktion für das Jahr 1952 (12.1.1953), S.2–3, *Volkswagen Archiv*, Z174/Nr.2037, Jahresbericht der Produktion für das Jahr 1953 (7.1.1954), S.2].

However, after 1954, Volkswagen worked on technical reshuffling with the objective of creating an external force for the work rhythm based on the takt time (effective working time in a period/demand in a period) of machines and conveyors. The time required for each process was calculated and set as the standard time for workers. This technical reshuffling in the Wolfsburg plant forced the labor organization to adapt from the outset and align with the US model (Wellhöner 1996, pp. 116–117). When investigating the representative cases of the introduction of a flow production system, in Hall 3 of the Wolfsburg Plant, the assembly of the body was completely synchronized with the final assembly of the vehicle after the transfer of four assembly conveyors in the 1955 fiscal year. Furthermore, in Hall 4 of this plant, one conveyor was newly installed for the production of the rear axle [*Volkswagen Archiv*, Z174/ Nr.2037, Jahresbericht der Produktion für das Jahr 1955 (27.1.1956), S. 2–3]. In the 1956 fiscal year, equipment was arranged in the new press plant of Hall 0, and six large components, such as doors and roofs, were produced at the same takt time, from the arrival of the sheet plate to the assembling group in the mechanized production line. As a result, production progressed without interruption [*Volkswagen Archiv*, Z174/ Nr.2037, Jahresbericht der Produktion für das Jahr 1956 (24.1.1957), S. 1].

Thus, the conveyor assembly line that began operating in 1946 produced only one model, the Beetle; by the beginning of the 1960s, a perfect flow had been developed for coordinated mass production (Tolliday 1995, p. 328). In the summer of 1961, two new assembly conveyors were completed that allowed Volkswagen to produce 250,000 VW1500 vehicles per year [*Volkswagen Archiv*, Z174/ Nr.2037, Jahresbericht 1961. Vorstandsbereicheich: Produktion (18.1.1962), S. 4, DWI-Berichte 1961, p. 19]. In the 1964 fiscal year, the body assembly conveyor and the final assembly conveyor in this plant were rebuilt so that they could produce Type 1 or Type 3 models. In addition, according to an annual report by the board of directors in 1968, the need for flexibility increased because of various types of products and the differences in their designs. Thus, improvement in flexibility characterized the Braunschweig Plant [*Volkswagen Archiv*, Z174/ Nr.2037, Jahresbericht 1968. Vorstandsbereich: Produktion (17.1.1969), S. 0.9]. In the 1970 fiscal year, the flexible mixed-model production of each product was created corresponding with the remarkable increase of variations in Type 1 produced at the Wolfsburg Plant. However, such production methods caused considerable losses of time and changes in the transport system [*Volkswagen Archiv*, Z174/Nr.2037, Jahresbericht 1970. Vorstandsbereich Produktion und Qualititätskontrolle (15.1.1971), S. 8].

In the new delivery van factory opened in Hanover in 1956, final assembly used a conveyor belt. Production was organized by deploying various new mechanized or partially automated routings to individual lines that fed the final assembly. Assembly using fully mechanized conveyor belts was typical, and the widespread use of these belts was characteristic of the production technology of this plant. Body production conveyors were synchronized with body panel production, thus reducing work time by 25% compared with stationary assembly (Automobiltechnische Zeitschrift 1957, pp. 116–117).

For deploying special-purpose machinery and automation technology, which was important for expanding the Ford system type of mass production methods, H. Nordhoff sought a "perfect new direction" by the spring of 1954. While the automation of body frame production and painting and plating areas was already well underway, press plants and machining departments were striving to gradually eliminate or substantially reduce manual work (Edelmann 2003, p. 184). Although many new, specialized machines were used until the mid-1950s [*Volkswagen Archiv*, Z174/ Nr.2037, Jahresbericht der Produktion für das Jahr 1951 (15.1.1952), S.2, *Volkswagen Archiv*, Z174/Nr.2037, Jahresbericht der Produktion für das Jahr 1952 (12.1.1953), S.3, *Volkswagen Archiv*, Z174/Nr.2037, Jahresbericht der Produktion für das Jahr 1953 (7.1.1954), S.2, *Volkswagen Archiv*, Z174/Nr.2037, Jahresbericht der Produktion für das Jahr 1954 (21.1.1955), S.3], automation efforts continued to expand, after which the company made significant investments in specialized machine tools and general automation as they replaced old multipurpose tools in 1955. The company's continuous flow production was developed by connecting the various stages of individual routings through the transfer machines of different workspaces. Wherever the planning of the production volume was possible without frequent design and structure coordination, multipurpose machinery was replaced with flexible specialized machinery. This type of automation was deployed early on for producing the Beetle economy car. Meanwhile, automation was not deployed for manufacturing delivery vehicles due to the relatively small demand for these vehicles (Abelshauser 1995, p. 284; Abelshauser 2018, p. 107).

Volkswagen's automation had two main technical aspects: the use of production lines for combining individual processing stages and the greater prominence of specialized machinery (Wellhöner 1996, p. 113). However, although Volkswagen possessed the most modern equipment among West German corporations by the end of the 1950s (Vgl. Eberhorst 1959, p. 7), manufacturing processes were automated very cautiously until the company was certain that markets could absorb the increased production enabled by the additional automation. This type of corporate intervention resulted from operating in product markets and factor supply conditions that evidently differed from those of the United States (Zeitlin 2000, p. 37).

However, the 1960s saw tremendous expansion in the automobile market, and full-scale deployment of American-style automation technology was attempted. For example, the 1963 annual report of the "Purchasing and Materials Management Department" for the board of directors mentioned the approval of various orders for presses, equipment, and transfer machines in the Kasel and Hanover plants (*Volkswagen Archiv*, Z174/Nr.2366, Jahresbericht 1963 des Vorstandsbericht "Einkauf und Materialverwaltung"). In the Wolfsburg Plant, transfer machines for the production of white bodies began operating, which replaced 210 workers [*Volkswagen Archiv*, Z174/Nr.2037, Jahresbericht 1963.Vorstandsbereich: Produktion (20.1.1964), S. 4–5]. In 1964, new transfer machines for the automated assembly of the 1200 and 1300 Beetles were in operation at the Wolfsburg plant (Seherr-Thoss 1979, p. 476). Furthermore, in the 1969 fiscal year, 56 new machines for the production of tools were introduced to increase the production capacity and replace old machines. Two of them were horizontal drill machines and vertical drill machines, both of which were advanced digital control machines [*Volkswagen Archiv*, Z174/Nr.2037, Jahresbericht 1969.Vorstandsbereich Produktion (14.1.1970), S. 12].

In the deployment of these types of production technology innovations within Volkswagen, Christian Kleinschmidt (2004, pp. 75–76) maintains that excluding companies such as Ford and Opel, Volkswagen was the only German automotive manufacturer capable of adapting the American model over the decades. Volkswagen strongly embraced the American model, particularly Ford's River Rouge plant; thus, the United States played a decisive role in Volkswagen's success in the 1950s.

However, Volkswagen's success could be attributed to its selective approach to the American model. While Volkswagen followed the US expansion, they used specialized know-how, such as highly mechanized proprietary transfer machines for body assembly, and could thus relax their stringent adherence to the American model (Kleinschmidt 2004, pp. 82, 88–89; Abelshauser 2018, p. 106). An example of this German approach to production technology innovation was Volkswagen's decision to replace the US style of automation called "Detroit automation," which impeded flexible production methods, with one adapted to the German context. As a follower, Volkswagen was able to learn from others' mistakes and avoid the challenges faced by early adopters of the automation process. In this way, a new mode of Germany-focused Fordism was born, enabling Volkswagen to survive the decline of the 1970s. This new mode engendered diverse, high-quality production that dominated the country in alignment with German-style labor relations that were critical to codetermination. This system of harmonious labor relations based on labor resource cooperation in distributing shop-floor power between labor and management represented the essential elements of a classic paradigm of highly skilled labor that values technical precision (Abelshauser 2003, pp. 130–133; Abelshauser 2004, pp. 376–377; Abelshauser 2005, pp. 100–102; Abelshauser 2018, pp. 108, 115).

9.2.2.2 Opel

Looking at the cases of Opel and K40, its new, large-scale body and assembly plants were in full operation by August 1956, and the company was working on production system innovations. Two basic chassis types for 1.5 L and 2.5 L engine vehicles were separately assembled on two conveyors in body assembly; these were then merged onto one conveyor to produce white bodies. After undercoating, painting, and installing the interiors, completed bodies were sent via conveyor to final assembly, where engines and chassis were also moved on conveyors. Two-thirds of the main assembly conveyors comprised overhead chain conveyors whose height could be adjusted on the basis of the work being conducted (Automobiltechnische Zeitschrift 1956, p. 351). A 1957 report mentions that only one 6,500-m-long main conveyor remained in the Rüsselsheim plant for body manufacturing, where all six types of vehicles were manufactured. Large belt conveyors can be used for production in two ways: continuous production using larger volumes of the same model or a mixed production environment for all models based on the assembly plan. Opel chose the latter method because of long work times that varied by model and as they could effectively use tools set up along the conveyor belt (Faensen 1957, p. 1425). The combined length of the plant's conveyor belts and assembly conveyors amounted to 28,000 m. A teletype system was created to manage the assembly of all models other than trucks on the same conveyor, making the plant one of the world's most modern automobile plants at the time (Der Volkswirt 1957, p. 1274; Seherr-Thoss 1979, p. 443). Opel primarily manufactured small cars and economy vehicles, and they put tremendous effort into deploying the Ford system. In 1962, conveyor belts were being used for mass production, with one automobile rolling off the line every 50 s (Adam Opel 1962, p. 73).

The Bochum Plant began production in 1962. The Number 2 plant produced engines and chassis parts and used conveyors for engine assembly. The Number 1 plant produced bodies and performed final assembly using overheard chain conveyors, assembly conveyors, and other transportation equipment; these machines totaled 31 km in length and comprised 227 pieces of equipment. The length of the conveyor and assembly conveyors in the Number 2 plant was 11 km. Bodies, pre-assembled chassis units, and engines converged on final assembly conveyors (Automobiltechnische Zeitschrift 1962, pp. 343–345; Stahl und Eisen 1962, p. 805).

In terms of the deployment of specialized machinery and automation at Opel, transfer machines and other automation equipment were implemented for crankshaft production in machining departments in the mid-1950s [*Mercedes-Benz Classic Archiv*, Konecke 122, Transferstraße für 4-Zyl.-Kurbelwelle für die Fa. Opel (5.7.1954)]. A characteristic of production during this period was the addition to the workflow of numerous pieces of equipment that could also monitor and control the work, rather than simply automating it (Hilf 1956, p. 5). At the end of 1958, a new, large investment project was begun, and the pace of investment accelerated (Der Volkswirt 1960, p. 1852). Around this time, Opel began using cylinder piston lines along with many general transfer machines, a phenomenon unique to this plant (*Bundesarchiv Koblenz*, B149/5697, Untersuchung sozialer Auswirkungen des technischen Fortschrittes, p. 1).

The Rüsselsheim Plant began using new equipment for producing engines and transmissions in August 1961. At the time, the plant had 55 transfer machines, 70 multi-axis lathes, and 1,175 individual pieces of machine tools (Seherr-Thoss 1979, p. 464). In 1962, the Bochum plant began producing engines, transmissions, axles, cardan shafts, and other components using 1,147 individual machine tools. The standard of technology was high, with 47 transfer machines making up a large portion of the equipment used for processing cylinder blocks and crankshafts and connecting rods, gearboxes, and the like (Automobiltechnische Zeitschrift 1962, pp. 343–344; Stahl und Eisen 1962, p. 805). Opel also stated in their 1962 corporate history document that they had begun using transfer machines to automatically transport all work in process inventories (Adam Opel 1962, pp. 77, 83–84).

When transferring production systems to a subsidiary of an American company, as was the case with Opel and Ford, it was sometimes necessary to understand subsidiary production system dynamics not present in the parent company. Even when the subsidiary was receptive, this transfer required innovation and flexibility (Tolliday 2000, p. 78). This issue also relates to the adaptation of methodologies to the conditions in postwar Germany. A huge gap could sometimes be observed between the potential power of GM and Ford's methods and their ability to effectively apply them. In Germany, Volkswagen illustrated the successful selective and skillful application of American expertise in the European context (Tolliday 2000, p. 117).

9.2.2.3 Daimler-Benz

In 1950, Daimler-Benz had begun work on production lines for the 220 and 300 model automobiles. The 220 model was produced using conveyor belts starting from the fall of 1951, whereas the 300 model adopted mass production gradually, beginning in November 1951 (Hiller 1952, p. 26). After the war, the Sindelfingen plant began final assembly work in addition to body production (Mercedes-Benz 1990, p. 100; Feldenkirchen 2004, p. 179). In the 1957 fiscal year, the company invested in production methods that would lower costs (Daimler-Benz 1957, p. 25) and worked on improving production methods for mass production along with complete process modernization.

However, even in the first half of the 1960s, there remained a serious gap in productivity between Daimler-Benz and the US corporations. In the United States, Ford produced a maximum of 2,500 cars per day, whereas Daimler-Benz required 17 manufacturing hours to assemble even the smallest passenger car. The high-production capacity of US factories was due to the complete mechanization of transportation using conveyors and conveyor belts. An important way for creating economies of scale included standardization based on the "unit system" principle that enabled model variety and economically viable production volumes. Daimler-Benz implemented standardized mass production using the unit system and cutting back on certain models in the passenger and commercial vehicle departments (Vgl. Hilger 2004, pp. 175, 177).

The applicability of standardized production factors based on the unit system principle and the integration work that increased their applicability was very important. When considering production methods from a work organization perspective, Daimler's case could be addressed by adopting an organized flow of work as found in the United States. However, the skills within the key production elements between design and production were significant. Thus, emphasis was placed on the development of high-quality production that encompassed labor process flexibility considering Daimler-Benz's reliance on skilled labor. Even in the period from 1957 to 1963, high ability of handicraft type was required for the assembly of Benz 300SL model (Feldenkirchen 2003, p. 213).

Examining the deployment of specialized machinery and automation, a survey conducted in August 1958 noted that production volumes were low at the Untertürkheim Plant and that its equipment did not meet the highest standards of modernization (*Bundesarchiv Koblenz*, B149/5697, Untersuchung sozialer Auswirkungen des technischen Fortschrittes, p. 1). An annual report on that plant in 1959 reported that further automation for larger-scale production had restricted potential because of the diverse models being produced (*Mercedes-Benz Classic Archiv*, Daimler-Benz AG, Jahresbericht 1959 des Werkes Stuttgart-Untertürkheim, p. 3). This factor alone demonstrates that standardization was critical in deploying the latest technology, even more so in the 1960s, when the deployment of automation technology began in earnest at Daimler-Benz. For example, the number of transfer machines purchased in the Untertürkheim plant was 4 in 1961, 13 in 1962, 1 in 1963, 7 in 1965, 1 in 1966, 10 in 1967, and 5 in 1970. The deployment scope was not limited to engine production; it also involved axles, transmissions, oil pans, bracing tubes, and other systems (*Mercedes-Benz Classic Archiv*, Daimler-Benz AG, Jahresbericht 1961 des Werkes Stuttgart-Untertürkheim, pp. 40–41, *Mercedes-Benz Classic Archiv*, Jahresbericht 1962 des Werkes Stuttgart-Untertürkheim, p. 35, *Mercedes-Benz Classic Archiv*, Jahresbericht 1963 des Werkes Stuttgart-Untertürkheim, p. 34, *Mercedes-Benz Classic Archiv*, Jahresbericht 1965 des Werkes Stuttgart-Untertürkheim, p. 35, Jahresbericht 1966 des Werkes Stuttgart-Untertürkheim, p. 33 *Mercedes-Benz Classic Archiv*,, Jahresbericht 1967 des Werkes Stuttgart-Untertürkheim, p. 34, *Mercedes-Benz Classic Archiv*, Jahresbericht 1970 des Werkes Stuttgart-Untertürkheim, p. 38). An annual report on the Untertürkheim plant listed machines and their years of use, but reports after 1959 provided a simple average of machines by year of purchase without accurately reflecting the aging of equipment because of the deployment of special-purpose machinery and increased use of high performance transfer machines for many machining processes (*Mercedes-Benz Classic Archiv*, Daimler-Benz AG, Jahresbericht 1959 des Werkes Stuttgart-Untertürkheim, p. 28, *Mercedes-Benz Classic Archiv*, Jahresbericht 1962 des Werkes Stuttgart-Untertürkheim, p. 36, *Mercedes-Benz Classic Archiv*, Jahresbericht 1965 des Werkes Stuttgart-Untertürkheim, p. 36).

Corporations such as Daimler-Benz, which were pursuing a product strategy emphasizing upper-class market segments, sought a German production model while deploying American-style mass production technologies and systems. Specifically, to ensure high-quality products and differentiate themselves in the marketplace, Daimler-Benz rolled out a system for diverse, high-quality production, relying on skilled labor that complemented the standards created by technical equipment and integration of production factors within the unit system. In this context, it could be said that they chose to "Germanize" the model differently from Volkswagen.

9.3 Reframing in the Deployment of the Ford System in Japan and Germany

Based on the foregoing discussions, this section explores the "reframing" in the deployment of the Ford system in Japan and Germany.

The adaptation of the American mass production system represented by the Ford system in Japan can be observed in the hybridization of the Ford system and the conventional craft production methods and in the introduction of a mix of foreign technologies and management methods based on particular logics. These included the withdrawal of needed parts by downstream processes, small lot production, and putting one worker in charge of multiple processes. Hybridization is also evident in the mix of specialized machines and in terms of the operation of multiple machines and multiple processes by one multi-skilled worker instead of single-skilled workers, as well as in the development of the flexible standard work system.

The reframing of American management principles in Japan was influenced by values and cultural factors which emphasized production spots, collectivism, and mutual trust between employees and management. Long-term and continuous trade relationships between large enterprises and small and medium enterprises under the subcontracting system also influenced the deployment of the Ford system.

Next, considering the institutional factors impacting the Japanese-style of adaptation in the process of Americanization, factors such as labor relations, the educational system, and postwar reforms were deeply concerned with reframing the process of Americanization. In Japan, the regulating powers of trade unions were weak despite new frameworks of industrial relations for labor democratization after World War II, which influenced the deployment and implementation of American management methods. Labor flexibility was pursued under the lifetime employment system and the weak regulations at workplaces by labor laws. Such cases can be seen with respect to multi-skilled workers and the flexible use of workers in the team working system. Just-in-time production was pursued not only between the processes of automobile enterprise but also between car makers and parts-producing companies under the multilayer subcontracting system peculiar to Japan.

Productive forces based on craft production and delay in mass production before the war experienced reform after the war. In prewar Japan, delay in the development of productive forces in heavy industries and the process and assembly industries was prominent. Although mass production based on the flow production system and automation was strongly invested in after the war, influences of prewar characteristics vis-à-vis productive forces and craft production were substantial.

Industrial structure also changed greatly with the rapid development and expansion of the heavy and chemical industries and the durable consumer goods industries that were the leading industrial sectors for mass production after the war. Durable consumer goods industries such as the automobile industry and the home appliance industry developed and expanded rapidly and their importance in the productive industrial sectors tended to grow. However, similarities between the industrial structures of the rapidly expanding industries and the competitiveness of key industrial sectors in postwar Japan and the United States influenced further reform of the mass production system in the 1970s and the 1980s.

Regarding the context of market structure characteristics, the labor market structures were influenced by factors such as lifetime employment, the seniority wage system, and internal promotion of personnel within companies. Labor formation based on the principle of "generalization," such as the flexible use of multi-skilled workers in team-based working systems, was pursued in the deployment of the Ford system in a labor market characterized by the lifetime employment system, which contributed to coping with changes in demand and realizing full use of workers as a fixed cost consideration.

The deployment of the Ford system in Japan was also influenced by, the small yet diverse domestic market, similarities between market structures in terms of emphasizing product quality between Japan and the United States as a core of export market, labor formation based on the principle of "generalization" in the context of a labor market established on lifetime employment. In Japan, the Ford system was modified to make it compatible with narrow and diverse domestic markets, which determined selective deployment and modification of a part of the Ford system, such as moving assembly lines, transfer machines, the system of synchronization of production processes, and the use of multi-skilled workers and the flexible standard work systems. However, the strongest market structure factor determining the development of Japanese-style business management was in the commodities markets.

Meanwhile, in Germany, concerning the aspect of hybridization of American and German elements, the following mix of American and German factors in the production system was seen. In the introduction of the Ford system in Germany, there was a combination of various American elements with those of Germany's own prewar production system such as the system based on "the flexible production concept with an emphasis on quality" as seen in the automotive industry (Stahlmann 1993). We can also see the modification of the Ford system with hybridization in the use of knowledge-intensive skills relying on skilled workers and linking standardization systems through the unit system. Economy of scale was pursued on the basis of using unit systems in Germany as well as mass production.

In looking at the deployment of the Ford system in Germany with regard to various factors determining the reframing of the American management method, regarding management values and cultural factors, influences of technology, quality, and functionality-oriented management values, management values, and manufacturing views based on understanding customer needs, and the tradition of prioritizing skilled engineers in the production management function were prominent.

Institutional factors that influenced the deployment of the Ford system can be observed in production systems with the foundation of the vocational education system and professional qualification system such as the Meister system.

Concerning the structure of productive forces, the pursuit of economies of scale based on lower production volumes since the prewar era and the development of production systems that ensured production flexibility and the prewar tradition of flexible quality production strongly influenced production system reform.

In the industrial structure, expansion of processing and assembly industries since the prewar period and further development and expansion of these industrial sectors after the war promoted German-style deployment of the Ford system.

Regarding the market structure factors, market characteristics of the German and European emphasis on quality and functionality and patterns of foreign trade based on complementary relationships among European industrial and product fields greatly influenced the German modifications of American methods.

Germany, in contrast to Japan, did not pursue a system of complete production process synchronization as Japan did. Although Germany did attempt to develop a mass production system that leveraged the workers' skills and technical abilities, the two countries had different markets, and so the workers' skills and abilities were different. Consequently, differences can be seen between the two nations' hybrid production systems based on Ford production methods and the artisan production system.

Regarding the conditions surrounding the introduction of the Ford system in Japan and Germany during the postwar boom years as well as "reframing" and the factors defining, Table 9.1 shows an inline comparison of the respective countries, based on the discussion so far in this chapter.

Table 9.1 Comparison of conditions surrounding the introduction of the Ford system in Japan and Germany

Deployment and factors affecting them	Management methods	
	The Ford system	
	Japanese management methods	German management methods
Overall conditions in the deployment of American management methods	• Deployment of flow production system mechanisms and production organization principles • Restricted and selective deployment of the Ford system	• Deployment of flow production system mechanisms and production organization principles
Deployment characteristics of American management methods	• "Compressed life cycle" in the transition from craft production to the flexible mass production system (simultaneous progress of the deployment of the Ford system and the development of flexible mass production methods) • Emphasis on securing flexibility in the production system compatible with the growth of automobile companies with diverse product models	• Differences in production systems among companies • The development of diversified quality production based on skilled or specialized labor • Case of deployments of mixed-model assembly line
Modifications in American management methods	• Use of elements of the conventional craft production methods • Pursuit of synchronization of production processes based on the just-in-time production method • Selective deployment and modifications of structural elements of the Ford system such as moving assembly lines or transfer machines) • Emphasis of charge of plural machines and multi-processes by one worker • Flexible use of multi-skilled workers	• The pursuit of economies of scale by using unit systems

(continued)

Table 9.1 (continued)

Deployment and factors affecting them		Management methods	
		The Ford system	
		Japanese management methods	German management methods
Amalgamation of American and Japanese elements		• Hybridization of the Ford system and the conventional craft production methods in Japan • Mix of introduced technology from foreign countries and meta-technology including peculiar logics (method of withdrawal of needed parts by downstream processes, small lot production, and charge of multi-processes by one worker) • Mix of introduction of special purpose machines and charge of plural machines and multi-processes by one worker • Use of multi-skilled workers instead of single-skilled workers and development of the flexible standard work system	• Linking unique prewar production system elements in Germany • Use of knowledge-intensive skills relying on skilled workers • Linking standardization systems through the unit system
Factors of Modification of American management method	Influence of traditions, cultural factors, and management values	• Management values emphasizing production spots • Long-term and continuous trade relationships between large corporations and small and medium enterprises under the subcontracting system • Management values focused on behavioral patterns based on collectivism	• Technology-, quality-, and functionality-oriented management values • Management values and manufacturing views based on understanding customer needs, rather than production perspectives • The tradition of prioritizing skilled engineers in the production management function

(continued)

Table 9.1 (continued)

Deployment and factors affecting them		Management methods	
		The Ford system	
		Japanese management methods	German management methods
	Influence of institutional factors	• Pursuit of labor flexibility under the lifetime employment system (multi-skilled workers and flexible use of workers) • Flexibility in the use of work forces under weak regulations at workplaces by labor laws • Development of just-in-time production based on the multilayered subcontracting system • Framework of labor relations as a foundation of the Japanese labor formation	• Production systems with the foundation of the vocational education system and professional qualification system (the Meister system)
	Influencing factors of the productive forces	• Productive forces based on craft production before World War II • Delay in mass production before World War II	• Pursuit of economies of scale based on lower production volumes since the prewar era and the development of production systems that ensured production flexibility • Prewar tradition of flexible quality production
	Influence of industrial structure factors	• Similarities of industrial structures between the rapidly expanding industries and sectors with international competitiveness in Japan after the war and the key industrial sectors in the United States	• Expansion of processing and assembly industries since the prewar period • Further development and expansion of the processing and assembly industries after World War II • Foundation of international industrial competitiveness based on a second industrial revolution
	Influence of market structure factors	• Small yet highly diverse domestic markets • Similarities of market structures in terms of emphasizing product quality between Japan and the United States • Labor formation based on the principle of "generalization" under labor market established on lifetime employment	• Market characteristics of the German and European emphasis on quality and functionality • Postwar expansion of the mass consumer market • Patterns of foreign trade based on complementary relationships among European industrial and product fields

Source This table was compiled by the author, based on discussions in this chapter

9.4 The Rollout of Mass Production Systems and Japanese and German Manufacturing

Based on the preceding discussions, this section examines the characteristics of the rollout of mass production systems in Japanese and German manufacturing in the postwar period.

9.4.1 The Rollout of Mass Production Systems and Japanese Manufacturing

Japan's small yet highly diverse domestic market, such as that of the automobile industry, necessitated revisions to the system. Postwar production system reforms progressed as a hybrid of the Ford production method and the traditional craft production system (Fujimoto 1997, pp. 100–101, 120). Such a system was formed by absorbing the essence of effective management that held universal validity and modifying it with a goal of adjusting American methods to Japanese-specific conditions in the processes of learning and deployment (Onizuka 1991, p. 261). It can be stated that the success of Japanese enterprises, as seen in their increasing international competitiveness after the 1970s, could primarily be attributed to management innovations implemented in the process of Japanese modification and adoption of American management techniques (Shimokawa 1990, p.114).

Japanese automobile companies pursued their own unique production system, while depending on the introduction of the Ford system. This was based on the assumption that eliminating waste from overproduction and producing many models in small quantities (instead of expansion) was highly necessary under the specific conditions of the domestic market in the postwar era that did not enable enterprises to realize scale merit and required many product models. If we regard "the general name of know-how and technique concerning the combination of the element technology" as "the meta-technology," then the development of the production system in the Japanese automobile industry had been performed on the basis of such meta-technology (Itami et al 1988, pp. 87–88, 91, 97–101, 104).

The basic framework of the Japanese production system represented by the Toyota Production System was practically created during the deployment of the Ford system, especially during the postwar period of high economic growth. However, such a production system brought high competitiveness in the international market by accomplishing further evolution under the structural change of capitalism after the 1970s. When the propensity to consume deteriorated with the shift toward low economic growth, the demand was not able to expand at the same pace as the increase in the number of product types induced by the strategy of diversification and differentiation of products. As a result, the average production lot per one type of product also deteriorated.

Therefore, it became difficult to secure an operating rate that could realize the economy of scale based on the American-style mass production system and the formation of production by the principle of "specialization." Under such circumstances, the mass production of many types of products, while maintaining low costs and responding to the demand fluctuation between product types became an important managerial problem. As a result, ever-greater flexibility was required in the production system. In the case that multiple products were manufactured in numerous specialized production lines, it was impossible to secure the flexibility required for such production and cope with the fluctuation in demand. In addition, not only had the mass production of the specific products become important but the market had to stabilize. If such conditions could not be secured, then realizing an economy of scale would be extremely difficult. As a result, satisfying the twin demand of viable costs and product flexibility became much more important issues for management.

Furthermore, under such conditions, improvement of flexibility was realized by the use of micro-electronic technology, which enabled effectiveness, the automation of facilities, and the generality of certain equipment. For instance, Toyota developed its automated processes by integrating new technology, such as industrial robots in the 1980s. Moreover, it introduced digital control machines for mass production in the machining process in 1978 and 1983. This enterprise also saw a significant increase in the use of robots for body assembly. Toyota also attempted to adopt assembly robots in 1986 (Toyota jidosha kabushikigaisha 1987b, pp. 114, 119, 131). Furthermore, mixed-model production, as seen in the mixed-model assembly line for various product types, was further developed. After 1975, the mixed-model production system was flexible enough to match demand fluctuations at Toyota. This production method became part of the total assembly line throughout the 1970s (Satake 1998, pp. 27, 154, 156, 166, 215–216; Nikkei sangyo shinbun 1975a, b).

Mixed-model production in the same line was pursued as a method of "management that could correspond to limit amounts" on the basis of the adoption of a new order entry system in 1974, which included a 10-day correction system (Satake 1998, pp. 154–156, 164–165). At Toyota, although an attempt to integrate mixed-model production into the assembly line facility was made before 1970, production volume was such small that only one model was produced in the same line at that time (Satake 1998, pp. 166, 216). In contrast, the necessity and significance of implementing the mixed-model production method at a higher level greatly increased after the 1970s in response to the decrease in the production of one car model and the necessity of securing the flexibility that enabled coping with demand fluctuation. The evolution of the Japanese production system after the 1970s had established the basis of international competitiveness by the end of the 1980s.

When examining the characteristics of Japanese manufacturing in relation to such a development of a mass production system, an important aspect is that various types of products with many variations can be produced in accordance with the change in demand for such products. The Japanese production system overcame difficult problems on the basis of the principle of "universalization (generalization)" instead of "specialization." Japanese enterprises pursued this principle through the mixed-flow system in the same production line and the use of various technologies (such as ME technology) as well as the universalization of the labor force, as seen in the use of multi-process workers and the synchronization between various production processes. As a result, Japanese enterprises became remarkably competitive after the latter half of the 1970s, especially in the capital goods and durable consumer goods markets. In addition, Japanese companies in these industries established an international competitive reputation in production costs, quality, accurate delivery schedules, and product variety.

An important characteristic of Japanese manufacturing can also be seen in the total systematization of production, development, purchasing, and sales. Regarding this aspect of Japanese manufacturing, Takahiro Fujimoto pointed out that a common pattern in Japanese companies after the war can be seen in their organizational capabilities, which are specific to the system of integrated-type manufacturing (Fujimoto 2004, p. 72). In addition, their capabilities for manufacturing of this kind were based on teamwork among multi-skilled workers (Fujimoto 2012, p. 112). Furthermore, an efficient troubleshooting cycle was established, based on the abilities of multi-skilled workers who not only carry out their jobs at their multiple workplaces but are also able to quickly cope with unusual situations occurring in the workplace (Fujimoto 2004, p. 193). Finally, Japanese integrated-type manufacturing is suitable for product types with "integrated-type architecture" that require mutual coordination in the workplace, where development and production processes are undertaken (Fujimoto 2004, p. 25, pp. 297–298; Fujimoto 2003, p. 24).

The foundation of Japanese manufacturing is also supported by a division of labor production structure unique to Japan, such as the subcontracting system. In addition, regarding assembly network within a company, Toyota, for example, does not produce all Toyota automobiles itself. It has, from the beginning, created a network of consignment assemblers and developed a production system based on this comprehensive and consistent approach of final assembly consignments. Toyota was also able to fine-tune a multilateral response to fluctuations in demand by utilizing its assembler network. Furthermore, this assembler network enabled Toyota to respond to and absorb short-term demand fluctuations, such as those influenced by seasonal variations and the vicissitudes of popular models.

However, a single, central managerial pivot was required for the dynamic operation of the assembler network. The regulation of production within the assembler network was undertaken centrally and hierarchically by Toyota's Production Management Department, which was established in 1960. After 1966, when the General Planning Department was created, this department was responsible for the planning of the transfers within the assembler network. Toyota developed the assembly network in order to disseminate the risk involved in capital investments and absorb the fluctuations in demand, taking into account the mass production of different models and the lack of managerial resources (Shiomi 1995, pp. 30, 41–5).

An important aspect of Japanese firms' international competitiveness in terms of quality was achieved by the workers' abilities to take charge of the multi-level production process through small group activities, such as the QC circle and the suggestion activities, and effective teamwork. Japanese enterprises emphasize product quality, as seen in the low defect rate of parts and breakdown of products. These are very different from the factors of product functionality, such as a safe driving experience and reliability, that German companies tend to emphasize. These differences also became an important factor in determining the competitive advantage of Japanese enterprises and the quality of their products in the eyes of the consumers. Finally, Japanese manufacturing had developed a unique production system while focusing on the generalization and total systematization of the important elements of such a system.

9.4.2 The Rollout of Mass Production Systems and German Manufacturing

As several examples have demonstrated, postwar Germany's deployment of mass production systems such as the Ford system centered on typical volume production industries such as the automobile and electrical industries. Overall, changes in production during the 1950s were not simply a "rebuilding" of the prewar state, as they also became more flexible and dynamic. Radkau (1993, p. 139) pointed out that rationalization along the lines of the Taylor-Ford model using an American-style, mass production model was integrated with the 1950s management climate and modified on the basis of collective experience. On this point, Ambrosius (1993, pp. 117–118) identifies two important factors in the failure of the Taylor-Ford model of rationalization in quickly spreading in 1950s West Germany. Consumer goods production at the time had secondary significance, and German managers had a traditionally skeptical attitude toward American-style Fordism. This was attributable to the need for wide-scale management units for rolling out this type of rationalization model as well as to the "Made in Germany" brand, combined with flexible labor- and knowledge-intensive production methods instead of globally standardized mass production.

Mass production did progress in Germany during the 1950s and 1960s, but even there it was limited to two types of companies. First are companies like Volkswagen, which pursued economies of scale through American-style mass production, owing to their corporate policy of producing affordable cars for their broad customer base (Der Volkswirt 1969, p. 55). In contrast, certain companies had developed management and product strategies that prioritized high-end market segments with outstanding quality and technology in the context of the relatively low price elasticity of upper segments in the market; these companies occupied an important position although their strategy was different (Vgl. Schmidt 1993, p. 94). Companies such as Daimler-Benz and BMW in particular implemented strategies to design high-quality, value-added products based on a relatively long-term model policy. From the manufacturers' perspective, product design concepts were based on users' functional needs of quality and durability, which differed from the needs of US consumers.

For example, in the 1950s, the corporate philosophy of Daimler-Benz was anchored in two production concepts: (1) manufacturing vehicles with a utility value created in response to the demands for uniqueness and luxury and (2) a broad and comprehensive supply of commercial vehicles. This philosophy proved highly successful (Sörgel 1986, p. 16). In the field of useful vehicles, the expansion of the products from small transport vehicles to large trucks, as well as the internationalization of production, was promoted to realize the synergy of proper, long-term production. In contrast, the conscious evasion of this step by concentrating on the passenger car market, which has high demand and technologically high value, and the maintenance of "the unity" of the Mercedes-Benz brand, as seen in the manufacturing of passenger cars being limited to Germany (excluding some knockdown assemblies), continued to exist. (Feldenkiruchen 2003, p. 202). Such product and production concepts are related to the production model.

According to W. Streeck, there were two types of auto manufacturers in postwar West Germany: mass production manufacturers in the north (Volkswagen, Ford, and Opel) and luxury car manufacturers, remnants of craft production, in the south (BMW, Daimler-Benz, and their competitors). These regional differences developed in response to differences in manufacturing principles and philosophies. Southern manufacturers exhibited technical creativity and engineering perfection (Streeck 1989, p. 119). For these manufacturers, specializing in these particular market segments with a value-added strategy of high quality and high performance meant that there was little need for establishing cost superiority through economies of scale (Kazama 1997, p. 69). Strategies for product design concepts and market positioning greatly influenced the important characteristics of quality and flexible production concept, an inherently German characteristic.

This focus on "quality and a flexible production concept" could be observed in prewar Germany as one method of production responding to market limits (Vgl. Stahlmann 1993). The basic principles of this production concept could also be observed in postwar Germany. We can see another attempt at production reforms before the war, which mainly occurred in the automobile, electrical, and machinery industries. More specifically, these industries attempted to secure a certain level of flexibility for dealing with demand fluctuations between products and obtaining some of the benefits of mass production, even under certain market constraints (Vgl. von Freyberg 1989; Siegel and von Freyberg 1991). Regarding the aspect of hybridization, there was a combination of various American elements in the introduction of the Ford system with those of Germany's own prewar production system as well as the standardized "unit system."

After WWII, both the domestic and export market conditions were equipped to introduce American-style mass production. However, Germany sought market positioning by pursuing competitiveness in European markets where product quality, in terms of functionality, was emphasized. For instance, in the European automobile market, brand loyalty of consumers tends to be stronger compared with that of the North American market consumers (Jürgens 2005. pp. 14–15). Given these circumstances, German companies pursued a suitable production system.

German characteristics in production methods and systems can be identified on the basis of product design concepts, such as avoiding price competition, positioning, and specific niche strategies in postwar international market expansion. Although work organization itself was a flow production system that may have been inspired by a US model and although these corporations pursued economies of scale in mass production, the elements of high-quality, knowledge-intensive production relying on skilled labor and German-specific systems of vocational education and specialist qualifications, such as the Meister system, were significant. The German production system was based on technical qualifications and vocational education, and production management was dominated by skilled engineers. Thus, production managers were highly skilled, thereby influencing the superiority of the design, development, production, and quality of German products (Lawrence 1980, pp. 131, 140–141, 150, 187, 190). German companies pursued production systems which corresponded with this advantage. They pursued the creation of a quality- and functionality-focused production system with the support of the German-specific method of specialized skill qualification system and vocational education system.

Thus, in Germany's case, quality in the form of product functionality, durability, dependability, and safety was heavily emphasized (Daimler-Benz AG 1980, p. 39; Daimler-Benz AG 1983, p. 39; Daimler-Benz AG 1984, p. 39; Volkswagen AG 1981, p. 21, Adam Opel AG 1971, p. 15), as was reliance on expert, skilled labor in certain jobs. This model differs from Japan's, where integration emphasizing operational capability was a major source of competitive advantage (Fujimoto 2004, Chap. 5). Germany did not pursue a system of complete production process synchronization as Japan did. Although Germany did attempt to develop a mass production system that leveraged workers' skills and technical abilities, the two countries had different markets, and so workers' skills and abilities were different. Consequently, differences can be seen between the two nations' hybrid production systems based on Ford production methods and the artisan production system. The distinct characteristics of German-style manufacturing are evident in production, which reflected an emphasis on quality, function, and branding in product design concepts against the background of the European market's competitiveness and factors of competitive advantage.

Despite the common perception of "Americanization," important German characteristics in German production and manufacturing can be observed in the context of postwar American influences. However, these characteristics are deeply rooted in market structures and differed from those of the United States, which had a highly standardized market. Because this phenomenon was born of the uniquely German and European market emphasis on quality and function, the German production and manufacturing model was a rational adaptation to adhere to the nature of these markets.

Regarding the background in which Japanese companies, such as Toyota, continued to pursue unique production methods, even after being introduced to the American Ford system and the mass production system after World War II, this chapter can still point out historical circumstances such as the domestic market's quantitative limitations, the lack of funds for equipment investment, and the insufficient technology (Fujimoto 1997, p. 74). There were also differences in the level of technology between Japan and Germany. For example, in Germany, the introduction of the Ford system advanced (to some extent) before World War II, but the full-scale introduction and the fixation of the Ford system were not realized, even though the technical level in Germany was higher than that in Japan. Therefore, German enterprises did not face such limited conditions as the Japanese companies did in the introduction of special-purpose machines, the use of automated technology, and the development of the flow production system. In comparison with Japan, it can be stated that the situations in Germany were still closer to those in the United States. This was one reason why German enterprises pursued reforms in its mass production system after the 1970s that emphasized on the use of the ME technology, rather than performing a "general systematization," as seen in Japan (see Chap. 13; Yamazaki 2013).

References

Abelshauser W (1995) Two kinds of fordism: on the differing roles of the industry in the development to the two German states. In: Shiomi H, Wada K (eds) Fordism transformed. Oxford University Press, New York, The development of production methods in the automobile industry, pp 269–296

Abelshauser W (2003) Kulturkamp. Der deutsche Weg in die neue Wirtschaft und die amerikanische Herausforderung. Kulturverlag Kadmos, Berlin

Abelshauser W (2004) Deutsche Wirtschaftsgeschichte seit 1945. C. H. Beck, München

Abelshauser W (2005) The dynamics of German industry. Berghahn Books, New York

Abelshauser W (2018) Zweierlei Fordismus. Zur Rolle der Automobilindustrie in der Wirtschaft der beiden deutschen Staaten. In: K Y, Laks T, Schramm M (eds) Regional Ressourcen und Europa. Dimensionen kritischer Industrie- und Unternehmensgechichtsschreibung. Duncker & Humblot, Berlin, S.93–117

Adam Opel AG (Hrsg) (1962) · · · auch das ist Opel.Adam Opel AG. Adam Opel AG, Rüsselsheim

Adam Opel AG (1971) Geschäftsbericht 1971. Adam Opel AG, Rüsselsheim

Ambrosius G (1993) Wirtschaftlicher Strukturwandel und Technikentwicklung. In: Schildt A, Sywottek A (eds) Modernisierung im Wiederaufbau. Die westdeutsche Gesellschaft der 50er Jahre. Die westdeutsche Gesellschaft der 50er Jahre. Dietz, Bonn, pp 107–128

Automobiltechnische Zeitschrift (1946) Das Volkswagenwerk. In: Automobiltechnische Zeitschrift 48(3):45

Automobiltechnische Zeitschrift (1956) Das neue Opel-Werk K-40, 2000000 Opelwagen. In: Automobiltechnische Zeitschrift 58(12):351

Automobiltechnische Zeitschrift (1957) Bildbericht vom VW-Transporter-Werk Hannover. In: Automobiltechnische Zeitschrift 59(4):116–117

Automobiltechnische Zeitschrift (1962) Das neue Opelwerk in Bochum. In: Automobiltechnische Zeitschrift 64(11):343–345

Bönig, J (1993) Die Einführung von Flieβbandarbeit in Deutschland bis 1933. Zur Geschichte einer Sozialinnovation. Teil I, LIT Verlag, Münster, Hamburg

Braun HJ (1995) Automobilfertigung in Deutschland von den Anfängen bis zu den vierziger Jahren. In: Niemann H, Hermann A (eds) Die Entwicklung der Motorisierung im Deutschen Reich und den Nachfolgestaaten. Stuttgarter Tage zur Automobil- und Unternehmensgeschichte. Franz Steiner, Stuttgart, pp 58–68

Daimler-Benz AG (1957) Geschäftsbericht 1957. Daimler-Benz AG, Stuttgart

Daimler-Benz AG (1980) Geschäftsbericht 1980. Daimler-Benz AG, Stuttgart

Daimler-Benz AG (1983) Geschäftsbericht 1983. Daimler-Benz AG, Stuttgart
Daimler-Benz AG (1984) Annual Report 1984. Daimler-Benz AG, Stuttgart
Der Volkswirt (1957) Opel in stetiger Entwicklung. 12(13) vH Dividende. In: Der Volkswirt 11(25):1273–1275
Der Volkswirt (1959) Riskovolle Kleinwagenproduktion. In: Der Volkswirt 13(38):2133
Der Volkswirt (1960) Hohe Gewinn bei Opel. Steiler Investitionsanstieg—200 (125) Mill. DM Dividende. In: Der Volkswirt 14(33):1851–1853
Der Volkswirt (1969) Hauptversammlungs-Ansprache des Herrn Dr. Kurt Lotz, Vorsitzender des Vorstandes der Volkswagen AG, in der Hauptversammlung 1969. In: Der Volkswirt 23(28):54–57
DWI-Berichte (1961) Die westdeutsche Automobilindustrie und die Entwicklung auf dem internationalen kapitalistischen Automobilmarkt. In: DWI-Berichte 12(22):13–19
Eberhorst E v (1959) Fortschritt im deutschen Kraftfahrzeugbau. In: Der Volkswirt, 13. Jg, Technische Fachbeilage zu Nr. 38 vom 19. September 1959, In: Wirtschaft und Technik, Kraftfahrzeug am deutschen Markt, pp 6–7
Edelmann H (2003) Heinz Nordhoff und Volkswagen. Ein deutscher Unternehmer im amerikanischen Jahrhundert. Vandenhoeck & Ruprecht, Göttingen
Faensen HH (1957) Lochkarten und Fernshreiber als Arbeitsvorbereitung. Beispiel der Adam Opel AG, Rüsselsheim. In: Der Volkswirt 11(27):1425–1427
Feldenkirchen W (2003) "Vom Guten das Beste." Von Daimler und Benz zur Daimler-Chrysler AG. Band 1, Die ersten 100 Jahre (1883–1983), 1. Aufl., F.A.Hebig Verlagsbuchhandlung GmbH, München
Feldenkirchen W (2004) DaimlerChrysle Werk Untertürkheim. Motorbuch-Verlag, Stuttgart
Fujimoto T (1997) Seisan Sisutemu no Sinka Ron (Evolution of production system). Yuhikaku, Tokyo
Fujimoto T (1999) The Evolution of a Manufacturing System at Toyota. Oxford University Press, New York, Oxford
Fujimoto T (2003) Noryoku Kochiku Kyoso (Competition over establishing of capability). Chuou Koron Shinsha, Tokyo
Fujimoto T (2004) Nihon no Monodukuri Tetsugaku (Philosophy of Japanese manufacturing). Nihon Keizai Shinbunsha, Tokyo
Fujimoto T (2012) Monozukuri karano Fukkatsu (Revival based on manufacturing). Nihon Keizai Shinbunsha, Tokyo
Fujimoto T, Tidd J (1993a) Ford sisutemu no donyu to genti tekiou. Nichi ei jidosha sangyo no hikaku kenkyu (The UK and Japanese Auto Industry—Adoption and Adaptation of Fordism, 1). In: Keizaigaku ronsgu (J Econ) 59(2):36–50
Fujimoto T, Tidd J (1993b) Ford sisutemu no donyu to genti tekiou: Nichi ei jidosha sangyo no hikaku kenkyu (2・kan) (The UK and Japanese Auto Industry—Adoption and Adaptation of Fordism, 2). In: Keizaigaku ronsgu (J Econ) 59(3):34–56
Goos G (1963) Spezielle Fertigungsfragen im Kraftfahrzeugbau. In: Werkstatt und Betrieb 96(3):151–152
Hilf HH (1956) Arbeitswissenschaftliche Beobachtungen in USA. In: Rationalisierung 7(1):3–8
Hilger S (2004) „Amerikanisierung“ deutscher Unternehmen. Wettbewerbsstrategien und Unternehmenspolitik bei Henkel, Siemens und Daimler-Benz (1945/49–1975). Franz Steiner Verlag, Stuttagart
Hiller H (1952) Alteste Automobilfabrik der Welt. Der einzigartige Wiederaufstieg der Daimler-Benz-Werke. In: Der Volkswirt 6(9):25–28
Homburg H (1991) Rationalisierung und Industriearbeit: Arbeitsmarkt—Management—Arbeiterschaft im Siemens-Konzern Berlin 1900–1939. Haude & Spener, Berlin
Isuzu jidosha kabushikigaisha syashihennsyu iinkai (1988) (ed) Isuzu gojyunenshi (50-year history of Isuzu Motores Ltd.). Isuzu jidosha kabushikigaisha, Tokyo
Itami H, Kagono T, Kobayashi T, Sakakibara K, Ito M (1988) kyoso to kakushin (Competition and innovation). Toyo keizai shinposya, Tokyo.

Iwagoshi T (1963) Jidosha kogyoron (Automobile industry). Tokyo daigaku shuppankai, Tokyo
Jürgens U (2005) Charakteristika der europäischen Automobilindustrie. Gibt es einen europäischen Entwicklungsweg? In: Schmidt G., Bungsche H., Heyder T, Klemm M (eds) Und es fährt und fährt...Automobilindustrie und Automobilkultur am Beginn des 21. Jahrhundert, Edition Sigma, Berlin, pp 11–71
Kazama N (1997) Doitsuteki Seisan Moderu to Furekisibiriti (German production model and flexibility). Chuo Keizaisha, Tokyo
Kern H, Schumann M (1984) Das Ende der Arbeitsteilung? Rationalisierung in der industriellen Produkution: Bestandnahme, Trendbestimmung. C. H. Beck, München
Kleinschmidt C (2004) Driving the West German consumer society: the introduction of US style production and marketing at Volkswagen, 1945–70. In: Kudo A, Kipping M, Schroter HG (eds) German and Japanese business in the boom year. Transforming American management and technology models. Routledge, London, pp 75–92
Klenke D (1996) "Wirtschaftswunder"-Weltmarkt-Westdeutscher Fordismus von V. Wellhoner. In: Zeitschrift Für Unternehmensgeschichte 41:219–220
Kohira K (1968) Jidosha (Automobile). Aki Shobo, Tokyo
Lauke (1956) Für und wider die Flieβarbeit. Ruckblick und Ausblick. In: REFA-Nachrichten 9(2):41–46
Lauke (1958) Tendenzen in der Weiterentwicklung des Fluβprinzips. In: REFA-Nachrichten 11(3):79
Lawrence P (1980) Managers and management in West Germany. Croom Helm, London
Liker JL (2004) The Toyota way: 14 management principles from the world's greatest manufacturer. McGraw-Hill, New York
Mennecke K (1956) Flieβende Fertigung durch Stetigforderer. In: Der Volkswirt 10(3):45–46
Mercedes-Benz AG (1990) Werk Sindelfingen. Karosserie- und Montagewerk der Mercedes-Benz Aktiengesellschaft. Ein historischer Uberblick. Mercedes-Benz AG, Sindelfingen
Nihon choki sinyo ginko chosabu dai ichika (1963) Jidosha buhin kogyo no genjyo to mondaiten (The present conditions and problems of the automobile parts industry). In: Chosa geppo (Monthly report of investigartion) 76:2–60
Nikkei sangyo shinbun (1975a) Toyota jiko senyo lain wo yameru (Toyota Motor Corporation cease special line). In: Nikkei sangyo shinbun (Nikkei Business Daily), 2.4.1975
Nikkei sangyo shinbun (1975b) Toyota no kojyo hisokani henkaku (Toyota's factory secretely attempts reform). In: Nikkei sangyo shinbun (Nikkei Business Daily), 30.4.1975
Nissan jidosha kabushikigaisha shashi hensaniinkai (ed) (1975) Nissan jidosha syashi 1964–1973 (History of Nissan Motor Corporation). Nissan jidosha kabushikigaisha, Tokyo
Nissan jidosha kabushikigaisha somubu chosaka (ed) (1965) Nissan jidosha sanjunenshi (30-year history of Nissan Motor Corporation), Nissan jidosha kabushikigaisha, Yokohama
Nohara H (2006) Gendai no bungyo to hyojyunka (Modern division of labor and standardization). Takasuga syuppann, Tokyo
Onizuka M (1991) Sengo nihon kigyo ni okeru seisan kanri no tenkai (Development of production management in postwar Japanese enterprise). In: Sengo nihon keiei kenkyukai (ed) Sengo nihon no kigyo keiie (Business administration in post war Japan). Bunshindo, Tokyo, pp 215–272
Ono T (1978) Toyota seisan hoshiki (Toyota production system). Daiyamondosha, Tokyo
Radkau R (1993) "Wirtschaftswunder" ohne technologische Innovation? Technische Modernitat in den 50er Jahren. In: Schildt A, Sywottek A (eds) Modernisierung im Wiederaufbau. Die westdeutsche Gesellschaft der 50er Jahre. Dietz, Bonn, pp 129–154
Satake H (1998) Toya seisan hoshiki no seisei · hatten · henyo (Birth, development, and change of the Toyota production system). Toyo keizai shinpo sha, Tokyo
Shimokawa K (1990) Nihon no Kigyo Hattenshi (Development history of Japanese enterprises). Kodansha, Tokyo
Shimokawa K (2004) Gurobaru Jidosha Sangyo Keieishi (Global history of the automobile industry). Yuhikaku, Tokyo

Shioji H (1994) Toyota sisutemu keisei katei no syotokusitsu (How has the Toyota production system been developed?). In: Keizai ronso (Econ Rev) 154(6):49–61
Shiomi H (1995) The formation of assembler networks in the automobile industry: the case of Toyota Motor Company (1955–80). In: Shiomi H, Wada K (eds) Fordism transformed: the development of production methods in the automobile industry. Oxford University Press, Oxford, pp 28–48
Schmidt V (1993) Die Mercedes-Benz AG als Dominant Firm auf dem Nutzfahrzeugmarkt—Zur wettbewerbspolitischen Problematik der Dominant Firmen. Vandenhoeck & Ruprecht, Gottingen
Schröter HG (2005) Americanization of the European economy. A compact survey of American economic influence in Europe since the 1880s. Springer, Dordrecht
Siegel T, von Freyberg T (1991) Industrielle Rationalisierung unter dem Nationalsozialismus. Campus, Frankfurt am Main
Sörgel A (1986) Daimler-Benz—der Multi im Musterländle. Progress-Institut für Wirtschaftsforschung, Bremen
Springer K (1963) Weibliche Arbeitskrafte am Fließband. In: Werkstatt und Betrieb 96(10):769–771
Stahl und Eisen (1962) Adam Opel AG, Bochum. In: Stahl und Eisen 82(26):805
Stahlmann M (1993) Die erste Revolution in der Autoindustrie. Management und Arbeitspolitik von 1900–1940. Campus, Frankfurt am Main
Steeger A (1953) Fließfertigung für Kurbelwellen während der Rationalisierungsausstellung. In: Rationalisierung 4(1):196–199
Streeck W (1989) Successful adjustment to turbulent markets: the automobile industry. In: Katzenstein PJ (ed) Industry and politics in West Germany. Toward the third republic. Cornell University Press, Ithaca, pp 113–156
Takeda H (1995) Jidosha sangyo (Automobile industry). In: Takeda H (ed) Nihon sangyo hatten no dainamizumu (Dynamism of development of Japanese industry). Tokyo daigaku shuppankai, Tokyo, pp 191–242
Tolliday S (1995) Enterprise and State in the West German Wirtschaftswunder. In: Bus History Rev 69:273–350
Tolliday S (2000) Transplanting the American model? US automobile companies and the transfer of technology and management to Britain, France, and Germany, 1928–1962. In: Zeitlin J, Herrigel G (eds) Americanization and its limits. Reworking US technology and management in post-war Europe and Japans. Oxford University Press, Oxford, pp 76–119
Toyota jidosha kabushikigaisha (ed) (1987a) Sozo kagirinaku (Unlimited creation). Toyota jidosha kabushikigaisha, Toyota
Toyota jidosha kabushikigaisha (ed) (1987b) Sozo kagirinaku. Shiryo hen (Unlimited creation. Material edition). Toyota jidosha kabushikigaisha, Toyota
Toyota jidosha kabushikigaisha (2013) Toyota jidosha nanajyugonen shi (70-year history of Toyota Motor Corporation). Toyota jidosha kabushikigaisha, Toyota
Toyota jidosha kogyo kabushikigaisha shashi henshu iinkai (ed) (1958) Toyota jidosha nijunenshi (20-year history of Toyota Motor Corporation), Toyota jidosha kogyo kabushikigaisha, Tokyo
Toyota jidosha kogyo kabushikigaisha shashi henshu iinkai (ed) (1967) Toyota jidosha sanjyunen shi (30-year history of Toyota Motor Corporation). Toyota jidosha kogyo kabushikigaisha Toyota
Toyota jidosha kogyo kabushikigaisha (ed) (1978) Toyota no Ayumi (History of Toyota). Toyota jidosha kogyo kabushikigaisha, Toyota
Tsuda M, Sumiya M (1963) Toyota jiko ni okeru gijyutsu kakushin (Technological innovation in Toyota Motor Corporation). Nihon jinbun kagaku kai (ed) Gijyutsu kakushin no shakaiteki eikyo (Social influence of technological innovation). Tokyo daigaku shuppankai, Tokyo, pp 32–57
Volkswagen AG (1981) Bericht über das Geschäftsjahr 1981. Volkswagen AG, Wolfsburg
von Freyberg T (1989) Industrielle Rationalisierung in der Weimarer Republik: Untersucht an Beispielen aus dem Maschinenbau und der Elektroindustrie. Campus, Frankfurt am Main
von Seherr-Thoss HCG (1979) Die deutsche Automobilindustrie. Eine Dokumentation von 1886 bis 1979, 2nd edn. Deutsches Verlagsanstalt, Stuttgart

Wada K (2009) Monozukuri no Guwa (A fable of manufacturing). Nagoya Daigaku Shuppankai, Nagoya

Wada K, Shiba T (1995) Nihonteki Seisan Sisutemu no Keisei (Formation of the Japanese production system). In: Yamazaki H, Kikkawa T (eds) "Nihonteki" Keiei no Renzoku to Danzetsu (Continuity and discontinuity of "Japanese" management). Iwanami Shoten, Tokyo, pp 125–157

Watanabe T, Hirao K (1972) Jidosha sangyo no yakushin to sono henbo (Advancement of the automobile industry and its changes). In: Sangyo to keizai shuppanbu (ed) Shuyo sangyo sengo nijyugonenshi (Postwar 25-year history of major industries). Sangyo to keizai shuppanbu, pp 421–472

Wellhöner V (1996) "Wirtschaftswunder"—Weltmarkt—Westdeutscher Fordismus. Der Fall Volkswagen. Westfalisches Dampfboot, Münster

Wittke V (1996) Wie entstand industrielle Massenproduktion? Diskontinuierliche Entwicklung der deutschen Elektroindustrie von den Anfängen der „groβen Industrie" bis zur Entfaltung des Fordismus [1880–1975]. Edition Sigma, Berlin

Yamamoto K (1994) Nihon ni okeru syokuba no gijyutsu · rodoshi—1854–1990nen— (Workshop technique and labor in Japan—1854–1990—). Tokyo daigaku shuppankai, Tokyo

Yamazaki T (2001a) Vaimaruki Doitsu gorika undo no tenkai (Rationalization movement in Germany during the Weimar era). Moriyama shoten, Tokyo

Yamazaki T (2001b) Natisuki Doitsu gorika undo no tenkai (Rationalization movement in Germany during the Nazi era). Moriyama shoten, Tokyo

Yamazaki T (2013) Gendai no Doitsu kigyo—Sono gurobaru chiikika to keiei tokushitsu —(Contemporary German enterprises—their global-regionalization and characteristics of business management—). Moriyama shoten, Tokyo

Yamazaki T (2015) Doitsu senzenki keieishi kenkyu (German business history until the end of World War II). Moriyama shoten, Tokyo

Zeitlin J (2000) Introduction: Americanization and its limits: reworking US technology and management in post-War Europe and Japan. In: Zeitlin J, Herrigel G (eds) Americanization and its limits. Reworking US technology and management in post-war Europe and Japan. Oxford University Press, Oxford, pp 1–50

Chapter 10
Deployment of Marketing Methods

Abstract The deployment of American methods for adapting to a mass market is examined in this chapter. Following World War II, Japan, Germany, and other European countries advanced in the development of mass production. As a result, how businesses adapt to the mass market through methods such as marketing has become critical. However, many factors influenced the adoption of these American methods in both Japan and Germany. Thus, this chapter first considers the deployment of American marketing methods in Japan as a representative measure for mass-market adaptation in relation to the postwar market and social structures, the distribution system, and the business strategy. Next, it examines Germany's deployment of American marketing methods in relation to various factors, including the characteristics of domestic and European markets, production- and technology-oriented management values, the composition of executive management, and changes in the structure of competition. Based on these discussions, Japanese and German characteristics in the introduction of American marketing methods are clarified. Finally, the role of reframing in the Americanization of business management will be investigated.

Keywords Advertising · Channel policy · Marketing · Management value · Market structure · Pricing policy · Product policy

From Chaps. 6–9, we discussed the deployment of American management education and American-style managements- and production systems in Japan and Germany. Introduction of the American management system post-WWII constituted a fundamental condition for the development of full-scale mass production. Eventually, in the 1950s and 1960s, the mass production system was established in both Japan and Germany. This was accompanied by an increase in the importance of adapting to the market. Under these circumstances, marketing became very significant as a means of supporting sales and adapting to the market. These techniques have also become an important method for supporting mass production systems. Under these conditions, the introduction of the American approach to marketing was also promoted in both Japan and Germany.

T. Yamazaki, *Japanese and German Enterprises*,
https://doi.org/10.1007/978-981-97-4880-8_10

In terms of the impact of American marketing measures, Schröter argued that, in terms of the Americanization of the European economy, changes such as marketing research and publicity were a logical result of mass production, mass distribution, and US direct investment (Schröter 2005, p. 97). Marketing was one of the core American management concepts that Europe began to adopt in the 1960s, along with divisional structure and management education. In the 1950s, many Europeans saw mass-produced goods as standardized, and mass production was antithetical to individualism. However, the American perspective suggests that mass production promotes individualism because it allows people to buy a wider range of goods. With further integration of the European national markets and an increase in consumer purchasing power, this perception began to spread throughout Europe (Schröter 2005, pp. 121–122).

After World War II, large manufacturing companies in Japan, especially in the consumer goods industries, had to deal aggressively with marketing in order to pursue the adoption of mass production, expand market share under intense competition, acquire correct information on market conditions, and correspond to the limits of the conventional distribution structure in distributing new mass-produced products (Sato 1983, pp. 131–132, 140).

This chapter discusses the deployment of American methods to adapt to a mass market with consideration for the connection to the changes in the postwar market and social structure.[1] The deployment of American marketing methods in Japan and Germany is considered in Sect. 10.1 and Sect. 10.2, respectively. Section 10.3 clarifies Japanese and German characteristics of the deployment of marketing method. Based on the analyses in these sections, in Sect. 10.4, reframing in the Deployment of American Marketing Methods in Japan and Germany is examined.

10.1 Deployment of Marketing Methods in Japan

10.1.1 Historical Stages of the Deployment of Marketing Methods

The use of American marketing methods as market adaptation measures that accompanied the evolution of postwar mass production in Japan is examined first. Marketing in postwar Japan can be divided into three periods: (1) the introductory period when leading manufacturers introduced American marketing (the latter half of the 1950s through the first half of the 1960s), (2) the period of modification of American marketing and the appearance of the distribution industry in which Japanese marketing was established as a part of Japanese management (the second half of

[1] The first content analysis related to Germany in this chapter is Chap. 8 of the author's book "*German Business Management: A Japanese Perspective on Regional Development Factors,*" which was published by Springer in 2013.

the 1960s through the first half of the 1970s), and (3) the period of modification of Japanese marketing toward the era of internationalization and technological innovation/digitalization (since the late 1970s).

In Japan, the technological innovation and capital investment boom were rather sudden. Managerial marketing, on the other hand, was developed as an overall marketing technique as a result of the introduction of American marketing techniques. As a result, Japan did not go through the historical steps that Americans did, such as (1) beginning with high-pressure marketing, (2) consumer-oriented marketing, and (3) managerial marketing. Rather, Japan introduced and implemented managerial marketing and high-pressure marketing simultaneously. In other words, despite emphasizing precise market research and product policies, Japanese enterprises relied on high-pressure marketing as competition among companies increased due to the rapid expansion of mass production capacity. To bridge the gap between rapidly increasing production capacity and the market, great efforts were made for high-pressure advertising, sales promotion, provision of consumer credit, and in particular, a great emphasis on controlling sales channels. However, in the Japanese market, where competition is fierce, product policies emphasizing the importance of applied research and improved new products in R & D and new product development were emphasized. As a result, product policies have tended to emphasize market segmentation and product differentiation. For example, in the automobile industry, a full-line policy and rapid model changes facilitated product differentiation and planned obsolescence. It was not pursued to increase the penetration rate of automobiles through mass production focusing on a single model. Rather, an unusually early combination of mass production and market segmentation policies occurred. This tendency has also been observed in other consumer goods such as household electrical devices and cameras.

Marketing focused on product policy was developed during the aforementioned "modification period." However, because of the specific trend of Japanese business management, there were various modifications to marketing, particularly the characteristics of organizational conduct. One of these was the previously mentioned preference for applied research and improved new products in new product development and R&D. Furthermore, because of collectivist behavior patterns, the characteristics of business organizations linked by multilayered informal human relationships within the organization, and horizontal communication among organizational departments accompanied by successful mutual adjustment, total marketing was developed with the goal of achieving overall integration in accordance with the marketing strategy (Shimokawa 1997, pp. 140–143, 155–157; Goji 1969, pp. 211–214, Arakawa 1960, p. 40; Zaiga 1980, p. 236).

In the 1965 recession, managerial marketing advanced significantly under the intensification of competition among oligopolistic companies in addition to integrated marketing that focused on strategic development. Thus, enterprises underwent a transition from production orientation or finance orientation (Akimoto and Watanabe 1983, p. 22). Moreover, some enterprises attempted to avoid dependence on the general trading company peculiar to Japan that had played a significant role in export and established marketing systems from an international perspective by promoting house brands and advertising activities based on them, thereby reinforcing sales and supporting the sales staff (Akimoto and Watabnabe 1983, p. 29). Managerial marketing, in which strategic decision-making processes are focused on marketing, was deployed in the United States after World War II. Although there was a delay in the spread of such marketing to Japan, manufacturing firms in the country eventually focused on this aspect after 1965 (Toba 1982, p. 4).

In the third period described earlier, Japanese-style marketing was formed in response to the era of internationalization and technological innovation/digitalization. Even in such cases, however, marketing techniques in Japan and those in America did not differ significantly; the only difference was in how they were implemented (Shimokawa 1997, pp. 140–141).

Another distinguishing feature of Japan is that the traditional wholesaler-led distribution system was revised under the leadership of large-scale consumer goods manufacturers. The distribution system led by large-scale consumer goods manufacturers took the form of restricted group-controlled distribution channels (Sato 1983, p. 168; Wakabayashi 1999, p. 21; Ogawa 2010, p. 208). One of the important problems in the latter half of the 1960s was the affliated distribution system which was determined by two necessities; (1) securing of certain choice by consumer in the final purchase and (2) evasion of the competition resulting from the handling of behavior with the product of other companies by the merchant wholesalers (Takaoka 1976, pp. 156–157; Sato 1983, pp. 151–152). The differences in marketing between Japan and the United States were due to the complexities of the distribution structure and the marketing achievements of wholesale dealers (Toba 1982, p. 5). During the period when large manufacturers played a leading role in the deployment of American marketing, the Japanese-style expansion of the mass market for consumer durables was pursued, which was characterized by a continuous and constant cycle of development, particularly sales promotion driven high-pressure marketing. In this progression, group-sales channels were particularly effective (Shimokawa 1997, p. 156). Such a trend toward the affiliated distribution system eventually brought about a specific style of distribution and marketing in Japan.

In this way, American marketing exerted a significant influence on Japan. However, it is important to clarify how Japanese companies, based on market conditions, performed original improvements, adapted American marketing methods, and followed the process of learning (Wakabayashi 1999, p. 17). Although some Japanese pioneer firms adopted and imitated American marketing techniques in the 1950s, the stage moved toward "application and innovation," with modifications corresponding to market and consumer needs and further advanced to the stage of "proficiency and emergence" (Ogawa and Hayashi 1997, pp. 6–7). The imitation process of American-style marketing was completed during the 1960s (Ogawa 2010, p. 207). American marketing methods diffused in such a process were revised according to Japanese circumstances.

10.1.2 General Conditions of the Deployment of Marketing Techniques

In the 1950s, marketing was introduced as one of the techniques for modern sales activities. Conversion from production-oriented to consumer-oriented management became inevitable due to mass consumption and mass production (Eguchi 1975, p. 175). Although attempts to introduce various methods were made under such conditions, the marketing approach introduced and deployed with initiatives of the Japan Productivity Center was managerial marketing. Managerial marketing began in the United States as a market improvement movement, emphasizing consumer-based principles and new techniques such as market research, advertising, and product development. However, around 1960, efforts were made to modify American techniques of long-term marketing planning and short-term problem-solving in order to adapt them to Japanese circumstances (Arakawa 1960, p. 39; Arakawa 1964, p. 88; Shirahige 1976, pp. 144–145; Shirahige 1962, p. 148; Murata 1981, p. 8). Since 1960, the main issues with regard to marketing management in leading companies have been developing appropriate procedures for product development and establishing effective control of marketing channels. In relation to these issues, questions have been raised about how to integrate marketing activities effectively and how to maintain proper coordination between marketing and other business activities (Arakawa 1964, p. 81).

Managerial marketing became the primary technique used by top management and other management in the competitive market (Ogawa 2010, p. 204) since it combined total management techniques with investment activities (Shimokawa 1976a, p. 89). However, due to the rapid advance of innovation and equipment investment, the differentiation of new products became an important factor affecting the introduction and use of managerial marketing techniques in Japan. In the postwar boom years, geared toward market expansion, sales strategies generally focused on advertising, publicity, and the affiliated distribution system rather than on determining the consumers' needs and demands (Takaoka 1976, pp. 154–155). The most prominent differences between the marketing policies of Japan and the United States were seen in their distribution channel policies, sales promotion policies, such as advertising and publicity, and price policies (Eguchi 1975, pp. 179, 181; Katagiri 2000, p. 37). Therefore, it is important to consider the main fields of marketing.

Market Research: Although market research was initially implemented after World War II in the form of public opinion polls, there was criticism of the method due to its textbook-like sampling survey from 1952 to 1955. Market research through public opinion polls was unable to satisfy the demand. Thus, additional techniques were required. However, market research was regarded as comprising methods related to public opinion polls or quality control and was not introduced as a marketing technique. Around 1954, market research departments were established in many companies, after which such marketing became a functional field in the business world (Goji et al. 1965, pp. 926–927, 934–935; Hayashi 1965, p. 31). Despite such improvements, it was not until the latter half of the 1950s that market research changed from simply collecting data and performing statistical analyses to incorporating psychological and calculative approaches (Goji et al. 1969, pp. 211–212). As competition between industries became more intense, market research through public opinion polls was unable to satisfy the demand (Arai 1961, p. 65).

From the end of the 1950s to the beginning of the 1960s, the study of consumption behaviors became an important part of new product development in addition to test marketing of limited products (Goji et al. 1969, p. 534). Eventually, marketing research became a functional part of business management that examined market trends and consumer behaviors (Iseda 1963, p. 40).

Distribution Channel Policy: An important characteristic of marketing in Japan after World War II was seen in the circulation of distribution. In most consumer goods industries, large wholesalers and trading companies occupied a pivotal position in the marketing system, and they played an important role in distribution functions prior to World War II. However, this situation underwent a radical change. One of the most significant developments in marketing after the war was the very extensive control attained by large manufacturers of selected consumer goods over their channels of distribution. Large firms in the manufacturing industries took over distribution functions through outright ownership of outlets or by controlling interdependent wholesalers and retailers under their control. In many consumer goods industries, a manufacturer-dominated centrally coordinated and vertically integrated distribution system was formed. The emergence of this type of distribution system resulted in a rather basic alteration of the power relationship between manufacturers and marketing intermediaries (Sato 1983, pp. 138–140; Yoshino 1971, pp. 109–110). Before World War II, wholesalers were channel leaders who had the powers of distribution control and price determination (Eguchi 1975, p. 192). In contrast, manufacturing companies became the main bearers of distribution control. In addition, maximizing market share, maintaining market prices and strong distribution dominance through a superior channel system, and gaining superiority in inter-firm competition were stressed upon. However, in Japan, the focus was on three particular aspects: (1) the length of the channel, (2) the manner in which the channel was evaluated on the basis of its handling of in-house goods, and (3) members' density within the specific region according to their business policy and the character of the goods treated by each enterprise (Eguchi 1975, pp. 181–182). Such movement was a necessary measure to secure the market of in-house products for manufacturing companies. On the other hand, some of the weakened distributors also expected such focus (Hayashi 1961, p. 17).

Although improvement and reorganization of the distribution system became an important issue after 1952 (Goji et al. 1965, p. 937), it was around 1962 that interest in the "distribution problem" became strong. Characteristics of the market policy at that time can be seen in various methods, such as supporting the intermediate sales organization, affiliating sales channel policies, and directing sales toward consumers. However, the market policy at that time generally focused on the manufacturer's perspective and not the consumers' viewpoint (Goji et al. 1969, pp. 215–217).

Affiliating sales channel policies were usually dealt with at the retail level. However, attempts to affiliate end-users became prominent in each company around

1957–1958. The most representative industries of such a movement included the durable consumer goods industries, such as automobiles, the household appliance industry, the cosmetic industry, and the medicaments industry (Goji et al. 1969, pp. 538–539; Nishimura 1995, pp. 154–155; Onaga 1995, p. 72).

In this way, the distribution channel policy established an original position that reflected the specific Japanese management climate (Eguchi 1975, p. 176). Above all, in the affiliated distribution system, as seen in the home appliance industry, one of the intentions was to prevent extreme underselling and price collapse, even under mass production (Niida and Mishima 1991, pp. 98, 115). However, the distribution channel policy itself did not function effectively as a marketing policy. Therefore, it became necessary that the distribution channel policy be promoted concurrently with other policies, such as price policies and sales promotion policies, both of which were different marketing elements (Eguchi 1975, p. 186).

Product Policy: After 1955, each firm earnestly promoted product development, both premeditatedly and systematically, by establishing a department that was in charge of production planning (Goji et al. 1965, p. 930; Hayashi 1965, p. 32). The planned obsolescence policy, as a means of demand reclamation and the restraint of competition, began to prevail, due to the shortening of the product life cycle, from around 1958 to the early 1960s. The 1955–1958 period was the take-off period for product planning (Goji et al. 1969, pp. 214, 533; Fujieda 1965, p. 35). Whereas the emphasis of product planning around the mid-1950s was based on the strengthening of merchandising, that from the end of the 1950s to the early 1960s was based on the development of new products and their market entry (Goji et al. 1969, pp. 531–532). Japanese companies had promoted the establishment and maintenance of a sales system that emphasized sales volume under the pursuit of expanding market share. However, criticism of such behavior appeared during the 1965 recession, after which the market segmentation strategy was widely employed (Uno 1969, pp. 26–27).

Large consumer goods makers in Japan eventually made product planning the main pillars of their marketing due to the necessity of product differentiation (Sato 1983, p. 136). This was based on the fact that Japanese industries had vigorously pursued new product introduction and diversification strategies, mainly through the import of foreign technology (Yoshino 1971, p. 102).

Price Policy: Important characteristics of the pricing policy of Japanese enterprises, particularly manufacturing companies in the postwar boom years, included the maximization of sales volume, profits, and market share. In other words, the pricing policy was mainly based on the superficial market quotations system. The pricing policy of manufacturing companies also emphasized an indirect complementary price policy with strategic intention. One of the typical policies developed with the intention to spread products in the distribution stage, while maintaining price by preventing underselling, was the rebate. However, in Japan, there were very few cases in which the price that was previously set was maintained with the exception of the resale price maintenance products under the business transactions that contained the conventional non-rationality (Eguchi 1975, pp. 193–194, 196).

In American enterprises, once a price that could secure a profit was set according to the strict principle of business management, such as the rate of return on investment (ROI), various measures, such as advertising, sales promotion, and product policies, were emphasized without using price as the competitive means. The reason for this was that price had become a type of contract that helped secure the company's foundation (Eguchi 1975, p. 180). Overall, in the Japanese enterprises that emphasized sales volume and market share, the price policy differed greatly from that in the United States.

Sales Promotion Policy: In Japan, the driving force behind sales promotions was always manufacturing companies. This important characteristic of marketing in Japan differed from that in the United States, where large retail companies performed sales promotions through widespread advertising. The main objective of sales promotion was in distribution, rather than the consumer, especially during the postwar boom years. This indicates that the distribution channel policy and sales promotion policy of manufacturing companies were always closely interconnected in Japan (Eguchi 1975, pp. 187–188).

Although there were advertising and publicity activities performed by Japanese companies before World War II (Mori 1976, p. 269), after the war, particularly after 1955, full-scale advertising and publicity activities continued (Takaoka 1976, p. 156). It was around 1958 that advertising and publicity came to be taken up politically, especially under the organic relations with other marketing activities. At that time, different market research techniques were beginning to be applied for advertising and publicity (Goji et al. 1969, pp. 214–215). The advertising expenses in each enterprise dramatically increased in correspondence with the expansion of the market around 1960. In addition, there was an emphasis on corporate advertising as well as on company-wide professionalization and mass advertising (Goji et al. 1969, pp. 535–536).

Based on the aforementioned points, various elements of marketing methods were deployed after World War II. However, marketing techniques were not systematically accepted. Until the early 1950s, there were many cases in which each technique was individually introduced. Therefore, establishment of a marketing mix, as seen in how some companies synthesized and coordinated marketing techniques, became an important issue. In addition, it is also important to realize how each firm adapted American marketing methods to the Japanese business climate (Arai 1961, p. 67).

Reformation of Retail Business Status: In the 1960s, significant modernization and innovation appeared in the distribution industry for the first time, after which the subject of focus was the issue of distribution in Japan. For example, prominent changes occurred in the rise of the supermarket and its rapid growth during that time (Sato 1971, pp. 2, 6, 10–11).

The so-called Japanization of the business system was indispensable for the acceptance of innovative American retail techniques. The innovative retail business status that was compatible with various conditions in the United States, such as motorization, large storage capabilities, inexpensive land value, and high wages, was incompatible with conditions in Japan. Thus, various improvements, such as store layout, choice of location, product development, merchandise assortment, and sales method, all based on Japanese circumstances, were indispensable for the introduction of an innovative retail store. Although the Japanization of the retail business status was not easily realized (Hashimoto 1998, p. 15), it can be seen in the case of supermarkets.

One of the changes in consumption lifestyle was the Westernization of eating habits. In Japan, although the Westernization of eating habits was advanced, the traditional structure of consumption remained. Such a consumption style was related to distribution, as seen in the rapid growth of supermarkets and the survival of small retailers and merchant wholesalers (Kikkawa 1998, pp. 109, 111, 116, 130). It was in the latter half of the 1950s that supermarkets established in the United States were transferred to Japan as a part of the Americanization of the business system. The function of the supermarkets, according to Japanese circumstances, was based on the pre-package system, which enabled self-service sales of perishable goods. This was a total system that included not only the issues of packaging techniques but also other aspects such as the quality of meat, the technique of the cooking service, and pricing that could reduce dead stock. As a result, the innovation of the system of supermarkets was realized by developing pre-packaged items suitable for Japanese consumption behaviors (Kikkawa and Takaoka 1998, pp. 280, 288, 291, 295).

In addition, regarding the retail store type, there is the Japanese characteristic in the dual control system of department stores and supermarkets. However, although there was originality in the development of chain-style management in large retail companies, this type of management did not prevail. Instead, it was promoted as a combination supermarket and discount store (Nakano 1983, pp. 13, 16). The full-scale development of chain stores began in the 1960s following the application of American theories and experiences under Japanese conditions, such as seen in the mass production of standardized products, the improvement and leveling of consumers' income levels, the homogenization of lifestyles, and the new accumulation of population in metropolitan areas (Suzuki 1974, pp. 377–37).

International Marketing: In Japan, trading companies played a significant role in exports before and after World War II. Dependence on trading companies was especially seen in the producer goods industry. In contrast, international marketing was independently developed in the durable consumer goods departments, such as the automobile industry and the electrical industry, and in the establishment of manufacturing companies' original international distribution channels. In contrast to the United States, in the automobile industry, Japanese firms made efforts to build a cooperative distribution channel with domestic dealers. This approach bore fruit as an effective channel in foreign countries and it eventually became a factor of international competitiveness. However, problems of "application" and "adaptation," as seen in the transfer of production systems and control methods to local factories, came to be an important factor for success or failure in international marketing (Obara and Yamanaka 1995, pp. 20, 32, 36, 42, 45). In this regard, the development of international marketing included its issues as the total issue in business management.

Even given the above-mentioned circumstances regarding the deployment of marketing methods in Japanese companies, there were differences between the producer goods industry and the consumer goods industry, and between the durable consumer goods industry and other general consumer goods industries. Industries that played the most important role in the development of marketing of durable consumer goods included the home appliance industry and the automobile industry. Furthermore, in the chemical industry, marketing activities were mainly performed in the consumer goods industry and the field of synthetic fiber, the latter achieving rapid growth after World War II. Therefore, the following sections will examine these industries.

10.1.3 Deployment of Marketing Techniques in Major Industrial Sectors

10.1.3.1 Chemical Industry

The active market development of synthetic fiber became indispensable in the 1950s, during which the marketing of chemical fiber producers became extremely active. For example, in 1952, Asahi Chemical Industry Co. Ltd. began to perform marketing activities with real development in the production and sale of nylon. Unlike the situation around 1950, in which publicity activities were not yet established or were performed sporadically, the system was improved by first setting up a technical service section and an advertising section, and then changing the latter into a sales service section. Thus, the company appealed to general consumers by developing various publicity activities. This was one of the new strategies that started in the postwar boom years. In addition, publicity activities through mass media, such as radio and television, played an important role, after which corporate image advertisements were introduced. However, as a result of diversification in the latter half of the 1960s, advertising that focused on individual products brought a different corporate image, which promoted the advertisement style for establishing corporate image.

There were three stages of marketing activities in this company during the decade after 1955: (1) fixation of the quality guarantee system for consumers in the latter half of the 1950s; (2) campaign marketing, which started around 1960; and (3) reinforcement of cooperation with retail stores corresponding to the consumption revolution in the first half of the 1960s. In particular, during the third stage, sales promotion activities that corresponded to the intensification of competition among the synthetic fiber makers included: the organization of end-users; the formation of sales teams; and the differentiation of brand labels for securing and enlarging the distribution channel. In addition, flexible pricing corresponding to the consumer use and the market became necessary in order to realize expansion of sales volume and reclaim the new market under the intensification of competition between materials. As a result, market quotations were nominally abolished.

In the decade after 1965, securing the distribution route through effective activities became necessary under the intensified competition among synthetic fiber manufacturers and the remarkable growth of the synthetic fiber market. Thus, in their sales promotions, pull marketing activities, such as improving market share, reclaiming new products and new markets, and performing countermeasures against other apparel makers, were expanded, based on the close cooperation between sales activities and publicity activities. Unlike the age of market research, which mainly centered on demand forecasting in the decade after 1955, market intelligence became the main issue. At Asahi Chemical Industry Co. Ltd., a market segmentation campaign was quickly proposed and implemented in order to secure the heavy demand in the field of new clothes. Furthermore, reorganization of the marketing system was required due to the changes in the consumption market around 1970, as well as changes in fiber production and the distribution structure. As a result, the sales promotion department that developed marketing activities according to the distribution channel was reorganized into the marketing department that did them in accordance with final product in 1971 (Nihon keieishi kenkyusho 2002, pp. 267, 365–366, 374, 390–395). Based on these points, the marketing activities of large enterprises in the chemical industry were broadly developed on the basis of the growth of the product field (which was directly connected to the final consumer market) and the characteristics of such products in relation to other industries.

10.1.3.2 Electrical Industry

In the home appliance department, how each company quickly established the mass production system and how they were able to sell mass-produced products while controlling the price were points of competition between Japanese firms during the postwar boom years. Thus, unlike the market segmentation strategy in the latter half of the 1970s, mass marketing was a fundamental characteristic. The transformation of strategies, from the production and improvement of standard products to the upgrading of products through the addition of new functions, significantly advanced (Ozaki 1995, pp. 77, 100–101). This reflected the tendency to emphasize new, improved products in the new product department, especially under circumstances such as being in a protected market with little foreign competition.

The situation in which merchandising of household appliances was performed by catching up to foreign technology, especially American technology, made the introduction of American methods relatively easy. In addition, policies emphasizing the release of new products (including improved versions of existing products), the promotion of planned obsolescence of existing products, and the shortening of service life, were adopted. The method of market segmentation was also formed as a new product policy. However, the development of new products by improving the existing product lowered the difference between the products of each company. Differentiation in various aspects, such as price, quality, and performance, increased costs in equipment investments. Since the risk of such a method was large without acquiring a very high market share, the significance of advertising as an effective means of differentiation also had to be significant (Miyazaki 1983, pp. 152–154).

In the home appliance industry, the necessity of the affiliated distribution system in manufacturing companies was strong, not only in the wholesale stage but also in the retail stage, due to the limitations of the merchants' sales power. As a result, unlike in the United States, where the majority of sales of household electrical appliances were made by discount stores that were not affiliated with manufacturers, Japanese commercial organizations were affiliated with the manufacturers and integrated into the specified agent contract system (with restrictions). Thus, the distribution system, led by the producing company, was established. Furthermore, the control of the distribution channel by the territorial system, which Japanese home appliance companies had completed around the mid-1960s, was a specific Japanese marketing method that greatly differed from the sales method of home appliance makers in the United States (Sato 1983, pp. 162–263, 167–168, 173, 182; Niida and Mishima 1991, p. 102; Zaiga 1980, p. 249).

The distribution channel eventually functioned as a stable and continuous system for product supply that enabled mass production (Niida and Mishima 1991, p. 110). At Matsushita Electric Industrial Co., Ltd., total marketing, such as price maintenance through the sales system at a set price, selling agents, federated stores, brand construction, and independent advertisements, was consistently performed. This process of establishing a distribution channel in this company, and its change, was a typical pattern in the development of marketing in Japanese firms (Obara 2010, p. 92).

The affiliated distribution system of house appliance manufacturers was combined with the full-line strategy. The competition between firms that adopted such a strategy brought about homogeneous competition. Such competition greatly differed from "the competition based on complementary relationships in the product field" seen in the United States. In addition, it strengthened the international competitiveness of Japanese companies and led to the conversion of the distribution system in home appliance products, which had a significant influence on the system in the United States (Kikkawa 1998, pp. 125, 127–128, 130).

10.1.3.3 Automobile Industry

In contrast to American automobile companies that generally made model changes every two or three years, Japanese automobile companies avoided such relatively short-term model changes as excessive marketing and pursued the maintenance of the products and their related investments. Another characteristic of marketing, in comparison with that in the United States, was seen in the dealer system, which was modified according to Japanese company culture (Shiraishi 1995, p. 118).

Toyota Motor Sales Co., Ltd. played the most important role in the deployment of marketing methods in the automobile industry. Although this company began adopting marketing techniques under the influence of American marketing methods, it established unique marketing methods based on Japanese modifications. Unlike the United States, where marketing was developed through trial and error of different sales methods, the franchise system (led by large manufacturing companies) was introduced without such experience in Japan. However, sales planning and production planning were coordinated, and profit planning was achieved by connecting sales forecasts with sales plans through the close communication system among Toyota Motor Co., Ltd., Toyota Motor Sales Co., Ltd., and various dealers. This system was based on the close interdependence and mutual trust between manufacturers and dealers, rather than the one-sided relationships of control and subordinates, as seen in the United States. The affiliated dealer network enabled companies to respond effectively to the rapid expansion of the market by performing business management based on the Japanese management of groupism (Shimokawa 1976b, p. 228; Shimokawa 1983, p. 137). Moreover, one important aspect of the Japanese marketing strategy was its cooperative and family-like posture, which treated dealers not as objects and subordinates but as "equal partners" (Shiraishi 1995, pp. 123, 126).

Furthermore, the greatest differences between the automobile sales systems of Japan and the United States (or Europe) included two aspects in particular: (1) Japanese firms adopted a principle emphasizing a large foothold and a limited number of shops (despite adopting the franchise system developed in the United States) and (2) the producing company was concerned with the inventory financing and retail finances of the dealer. In the early 1960s, Toyota Motor Sales Co., Ltd. conducted an American-style full-scale release of the Toyota Publica. However, this company transformed its policy to the system of a limited number of shops based on the fact that the open territory system, which emphasized door-to-door sales, was not suitable for Japanese conditions (Toyota jidosha hanbai kabushikigaisha shashi henshu iinkai 1970, pp. 280–283; Toyota jidosha hanbai kabushikigaisha shashi hensan iinkai 1980, pp. 109–113). The integration of distribution, sales finance, and the system of affiliating dealers into Toyota Motor Sales Co., Ltd. were also adopted by most Japanese automobile companies (Shimokawa 1976b, p. 227). In the automobile industry, most of the sales and service networks were established under the affiliating policy in which the distribution channel was under the complete control of the manufacturer. In other words, the control system of the affiliation was a manufacturer-led distribution system (Sato 1983, pp. 160–161).

In this way, the American franchise system was revised by the manufacturer-led approach, based on Japanese trade practices (Shimokawa 1983, pp. 126, 137). In Japan, unlike the United States, high-pressure marketing and the sales method using many dealers did not prevail. The main reason was that many companies used this approach to maximize their economies of scale, while promoting the coordination of production volume according to changes in demand (Shioji 2002, p. 51). As seen in the example of Toyota Motor Sales Co., Ltd., establishing a production system that considered production volume (depending on changes in demand) had significant meaning. Therefore, the development of the distribution system and marketing in the Japanese automobile industry was directly connected to the original production system.

10.2 Deployment of Marketing Methods in Germany

Based on the foregoing analysis, this section will next examine the introduction of marketing methods in Germany. First, in Sect. 10.2.1, the influence of American marketing in Germany is reviewed followed by a discussion of the channels through which marketing methods were learned and introduced in Sect. 10.2.2. In Sect. 10.2.3, the general conditions of the introduction of marketing methods are considered.

10.2.1 Influence of American Marketing in Germany

First, the German response to sales problems and the impact of American marketing are considered. There was a greater lag in distribution in Europe than in production, so the subconscious potential for learning and transfer in the former was much greater (Schröter 2005, p. 78). Germany traditionally had strong production and technology orientations. As a result, it was assumed that a demand for a marketing "revolution" in German enterprises would necessitate a behavioral shift that would be accompanied by a radical shift in mental attitude and traditional management practices (Kleinschmidt 2002, p. 226). During the postwar boom period, rationalization efforts were entirely focused on the field of production, with no forewarning of any problems with product sales (Remele 1963, p. 113). Even in the mid-1950s, Germany was far behind the United States in market research, according to American observers (*Rheinisch-Westfälisches Wirtschaftsarchiv zu Köln*, Abt 1,517.6, Stand der Rationalisierung in Deutschland, p. 14). At the time, European corporations did not place a high value on salespeople's abilities, and Germany was no exception (OEEC 1954, p. 16).

In these situations, it became clear in the many programs supported by the United States Technical Assistance and Productivity Program (USTA&P) on the topic of sales and marketing that knowledge of modern sales economics and various methods was insufficient in Germany. As a result, interest in American marketing methods grew, and the negative perception of American sales and market research methods began to fade (Kleinschmidt 1998, p. 181). Until the 1960s, in particular, the situation of emphasizing rationalization efforts in only the production area underwent a critical change. Furthermore, changing consumer needs have shifted the focus of the sales function back to the original theme (Remele 1963, p. 114).

10.2.2 Learning and Introducing Channels of Marketing Methods

Following that, the avenues for learning and introducing American marketing techniques were investigated. The primary channels include study trips to America sponsored by the USTA&P, the invitation of experts from the United States to Germany and their participation in various events, learning through books and other published materials, the involvement of advertising agencies, and direct investment by American enterprises.

The efforts of USTA&P were the most successful of the United States' efforts in the field of marketing [*National Archives,* RG469, Productivity and Technical Assistance Division, Office of the Director, Technical Assistance Country Subject Files, 1949–1952, German-General, A letter to the Economic Cooperation Administration from Dr. C. Kapfner (20.9.1950)]. A large number of businessmen who traveled to the United States with the assistance of the Mutual Security Agency, the Foreign Administration Organization, and the Rationalisierungs-Kuratorium der Deutschen Wirtschaft (RKW) began to request to learn about the most recent marketing and advertising techniques (Kleinschmidt 2004, p. 83). During a trip to the United States in the 1950s as part of a delegation of productivity missions, German entrepreneurs and engineers investigated sales and marketing issues to the same extent that they observed the latest technology and manufacturing methods (Kleinschmidt 1998, p. 181). Even in the programs at the European Productivity Agency, marketing and distribution issues were discussed (*National Archives*, RG469, Productivity & Technical Assist Division Labor Advisor Subject Files 1952–1954, TA-Work, Program Suggestions of PTAD/FOA for the EPA second annual Program).

In addition, inviting experts from the U.S. was one of the channels. Exchange programs for studying American marketing techniques and PR were planned and implemented as part of the Technical Assistance Plan's *B-Project* [*National Archives*, RG469, Productivity & Technical Assist Division Labor Advisor Subject Files 1952–1954, TA-Work, TA-B-Project Berlin 09–215—Marketing and Public Relations Team Berlin (24.11.1953)]. In 1953, for example, the person in charge of marketing at Westinghouse's Electric Appliance Division was invited to a management seminar in Berlin. There were group discussions about marketing research, product planning, sales planning, advertising/distribution, publicity, product service, consumer goods distribution methods, marketing personnel development, factory organization, and PR at this seminar [*National Archives*, RG469, Mission to Germany, Productivity and Technical Assistance Division, Subject Files of the Chief, 1953–1956, Report on Experiences German-American Management Seminars in Berlin (2.11.1953)].

Events such as lectures and conferences were also important in the 1950s. In the mid-1950s, the Federation of German Industries, RKW, and the Foreign Operations Administration used the Baden–Baden seminar to stage an event called "New Methods of Sales Economy" in which there were 140 participants. The challenge was to cope with transitioning from a seller's market to a buyer's market while using new methods of sales, publicity, and marketing. The relationship between the American and German experts in these events was analogous to that between a teacher and a student (Kleinschmidt 2002, p. 225).

Furthermore, almost all of the German commercial publications dealing with distribution referred to the American model of selling styles, salesmanship, or organization in the case of books and commercial magazines. In addition, in many cases, related books were translated and published under the editorship of well-known Germans in the business world (Schröter 2005, p. 82).

Working with advertising agencies and consulting firms provided German corporations with knowledge about the practice of American marketing (Hilger 2004a, p. 203), and this method played a significant role. In the 1950s, it became clear that American-style advertising agencies that provided full service represented a more economically successful model. Under these conditions, German businesses began to increasingly rely on the diverse services provided by such advertising agencies (Schröter 1997, pp. 98–99). For example, in the case of Henkel products, the Stanford Research Institute (SRI) and McCann-Erickson advertising agency were the most important facilitators of American know-how. In contrast to American competitive enterprises such as GM, Daimler-Benz was initially critical of questionnaire surveys. However, after meeting with Ogilvy, an expert in American advertising, in the early 1960s, they changed their evaluation method, and with the help of the country's experts, unlocked new marketing know-how (Hilger 2004a, pp. 187–188).

The introduction of advertising agencies in Europe that provided full service, from marketing research to the organization and execution of advertising campaigns, including the evaluation of research results, exemplified the Americanization of this industry. European employees' experience at American advertising agencies also aided in the transfer of American methods and attitudes (Schröter 2005, pp. 118–119).

Direct investment by American corporations was also an important channel for knowledge transfer. The marketing activities of American subsidiaries in Germany in the field of consumer goods frequently had a very strong direct influence on the adoption of similar methods by German enterprises (Dyas and Thanheiser 1976, p. 112). In some American subsidiaries and branches surveyed by Hartmann et al., the independent position of marketing director, which had jurisdiction over sales and publicity, was created. It can be confirmed in other subsidiaries and branch offices, that while both sales and advertising functions were relatively independent, they tended to be integrated in the form of work teams such as marketing groups and committees (Hartmann 1963, p. 109). Many advertising agencies were established in the United States capital, particularly in the late 1960s. To better adapt to the market, many of the agencies accepted German partners or formed liaisons with existing local agencies (Schröter 1997, p. 107). This also helped to promote the introduction and transfer of American know-how.

10.2.3 General Conditions of the Deployment of Marketing Techniques

Following that, the overall situation of the implementation of marketing techniques is considered. The introduction of American marketing methods was a broad movement that influenced many businesses at the same time in the 1950s. For example, the motto "From Sales to Marketing" at the first Sales and Marketing Conference in Germany in 1958 summed up what was going on throughout Europe at the time. Managers in the European manufacturing industry, on the other hand, were skeptical of the new methods and their significance. Marketing, according to the directors who focused on production issues, required not only a thorough transformation of their way of thinking but also represented a loss of authority within their enterprises. Under these conditions, widespread acceptance of American marketing and related management methods did not occur until a generational shift in management occurred in the early 1960s (Schröter 2005, p. 106).

Until the late 1950s, German enterprises conducted sales policy activities independently without a master plan, with the exception of certain sales, advertising, and publicity departments (Hilger 2004a, p. 186). In the 1950s, many European executives established a small marketing unit within the sales department. In the US corporations, the marketing department developed the company's long-term strategy, whereas the sales department is responsible for short-term tactics. Such a division did not occur in Germany until the late 1960s. According to a study, by 1968, 79% of German businesses had established a clear division between the two departments within the organization (Schröter 2005, p. 107).

Thus, from the beginning of the 1960s, the introduction of American marketing methods had proceeded earnestly. Following that, the application of the primary marketing techniques is examined.

Advertising and Publicity: In 1945, there was a significant difference between the United States and Europe in terms of advertising and publicity, the most significant of which was the attitude toward advertising. For example, American advertisers used highly sophisticated techniques that adopted modern scientific methods, and advertising was observed everywhere. For several years, American advertising had been organized on a much larger scale compared with European advertising. While full-service advertising agencies were common in the United States, they were uncommon in Europe (Schröter 2005, p. 118). Advertising agencies of this type were founded in Germany in 1947 on the basis of the American model (Schindelbeck 1995, p. 247). Advertising under the influence of the American model was increasingly regarded as a part of the marketing sphere in the 1950s (Kleinschmidt 2002, p. 224).

In the field of advertising and publicity, two waves of Americanization can be seen. The role of American-style advertising agencies providing full service was a feature of the first wave in the 1950s. However, at this stage, there was considerable social antipathy toward American advertising among Germans. Measures such as publicity campaigns based on planned obsolescence had not been introduced in Germany then. As for the 1950s, it has been pointed out that the degree of the catalytic effect of the American model and Americanization should not be overestimated. The American influence was also limited to the organizational structure of German advertising firms. This type of stuttering in the Americanization process was caused by economic factors, such as the existence of the seller's market and the much stronger development of the traditional producer goods industry compared with that of the consumer goods industry. The second wave of Americanization, on the other hand, can be seen beginning in the 1960s, and at this point, the introduction of American marketing concepts and techniques advanced (Schröter 1997, pp. 98–103).

Even in the middle of the 1960s, administrators of publicity were in the middle or lower management (Vgl. Hölzer, 1964; Korte 1964, pp. 26, 30). This differed significantly from the situation in the United States, where the person in charge of the advertising department reported directly to the vice president of marketing in several cases (Hallig 1965, p. 64). The American system was followed by the subsidiaries and branch offices of American companies in Germany. In such subsidiaries and branch offices, the role of the administrators in charge of advertising differed from their typical role in a German enterprise, commonly that of a director. This point is the most noticeable difference between these companies and companies of German capital (Hartmann 1963, p. 111). Several German enterprises underwent reorganization based on the American model, particularly in the early 1970s. Previously, there had been a lack of trust and conflict between the publicity departments and advertising agencies. However, this situation improved fundamentally with the new generation of managers. The marketing department, along with management, determined the corporate goals, publicity goals, concepts, publicity planning, and to a certain extent the budget and implemented these decisions primarily in collaboration with the agencies (Schröter 1997, pp. 105, 107).

In this way, publicity of sales was one area in the German economy from the 1960s that was most strongly "Americanized" (Hilger 2004a, p. 202). This can be seen in the fact that, by the mid-1960s, the American-style advertising agency had taken over (Schindelbeck 1995, p. 235). In 1960, the per capita expenditure on advertising in Germany was approximately one-third that in the UnitedStates, but by 1970, it had increased to approximately 72% of the United States. This was approximately 3.1 times greater than the amount in England, 3.8 times greater than that in France, and the largest in Europe (Schröter 1998, pp. 28–29; Schröter, 2005, p. 120).

However, in the 1960s, the United States still dominated the selection of advertising media, particularly television advertising (Schröter 1997, p. 108). For instance, in 1960, P&G was already spending 90% of its publicity budget in the UnitedStates on television advertising. Henkel's delegation to the United States also showed a strong interest in such advertising efforts (Hilger 2004b, p. 202). Following that, with the spread of television, this new advertising medium came to play a more significant role in publicity in Germany, albeit slightly later than in the United States.

Marketing Research: Next, when it comes to the deployment of marketing research, even in 1960, the increase in consumer diversity and increasing consumer demands frequently hampered the various efforts to achieve large-lot rationalized production. Under these conditions, product testing and long-term sales forecasting methods used in modern market research encouraged the use of basic data required for determining the type of products that made optimal sales engagement (Strotmann 1960, p. 12).

Marketing research activities had already been observed in Europe prior to 1945. However, the United States' leading position in this field was due to the combination of scientific techniques such as OR and office equipment technology, as well as the innovative application of new statistical techniques with polling methods. The most important of these techniques was consumer panels, which were used in Germany after the mid-1950s.

Furthermore, beginning in the early 1950s, American marketing research firms also established subsidiaries and offices in Germany, which aided in the spread of these methods. However, the majority of the demand for these companies came from American subsidiaries or businesses looking to expand into the European market. Thus, the major part of the expansion of marketing research was from American direct investment. During the establishment of marketing research in Europe, the American model was so prominent that exact imitations of the model were common (Schröter 2005, pp. 111–114, 117).

Product Policy and Pricing Policy: In terms of additional product and pricing policies, German suppliers, in contrast to American companies, frequently prioritized product policies with an emphasis on traditional brand awareness. This was especially true for businesses that focused on brand strength acquired through high quality, such as the case with Daimler-Benz. Hilger characterized this tendency as a "model policy that is not constrained by the stream of the times." Since the late 1950s, Daimler-Benz pursued a product strategy that sought to vary in the appearance of its vehicles at the lowest possible cost by making only minor changes to the cars' bodies. By promoting such concessions, this automobile company repressed American customs and thus hampered further shortening of model change cycles in the European market. However, even in this case, Europe tended to regard high development costs associated with the sales technique of frequent model changes as a wasteful policy and criticized it as "planned obsolescence." This tendency was not limited to Germany and should instead be considered a European characteristic (Hilger 2004a, pp. 190, 192–193). Given Germany's reliance on the European market, this market characteristic laid the groundwork for Germany's product policy to be effective in this sector.

In terms of pricing policy, it can be seen that American pricing policies closely tracked the effects of free-market forces. In contrast, in Germany, there were influences such as price-fixing for brand products, and the regulation of national policies such as the gift regulations and the rebates act. Furthermore, German enterprises that prioritized the traditional mild competition policy that was part of the market agreements such as cartel or syndicate prior to the war were less able to adopt American business practices. After the war, American companies coped with the disturbance of the European market with discounts and low prices. In contrast, German firms sought to maintain normal, high prices in the face of slow growth in the late 1960s. However, under the conditions of increased price competition, there was an even greater shift in Henkel's obstinate attitude as a result of constant discounting and exceptional price cuts in the cleaner and detergent business beginning in the late 1960s. Henkel came to a compromise solution as a result of intense competition with P&G, Henkel's strongest competitor, which was a middle path between American competition policies and traditional pricing policies. Only major brands, such as Persil, implemented discounts and sales to the extent that was absolutely necessary, while other products pursued a strategy to protect their overall market share by adjusting their supply to meet the state of competition (Vgl. Hilger 2004a, pp. 195–197, 201).

In this way, the American marketing strategy had a lasting effect on the concept of German enterprises' sales policies. American companies' techniques and know-how were introduced in various product policies and publicity. The degree of acceptance depended on the intensity of competition. Not considering the content of advertising, there was a considerably more powerful systemization of sales policies depending on the new techniques of market research and opinion surveys from the late 1950s. However, in terms of German producers' price and terms policies, which were also influenced by competition policies, it was clear that corporations found it difficult to break away from their existing tradition (Vgl. Hilger 2004a, pp. 211–212).

Despite the above circumstances, there were intercompany differences in the shift to market-oriented management in the 1950s and 1960s. Furthermore, regarding the transition from a seller's market to buyer's market after the war, there was a difference between the raw materials and consumer goods industries. In addition, the perceptions about issues related to sales, publicity, marketing, and consumers varied among industrial sectors and even within individual companies. Individual experiences, perceptions, and attitudes all played important roles in this case. In the heavy industry, because of historical reasons such as the existence of cartels, sales, publicity, and marketing were considered of only secondary significance until the mid-1960s. In contrast, top management in the chemical and artificial fiber industries paid much more attention to marketing, and the implementation of marketing methods and techniques had already begun at an early stage (Kleinschmidt 2002, pp. 226–227; Kleinschmidt 2004, pp. 83–84). In addition, according to the early 1970s Booz Allen & Hamilton report, the American marketing concept had been understood and introduced, particularly in progressive enterprises in the consumer goods industry, and the function consisting of marketing such as market research, sales, and sales promotion, and advertising had somewhat developed. In contrast, in numerous enterprises in the producer goods industry, the focus was on production instead of market needs, as it had been before (Booz-Allen and Hamilton 1973, p. 35).

Furthermore, there were the strong differences that existed in marketing methods from one industry to another. There are some good contrasting examples in the automobile and mechanical engineering industries, particularly with regard to the types of products that they sold, the types of consumers, and the basic industrial structures. The German automobile industry consisted of a handful of companies, whereas there was a multitude of companies in the mechanical engineering industry. Moreover, the mechanical engineering industry sold to other industries, whereas the automobile industry sold directly to the general public (Vogel 1973, p.116, 120). Hence, next, the introduction of marketing techniques in the main industries and their representative companies will be analyzed.

10.2.4 Deployment of Marketing Techniques in Major Industrial Sectors

10.2.4.1 Chemical Industry

This section looks at the chemical industry as one of the industries where marketing became an important issue during the post-World War II expansion of consumer goods and products. It examines this industry through the lens of specific individual businesses.

First, the **Henkel** example is used as a representative case. The postwar publicity activities for Persil began in 1950 (*Siemens Archiv Akten*, 49/Lb457, Gömmel R, Werbeverhalten im Konsum und Investitionsgüterbereich von 1945 bis 1980, gezeigt an frei gewählten Beispielen, p. 16). However, according to internal documents dating back to September 1953, advertising was not considered a modern method, and the competition's publicity was also superior [*Henkel Archiv*, 153/9, Niederschrift uber die Postbesprechung vom 18.9.1953 (19.9.1953), p. 7]. In the fall of 1956, Henkel introduced its television publicity of Persil, thus becoming the first West German enterprise to begin television advertising. The advertising served as a deterrent to P&G's extraordinary publicity efforts in the expanding all-temperature cleaner and detergent market. However, as a traditional German brand product company, Henkel's management team, even after this, remained distant from such content (Hilger 2004a, pp. 208–209).

Given the increasing demand for advertising in the period from the second half to the end of the 1950s, external experts such as market advertising agencies and research organizations became involved in such situations. Troost-Campbell-Ewald GmbH, the advertising agency, was tasked with the Persil campaign for the first time in 1959. The same year, a marketing department in charge of advertising and product planning was established, and the advertising and publicity center took over responsibility for the conception and execution of all advertising and publicity activities (*Siemens Archiv Akten*, 49/Lb 457, Gömmel R, Werbeverhalten im Konsum und Investitionsguterbereich von 1945 bis 1980, gezeigt an frei gewahlten Beispielen, p. 39). However, due to a lack of capital, the management team was almost entirely unable to investigate implementing a strategy for advertising and pricing policies similar to that of the competition until the early 1960s (Hilger 2004b, p. 211).

An analysis of market research data and their competitors provided stimulus to sales policies in the face of increasing competitive pressures from their American competitors. In the early 1960s, a central department within the marketing department was established to collect materials related to the introduction of new American brand products and to transfer such materials to the section in charge (Hilger 2004a, pp. 188–189). Henkel participated in the Ministry of Economic Affairs' productivity subsidiary program in 1961 and 1962 to train personnel with expertise in market research [*Henkel Archiv*, 153/20, Niederschrift uber die Postbesprechung Henkel vom 31. Juli 1962 (2.8.1962), p. 3]. Furthermore, they aimed to obtain information on new trends in sales methods and marketing with the cooperation of representative producers of American brand products, sales enterprises, and merchandizers (Hilger 2004b, p. 200). Henkel had been introducing a wide range of products in collaboration with German advertising agencies. This chemical company, on the other hand, entrusted the advertising campaign for the new detergent "Amba" to an American advertising agency in 1963 (Hilger 2004a, p. 203).

Following that, the competition in the European market became a battle between two companies, Henkel and P&G. As a result, since the mid-1960s a thorough investigation of P&G's management policies has been underway (Hilger 2004a, p. 189). As a result, it was proposed that Henkel would pursue a smooth and consistent handling of all marketing factors comparable to that of their competitor P&G [*Henkel Archiv*, 451/55, Auszug aus dem Protokoll Nr. 3/1968 über die Sitzung des Verwaltungsrates der Persil GmbH am 4. April 1968, *Henkel Archiv*, 153/42, Niederschrift über die gemeisame Post PERSIL/HENKEL/Bohme/HI vom 9.1.1968 (10.1.1968), p. 7]. To prepare for future competition, Henkel needed a detailed analysis of P&G's methods, goals, and organization; in the late 1960s, a committee was formed to investigate P&G's sales [*Henkel Archiv*, 451/55, Auszug aus dem Protokoll Nr. 1/68 über die gemeinsame Post vom 9. Januar 1968, p. 2, *Henkel Archiv*, 153/42, Niederschrift über die gemeisame Post PERSIL/HENKEL/Bohme/HI vom 9.1.1968 (10.1.1968), p. 7]. Around that time, there was a decline in brand value due to increased competition, and because it was predicted that brand differentiation would be even weaker, countermeasures to drastically reduce the number of product items were implemented (*Henkel Archiv*, 451/55, Auszug aus dem Protokoll Nr. 1/68 über die gemeinsame Post vom 9. Januar 1968, p. 1). Under these conditions, the American consulting firm SRI proposed in 1968 that separate cost centers be established for each unit and group within the marketing organization, as well as that existing sales-oriented activities be transformed into an all-inclusive customer-oriented marketing program (*Henkel Archiv*, 251/2, Stanford Research Institute, Langfristigen Planung fur Persil/Henkel, Phase II: Strategische Plaung, 2. Bd, Juli 1968, pp. 339, 344–346).

Next, we examine the case of **Glanzstoff**. The company pursued a strict market-oriented sales strategy, indicating a shift in the traditional sales concept. American marketing and publicity techniques introduced a completely new concept, and Du Pont served as a model for both. The organization was also influenced by the increased importance of marketing. The advertising department was separated from the sales department in 1954, and the former was placed under the direct control of the managing board. A publicity committee responsible for decisions related to publicity methods was concurrently established. The committee conducted local research on American advertising and publicity techniques, visited American businesses and organizations, and examined publications and magazines. The polyester fiber Diolen was widely publicized from the late 1950s to the early 1960s. In 1959, a new sales promotion section and team were established for this product. Orientation toward America was also introduced, as evidenced by television commercials (Kleinschmidt 2002, pp. 229–231; Kleinschmidt 1998, p. 182). Glanzstoff is an example of a company that introduced American marketing methods more directly. The adoption of American terminology by German management teams, as well as the transfer of corporate culture, demonstrates the pervasiveness of such techniques (Kleinschmidt 1998, p. 183).

In addition, the case of **Hüls** is examined. Immediately after the war, the concept of marketing did not play a role in this company (Kleinschmidt 2002, p. 233). However, as the ratio of exports increased in the early 1950s, the division of the advertising budget for domestic and foreign purposes became an important issue, as did the type of advertising media to be used (*Hüls Archiv*, VII-7–1/1, CWH-Werbung im Jahr 1952). Nonetheless, they were still lagging behind the United States at this point [*Hüls Archiv*, VII-7, Neugestaltung der Industriewerbung (7.6.1951)]. Unlike Glanzstoff, there was a lack of personnel pursuing an appropriate marketing concept, and even in the late 1950s, there was little attention paid to the American model. However, with the introduction of Vestan polyester fiber in the early 1960s, the situation changed. A large-scale marketing campaign for Vestan, similar to Glanzstoff's Diolen campaign, was launched in response to increased competition from other manufacturers and their brand products, as well as the greater need to adapt to other market needs. However, this campaign was carried out without accepting American marketing sales policies based on direct human contact or the terminology of American management methods (Kleinschmidt 2002, pp. 234–235).

As a result of the increased competition in the chemical industry that resulted from progress in mass production in the consumer goods products industries and America's export stance, responding to the marketing methods became an even more significant theme. However, in this situation, in addition to businesses that emphasized these issues through close contact with America, including the use of advertising agencies, there were also businesses that addressed these issues from a distance.

10.2.4.2 Electrical Industry

In the electrical industry, such as **Siemens**, an advertising center was already founded in 1938 to support sales promotion. The focus of this organization's activities shifted with the 1948 currency reform. In the 1950s, publicity research enabled empirical investigation of the various factors influencing the effect of publicity [*Siemens Archiv Akten*, 9871, Schwabenthan O, Unternehmenskommunikation für Siemens 1847 bis 1989, München, 1995 (Selbstverlag), pp. 62–63, *Siemens Archiv Akten*, 49/Lb457, Gömmel R, Werbeverhalten im Konsum und Investitionsgüterbereich von 1945 bis 1980, gezeigt an frei gewählten Beispielen, pp. 6, 8]. There was a unified style created in the establishment of the advertising media for Siemens to verify their technological nature and to secure trust in their products. In 1954, illustrative advertising to the masses was launched in response to the intense competition in the consumer goods market. Due to numerous new technological developments in the investment goods sector, it was essential for sales staff to have excellent information measures to support the development of human relations. There was a focus on printed materials, publicity brochures, and advertising in media such as newspapers in this (*Siemens Archiv Akten*, 49/Lb457, Gömmel R, Werbeverhalten im Konsum und Investitionsgüterbereich von 1945 bis 1980, gezeigt an frei gewählten

Beispielen, pp. 7–9). According to the company's internal documents from 1961, the challenges of sales promotion, marketing research, production planning, and sales planning arose as competition increased (*Siemens Archiv Akten*, 37/Lk975, Illmer H, Warum materialorientierter Vertrieb? p. 30).

The general economic breakthrough, an increase in market dynamism combined with the use of more powerful advertising, and progress made in international competition, in particular, resulted in a movement toward modern American marketing, which is defined as product and sales policies oriented toward market conditions and customer needs. Beginning in 1962, specialized units other than advertising and publicity groups were established to ensure the effective generation of required publicity techniques and the maintenance of Siemens advertising style [*Siemens Archiv Akten*, 9871, Schwabenthan O, Unternehmenskommunikation für Siemens 1847 bis 1989, München, 1995 (Selbstverlag), pp. 85, 87, 92].

The results of image analysis began to provide the foundation for the establishment of a modern advertising style and a corporate identity strategy in the 1960s. In Germany, scientific analysis was first used for advertising goals in the 1950s (Feldenkirchen 2004b, p. 130). However, in the 1960s, a neutral institution conducted scientific research on Siemens' corporate image. Furthermore, activities such as research on the corporate brand and its symbolic characteristics, an analysis of the enterprise's and its products' popularity in comparison with its competitors, and a comparison of Siemens and AEG advertising expenditures were implemented. Furthermore, market research, market observations, and publicity research were used to supplement planning (*Siemens Archiv Akten*, 49/Lb457, Gömmel R, Werbeverhalten im Konsum und Investitionsgüterbereich von 1945 bis 1980, gezeigt an frei gewählten Beispielen, p. 25). GfK Nürnberg, a consumer, sales, and marketing research firm, was tasked with conducting a survey on the concept of "Siemens' product series" in the late 1960s. Siemens obtained survey results in three categories: visibility, image, and information [Vgl. *Siemens Archiv Akten*, 37/Lk975, Siemens-Serienfabrikate. Eine Untersuchung bei ausgewählten Abnehmerkreisen von Siemens-Erzeugnissen].

Furthermore, Siemens' electrothermal equipment enterprise, which manufactured and sold home appliance electric products, conducted a research trip to the United States in 1968 in order to apply the knowledge gained from investigating the American small electric products market to the conditions of the European market and demonstrate the possibility of expanding their business. It conducted a questionnaire survey there, covering six topics: (1) market conditions, (2) product characteristics, (3) product planning and development, (4) production, (5) sales, and (6) advertising and sales promotion. In addition to meeting with top management at SMEs, it visited larger enterprises and held discussions with the people in charge of small electrical products, as well as exploring topics such as sales and organizational methods by visiting companies such as Westinghouse (*Siemens Archiv Akten*, 68/Li137, Analyse des USA-Kleingeratenmarktes. Reise der Herren Fromm, Prahl und Dr. Rumswinkel vom 15.5. bis 29.6.1968).

Thus, in the 1960s, Siemens' advertising activities had developed into important components of marketing and were able to adapt to the changing market conditions.

However, at the beginning of the 1970s, advertising moved beyond its function as part of the marketing mix in sales issues, as it had done since the 1960s, and began to function as part of the enterprise-wide communication mix (*Siemens Archiv Akten*, 49/Lb457, Gömmel R, Werbeverhalten im Konsum und Investitionsgüterbereich von 1945 bis 1980, gezeigt an frei gewählten Beispielen, pp. 49, 57).

10.2.4.3 Automobile Industry

In the automobile industry, **Volkswagen** was one of the most advanced corporations in terms of its various marketing polices, with a strong customer and sales orientation. H. Nordhoff received impetus from American know-how, and the company began meticulously planning a large-scale and broad-reaching organization as early as 1948–1950 (Vogelsang 1961, p. 6; Hiller 1952, pp. 26–27). Thereafter, the establishment of a national and international sales network was actively facilitated. In 1947, the company's sales network merely consisted of 10 core distributors and 14 dealers, and no factory-authorized repair shops existed. Two years later, the sales organization had grown to include 16 core representative agents, 31 wholesale distributors, 103 dealers, and 84 authorized repair shops. (Kleinschmidt 2004, p. 84).

In contrast to other German automobile companies, Volkswagen was unable to rely on its existing dealership network after World War II, and the development of a sales network became a major issue. Following the 1948 currency reform, the number of sales locations increased significantly, and they expanded their customer service network in addition to developing a system of independent retailers who also handled wholesale. In the 1960s, they used the method of acquiring other companies to maintain their sales points (Borgward and Auto Union) (Vgl. Linne 2008, pp. 8, 25–26, 31).

Volkswagen was early in emphasizing the importance of advertising, market analysis, and the customer service function in each issue of the public relations magazine "*VW Information Service*" ("*Volkswagen Informationsdienst*") which was launched in August 1949, and this enterprise worked on the development of survey questionnaires, statistics, and the customer service function [*Volkswagen Archiv*, 61/2036, Volkswagen G.m.b.H., *Volkswagen Informationsdienst*, Nr. 1 (1.8.1948), Nr. 2 (5.10.1948), Nr. 3 (16.12.1948), Nr. 4 (10.2.1949), Nr. 5 (20.5.1949), Nr. 6 (1.9.1949), Nr. 7 (16.12.1949), *Volkswagen Archiv*, 174/1588, Nordhoff H, Ein offenes Wort zu unserer Situation, *Volkswagen Information*, Nr. 19, September 1954]. Customer service department had already been re-established by the fourth quarter of 1945, and the organization was expanded the following year to include the three departments of technique, replacement parts, and customer service training (*Volkswagen Archiv*, 174/1033, Bericht der Verkaufs- und Kundendienstorganisation für das Geschäftsjahr 1946). In 1948, the center for sales and customer service was organized with sections for domestic sales, advertising, technology, and trade service. In July of this year, publicity departments were established (*Volkswagen Archiv*, 174/1033, Tätigkeitsbericht der Hauptabteilung VERKAUF und KUNDENDIENST für das Jahr 1948).

The sales promotion department was established in the fiscal year of 1950 as part of the restructuring of the department responsible for domestic sales, Not only was the publicity department integrated into the organization but also sales statistics techniques and various sales promotion policies were implemented. This fiscal year was the first time that the development of aggressive publicity existed on a considerable scale (*Volkswagen Archiv*, 174/1033, Geschäftsbericht 1950 der Hauptabteilung VERKAUF und KUNDENDIENST, p. 13).

The sales promotion/publicity section carried out systematic and planned activities for the first time in the 1951 fiscal year (*Volkswagen Archiv*, 174/1033, Geschäftsbericht 1951 der Hauptabteilung VERKAUF und KUNDENDIENST, p. 17). Among these movements, direct publicity methods began to be focused in 1953 (*Volkswagen Archiv*, 174/1588, Direktwerbung—methodisch betrieben, *VW Informationen*, Nr. 14, 1953.8, Sonderheft: Die hohe Kunst des Verkaufens und des Umgangs mit Menschen), and great emphasis was also placed on advertising and publicity. In addition, in the 1958 "*Volkswagen Information*," the emphasis on sales promotion and publicity as basic advertising principles was stressed (*Volkswagen Archiv*, 174/1588, Grundsätzliches zur VW-Werbung, *Volkswagen Informationen*, Nr. 14, August 1958, Sonderheft: Die hohe Kunst des Verkaufens und des Umgangs mit Menschen), and policies such as training of sales staff were performed on a larger scale (Vgl. *Volkswagen Archiv*, 174/1035, Geschäftsbericht 1958 der Hauptabteilung VERKAUF und KUNDENDIENST, pp. 7–8; Linne 2008, pp. 20–21). In the 1959 fiscal year, the dealer and repair shop networks were strengthened, and regional customer service, particularly in major cities, was expanded (Der Volkswirt 1960, p. 2047). Furthermore, support policies for contractual dealers were actively pushed. Among these efforts are the retention of the 1962 dealer advisory council and the dealer financial advisory system (Vgl. *Volkswagen Archiv*, 174/742, Remarks by Professor Nordhoff at Dealer Advisory Council Breakfast, *Volkswagen Archiv*, 174/1043, Jahresbericht 1960 der Hauptabteilung VERKAUF und KUNDENDIENST, *Volkswagen Archiv*, 174/1035, Geschäftsbericht für das Jahr 1962 der Hauptabteilung VERKAUF und KUNDENDIENST, *Volkswagen Archiv*, 174/1035, Geschäftsbericht für das Jahr 1964 der Hauptabteilung VERKAUF und KUNDENDIENST, *Volkswagen Archiv*, 174/1035, Geschäftsbericht für das Jahr 1965 der Hauptabteilung VERKAUF und KUNDENDIENST).

Establishment and expansion of such sales networks and service systems were also pursued on a global scale in order to increase exports. In 1950, Nordhoff already pointed out the importance of exports to the United States and based on a market analysis of the United States, Volkswagen chose a good time to begin this activity (*Volkswagen Archiv*, 174/1588, Ansprache von Generaldirektor Dr.-Ing.e.h. HEINZ NORDHOFF anläβlich der Presskonferenz am 14. Oktober 1950, *Volkswagen Information*—Ausschnitt zu Heinrich Nordhoff). In 1955, there were 2,800 retailers and repair shops worldwide, and the "*Volkswagen Information*" of the time stated that they had the best sales and customer service organization in Europe as well as being ahead of their American counterparts (*Volkswagen Archiv*, 174/1588, Ansprache von herrn Generaldirektor Prof. Dr. Nordhoff zur Presskonferenz am 6. August 1955 anläβlich der Fertigstellung des millionsten Volkswagen, *Volkswagen Information—* Ausschnitt zu Heinrich Nordhoff, p. 4; Der Volkswirt 1955, p. 11). The source of the enterprise's competitive power in the US market was primarily due to the quality of service network and high productivity developed after the war (Abelshauser 1995, p. 289; Abelshauser 2018, p.111).

Nonetheless, Nordhoff concentrated on the expansion of customer service; hence, advertising continued to be limited and played a minor role until the end of 1950 (Kleinschmidt 2004, pp. 84–85). There was still a strong emphasis on production. He had maintained a cautious attitude toward modern marketing, and until 1963, there was no such thing as a publicity budget in the sense that we know it today. However, with the beginning of the 1960s, the automobile market in the West Germany slowly transformed from a seller's market to a buyer's market, and Volkswagen intended to enter the advertising market and expand as a response to the changing economic environment (Wellhöner 1996, p. 130).

The German automobile industry's growth rate began to slow in the early 1960s. The reason for this was the greater inroads made into the German market by foreign suppliers through various aggressive marketing policies as well as changes in the domestic market (Feldenkirchen 2004a, p. 158). Under such conditions, the adoption of American marketing methods was eagerly pursued. In the 1960s, the scale of advertising activities using publicity agencies increased further. For example, in the 1964 fiscal year, the new style of advertising and publicity established in 1963 was strictly maintained, and advertising of new cars and spot commercials were carried out in collaboration with various advertising agencies (*Volkswagen Archiv*, 174/1043, Jahresbericht für den Vorstandsbereich VERKAUF 1964, *Volkswagen Archiv*, 174/1043, Jahresbericht für den Vorstandsbereich VERKAUF 1965; Köhler, 2008, pp. 232–233).

In general, the top management at Volkswagen headquarters only gradually gained confidence in the quality of American advertising and publicity and gradually began to accept American methods. The American impact, on the other hand, was enormous and significant. In German advertising, new ways of thinking, terminology, knowledge, and elements of new styles were introduced. Volkswagen began advertising in illustrations, women's magazines, and television magazines for the first time in 1960, in addition to television publicity. For the first time in 1966, the annual report of the sales/customer service department referred to sales promotion, publicity, and customer service as "marketing" and expressed these elements as a unified strategy combining these elements. Two years later, the corporate group's sales department and subsidiary enterprises created a unified marketing plan that determined the necessary means to meet the set sales targets based on a thorough examination of domestic and foreign market factors. As a result, the company's new sales strategy and publicity methods were closely linked to the American model, as they used American publicity and marketing methods as a standard or "role model" (Vgl. Kleinschmidt 2002, pp. 250, 255–256).

Exports to the United States were a significant driving force in the reinforcement and implementation of publicity at Volkswagen. This company was oriented toward the international market from the beginning, and the US market was a substantial component of its growth strategy based on Fordism. The "Beetle" found its niche in the US market owing to the lack of compact cars provided by US automobile enterprises until 1959 (Abelshauser 2018, pp. 109–111). Therefore, measurements such as publicity and building of service network had great significance. C. H. Hahn, the president of Volkswagen of America, played an important role in developing publicity. Under the pressure of wholesalers and American enterprises' first introduction of a small-sized car in 1959, a publicity committee was formed to promote a stronger deployment of advertising and publicity in the United States. The publicity for the "Beetle," which was handled by a local advertising agency, marked the first time that sophisticated American advertising methods were used. In the late 1950s, in contrast to the wide use of professional advertising agencies for publicity in the United States, this was an exception in case of German enterprises. Given this situation, it is reasonable to conclude that Volkswagen was ahead of its time in introducing American marketing methods and techniques (Kleinschmidt 2002, p. 254; Kleinschmidt 2004, p. 80). Unlike some American companies, German companies generally used the leading national advertising agencies in the countries where they aimed to sell their products, rather than employing German advertising companies to make foreign sales campaigns. F. Vogel pointed out that "the skill of carefully choosing the best foreign advertising agencies has possibly been best demonstrated by Volkswagen in the United States" (Vogel 1973, p.112).

It became an even more important theme, particularly during Volkswagen's export expansion in the 1960s, to develop marketing for promoting exports. For example, because of the development of a planned supply of advertising materials to importers, financial support for several markets, and the introduction of international merchandising catalogs, there was an effort for sales promotion activities to be as close to international levels as possible (*Volkswagen Archiv*, Z174/N.2366, Jahresbericht 1966 des Vorstandsbereich Verkaufs, p. 18, *Volkswagen Archiv*, 174/1039, Jahresbericht 1969 der Hauptabteilung Verkauf und Kundendienst).

In this way, Volkswagen adopted a distinct and independent marketing strategy, whereas in their efforts to enter the US market and expand exports, the company relied heavily on individuals such as Hahn (Kleinschmidt 2004, p. 85). In addition, the introduction of American marketing methods progressed in their use of advertising agencies. The use of such techniques in the company's development in the German domestic market also expanded. In the 1960s and 1970s, the scattered individual marketing functions were integrated within the enterprise, and in this process, marketing evolved from an auxiliary function of operational planning into a strategic planning method for business policies. However, in the 1970s and 1980s, when the business environment became much more rigorous, consumer-oriented marketing management, which integrated the various functions of sales, product, pricing policy, and advertising, developed even more vigorously (Vgl. Köhler 2008, pp. 216–239).

10.2.4.4 Iron and Steel Industry

In comparison with the industries discussed thus far, the following subsection examines a producer goods industry, the iron and steel industry. The Federation of German Iron and Steel Industry's implementation of a study trip to the United States in October 1954, within the framework of Technical Assistance Project, was an example of a coordinated effort to learn about American marketing measures. The trip was related to marketing research, management organization, and industrial relations. During the trip, participants learned about sales management enterprises, various staff departments such as the department of general production planning, pricing department, advertising department, claims department, and market research in relation to the organization of sales of commercial transactions. In this case, US Steel served as a model [thyssenkrupp Corporate Archives, WVS/148, USA-Reise Oktober 1954: Marketing Research, Management Organisation, Industrial Relations (TA Projekt 09–288) (8.12.1954)]. In addition, there were efforts of individual enterprises. For example, in 1955, Thyssen implemented a study trip to their affiliate Armco in relation to the former's sales organization and market development department (thyssenkrupp Corporate Archives, A/1207, Untersuchung über die Organisation des Verkaufs und der Abteilung Market Development). Following this, Thyssen signed an agreement with Armco in 1956 to establish a market research and sales enterprise. [thyssenkrupp Corporate Archives, A/34272, Vertrag mit der Armco über die Marktforschungs- und Vertriebs GmbH (14.1.1956)].

However, because steel industry products are producer goods, market characteristic issues are different from those of the consumer goods industry where purchaser needs and tastes vary. Furthermore, the nature of marketing development differs from that of the previously examined industrial sectors. As previously stated, until the mid-1960s, companies in heavy industries had a tendency to show only secondary interest in sales, advertising, and marketing (Kleinschmidt 2002, p. 226; Kleinschmidt 2004, p. 84). The iron and steel industry is a representative of one of these industries.

10.3 The Characteristics of Japanese and German Deployment of American Marketing Methods

Building on the foregoing analysis, this section clarifies the Japanese and German characteristics in the deployment of American marketing methods, as well as examines them by considering the market and social structures in the United States.

10.3.1 Japanese Deployment of American Marketing Methods

10.3.1.1 Management Emphasizing Sales Volume and Market Share in Japanese Marketing

Marketing policies in Japanese manufacturing companies during the postwar boom years aimed at realizing the mass distribution of products in order to maximize sales volume and market share. Thus, many firms concentrated their greatest efforts in market policy on "the control of distribution," as seen in vertically integrated distribution channels, price policies using excessive rebates, sales promotions, and sales staff. In addition, manufacturing companies developed marketing policies for the control of distribution in order to distribute products as much as possible under conditions of overproduction (Eguch 1975, pp. 198, 200).

In the manufacturing industry, large Japanese enterprises introduced marketing techniques to overcome intensive competition with other domestic companies and to respond to foreign competition through the liberalization of capital transactions. However, as seen in the distribution channel and the price policy in particular, a specific Japanese structure and form was created, which differed from that in many foreign countries, especially in regard to the intensive competition among firms, the liberalization of capital transactions, the conventional trade practice, and the posture of business management (Eguchi 1975, p. 177).

Among the greatest characteristics of the American mass market were its homogeneity and size. This was due to the remarkable increase in the intermediate-income hierarchy and the similarity of their orientation of consumption (Nihon seisansei honbu 1957, pp. 7–8). In the United States, the maturity market emerged earlier than in other countries. Since the market growth rate was generally low and the position of powerful companies in the market was established in many industries, many firms attempted to find and develop new markets rather than compete for market share in the existing market. Thus, marketing activities that focused on product innovations and sales, as well as on diversification strategies, were developed in order to reclaim the new market. Conversely, the importance of acquiring market share in the existing competitive market, through sales promotions and distribution control, remained high in Japan (Eguchi 1975, pp. 178–179; Nihon seisansei honbu 1960, p. 23).

Even from the end of the 1960s to the 1970s, whereas American marketing was dry, large-scale, and strategic, with a focus on profitability, Japanese marketing was wet, small-scale, and non-strategic, with a focus on sales volume. In fact, the production-oriented manner of thinking was still considerable in Japan (Mogi 1969, pp. 46–49; Keizai doyukai sogo keiei koritsu kenkyukai 1970, pp. 16–18). The following points explain the reasons for such differences. In the American marketing approach, which focuses on profitability, the idea that a company should sell products at prices that buyers expect, rather than cost-plus pricing, was strong (Nihon seisansei hobu 1957, p. 15; Mogi 1969, p. 48). Conversely, in Japan, the idea that the management of a company was based on return on investment (ROI) was not sufficiently established under the consideration of sales volume and market share. Even among Japanese companies that adopted the divisional structure, there were many cases in which the ratio of profit to net sales was emphasized as a basic standard of performance, rather than the ROI (Fushimi 1997, p. 8).

Regarding the sales strategies of Japanese companies, an important characteristic can be seen in the way that each company attempted to acquire market share through low-price policies (Takeda 1985, p. 133), and that management emphasized market share data reflecting such strategies. Such management practices and behavior patterns had a significant influence on the deployment of American marketing techniques. According to Ikeo (1999), Japanese-style marketing assumed that consumers were interested in purchasing products that helped them achieve an "American lifestyle." It had characteristics such as affiliated distribution systems, name brands, homogeneous marketing, and the continuous injection of products. The competition between companies intensified under the development of such marketing. In the period of low economic growth following the first oil crisis in 1973, the basis of marketing changed greatly (Ikeo 1999, pp. 54–57, 61, 63, 70–73, 249). Such conditions in the postwar boom years were due to the developments in Japanese marketing. This was also related to the competitive oligopolistic system in which cooperative stability was missing and mutual competition was intense despite the high degree of concentration. Thus, the entry of latecomers into the new product field was intense (Hashimoto 1973, pp. 96, 98–99).

Under such situations, an important characteristic of Japanese marketing in the period of high economic growth was seen in "the marketing as means of competitive advantage." In the durable consumer goods industry in particular, marketing was developed in order to realize product advantages through the following: full-line policies and constant model changes; price advantages through mass production and various cost reductions; channel advantages by establishing sales networks; image improvements and sales promotions through mass advertising and promotion measures; and competitive advantages. Therefore, marketing occupied a strategically important position for competitive dominance (Obara 1994, pp. 192–195, 283–284).

10.3.1.2 Affiliated Distribution System Based on the Relationship of Mutual Trust in Japanese Marketing

Another important characteristic of Japanese marketing was the affiliated distribution system. In the United States, whereas the mass production of durable consumer goods was performed in large manufacturing companies, the system in which sales were made through a network of independent small- and medium-sized retailers or discount stores was dominant. There are two main pillars in marketing: product planning aiming at product differentiation and various measures, such as mass advertising and sales promotions, for the penetration of the brand. In Japan, a third method was added, namely, affiliated distribution, since control of the market and distribution by

Japanese producers exceeded that of the United States (Sato 1983, pp. 168, 173). This is an important point regarding the development of Japanese marketing.

Under the distribution control by the affiliated distribution system, intense competition among manufacturing companies was developed not on price but around new products, advertisements, publicities, and rebates. Planned obsolescence was strongly promoted in the process of such competition, while modern marketing techniques and methods were still being applied (Sato 1983, p. 186). The original product policy and the system of marketing that aimed at "securing a wide line of products" and the "quick and continual development of products" became indispensable. In Japanese marketing, particularly in the development of a new product, this relatively small improvement became a prominent characteristic (Katagiri 2000, pp. 38–40). Developing homogeneous competition with rival companies by strengthening the affiliated distribution channel was a pattern of excellence in Japanese marketing (Ikeo 1999, p. 94). How planned obsolescence was promoted had an important meaning for the industry because of homogeneous competition.

The movement toward the affiliated distribution system in Japan had a significant influence on the fixation of American managerial marketing. Such marketing was introduced while being accompanied by technical characteristics, such as the emphasis on market research, sales promotions through advertisements using mass media, and sales principles. However, in Japan, affiliating stores had already advanced and American managerial marketing was deployed, assuming that such development occurred. There were also certain limitations during this period. Moreover, since price competition was significantly affected, under the condition that the competition structure had not yet become an oligopoly, affiliating stores emerged to control prices (Shirahige 1976, pp. 144, 147). This situation also greatly differed from that in the United States.

Furthermore, the vertical cooperation between manufacturing companies and wholesalers or retailers was promoted by the leadership of the manufacturers, which made vertical integration an important characteristic of the Japanese-affiliated distribution system. The Japanese practice of maintaining a continuous business relationship based on mutual trust was also important (Nishimura 1995, p. 155). In other words, "human relations based on personal trust," rather than "contract relationships with high transparency based on economic rationality," was emphasized (Iwanaga 2005, p. 213).

For example, the vertical affiliated policy in the home appliance industry was the Japanese policy that reflected this Japanese trading practice. Although the United States was the first country to promote and market household appliances, such a policy did not exist at that time. One prominent characteristic of the Japanese policy can be seen in the home appliance manufacturers that base their business relationships on mutual trust and utilize this approach as the most effective means for monopolistic control (Miyazaki 1983, pp. 158–159). However, in the household appliance industry, the acceptance of American large-sized, durable consumer goods was difficult due to the differences between the residential environments of Japan and the United States. As a result, the development of products in accordance with Japanese needs became important (Hashimoto 1998, p. 16). Based on these aforementioned points, the general balanced development of marketing was required.

The rapid change in the environment due to the low economic growth in the 1970s had a significant influence on the affiliated distribution system. However, the affiliated distribution system did not match the actual conditions under the changing market environment. An important characteristic can be seen in the decline of affiliated stores' market share because of the rapid growth of independent mass-sales stores. Thus, there was a shift to the compound system, emphasizing selling through independent mass sales stores as well as affiliated stores (Nakano 1983, pp. 31–33; Niida and Mishima 1991, p. 99). Through this transformation, channel maintenance became an important problem during this period, after which primary consumer orientation emerged (Obara 1994, pp. 214, 283).

10.3.1.3 Development of Bottom-Up Marketing Based on the Role of Human Factors

In the introduction of mass production marketing in the consumer goods industry, Japanese modifications emphasized human factors, consumer services, and development related to market needs. In addition, other Japanese characteristics can be seen in the traditional distribution system, the late start of the innovation of distribution, the progress of affiliated sales and its historical change, the advancement of marketing for adaptation to the situation, the shift from marketing with the emphasis on product improvement to that focusing on new product development, the influence of the Japanese production system supporting the Japanese adaptation to the situation, and the influence of the general trading firm on distribution innovation and its historical role in international marketing (Shimokawa 1991, p. 299).

In Japan, the personal connection and the human element in sales activities were stronger than those in the United States. Thus, Japanese marketing had a special characteristic of "wet" marketing in this meaning (Mogi 1969, p. 48). The significance of the human factor was also seen in industry, except in the mass production of consumer goods. According to Takeda (1995), in the light machines industry, there were three Japanese aspects that appeared through the intensive inter-firm competition in the domestic market: (1) product development that closely fit the customers' needs; (2) positive support that included the affiliating business; and (3) correct delivery and courteous service. Such aspects were deeply rooted in Japan, while American marketing established the idea of "the person" during periods of high economic growth (Takeda 1995, pp. 68–69).

Japanese marketing that developed under the market with various needs includes the important characteristic of providing courteous service, grasping the needs of consumers, and feeding them back into the production, which has a positive effect on production and sales. This was the bottom-up marketing approach that was heterogeneous with marketing in the United States. It enabled Japanese companies to perform marketing based on the customers' needs, while allowing cooperation to coexist with the competition (Toba 1982, pp. 11–13, 18).

10.3.1.4 Japanese Characteristics of Marketing in Relation to Strategy

In regard to marketing strategy, there is a fundamental characteristic of the strategy in that Japanese companies attempt to realize price leadership by supporting the sales staff in their collection of information and the harmonious personal relations, and developing product strategies based on the strong sales organization. The effectiveness of this approach relied on more long-term strategies, such as the product and channel strategies, rather than the price and sales promotion strategies (Tamura 1983, pp. 164–166). However, in the development of the marketing strategy in Japan from the latter half of the 1960s to the 1970s, whereas totalization was emphasized, the era of the product planning strategy (in which new products were produced during the period of high economic growth after 1955) had come to an end. In the period of maturity after 1965, the sales promotion strategy, based on information developed by the producing company and the large store, was stressed (Nihon keiei seisakun gakkai 1970, p. 8).

However, in the early 1970s, despite the appearance of characteristics that were generally associated with marketing-oriented firms, many large Japanese manufacturing companies did not have a sufficient plan to become truly marketing-oriented. Despite their technical sophistication, it was uncommon to find firms (even among the leading companies) that had clearly defined and integrated marketing objectives and strategies. Despite the prevalence of organizations that specialized in marketing research for large firms, only a limited number were used in strategic decision-making. Even in the most progressive manufacturing companies, the coordination of various individual elements in the marketing mix was insufficient. In addition, among large Japanese firms, there were many that lacked total marketing orientation in their approaches to diversification. In determining the direction of diversification, the tendency (even among the more progressive companies) was to do so on the basis of their production and manufacturing capabilities (Yoshino 1971, pp. 125–127).

One of the marketing behaviors in Japanese companies, compared to that in the United States, was to respond to the irreversible accumulation of the production supply. These attempts also promoted the accumulation of marketing resources in itself. As a result, marketing resources were integrated by the company or immobilized through long-term employment or trade contracts. In addition, certain characteristics, such as the mobility of marketing resources means the possibility to change allocation of resources flexibly in accordance with changes in the product market or the cost of marketing resources, were lost (Ishii 1993, p. 155).

In the deployment of American management methods, creative absorption (by adjusting to Japanese actual conditions) had been performed. This was brought about by applying the deployed management methods and techniques, gaining feedback regarding such deployment, and sharing the findings with the company. It also greatly depended on the fact that Japanese enterprises coped with the situation by not applying the European and American models (based on the principle of personal responsibility), but by emphasizing collective responsibility (Shimokawa 1991, p. 295).

10.3.2 German Deployment of American Marketing Methods

Based on the above discussion, the German characteristics of the introduction of American marketing techniques are discussed. Germany did not have the same advancement in standardization of consumption as in America. The market characteristics and consumer behavior trended toward emphasizing technology, quality, and functionality, and the focus was put on competition in terms of quality. These market characteristics are not just seen in Germany, but also at the European level, the core market for German exports.

In Germany's case, the main influences were the characteristics of the domestic and European market, which was the main recipient of exports, as well as the production- and technology-oriented management values, which were reflected in the composition of top management. There were certain aspects of the various types of American measures that were strongly incompatible with German traditions and management values, emphasizing technology, quality, and production, as well as with managerial philosophy related to personnel structure, populated by managers with technological backgrounds. With management values that only emphasized technology in the background, and under German-style management values, rather than following producer-oriented measures such as planned obsolescence, a typical oligopolistic behavior, German companies tended to emphasize sales policies that prioritized consumer interests. Traditional influences from the pre-WWII period were also seen, such as priority given to moderate pricing policies based on market agreements. In addition, the product policy emphasized quality and functionality, which enabled the differentiation of high-priced policies and stressed the stability of prices. Therefore, even in the introduction of the various measures that form the important components of marketing, Germany pursued distinctive methods. Overall, because of the differences in corporate management values, the structure of the market and competition, and the introduction of American-style marketing, the introduction of marketing measures in Germany was not as extensive as in Japan; on the other hand, there was a special evolution in terms of the scope of the introduction and extent of its prevalence.

In terms of the introduction of advertising and publicity, the scale of the second wave of Americanization from the mid-1960s to the early 1970s, particularly the acceptance of mass consumption marketing, was so large that it cannot be compared with the first wave of Americanization in the 1950s. It had an impact on almost all large and medium-sized businesses. Although American influence in the 1970s was not as strong as it had been previously, there was a steady flow of American ideas and concepts. However, significant differences between American and German advertising and publicity remained in many areas even after the 1970s. Americanization does not imply that traditional German behavior has been replaced by American behavior. It has been pointed out that the respect for individuality in advertising was never Americanized (Schröter 1997, p. 114).

The adoption of American marketing and advertising techniques was not a natural process of movement toward convergence; rather, it required active and innovative entrepreneurs and managers. Even in the 1950s, such entrepreneurs and managers were opposed to certain practices in their own enterprises, such as the cartels and syndicates' model-oriented, traditional sales policies. Based on their discoveries and experiences in the United States, they influenced the transition of the country toward the market-oriented American model. However, it was not uncommon for them to face opposition from within their organizations (Kleinschmidt 2002, pp. 258–259).

There was hardly any economic field that felt the innovative pressure from the United States as intensely as the advertising and publicity sector. No model was more characteristically American in economic and cultural history than the advertising agency model. There was, however, a vocation with as much widespread antipathy toward the United States as the German advertising experts. According to the history of American advertising in Germany, there was a 40-year fusion process between German tradition and modern American methods which began in the mid-1920s and lasted until the mid-1960s, with a brief interruption during the Nazi era (Vgl. Schindelbeck 1995, p. 236).

Indeed, as competitive pressures increased, the need for marketing became more pressing. However, there were sales function expectations in terms of quality, delivery, and after-service in German firms, as well as the mindset that quality products and services would be purchased. Because of the emphasis on providing high-quality products and services, concerns about distribution channels and pricing policies were generally minor (Lawrence 1980, p. 94). These points were also reflected in Germany's approach of introducing American marketing methods. In 1973, F. Vogel pointed out that German companies increasingly stressed the qualities of their products, rather than the prices, so that customers might be willing to purchase German goods at slightly higher prices than similar products made in other countries. This approach was based on the concept that German goods were of superior quality (Vogel 1973, p. 129). Such recognition reflected a German-style adaptation of the American marketing method. However, as Michael Porter pointed out, German enterprises were behind in sophisticated marketing techniques (Porter 1990, p. 717).

In this way, in contrast to America's strong tendency toward pragmatic thinking, consumer purchasing characteristics and behavior that emphasize technology, quality, and function can be observed in the German product market. There were trends, management practices, and management cultures that emphasized quality, technology, and production in the case of businesses as well. In these circumstances, intense price competition tended to be suppressed, and quality competition was more pronounced in Germany than in other countries. This German trait, which could be seen in areas such as product strategy, was a major background factor in the introduction and growth of marketing methods and techniques in the development of postwar mass production.

Building upon the aforementioned discussion, the majority of German enterprises constantly strived for technical perfection while maintaining a high level of concern for quality. This is not surprising, since the top management of many German firms consisted of individuals with technical backgrounds (Porter 1990, pp. 108, 375–376, Lawrence 1980, pp. 80, 83, 96–100, 186, 190, Eberwein and Tholen 1993, p. 173), and management value emphasizing on quality, technology, and production reflects the composition of executive management. Under such circumstances, intense price competition was restricted and quality competition had a more important meaning, compared to other countries. In Germany, price competition is not typical, but active rivalry on product performance, features, and services has sustained strong competitive advantages in many German industries (Porter 1990, p. 118). In addition, the technical orientation of German firms has almost inevitably led them to compete on the basis of differentiation instead of cost (Porter 1990, pp. 375, 715).

Following World War II, marketing, PR, and OR maintained their management foundation for supporting the large enterprise constitution based on oligopolistic market and big business market control. However, in contrast to the German tradition of quality and technology-oriented management, values/management culture, and market characteristics, American management methods, which were created and developed during the advanced stage of standardization of both production and consumption in the United States based on the pragmatic tradition emphasizing the efficiency principle, were not always compatible with German conditions. For example, "planned obsolescence," a typical oligopolistic behavior that has been widely promoted in the United States as a sales policy technique that contributes to achieving of competitive advantage (Busch 1966, p. 159), was not appropriate in Germany. W R. Smyser points out "Germans do not believe in planned obsolescence" and "they expect their products to be good and to be respected" (Smyser 1992, p. 68). Enterprises such as Daimler-Benz had a product development-oriented strategy that reflected their social responsibility of providing the highest quality in terms of safety and comfort regardless of whether the vehicle was a luxury car, utility vehicle, passenger car, or commercial vehicle (Vgl. Daimler-Benz 1972, pp. 196, 202, 210; Daimler-Benz 1983, p. 127; Walz and Niemann 1997, p. 178). Similarly, in companies such as Volkswagen that had a mass production orientation from the early stages of the postwar period, the emphasis on quality ensured their competitive strength in the international market (Volkswagen 1955, p. 26). The market characteristic that emphasized quality and functionality, in particular, was seen not only in Germany but also elsewhere in Europe as the core market for German exports. For example, in the European Economic Community (EEC), German automobile firms applied the same sales approaches that they used in their home market. As seen in the case of Volkswagen, Daimler-Benz, and BMW, these efforts were supported by heavy advertising that stressed the technical excellence of their products as well as their reliable service (Vogel 1973, pp. 123–124).

The American market has been more homogeneous compared to other countries (Chandler 1977, p. 498), and, thus, the standardization of consumption advanced. Generally, the differences in the American and European market conditions are important factors in defining the nature of business management in Germany. The impact from these market structure factors are also observed in the areas of market adaptation, such as marketing, as well as in the area of production.

As seen in the cases of the automobile firms, German enterprises invested heavily in order to ensure that their products were always technically competitive with those of the best foreign rivals (Vogel 1973, p. 112). The characteristics of German management behavior were also seen in these types of situations, and market characteristics, consumer purchasing characteristics, and corporate behavior principles based on these characteristics can be said to have influenced the German way of adapting to the market under the development of mass production.

Looking at this from a more contemporary perspective, the most important fields for sales, especially in a high-wage country such as Germany, include the upper market and the premium market. Its representative cases can be found in the clothing, machine tools, and automobile industries. Above all, in the machine tools industry and the automobile industry, technical innovation and quality were highly emphasized (Becker 1995, p. 549), which continues to be an important marketing strategy today.

However, this type of German development and way of life was more than just a reflection of the market's structure and characteristics. The fact that the problem was not identified during favorable historical conditions, as seen in the competitive structure and relationship between market and productive forces during the boom years of the 1950s and 1960s, is also significant. German companies achieved record-breaking sales during the 1950s and 1960s through the marketing of high-quality products at competitive prices. However, the competitiveness of German industries dramatically decreased due to currency factors and the swift rise in wage costs in the 1970s. As a result, German managers had to devise radically new marketing strategies in order to cope with such situations (Vogel 1973, p. 108).

10.4 Reframing in the Deployment of American Marketing Methods in Japan and Germany

Finally, based on the preceding analysis, this section investigates "reframing" in the deployment of American marketing methods in Japan and Germany, as well as some factors influencing such modification.

When examining the fusion of American and Japanese elements, hybridization can be seen in the combination of the American supermarket system with the Japanese pre-packaged system of perishable goods that was suitable for Japanese consumption behaviors. The hybridization of elements from each country was also visible in the incorporation of the Japanese way of forming groups based on mutual trust relationships in the affiliation of distribution systems.

When considering the deployment of marketing in Japan in relation to important factors that influenced the implementation of such American marketing methods, the following influences of management values, management traditions and cultures can be observed: (1) management values emphasizing sales volume and market share differed from those in the United States, which viewed price as "a contract between enterprise and customer," (2) management values regarding inter-firm relationships based on mutual trust and collectivism as well as contract, (3) management traditions emphasizing collectivism and close departmental coordination, and (4) long-term continuous trade customs between enterprises.

In terms of the institutional factors that determined reframing in Americanization, social structures other than those emphasizing contracting relations in the United States, and social structures emphasizing collectivism based on social reliance through close relationships among members, greatly influenced the implementation of marketing techniques developed in the United States.

When considering the influence of Japanese capitalism's structural characteristics, the effect of a productive force structure is seen in the development of productive forces based on the rapid progress of mass production, including changes in productive force structures and the progress of mass production in these industries, particularly the durable consumer goods industries. After the war, the rapid progress of mass production in Japan, as well as the increasing need to cope with mass market with it, became important factors in determining Japanese-style marketing.

The influence of industrial structure factors was also significant. It is reflected in the delay in the development of heavy and chemical industries prior to the war, as well as the rapid development and expansion of consumer goods industries and the growing importance of durable consumer goods departments in the production industrial sectors.

Furthermore, four points can be observed in terms of the influence of marketing structure factors: (1) differences in marketing deployment across industrial sectors due to competitive conditions and a competitive structure, (2) characteristics of domestic markets, such as narrow and diverse markets, (3) rapid expansion of consumer goods industries, particularly durable consumer goods industries, and (4) importance of planned obsolescence due to the development of home appliance market in the form of catching up with US technologies.

Next, when examining the reframing of American marketing methods in Germany, an amalgamation of American and German elements can be seen in the combining of US-style thinking and mass marketing methods with product and price policies that emphasize Germany's respect for individuality, quality, functionality, and brand.

In terms of management values and cultural factors in business management, the influence of management values emphasizing technology, quality, and production, as well as a historical tendency to dismiss sales and marketing viewpoints were important factors in determining the reframing. A large proportion of executives in technical fields was deeply concerned about such management values. The prewar tradition of prioritizing moderate competition policies based on cartels had an impact on German enterprises' price policies. The persistent influence of traditional pricing and terms policies on German corporations hampered the spread of American marketing methods and thinking.

Institutional factors influencing the deployment of marketing methods can be found in the prewar acceptance of cartels and state regulations such as gift regulations and the Rebate's Act. The historical influence of traditional cartels on heavy industry's low marketing value recognition was significant.

When considering the impact of German capitalism's structural characteristics, the impact of the structure of productive forces is indicated in the foundation of product differentiation based on a structure with diversified quality production. Since the prewar period, industrial structures centered on producer goods industries, and relatively high proportions of producer goods industries in the postwar period, have influenced the deployment of American marketing measures.

In terms of market structure factors, market characteristics emphasizing quality and functionality, consumer resistance to product standardization, resistance to planned obsolescence as a product policy, and differences in marketing and deployment recognition across industrial sectors due to competitive conditions and a competitive structure were significant. In Germany's case, the main influences were the characteristics of the domestic and European markets, which were the primary recipients of exports, as well as the production and technology-oriented management values, reflected in the composition of top management. Prioritization of long-term product policies, as well as focus on quality and functionality rather than planned obsolescence, were prominent features in the deployment of marketing methods in Germany, and premium pricing policy through product differentiation was emphasized under the European market as a core export market.

As a result, even in the implementation of the various measures that are important components of marketing, Germany pursued distinct methods. Overall, because of the differences in corporate management values, market structure, and competition, the introduction of American-style marketing in Germany was not as extensive as in Japan; however, there was a distinct evolution in terms of the scope of the introduction and the extent of its prevalence.

Regarding the conditions surrounding the introduction of American marketing methods in Japan and Germany during the postwar boom years as well as "reframing" and the factors defining, Table 10.1 shows an inline comparison of the respective countries, based on the discussion so far in this chapter.

Table 10.1 Comparison of conditions surrounding the introduction of marketing in Japan and Germany

Deploymen and factors affecting them	Management methods	
	Marketing	
	Japanese management methods	German management methods
Overall conditions in the deployment of American management methods	• Simultaneous deployment and implementation of managerial marketing and high-pressure marketing • Marketing emphasizing product policy • Deployment of integrated marketing focused on strategic development • Affiliated distribution systems as large manufacturing company-led distribution channel policy • Completion of imitation processes of American-style marketing during the 1960s • Development of international marketing in the durable consumer goods departments, such as seen in the establishment of their own distribution channels	• Deployment of divisions of labor between sales (short-term strategy) and marketing (long-term strategy) departments • Basic marketing philosophies and principles, and the deployment and spread of advertising and publicity methods • Progress of deployments in the consumer goods sector and sluggishness in the production sector

(continued)

Table 10.1 (continued)

Deploymen and factors affecting them	Management methods	
	Marketing	
	Japanese management methods	German management methods
Deployment characteristics of American management methods	• Development of total marketing that reflected Japanese characteristics of company organization, such as informal and dense human relations and behavioral patterns based on collectivism • Price policies emphasizing sales volume and market share • Development of wet, small-scale, and non-strategic marketing focused on sales and production orientations • Bottom-up marketing based on the role of human factors • Emphasis on planned obsolescence as a product policy in the durable consumer goods sectors • Marketing focused on non-price competition under the distribution control by affiliated distribution system • Marketing based on product policy emphasizing market segmentation and product differentiation	• Marketing was the most successful field among the various efforts undertaken by the US Technical and Productivity Program • Role of US advertising agencies and consulting firms • Low status of the head of publicity in the corporate hierarchy • Differentiated product strategy emphasizing quality and functionality

(continued)

Table 10.1 (continued)

Deploymen and factors affecting them	Management methods	
	Marketing	
	Japanese management methods	German management methods
Modifications in American management methods	• Japanization of business systems in the deployment of retail techniques • Modification of American automobile dealer systems by making use of the close interdependent relationships between producing company and dealer • Marketing focused on human factors and consumer service • Development of marketing cohered with the market needs in the product strategy	• Prioritization of long-term product policies and focus on quality and functionality rather than planned obsolescence • Premium pricing policy through product differentiation
Amalgamation of American and Japanese elements	• Combining the American super-market system with Japanese pre-package system of perishable goods that was suitable for Japanese consumption behaviors • Integration of Japanese way of forming groups based on relationships of mutual trust in the affiliation of distribution systems	• Combining US-style thinking and methods of mass marketing, with product and price policies that emphasize Germany's respect for individuality, quality, functionality, and brand

(continued)

Table 10.1 (continued)

Deploymen and factors affecting them		Management methods	
		Marketing	
		Japanese management methods	German management methods
Factors of modification of American management method	Influence of traditions, cultural factors, and management values	• Management values emphasizing sales volume and market share that were different from those in the United States which regarded price as "a contract between enterprise and customer" • Management values regarding inter-firm relationships based on mutual trust and collectivism as well as the contract • Management traditions emphasizing collectivism and close coordination between departments • Long-term and continuous trade customs between enterprises	• Management values emphasizing technology, quality, and production • High proportion of executives from technical fields • Prewar tradition of prioritizing moderate competition policies based on cartels • Historical tendency to take sales and marketing viewpoints lightly • German corporations' persistent influence of traditional pricing and terms policies
	Influence of institutional factors	• Social structure different from that emphasizing contracting relations in the United States • Social structure emphasizing collectivism based on social reliance through the close relationships among members	• Historical influence of traditional cartels on heavy industry's low recognition of marketing value • Influence of state regulations such as gift regulations and the Rebates Act • Influence of competition order in the prewar acceptance of cartels

(continued)

Table 10.1 (continued)

Deploymen and factors affecting them		Management methods	
		Marketing	
		Japanese management methods	German management methods
	Influencing factors of the productive forces	• Development of productive forces based on rapid progress of mass production • Changes in structure of productive forces in the durable consumer goods industries and progress of mass production in these industries	• Progress of mass production and reforms to the structure of productive forces in the durable consumer goods sector • Foundation of product differentiation based on a structure with diversified quality production and the structure of productive forces
	Influence of industrial structure factors	• Delay in development of the heavy and chemical industries before World War II • Rapid development and expansion of consumer goods industries and the growing weight of the durable consumer goods departments in the production industrial sectors	• Characteristics of industrial structures centered on producer goods industries since the prewar period • Relatively high proportions of producer goods industries in the postwar era

(continued)

Table 10.1 (continued)

Deploymen and factors affecting them		Management methods	
		Marketing	
		Japanese management methods	German management methods
	Influence of market structure factors	• Differences in the deployment of marketing among industrial sectors due to competitive conditions and a competitive structure • Characteristics of domestic markets, such as narrow and diverse markets and tendency of concentration of population in large city areas • Rapid expansion of consumer goods industries, in particular, the durable consumer goods industries • Importance of planned obsolescence due to the development of home appliance market in the form of catching up to US technologies	• Market characteristics emphasizing quality and functionality • Consumer resistance to product standardization • Resistance to planned obsolescence as a product policy • Differences in recognition of marketing and deployment among industrial sectors due to competitive conditions and a competitive structure

Source This table was compiled by the author, based on discussions in this chapter

References

Abelshauser W (1995) Two kinds of Fordism: on the differing roles of the industry in the development to the two German states. In: Shiomi H, Wada K (eds) Fordism transformed. The development of production methods on the automobile industry. Oxford University Press, New York, pp 269–296

Abelshauser W (2018) Zweierlei Fordismus. Zur Rolle der Automobilindustrie in der Wirtschaft der beiden deutschen Staaten. In: K Y, Laks T, Schramm M (eds) Regional Ressourcen und Europa. Dimensionen kritischer Industrie- und Unternehmensgechichtsschreibung. Duncker & Humblot, Berlin, S 93–117

Akimoto I, Watanabe M (1983) Gendai nihon shihonshugi to sijyo mondai (Modern Japanese capitalism and market problems). In: Akimoto I, Kadomatsu M, Shimokawa K (eds) Gendai nihon dokusen no maketingu (Marketing of modern Japanese monopoly). Otsuki shoten, Tokyo, pp 7–39

Arai K (1961) Sengo maketingu no shokeitai (Forms of postwar marketing). In: Keizai semina (Keizai Semin) 52:64–67

Arakawa Y (1960) Gendai haikyu riron (Modern distribution theory). Chikura shobo, Tokyo

Arakawa Y (1964) Distributive trade and marketing in Japan. Chikura Shobo, Tokyo

Becker J (Translated by Oda) (1995) Doitsu ni okeru maketingu senryaku (Marketing strategy in Germany). In: Ohashi S, Oda A, Schanz G (eds) Nihonteki keiei to doitsuteki keiei (Japanese mamagement and German management). Chikura shobo, Tokyo, pp 540–564

Booz-Allen & Hamilton (1973) Herausforderungen des deutschen Managements und ihre Bewaltigung. Otto Schwartz, Göttingen

Busch KW (1966) Strukturwandlungen der westdeutschen Automobilindustrie. Ein Beitrag zur Erfassung und Deutung einer industriellen Entwicklungsphasen im Ubergang vom produktionsorientierten zum marktorientierten Wachstum. Dunker & Humblot, Berlin

Chandler AD Jr (1977) The visible hand: managerial revolution in American business. Harvard University Press, Cambridge

Daimler-Benz AG (ed) (1972) Chronik. Mercedes-Benz Fahrzeuge und Motoren, 5th edn. Daimler-Benz, Stuttgart

Daimler-Benz AG (1983) Werk Unterturkheim. Stammwerke der Daimler-Benz Aktiengesellschaft. Ein historischen Überbild. Daimler-Benz AG, Stuttgart

Der Volkswirt (1955) Eine Million Volkswagen. In: Der Volkswirt 9(32):10–11

Der Volkswirt (1960) Volkswagenwerk mit hohen Zuwachsraten. Rund 256 Mill.DM Gewinne—Auflosung stiller Reserven. In: Der Volkswirt 14(36):2046–2050

Dyas GP, Thanheiser HT (1976) The emerging European enterprise. Strategy and structure in French and German industry. Macmillan, London

Eberwein W, Tholen J (1993) Euro-Manager or splendid isolation? International management—an Anglo-German comparison. Walter de Gruyter, Berlin, New York

Eguchi Y (1975) Maketingu katsudo (Marketing activity). In: Noda K (ed) Nihon no keiei (Japanese management). Daiyamondosha, Tokyo

Feldenkirchen W (2004a) DaimlerChrysler Werk Untertürkheim. Motorbuch-Verlag, Stuttgart

Feldenkirchen W (2004b) The Americanization of the German electrical industry after 1945. Siemens as a case study. In: Kudo A, Kipping M, Schröter HG (eds) German and Japanese business in the boom years. Transforming American management and technology models. Routledge, London, pp 116–137

Fujieda T (1965) Maketingu no dainamizumu (Dynamism of marketing). In: Bijinesu (Business) 9(4):34–35

Fushimi T (1997) Jigyobusei manejimento · kontororu ni okeru "nihongata" no kenkyu (Study of Japanese type of divisional management control). In: Nihon kanri kaikei gakkaishi (J Jpn Assoc Manag Account) 5(1):3–14

Goji K et al (supvr), Noda K (ed) (1965) Sengo keieishi (Postwar business history). Nihon seisansei honbu, Tokyo

Goji K et al (supvr), Noda K (ed) (1969) Gendai keieishi (Modern business history). Nihon seisansei honbu, Tokyo

Hallig K (1965) Amerikanische Erfahrungen auf dem Gebiet der wirtschaftswerbung im Hinblick auf ihre Anwendung im westeuropaischen Raum. Duncker & Humblot, Berlin

Hartmann H (1963) Amerikanische Firmen in Deutschland: Beobachtungen über Kontakte und Kontraste zwischen Industriegesellschaften. Westdeutscher Verlag, Koln

Hashimoto I (1973) Gendai Maketingu ron (Modern marketing). Shinhyoron, Tokyo

Hashimoto J (1998) Amerika no inpakuto to shisutemu no kakuran (Impact of the United States and disruption of the system). In: Tokyo daigaku shakaikagaku kenkyusho (ed) 20 seiki shisutemu 3 Keizai seicho III Juyo to taiko (20th century system 3 Economic growth III acceptance and opposition). Tokyo daigaku shuppankai, Tokyo, pp 1–25

Hayashi S (1961) Nihon no kigyo to maketingu (Japanese enterprises and marketing). Nihon seisansei honbu, Tokyo

Hayashi S (1965) Henyo suru nihon no maketingu (The changing Japanese marketing). In: Bijinesu (Business) 9(4):30–33

Hilger S (2004a) „Amerikanisierung" deutscher Unternehmen. Wettbewerbsstrategien und Unternehmenspolitik bei Henkel, Siemens und Daimler-Benz (1945/49–1975). Franz Steiner Verlag, Stuttgart

Hilger S (2004b) Reluctant Americanization? The reaction of Henkel to the influences and competition from the United States. In: Kudo A, Kipping M, Schröter HG (eds) German and Japanese business in the boom years. Transforming American management and technology models. Routledge, London, pp 193–220

Hiller H (1952) Das Volkswagenwerk Legt Rechnung. In: Der Volkswirt 6(22):26–29

Hölzer H (1964) Werbung ist Führungsaufgabe. In: Der Volkswirt, 18. Jg, Beiheft zu Nr. 39 vom 25 September 1964. Werbung ist Führungsaufgabe, p 5

Ikeo K (1999) Nihongata maketingu no kakushin (Reform of Japanese-type marketing). Nihon keizai shinbunsha, Tokyo

Iseda Y (1963) Tekkogyo ni okeru maketingu · risachi (Marketing research in the iron and steel industry). In: Tekkokai (Iron and Steel World) 13(6):40–45

Ishii J (1993) Maketingu no Shinwa (Myth of marketing). Nihon keizai shinbusha, Tokyo

Iwanaga T (2005) Maketingu senryaku ron (Marketing strategy), enlarged revised edn. Gokosha, Tokyo

Katagiri S (2000) Nihon no maketingu no tenkai to tokushitsu (Development of marketing in Japan and its characteristics). In: Katagiri S, Takamori T, Azuma T (eds) Gendai maketingu no kozu (Structure of modern marketing). Sagano shoin, Kyoto, pp. 33–46)

Keizai doyukai sogo keiei koritsu kenkyukai (1970) Sogoteki na keiei koritsu kara mita nanajunendai nihon no keiei kadai (Management tasks in the 1970s from the viewpoint of total management efficiency). In: Keizai doyu (Econ Comrade) 25(9):3–39

Kikkawa T (1998) "Shohi kakumei" to "ryutsu kakumei" ("Consumption revolution" and "distribution revolution"). In: Tokyo daigaku shakai kagaku kenkyusho (ed) 20 seiki shisutemu 3. Keizai seicho III, Juyo to taiko (20th century system 3 Economic growth III acceptance and opposition). Tokyo daigaku shuppankai, Tokyo, pp 99–137

Kikkawa T, Takaoka M (1998) Supa · maketto · shisutemu no kokusai iten to nihonteki juyo (International transfer of super-market system and Japanese change). In: Morikawa M, Yui T (eds) Kokusai hikaku · kokusai kankei no keieishi (Business history of international comparison and international relations). Nagoya daigaku shuppankai, Nagoya, pp 279–304

Kleinschmidt C (1998) An Americanized company in Germany. The Vereinigte Glanzstoff Fabriken AG in the 1950s. In: Kipping M, Bjarnar O (eds) The Americanization of European business. The Marshall plan and the transfer of US management models. Routledge, London, pp 171–189

Kleinschmidt C (2002) Der produktive Blick. Wahrnehmung amerikanischer und japanischer Management- und Produktionsmethoden durch deutsche Unternehmer 1950–1985. Akademie Verlag, Berlin

Kleinschmidt C (2004) Driving the West German consumer society: the introduction of US style production and marketing at Volkswagen, 1945–70. In: Kudo A, Kipping M, Schröter HG (eds) German and Japanese business in the boom year. Transforming American management and technology models. Routledge, London, pp 75–92

Köhler I (2008) Marketingmanagement als Strukturmodell. Der organisatorische Wandel in der deutschen Automobilindustrie der 1960er bis 1980er Jahre. In: Zeitschrift für Unternehmensgeschichte 53(2):216–239

Korte FK (1964) Der Werbeleiter in der Unternehmens-Hierarchie. In: Der Volkswirt, 18. Jg, Beiheft zu Nr. 39 vom 25 September 1964, pp 26–31

Lawrence P (1980) Managers and management in West Germany. Croom Helm, London

Linne K (2008) «[...] bisher nur Sonnentage [...] ». Der Aufbau der Volkswagen-Händlerorganisation 1948 bis 1967. In: Zeitschrift für Unternehmensgeschichte 53(1):5–32

Miyazaki A (1983) Taikyu shohizai dokusen no marketingu (B Kaden) [Marketing of monoploly in the durable consumer goods industry (B. home appliance)]. In: Akimoto I, Kadomatsu M, Shimokawa K (eds) Gendai Nihon dokusen no maketingu (Marketing of modern Japanese monopoly). Otsuki shoten, Tokyo, pp 147–164

Mogi T (1969) Maketingu koritsu no nichibei hikaku (Comparison of marketing efficiency in Japan and the United States). In: Bijinesu (Business), Sept 1969:46–49

Mori M (1976) "Maketingu" no senkuteki Keisei (Pioneering formation of "marketing"). In: Kobayashi M, Simokoawa K, Sugiyama K et al (eds) Nihon keiieshi wo manabu, 2. Taisho · showa keieishi, vol 2. (Learning Japanese business history, 2.) Yuhikaku, Tokyo, pp 266–281

Murata S (1981) Maketingu towa nanika (What is marketing?). In: Tauchi K, Murata S (eds) Gendai maketingu no kiso riron (Fundamental theory of modern marketing). Dobukan shuppan, Tokyo, pp 3–68

Nakano Y (1983) Gendai nihon shihonshugi to ryutsu kiko (Modern Japanese capitalism and distribution system). In: Itozono T, NakanoY, Maeda J et al (eds) Gendai nihon no ryutsu kiko (Modern Japanese distribution system). Otsuki shoten, Tokyo, pp 7–43

Nihon keiei seisaku gakkai (ed) (1970) Keiie shiryo shutaisei IV (Compiled management materials IV). Nihon sogo shuppan kiko, Tokyo

Nihon keieishi kenkyusho (ed) (2002) Asahi kasei hachijunenshi (80-year history of Asahi Kasei Corporation). Asahi kasei kabushikigaisha, Tokyo

Nihon seisansei honbu (ed) (1957) Maketingu—Marketingu senmon shisatsudanhokokusho—(Marketing—Report of the special inspection team for marketing—). Nihon seisansei honbu, Tokyo

Nihon seisansei honbu (ed) (1960) Amerika tekkogyo ni okeru maketingu risachi (Marketing research in the US iron and steel industry). Nihon seisansei honbu, Tokyo

Niida H, Mishima M (1991) Ryutsu keiretsuka no tenkai (Development of affiliated distribution). In: Miwa Y, Nishimura K (eds) Nihon no ryutsu (Japanese distribution). Tokyo daigaku shuppankai, Tokyo, pp 97–130

Nishimura E (1995) Iyakuhin no maketingu (Marketing of pharamaceuticals). In: Maketingushi kenkyukai (ed) Nihon no maketingu (Japanese marketing). Dobunkan shuppan, Tokyo, pp 129–157

Obara H (1994) Nihon maketingushi (Marketing history in Japan). Chuo keizasha, Tokyo

Obara H (2010) Panasonic (Matsushita denki sangyo) no maketingu [Marketing of Panasonic (Matsushita Electric Industrial Co. Ltd.). In: Maketingushi kenkyukai (ed) Nihon no maketingu (Japanese marketing). Dobunkan shuppan, Tokyo, pp 76–94

Obara H, Yamanaka T (1995) Nihon no maketingu (Marketing in Japan). In: Maketingushi kenkyukai (ed) Nihon no maketingu (Japanese marketing). Dobunkan shuppan, Tokyo, pp 3–50

OEEC (1954) Problems of business management. OEEC, Paris

Ogawa K (2010) Nihonteki maketingu no genryu to sono sengoshi (Origin of Japanese marketing and its postwar history). In: Kikkawa T, Kubo F (eds) Gurobaruka to nihongata kigyo shisutemu no henyo—1985~2008—(Globalization and changes in the Japanese corporate system—1985–2008—). Mineruva shobo, Kyoto, pp 199–220

Ogawa K, Hayashi H (1997) Beinichikan deno maketingu gijutsu no iten moderu (Transfer model of marketing techniques between the US and Japan). In: Kikan marketing journal (Market J Q) 67:4–22
Onaga K (1995) Shiseido no maketingu (Marketing of Shiseido Company). In: Maketingushi kenkyukai (ed) Nihon no maketingu (Japanese marketing). Dobunkan shuppan, Tokyo, pp 57–75
Ozaki K (1995) Kaden seihin no maketingu (Marketing of home appliances). In: Maketingushi kenkyukai (ed) Nihon no maketingu (Japanese marketing). Dobunkan shuppan, Tokyo, pp 73–104
Porter ME (1990) The competitive advantage of nations. The Free Press, New York
Remele H (1963) Rationalisierungsreserven in Klein- und Mittelbetrieben. Ergebnisse einer Analyse des RKW-Betriebsbegehungsdienstes. In: Rationalisierung 14(5):113–115
Sato H (1971) Ryutsu sangyo kakumei (Revolution in distribution industry). Yuhikaku, Tokyo
Sato H (1983) Nihon no ryutsu kiko (Japanese distribution system). Yuhikaku, Tokyo
Schindelbeck D (1995) "Asbach Uralt" und "Soziale Marktwirtschaft." Zur Kulturgeschichte der Werbeagentur in Deutschland am Beispiel von Hannes W. Brose (1899–1971). In: Zeitschrift für Unternehmensgeschichte 40(4):235–252
Schröter HG (1997) Die Amerikanisierung der Werbung in der Bundesrepublik Deutschland. In: Jahrbuch für Wirtschaftsgeschichte, 1997/1:93–115
Schröter HG (1998) Advertising in West Germany after World War II. A case of an Americanization. In: Schröter HG, Moen E (eds) Une Américanisation des Enterprises? Eska, Paris, pp 15–33
Schröter HG (2005) Americanization of the European economy. A compact survey of American economic influence in Europe since the 1880s. Springer, Dordrecht
Shimokawa K (1976a) Maketingu no hatten (Development of marketing). In: Shirahige T, Shimokawa K (eds) Maketingu ron (Marketing). Nihon hyoronsha, Tokyo, pp 61–92
Shimokawa K (1976b) Toyota jihan no maketingu (Marketing of Toyota Sales Corporation). In: Kobayashi M, Shimokawa K, Sugiyama K et al (eds) Nihon keiieshi wo manabu 3. Sengo keieishi (Learning Japanese business history 3. The postwar business history), vol 3. Yuhikaku, Tokyo, pp 218–229
Shimokawa K (1983) Taikyu shohizai no maketingu (A Jidosha) [Marketing of durable consumer goods (A automonbile)]. In: Akimoto I, Kadomatsu M, Shimokawa K (eds) Gendai Nihon dokusen no maketingu (Marketing of modern Japanese monopoly). Otsuki shoten, Tokyo, pp 119–146
Shimokawa K (1991) Sengo nihon keieishi kenkyu no kaiko to tenbo (Retrospective study of Japanese business history). In: Yonekawa S, Shimokawa K, Yamazaki H (eds) Sengo keieishi Dai III Kan (Postwar business history), vol 3. Toyo keizai shinposha, Tokyo, pp 281–301
Shimokawa K (1997) Maketingu (Marketing), 2nd edn. Bunshindo, Tokyo
Shioji H (2002) Jidosha ryutsu no kokusai hikaku (International comparison of automobile distribution). Yuhikaku, Tokyo
Shirahige T (1962) Gendai no maketingu (Modern marketing). Zeimu keiri kyokai, Tokyo
Sirahige T (1976) Nihon no maketingu (Japanese marketing). In: Sirahige T, Shimokawa K (eds) Maketingu ron (Marketing). Nihon hyoronsha, Tokyo, pp 141–157
Shiraishi Y (1995) Jidosha no maketingu (Marketing of automobiles). In: Maketingushi kenkyukai (ed) Nihon no maketingu (Japanese marketing). Dobunkan shuppan, Tokyo, pp 105–127
Smyser WR (1992) The economy of United Germany: colossus at crossroads. St. Martin's Press, New York
Strotmann K-H (1960) Marktforschung als Voraussetzung für Typenbeschränkung. In: Rationalisierung 11(1):12–14
Suzuki Y (1974) Kourigyo no shokeitai (Forms of retail industry). In: Kubomura T, Arakawa Y (eds) Shogyogaku (Commercial science). Yuhikaku, Toky, pp 365–388
Takaoka S (1976) Maketingu to ryutsu keiretuka (Marketing and formation of affiliated distribution). In: Kobayashi M, Shimokawa K, Sugiyama K et al (eds) Nihon keiieshi wo manabu 3. Sengo keieishi (Learning Japanese business history 3. The postwar business history), vol 3. Yuhikaku, Tokyo, pp 152–166

Takeda S (1985) Nihon kigyo no kokusai marketing (International marketing of Japanese enterprises). Dobunkan shuppan, Tokyo
Takeda S (1995) Keikikaihin no marketing (Marketing of light machines). In: Maketingushi kenkyukai (ed) Nihon no maketingu (Japanese marketing). Dobunkan shuppan, Tokyo, pp 51–71
Tamura M (1983) Nihon kigyo no maketingu senryaku (Marketing strategy of Japanese enterprises). In: Bijinesu rebyu (Bus Rev) 30(3 · 4):147–167
Toba K (1982) Nihon no maketingu (Japanese marketing). In: Keieishigaku (Jpn Bus Hist Rev) 17(1):1–21
Toyota jidosha hanbai kabushikigaisha shashi henshu iinkai (ed) (1970) Motarizeshon to Tomoni (With motorization). Toyota jidosha hanbain kabushikigaisha, Nagoya
Toyota jidosha hanbai kabushikgaisha shashi hensan iinkai (ed) (1980) Sekai heno ayumi. Toyota jihan sanjunenshi (Step toward the world. 30-year history of Toyota Sales Corporation). Toyota jidosha hanbai kabushikigaisha, Nagoya
Uno M (1969) Maketingu vijyon no tenkai (Development of marketing vision). In: Uno M (ed) Nihon no maketingu (Japanese marketing), Dobunkan shuppan, Tokyo, pp 1–30
Vogel F (1973) German business after the economic miracle. Macmillan, London
Vogelsang G (1961) Über die technische Entwicklung des Volkswagens. In: Automobiltechnische Zeitschrift 63(1):1–13
Volkswagen GmbH (ed) (1955) Ein Rechenschaftsbericht für die Belegschaft und für die Außenenorganisation des Volkswagenwerks. Geschäftsverlauf und Rechnungsabschluß 1951 bis 1954, Werks-Chronik bis 1955. Volkswagen GmbH, Wolfsburg
Wakabayashi Y (1999) Nihon no maketingshi kenkyu no igi to kenkyu wakugumi (Significance of marketing study in Japan and research framework). In: Kondo F, Wakabayashi Y (eds) Nihonkigyo no masu · maketingushi (History of mass marketing of Japanese enterprises). Dobunkan, Tokyo, pp 3–24
Walz W, Niemann H (1997) Daimler-Benz. Wo das Auto anfing, 6th edn. Friedr. Stadler, Konstanz
Wellhöner V (1996) „Wirtschaftswunder"—Weltmarkt—Westdeutscher Fordismus. Der Fall Volkswagen. Westfälisches Dampfboot, Münster
Yoshino M (1971) The Japanese marketing system: adaptations and innovations. The MIT Press, Cambridge, Massachusetts
Zaiga E (1980) Katei denki to maketingu (Home appliances and marketing). In: Aritomi S, Kasio M (eds) Nihon no sangyo kozo to maketingu (Industrial structure and marketing in Japan). Shin hyoron, Tokyo, pp 224–266

Chapter 11
Deployment of a Divisional Structure

Abstract This chapter investigates the implementation of a divisional structure in light of changes in business strategies, management systems and practices, and managers' traditional attitudes. The deployment of a divisional structure in Japan and Germany, the advancement of diversification in large companies and its relationship to organizational structure reforms, and the overall actual conditions after the deployment of the divisional structure are all examined. Furthermore, this chapter examines case studies of representative enterprises in major industrial sectors such as the chemical, electric, and machinery industries, the precision instrument industry, the heavy engineering and shipbuilding industries, and the iron and steel industries. These discussions clarify various aspects of the deployment of Japanese and German-style divisional structures, including (1) the degree of self-sufficiency of divisions, (2) the level of influence of delegation of authority and responsibility, (3) the traditions and roles of the board of directors and collegiate management, (4) the characteristics of the board-majority system, (5) the use of a compensation system linked to divisional results, and (6) the significance of divisional results.

Keywords Decentralization · Diversification strategy · Divisional structure · Functional structure · Self-sufficiency of divisions · Self-supporting accounting system

From Chaps. 6–10, we analyzed management education, management- and production systems, and marketing methods as methods of adapting to the mass market regarding changes in business management and the significance of the deployment and transfer of US management methods in Japan and Germany. In this chapter, the deployment of divisional structure will be discussed.[1]

Following World War II, the expansion of domestic markets and market opportunities as a result of advances in mass production laid the foundation for business diversification, which in turn prompted changes in organizational structure. Once

[1] The first content analysis related to Germany in this chapter is Chap. 9 of the author's book "*German Business Management: A Japanese Perspective on Regional Development Factors,*" which was published by Springer in 2013.

T. Yamazaki, *Japanese and German Enterprises*,
https://doi.org/10.1007/978-981-97-4880-8_11

again, the American-style management system was established as an effective model. A prime example was the decentralized divisional structure, which was first implemented in several pioneering enterprises in the 1920s (Chandler 1962, 1977, 1990) and spread after the war. Moreover, in Germany, IG Farben, in the chemical industry, built an organizational structure similar to the product divisional structure seen in Du Pont after World War I, thus corresponding to the change in the business structure around the same time. However, the new organization in this German company could not solve certain management problems; therefore, it had significant limitations (Yamazaki 1997, 2001, 2015; Chaps. 4, 7 and 8). In Japan, there was a case in which organizational structure (similar to the divisional structure) was established without direct American influence before World War II, as seen in Matsushita Electric Industrial Co., Ltd. (Matsushita denki sangyo kabushikigaisha sogyo gojushunen kinen iinkai 1968, pp. 111–114; Ono 1979, pp. 306–308; Hiramoto 2000; Nishikawa 1996, p. 77; Shimotani 1998, pp. 56–64). In both Germany and Japan, diffusion of the divisional structure advanced after World War II, especially when business diversification progressed and American influence appeared strongly.

Japanese and German corporations also sought to restructure organizations along the lines of the American model. Even in the process of such Americanization, the introduction of the divisional structure in both Japan and Germany was not always a direct import from the United States. Therefore, it is important to clarify the type of organizational innovation that occurred in both countries while requiring a model from the United States, the factors that determined such conditions, and the characteristics that this development possessed.

This chapter considers the deployment of divisional structures using case studies of typical corporations from major industries in order to understand Japanese and German characteristics of management organization structure. These deployments based on their relationship to the traditional attributes of Japanese and German business management will be examined.

The deployment of divisional structure in Japan and Germany will be considered in Sect. 11.1 and Sect. 11.2, respectively. In Sect. 11.3, characteristics of Japanese and German deployment of divisional structures will be examined. Based on these discussions, Sect. 11.4 clarifies "reframing" in the deployment of divisional structure in both countries.

11.1 Transformation of Business Strategy and Deployment of Divisional Structure in Japan

11.1.1 Transformation of Business Strategy

This section first considers the transformation of business strategy and deployment of divisional structure in Japan. Observing the situation in Japan for comparison of these organizational changes, it can be observed that the deployment of organizational divisional structure was facilitated by diversification of business. With regard to the development of strategy in large enterprises during the postwar boom years, according to a survey by Hideki Yoshihara et al., which investigated changes in strategy and structure of 118 large businesses in Japan during the 1958–1973 period, there was a trend toward diversification. However, with Japan's high economic growth, one could notice not only diversification in large corporations but also an increase in corporations taking the opposite approach of vertical integration. In addition, there were a large number of companies that showed movement toward the concentration of businesses. Therefore, the level of diversification was low compared to that of US corporations, and the pace of diversification was slow (Yoshihara et al. 1981, pp. 58, 64–65). There was also a time lag in the aforementioned trend in comparison with European and American companies. Furthermore, the necessity of promoting diversification was not very high in Japan since it had achieved a remarkably high rate of economic growth compared to that of the United States and other European countries (Yoshihara et al. 1981, pp. 39, 57–58, 64–65).

When comparing the type of strategy used in the 118 large Japanese enterprises between 1958 and 1973, the rate of single-type firms significantly decreased from 26.3% to 16.9%. In contrast, the rate of vertical-type firms increased from 13.2% to 18.6%. Meanwhile, the weight of dominant-constrained-type firms slightly increased from 6.1% to 6.8%. While the rate of related-constrained-type firms decreased from 14.9% to 14.4%, that of related-linked-type firms greatly increased from 15.8% to 25.4%. In this period, the increase of vertical-type firms and related-linked-type firms was remarkable. Conversely, the ratio of unrelated-type firms decreased from 8.8% to 6.8% (Yoshihara et al. 1981, p. 36).

The strategic elements of single-type and related-type firms reveal "the difference at the quantitative level between the product market fields." In addition, the elements of constrained-type and linked-type firms represent not only "the difference of the related pattern between the product market fields in the company" but also "the difference of the method employed for the use and accumulation of resources." Shifts in the strategy of vertical-type firms and in diversification were fundamental characteristics of the change from dominant-constrained-type firms. On the other hand, related-linked-type firms indicated the highest rate in 1973, and the tendency toward this type clearly revealed a diversification trend in Japan. In addition, upon examining the movement of strategic-type firms from the perspective of constrained-type or linked-type firms, movement between the strategic types that included the same elements was frequent, as seen in between the dominant-constrained and related-linked types. In contrast, movement between strategic types that included different elements was rare, as seen between dominant-constrained types and related-linked types. In this way, there were relatively few examples of qualitative, aggressive diversification in Japanese corporations focusing on changing patterns of resource accumulation and utilization (Yoshihara et al.1981, pp. 49–50, 65). With regard to the route of diversification, there were two main routes: (1) "single type → dominant-constrained type → related-constrained type → related-linked type," and (2) "single type → dominant-linked type → related-linked type" (Yoshihara et 1981, p. 55).

With regard to the subsequent changes, according to a 1980 survey by the Japan Association of Corporate Executives, the rates of firms that diversified into the conventional market-related field and the conventional product technology-related field from 1974 to 1979 were 34.6 or 35.8%, respectively. The total for both types of diversification amounted to approximately 70%; therefore, diversification into the main profession-related fields was dominant. Conversely, the rates of companies that did not diversify, and the firms that withdrew from the diversified field, were 14.4% and 5.7%, respectively (Keizai doyukai 1980, pp. 2, 30–31).

11.1.2 Deployment of Divisional Structure

11.1.2.1 Overall Circumstances of the Deployment of Divisional Structure

Next, the deployment of a divisional structure is considered. According to Yoshihara et al. (1981), whereas the rate of functional structure declined from 55.9% in 1963 to 45.8% in 1968, further to 40.7% in 1973, the rate of divisional structure rose from 28.3% to 33.9%, further to 41.5% in the same period. Although the rate of the mixed form of functional and divisional structure rose from 15.3% in 1963 to 20.3%, it declined to 17.8% in 1973 slightly. However, in this type of structure, there was not change seen in the functional structure and the divisional structure (Yoshihara et al. 1981, p. 198). Organizational structures that were a mixed form of functional and divisional structures were a combination of divisional and functional structure wherein functional structures were retained for core business lines, while non-core businesses were organizations of independent divisions (Yoshihara et al. 1981, p. 191).

Let us now examine the changes in structure in relation to business strategy. Diversification caused significant changes in the organizational structure. With increased diversification, the adoption rate of functional structures became lower and that of divisional structures had an almost equally inverse growth (Yoshihara et al. 1981, pp. 205–207, 225). While in the group that adopted the specialization strategy, 80–90% of the companies introduced the functional structure, among the firms that adopted the unrelated diversification strategy or the related-linked diversification strategy, more than 70% used the divisional structure. On the other hand, in the group that developed the vertical-integration strategy, the companies that adopted the functional structure or a mixture of functional and divisional structures occupied the majority. Thus, generally speaking, the proposition that "structure follows strategy" has sufficient validity. However, the relationship between diversification strategies and the shape of an organization was not so strong that a particular strategy would require to use a particular organization form. In fact, there was a great deal of freedom of choice in the selection of organization form. This is particularly true for a moderate scope of diversification. Thus, this proposition reveals that the correspondence is valid from a broader perspective as far as the organization's form is concerned (Yoshihara et al. 1981, pp. 205–207).

Regarding the industrial characteristics, industries with a high adoption rate of the divisional structure were those with a high degree of advancement of the diversification strategy. In contrast, industries with a high adoption rate of the functional structure were industries that generally had a low degree of advancement of such a strategy (Yoshihara et al. 1981, p. 209). The representative industries with a high adoption rate of the divisional structure were the chemical and electrical industries. In the heavy engineering and shipbuilding industries, companies that adopted the divisional structure were overwhelmingly large enterprises that diversified in the business field, such as manufacturing of machines used for work on the ground in order to utilize the production equipment and the excessive capacity for shipbuilding (Urabe 1969, pp. 59–60, 62, 65, 68, 75). In Japan, there was a trend of adopting the divisional structure under the circumstance that the technology-related diversification brought diversification of the task environment (Kagono 1978, pp. 86–87). In the industries where such diversification advanced, there were cases of the adoption of the divisional structure.

However, compared to foreign countries, the adoption rate of divisional structures by Japanese corporations was relatively lower than that in Europe, and especially lower than in the United States. In fact, there was a time lag of approximately 15 years. A major reason for the lower adoption rate of the divisional structure was the low level and slow pace of diversification. In addition, 12.5% of the firms that adopted the divisional structure moved to a more centralized organizational structure in the five years from 1968 to 1973. Such movement also indicates a fundamental characteristic regarding the selection of organizational form in comparison with the United States and Europe (Yoshihara et al. 1981, pp. 58, 64–65, 201, 203, 225). In Japan, there were corporations that adopted the divisional structure rather well, although the necessity was not strong. Among corporations that adopted the divisional structure, many deployed trendy divisional structures rather than those based on a rational comparison of the relative merits and demerits of divisional and functional structures. However, from 1965 onward, corporations began to examine the strengths and weaknesses of divisional structure and reflect more carefully on the shape of the organization. During this period, some companies discontinued their divisional structures and returned to a centralized functional structure. A characteristic of this period was a trend toward recentralization (Yoshihara et al. 1981, pp. 200, 203, 224–225; Ono 1979, pp. 125–128; Imanishi 1988, p. 61). According to an investigation by the Kansai Productivity Center, the rates of firms that abolished the divisional structure in 1970, 1975, 1980, and 1985, were 2.2%, 3.6%, 2.2%, 7.9%, and 2.8%, respectively. Among them, there were many companies that abolished the divisional structure after the first oil crunch (Kansai seisansei honbu 1976, p. 51; kansai seisansei honbu 1981, pp. 38–39; Kansai seisansei honbu 1986, p. 24). The movement to abolish the divisional structure also appeared in the latter half of the 1980s. In the industries that were not suitable for the adoption of the divisional structure, there were firms that abolished this type of organizational structure after it was introduced (Tsunoda 1993, pp. 13–14, 16–17).

In Japan, there were cases in which the division headquarters system was adopted. There were also cases where the duplication of staff occurred with the segmentation of each division, according to the product and the division headquarters that was in charge of coordinating the mutually related divisions. However, the true profit center was each division under the divisional headquarters, the latter of which only engaged in coordinating the decision-making processes of each division (Urabe 1969, p. 372). This was due to the advancement of each subdivision based on the characteristics of various markets. In this regard, the divisional headquarters system was not only introduced to control each division but it was used to re-examine the introduction of the divisional structure (Omori 1975, pp. 178–179). For example, in the latter half of the 1980s, the majority of the companies that adopted the divisional structure reinforced the system for control of each division. In addition, company split-ups became the new trend in Japanese enterprises. Based on these discussions, the following section will consider case studies of several major corporations in Japan.

11.1.2.2 Deployment of Divisional Structure in Major Industries

11.1.2.2.1 Deployment of Divisional Structure in the Chemical Industry and Its Characteristics

First, the chemical industry as the most typical case of the expansion of diversification and deployment of divisional structure is considered.

11.1.2.2.1.1 ***Asahi Kasei***

Asahi Chemical Industry Co., Ltd., a representative company in the chemical industry, diversified into many new fields, such as synthetic fibers and petrochemistry, and its organizational structure was revised after World War II. In 1959, the company introduced the divisional structure by integrating both the production and the sales departments according to product group. Profitability of each product was clarified and the competence of each general manager concerning the management of each division was centralized as much as possible. In this case, five divisions were established as product divisions: (1) Cashmilon; (2) rayon; (3) Bemberg; (4) formation products; and (5) gunpowder.

However, because problems such as the duplication of personnel in indirect departments and incompatibility with the divisional structure existed, a more flexible management organization with high mobility was required to implement strategies aimed at business expansion. The divisional headquarters was introduced as the upper organization for control of plural divisions in 1971, for the purpose of developing unified sales, by cooperating with other business fields, training employees through planned rotations, securing fund efficiency, and the delegation of authority and responsibility. Three divisional headquarters were established: textiles, formation products, and plastics. In addition, for the macromolecule business, which includes synthetic resin and synthetic rubber, divisional headquarters were introduced. However, the food and zymurgy division, as well as the building materials division, remained the same.

In 1982, the divisional headquarters structure was changed to the headquarters system, and the profit and loss management unit shifted from the divisional headquarters to the division itself. However, the independence of the division was not necessarily established. In 1982, the Asahi Chemical Industry changed its organizational structure significantly following its merger with Asahi Dow. Overall, there were two objectives: (1) to reorganize the factory, research and development (R&D), and production technology departments, while maintaining the safety and environment department (i.e., unifying the R&D and production technology departments) and (2) to divide the formation product and resin headquarters into 11 divisions while maintaining the fiber headquarters as the headquarters in order to secure a single-body administration. The latter also aimed at promoting marketing activity in the division and establishing an independent organization.

Eventually, the headquarters system was changed to the divisional structure in order to increase the independence of each division. Moreover, to reinforce sales in technology, an engineering department was established in each division. However, with the rapid promotion of the technology department and the increasing importance of the electronics and life science fields, the drafting of overall business strategies including these new fields became necessary. In 1986, the divisional department structure was further divided into four divisional departments: (1) formation products and rubber; (2) resin; (3) building materials and chemicals; and (4) housing. The aim of such organizational reform was to strengthen each division to better correspond to the overall strategic goal, and to have the R&D department consider the organic linkage of various policies and measures (Zaidanhojin nihon keieishi kenkyusho 2002, pp. 263–266, 364–365, 367–368, 468–470, 629–630).

11.1.2.2.1.2 ***Toray Industries***

In Toray Industries, Inc., the divisional structure was adopted in 1970 instead of the functional structure that was in existence until that point to promote flexible business management corresponding to the expansion of the scale of business, diversification of business, and the further development of the internationalization of management. It was an organization that was mainly composed of three divisional headquarters (fiber, plastic, and formation products) and eight central departments. This structure included two main goals: (1) to clarify profit responsibility in order to increase the independence of each division, strengthen profit control, and establish the flexible management of the administrative system and (2) to build up profit responsibility for the purpose of shifting from authority-based thinking to responsibility-based management (Tore kabushikigaisha shashi hensan iinkai 1977, pp. 240–245, 370; Baba 1975, pp. 283–285).

In this company, thorough profit control was consistently emphasized under the characteristics and limitations of the chemical industry such as the interrelations regarding the aspects of raw materials, processing, and technology, and the regional complication in that a certain business was concerned with plural business establishments. Although the control unit for profit management was the divisional headquarters, the profit center in the divisional headquarters was each division. In addition, the general manager not only had direct control of the sales department but he also gave instructions about business activities to the manufacturing department (through the chief of the business establishment). Moreover, the management section in the division was responsible for profit control, the chief of the business establishment received instructions about production from the general manager, followed technical instructions from the manager of the production department, and received directions regarding local measures from the president. Although the effect of such a "matrix-like" divisional structure was established through the unification of production and sales, the importance of profit-minded thinking still remained (Baba 1975, pp. 286–291).

However, in 1976, this company changed the divisional headquarters structure to the functional structure after which its organizational structure consisted of 11 departments for the purpose of utilizing resources and flexible business management that corresponded to the shift from the high-growth economy to the low-growth economy. Furthermore, the organization of top management was reinforced and the general planning office was newly established (Tore kabushikigaisha shashi hensan iinkai 1977, pp. 240, 245).

11.1.2.2.2 **Deployment of Divisional Structure in the Electrical Industry and Its Characteristics**

Next, this subsection examines the deployment of a divisional structure in the electrical industry, where diversification proceeded as in the chemical industry, and the divisional structure was important because of the nature of the industry.

11.1.2.2.2.1 ***Matsushita Electric Industrial***

In Matsushita Electric Industrial Co., Ltd., the divisional structure was introduced in 1933 (Matsushita denki sangyo kabushikigaisha sogyo gojushunen kinen junbi iinkai 1968, pp. 111–114; Ono 1979, pp. 306–308; Hiramoto 2000, pp. 29–30, 36, 40; Nishikawa 1996, p. 77; Shimotani 1998, p. 56). It carried out the first organizational reform after World War II, in 1949. In this case, a system was introduced in which 19 factories took charge of a portion of production, the sales departments in eight locations were in charge of sales, and the production department and the sales department at the central office were in control of the line functions of manufacturing and sales. In addition, engineering, materials, general affairs, and personnel departments were also set up at the central office. Such an organization represented the abandonment of the divisional structure and the complete return to the functional structure.

However, in 1950, the firm returned to the divisional structure and formed three divisions. The first division focused on radio and communications equipment, vacuum tubes, and electric lamps, while the second division took charge of dry cells and electric heating apparatuses. Meanwhile, the third division included electric machine equipment and storage batteries. In 1953, the number of divisions increased to seven, and each division was in charge of product planning and production. However, the sales office was not part of each division. In addition, although each division was engaged in the planning of production and sales, the original divisional structure in which production and sales were directly connected was not necessarily maintained (Matsushita denki sangyo kabushikigaisha sanjunenshi henshu iinkai 1953, pp. 96–97, 116–124; Matsushita denki sangyo kabushikigaisha sogyo gojunen kinen junbi iinkai 1968, p. 245; Omori 2007, pp. 44, 46; Kigyo soshiki kebkyukai 1962, p. 193).

In 1954, Matsushita Electric Industrial adopted the functional headquarters structure with four headquarters and ten divisions. In addition, the departmental structure included department directors who controlled several departments according to function. Thus, the dispersal of operating units occurred by decentralizing each department, and the top management organization was improved by establishing the department director's council. Moreover, the management headquarters, engineering headquarters, and sales headquarters were built up, and the divisional headquarters was only in charge of production. The aim of this organizational reform was to promote positive business activities that were adapted to the current circumstances and to sufficiently display the collective strength of the specialized subdivisions and the management. Furthermore, the internal capital system was introduced in each division and the sales office for the purpose of maintaining a self-supporting accounting system.

After 1955, this company promoted business efficiency by reforming its organizational structure. This was seen in the development of high-value-added products, the construction of new factories, the increase in new divisions, and the integration of related businesses into one divisional headquarters. However, each department director still took charge of duties at both the operating and top management levels. Thus, there was no differentiation between strategic decisions and static decisions at that point. In addition, the sales function was not integrated into each division.

The direct sale system was adopted in 1965 (Matsushita denki sangyo kabushikigaisha sanjugonenshi henshu iinkai 1955, p. 3; Matsushita denki sangyo kabushikigaisha sogyo gojunen kinen junbi iinkai 1968, pp. 262–267; Ono 1979, pp. 313–316; Ozawa 1971, pp. 93, 100; Nishikawa 1996, pp. 78–79; Shimotani 1998, pp. 135–136). In the first half of the 1960s, each division did not have production equipment, and production line functions were performed by the affiliated companies or subsidiaries, as seen in the following divisions: refrigerators, electric bulbs, pumps, photographic equipment, electric fans, and bicycles. In this case, the divisions in this corporation lacked a high degree of self-sufficiency. However, since each division was responsible for the sales and profit of the products that they produced, the sales headquarters system was adopted, after which the sales of products in each division produced were performed by each sales office (Urabe 1969, pp. 372–373).

In 1965, Matsushita Electric Industrial Co., Ltd. returned to the divisional structure and each division performed direct sales, thus excluding the sales company. As a result, each division became an independent department responsible for all production and sales activities regarding products that it treated (Matsushita denki sangyo kabushikigaisha sanjugonenshi henshu iinkai 1955, p. 3; Ono 1979, pp. 317–319; Ozawa 1971, p. 93). This structural reorganization was a return to the original divisional structure that adhered to the market and directly connected production to sales (Omori 2007, p. 52).

In 1972, the production divisional headquarters was abolished and changed into the production group structure. The clarification of the responsibility and authority of each division, as well as the establishment of the system, highlighted the advantages of the divisional structure in all situations. However, although the production divisional headquarters was established by integrating divisions that, to some extent, corresponded to an increase in the number of divisions, the self-supporting accounting system of each division was insufficient due to the interdependence between the divisions and the divisional headquarters. As a result, a total of 17 production divisional headquarters were abandoned, whereas 12 product groups and one direct control department were established in order to make the divisions completely independent. In 1973, this company returned to the original divisional structure (Matsushita denki sangyo kabushikigaisha shashisitsu 1978, pp. 37–38, 376–378, 389, 392, 395). In this way, the organizational reform at Matsushita Electric Industrial Co., Ltd. was not based on the new principle, but ultimately, the foundation of organizational management in the divisional structure (Shimotani 1998, p. 32).

11.1.2.2.2.2 ***Mitsubishi Electric***

The Mitsubishi Electric Corporation introduced a divisional structure in 1958 in order to increase sales by directly connecting production with sales. Before then, management development, the sales department, and manufacturing (factory) department were under the control of the representative body in the board of directors (*jomukai*), and each production and sales department was not individually integrated. Thus, the divisional structure was adopted on the basis of the following three reasons: (1) the advancement of diversification; (2) the difficulty in drafting a unified management policy, due to the lack of differentiation of the line function and the staff function; and (3) the difficulty of developing a new model, based on the fact that the sales department controlled the sale of all production models. In addition, the necessity for correspondence on the organizational side between production and sales became enormous. As a result, four divisions (heavy electrical machinery, electronics, appliances, and an overseas department) were established, of which this organizational reform focused on the administration of three divisions (heavy electrical machinery, electronics, and appliances), based on the self-supporting accounting system. Each division was given independent responsibility for production, sales, and profit and loss, that is, each division became a profit center. In addition, each division focused on market research, sales promotion, production control, and the development of new product models. Furthermore, the system in which the capital return rate was calculated according to each division was adopted. Thus, all functions of planning, production, and sales of products were integrated into each division and were under the control of a general manager. Since the point of implementing the divisional structure was to reinforce the organization for sales in the appliance division, which included home appliances and standard electrical equipment, not only was the product planning department established but also the expansion of the sales office. Such improvements in sales functions were also pursued in the heavy electrical machinery division and the electronics division.

With regard to top management organization, administration departments, such as general affairs, planning, personnel affairs, work, accounting, audit, sales management, material, and engineering, were established. These departments functioned as staff departments that took charge of providing advice and assistance on drafting and executing plans in each division, as well as on offering support for top management in regard to the company's policies and objectives. Meanwhile, the planning department was mainly in charge of long-term planning and providing advice related to the planning and execution in each division. In addition, the planning department was in charge of public relations outside of the company, while the sales management department focused on publicity, revenues and expenditures, accounting, and sales management. Furthermore, the staff organization of each division was only in charge of manufacturing and sales, and all other staff functions were integrated into the management departments at the head office (Mitsubishi Historical Archives, MEL-00156, Mitsubishi denki news, No.41, pp. 4–5; Mitsubishi denki kabushikigaisha shashi hensansitsu 1982, pp. 117–118, 260, 295–297, 308–309; Urabe 1960, pp. 195–198; Watanabe 1960, pp. 96–97; Kigyo sosiki kenkyukai 1962, p. 155; Keiei kenkyusho kenkyubu 1967, p. 82).

However, in the divisional structure of the Mitsubishi Electric Corporation at that time, the sales of home appliances were made by the agency system without establishing a sales company. Concerning their production, in the case that some types of products were manufactured in the factory, there were conditions in which the products were related to plural divisions. Possible reasons behind this include the necessity of a lot of sales personnel in the case of integrating the sales function into each division, the poor economy arising from adopting the same system regardless of sales size of each product field, the need for a local office that serves as the common department that helps unify the organization, and the fear of losing customers due to the various sales departments (Watanabe 1960, pp. 97–98; Keiei kenkyusho kenkyubu 1967, pp. 84–85). In this way, the Mitsubishi Electric Corporation did not just introduce a textbook example of divisional structure; it emphasized deployment that was compatible with the traditions and unique characteristics of the company (Mitsubishi denki kabushikigaisha shashi hensansitsu 1982, pp. 260, 295–296).

In 1977, a significant revision of the company's organizational structure took place, based on the following needs. First, organizational reform that exceeded the framework of the conventional divisional structure in order to respond to the demands of the market as well as to develop flexible management strategies that correspond to changes in the market. Second, an organization that enabled the development of fiber products by reinforcing sales power and grasping the market's needs quickly. Third, the establishment of the system made it possible to lead the technological development of the company toward rapid commercialization and industrialization. Thus, organizational reforms were carried out with three main goals: (1) to reinforce the sales system; (2) to utilize resources; and (3) to strengthen the R&D system. Regarding the first goal, the sales department was integrated into the division, its responsibilities were clarified, and the profit and loss responsibility was given to each division. Concerning the utilization of resources, the division that integrated production and sales was dismantled, after which four divisional headquarters were established: (1) heavy electrical machinery; (2) electronics; (3) apparatuses; and (4) appliances. Each headquarters included the sales division, the sales office, and factories under its influence. Although each division exceeded the conventional divisional structure, the most important goal of the organizational reforms was to improve business structure toward sales and market orientation (Mitsubishi denki kabushikigaisha shashi hensan iinkai 1982, pp. 297–300).

The introduction of the divisional structure in the electrical industry was deeply related to the household appliance market. For example, Mitsubishi Electric, the Toshiba Electric Corporation, and Hitachi, Ltd. reached a certain stage of completion of divisional structure around the middle of the 1960s. The commonality of these three companies was that they wanted to transform the conventional divisional structure to emphasize the direct connection between production and sales, and integrate the sales function into each division, both of which were especially important around 1963 during the shift from a seller's market to a buyer's market (Ozawa 1971, pp. 101–103).

11.1.2.2.3 Deployment of Divisional Structure in Other Industries and Its Characteristics

We considered the deployment of divisional structures in the chemical industry and the electrical industry as typical industries where divisional structures were deployed. For comparison, the machine industry, the precision instrument industry, the heavy and shipbuilding industries, and the steel and iron industry will be examined.

11.1.2.2.3.1 The Machine Industry

As a case study of the machine industry, Kubota Ltd. is considered. This company introduced a divisional structure and developed its diversification strategy, which brought about four business fields: (1) casting; (2) machinery; (3) lead pipes; and (4) equilibrium instruments. Although the functional structure was adopted until 1950, five product divisions were established: (1) iron tubes; (2) casting; (3)

internal combustion engines; (4) machinery; and (5) equilibrium instruments. Each general manager supervised employees in sales, in design, and in the factory. Each division consisted of the three sections of production, sales, and engineering, to which the product factory and the sales department belonged. These divisions were autonomously administrated by unifying the production and sales of the products within each division. The business results of each division were then reflected in the employees' salaries. In addition, each division served as the profit center of the self-supporting accounting system, and production and sales were integrated into each division, excluding the sales division. In management functions, such as budget control, cost control, market research, sales planning, and production planning, broad decentralization was implemented. Each division also took responsibility for R&D of the product field of which it was in charge. Furthermore, various departments, such as the administrative department, the audit department, the planning, production engineering, general control, and accounting departments were created at the head office (Kabushikigaisha Kubota 1990, pp. 104, 149, 360, 362–367; Kubota tekko kabushikigaisha 1970, pp. 333–334, 1980, p. 145; Urabe 1969, pp 380–383, 388; Hara 1960, pp. 92–94). In this company, the right of nullification was accepted in trade between each division, and the most effective method of decentralized management was introduced on the basis of this point (Hara 1960, p. 93).

Finally, the divisional headquarters was newly established in 1971 in order to further subdivide the divisions, correspond to the market, and develop strategies that generalized each group. Organizational structure was changed from 13 divisions to a structure that consisted of six divisional headquarters (pipes, casting, machinery, internal combustion engines, environmental equipment, and housing), 15 product divisions, and an overseas division. Under such a system, the general manager of the divisional headquarters was entirely responsible for the company's profit and growth (Kubota tekko kabushikigaisha 1980, pp. 31–34).

11.1.2.2.3.2 ***The Precision Instrument Industry***

Regarding the precision instrument industry, let us examine Canon Inc. From the 1960s to 1970, this company changed from a functional structure to a divisional structure. As a result, the basis for five business fields was established: (1) cameras; (2) calculating machines; (3) copiers; (4) micro-equipment; and (5) optical special machines (Omori 1975, pp. 181–182). However, the responsibility for profits and costs became vague due to the development of diversification and specialization, as well as the dispersion of authority under the conventional functional structure. Thus, establishing the responsibility system of the division through the divisional structure became the subject of focus in the organization (Sasaki 1975, pp. 190–2). In 1972, the company promoted organizational reform on the basis of the principle that it would shift to the divisional structure as quickly as possible in the business field in which the adoption of such a structure would be possible and integrate factories according to product field. Based on this fundamental policy, a division was established only for the field of special optical machines (Omori 1975, pp. 181–182).

In 1978, the divisional structure at Canon Inc. reached tentative completion, meaning that such a structure covered all business fields of the company. The structure at that time consisted of three product divisions: (1) cameras; (2) office equipment; and (3) optical machines. However, the divisional structure showed considerable imperfections, one of which was that the sales department was not integrated into the division, thus forcing a certain level of coordination between the divisions and each section of the sales company. Regarding the divisional structure in Japanese enterprises, in addition to Canon Inc., there have been many cases in which such a structure prevailed even though its form differed from the original (Harasawa 1987, pp. 19, 22, 28–29).

11.1.2.2.3.3 ***The Heavy Engineering and Shipbuilding Industries***

From 1945 to 1957, the centralized functional structure was generally adopted in response to the needs of the heavy engineering and shipbuilding industries. One of the most important reasons behind the adoption of such a structure was the specialization strategy focusing on the shipbuilding business. From 1958 to 1973, the divisional structure was introduced when diversification toward related product fields advanced, with the exception of Mitsubishi Heavy Industries, Ltd. (Mizota 1997, pp. 94–95, 210–211, 349, 353). However, after 1974, there were companies that abolished the divisional structure or the divisional headquarters structure, as seen in Ishikawajima-Harima Heavy Industries Co., Ltd., and Hitachi Shipbuilding & Engineering Co., Ltd. (Ishikawajima harima kogyo kabushikigaisha somu sokatsubu shashi hensan tanto 1992, pp. 180, 199; Hitaci zosen kabushikigaisha 2012, pp. 35, 50; Mizota 1997, p. 353).

Mitsubishi Heavy Industries: In order to reinforce international competitiveness and pursue the merits of the divisional structure, this company established five product divisions: (1) ships; (2) heavy machines; (3) machinery; (4) automobiles; and (5) aircraft and special vehicles in 1957. The functions of business planning, product development, and sales were under the direct control of a general manager. Whereas the functions related to production were under the control of the chief of the business establishment (who was under the direct control of the president), the general manager was in charge of the aforementioned functions, as well as their administration. The power of each general manager was not uniformly but differently established according to the special characteristics of each product field. In this way, the divisions within the company were not established as unified profit centers that included the functions of business planning, sales, and production. The division and business establishments and functions, including profit and loss, were considered to be the responsibilities of the general manager and the chief of the business establishment. This was the company's original structure, which was in line with diversified management practices. The overall production system included 16 business establishments. In addition, there was the head office that consisted of the president's office, seven departments, and four management offices responsible for functions, such as general affairs, personnel, accounting, and purchasing. In 1967, two divisions (heavy machines and machinery) were reorganized into three divisions:

(1) motors; (2) first division of machines; and (3) second division of machines. In 1969, the automobile division was moved to the divisional headquarters.

However, as the size of the management increased with the expansion of market size, the establishment of a suitable business system became necessary. With the separation and independence of the Mitsubishi Motors Corporation, specialization in the division was promoted in June 1970. The organizational structure was reorganized into four divisional headquarters (ships, motors, machines, and aircraft) and six divisions: vehicles and transport machines; precision machines; construction machines; refrigeration machines; apparatuses; and special vehicles. Specialization according to product was promoted, and business responsibilities were clarified by integrating divisions with large production into the divisional headquarters, while maintaining those with relatively small production as independent divisions.

In the 1970s, it became necessary to perform administrative tasks more flexibly according to various aspects: the product field itself; special characteristics; the scale under conditions of low economic growth; the diversification of the sense of values; the dramatic change of the industrial structure; and the intensification of competition. Thus, faster decision-making processes were required. For example, two business establishments of the Kyoto precision machine factory and the Akashi factory, two plants of the Hiroshima machine factory, and the Nagoya air-conditioning and refrigeration machinery works came to be under the direct control of the mass production product control headquarters in 1982. Such direct control enabled the company to clarify the responsibility for profit and loss and to speed up the decision-making process. Furthermore, around the mid-1980s, the divisional headquarters and business establishment were unified and placed to reinforce the company's collective strength (Mitsubishi juko kabushikigaisha shashi hensan iinkai 1990, pp. 68–71, 125–126, 193–195, 279–281).

Kawasaki Heavy Industries: In 1961, the structure of this company consisted of five divisions: (1) shipbuilding; (2) machinery; (3) industrial machines; (4) precision machines; and (5) steel structure. In 1962, the five divisions became four through the integration of the machinery and the industrial machines divisions. The divisional structure of this company was organized according to the market, and each organization was individually responsible for profit and loss. Profit goals were set for each division so that they could allocate a profit of 10% on investment. With the birth of New Kawasaki Heavy Industries (through a merger in April 1969), five divisional headquarters (groups) were established: (1) ships; (2) vehicles; (3) aircraft; (4) machinery; and (5) motors and motorcycles. In addition, three divisions were created: (1) steel structure; (2) oil pressure machines; and (3) Akashi machinery. Such a structure was changed to the system of seven divisional headquarters and two divisions in October 1970. Moreover, the central office departments consisted of the general planning office, the company development headquarters, and the technology development headquarters, all of which supported the activities in each division. In 1973, a partial change was made, as seen in the establishment of the plant divisional headquarters and the construction machine divisional headquarters.

In 1977, the headquarters system was adopted and this organizational reform included three main changes: (1) new establishment of the headquarters system at the central office (general affairs, personnel, finance, and materials); (2) consolidation of eight divisional headquarters into six divisional headquarters and the integration of the plant division and the steel structure division; and (3) formation of the sales generalization headquarters and the technology development headquarters by reorganizing the development headquarters and the engineering headquarters. This reform was aimed at overcoming problems with the divisional structure, as seen in the lack of cooperation between the different divisional headquarters. In addition, the sales generalization headquarters was established to reinforce cooperation between the divisional headquarters and the control of sales. This organization also aimed at drafting and promoting measures that supported general sales power, sales activities of each divisional headquarters, and public relations activities related to sales. Furthermore, the technology development headquarters was established in order to focus specifically on promising projects for the future (Kawasaki jukogyo kabushikigaisha hyakunenshi hensan iinkai 1997a, pp. 75, 84–85, 123–125; Kawasaki jukogyo kabushikigaisha hyakunenshi hensan iinkai 1997b, pp. 46, 50–52; Kawasaki jukogyo kabushikigaisha kiko jigyobu sanjunenshi hensan iinkai 1997c, p. 8).

11.1.2.2.3.4 ***The Iron and Steel Industry***

The final case that this section will consider is Kobe Steel Ltd. in the iron and steel industry. This company changed its organizational structure from a functional structure to a divisional structure, after which it established the iron and steel division and the machinery division in 1955. Four factories, including the central office factory, belonged to each division. In regard to the adoption of the divisional structure, this enterprise was a pioneer in the industrial world at that time. The self-supporting accounting system of each factory was also adopted. In 1957, the alloy division was created through a merger with Shinko Metal Industry. In 1958, the managing directors' meeting (*jomukai*), the representative executive organ of the board of directors, was established. In the same year, authority was largely delegated to each division and the locus of responsibility was clarified. In 1959, the welding electrode division was separated from the iron and steel division and formed into a fourth division. In 1968, the product headquarters structure was introduced in response to the expansion of activities in each product field. The organization was then divided according to the product group and reorganized into three headquarters: (1) industrial machines; (2) processing machines; and (3) cast and forged steel (Kabushikigaisha kobe seikosho hatijunenshi hensan iinkai 1986, pp. 116, 120–121, 124–125, 169; Kabushikigaisha kobe seikosho somubu and Kyodo PR kabushikigaisha 1974, pp. 17–19; Kobe seikosho soritsu hyakushunen kinen jigyo iinkai 2006, p. 88). Furthermore, the divisional headquarters, established in 1987, consisted of five departments: (1) new product business planning department; (2) new materials department; (3) information electronics department; (4) advanced separation systems department; and (5) business development department. This headquarters controlled all activities, from conception to development, and the commercialization to sale of new products (Kobe seikosho soritsu hyakushunen kinen jigyo iinkai 2006, p. 144).

At this point, this chapter has analyzed the deployment of the divisional structure in Japan by examining several representative cases. Based on the foregoing discussions, the following section will consider the transformation of business strategies and the deployment of the divisional structure in Germany.

11.2 Transformation of Business Strategy and Deployment of Divisional Structure in Germany

11.2.1 Transformation of Business Strategy

11.2.1.1 Socio-Economic Background of Postwar Diversification

This section examines the evolution of diversification, which is one of the most important factors in postwar management organization reforms. Diversification in German firms was regulated and influenced by changes in the environment of industry competition at the time. Changes in demand patterns and the rate of technological advancement, in particular, resulted in changes in competition, with innovations in products and marketing methods replacing traditional factors such as pricing and quality. Furthermore, increased consumer opulence as a result of technological potential led to the development of many new products and market opportunities, allowing corporations in various industries to experience rapid growth and high profits. Major enterprises operating within more traditional boundaries, with no opportunity for absolute or relative growth, were forced to make a difficult decision. For example, at the chemical firm Hüls, the revenue and profit declined at the start of the 1960s far exceeded that of IG Farben's three major successor enterprises, emphasizing the need for diversification [Vgl. *Hüls Archiv*, I-5–8, Aktennotiz (8.8.1962), S 1]. Moreover, many companies that had quickly accumulated resources rather than reinvesting in mature products or markets, particularly the most successful corporations, needed to find growth opportunities outside their own industrial sector. Diversification was an important element in the strategic response to these circumstances (Dyas and Thanheiser 1976, p. 132). Especially at the end of the 1960s, competition due to the opening up of new markets and the lowering of tariffs in EEC nations was an important factor in this reorientation toward diversification (Wengenroth 1997, p. 162).

However, the characteristics of German corporate ownership, particularly financial and management constraints in family-owned businesses, hampered diversification (Dyas and Thanheiser 1976, p. 133). Other factors limiting diversification include the need to rebuild in the postwar years, extremely rapid growth in the automobile, electrical, and capital goods industries, a tradition of cartels and trusts linked to relatively weak anti-trust laws, and tax laws (Dyas and Thanheiser 1976, p. 100). Technological relevance was a major factor influencing Germany's diversification movement. However, analysis of the top 100 industrial enterprises reveals that diversification was not the only direction taken after World War II. In fact, diversification also occurred along with horizontal and vertical integration (Dyas and Thanheiser 1976, pp. 90, 101).

11.2.1.2 Advancement of Diversification and Its Characteristics

Next, considering strategic changes in the progress of diversification, 34 of the top 100 industrial enterprises' business structures in 1950s Germany were single types, while 26 were dominant types. In contrast, 32 companies were related types and seven were unrelated types. Although single-type firms decreased to 22 by 1960, the most important change in the 1950s was the diversification that was observed in 12 such firms, in which nine firms became dominant types, two related types, and one an unrelated type. As a result, the number of dominant-type firms increased to just 28 by 1960. From 1950 to 1960, nine enterprises diversified away from being dominant types, with eight of these becoming related types and one an unrelated type. Whereas 40 companies had become related types by 1960, unrelated types had increased slightly to nine, a minor shift.

In contrast, in 1960 and 1970, the greatest changes can be seen in diversification to related types (5) and unrelated types (10). In 1970, 56% of enterprises had significantly diversified in this manner. Although related types had decreased slightly to 38, unrelated types had greatly increased to 18.

Furthermore, as evidenced by our examination of changes over a 20-year-period between 1950 and 1970, the channel diversification most frequently was from a single type to a dominant type to a related type to an unrelated type. It was uncommon for a corporation to deviate from this channel and transition from a single type to a highly diverse related or unrelated type. That is, 35% (nine of 26) of the firms that were dominant types in 1950 had changed over 10 years, and 25% (seven of 28) of the dominant types changed by 1970 (Dyas and Thanheiser 1976, pp. 26, 63–72. For an index on types and classifications of diversification, refer to Rumelt 1974, Chap. 1).

Thus, in Germany, the remarkable expansion of diversification to unrelated types, such as that among US conglomerates, had not occurred in the 1960s as Germany had emphasized diversification in related types.

11.2.2 Deployment of Divisional Structure

11.2.2.1 Overall Conditions of the Deployment of Divisional Structure

This section examines the changes in organizational structure and their relationship with the expansion of strategy. Comparing the number of top 100 industrial firms using a functional structure in the years 1950, 1960, and 1970, 36 companies used a functional structure, which then decreased to 21 and finally to 20. In 1950, 15 enterprises had a holding company structure, which fell to 14 and then to 12. Companies with a mix of functional and holding company structures increased from 43 to 48 and then fell substantially to 18. In contrast, corporations with a divisional structure numbered a mere five in 1950, tripled to 15 in 1960, and dramatically increased to 50 by 1970. Considering the 78 German capital enterprises, firms with a divisional structure were unheard of in 1950, and by 1960 there were still only three; however, by 1970, they accounted for approximately 40% of the total. Nevertheless, compared to the 78% and 72% adoption rates of the United States and the United Kingdom, respectively, Germany's rate remained low.

Between 1950 and 1960, 25 of the top 100 enterprises implemented organizational structure reforms, with a shift from a functional structure to a combination of functional and holding company structures (12 companies) being the most common change, while a shift to a divisional structure was not widely observed. Deployment of divisional structures progressed greatly in the 1960s, and between 1960 and 1970, 36 out of 47 corporations chose to adopt this type of organization. Between 1950 and 1970, the most common pattern was a shift from a functional structure to a combination of functional structure and holding company, and then to a divisional structure. Of the 45 enterprises that adopted a divisional structure, only four transitioned from a functional structure and six from a holding company structure. In contrast, 35 enterprises transitioned from a functional structure/holding company combination to a divisional structure (Dyas and Thanheiser 1976, pp. 65–73).

E. Gabele emphasized that, among the overall changes to organizational structure, change processes resulting in divisional structures were extremely common. However, there was a great difference in adoption between large companies and small- and medium-sized companies. For example, while 46.7% of large enterprises had adopted a divisional structure by the end of 1974, only 38% of medium-sized enterprises had done so (Gabele 1981, S 1–2; Kirsch et al. 1999, pp. 3–4). Harrmann had observed in 1982 that many companies had restructured during the previous decade, with one of the characteristics of this change being visible in operational fields, divisions, and product-oriented organizations. However, when viewed overall with small- and medium-sized enterprises, many firms did not replace their functional structures with divisional structures. Among the large corporations that primarily transited to a divisional department or divisional structure in the late 1960s and early 1970s, some had product divisions and regional divisions, with overseas and European division regions posing challenges (Harrmann 1982, pp. 202–203).

Next, in analyzing the relationship between strategy and organizational structure, in 1950, only 7% of the top 100 industrial enterprises that had implemented diversification (both related and unrelated) used a divisional structure. By 1960, the ratio had risen to 20%, and by 1970, this ratio had risen to 67%. In 1960, only 8% of the 78 West German capital companies had this type of structure, which increased to 63% by 1970 (Dyas and Thanheiser 1976, p. 66). However, in comparison with the 500 largest US corporations, there was a difference in the adoption rate of divisional structures as well as a time lag in implementing diversification and divisional structures. Of the 40 firms that had shifted to this organizational form between 1950 and 1970 with a time lag between the implementation of a diversification strategy and the adoption of a divisional structure, 14 had made the change within 10 years, seven between 10 and 20 years, and 19 required more than 20 years to change. In addition, 60% of companies that had expanded to include greater varieties in products and markets during the 1950s had adopted a divisional structure during this 10-year-period. Although this figure increased to 75% by the 1960s, the largest wave of divisional structure deployment was witnessed in the late 1960s (Dyas and Thanheiser 1976, pp. 73–74). The domain of corporate organization was regarded as a new frontier in 1967 (REFA-Nachrichten 1967, p. 263), and deployment of divisional structures in more than half of the 100 largest industrial enterprises occurred after that year (Dyas and Thanheiser 1976, p. 129). According to H. Siegrist, divisional structures first began to truly penetrate German companies in the late 1960s, approximately 10 years after overall diffusion in the United States (Siegrist 1980, p. 88).

11.2.2.2 Generational Change in Management and Deployment of Divisional Structures

Divisional structure deployment in German firms was substantially influenced by management systems and practices as well as managers' traditional attitudes. Compared with a nation such as the United States, where management had evolved, business management specialization in German companies was stagnant, and there was a significant difference between daily operational and top executives, who were highly autonomous (Vgl. Hartmann 1968, pp. 47, 75, 78, 91, 281, 291). The ideological foundation of top management authority, which had become entrenched as a traditionally strict gap kept between executives at the managing board level and the lower laborer level was diametrically opposed to the broader delegation of authority and responsibility, and strategic information sharing between vertical strata required by a divisional structure. In such cases, the adoption of a new form of organization typically depended on one person or alternatively a group of a few people. The departure of certain individuals from the ranks of top management, as well as handovers to successors, became critical determinants in the timing of organizational change (Dyas and Thanheiser 1976, p. 136).

The fact that organizational restructuring occurred after the beginning of the 1960s was generally due to opposition by one or two key individuals in a given enterprise's power structure, rather than a lack of top management knowledge on divisional structures or confidence in its appropriateness and effectiveness for solving problems in their organization. As a result, a change in corporate control as a result of a generational change in management was an important measure for removing impediments to organizational restructuring (Dyas and Thanheiser 1976, p. 114). In contrast to Japan, which witnessed a shift between generations (due to the removal of top business leaders from older generations), in West Germany, despite post-WWII reforms, legislations involving corporations were maintained. As a result, the supervisory board authority retained its previous power and the older generation of managers continued to be active; thus, no comparison can be made with the situation in Japan (Kudo et al. 2004, pp. 19–24, Schröter 2005, p. 219). The post-WWII institutional reforms had a significant impact on the configuration of management and were strongly associated with traditional management philosophy and values. In 1950s and 1960s Germany under the American influence, a pragmatic model of behavior gradually evolved. However, representatives of the old elite tended to stick to the uniqueness of the "German spirit" (Lüdtke et al. 1997, p. 25). As V. Berghahn pointed out, the generational change in management began slowly at the beginning of the 1960s (Berghahn 1985, p. 293), and due to a company's reliance on generational changes, shifts from a functional structure to a divisional structure occurred relatively slowly (Hilger 2004, p. 278).

11.2.2.3 Deployment of Divisional Structure in Major Industries

11.2.2.3.1 Deployment of Divisional Structure in the Chemical Industry and Its Characteristics

Based on the previous overview of the deployment of divisional structures, this section will next consider case studies of typical corporations in major industries.

11.2.2.3.1.1 **Henkel**

First, the chemical industry, an archetype of the expansion of diversification and deployment of divisional structures is analyzed.

Henkel was an example of a company that used a proposal from the Stanford Research Institute (SRI), a US consulting firm, to implement organizational restructuring. SRI made three proposals regarding long-term business planning, strategic business planning, and organizational structure [Vgl. *Henkel Archiv*, 251/1, Stanford Research Institute (SRI), Einführung einer verbindlichen langfristigen Planung in die Persil/Henkel Gruppe—Phase I, April 1967, *Henkel Archiv*, 251/2, SRI, Langfristigen Planung für Persil/Henkel, Phase II: Strategische Planung, 1.Bd, Bd.2, Juli 1968, *Henkel Archiv*, 314/133, SRI, Langfristigen Planung für Persil/Henkel, Phase III: Organisationsstruktur der Unternehmensspitze und des leitenden Management, Dezember 1968]. In 1969, the proposal for organizational reform made in December 1968 was acknowledged (Henkel GmbH 1969, p. 33), and on this basis, a new organizational structure was deployed. At Persil/Henkel, where diversification was underway to some extent, top management faced extraordinary challenges in operating the enterprise at peak efficiency with middle and lower levels of management organized by function (*Henkel Archiv*, 251/2, Stanford Research Institute, Langfristigen Planung für Persil/Hen kel, Phase II, p. 315). Persil/Henkel had already reached the point in SRI's proposal where they needed to make fundamental changes to their organizational structure due to corporate scale and diversity (*Henkel Archiv*, 314/133, Stanford Research Institute, Langfristigen Planung für Persil/Henkel, Phase III, pp. 3, 24).

Special impediments had become apparent in Henkel's existing functional structure, including the delegation of profit responsibility, manufacturing methods to reduce overall company costs, cost optimization for marketing and other functions, and insufficient information exchange among various functional units during operational planning. Major issues arose as a result of a lack of clarity on responsibilities and authority, as well as a scarcity of the delegation of authority at all levels of the enterprise. As a result, top management was forced to deal with issues in minute detail, which caused issues because there was insufficient time for basic corporate policy decision-making and planning [*Henkel Archiv*, 314/133, Stanford Research Institute, Langfristigen Planung für Persil/ Henkel, Phase III, pp. 24–26, 28–30, *Henkel Archiv*, 314/96, SRI-Besprechung am 16. Oktober 1968 (17.10.1968), p. 3, *Henkel Archiv*, 251/10, SRI. Mündliche Präsentation. Struktur der Unternehmensorganisation von Persil/Henkel].

It was recognized and decided that decreasing costs and increasing profits necessitated the establishment of cost and profit centers in lower groups with delegated authority and responsibility (*Henkel Archiv*, 251/2, Stanford Research Institute, Langfristigen Planung für Persil/Henkel, Phase II, 2. Bd, p. 440). As a result, specific market responsibilities were delegated to each division, and organizational restructuring was implemented with the idea that various activities such as product development, production, and marketing in any given market orientation should be integrated into divisions (Zeitschrift für Organisation 1970c, p. 199). The restructuring resulted in (1) six product divisions, (2) regional departments, (3) eight functional departments, and (4) an executive committee that acted as the representative executive organ of the board of directors.

The organization comprised six divisions: (1) detergent and cleaners, (2) packaging materials, (3) organic chemical products, (4) home care pharmacology, (5) toiletries, and (6) inorganic chemical products and adhesive substances. Each division's operational management was responsible for the authority delegated to them by the executive committee, as well as operations as defined by a policy framework. Each division was in charge of the various operational functions required for the efficient execution of divisional business activities and operational functions such as new product development through product release, production, marketing, and exportation. Responsibility for all necessary operations in the division rested with a general manager, and each division was organized as an independent profit center.

Considering regional departments, the SRI suggestions contained the establishment of two departments: one for Europe and the other for non-European regions. However, in reality, only the department responsible for non-European regions was created. Furthermore, functional departments were established with the primary responsibilities of (1) advising and supporting divisions, other operational departments, and regional departments; (2) assisting and informing executive committees on various functional areas and issues; and (3) developing policies, standards, and processing methods for the enterprise as a whole, providing major service functions, and estimating each functional activity. Functional departments were organized for

(1) production and engineering, (2) R & D, (3) logistics, (4) organizations and scientific management, (5) business planning, (6) human resources and social affairs, (7) finance and accounting, and (8) legal affairs. These were all cost centers.

Henkel GmbH became the executive body acting as general office managing and controlling all domestic and foreign operations as a result of top management organization reforms. This office was in charge of Henkel & Cie GmbH, which was in charge of European operations and Henkel International GmbH, which was in charge of non-European regions. By establishing a headquarters' organization as well as divisions, the executive team, which included the headquarters' managing board, was liberated from individual operational problems of each division and was able to devote its time and energy to activities such as general issues in operational management of each division, as well as planning, management, and control. Furthermore, in order to support their activities, these executives established five corporate-wide staff departments: (1) management assistance, (2) European industry, (3) international public relations, (4) audits, and (5) secretarial [Vgl. *Henkel Archiv*, 314/133, Stanford Research Institute, Langfristigen Planung für Persil/Henkel, Phase III, pp. 1–114, *Henkel Archiv*, 314/96, Niederschrift über eine auβerordentliche gemeinsame Postbesprechung am 20. Februar1969 (20.2.1969), *Henkel Archiv*, 251/10, Einrichtung von Sparten und Funktionen (31.10.1968), *Henkel Archiv*, 251/10, Faktoren, die für eine produktionorientierte Organisationsstruktur sprechen (11.7. 1968), *Henkel Archiv*, 153/42, Niederschrift über die gemeinsame Post PERSIL/HENKEL/BÖHME/HI vom 12.11.1968 (14.11.1968), *Henkel Archiv*, 251/10, Neuorganisation. Unterlage für Gemeinsame Post am 12.11.1968 (9.11.1968), *Henkel Archiv*, 251/10, Oranisation der Unternehmensspitze (30.5.1968), *Henkel Archiv*, 153/42, Präsentation einer Organisationsstruktur für das Management Persil/Henkel durch das Stanford Research Institut (SRI), *Henkel Archiv*, 314/96, Zentral-Geschäftsführung Henkel GmbH, *Henkel Archiv*, 314/96, Die Unternehmensorganisation nach Sparten (18.7.1968), *Henkel Archiv*, 314/96, Neuordnung (10.3.1969), *Henkel Archiv*, 314/96, Neuordnung. Organisationsvorschlag für Funktionen—Produktion/Ingenieurwesen—Besprechung am 12. Februar 1969 (13.2.1969), *Henkel Archiv*, 251/9, Kurz-Referat. Gewinn- und Kosten-Verantwortung der Sparten/Funktionen (6.5.1969), *Henkel Archiv*, 251/9, Kostenverantwortung der Funktionen, insbesondere der Funktion Finanzen/Rechnungswesen. Notiz Mr.Cavender vom 17.4.1969 (23.4.1969), Henkel GmbH 1968, Feldenkirchen and Hilger 2001, pp. 200–202, Zeitschrift für Organisation 1970b, pp. 196–198].

SRI had communicated the principle of return on investment (ROI) by 1967, an important concept and method for management in a divisional structure requiring a self-support account system (Hilger 2004, p. 233). This provided a solid system foundation for profit planning and budgetary control.

11.2.2.3.1.2 ***BASF***

The case of BASF is then examined. From the late 1960s to the early 1970s, this company was busy restructuring its organization, and in June of 1970, they instituted a new organization (*BASF Archiv*, C0, Organisatiorische und personelleänderungen bei

AOA (5.6.1970), p. 1, Koch 1970). After the war, BASF adopted a functional structure covering production, sales, engineering, research, human resource and social issues, finance, and legal affairs [*BASF Archiv*, C0, Die Neuorganisation der BASF unter Marketingssichtspunkten, p. 2, *BASF Archiv*, C19/14, Organisatorische Maβnahmen (19.12.1961), *BASF Archiv*, C19/14, Organisatorische Maβnahmen (21.12.1961), *BASF Archiv*, C19/13, Organisation im Verkauf (24.6.1960)]. In addition, by the early 1960s, manufacturing department was divided into four sections by product line [*BASF Archiv*, C0, Organisation der BASF (1.1.1964), *BASF Archiv*, C19/14, Werksinterner Verteiler (25.1.1962), *BASF Archiv*, C19/15, Rundschreiben an alle Abteilungen des Werkes (20.12.1963), *BASF Archiv*, C19/15, Die Schrift an alle Vertrauensleute (22.7.1963). For information on organization changes at this level, refer to Abelshauser 2002, pp. 571–573].

However, the scope and rate of growth of the chemical industry made a review of the functional domain of a functional structure impossible. At BASF, as at Bayer, Hoechst, and Siemens, the only way to regain visibility was to divide the enterprise into relatively independent divisions and delegate responsibilities for the production and sales of specific product lines to divisions (*BASF Archiv*, C0, Die Neuorganisation der BASF unter Marketingssichtspunkten, p. 2). Not only did BASF's revenues more than double between 1960 and 1970, other group firms' earnings also increased to 20 times during the same period, thanks to additional progress made through business expansion and external acquisitions. Furthermore, with the enterprise's forward and backward integration into the oil and gas areas, the corporation's dramatic growth, and the expansion of industry scope and business lines, it became impossible to maintain the enterprise's existing organization management. The first profit and finance crisis occurred in mid-1967, forcing the firm to recognize the need for organizational restructuring (Selinger 1977, p. 17; Abelshauser 2002, pp. 570, 574).

The organizational restructuring was designed to address these issues by transferring management functions from the board of directors to operational divisions. The general manager of a division was responsible for implementing and realizing optimal production and sales strategies that could achieve planned revenue goals. The general manager was given domains worth between 100 and 600 million Deutsche Marks, and it was highly valued that they act as actual managers. As a result, each division was given extensive technical and commercial responsibilities (Koch 1970). There were four product divisions at the operational activity level: (1) basic chemicals, oil, gas, and agricultural chemical products; (2) plastics and textiles; (3) dyes, chemicals, and pharmaceuticals; and (4) consumer products and sales coordination. The responsibilities of these product divisions, as well as the domains of production and sales, included planning, development, and applications engineering functions, as well as serving as profit centers with revenues and profits responsibility [*BASF Archiv*, C0, Neuorganisation der BASF-Gruppe (in: *BASF Information*, Sonderausgabe, Oktober 1969)]. BASF's own internal documents on this organizational reform focused on one major issue the organization had been dealing with up to that point with operational departments, namely that, while operational departments were responsible for costs, they were not responsible for profits (*BASF Archiv*, C0, Die Neuorganisation der BASF unter Marketingssichtspunkten, pp. 3–4).

As a result, with that issue in mind a divisional general manager was assigned a division built as a profit center under the direction of the managing board and each division was consolidated according to their group under the purview of an executive director [*BASF Archiv*, C0, Bemerkungen von Professor Dr. Timm über die Neuorganisation der BASF (29.8.1973), p. 6]. The board of directors had nine members, seven of whom were divisional general managers [*BASF Archiv*, C0, The Badische Anilin- und Soda-Fabrik AG (BASF), Some Information Worth Knowing, p. 5. For more information on personnel changes in primary BASF departments and positions, refer to *BASF Archiv*, C0, Organisation der BASF (Stand: Juli 1975)]. Furthermore, the divisions were in charge of developing and implementing long-term strategies for not only operational planning but also other areas of activity. Planning systems, transfer pricing, and a common sales network were used to ensure inter-divisional connections in production and sales (Selinger 1977, p. 17).

Internal divisional structures such as basic chemicals, oil and gas, and agricultural products were narrowed down to product lines such as basic chemical products, oil and gas, chemical fertilizers, and plant protection chemicals. Each unit held a staff organization and a support system for operational activities. The consumer products and sales coordination division had three departments: (1) dyes and paints, (2) magnetic technology and printing plates, and (3) sales coordination. Unlike the previous two product departments, the sales coordination department was in charge of marketing methods, sales staff coordination, publicity, organization, and European branches (including customer coordination) [*BASF Archiv*, C0, Neuorganisation der BASF-Gruppe (Juni 1970)].

In addition, regional departments responsible for non-European regions were established in response to the growing importance of overseas operations. Regional departments were divided into four regional sections: (1) North America, (2) Central and South America, (3) Africa and West Asia, and (4) South Asia, Southeast Asia, and Australia. Each had its own staffing structure [*BASF Archiv*, C0, Neuorganisation der BASF-Gruppe (Juni 1970) pp. 12–13, Neuorganisation der BASF-Gruppe, *BASF Information*, Sonderausgabe, Oktober 1969 (*BASF Archiv*, C0)]. Product divisions had responsibility for products primarily limited to Europe, whereas the four regional departments were responsible for all products in their region. BASF's international activities were always overseen by legally independent enterprises; thus, the primary function of regional departments was to coordinate the revenue goals of these firms. Regional departments, as well as product divisions, were evaluated on the basis of their performance (Selinger 1977, p. 19). Regional departments served as regional divisions in areas outside of Europe, and product divisions focused on Europe, as well as regional departments responsible for non-European districts, had integrated management organizations.

At the top management level, executives were responsible for managing corporate group strategy as well as direct responsibility for parts of new organizational subsets. The activities of the managing board were supported by a new staff group called the "headquarters planning department." For the selection and processing of information, modern technologies such as management information systems (MIS) were used. Moreover, their use enabled management activities that were informed by data-based planning and the clear delegation of authority within large work domains at appropriate management levels (*BASF Archiv*, C0, Direktionssitzung am 17.10.1969 zum Thema "Neugestaltung der Organisation der BASF-Gruppe," pp. 1–3). This headquarters planning department had five sections: (1) planning systems, (2) strategic planning and investment, (3) investment appraisal, (4) annual planning and budgeting, and (5) national economy. Work on the planning function was divided, with a unit responsible for market analysis placed in the national economy [*BASF Archiv*, C0, Dem Vorstandsvorsitzenden direkt unterstellte Einheiten, pp. A, 2A, *BASF Archiv*, C0, Organisation der BASF-Grupe (Dezember 1972), p. 3, *BASF Archiv*, C0, Neuorganisation der BASF-Gruppe (Juni 1970), p. 3]. The production, sales, and investment plans developed by the various departments of each division were investigated and elaborated on in these planning departments, and alternative plans were also developed. Many more company strategy and investment plans were submitted to directors as a result of this process, allowing them to select a plan that is more likely to be considered optimal (Koch 1970). The development of such headquarters mechanisms enabled by these planning departments was a response to the need for delegation of operational authority and connecting functions in the centralized elements that followed decentralization [*BASF Archiv*, C0, Neuorganisation der BASF-Gruppe, *BASF Information*, Sonderausgabe, Oktober 1969 (*BASF Archiv*, C0)]. At the headquarters level, functional staff departments were established to provide corporate group services. These four departments were (1) research, (2) human resources and social issues, (3) finance, and (4) legal and tax affairs [*BASF Archiv*, C0, Die Schrift an die Mitarbeiter (2.2.1970), Neuorganisation der BASF-Gruppe, *BASF Information*, Sonderausgabe, Oktober 1969 (*BASF Archiv*, C0)].

McKinsey & Company, a powerful US management consulting firm, collaborated and advised on the development of these new forms of organization (*BASF Archiv*, C0, Direktionssitzung am 17.10.1969 zum Thema "Neugestaltung der Organisation der BASF-Gruppe," pp. 2–3). This US consulting firm had a significant impact on BASF's subsequent organizational restructuring.

11.2.2.3.1.3 **Bayer**

Furthermore, case of Bayer is examined. Bayer had no need to move away from a functional structure until the beginning of the 1960s. However, as with Henkel, corporate expansion and competition led to a shift in company management on a new path (Kleinschmidt 2002, pp. 266–268). To reduce the operational burden of executives, it was proposed that daily operational management be delegated to lower-level managers and it was decided that these operations would be carried out by divisions. The separation of production and sales organizations came to an end, and the consolidation of production and sales resulted in the formation of "partial companies" which were defined in the same terms as US-style divisions [*Bayer Archiv*, 001–004-003, Vorschlag für einen Organisationsplan der FFB (ohne Agfa), pp.1–2, 4].

The deployment of a divisional structure in Bayer began with the restructuring in February 1970 [*Bayer Archiv*, 001–004-002, Die Schrift von Kurt Hansen an die Leitenden Angestelltender Werke Leverkusen, Dormagen, Elberfeld und Uerdingen sowie der deutschen Aueβnstellen (25.2.1970), p. 1, *Bayer Archiv*, 001-004-002, Neuorganisation der Farbenfabriken Bayer AG—(3.2.1970), *Bayer Archiv*, 010-004-005, Neuorganisation der Bayer AG, p.1, *Bayer Archiv*, 010-004-005, Die Schrift von Kurt Hansen an die Leitenden Angestellten der Werke Leverkusen, Dormagen, Elberfeld und Uerdingen (2.9.1965), *Bayer Archiv*, 001-004-003, Neuorganisation)], and the new organization was adopted on January 1, 1971 [*Bayer Archiv*, 001-004-002, Vorstandsrundschreiben Nr.63 (14.10.1970), p. 1]. Three essential components were included in the new organization (*Bayer Archiv*, 010-004-005, Neuorganisation der Bayer AG, p. 2): divisions, a central staff department, and staff for the board of directors. Bayer established a thorough division of labor and pursued delegation of authority, allowing managers to focus more on managerial activities (Vgl. *Bayer Archiv*, 210-001, Führungsgrundsätze der Bayer AG, p. 4).

The overreaching goal of the new organization conceived by Bayer's W. Knauff was to take steps to address the changes brought about by rapid growth, technological development, and market expansion, putting Bayer in a position to effectively manage the growing number of operations in the future. Maximizing flexibility and efficiency became an important goal in this endeavor. In addition to creating sales-oriented divisions, Bayer clearly defined administrative boundaries; delegated authority and responsibilities; established an efficient information system suitable for the new organizational structure; created a corporate group-wide integrated planning system; and clearly divided functions within lines, staff, and committees.

Bayer's product divisions were as follows: (1) inorganic chemical products, (2) organic chemical products, (3) rubber, (4) plastics and lacquer, (5) polyurethane, (6) dyes, (7) textiles, (8) pharmaceuticals, and (9) plant protection chemicals. These divisions were managed in accordance with policies established by the management board, from which general managers sought approval for their division plans at the appropriate time each year. They then accepted the responsibility delegated by the board of directors to achieve the goals outlined in those plans. The division into nine product divisions was deemed necessary in order to provide relevant operational scale to the divisions. Each division had a unified set of functions that included production, sales, research, and application engineering. Division management was generally delegated by the managing board to two people: an individual responsible for commercial affairs and the other responsible for technological affairs. Each was a director possessing equal authority.

Manufacturing plants and their associated auxiliary plants (such as drying plants) were integrated on a division production basis, which was appropriate for their locations. Insofar as the various departments within each division were not consolidated into service departments that worked across divisions (such as central staff departments), a specific division's sales oversight included all other departments or groups required for the success of the respective division's marketing, such as marketing research, market development, customer support, and order processing.

Furthermore, research operations were integrated into divisional research departments, with research groups working in divisional research departments as well as with researchers outside the central scientific research laboratories consolidated into the division's research department. Bayer aimed to promote close contact between sales, development, research, and production by dividing technology departments into divisions. In terms of divisional staff departments, division offices were made up of staff units that were managed by a single person who oversaw both technical and commercial staff. These staff organizations served as planning, direction, and control organizations, providing services within the division's purview.

The board of directors had company-wide operational management responsibility and was in charge of divisional and central staff department operation management; corporate policy; setting enterprise-wide or semi-enterprise-wide goals; decision-making for investments or other basic organizational issues; decision-making and acknowledgment for opening up negotiations on stock acquisition and sale; and important personnel issues such as manager selection and support for appointment, advancement, and transfer. Even among directors, there was a division of labor for production, sales, corporate group adjustment, research, engineering, finance and accounting, legal and tax affairs, and human resources and social issues.

Furthermore, a staff for the managing board was established to assist directors in their work. This staff organization served several functions, including prioritizing activities and preventing information loss; jointly conducting staff functions between those responsible for commercial and technical areas as a measure for planning, direction, and control for the board of directors to provide company-wide management; and establishing and allocating staff functions appropriate for new organizations. Furthermore, central staff departments were established. Their functions were to provide services to divisions as well as the entire company, and each of them was overseen by a single person who reported to the management board. These staff departments were (1) purchasing, (2) engineering, (3) central research, (4) patents and licensing, (5) advertising, (6) human resources and social issues, (7) finance and accounting, (8) legal and tax affairs, and (9) applications engineering. These central staff departments, along with the board of directors' staff, served as vital connecting points for the company's nine divisions, both domestic and international. Executives representing specialized fields were in charge of specialized management for each central staff department. In addition, extra-divisional committees and council organizations were established to facilitate effective information exchange. In 1972, 10 committees and council organizations were established: (1) general manager council, (2) investment council, (3) central production committee, (4) plant manager council, (5) central technical committee, (6) central engineering committee, (7) central research committee, (8) central sales committee, (9) central personnel committee, and (10) central corporate group coordination committee [*Bayer Archiv*, 001–004-002, Neuorganisation der Farbenfabriken Bayer AG (3.2.1970), *Bayer Archiv*, 001-004-002, Organizational Rearrangement of Farbenfabriken Bayer AG—Objectives, Functions and Tasks—, *Bayer Archiv*, 001-004-002, Organisationplan der Farbenfabriken Bayer AG, Leverkusen, Stand: 1.4.1971, *Bayer Archiv*,001–004-001, Farbenfabriken Bayer A.G., Leverkusen-Bayerwerk. Organisationspläne der

Verkaufsabteilungen, *Bayer Archiv*, 001–004-002, Vorstandsrundschreben Nr. 64 (22.10.1970), *Bayer Archiv*, 001-004-003, Die Schrift von Kurt Hansen an W. Knauff über den Vorschlag des Organizsationsplanes von Knauff (24.2.1964), pp. 3–4, 8, *Bayer Archiv*, 010–004-005, Organisatiorische Gliederung der Bayer AG, Stand: 1.7.1972, *Bayer Archiv*,010-004-005, Neuorganisation der Bayer AG, *Bayer Archiv*, 001-004-002, Die Schrift von Kurt Hansen an die Leitenden Angestellten der Werke Leverkusen, Dormagen, Elberfeld und Uerdingen sowie der deutschen Aueβnstellen (25.2.1970), pp. 2–3].

Overall, the new organizational structure aided the enterprise's competitiveness in global markets. Furthermore, the organization aimed to improve the workforce's awareness of revenues and costs, delegate authority and personnel management, and strengthen market consciousness throughout the organization (Kleinschmidt 2002, p. 269).

11.2.2.3.1.4 ***Hoechst***

Hoechst's organizational restructuring of 1952 divided all the enterprise's domestic and foreign plants and subsidiary companies into five divisions: (1) inorganic chemical products, nitrogen fertilizer, and plant protection chemicals, (2) pharmaceuticals, (3) dyes and other materials and textile auxiliaries, (4) plastics and solvents, and (5) textiles and film. That organizational structure would later be further reorganized into seven divisions. Each division was placed under a director responsible for technology. Coordinating departments were established for sales; plant management; research; engineering; finance and accounting; legal affairs, patents, and tax affairs; and technology (which was later abolished). A technical management department and a commercial management department were also established. In this way, Hoechst implemented broad management decentralization, even though one domain was always concerned with a division and a coordinating department at the same time. Because of this structure, all major decisions required the approval of at least two directors, which was a joint responsibility [Farbwerke Hoechst 1969, p. 14, Winnacker 1972, pp. 178–179, 504, *Hoechst Archiv*, H0136347, Organisationsplan des Finanz- und Rechnungswesen der Farbwerke Hoechst (19.1.1952), *Hoechst Archiv*, H0136339, Vorläufigen Organisationsplan für das Rechts- und Steuerwesen der Farbwerke Hoechst AG. (26.5.1952), *Hoechst Archiv*, H0136339]. Workgroup committees with broad decision-making authority were established under the directors, which could include administrative directors and important engineers in the plant, for example. In this structure, Hoechst followed IG Farben AG's model (Winnacker 1972, p. 184).

However, with the increase in global revenues, continually expanding operations, greater number of manufacturing facilities, and additional domains that came with Hoechst's rapid growth in the 1960s, enterprises could no longer be effectively managed within the existing organizational framework. As a result, Hoechst decided to implement an organizational reform, attempting to delegate authority more broadly and clearly so that the board of directors could spend more time considering fundamental issues and making decisions. To that end, all operations were separated into

14 distinct divisions. Production, research, applications engineering, sales, planning, and profit and loss accounting were all integrated functions in each division. The divisions operated within a predetermined operational scope for which they were responsible globally. Each division's management groups were made up of scientists and technologists in addition to sales and production management personnel, and domains were restructured with clearly defined operations.

Half of the directors were in charge of divisions while the other half was in charge of the 10 coordination departments: (1) procurement; (2) domestic plant and technical management; (3) international production; (4) research; (5) engineering; (6) applications engineering; (7) sales; (8) finance and accounting; (9) legal affairs, patents, and taxes; and (10) human resources and social issues. Performance evaluations for each division were in principle performed by two directors who were entrusted by the managing board to audit each division as a component of their overall set of responsibilities. Additional staff departments were established, with two critical roles: producing preparatory communications for all work committees and ensuring broad collaboration within the company [*Hoechst Archiv*, H0136364, Organisationsprinzip der Farbwerke Hoechst AG (Änderung Okt.70), *Hoechst Archiv*, H0136364, Geschäftsberichte der Farbwerke Hoechst AG (Änderung Okt.70), Farbwerke Hoechst 1969, pp. 14–17, Winnacker 1972, pp. 451, 463–464, 505, Generationswechsel. Von Winnacker zu Sammet, *Weilheimer Tagesblatt* (in: *Hoechst Archiv*, H0028468)].

As a result, s system of collegiate management for the divisions was established. The benefits of this organization, which began operations on January 1, 1970, included ensuring effective cooperation in each division, logically allocating functions, global coordination, and facilitating attention to any adjustments required in intra-divisional areas of small groups (Farbwerke Hoechst 1969, pp. 14–15). At this point, the board of directors decided to return to the specialization of production and sales held by members of the managing board for all divisions reporting to them (Dyas and Thanheiser 1976, pp. 122–123).

11.2.2.3.1.5 ***Hüls***

Hüls had begun to deploy a divisional structure by the mid-1950s in the areas of rubber, catalysts, and textiles (Kleinschmidt 2002, p. 270). Until a divisional structure was fully deployed in the 1970s, they used what was a fundamentally functional structure, comprising four functional departments: (1) production, (2) research, (3) commerce, and (4) human resources and legal affairs (Der Lichtbogen 1970, p. 26, Lorentz and Erker 2003, p. 270). However, due to increased competition in the global markets, increased production scale, and rapid advances in science and technology, greater changes in production and marketing became necessary (Der Lichtbogen 1970, p. 26). Along with these changes, serious problems that arose in postwar period under the existing organizational structure, particularly with diversification during the 1960s, were a major factor in restructuring. The restructuring created a critical need for directors to be freed from daily activities and detailed matters in order to be absorbed in more fundamental duties with a broader scope, a need for stronger efforts to mobilize workers with specialized knowledge in managing plant groups, and a need to entrust these workers with details in order for them to participate in decision-making systems and processes [*Hüls Archiv*, I-5–8, Einige Überlegungen zu den Möglichkeiten einer Organisationsänderung bei CWH, p. 1, *Hüls Archiv*, ohne Signatur, Niederschrift über die Sitzung des Vorstands am 3. April 1970 in Münster, Sitzungssaal der Landesbank (11.5.1970)].

As a result, the process of deploying divisional structures accelerated in the early 1970s (Kleinschmidt 2002, p. 270), and it was finally implemented in 1972 (*Hüls Archiv*, ohne Signatur, Niederschrift über die Besprechung in Hüls am 14. Juni 1971, p. 2, *Hüls Archiv*, ohne Signatur, Vorstandssitzung vom 6.7.70, p. 4, Der Lichtbogen 1970, p. 26). The organizational structure deployed to achieve these goals was a product divisional structure with six divisions: (1) raw materials and inorganic chemicals, (2) organic chemicals, detergents, and cleaners, (3) rubber, (4) thermoplastics, (5) polycondensates and paint materials, and (6) energy (later nitrogen and agricultural chemicals). These divisions were created to function as technically and financially independent units, each with its own production and sales operations. Each division operated as a quasi-independent enterprise with the managing board establishing business policies. The management of their scopes of operations was delegated to two people, a production and sales specialist, resulting in a collegiate management structure based on a board-majority system. Furthermore, the organization had 10 central corporate departments that operated on a company-wide basis, such as R&D, patents, finance and accounting, and legal and tax affairs. The board of directors, divisions, and the central company departments received an advice and assistance from seven staff departments. In this way, broad areas of authority and responsibility for short-term, daily operations were delegated to the divisions, and top management created an organization in which they could focus on long-term planning, their essential job, rather than daily operational work [*Hüls Archiv*, ohne Signatur, Niederschrift über die Sitzung des Vorstands CWH am 17. Juli 1970 in Schloβ Raesfeld (5.8.1970), Der Lichtbogen 1970, pp. 26–7, Lorentz and Erker 2003, pp. 270–271]. Furthermore, a new business planning and control concept was implemented, with a standing corporate planning committee. This committee was involved with deploying new control mechanisms and in improving short-, mid-, and long-term planning [Vgl. *Hüls Archiv*, VI-8–3/1, Die Schrift über die ständige Kommission "Unternehmungsplanung" und Sachbearbeiter für die Planung (15.12.1969), *Hüls Archiv*, VI-8–3/1, Besprechungsbericht von 1.Sitzung der Kommission "Unternehmungsplanung" (5.2.1970), *Hüls Archiv*, VI-8-3/1, Besprechungsbericht von 2. Sitzung der Kommission "Unternehmungsplanung" (27.2.1970), *Hüls Archiv*, VI-8-3/1, Besprechungsbericht von 3. Sitzung der Kommission "Unternehmungsplanung" (1.10.1970), *Hüls Archiv*, VI-8-3/1, Langfristige Unternehmungsplanung (11.12.1969), Lorentz and Erker 2003, p. 271].

As we have seen, US consulting firms played a significant role in the implementation of a divisional structure at BASF and Henkel. In contrast, Hüls used Bayer, BASF, and Hoechst as examples to follow [*Hüls Archiv*, ohne Signatur, Niederschrift über die Sitzung des Vorstands am 3. April 1970 in Münster, Sitzungssaal der Landesbank (11.5.1970), pp. 1, 5, Lorentz and Erker 2003, pp. 270–271], and this was a primary difference.

11.2.2.3.1.6 ***Glanzstoff***

Furthermore, the developments noted in the aforementioned three companies were observed at Glanzstoff from the late 1960s through the early 1970s, when Glanzstoff also deployed a product divisional structure. In examining the feinchemical division, for example, two integral principles were applied. One was a concept of divisions organized vertically by product domain, integrating all activities in Glanzstoff as well as AKU and other affiliated enterprises. The other principle sought international business structures for sulfur-containing chemical products and feinchemicals. This division was in charge of organic and inorganic sulfide products, with the exception of intermediate products resulting from Viscose production, agricultural chemical products, feinchemical, and products related to these three areas. Production and R & D of these products in various EEC nations as well as all sales and marketing activities globally were consolidated in this division. Divisions coordinated engineering and other various activities in the other operational fields of AKU and Glanzstoff's central department.

Each division was assigned a general manager who was responsible for its operational results as well as the coordination of all divisional functions, such as production, sales, and revenue, including the division's further expansion. General managers had authority over all departments and specialized buildings in AKU and Glanzstoff in order to perform their duties and obtain various reports, statistics, and other materials critical to their divisions. Furthermore, each division had a deputy general manager who served as a proxy in the absence of the general manager or when problems arose. A governing body comprised of three AKU and Granzstoff executive team members oversaw divisional activities.

For division investments, the general manager presented the governing body with the following year's investment plan each year. Authority for a discretionary amount of money was granted in an investment plan framework approved by the governing body that reviewed each investment application. The amount differed by position. The discretionary scope of a divisional general manager was between 20,000 and 100,000 Deutsche Marks, and anything above that amount required the approval of the governing body. Investment limits within the discretionary amount were set at a maximum of 20,000 Deutsche Marks for production or sales divisional operations managers and a maximum of 10,000 Deutsche Marks for anyone lower in the divisional hierarchy [*Rheinisch-Westfälisches Archiv zu Köln*, Abt 195, F7-4, Vorschlag über die Bildung einer gemeinsamen AKU-Glanzstoff Schwefelchemie-Division unter der Bezeichnung Feinchemikalien-Division (FCD) (1.10.1968)].

Similarly, all AKU and Glanzstoff wool domain activities were integrated into a vertically organized wool division that was an independent business division. The function of the division, authority and responsibility of its general manager, and discretionary investment amount were almost identical to those of the feinchemical division [*Rheinisch-Westfälisches Archiv zu Köln*, Abt 195, F7-5, Vorschlag über den Aufbau einer gemeinsamen AKU/Glanzstoff Vliesstoff Division unter der Bezeichnung Colbond Division (1.12.1968)].

Moreover, although other chemical corporations such as Freudenberg and Continental deployed divisional structures, these deployed structures had unique characteristics defined by their companies. As previously stated, generational shifts in top management served as important mechanisms for implementing organizational restructuring. For example, Glanzstoff's transition to a divisional structure was facilitated by older entrepreneurs such as R. Vits and L. Vaubel. Other firms accepted the advice of US consulting companies; however, they adopted an organizational structure that was different from an American-style divisional structure. Continental, for example, was advised by McKinsey and restructured with their help, establishing divisions that were an amalgamated organization that maintained functional departments. As a result, cases of different structures, as well as combined divisional and functional structures, can be found even in businesses that have deployed divisional structures and undergone decentralization (Kleinschmidt 2002, pp. 269–270).

That said, the following management issues inevitably emerged under functional structures as diversification advances. One issue was the difficulty encountered by each department's head manager in keeping pace with basic functions such as the production, sales, and procurement of a division where multiple and vastly different product lines are managed together. Another was the top management's frustration with making administrative decisions rather than entrepreneurial, executive decisions, such as allocating corporate or long-term business resources (Kroos and Gilbert 1972, p. 253). As Michel Aglietta pointed out, "the need now was to subject capital to an overall objective of valorization, in various fields of commodity production in which completely different conditions of production and exchange prevailed" and "this problem exerted insurmountable tensions on the centralized functional structure" (Aglietta 1979, p.255). As seen in these case studies of representative companies, most corporations that underwent diversification were forced to pursue organizational restructuring in order to address these managerial issues. Therefore, reforms based on restructuring principles found in the divisional structure were the norm.

11.2.2.3.2 **Deployment of Divisional Structures in the Electrical Industry and Its Characteristics**

This section then examines the use of divisional structure in the electrical industry, where diversification occurred in the same way it did in the chemical industry, and divisional structure was important due to the nature of the business.

11.2.2.3.2.1 **Siemens**

Organizational principles from the United States played a significant role in Siemens' organizational reforms in the 1960s. After World War II the rapid expansion of all Siemens' business units not only facilitated the integration of low-voltage technology and power engineering but also resulted in redundancies in production and development. This proclivity eventually necessitated organizational restructuring. In 1966, the three parent companies of Siemens & Halske, Siemens–Schuckert, and Siemens–Reininger–Werke were merged into one business enterprise known as Siemens AG. This audacious attempt helped to create a very positive corporate image for global markets. However, Siemens discovered the need to create manageable business units with no redundancies in order to respond to rapid technology advances (Feldenkirchen 2004, pp. 126–127).

Furthermore, market conditions stimulated organizational reform at Siemens (Zeitschrift für Organisation 1970a, p. 338). In the latter half of the 1960s, Siemens' scale grew to the point where centralized management was no longer possible, and the diversity and breadth of product programs necessitated the formation of divisions. It was already becoming impossible to keep the traditional split between the heavy current sector and low-voltage current sector, and a significant amount of redundancy would result between these two sectors. Furthermore, there were redundancies in authority engendering conflict between the sectors. As a result, reinforcing cooperation became necessary for achieving a synergistic effect. Moreover, the growth of the group required greater transparency in operations, making organizational restructuring an urgent issue (Hilger 2004, pp. 214–215).

The new enterprise was reorganized into six groups on October 1, 1969, with regional offices and regional companies as well as five corporate departments. Siemens' divisional structure into six business domains was composed of (1) components, (2) installation, (3) energy engineering, (4) data systems technology, (5) communications technology, and (6) medical technology, with each of these divisions being given the most independence in business affairs. Further, the organization had five functional corporate departments which dealt with company-wide affairs: (1) sales, (2) technology, (3) human resources, (4) finance, (5) managerial economics. These departments functioned in an advisory and coordinating capacity, and the organization as a whole took on a matrix-like character [*Siemens Archiv Akten*, 33/Ld603, Neuorganisation der Siemens AG (16.9.1969), *Siemens Archiv Akten*, 33/Ld603, V-Rundschreiben Nr.18/69 (30.9.1969), *Siemens Archiv Akten*, 33/Ld603, Z-Rundschreiben Nr.4/70 (22.12.1969), *Siemens Archiv Akten*, 33/Ld603, Z-Rundschreiben Nr.5/70 (22.12.1969), *Siemens Archiv Akten*, 4/Lr302-20, A-Rundschreiben Nr.3/69 (12.12.1968), *Siemens Archiv Akten*, 33/Ld603, A-Rundschreiben Nr.4/69(11.8.1969), Siemens 1969, pp. 14–15, Zeitschrift für Organisation 1970a, p. 338, Siemens-Mitteilungen 1969, Feldenkirchen 2004, p. 127, Hilger 2004, p. 216].

Each business domain or component unit within a domain was organized on the basis of technological and market relationships, and with the decentralization of decision-making according to products and product groups, much effort was put into making themselves self-sufficient, bearing responsibility for everything from development to sales [*Siemens Archiv Akten*, 33/Ld603, Z-Rundschreiben Nr.5/70 (22.12.1969), Zeitschrift für Organisation 1970a, pp. 338–340]. Business domains held profit responsibility along with authority over investment and human resources within the scope of company policy (Yamamoto 1993, pp. 152–153). The slow-down in Siemens' growth in the latter half of the 1960s motivated the adoption of profit centers as they were critical for decentralized management (Hilger 2004, p. 229). In contrast, the five corporate departments were there to secure cooperation and control conflict between the six business domains [*Siemens Archiv Akten*, 33/Ld603, A-Rundschreiben Nr.3/69 (12,12,1968), *Siemens Archiv Akten*, 33/Ld603, V-Rundschreiben Nr.18/69 (30.9.1969), S.3–4, Yamamoto 1993, p. 152]. Though they lacked command authority, the five corporate departments served as advisers to both the managing board and the business domains (Tacke 1977, p. 277).

Siemens' organizational reform was intended to promote "independence" as a concept and as a measure for organizational restructurings; as a result, Siemens distinguished itself from other enterprises by refusing to use outside consultants. This resulted in disparities between Siemens' organizational reform during the 1960s and the use of divisional structures by US companies (Hilger 2004, p. 215). New organizational concepts were based on principles of responsibility for products, functions, and regions, and the Siemens organization matrix differed significantly from the typical divisional structure used in US corporations in several aspects (Feldenkirchen 2004, pp. 127–128). Although Siemens adhered to basic divisional structure principles developed in the United States, they tried their organizational changes on different German circumstances and focused on maintaining their integrated Siemens culture, prioritizing the enterprise as a whole over individual components (Feldenkirchen 2004, p. 131).

11.2.2.3.2.2 **AEG**

At the time that AEG restructured its corporate group after World War II the decision-making structure was based on principles of centralization. The management board or the chairman himself was in charge of all major decisions. Production management was simply organized into work domains, with little authority (Hautsch 1979, p. 151). However, the breadth of these functions grew dramatically over time, both in terms of scale and the addition of new activities, and the first postwar organizational reform began in 1957. AEG was in danger of losing its ability to gain a clear overall picture of the company because the organization had previously accommodated small, simple corporations. Each product group was reorganized vertically in their organizational restructurings, operational departments were integrated into divisions, and authority for business execution was delegated to the division's general manager. However, they lacked horizontal departments for the management of such functions as managerial economics of overall corporate group finance, marketing, or human resources, for example (Strunk 2000, p. 70). Divisions were responsible for overall operations in their domains of specialization, in particular development, factory worker placement, production planning, production, sales planning, sales strategies, and pricing policies. The goal of this organization was to deal with the various needs that were derived from the increasing amounts of business by (1) enabling divisions to make their own business policies based on a clear overview of the entire business from a technical and commercial perspective, (2) accurately grasping the overall costs and performance for each division, (3) more clearly defined responsibilities, (4) simplified operations, (5) creating unified pricing policies, and (6) a strict integration of activities related to shared technology [*Historisches Archiv des Deutschen Technikmuseums*, GS839, Rundschreiben Nr.14/57, Neue Organisation der AEG (9.7.1957), pp. 1, 3].

However, changes beginning in the late 1950s made organizational restructuring vital, such as expansion of activities, rapid technological advances, more products, expanded sales channels, the development of business policies more focused on the creation of demand for new products and greater competition due to internationalization efforts in a better integrated EEC (AEG 1963, p. 53, Hautsch 1979). With the revenue situation worsening at the end of the 1950s, implementing corporate group reorganization became a critical issue, and the use of US consulting firms' experience was deemed necessary. However, the new organization established on October 1, 1963, employed a new management structure based on the one used by GE in the United States, with small- and medium-sized business units empowered with authority and an executive team that simply acted as a coordinating unit. The organization was vertical in terms of business domains, rather similar to those seen in the United States or the United Kingdom. The new organization had five departments: (1) energy production and distribution, (2) energy use, (3) home appliances (4) industrial supply, and (5) transportation. These departments each managed their own procurement, research, production, and sales. Therefore, reinforcing the department head's responsibility, greater flexibility and stricter management in each division were pursued [*Historisches Archiv des Deutschen Technikmuseums*, GS839, Rundschreiben RO2, Bildung von Horizontalen und Vertikalen Bereichen (30.5.1963), *Historisches Archiv des Deutschen Technikmuseums*, GS839, Ausführung von Dr.-Ing. E.h. Dr.-Ing. Hans Heyne, Vorsitzer der Vorstände der AEG und der Telefunken AG, in der Hauptversammlung der AEG am 25. Juni 1964 in der Berliner Kongreβhalle, *Historisches Archiv des Deutschen Technikmuseums*, Ü-V0438, Niederschrift über eine Sitzung des Personalausschusses am 20. Februar 1963, 10 Uhr., *Historisches Archiv des Deutschen Technikmuseums*, U0438, Niederschrift über eine Sitzung des Personalausschusses am 20. Februar 1963, 10 Uhr., *Historisches Archiv des Deutschen Technikmuseums*, U0438, Niederschrift über eine Sitzung des Personal-Ausschusses der AEG am 1. Dezember 1965 in Frankfurt/M., S.5, *Historisches Archiv des Deutschen Technikmuseums*, U0438, Niederschrift über eine Sitzung des Aufsichtsrates am 28.11.1963, 10.30 Uhr, S,8, S.11, *Historisches Archiv des Deutschen Technikmuseums*, U0438, Niederschrift über eine Sitzung des Aufsichtsrates am 25. Mai 1964, 15 Uhr., *Historisches Archiv des Deutschen Technikmuseums*, Ü-V0438, Niederschrift über eine Sitzung des Aufsichtsrats der AEG und Tfk am 25. Mai 1965 in Frankfurt/M., S.12, *Historisches Archiv des Deutschen Technikmuseums*, U0438, Niederschrift über eine Sitzung des Aufsichtsrates am 28. September 1962, 12 Uhr., S.3–4, AEG 1963, pp. 53, 55, Strunk 2000, pp. 70–74, Hautsch 1979, p. 151, Der Volkswirt 1963, p. 492, Reindl 2001, p. 138, Der Volkswirt 1964, p. 1241]. In addition to these five vertical departments, the new organization featured eight horizontal departments: (1) R&D, (2) production, (3) marketing, (4) commercial business, (5) exporting, (6) public relations, (7) finance, and (8) a general secretariat. Excluding the exporting department, these departments were responsible for assisting and coordinating with the entire corporation, though they had no command authority over the divisions [*Historisches Archiv des Deutschen Technikmuseums*, GS839, Rundschreiben RO2, Bildung von Horizontalen und Vertikalen Bereichen (30.5.1963), *Historisches Archiv des Deutschen Technikmuseums*, GS839, Rundschreiben RO3, Verantwortliche Leiter der Horizontalen und Vertikalen Bereiche (30.5.1962), *Historisches Archiv des Deutschen Technikmuseums*, U0438, Niederschrift über eine Sitzung des Personalausschusses am 20. Februar 1963, 10 Uhr., *Historisches Archiv des Deutschen Technikmuseums*, U0438, Niederschrift über eine Sitzung des Personal-Ausschusses der AEG am 1. Dezember 1965 in Frankfurt/M., S.5, *Historisches Archiv des Deutschen Technikmuseums*, Ü-V0438, Niederschrift über eine Sitzung des Personalausschusses am 28. September 1962, 10.30 Uhr., S.2, *Historisches Archiv des Deutschen Technikmuseums*, Ü-V0438, Niederschrift über eine Sitzung des Aufsichtsrates am 28. September 1962, 12 Uhr., S.3, AEG 1963; pp. 53, 55].

Though the board of directors remained the organ in charge of making final decisions on various management issues, operational functions were further decentralized. In each of the five divisions, sixteen departments were established, and each division functioned as a quasi-independent enterprise solely responsible for all actions related to development, production, commerce, and sales within the scope of each division's policies (AEG 1963, p. 54). The reorganization maintained the independence of subsidiaries and decentralized at a high level. However, coordination among the various departments and subsidiary companies alone was insufficient, and it was evident that the extremely decentralized organization had exceeded its objectives. Therefore, the latter half of the 1960s brought a retrenchment of the relative independence at the division level, with departments and subsidiary enterprises being consolidated into divisions. Divisions were integrated into five fields (mass-produced goods, consumer goods, energy, and industrial technology, office technology, and communications and transportation technology), and the newly integrated subsidiaries were integrated into these fields as departments. Control over the horizontal departments of (1) planning and control, (2) technology, (3) finance, (4) human resources, and (5) regional affairs and materials was divided among five directors. As a result, the corporate managing board was able to maintain direct control of everything down to the field level, and decision-making mechanisms were put in place (Hautsch 1979, pp. 151–152).

Later, in 1967, three additional business fields were added for a total of eight: components; communications equipment; and radio, television, and recording equipment (AEG-Telefunken AG 1967, pp. 33–44). In 1969, these were once again reorganized into seven product divisions: (1) energy engineering, (2) transportation, (3) communications and data systems technology, (4) components, (5) industrial supply, (6) home appliances, and (7) radio, television, and recording equipment. In addition, horizontal departments were reorganized into seven groups: (1) R&D, (2) production, (3) marketing, (4) human resources and social issues, (5) finance, (6) office management, and (7) international affairs [*Historisches Archiv des Deutschen Technikmuseums*, GS3501, Struktur-Organisation, Gesamt-Stellen-Übersicht Ausgabe 1970 Organisationsplan (Stand 1.11.1969), AEG-Telefunken AG 1969, pp. 39–50].

11.2.2.3.3 Deployment of Divisional Structure in Other Industries and Its Characteristics

Based on the preceding analysis, diversification occurred at a high level in the chemical and electrical industries, and the deployment of a divisional structure was significant if only for that reason. This subsection compares the iron and steel industries where diversification did not occur to the chemical and electrical industries.

In the late 1960s, Mannesmann implemented organizational restructurings, dividing their corporate group into autonomous groups on the basis of the US model. A change of top executive at Rheinische Stahlwerke AG in August 1968 (making T. Schmücker the company's CEO) facilitated organizational reform. The organization had previously been that of a holding company, managing only financial control and performing no other functions. The management of this multilayered corporate group faced numerous redundancies in production and sales as a result of its more than 30 subsidiary companies. Mannesmann believed that a top-down, rather than bottom-up, "attack" management style was not feasible. A wide range of activities were divided into the lowest level production domains and then integrated them into 15 divisions on the basis of the new organization plan. The alignment of domains with markets and technological commonalities, as well as the desire to eliminate disruptions and redundancies, were decisive factors in division appropriation. Divisions were organized into five integrated groups at the top, each led by a corporate group director. The goal of forming a new group was to clarify responsibility and management at the production domain, divisional, and corporate group board of directors' levels, in terms of management results, as well as to enable faster decision-making and greater flexibility.

Likewise, Krupp that worked in the iron and steel industry, went through an organizational restructuring as well as management change in 1968. Krupp, like Rheinische Stahlwerke AG, suffered from structural flaws in their manufacturing enterprises, which were made up of many parts, and sales companies, which had many redundancies. As a result, they decided to adopt organizational principles used by major US corporate groups and to integrate similar or identical activities on an organizational level. They aimed for a more effective product classification than other corporate groups, as well as the formation of a small number of large-scale business units, with each member of the Krupp group given a high level of managerial responsibility (Der Volkswirt 1969, p. 70).

11.3 The Characteristics of Japanese and German Deployment of the Divisional Structure

11.3.1 Japanese Deployment of Divisional Structure

11.3.1.1 Japanese Characteristics in the Self-sufficiency of Divisions and Decentralization of Management

Based on the foregoing analysis, Japanese and German characteristics regarding the deployment of the divisional structure will be examined. With regard to Japanese characteristics, there were several cases in which the divisional structure was introduced without comparing the structure's advantages and disadvantages. In addition, despite the promotion and adoption of the divisional structure after 1958, there were companies that returned to the functional structure after 1965 (Yoshihara et al. 1981, pp. 200, 203; Urabe 1969, p. 6; Gohara 1968, p. 143; Ono 1979, pp. 123, 126; Imanishi 1988, p. 61). Cases in which companies attempted to imitate the American-style divisional structure were also not rare (Sakakibara 1980, p. 65).

Moreover, the postwar boom years were characterized by a certain percentage of organizational structures that included a mixture of the divisional and functional structures in which the latter were retained for core business lines. Within this form of organization, business decision-making power for non-core businesses was left to the division, whereas for core business lines, no differentiation was made between headquarters and the organization conducting the business (Yoshihara et al. 1981, pp. 191–192, Kagono 1980, pp. 205, 271). In this case, decentralization was inconsistent.

Regarding decentralization of management, Japanese corporations had many "pseudo" divisions that were unlike the typical US divisional structure. In US divisional structures, the division typically bore profit responsibility as an autonomous unit. However, in Japanese corporations, many divisions lacked the requisite functions for autonomy (Ishii et al. 1996, pp. 132–133). Traditionally, for an organization to be autonomous, it had to have production, sales and marketing, technology, R&D, and other functions necessary for business—a rare situation for a Japanese corporate division (Yoshihara et al. 1981, p. 193).

According to a survey in 1961, the ratio of companies that delegated most of the authority to the divisions to companies that adopted a divisional structure was 48.6%, while the ratio of firms that transferred some authority was 45.9%. In addition, the rate of firms in which most of the authority was reserved by the head office was only around 5% (Fujiyoshi 1962, pp. 42–42). A 1963 investigation by the Japan Association of Corporate Executives (overlapping answers) pointed out that the ratio of enterprises that engaged in purchasing, production, and sales in each division to enterprises that adopted the divisional structures was 50.4%, while the rate of firms in which a purchasing department was common in each division was 27.3% (Shadan hojin keizai doyukai 1964, pp. 3–7, 103–105, 107). According to Ogawa (1969), the divisional structure in which the person in charge of the division had authority over production, purchasing, and finance rarely existed in Japan (Ogawa 1969, p. 30). According to a survey by Hiroshi Gohara in 1968, many of the divisional structures in Japan were those organized according to function, even though the form was decentralized according to the business field at that time. The fundamental reason for such a phenomenon was that only the form of the divisional structure was introduced without the prevalence of the management methods of such structure at that time. In addition, there were many cases in which organizational structure jumped from the centralized functional structure to the decentralized divisional structure, according to the business field despite the low necessity to adopt a divisional structure. In cases where the formal decentralization to the division occurred regardless of the necessity, there were numerous cases in which purchasing by the headquarters and by the divisions were combined (Gohara 1968, pp. 140, 142–143). According to a survey by Kunizo Nakkahashi in 1980, the self-sufficiency rates for the divisions that adopted the divisional structure were 74% in production, 72% in sales, 65% in R&D, and 47% in physical distribution. The relevant numerical values of sales and physical distribution in the United States were 82% and 79%, respectively.

In general, the degree of self-sufficiency among the divisions in Japanese corporations was relatively low. The historical differences between Japan and the United States in diversification and adoption of the divisional structure were related to this point. In Japan, although diversification began later than in the United States, it progressed rapidly after the 1960s. Furthermore, Japanese enterprises faced various problems, such as delegating duties between the main office and the divisions, and the shortage of human resources during the shift from the functional structure to the divisional structure. As a result, many functions remained in the head office (Nakahashi 1981, pp. 41, 43, 53–55, 74).

In Japan, there were a few cases in which production and sales were integrated even though the divisional structure was adopted. There were also many cases in which the sales departments were placed outside the divisions. In these instances, the sales departments were either centralized in the main office or established as another company. One reason for this was that sales activities performed at the head office in a concentrated manner (rather than separately by each division) under the affiliated distribution channel were favorable for strengthening the distribution channel (Kono 1985, pp. 20–21; Aoki 1960, p. 84). In Japan, there were also industries where it was necessary to perform sales activities by separating them from the divisions (Gohara 1968, p. 111). Moreover, the span of general managers' power concerning personnel affairs, equipment investments, and sales promotions was extremely narrow (Suzuki 1961, p. 63).

There were many cases in Japan in which one division would specialize in production and product development, while another division would focus on sales and marketing. However, the actual situation of such functional divisions varied greatly. Unlike Europe and the United States, where the divisions that integrated production and sales were numerous, the structural characteristic also determined some special features concerning the operation of the division. The internal market of the functional divisional structure was not only where commodities were traded, but also where strategic initiatives were transacted and where cooperation of other divisions occurred under the trade relationship between the production divisions and the sales divisions. Strategic initiatives denote the activities that propose the ideas and concepts generated toward various sections within the company and induce cooperation with other divisions. The functional divisional structure was the organizational structure that was suitable for the creation and transaction of strategic initiatives. In addition, the personnel network within the company was indispensable for creating and evaluating strategic initiatives. Long-term experience in an organization is required for the purpose of building such a network.

The appearance of the functional divisional structure in Japan reflected the conditions of long-term employment (Kagono 1993, pp. 35, 37, 39, 47, 49–50; Kagono 1992a, b, c, d). In Japan, although the deconcentration of the authority of sales advanced, there were many cases in which the decisive power of pricing was reserved for the main office. These situations were brought about by the following: the partial nature of the divisional structure; the difficulties of decentralizing the sales and purchasing business under the narrowness and concentration of the sales market, and the dependence on heavy exports during a poor economic period; and the problems arising from arranging a lot of staff members in each division in order to suit the divisional structure (Yamada 1961, pp. 48, 50–51).

Thus, in Japan, the divisions were never granted complete authority, and even with the adoption of the divisional structure, the various headquarters provided significant direction and exerted control over the divisions, which was a characteristic of headquarters-driven centralization (Choki 1993, p. 44, Kagono et al. 1983, p. 37, Urabe 1960, p. 198). In the Japanese divisional structure, even in the case where the authority of the functional management was delegated to the division manager, top management generally participated in administrative activities, even though the department was under the control of the division (Fushimi and Watabnabe 1995, p. 8). Even if considerable authority was given to each division, the delegation of power to the general manager was inconsistent, especially in matters that influenced profit such as personnel affairs, materials, and budgets. In such cases, the authority that was reserved for the head office was significant (Takamiya et al. 1962, pp. 13–14; Gohara 1968, pp. 136–142; Harasawa 1981, pp. 134–135). According to a survey by Kagono et al. in 1980, whereas the possession rates of the personnel function and the accounting and control function (by division) in the United States were 84.4% and 82%, respectively, the relevant numerical values in Japan were 35.5 and 40.1%, respectively (Kagono et al. 1983, pp. 18, 37).

11.3.1.2 Japanese Characteristics of the Contract Relations Regarding the Consignment and Trust of Management Rights and the Self-supporting Accounting System

The low self-sufficiency and the incompleteness of the decentralization process also had a negative effect on the introduction of the self-supporting accounting system in the divisions. For instance, according to a survey in 1961, the ratio of companies that introduced such a system to companies that adopted the divisional structure was 42.5%. In addition, few companies established divisions as autonomous profit centers, even though the self-supporting accounting system was regarded as an aim (Fujiyoshi 1962, pp. 43–44). An investigation by the Japan Association of Corporate Executives in 1963 pointed out that the ratio of enterprises that used the self-supporting accounting system to companies that adopted the divisional structures was 52.9% (Shadan hojin keizai doyukai 1964, pp. 106–107). After 1965, importance began to be placed on divisional independence and their traditional status as profit centers because customer- or market-oriented management systems responded to changes in corporate environments, which necessitated restructuring (Ono 1979, p. 128). However, according to a survey by the management department of the Industrial Structure Council in 1968, the rate of firms that introduced the self-supporting accounting system to firms that adopted the divisional structure was only 50.9% (Tsushosangyo sho kigyokyoku 1969, pp. 136–137, 230–231).

Conversely, there were many cases in which the divisions served as investment centers, as well as cases where they were regarded as profit centers in the United States. For example, according to a survey by Reece and Cool in 1978, 21.8% of 620 companies (including Fortune 1000 industrial companies) included profit centers, while 74% had investment centers. The rate of firms that used the return on investment (ROI) as a method for evaluating the performance of their investment centers was 93% (Reece and Cool 1978, pp. 28–30). In the United States, there were many cases in which the authority regarding investments was given to division managers in order to oversee business processes from production to sales. In contrast, in Japan, most enterprises included profit centers, but such authority was not delegated to division managers (Motizuki 2011, pp. 123, 126–127). In addition, there were many firms that shifted to the divisional headquarters structure during the period of low economic growth after the 1970s. However, even the divisional headquarters were generally profit centers with no investment authority (Torii 2007, p. 6). According to a survey by Takeo Yoshikawa in 1996 on the divisional structure in the manufacturing industry, the rate of companies that included profit centers was 74.82%, whereas the rate of firms that included investment centers was only 20.14%. The relevant numerical values in the non-manufacturing industry were 76.8% and 14.7%, respectively (Yoshikawa 1996, p.124).

In the Japanese enterprises that adopted the divisional structure, the concept of the investment center as the responsible unit for ROI did not prevail, even in the large companies. Among the divisional firms that adopted the system of the investment center, cases in which the residual income method, rather than the ROI, was used as the standard of evaluating divisions were far more abundant. In addition, there were many cases that emphasized the ratio of profits to net sales as the standard of performance in companies that adopted either the investment center or profit center system (Fushimi 1997, p. 8).

In Japanese enterprises, the American approach of social contracts, in which general managers assume the responsibility for achieving certain business goals in exchange for decision-making authority (from development and production to sale), is not normally used. The American-style management of the divisional structure is constructed on the fundamental premise that the shareholders have certain power, and that there is the relationship of the consignment and trust of capital that exists between top management and general managers as well as between the shareholders and the top management. In this regard, there is an important difference in the infrastructure concerning such a system (Fushimi and Yokota 1993, pp. 34, 36–37, 40–41; Fushimi and Watanabe 1995, pp. 7, 9). Many Japanese companies introduced this American-style management system as a new and superior approach. However, there were many cases in which various changes were performed in the actual administration process. In fact, there were many common characteristics in the way such changes were made between the various companies (Fushimi 1997, pp. 3, 6).

Given the above-mentioned conditions, the connection between results and compensation was also weak compared to the United States (Ishii et al. 1996, p. 133). In the United States, bonuses for general managers were generally seen as a reward for their achievements, which were directly related to the profits of their divisions. However, in Japan, the majority of such bonuses were included as part of the normal salary and were not directly related to performance. Although there were many companies that used the amount of profit as the standard of achievement, other firms used multiple standards for evaluating achievement. This not only led general managers to focus on positive growth, but it also contributed to building the company's power that could become the basis of long-term profitability (Nakahashi 1981, pp. 67, 73–74). In this way, divisions in Japanese corporations lacked a high degree of self-sufficiency, division performance evaluations were simpler, and divisional structures tended to be adopted after a revision of their traditional form (Kagono et al. 1983, p. 38). Furthermore, in the shift to the American-style divisional structure, there were many cases in Japan in which the characteristic of the division as an investment center and the internal transfer price system based on market price did not apply (Torii 2007, p. 8).

In Japanese companies, there were also cases in which the internal capital system was adopted in the divisional structure. This system aimed at clarifying the amount of working capital and improving capital operation efficiency by evaluating the activities of each division (Nishikawa 1996, p. 78). The internal capital system was adopted by Matsushita Electric Industrial Co., Ltd. in 1954 (Miura 2010, p. 47), after which the company was able to clarify the amount of capital employed, calculate the debt of each division and the acquired profit, and evaluate business performance from the perspectives of the capital amount to be maintained and the profit to be achieved (Kimura 1999, p. 147). Around 1970, the internal capital system had become widely known. However, it was not until the latter half of the 1990s that the implementation of this system was more widespread (Miura 2010, p. 45). For instance, according to a survey by Takayuki Tani in 1984, the adoption rate of the internal capital system in companies that introduced the divisional structure was 25.8% (Tani 1987, p. 141), whereas the relevant numerical value, according to a 1995 survey by Fumiko Hiki, was 52.1% (Hiki 1997, pp. 72, 76).

11.3.2 German Deployment of Divisional Structure

Building upon the foregoing examination, next, German characteristics of the deployment of the divisional structure are examined. The level of delegation of authority and responsibility, the traditions of the board of directors along with collegiate management and the board-majority system, the role of top management in divisions, the use of a compensation system linked to company results, and the high number of holding companies among the largest manufacturing companies greatly influenced changes in the organization structure.

11.3.2.1 Divisional Structure Mechanisms and Their German Characteristics

This section discusses German characteristics from the perspective of divisional structure mechanisms. In the top management, there are different applications of collegiate management in new organizations with three main alternatives. The first step was to make directors act as divisional general managers. This option was most frequently seen in relatively small-scale enterprises among the largest 100 companies. The responsibility for divisional profits in these cases rested upon top management, who were also collectively responsible for company-wide results. In these firms, there was a controller or a position with an equivalent function, which was filled by a member of the top management. The second option was to place divisions beneath directors who specialized in specific functions, with joint management of divisions performed further by managers who specialized in specific functions. This was primarily implemented in the chemical industry, where profit responsibility was vested in specialized management teams that were collectively accountable for directors. The directors were typically in charge of a division's technical or commercial aspects, as well as coordinating with staff or were in charge of both aspects. The third option was to have directors manage a group of divisions, as is common in extremely large enterprises such as Siemens, AEG, and Bayer. In these cases, two or more directors managed the group jointly, though the group was occasionally managed by a single director. Directors were usually the heads of either the division group or staff and sometimes both (Dyas and Thanheiser 1976, pp. 123–125).

In terms of compensation systems, unlike the United States, where the compensation of a general manager responsible for a division's profit is frequently tied to that division's profits, the use of performance-linked financial incentives for general managers based on profit and profit responsibility were extremely rare. The introduction of these types of incentives was often deemed undesirable (Dyas and Thanheiser 1976, p. 138). All of the 19 capital companies with divisional structures for which data is available had some type of payment system for special allowances. However, in an overwhelming number of cases, these incentives neither built a large portion of the general managers' net income nor showed a clear connection with divisional profits. Except for one firm that paid special allowances based on actual performance versus target performance and two firms that considered division results through a special allowance system that included corporate profits and divisional profits, the remaining sixteen paid special allowances based on corporate-wide profitability. The US concept of divisions as profit centers had not been adopted or implemented in any case. As a result, German companies in general followed their own path in taking advantage of opportunities inherent in divisional structures. The possibility of reinforcing profit orientation through compensation systems or methods of generating internal competition, both based on divisional profits was not consciously considered in nearly all the top 100 companies. Some of the reasons for the rejection of such concepts can be seen in that German managers felt that establishing direct links between divisional profits and a general manager's compensation was incompatible with corporate tradition or that the profit base was too volatile (Dyas and Thanheiser 1976, pp. 126–127).

Even in cases where management responsibility was delegated to a general manager who reported to the board of directors, there was considerable opposition to providing the general manager with sufficient freedom and authority, as well as profit responsibility (Dyas and Thanheiser 1976, pp. 118–119). Of course, only a few of the largest companies had delegated division management to lower levels and abolished the strict collegiate management tied to divisional management responsibility at the director level. The characteristics of the divisional structure in Germany and the United States became increasingly similar using these methods. However, there were also many other businesses that retained the authority of division management and the profit responsibility at the managing board level (Dyas and Thanheiser 1976, p. 129).

In terms of the nature of management decentralization, holding companies were adopted at a higher rate in the largest German manufacturing firms (see Sect. 11.2.2.1) than in the United States [The percentage of companies using a holding company as a management structure in the largest US industrial firms (189 in 1949; 207 in 1959; 183 in 1969) was no more than 3.7% in 1949; 1.4% in 1959; 2.4% in 1969; Rumelt 1974, p.65]. The holding company expanded and strengthened its control over subsidiary enterprises as it transitioned from a holding company to a divisional structure. Changes of this type were characteristic of the aggressive contribution of holding companies to subsidiaries' internal issues. Departments responsible for operations tended to have relatively low independence, as seen in transitions from functional structures to divisional structures. A change from a holding company structure to a divisional structure could be observed in the 1960s; however, in several cases, such as Gutehoffnung, these were incomplete as of 1971 (Dyas and Thanheiser 1976, pp. 115–117). The high rate of holding companies was based on the characteristics of large German firms (see Chap. 4), wherein "corporate group structures developed around a single industrial system as its foundation." A holding company style management structure was simply the most compatible in such cases.

11.3.2.2 Management Traditions in German Corporations and Their Influence on the Deployment of Divisional Structures

Examining traditional management in German companies, as seen in all examples of "Americanization" up to that point, one feature can be seen in the new wave of organizational reforms implemented along German traditions of collaborative corporate culture that emphasize technical skills (Wengenroth 1997, p. 162). Similarities in organizational structure to that in the United States undoubtedly reflected the relatively competitive, open business environment that resulted in high technical standards in abundant markets, as well as industrial companies' strategies that leaned toward increasing product and market diversity. However, cultural differences between the United States and Germany played a significant role in organizational differences. Some of these distinctions are as follows. Management authority that was foundational to functions in US enterprises and had widely spread with decentralization contrasted sharply with the hierarchical relations and highly centralized hierarchies that were a cornerstone in German companies in the first few years after the war (Dyas and Thanheiser 1976, p. 128). Management authority in Germany used to be exclusive, closely held by the managers themselves, because authority based on trust in top management was thought to be superior to authority based on function. As a result of the impact of the United States, these ideas tended to decrease and the exclusivity of management status waned (Hartmann 1968, pp. 271–272, 282–283, 286–289, Hartmann 1959, pp. 261, 271–272, 274–277). However, traditions like these, which are deeply embedded in the ideological foundations of management authority, have had a significant impact on the adoption and operation of divisional structures.

Another factor in the influence of traditional culture on German corporate management was the tradition of collegiate management and the board-majority system, which were unheard of in US enterprises. In German enterprises, the position of CEO, with one person having the independent authority to make decisions for the company as a whole, did not exist. The collegiate management tradition (Dyas and Thanheiser 1976, pp. 106–107), with the managing board generally making decisions based on a majority vote, differed greatly from that of the United States in terms of delegation of responsibility as well as the relationship with reporting and management mechanisms (Dyas and Thanheiser 1976, p. 137). For the allocation of assignments and responsibilities, the practice of collegiate management was applied to not only top management but also to the division management level. This form of management was important in the cultural differences that emerged in organizational development (Dyas and Thanheiser 1976, p. 129).

Financial incentives for general managers based on compensation systems linked to division results were extremely rare, reflecting the cultural and value differences between the United States and Germany. US compensation systems could potentially cause a general manager to lose objectivity in business judgment, with the plans negotiated between the division and corporate intensely conflicting with the interests of the division. However, it has been pointed out, in general, that such notions are not based on actual experience with such compensation systems, but rather on cultural values and attitudes that clearly differ between the two nations (Dyas and Thanheiser 1976, pp. 137–138). In such cultural factors, German corporate management traditions such as collegiate management were particularly influential.

Regarding the impact of these cultural and systemic factors, research of S. Hilger's case studies on Henkel, Siemens, and Daimler-Benz based on varying economic, political, cultural, and systemic conditions demonstrates that the adoption of the divisional structure in German companies frequently resulted in conditions that differed from those in the United States (Hilger 2004, p. 213). Although Germany heavily relied on US know-how, when it came to implementing the divisional structure, German firms did not see it as a simple imitation of a process, rather, to some extent, as an adaptation to local circumstances. The unquestioned acceptance of American knowledge had become a thing of the past and was replaced by greater selectivity and confidence inspired by German managers' own ways of thinking and methods (Dyas and Thanheiser 1976, p. 138). Thus, organizational changes were not merely adaptations to strategy but a cultural phenomenon (Dyas and Thanheiser 1976, p. 102). The continued development of new organizations in the late 1960s indicates a generally decreased reliance on US innovations by German management, demonstrating that unquestioning acceptance of US solutions was not yet seen. The emphasis has shifted from seeking US models and knowledge to carefully selecting only those US ideas deemed valuable to Germany from the many offered by research literature and consultants (Dyas and Thanheiser 1976, p. 129).

Our discussions till now have examined the deployment of divisional structures in Japanese and German corporations. One similarity is that a certain percentage of corporations in the largest industries had a mixed organization that differed from a divisional structure. Another is the low level of self-sufficiency resulting from the weak connection between the delegation of authority, results, and compensation. However, regarding various factors in which Germany and Japan differed from the United States, such as delegating authority to divisions, and correlating general manager compensation to division results, there were differences between Germany and Japan reflecting circumstances behind decentralization, and Germany's traditions of collegiate management and the board-majority system.

In addition, the consignment and trust of management rights, such as that seen in the United States, was weaker in Japan than in Germany. Thus, the structure was not the self-concluding type, as seen in the functional divisional structures in Japan. Such effectiveness was necessary for networking and evaluating strategic initiatives, both of which were indispensable for long-term growth.

In considering the compatibility of a new corporate structure based on the expansion of business domains in conjunction with diversification and the benefits of product division restructuring for an organization, we see that a German method of performing tasks was used in conducting such considerations. Specifically, a corporation's actual structure, management mechanisms and systems, and the use thereof reflect a corporate culture. It emphasizes technology rather than a sales and marketing point of view, a culture of collegiate management by a board of directors, the board-majority system tradition, the historical arc of delegation of authority, and a single large corporate group structure founded on a single industry structure.

In the deployment of management organizations such as the divisional structure, there was in fact a method compatible with the German method, and German corporations pursued those elements that could be adapted to German corporate culture. Even after the introduction of the divisional structure, there were still many cases wherein strong influences were exerted by the operational traditions of collegial management and the principle of board-majority system in the board of directors. While inheriting organizational structural principles, German companies sought to develop their own structure that differed from the American one. In the introduction of divisional structures and the formation of a matrix organizational structure, there was a fusion between the principles of the American-style product-based divisional structure and the German-style regional and functional departments.

11.4 Reframing in the Deployment of Divisional Structure in Japan and Germany

Finally, based on the preceding analyses, the deployment of divisional structure is investigated in terms of the factors determining the "reframing" of such American management methods.

Given the fusion of American and Japanese elements, hybridization can be seen in the mix of divisions and divisional headquarters as well as the introduction of an internal capital system in divisional structures.

In examining conditions in Japan with regard to factors that determined the reframing in the Americanization of business management in terms of management values and cultural factors, the weakness of American-style management values based on shareholder-oriented concepts—as seen in the consignment and trust of capital and management power, management values based on collectivism and egalitarianism, and management traditions emphasizing collectivism rather than individualism—influenced the modification of American-type contract-oriented divisional structure. Some management measures based on divisional structure were unsuitable in Japanese corporations due to management values emphasizing long-term enterprise growth and cooperative management values based on a mutual trust relationship.

Institutional factors that influenced the deployment of divisional structures can be found in social structures other than those found in the United States, where the company is regarded as a "contract nexus." Significant roles in developing personnel relationships based on long-term experiences under the lifetime employment system in functional divisional structures also influenced Japanese divisional structure development. The importance of personnel relationships in developing and evaluating strategic initiatives was emphasized in such an organization.

In terms of industrial structure, the rapid and strong development of industries compatible with business field diversification, such as durable consumer goods industries, which are primarily composed of electrical and chemical industries, aided in the deployment of divisional structure. However, the main office's retention of personnel affairs functions was emphasized for employment adjustment through personnel changes between divisions under the labor market's lifetime employment system. Difficulties in decentralizing sales and purchasing functions into divisions and retaining price-setting authority in the headquarters as a result of a small domestic market and heavy reliance on exports also determined Japanese development that different from that of the United States in the deployment of divisional structure. This can be seen in divisional structure developments that were not self-supporting account systems, as well as the deployment of compensation systems for general managers that were linked to divisional performance.

Meanwhile, in Germany, the following mix of American and German factors in production system can be seen in terms of hybridization of American and German elements: (1) Combining of mechanisms based on the principles of German collegiate management under a board of directors and the board-majority system with mechanisms in US-style divisions, (2) combination of principles of US-style product division system and principles of German-style functional and regional departments, and (3) cases involving the combination of prewar German corporate organizations with a subcommittee in the board of directors and US committee organizations.

In terms of important factors that determined the reframing in the Americanization of business management, the influence of management values, tradition, and cultural factors was significant in Germany. Ideological foundation of top management authority that strictly separates the board of directors from the overall labor hierarchy that is below middle management, tradition and practice of collegiate management principles under the board of directors and the board-majority system, and tradition of cooperative corporate culture emphasizing technology determined German-style deployment of divisional structure. Extensive resistance to delegating sufficient authority and responsibility to general managers was also a major impediment to the decentralization of management rights, the implementation of the self-support account system, and the deployment of compensation systems for general managers that were linked to the division's performance.

Concerning the impact of institutional factors, the decentralization system of management and ownership structure of the enterprise had a significant impact on the deployment of divisional structure. Such influence can be seen in the slow pace of delegation of authority and decentralization of management in German enterprises, the slow progress of business management specialization such as strong differentiation between top management and daily management, and the suppressive effects of diversification through characteristics of ownership, particularly family ownership in German corporations and its influence on divisional structure implementation. The institutional characteristics of large German corporations in large corporate group structures as a basis for industrial structures determined the relatively high proportion of holding company structures among the largest corporations.

In terms of the effects of German capitalism, the influence of industrial structure characterized by the high proportion of producer goods industries on the industrial sector composition of the largest corporations was seen in the adoption rate of each type of organizational structure. This is closely related to the relatively low rate of divisional structure introduction when compared with the largest US enterprises.

The deployment of divisional structure was also influenced by market structure. Market characteristics of quality and functionality, as well as their reflection of a collaborative corporate culture that emphasized technology, had an effect on German enterprise management values, determining German-style adaptation in the deployment of divisional structure. The impact of German corporations' heavy reliance on exports to Europe can be seen in cases of European operations in product divisions and the separation of operations in other regions in regional departments.

Regarding the conditions surrounding the introduction of divisional structure in Japan and Germany during the postwar boom years as well as "reframing" and the factors defining, Table 11.1 shows an inline comparison of the respective countries, based on the discussion so far in this chapter.

Indeed, in both Japan and Germany, diversification caused significant changes in the organizational structure. However, in considering the compatibility of a new corporate structure based on the expansion of business domains in conjunction with diversification and the benefits of product division restructuring for an organization, we see that a German or Japanese method of performing tasks was used in conducting such considerations. Specifically, a corporation's actual structure, management mechanisms and systems, and the use thereof reflect a corporate culture. It emphasizes technology rather than the sales and marketing point of view, a culture of collegiate management by a board of directors, the board-majority system tradition, the historical arc of delegation of authority, and a single large corporate group structure founded on a single industry structure.

There was, in fact, a method compatible with the Japanese or German methods in the deployment of management organizations such as the divisional structure, and corporations in both countries pursued those elements that could be adapted to each nation's corporate culture. Even after the introduction of the divisional structure, there were still many cases wherein strong influences were exerted by the operational traditions of collegial management and the principle of board-majority system in the board of directors. While inheriting organizational structural principles, Japanese and German companies sought to develop their own structure that differed from the American one. Thus, organizational reform such as seen in the deployment of a divisional structure was a cultural phenomenon.

Table 11.1 Comparison of conditions surrounding the introduction of divisional structure in Japan and Germany

Deployment and factors affecting them	Management methods	
	Divisional structure	
	Japanese management methods	German management methods
Overall conditions in the deployment of american management methods	• Expanding deployment of principles for modifying divisional structures • High adoption rate of divisional structures in large enterprises compared with other organizational structures • High adoption rate of divisional structures in enterprises where diversification progressed • Low adoption rate and delay in adoption of divisional structures compared with the United States and United Kingdom • Existence of mixed forms of divisional structures and the organizational structure • Cases of adoption of the divisional headquarters system • Re-concentration in companies that once adopted divisional structures (return to centralized functional structures)	• Expansion of deployment of principles for modifying divisional structures • Low rate of divisional structure adoption compared to the United States and United Kingdom • Vast differences in divisional structure deployment among large corporations and small- or medium-sized businesses • High proportion of holding company structures in the largest companies compared with that in the United States

(continued)

Table 11.1 (continued)

Deployment and factors affecting them	Management methods	
	Divisional structure	
	Japanese management methods	German management methods
Deployment characteristics of american management methods	• Cases of adoption of divisional structures in the form of imitation as a fashion • Cases of "pseudo" divisions that did not have necessary autonomous functions • Characteristics of centralization led by the main office in divisional structures (big headquarters) • Cases of functional divisional structures • Mixed divisional and functional structures • Divisional structure alternatives through the development of business fields by establishing other companies, such as subsidiary companies and affiliated companies	• Existence of matrix organizations in divisions and regional and functional departments • Amalgamations of divisional and functional structures • Deployments dependent on US consulting firms and corporations • Relatively less impact of consulting firms in Germany than in the United States and United Kingdom • Specific motives for changing the structure from a holding company to a divisional structure (more efficient strategies and better coordination in formerly independent subsidiaries

(continued)

Table 11.1 (continued)

Deployment and factors affecting them	Management methods	
	Divisional structure	
	Japanese management methods	German management methods
Modifications in American management methods	• Cases of divisional structure deployments that were not self-support account systems • Deployment of compensation systems for general managers not linked to divisional performance • Adoption of easier evaluation standards of division than those in the United States • Cases that adopted the residual income method or the rate of profit to net sales as a standard of evaluating performance of division • Insufficient relations between authorities and responsibilities due to lack of infrastructure concerning management control in divisional structures, such as seen in contract with the consignment and trust of management power between top management and general managers	• Operations based on principles of collegiate management under a board of directors and a board-majority system • Systems of collegiate management within divisions • Cases of divisional structure deployments that were not self-support account systems • The deployment of compensation systems for general managers not linked to the division's performance • Points where the controlling function was responsible at the operational level as well as in headquarters

(continued)

Table 11.1 (continued)

Deployment and factors affecting them	Management methods	
	Divisional structure	
	Japanese management methods	German management methods
Amalgamation of American and Japanese elements	• Mixture of division and divisional headquarters • Introduction of internal capital system in divisional structure	• Combining mechanisms based on the principles of German collegiate management under a board of directors and the board-majority system with mechanisms in US-style divisions • Combining of principles of US-style product division systems and principles of German-style functional and regional departments • Cases on combinations of prewar German corporate organizations with a sub-committee in the board of directors and US committee organizations

(continued)

Table 11.1 (continued)

Deployment and factors affecting them		Management methods	
		Divisional structure	
		Japanese management methods	German management methods
Factors of modification of American management method	Influence of traditions, cultural factors, and management values	• Weakness of American-style management values based on the shareholder-oriented concepts, such as seen in the consignment and trust of capital and management power • Management values based on collectivism and equalitarianism • Management traditions emphasizing collectivism rather than individualism • Management values emphasizing long-term growth of company • Cooperative management values based on a relationship of mutual trust	• Ideological foundation of top management authority that strictly divides the board of directors from the overall labor hierarchy that is below middle management • The tradition and practice of collegiate management principles under the board of directors and the board-majority system • Executive resistance to providing sufficient authority and responsibility toward general managers • The tradition of cooperative corporate culture emphasizing technology

(continued)

Table 11.1 (continued)

Deployment and factors affecting them		Management methods	
		Divisional structure	
		Japanese management methods	German management methods
	Influence of institutional factors	• Social structures different from those in the United States where enterprise is regarded as a "nexus of contract" • Significant roles in establishing personnel relationships based on long-term experiences under the lifetime employment system in the functional divisional structures (roles of personnel relationships in creating and evaluating strategic initiatives)	• German corporations' slow pace of delegation of authority and decentralization of management • Slow pace of business management specialization (strong differentiation between top and daily management) • Diversification's suppressive effects through characteristics of ownership (particularly family ownership) in German corporations and their influence on divisional structure implementations • Large German corporations' institutional characteristics in large corporate group structures as a basis for industrial structures and the influence of the proportion of holding company structures among the largest corporation

(continued)

Table 11.1 (continued)

Deployment and factors affecting them		Management methods	
		Divisional structure	
		Japanese management methods	German management methods
	Influencing factors of the productive forces	–	–
	Influence of industrial structure factors	• Rapid and strong development of industries compatible with diversification of business fields (consumer goods industries, such as electrical and chemical industries)	• Influence of a high proportion of producer goods industries on the largest corporations' industrial sector composition (and its influence on adoption of each type of organizational structure)
	Influence of market structure factors	• Retention of personnel affairs functions by the main office for employment adjustment through personnel changes between divisions under the labor market based on lifetime employment system • Difficulties in decentralization of sales and purchase functions into division and retention of rights of price determination in the headquarters due to narrow domestic market and heavy dependence on exports	• Market characteristics of quality and functionality and their reflection of the collaborative corporate culture that emphasized technology • Great reliance on exports to Europe (cases of European operations in product divisions and the separation of other regions' operations in regional departments)

Source This table was compiled by the author, based on discussions in this chapter

References

Abelshauser W (2002) Die BASF seit der Neugründung von 1952. In Abelshauser W (ed) Die BASF: Eine Unternehemensgeschichte. C. H. Beck, München, pp 359–637, 688–713
AEG (1963) Bericht über das Geschäftsjahr vom 1. Oktober 1962 bis 30. September 1963. AEG, Berlin
AEG-Telefunken AG (1967) Bericht über das Geschäftsjahr 1967. AEG-Telefunken AG, Berlin
AEG-Telefunken AG (1969) Bericht über das Geschäftsjahr 1969. AEG-Telefunken AG, Berlin
Aglietta M (1979) A theory of capitalist regulation. The US experience. NLB, London
Aoki S (1960) Jigyobusei no mondaiten (Problems of divisional structure). In: Kigyo kaikei (Accounting) 12(6):84–88
Baba H (1975) Senryaku keiei no sosiki to unei (Organization and operation of strategic management). In: Takamiya S (supvr), Nihon seisansei honbu soshiki kenkyukai (ed) Kigyo senryaku to keiei soshiki (Corporate strategy and management organization). Nihon seisansei honbu, Tokyo, pp 280–296
Berghahn V (1985) Unternehmer und Politik in der Bundesrepublik. Suhrkamp, Frankfurt am Main
Chandler AD Jr (1962) Strategy and structure: chapters in the history of the industrial enterprise. MIT, Cambridge
Chandler AD Jr (1977) The visible hand: managerial revolution in American business. Harvard University Press, Cambridge
Chandler AD Jr (1990) Scale and scope: the dynamics of industrial capitalism. Harvard University Press, Berkeley
Choki T (1993) Sengo hattenki no nihon kigyo no keiei genri (Management principles of Japanese enterprises in the post boom years). In: Gendai keieigaku kenkyukai (ed) Gendai keieigaku no kihon kadai (Fundamental problems of modern business administration study). Bunshindo, Tokyo, pp 37–56
Der Lichtbogen (1970) Neue Organisation bei Hüls. In: Der Lichtbogen 22(160):26–27
Der Volkswirt (1963) Reorganisation bei wachsender Rentabilitat. Relativ geringe Exportquote—Bau eines Atomkraftwerkes. In: Der Volkswirt 17(1):492–495
Der Volkswirt (1964) AEG. Ein Konzern wird neu organisiert. Geschäftsjahr umgestellt—Verlustauftrage bei Schwermaschinen. In: Der Volkswirt 18(25):1240–1243
Der Volkswirt (1969) Wachablösung an der Ruhr. Bewährte Sechziger und nüchterne Vierziger. In: Der Volkswirt 24(45):70–72
Dyas GP, Thanheiser HT (1976) The emerging European enterprise. Strategy and structure in French and German industry. Macmillan, London
Farbwerke Hoechst AG (1969) Geschäftsbericht 1969. Farbwerke Hoechst AG, Frankfurt am Main
Feldenkirchen W (2004) The Americanization of the German electrical industry after 1945. Siemens as a case study. In: Kudo A, Kipping M, Schroteret HG (eds) German and Japanese business in the boom years. Transforming American management and technology models. Routledge, London, pp 116–137
Feldenkirchen W, Hilger S (2001) Menschen und Marken. 125 Jahre Henkel 1876–2001. Stürtz, Düsseldorf
Fujiyoshi S (1962) Jigyobusei no jittai to sono doko (The present condition of divisional structure and its trend). In: Seisansei (Productivity) 182: 38–44
Fushimi T (1997) Jigyobusei manejimento · kontororu ni okeru "nihongata" no kenkyu (Study of "Japanese type" of management and control in the divisional structure). In: Nihon kanri kaikei gakkaishi (J Jpn Assoc Manag Account) 5(1):3–14
Fushimi T, Watabnabe Y (1995) Kanpani sei manejimento · kontororu to nihongata jigyobusei (Management and control in the company-system and Japanese-type divisional structure). In: Sangyo keiri (Financ Cost Account) 54(4):2–11
Fushimi T, Yokota E (1993) Jigyobusei manejimento · kontororu ni okeru nihonteki tokushitsu (Japanese characteristics of divisional management and control). In: Nihon kanri kaikei gakkaishi (J Jpn Assoc Manag Account) 2(2):25–45

Gabele E (1981) Die Einführung von Geschäftsbereichsorganisation. Mohr, Tubingen

Gohara H (1968) Nihon no keiei soshiki (Japanese management organization). Toyo keizai shinposha, Tokyo

Hara K (1960) Jigyobusei heno taido (Attitude to divisional structure). In: Sangyo keiri (Financ Cost Account) 20(4):90–95

Harasawa Y (1981) Sengo ni okeru toppu · manejimento to jigyobusei (Top management and divisional structure after World War II). In: Keizaigaku (Annual report of the Economic Society, Tohoku University), vol 42, no 4, pp 127–139

Harasawa Y (1987) Nihonteki jigyobusei no seiritsu katei (Formation process of the Japanese divisional structure). In: Keizaigaku (Annual report of the Economic Society, Tohoku University): 48(6): 17–33

Harrmann A (1982) Steigert ein Wechsel der Strukturorganisation die Unternehmenseffektivitat? In: REFA-Nachrichten 35(4):202–204

Hartmann H (1959) Authority and organization in German management. Princeton University Press, Princeton

Hartmann H (1968) Der deutsche Unternehmer: Autorität und Organisation. Europäische Verlagsasnstalt, Frankfurt am Main

Hautsch G (1979) Das Imperium AEG-Telefunken: Ein multinationaler Konzern. Verlag Marxistische Blätter, Frankfurt am Main

Henkel GmbH (1968) Geschäftsbericht 1968. Henkel GmbH, Düsseldorf

Henkel GmbH (1969) Geschäftsbericht 1969. Henkel GmbH, Düsseldorf

Hiki F (1997) Nihon kigyo ni okeru jigyobusei kaikei no kenkyu (1) (Study of accounting in divisional structure in Japanese enterprise, 1) In: Wako keizai (The bulletin of the faculty of economics and business) 29(2 · 3):67–84

Hilger S (2004) „Amerikanisierung" deutscher Unternehmen. Wettbewerbsstrategien und Unternehmenspolitik bei Henkel, Siemens und Daimler-Benz (1945/49-1975). Franz Steiner Verlag, Stuttgart

Hiramoto A (2000) Matsushita no rajio jigyo sinshutsu to jigyobusei no keisei (Entry into radio business and building of divisional structure in Matsushita Electric Industrial Co. Ltd.). In: Keieishigaku (Jpn Bus History Rev) 35(2):22–45

Hitachi zosen kabushikigaisha (ed) (2012) Hitachi zosen hyakusanjunenshi 1881–2011 (130-year history of Hitachi Zosen Corporation 1881–2011). Hitachi zosen kabushikigaisha, Osaka

Imanishi S (1988) Jigyobusei no kaimei (Clarifying divisional structure). Manejimentosha, Tokyo

Ishii J, Okumura A, Kagon T et al (1996) Shinban keiei senryaku ron (Business strategy), New edn. Yuhikaku, Tokyo

Ishikawajima harima jukogyo kabushikigaisha somu sokatsubu shashi hensan tanto (ed) (1992) Isikawajima harima jukogyo Shashi (History of Ishikawajima-Harima Heavy Industries Co. Ltd.). Isikawajima harima jukogyo kabushikigaisha, Tokyo

Kabushikigaisha Kobe seikosyo hachijunenshi hensan iinkai (ed) (1986) Kobe seiko hachujunen (80-year history of Kobe Steel Ltd.). Kabushikigaisha Kobe seikosho, Kobe

Kabushikigaisha Kobe seikosho somubu, Kyodo PR kabushikigaisha (ed) (1974) Kobe seiko nanajunen: Shiryo hen (70-year of Kobe Steel Ltd. Data edition). Kabushikigaisha Kobe seikosho, Kobe

Kabushikigaisha Kubota (1990) Kubota hyakunen (100 years of Kubota Tekko). Kabushikigaisha Kubota, Osaka

Kagono T (1978) Jigyobusei to shokunosei (Divisional structure and functional structure). In: Kokumin keizai zasshi (J Econ Bus Adm) 137(6):68–93

Kagono T (1980) Keiei soshiki no kankyo tekio (Adaptation of management organization to circumstance). Hakuto shobo, Tokyo

Kagono T (1992a) Nihon no jigyobusei, 1 (Japanese divisional structure, 1). In: Nihon keizai shinbun (Japanese economic newspaper), 11.7.1992

Kagono T (1992b) Nihon no jigyobusei, 2 (Japanese divisional structure, 2). In: Nihon keizai shinbun (Japanese economic newspaper), 13.7.1992

Kagono T (1992c) Nihon no jigyobusei, 5 (Japanese divisional structure, 5). In: Nihon keizai shinbun (Japanese economic newspaper), 16.7.1992
Kagono T (1992d) Nihon no jigyobusei, 6 (Japanese divisional structure, 6). In: Nihon keizai shinbun (Japanese economic newspaper), 17.7.1992
Kagono T (1993) Shokunobetsu jigyobusei to naibu shijo (Functional divisional structure and internal market). In: Kokumin keizai zasshi (J Econ Bus Adm) 167(2):35–52
Kagono T, Nonaka I, Sakakibara K et al (1983) Nichibei kigyo no keiei hikaku (Comparison of management in Japan and the United States). Nihon keizai shinbunsha, Tokyo
Kansai seisansei honbu (1976) Keiei soshiki no shindoko (New trend of management organization). Kansai seisansei honbu, Osaka
Kansai seisansei honbu (1981) Keiei senryaku to keiei soshiki no shindoko (New trend of business strategy and management organization). Kansai seisansei honbu, Osaka
Kansai seisansei honbu (1986) Keiei no shintenkai (New development of management). Kansai seisansei honbu, Osaka
Kawasaki jukogyo kabushikigaisha hyakunenshi hensan iinkai (ed) (1997a) Yume wo katachi ni. Kawasaki jukogyo kabushikigaisha hyakunenshi 1896–1996 (Realization of dreams. 100-year history of Kawasaki Heavy Industries, Ltd. 1896–1996). Kawasaki jukogyo kabushikigaisha, Kobe
Kawasaki jukogyo kabushikigaisha hyakunenshi hensan iinkai (ed) (1997b) Yume wo katachi ni. Kawasaki jukogyo kabushikigaisha hyakunenshi 1896–1996 (Shiryo · nenpyo) [Realization of dreams. 100-year history of Kawasaki Heavy Industries, Ltd. 1896–1996 (Data and chronological table)]. Kawasaki jukogyo kabushikigaisha, Kobe
Kawasaki jukogyo kabushikigaisha kiko jigyobu sanjunenshi hensan iinkai (ed) (1997c) Kiko jigyobu sanjunen no ayumi (History of machinery division). Kawasaki jukogyo kabushikigaisha kiko jigyobu, Kobe
Keiei kenkyusho kenkyubu (1967) Denki kikai seizo kigyo no soshiki kenkyu (Organization study of electric machine producing enterprises). In: Sosiki kagaku (Organ Sci) 1(1):78–88
Keizai doyukai (1980) 1980 nendai no kigyo keiei (Business administration in the 1980s). Keizai doyukai, Tokyo
Kigyo soshiki kenkyukai (ed) (1962) Ote kigyo no soshiki kenkyu (Organization study of major enterprises). Nikkan denki janarusha, Tokyo
Kimura I (1999) Gurupu kigyo ni okeru keiei soshiki to kanri kaikei jyoho (Management accounting information of group company organizations). In: Nihon kanri kaikei gakkaishi (J Jpn Assoc Manag Account) 7(1 · 2):137–158
Kirsch W, Esser W-M, Gabele E (1999) Das Management des geplanten Wandels von Organisation. Poeschel, Stuttgart
Kleinschmidt C (2002) Der produktive Blick. Wahrnehmung amerikanischer und japanischer Management- und Produktionsmethoden durch deutsche Unternehmer 1950–1985. Akademie Verlag, Berlin
Kobe seikosho soritsu hyakushunen kinen jigyo jikkko iinkai, Koberuko bijinesu sapoto kabushiki gaisha (eds) (2006) Kobe seiko hyakunen 1905–2005 (100 years of Kobe Steel Ltd. 1905–2005). Kabushikigaisha kobe seikosho, Kobe
Koch E (1970) Offene Tore für das schöpferische Potential. Neuorganisaton der BASF—Die WELT sprach mit Vorstandsvorsitzen dem Bernhard Timm. In: *Die Welt* 193
Kono T (1985) Honsha sosiki no kibo to kino ni tsuite no jittai chosa. Soshiki kagaku (An investigation of scale and functions of head office organization). In: Sosiki kagaku (Organ Sci) 19(3):15–24
Kroos HE, Gilbert C (1972) American business history. Prentice-Hall, Englewood Cliffs
Kubota tekko kabushikigaisha (ed) (1970) Kubota tekko hachijunen no Ayumi (80 years of Kubota Tekko corporation). Kubota tekko kabushikigaisha, Osaka
Kubota tekkko kabushikigaisha (1980) Kubota tekkko saikin junen no Ayumi (The last ten years of Kubota Tekko Corporation). Kubota tekko kabushikigaisha, Osaka

Kudo A, Kipping M, Schröter HG (2004) Americanization. Historical and conceptual issues. In: Kudo A, Kipping M, Schröter HG (eds) German and Japanese business in the boom years. Transforming American management and technology models. Routledge, London, pp 1–29
Lorentz B, Erker P (2003) Chemie und Politik. Die Geschichte der Chemischen Werke Hüls 1938–1979: Eine Studie zum Problem der Corporate Governance. C. H. Beck, München
Lüdtke A, Marβolek I, Saldern AV (1997) Amerikanisierung: Traum und Alptraum im Deutschland des 20.Jahrhunderts. In: Jaraush K, Siegrist H (eds) Amerikanisierng und Sowjetisierung in Deutschland 1945–1970. Campus, Frankfurt am Main, pp 7–33
Matsushita denki sangyo kabushikigaisha sanjugonenshi henshu iinkai (ed) (1953) Matsushita denki sangyo kabushikigaisha sogyo sanjugonenshi (35-year history of Matsushita Electric Industrial Co., Ltd.). Matsushita denki sangyo kabushikigaisha sanjugonenshi henshu iinkai, Osaka
Matsushita denki sangyo kabushikigaisha sanjugonenshi henshu iinkai (ed) (1955) Matsushita denki sangyo kabushikigaisha sogyo sanjugonenshi: Tsuiho (35 years history of Matsushita Electric Industrial Co., Ltd. Supplement). Matsushita denki sangyo kabushikigaisha sanjugonenshi henshu iinkai, Osaka
Matsushita denki sangyo kabushikigaisha shashisitsu (1978) Shashi Matsushita denki. Gekido no junen: Showa 43 nen-52 nen (Company history of Matsushita Electric Industrial Co. Ltd.: 1968–1977). Matsushita denki sangyo kabushikigaisha shashisitsu, Kadoma
Matsushita denki sangyo kabushikigaisha sogyo gojushunen kinen jyunbi iinkai (ed) (1968) Matsushita denki gojunen no ryakushi (50-year brief history of Matsushita Electric Industrial Co. Ltd.). Matsushita denki sangyo kabushikigaisha sogyo gojushunen kinen jyunbi iinkai, Osaka
Mitsubishi denki kabushikigaisha shashi hensansitsu (ed) (1982) Mitsubishi Denkishi (History of Mitsubishi Electric Corporation). Mitsubishi denki kabushikigaish, Tokyo
Mitsubishi jukogyo kabushikigaisha shashi hensan iinkai (ed) (1990) Umi ni riku ni soshite uchu he (To sea, land, and the universe). Mitsubishi jukogyo kabushikigaisha, Tokyo
Miura K (2010) Jigyobusei ni yoru rieki kanri sairon (Profit management by divisional structure. A reexamination). In: Shokei ronso (Ann Rev Econ Bus Law) 61:27–54
Mizota S (1997) Zosen jukikai sangyo no kigyo shisutemu (Corporate system in the shipbuilding and heavy machinery industry), 2nd edn. Moriyama shoten, Tokyo
Motizuki N (2011) Nichibei ni okeru jigyobusei sosiki to gyoseki hyoka sihyo no soui (Differences of divisional structure and indicators for performance evaluation in Japan and the US). In: Adominisutoreshon (Administration) 18(1 ・2):123–139
Nakahashi K (1981) Jigyobusei kigyo ni okeru soshiki sekkei (Organization design in company with divisonal structure). In: Shogaku tokyu (Econ Rev) 31(3 ・4):41–79
Nishikawa K (1996) Matsushita denki no jigyobusei (Divisional structure in Matsushita Electric Industry Co. Ltd.). In: Tezukayama keizaigaku (Tezukayama economic papers), vol 5, pp 75–85
Ogawa K (1969) Shanai sihonkin seido donyu no igi (Significance of introducing the internal capital system). In: Sangyo keiri (Financ Cost Account) 29(11):29–34
Omori H (2007) Jigyobusei no soshikishi (Organizational history of divisional structure). In: Ronso Matsushita konosuke (J Matsushita Kōnosuke Stud) 8:36–59
Omori K (1975) Kigyo senryaku ni motozuku soshiki Kaihatsu (Organizational development based on corporate strategy). In: Takamiya S (supvr), Nihon seisansei honbu soshiki kenkyukai (ed) Kigyo senryaku to keiei soshiki (Corporate strategy and management organization). Nihon seisansei honbu, Tokyo, pp 164–189
Ono T (1979) Nihon kigyo no soshiki senryaku (Organizational strategy of Japanese enterprises). Manejimentosha, Tokyo
Ozawa K (1971) Nihon no denki kikai sangyo ni okeru keiei senryaku to soshiki (Busness strategy and organization in Japanese electric machine producing companies). In: Nigata daigaku keizai ronshu (J Econ Niigata Univ) 9: 87–103
Reece JS, Cool WR (1978) Measuring investment center performance. In: Harvard business review 56(3):28–46, 174
REFA-Nachrichten (1967) Wo liegen noch Rationalisierungsmöglichkeiten im Betrieb? In: REFA-Nachrichten 20(6):259–263

Reindl R (2001) Wachstum und Wettbewerb in den Wirtschafyswunderjahren. Die elektorotechnische Industrie in der Bundesrepublik Deutschland und in Groβbritannien 1945–1967. Ferdinand Schöningh, Paderborn

Rumelt RP (1974) Strategy, structure and economic performance. University Press, Boston, Harvard

Sakakibara K (1980) Moho no soshiki ron (*Imitative organizational theory*). In: Soshiki kagaku (Organ Sci) 14(2):62–68

Sasaki T (1975) Canon · reporto ni kansuru komento (Comment on the Canon report). In: Takamiya S (supvr), Nihon seisansei honbu soshiki kenkyukai (ed) Kigyo senryaku to keiei soshiki (Corporate strategy and management organization). Nihon seisansei honbu, Tokyo, pp 190–195

Schröter HG (2005) Americanization of the European economy. A compact survey of American economic influence in Europe since the 1880s. Springer, Dordrecht

Selinger K (1977) Die Organisation der BASF-Gruppe. In: Zeitschrift für Organisation 46(1):17–22

Shadan hojin keizia doyukai topu · manejimento chosakai (1964) Keiei rinen to kigyo katsudo (Management philosophy and corporate activity). Keizai doyukai, Tokyo

Shimotani M (1998) Matsushita gurupu no rekishi to kozo (History and structure of the Matsushita corporate group). Yuhikaku, Tokyo

Siegrist H (1980) Deutscher Groβunternehmen vom späten 19. Jahrhundert bis zur Weimarer Republik. In: Geschichte und Gesellschaft 6(1):60–102

Siemens AG (1969) Bericht über das Geschäftsjahr vom 1. Oktober 1968 bis 30. September 1969. Siemens AG, München

Siemens-Mitteilungen (1969) Die neue Organisation der Siemens AG ab 1. Oktober 1969. In: Siemens-Mitteilungen 44(9):9–12

Strunk P (2000) Die AEG. Aufstieg und Niedergang einer Industrielegende, 2nd edn. Nicolai, Berlin

Suzuki T (1961) Jigyobusei no honsitsu (Essence of divisional structure). In: Keizai semina (Econ Semin) 52:59–63

Tacke G (1977) Ein Beitrag zur Geschichte der Siemens AG. Gerd Tacke, München

Takamiya S, Fujita F, Hosono Y et al (1962) Jigyobusei no saikento (Re-consideration of divisional structure). In: Bijinesu (Business) 6(5):12–19

Tani T (1987) Jigyobu gyoseki no sokutei to kanri (Measurement and management of divisional performance). Zeimu keiri kyokai, Tokyo

Tore kabushikigaisha shashi hensan iinkai (ed) (1977) Tore gojunenshi 1926–1976 (50-year history of Tore 1926–1976). Tore kabushikigaisha, Tokyo

Torii H (2007) Nihon ni okeru jigyobusei kaikei no hatten ni kansuru ichi kosatsu (A study of development of divisional accounting in Japan). In: Keizai kenkyu (The papers and proceedings of economics), vol 138, pp 1–11

Tsunoda R (1993) Nihon no kigyo no senryaku to soshiki (Strategy and organization of Japanese enterprises). In: Kagono T, Tsunoda R, Yamada K et al (eds) Risutorakutyaringu to soshiki bunka (Restructuring and organizational culture). Hakuto shobo, Tokyo, pp 5–30

Tsusho sangyosho kigyokyoku (ed) (1969) Kokusaika jidai ni okeru wagakuni kigyo keiei no kodoka ni tsuite (Sophisicated mangemet of Japanese companies in the era of internationlization). Tsusho sangyosho kigyokyoku, Tokyo

Urabe K (1960) Jigyobusei to kindai keiei (Divisional structure and modern management). Daiyamondosha, Tokyo

Urabe K (1969) Jigyobuse to rieki kanri (Divisional structure and profit management). Hakuto shobo, Tokyo

Watanabe Y (1960) Jigyobusei heno tenkan to mondaiten ni tsuite (Development of divisional structure and problems). In: Sangyo keiri (Financ Cost Account) 20(4):96–100

Wengenroth U (1997) Germany: competition abroad—cooperation at home, 1870–1990. In: Chandler AD Jr, Amatori F, Hikino T (eds) Big business and the wealth of nations. Cambridge University Press, Cambridge, pp 139–175

Winnacker K (1972) Nie den Mut verlieren. Erinnerungen an Schicksalsjahr der deutschen Chemie. Econ Verlag, Düsseldorf

Yamada I (1961) Jigyobusei no genjyo to mondaiten (The present condition and problems of divisional structure). In: Keizaikei (Quartery journal of the Economic Research Institute of Kanto Gakuin UniversityEconomics), vol 50, pp 42–68
Yamamoto K (1993) Gendai Doitsu no chiiki Keizai (Modern German regional economy). Hosei daigaku shuppankai, Tokyo
Yamazaki T (1997) Doitsu kigyo kanrishi kenkyu (History of business management in Germany). Moriyama syoten Tokyo
Yamazaki T (2001) Vaimaruki Doitsu gorika undo no tenkai (Rationalization movement in Germay durng the Weimar era). Moriyama shoten, Tokyo
Yamazaki T (2015) Doitsu senzenki keieishi kenkyu (German business history until the end of World War II). Moriyama shoten, Tokyo
Yoshihara H, Sakuma A, Itamai H et al (1981) Nihon kigyo no takakuka senryaku (Diversification strategy in Japanese enterprise). Nihon keizai shinbunsha, Tokyo
Yoshikawa T (1996) Jigyobusei (Divisional structure). In: Kaikeigaku Kenkyu (Study Account) 8:123–130
Zaidan hojin nihon keieishi kenkyusho (ed) (2002) Asahi kasei hachijunenshi (80-year history of Asahi Kasei Corporation). Asahi kasei kabushikigaisha, Tokyo
Zeitschrift für Organisation (1970a) Die Neuorganisation des Hauses Siemens. In: Zeitschrift für Organisation 39(8):337–342
Zeitschrift für Organisation (1970b) Die organisatorische Neuordnung der Henkel-Gruppe "Sparten, Funktionen und Regionen." In: Zeitschrift für Organisation 39(5):196–198
Zeitschrift für Organisation (1970c) Interview der Z für O zur Reorganisation der Henkel-Gruppe. In: Zeitschrift für Organisation 39(5):199–200

Chapter 12
"Reframing" in the Americanization Process and Japanese-Style Management and German-Style Management from the Postwar Period to the Early 1970s

Abstract Based on the previous chapters' topics in Part III, this chapter recaptures the changes in business management in Japan and Germany during economic growth up to the early 1970s by applying the framework "reframing" depicted in Chap. 1. Problems stemming from the Japanese and German approaches to conforming to American methods are explored as influenced by cultural and traditional factors in business management and institutional factors. Moreover, influences of the structural characteristics of Japanese and German capitalism, such as the structures of productive forces, industrial structure, and market structure, are examined. This chapter also elucidates the development of Japanese-style business management and German-style business management in relation to capitalism's reproduction (accumulation) structure in each country.

Keywords Americanization · Hybridization · Industrial structure · Management value · Market structure · Reframing

Following the preceding chapters in Part III, this chapter reevaluates changes in Japan and Germany's business management in the postwar period through the early 1970s. It also clarifies how Japanese business management style and its particular characteristics were created, conforming to Asian circumstances, and how German-style business management and its peculiar characteristics were determined, conforming to European conditions while still bearing on a country-specific management style during the deployment of American management methods. This chapter does so by using the original framework, that is, "reframing of Americanization," as described in Chap. 1.

This chapter analyzes the development of business management by the introduction of the American management method from the perspective of the author's original analytical framework, that is, "reframing." This issue was explained in Chap. 1. "Reframing" is defined by the following five factors: (1) business management traditions and cultural factors such as management values, (2) institutional factors, (3) structure of productive forces, (4) industrial structure, and (5) market structure.

T. Yamazaki, *Japanese and German Enterprises*,
https://doi.org/10.1007/978-981-97-4880-8_12

Factors (3), (4), and (5) are structural characteristics of Japanese and German capitalism. This chapter discusses the problems stemming from the conformity of the Japanese and German methods to the American model as affected by cultural and traditional factors in business management as well as institutional factors and its relation to the structural characteristics of Japanese and German capitalism.[1]

In Sect. 12.1, Japanese- and German-Style Adaptations in the "Americanization" of business management during the postwar boom years are examined. Sections 12.2 and 12.3 consider the "reframing" in the Americanization process in both nations and how Japanese-style or German-style management was built in such a process.

12.1 Japanese- and German-Style Adaptations in the "Americanization" of Business Management

First, in considering the Japanese-style and German-style adaptations of Americanization in terms of the post-WWII introduction of American technology and management methods, business management traditions, the management value in Japanese and German capitalism, and cultural and institutional factors exerted relatively little influence on the introduction of technology. From a comprehensive perspective, the introduction of American technology, for which intense endeavors were made, was considered an effective method to develop productive forces. In contrast, various factors related to "reframing" affected the introduction of American management methods, which were unavoidable and thus strongly expressed. Additionally, differences were observed among industries and enterprises and in each field and method.

From the viewpoint of this book, improving productivity at the time through introducing the American management method, the measures and elements which were directly concerned with improving "efficiency" (economic efficiency) were related to the development of productive forces; therefore, these principles were relatively, proactively, and widely introduced. These can be seen in (a) the basic principles of industrial engineering, such as production management and labor management; (b) Ford's assembly line system of mass production; (c) the basics of marketing philosophy and measures; and (d) organizational principles compatible with enterprises' diversified businesses and divisional structures.

However, numerous aspects of American-style management were not applied to the situations in Japan and Germany at the time. These included productive forces and conditional and environmental factors supporting market adaptation measures, especially aspects with American characteristics, such as the management style, management culture/tradition, and the culture and relationships shared among labor and management. Therefore, strong resistance and opposition occurred in many cases,

---

[1] The first content analysis related to Germany in this chapter is Chap. 10 of the author's book "*German Business Management: A Japanese Perspective on Regional Development Factors*," which was published by Springer in 2013.

which hindered the introduction of these aspects. They can only be introduced by modifying and adapting them to local conditions in the process. These problems were most outstanding in the areas of management education and human relations, which together were the most emphasized in America to transfer to the European nations under the US-led productivity movement.

Moreover, in many cases, the Japanese or German management method was pursued, concerning productive factors and market adaptation measures, even if principles and mechanisms for improving efficiency were introduced. In particular, because of the influence of German corporate traditions and management values and various systemic factors within enterprises, labor relations, and market characteristics, many German firms sought the German-style adaptation. Such cases were observed in marketing and public relations (PR) and the introduction of divisional structure and the Ford System. Similar conditions can be observed in Japan, as well.

The spread of the consumer society to technical and cultural adaptation, or more accurately the American impact in terms of adopting American management and production methods within German companies were generally contained in the concept of "Americanization"; Kleinschmidt notes that the expressions "America-Concentrated" or "American Model" are better reflected in the concept.

America represents technological progress, rationalization, and modernization, with one of the most successful economic models (Kleinschmidt 2004b, p. 75). Additionally, Feldenkirchen emphasizes that to keep up with international development in technology, German enterprises relied on relationships with their international partners, particularly technologically leading American companies. In contrast, in areas such as human resources, marketing and sales, and organization, the American methods were not directly incorporated; rather, the American model served as a useful guide for developing enterprise strategies within these fields (Feldenkirchen 2004, p. 131).

This trend can be also observed in the other European nations. For instance, in their research, Bjarnar and Kipping note that the fundamental results of Americanization were not the consummate adoption of the American management model, but rather a selective and partial adaptation. These authors note both the effectiveness and limitations of the process (Bjarnar and Kipping 1998, p. 14), and they specified that Europeans rarely imitate the American model; they do not perceive the model as good or excellent; rather, they select those aspects they feel are appropriate for the surroundings in their countries (Schröter 2005, p. 59). Zeitlin's research stresses the active altering of the American Model. Here Zeitlin points out the selective adaptation of American technology and management that was tailored to the local environment. He also observed creative modifications and innovative hybridizations. However, these modifications and hybridizations should not be regarded as a negative phenomenon or indications of domestic resistance to the transfer process, or even as the mark of inevitable compromise. Rather, they should be realized in a positive light, that is, the modifications originate from innovative learning and experimental work (Zeitlin 2000, pp. 11, 15–20). Thus, the people involved in the industry made the most of their experience and deconstructed, modified, and recombined various elements of the American model to best fit the local circumstances. By doing so, they reinterpreted and modified their country's practices and systems (Zeitlin 2000, pp. 38, 40–41).

However, not all practical modifications were equivalently successful. Consequently, European and Japanese industrialists had momentous existing knowledge of American-style practices. Zeitlin emphasizes that "European and Japanese industrialists' prior familiarity with American-style practices enabled them to treat US technology and management not as a unitary model to be imitated wholesale, but rather as a suggestive point of departure for selective adaptation, creative modification, and innovative hybridization" (Zeitlin 2000, pp. 38, 40–41).

Thus, certain limitations exist in adaptation, and hence, Japan and Germany did not wholly adopt and implement the American management model. While modifying the American management model to match the environments in their nation, both countries developed their own management style that had specific developmental characteristics. A mixed form was created because of the hybridization of the American and German management practices and factors. By the late 1960s to the early 1970s, definite discrimination between aspects, which were originally German, and those that were foreign could no longer be drawn. This was because American management practices had been widely integrated into German enterprises' beliefs and actions. Thus, in the 1970s, German managers were no longer oriented toward the American model to the same extent that they were 20 years ago. In particular, the adaptation of American management and production methods was successful as it was possible to combine American and German technology and management methods (Kleinschmidt 2002, pp. 120, 398–399). Although the will of most managers and technology experts in Japan to introduce various aspects of American management practices and technology was stronger than the counterparts in Germany (Kudo et al. 2004, pp. 20, 22; Schröter 2005, p. 219), similar conditions can be at least somewhat observed in Japan.

With regard to hybridization and examination of the results in this book, the following mix of American and German factors in management and production systems could be observed. First, industrial engineering methods such as Methods Time Measurement (MTM) and Work-Factor Method were incorporated into the traditional German REFA system. Second, there was a coalition of human relations aiming to improve the "working atmosphere" with the perspective of the prewar labor science research in Germany. Third, the American orientation of corporate personnel policies and managerial social policies such as human relations was combined with the German orientation of the prewar work community philosophy. Fourth, management education promoted manifestations of fusions, such as the exchange of opinions and transfer of knowledge between different generations and the network of managers centered in business and industrial associations, using American educational materials and methods. Finally, various American elements in the introduction of the Ford system are combined with those of Germany's own prewar production system and the standardized "unit system."

Moreover, a mixture of American and German methods existed in marketing. To give an example, cases in which the development of American-style marketing while German factors were incorporated can be observed. An example of this is the approach to sales and marketing, which combines market characteristics with an emphasis on values (respect for individual characteristics and quality). This was already diffused since before World War II and was a product policy that emphasized quality and function. Combination in PR was also observed to occur, for example between the American methods based on new social science methodology and the tradition of prewar German publicity activities and company image advertising (Yamazaki 2013, 8.3). Furthermore, in introducing divisional structures and forming a matrix organizational structure, a mixture exists between the principles of the American-style product-based divisional structure and the German-style regional and functional departments. This was in addition to the German-style structure based on the principle of the board-majority system in the managing board and collegial management.

The following mix of American and Japanese factors in management and production systems can also be discerned. First, the deployment of suggestion systems combined with TWI, Japanese job instrument activities, and a mix of American methods and Japanese concepts emphasizing production spots. Second, hybridization of American human relation methods and human relationships based on Japanese familyism and a mix of American methods based on cold contractive human relationships and Japanese methods emphasizing behavioral patterns based on collectivism. Third, the introduction of the job-based wage under the deployment of the work-factor method. Fourth, the hybridization of the Ford system and conventional craft production methods in Japan, a mix of introduced technology from foreign countries and meta-technology including peculiar logics, such as that seen in the method of withdrawal of needed parts by downstream processes, small lot production, and the administration of multiple processes by one worker. Fifth, combining the American supermarket system with the Japanese pre-package system of perishable goods that was suitable for Japanese consumption behaviors and integration of the Japanese way of forming groups based on relationships of mutual trust in the affiliation of distribution systems. Finally, the mixture of division and divisional headquarters and the introduction of internal capital systems in divisional structures.

12.2 "Reframing" in the Americanization Process and Japanese-Style Management

12.2.1 Japanese-Style Adaptation and the Influence of Business Management Tradition and Culture in the Americanization Process

Having examined Japanese- and German-style adaptations in the process of Americanization, let us now explore the influence of cultural factors such as Japanese business management traditions and values.

In Japan, the introduction of American management methods had more significance than in Germany under the necessities to overcome limits of management based on familyism and paternalism before the war. However, organizational operations in which relations of authorities and responsibilities were unclear were characteristic due to management values emphasizing relationships between management and labor based on a weak contracting view. Management values based on Japanese collectivism and mutual trust between company members strongly influence the deployment of American management methods under the climate of lifetime employment and seniority wage. Long-term and continuous trade customs between enterprises were also important factors that affected the deployment of American management methods.

Influences of such management values and management traditions and cultures can be seen in the following points. Work standards tended to be used not as the terms of workers' contracts but as a loose standard, which was deeply concerned with characteristics of Japanese improvement activities. Standard work time was used as a benchmark in establishing goals of job improvement by general foremen and evaluating the results. Japanese norms vis-à-vis the deployment of human relations, such as seen in methods of human relations management including the entity family, a mix of managerial familyism and human relations management, the hybridization of American methods based on cold contracting human relations in the United States, and Japanese methods emphasizing collective behavioral patterns were also examples of the influence of management values based on collectivism. The role of production spots and collective behavioral patterns were emphasized in the deployment of the Ford system. In the deployment of American management education, American methods were mixed with Japanese concepts emphasizing production spots. Such cases can be observed in the emphasis placed on improvement activities, self-development, and the instigation of suggestion systems combined with TWI and job improvement activities.

Regarding marketing, influences of management values emphasizing sales volume and market share that were different from those in the United States which regarded price as "a contract between enterprise and customer" were significant. Management values regarding inter-firm relationships based on mutual trust and collectivism as well as contracts and long-term and continuous trade customs between enterprises were also important factors that affected Japanese deployment of American marketing methods. Such cases can be seen in small-scale non-strategic marketing focused on sales and production orientations, bottom-up marketing based on the role of human factors, and Japanese development of the affiliation of distribution systems based on relationships of mutual trust relationships between large producing companies and sales enterprises. In the deployment of divisional structures, weaknesses of American-style management values can be discerned on the basis of shareholder-oriented concepts, such as seen in the relationships between consignment and trust of capital and management power, management values based on collectivism and equalitarianism rather than individualism, and those emphasizing long-term company growth. Such influences can be seen in cases of "pseudo" divisions that did not have necessary, autonomous functions, divisional structure deployment that was not self-supporting account systems, deployment of compensation systems for general managers not linked to divisional performance, cases of insufficient relations between authorities and responsibilities in divisions, and the existence of functional divisional structures.

12.2.2 Japanese-Style Adaptation and the Influence of Institutional Factors in the Americanization Process

Next, examining the institutional factors impacting the Japanese-style of adaptation in the process of Americanization, factors such as labor relations, the educational system, and postwar reforms were deeply concerned with reframing in the process of Americanization.

New frameworks of labor relations were formed in Japan after World War II to overcome prewar weaknesses in this respect and to enhance both labor democratization and labor mobility. However, weak regulating powers of trade unions influenced the deployment and implementation of American management methods. There had not been legal institutions that facilitated communication between management and labor, such as the work councils that existed in Germany. The framework of collective agreement and its Japanese characteristics led to a tendency to avoid collective bargaining by using the claim disposition system. In large companies, human relations methods were deployed as a mechanism for increasing corporate consciousness and countermeasures to trade unions under labor relations with the three basic pillars of lifetime employment system, seniority wage system, and enterprise trade unions. Such Japanese cooperative labor relations promoted the deployment of human relations with the purpose of rationalization such as job improvement and increase of work efficiency at workplaces based on close relationships between supervisors and subordinates. In the deployment of the Ford system, labor flexibility was pursued under the lifetime employment system and the weak regulations at workplaces by labor laws. Such cases can be seen with respect to multi-skilled workers and flexible use of workers in the team working system. Japanese labor-management systems based on Japanese labor relations, such as employment, personnel changes, and promotion also influenced the deployment of human relations.

In addition, the Japanese social structure emphasizing collectivism based on social reliance through close relationships between companies and among members was different from that emphasizing the contracting relations in the United States, which was concerned with the reframing of the Americanization process. Such cases can be seen in bottom-up marketing based on the role of human factors and the integration of the Japanese way of forming groups based on relationships of mutual trust in the affiliation of distribution systems between large producing companies and sales companies. Such influences of social structures can be observed in the deployment of divisional structures. Cases of "pseudo" divisions that did not have necessary functions as an autonomous unit and deployment of divisional structure that were not self-support account systems, and compensation systems for general managers not linked to the division's performance in divisional structures reflected the social structures of different from those in the United States where enterprise is regarded as a "nexus of contract."

Furthermore, special systems such as subcontracting systems also influenced the deployment of American management methods. Such cases can be seen in the deployment and modifications of IE in subcontracting firms and affiliated companies under the guidance of large enterprises that were at the top of the pyramid of subcontracting system. Large corporations pursued the deployment of just-in-time production based on the multilayered subcontracting system and attempted to expand it to companies in the position of the upper class of such a system (see Chap. 13).

Regarding the influences of postwar reforms, in contrast to Germany, in Japan, the business world experienced a shift between generations due to the removal of the top business leaders from older generations. Many new managers of postwar "zaibatsu"-type companies were promoted from the ranks of middle management. There were many cases in which they had not received sufficient training as top management at the time of their promotion (Miyajima 1991, pp. 139–140; Miyajima 1992, pp. 212–213; Miyazaki 1966, p. 224), which was one of the factors that called for the active introduction of American management methods.

12.2.3 The Structural Characteristics of Japanese Capitalism and the Development of Postwar Japanese Business Management

Based on previous discussions, the next issue to be considered is how the structural characteristics of Japanese capitalism defined the development of post-WWII business management in that country. In particular, the relationship between Japanese characteristics and their structure of productive forces, industrial structure, and market structure will be examined.

12.2.3.1 Impact of the Characteristics of the Structure of Productive Forces

First, in relation to the characteristics of the structure of productive forces prior to WWII, delay in the development of productive forces in the heavy industries and the process and assembly industries before the war was prominent. These industrial sectors rapidly expanded after the war. Introduction of the flow production system and innovations including automation promoted the deployment of IE methods. IE was implemented as various rationalization measures, such as production control and cost control for the modernization of production and to decrease costs via rapid development of productive forces. Although mass production based on the flow production system and automation was strongly pursued after the war, influences of prewar characteristics vis-à-vis productive forces and craft production were substantial. The Ford system and elements of conventional craft production in Japan were hybridized with a view to establishing a more flexible production system than the Ford system under restricted market conditions, such as the narrow and diverse domestic markets (Fujimoto 1997, pp. 57, 59, 74, 100, 120; Hashimoto 2001, pp. 241–242).

Changes in the structure of productive forces after the war also influenced the deployment of marketing in the consumer goods industries. Planned obsolescence was emphasized as an important product policy measure for creating demand due to the rapid development of productive forces in the durable consumer goods sectors, such as the electrical and automobile industries. Movements to build affiliated distribution systems were pursued in the form of large manufacturing company-led distribution channels. The American automobile dealer system was modified by making use of the close interdependent relationships between producing companies and dealers with a view to realizing mass sales and distribution.

12.2.3.2 Impact of the Industrial Structure Characteristics

Industrial structure changed greatly with the rapid development and expansion of the heavy and chemical industries and the durable consumer goods industries that were the leading industrial sectors for mass production after the war. The iron and steel industries as well as the electrical and automobile industries were the most representative industrial sectors. Durable consumer goods industries developed and expanded rapidly and their weight in the productive industrial sectors tended to grow. However, industrial structures between the rapidly expanding industries and sectors with international competitiveness in Japan after the war and the key industrial sectors in the US tended to be similar. Japanese enterprises were forced to pursue Japanese development of mass production systems including the original elements peculiar to this country in the 1970s and the 1980s due to such similarities in industrial structures between Japan and the United States, which resulted in trade friction with the United States, the core of Japan's exports.

Such rapid development and expansion of consumer goods industries and the growing weight of durable consumer goods in the industrial sectors were important factors that determined reframing in the deployment of American marketing methods. Marketing cohered with market needs and establishment of the original affiliated distribution system were pursued. In addition, international marketing, such as seen in the establishment of their own distribution channels was performed in the durable consumer goods departments while the trading companies continued to play significant roles in the export of enterprises in many industries.

Rapid and strong development of industries where diversification of business fields gave opportunities of great development and growth, such as the chemical industry and the electrical industry promoted the deployment and fixation of product divisional structures compatible with enterprises that had various business fields. However, such situations led to the adoption of divisional structures in the form of imitation as a fashion without sufficient consideration of the merits and demerits of divisional structures. As a result, there were "pseudo" divisions that did not have the necessary autonomous functions. There were also cases of abolishing divisional structure once adopted and movements of recentralization by return to functional structures.

12.2.3.3 Impact of the Market Structure Characteristics

Structural characteristics of the labor market were influenced by factors such as lifetime employment, the seniority wage system, and the internal promotion of personnel within companies. Hence American-style business schools for management training were incompatible with the Japanese context. These labor market characteristics became the factors defining Japanese-style management training. Labor formation based on the principle of "generalization," such as the flexible use of multi-skilled workers in team-based working systems, was pursued in the deployment of the Ford system under labor markets based on lifetime employment system, which contributed to coping with changes in demand and realizing full use of workers as a fixed cost consideration. Influences of labor market structure can be seen in the deployment of divisional structures. In Japanese enterprises, there were tendencies that the main office retained personnel affairs functions with a view to securing the possibility of employment adjustment through personnel changes between divisions, which was deeply connected with characteristics of the labor market based on the lifetime employment system. In addition, establishing personnel relationships based on long-term experiences under the labor market based on the lifetime employment system had significant roles in creating and evaluating strategic initiatives in the functional divisional structures.

However, the strongest market structure factor determining the development of Japanese-style business management was in the commodities markets. The Ford system was modified to make it compatible with small yet highly diverse domestic markets, as seen in the automobile industry. Although flow production system mechanisms and production organization principles were deployed the Ford system was hybridized with conventional craft production methods in Japan and was combined with meta-technology including peculiar logics, such as the method of withdrawal of needed parts by downstream processes, small lot production, and charge of multi-processes by one worker. Such reframing in the deployment of American management methods greatly contributed to establishing and reinforcing Japanese companies' competitiveness. Similarities in characteristics of market structures in terms of emphasizing product quality between Japan and the United States, were significant for such competitive advantages.

Influences of commodity market structure can be seen in the deployment of marketing and divisional structures. Planned obsolescence was regarded as an important product policy measure in durable consumer goods enterprises due to the narrow and diverse domestic markets that were different from the highly standardized markets in the United States. Marketing cohered with market needs, movement to pursue the distribution control by the large manufacturer-led affiliated distribution system, and marketing focused on nonprice competition under such distribution channels were also determined by Japanese market structures as well as the rapid expansion of the durable consumer goods markets. Japanese affiliated distribution system based on the close interdependence and mutual trust between manufacturers and sales companies, rather than the one-sided relationships of control and subordinates, as seen in the United States was compatible with the domestic market conditions in Japan. Further, in the deployment of the divisional structures, Japanese companies were confronted with difficulties in decentralization of sales and purchase functions into divisions due to the narrow and diverse domestic markets and heavy dependence on exports. In Japan, there were cases in which the headquarters retained rights of price determination under such conditions.

"Reframing" in the "Americanization" of business management was the process in which business management methods and systems that are defined by structural characteristics of American capitalism were adapted, modified, and made compatible with the structural characteristics of capitalism in Japan as a country to which they were transferred. It was a process to build more favorable and compatible foundations for the development of long-term-oriented management emphasizing on sales volume and market share that was different from the systems based on the radical "efficiency-first principle" in the United States while making the Japanese market and the US market as the core target of the markets.

The conditions surrounding the introduction of major methods of the American management system in Japan as well as "reframing" and the factors defining it were explained in each table in Part II, based on the discussion so far in this book.

12.3 "Reframing" in the Americanization Process and German-Style Management

12.3.1 German-Style Adaptation and the Influence of Business Management Tradition and Culture in the Americanization Process

Next, this subsection considers "reframing" in the Americanization process. German managers' and entrepreneurs' willingness and speedy acceptance of American business management and production methods were not merely the consequence of objective political and economic conditions. Instead, they primarily resulted from the existence of dynamic and nimble managers and entrepreneurs holding qualities of openness, adaptability, and orientation toward global markets (Kleinschmidt 2002, pp. 312, 396). The absence of fundamental Americanization of business management was due to Germany's strong culture combined with its tradition of skepticism and noncompliance with the "American vogue." Additionally, encountered the situation of having to keep pace with technological innovation and regain lost markets, German enterprises demonstrated a relatively high level of readiness to accept American know-how.

When considering the changes in the European market from the 1950s, i.e., the midst of the progress of mass production, mass marketing, and mass consumption, we can confirm a change in the disposition of entrepreneurs.

However, in the Americanization process, tension occurred because of the conflict between the high interest toward and readiness to accept American ideas and cautious skepticism. American management systems and thinking were and still are firmly rooted in American economic culture (Hilger 2004, pp. 279–282). However, in Germany as in Japan, despite initial enthusiasm, their appearance of management continued to be uncertain (Locke 1996, p. 54). Kleinschmidt highlights that "a broad adoption of values, behavior, norms, and behavior and their implementation on the corporate level did not occur" (Kleinschmidt 2004a, p. 172). According to McCreary's (1964) research on the phenomenon of Americanization in Europe, the answer is "Yes" when American goods, methods, and organizational forms are considered and "No" when American philosophy and attitudes are taken into account (McCreary 1964, p. 23).

As to these points, Berghahn (1985) stressed that in the Americanization of industrial capitalism in West Germany, a fusion between the elements of American industrial culture and those of Germany was created (Berghahn 1985, p. 330). The successful synthesis of modern American industrial culture and traditional West German economic spirit and structure established one of the important foundations for sustained growth of the postwar economy (Neebe 1989, p. 75). According to Hilger (2004), the Americanization of German enterprises can be understood as the appropriate and selective adaptation to market changes based on the use of America's new technology, modern managerial methods, and product innovation. However, such adaptation, simultaneously, reinforced the unique German-style corporate culture, which in a way was a limited movement (Hilger 2004, p. 287).

The important aspect regarding these types of traditions, values, and cultural factors of German business management is the impact of management values which emphasize technology, quality, and production. In postwar Germany, a tendency exists toward a contemptuous perception of the prevalence of American consumer-oriented management practices (Wengenroth 1997, p. 161). Rather than an orientation toward marketing and more direct pursuits of profit, the production orientation emphasizing technology and quality shows a strong trend. This exerted a great influence on the introduction of American-style management methods and led to the birth of German-style business management characteristics.

This type of management orientation is observed in a high proportion of engineers who are also directors and managers and in individuals at relatively high positions in their companies. In addition, their appointment and positions regulate the methods of German-style management. In Germany, knowledge, skills, and expertise related to production tends to be emphasized; there are numerous engineers who have higher levels of expertise and more vocational qualifications than other professional managers. Management values and technology-oriented thinking support the important role of engineers in industrial management. The emphasis on technology also influences the disposition of typical German corporations in general and is related to top management ideas regarding goals and the methods for achieving them (Lawrence 1980, pp. 80, 83, 96–100, 186, 190).

This influence can be observed in the introduction of various management methods and values. For instance, American pragmatic management forms the background for the introduction of management methods related to labor and human relations. This method emphasizes the management principle of "increased efficiency" in corporate behavior mechanisms for management practices and the labor environment. Thus, certain aspects of the various types of American measures were highly incompatible with German management values and traditions that emphasize technology, quality, and production as well as with managerial philosophy related to personnel structure and populated by managers with technological backgrounds. With management values only emphasizing technology in the background, modern technologies of planning and control, for instance, the use of mathematical methods for decision-making such as OR, did not interest German enterprises (Lawrence 1980, p. 98). It was the same in the case of marketing. Under German-style management values, German enterprises tended to emphasize sales policies prioritizing consumer interests, as opposed to planned obsolescence, a typical oligopolistic behavior, rather than following producer-oriented measures. Traditional influences from the pre-WWII period were also observed, such as priority given to moderate pricing policies based on market agreement measures such as cartel and syndicate. Moreover, a look at the introduction of management education methods also demonstrates that methods such as TWI were unsuccessful because of the tradition of the German firms' managerial social policy and actual management behavior; this was because the education methods were not necessarily compatible with German personnel philosophy and management values.

In Germany, management values and culture with long-term orientation and emphasis on technology existed. They greatly differed from the management values that were based on the American vogue of pragmatism and reflected in radical "efficiency-first principle" personnel policies. Even under strong American influence, these German management culture and values could not be reversed instantly. Furthermore, even after introducing the divisional structure, still several cases show that significant influences were exerted by the operational traditions of collegial management and the principle of board-majority system in the management board. While inheriting organizational structural principles, German enterprises sought to adopt unique structures that differed from American ones. With regard to organizational reforms, the influence of traditional authority was evident in the strict separation between top and middle management or those at the lower level. In Germany, traditional family-controlled firms tended to be widely maintained, demonstrating greater continuity of management and manager values compared with firms in Japan. Thus, there was strong resistance and hesitation toward the introduction of the American way of thinking, management, and technology (Kudo et al. 2004, pp. 20–21).

However, these types of German management values, management traditions and cultural factors do not simply reflect culture in general; rather, they reflect market characteristics and are suitable for the German and European markets as a core export market. This reveals the significance of German-style business management. This point will be considered in more detail in Sect. 12.3.3.3.

12.3.2 German-Style Adaptation and the Influence of Institutional Factors in the Americanization Process

Analyzing the institutional factors influencing the German style of adaptation during the Americanization process of business management, aspects of labor relations were an important issue. The deep-rooted differences between the United States and Europe in terms of comprehending and implementing working participation in the management process were an obstacle in the Americanization of European economic life (Schröter 2005, p. 193). In Germany, the legally ordained codetermination system was one of the most significant factors. The labor agreement that was complementary relations with codetermination at the top management and plant levels built the framework of industrial relations during the post-WWII period. Thus, the politically motivated attempt by America to promote the introduction of human relations to transform industrial relations did not come off. The traditional German-style labor relations, emphasizing technology and skills, were a significant background in the quest to design a method appropriate to the German adaptation of the American management system and style. This can be said to have had a strong impact on the view of management of enterprises and the issues of management, in general, based on the "efficiency principle."

For the influence of institutional factors such as labor relations, two aspects are important in the analysis: (a) the harmonious nature of industrial relations hastening the introduction of management measures proposed by the enterprises and (b) the necessary changes in the process of "reframing" of the American-style system facilitated by the power exerted by industrial relations regulations. Thus, a system with a management nature needs to be compatible with Germany's circumstances such that strategic responses could be produced among the impacts of regulatory functions and promotional efforts.

For instance, the introduction of human relations was greatly limited by the labor relations traditions dating back before WWII and the resistance of labor. Furthermore, there were factors such as the new framework of industrial relations stemming from the codetermination system. However, employment and wage security based on the dual system and the characteristics of German-style labor relations were factors facilitating investment in vocational education, particularly for the labor force within companies. Such investment in education and training established the foundation for developing diversified and high-quality production relying on skilled workers. Securing labor flexibility was of significance in terms of the development of diversified and high-quality production. Moreover, it was essential to form the type of skill and expertise required to complement the level of technical facilities and achieve high quality hastened by the development of the German-style production system. Kathleen Thelen points out "vocational training institutions are seen as part of a larger institutional package that, along with centralized collective bargaining, strong bank-industry links, and encompassing employer associations and labor unions, underpins Germany's high-skill, high wage, high-value-added ("high everything") economy" (Thelen 2003, p. 223).

In more than a few cases, the nature of labor relations was harmonious with promoting the introduction of management measures proposed by the enterprises. For instance, in firms that used the method of job evaluation in the payment of wages, the introduction of the method was performed only with the agreement of the work council and not with the trade unions (Vgl. Industriegewerkschaft Metall 1956, pp. 97, 101, 104). There were also cases in which IE methods were introduced by work councils in the form of work agreements (refer Chap. 8).

One institutional factor influencing the Americanization process after World War II was the education system. The traditions and nature of the German university educational system tended to emphasize and focus on the reasoning and understanding of the topics and had a great impact on management education. The institutional characteristics of these German universities greatly influenced the introduction of a more practical American-style management education method. Specialized skills and qualifications systems, such as the vocational education system and the Meister system, which were weighty for training skilled workers, were closely concerned with the introduction of the American production system and German-style production. In the United States, enterprises tend to value low costs and high flexibility in employee recruitment. For example, the training of engineers greatly emphasizes theoretical aspects and intermediates wider ability. It facilitates changes in occupational fields (Soskice 1999, pp. 208–209).

In comparing the situation in Japan, in terms of the influence of institutional factors on the process of Americanization, several significant issues may be mentioned. Generally, the scope of Americanization, on both company and national economy levels, was much broader and deeper in Japan than in Germany. Therefore, the shock of America's superiority was even greater. Most technology experts and managers in Japan desperately attempted to introduce all the aspects of American management practices and technology; moreover, learning and re-learning became company-wide movement. In contrast, in Germany, the volition for such practices was very limited, and the nation tried to incorporate American management methods and technology into their existing methods. During the productivity movement, the impact exerted by country-specific systems in Germany was far more extensive than in Japan, both on the scale of Americanization and the influence of adapting selective American management practices and thinking, given the nation's peculiar systems. The factors defining the difference between the two countries, regarding the scale of Americanization, were the differences in willingness to learn and study, and the difference in levels of the introduction of American methods as defined by the level of development in each nation. Moreover, differences in the scale of postwar reforms during the occupation and reconstruction period were of significance. In West Germany, legislation involving corporations was maintained despite postwar reforms. Thus, the supervisory board authority retained its earlier powers and the older generation of managers continued to be active, such that the situation cannot be compared with that in Japan (Kudo et al. 2004, pp. 19–24; Schröter 2005, p. 219).

Concerning the differences between Japan and Germany, Kudo (1999) pointed out two factors regarding the acceptance of American-style management: (1) "the difference in the development stage between Germany, which was a leader in the secondary industry revolution, and Japan which was a late developing country" and (2) "the wave of extensive institutionalization in Germany during the 1950s." With respect to the latter, he stressed that "the institutionalization brought about in the 1950s along the length and breadth of corporate society, including inter-firm relationships, internal organizational structure, and industrial relations, gave power to the traditional management philosophy and subsequently constrained the new generation of managers" (Kudo 1999, pp. 507–508). Thus, the post-WWII institutional reforms had a significant effect on the configuration of management and were deeply concerned with traditional management philosophy and values.

In the 1950s and the 1960s, a pragmatic model of behavior was gradually formed in Germany under the American impact. However, representatives of the old elite tended to adhere to the uniqueness of the "German spirit" (Lüdtke et al. 1997, p. 25). The monopoly and exclusivity of management revealed that authority was bestowed upon the managers themselves, but after World War II this changed under America's influence, reducing the exclusivity of manager positions. However, at the end of the 1950s "authority based on credentials" still dominated over "authority based on function" typically observed in the United States (Hartmann 1959, pp. 261, 271–272, 274–277; Hartmann 1968, pp. 271–272, 282–283, 286–289). The German method in terms of authority was also a factor that greatly affected the decentralization and delegation of authority. In the development of postwar Americanization, the significance of a generational shift in management was great. According to Berghahn, this process began in the early 1960s (Vgl. Berghahn 1985, pp. 249–252, 255–257, 293). However, it should also be taken notice that the promotion of Americanization occurred in some cases, regardless of a generational shift in management, as seen in the role of the Vaubel initiative in Glanzstoff (Kleinschmidt 1998, p. 186).

12.3.3 The Structural Characteristics of German Capitalism and the Development of Postwar German Business Management

Based on previous discussions, this subsection examines how the structural characteristics of German capitalism influenced the development of post-WWII German business management. In particular, the relationship between German characteristics and their structures of productive forces, industries, and markets are considered.

12.3.3.1 Impact of the Characteristics of the Structure of Productive Forces

First, as to the context of the characteristics of the structure of productive forces in Germany before World War II, a tradition existed wherein "the flexible production concept with an emphasis on quality" was observed in the automobile industry (Vgl. Stahlmann 1993). German companies had attempted various methods of mass production, mainly in the automotive, electrical, and machinery industries, that aimed to secure a certain level of flexibility for dealing with demand fluctuations between products and to gain some of the benefits of mass production even with a decreased production output under the conditions of market constraints (Vgl. von Freyberg 1989; Siegel and Freyberg 1991). After the war, both the domestic and export market conditions were equipped to adopt American-style mass production. However, Germany sought to optimize its market positioning by developing its competitive strength in Europe's relatively high share of exports owing to the high quality of European goods. Given these circumstances, German enterprises pursued a suitable production system. Here, they made efforts to construct a quality- and functionality-focused production system with the support of the German-specific method of specialized skill qualification system and vocational education system.

As will be discussed later, the German-specific method since before World War II was more suitable for the market structure and conditions given that a large portion of sales went to the European markets, including Germany. The German method served as an alternative of sorts, even while the nation's firms continued to accept American-style methods. The foundation of product differentiation based on the postwar diversified, and a high-quality production system, particularly with respect to product and price policies, influenced the introduction and development of marketing methods. In this way, the characteristics of the structure of productive forces influenced the broad reframing of American management methods in relation to increasing production capacity and ensuring adjustment to the market.

12.3.3.2 Impact of the Industrial Structure Characteristics

The characteristics of the structure of productive forces define the characteristics of the industrial structure. Therefore, this subsection examines the context of the industrial structure. In pre-WWII Germany, the core of the industrial structure was composed of the coal, iron, and steel industries, the chemical industry, the electrical industry, and the machinery industry, which was the cornerstone of the producer goods industry. In addition, the gradually expanding automobile industry contributed to the industrial structure. Consequently, this slow start of the consumer goods industry became a distinguishing character. After World War II, the development of the automotive industry and the home appliances of the electrical industry rapidly went ahead.

However, as pointed out by Wengenroth in 1997, despite the universal Americanization of the consumer goods market and the management style, the traditional dominance of the producer goods industry in West Germany was reinforced rather than weakened because of the new competitive advantage pattern among postwar European manufacturers. Of course, a mass consumer society was established after the war; however, certain industrial structure characteristics enabled Germany to keep its own consumer society without developing a consumer goods industry that was strong enough to rival America (Wengenroth 1997, p. 161).

Under such conditions, and for these reasons, strengthening the producer goods industries' international competitive power became significant. As in the case of the machine tool industry, the quality and functionality of the producer goods contributed immensely to improving the quality of final products and pursuing competitiveness by differentiating quality and functionality. Similarly, it was important to expand production systems by maintaining reliance on skilled workers. This is also valid in the automobile industry, a durable consumer goods sector. These industrial sectors are ones where Germany has a high level of export competitive strength in terms of quality. Here, a different production system was developed from the American-style mass production systems.

Thus, the development of heavy industries, processing, and assembly industries, prior to World War II, and the further development of these industries, postwar, proceeded and facilitated the German-style development of management and production systems within the American management system. After the war, the industries that established the foundation for the secondary industry's revolutionary development became the most likely basis of international competitive power. In these industries, the production methods, which emphasized quality and functionality to make product differentiation possible, were significant for building a competitive advantage. These factors influenced the "reframing" of American-style methods. Having the producer goods industry at the core of the industrial structure from the pre-WWII period and the notable role of the producer goods industry even after the development of the postwar consumer goods sector were defining factors in the delay of marketing in the producer goods industry. These factors also engendered German-style development with its emphasis on production rather than marketing.

12.3.3.3 Impact of the Market Structure Characteristics—European Market Structure and German Business Management

Considering the context of market structure characteristics, the labor market structure characteristics are impacted by labor market factors, such as talents needed by the managers and directors and the enterprises' internal promotion systems. Hence, American-style business schools for management development training were not suitable for Germany. These labor market characteristics became the factors determining German-style management training. However, the strongest market structure factor defining the development of German-style business management can be seen in the commodity markets.

Historically, the United States has emphasized efficiency based on standardization. This stemmed from a strong necessity for the unification of procedures owing to the large immigrant population, potential demand expansion due to the vast domestic market, and pragmatic cultures or values and customs defined by these conditions. For many years, the American market has remained more homogeneous compared with other nations (Chandler 1977, p. 498); thus, the standardization of consumption has progressed. Given these market and consumption characteristics, mass production and market competition aiming at fully standardizing production, and consumption became a prerequisite. American management methods and styles based on the principle of "efficiency improvement" were created to reflect free competition and are suitable for those situations in such markets.

By contrast, Germany did not have the same progress in the standardization of consumption as in the United States. The market characteristics and consumer behavior trended toward emphasizing technology, quality, and functionality, and the focus was placed on competition in terms of quality. These market characteristics are observed in Germany as well as across Europe, the core market for German exports.

Thus, unlike the aggressive American-type price competition (Streeck 1997, pp. 39–40), where efficiency is the primary management issue, Germany placed greater emphasis on product differentiation based on technology, quality, and functionality. This German method of management is also compatible with the European market. On this point, similarities were seen in German and European markets, for instance, in the negative perceptions and resistance toward planned obsolescence, one of the important American marketing measures, and in the strong reluctance of consumers toward standardized products. Of course, the terms for a technological and qualitative competitive advantage are greatly different depending on the product, and in product groups in which differentiation is difficult, the American method has more significance. However, the differences in the American and European market conditions are generally important factors in determining business management in Germany. The influences of these market structure factors are seen in the fields of market adaptation, such as marketing and PR, and in the area of production.

After World War II, international competitive power was divided on the basis of the types of market structures, which eventually led to the development of compatible product strategies and production systems supporting these strategies. It became meaningful for German enterprises during the development of this type of management to have a high degree of dependency on exports to the European market (Vgl. Statistisches Bundesamt 1956, pp. 282–283; Statistisches Bundesamt 1961, pp. 316–317; Statistisches Bundesamt 1971, pp. 296–297, 299–300; Statistisches Bundesamt 1981, pp. 258–259) with a relative importance placed on having basic similarities in market conditions and characteristics. The postwar Americanism-led free trade market system and the international monetary system enabled the establishment of an international economic system of the capitalist bloc. Furthermore, the formation of the common market in Western Europe has supported the conditions for favorable trade; as a result, Germany's export structure is even more dependent upon Europe. Under conditions that greatly differ from those in the pre-WWII period, a complementary relationship has been built in industrial sectors and goods areas. Overall, in addition to automobile, machinery, and chemical products, Germany has international competitive strength in areas and products that have industrial and product characteristics based on technology, quality, and functionality, particularly capital goods, investment goods, and consumer durable goods, and has established a competitive advantage.

Germany's trend has been to establish competitive power in exports by specializing in sectors based on the so-called med-ranking technology (Lindler and Holtfreich 1997, pp. 418, 420–421). "West Germany specialized in the production of highly income-elastic goods and her main markets were in West Europe, where trade expansion outpaced the growth of world trade itself" (Vonyó 2018, p. 140). German manufacturers specialized even more intensely in the production of high-valued-added capital goods in the 1960s owing to a highly income-elastic characteristic of demand for quality engineering products in world markets (Vonyó 2018, p. 170; Abelshause 2004, p. 262).

With a principal focus on the competitive force of the key industrial sectors in the European market, a division of labor was built to supplement existing industries and products. For instance, even observations during the period leading up to the formation of the European Economic Community (EEC) show that West Germany's competitive power leveraged the disparity in productive forces among the neighboring high-income level countries, particularly in the heavy and chemical industrial sectors. This facilitated penetration in the Western European export market, and later, with the expansion of imports from the ECC nations, a horizontal multilayered trade structure was established (Furuuchi 2007, pp. 89–100). Following World War II, against the background of Germany's highly nonprice competitive industrial products, a trade structure was built among the surrounding advanced economies that was based on the mutually complementary division of labor of trade goods (Sato and Hermann 1997, p. 218). In that sense, West Germany succeeded in extracting maximum profits not by building an industrial structure within the country's boundaries but by relying on the principle of optimal division of labor within the EEC (NHK Shuzaihan 1988, p. 91). Accordingly, within the product and industrial competitive structure, the dominance of German enterprises was reinforced. By doing this, the development of German-style management, job security based on the codetermination system, and the foundation of capital accumulation under the high-cost structure of wages were supported.

European-style development reflects characteristics of the European market; it entails high dependency on the regional market of German firms, German-style development of business management within the Americanism movement, and the German capitalist reproduction structure (accumulation structure). The post-WWII accumulation system or so-called "German model" is supported by a quality competitive sector as a core, industrial structure differences among European countries, and a trade structure that is closely related (Furuuchi 2007, pp. 89–101). Such European-style reproduction (accumulation) structures differ substantially from the Japanese case. In the period following WWII, given many Asian countries had been colonies, Japan did not seek out Asia as an export base, as was the case with Germany and Europe; in turn, Japan depended on exports to the United States, and this dependency continued to deepen. Therefore, Germany's business management must be analyzed and grasped by considering phrases such as "Germany in Europe" and "Europe for Germany."

In this manner, the German domestic market and structure of the European market that accounts for the major part of Germany's exports act as important factors that have a complex relationship with the problem of "reframing" in introducing the American management style. These facts have substantially defined the German-style development of business management. Under Germany's capitalistic reproduction structure, a business management style compatible with European circumstances was pursued. This type of business management style was also an important linchpin of Germany's capitalistic reproduction structure (accumulation structure).

References

Abelshause W (2004) Deutsche Wirtschaftsgeschichte: seit 1945. C. H. Beck, München

Berghahn V (1985) Unternehmer und Politik in der Bundesrepublik. Suhrkamp, Frankfurt am Main

Bjarnar O, Kipping M (1998) The Marshall plan and the transfer of US manage ment models to Europe. In: Kipping M, Bjarnar O (eds) The Americanization of European Business. The Marshall plan and the transfer of US management models. Routledge, London, pp 1–17

Chandler AD Jr (1977) The visible hand: managerial revolution in American business. Harvard University Press, Cambridge

Feldenkirchen W (2004) The Americanization of the German electrical industry after 1945. Siemens as a case study. In: Kudo A, Kipping M, Schröter HG (eds) German and Japanese business in the boom years. Transforming American management and technology models. Routledge, London, pp 116–137

Fujimoto T (1997) Seisan Sisutemu no Sinka Ron (Evolution of production system). Yuhikaku, Tokyo

Furuuchi H (2007) Gendai Doitsu keizai no rekishi (A history of the modern German economy). Tokyo daigaku shuppankai, Tokyo

Hartmann H (1959) Authority and organization in German management. Princeton University Press, Princeton

Hartmann H (1968) Der deutsche Unternehmer: Autorität und Organization. Europäische Verlagsanstalt, Frankfurt am Main

Hashimoto J (2001) Sengo Nihon keizai no seicho kozo (Growth structure of postwar Japan). Yuhikaku, Tokyo

Hilger S (2004) „Amerikanisierung" deutscher Unternehmen. Wettbewerbsstrategien und Unternehmenspolitik bei Henkel, Siemens und Daimler-Benz (1945/49-1975). Franz Steiner Verlag, Stuttgart

Industriegewerkschaft Metall (1956) Geschäftsbericht 1954/1955 des Vorstandes der Industriegewerkschaft Metall für d ie Bundesrepublik Deutschland. Industriegewerkschaft Metall, Frankfurt am Main

Kleinschmidt C (1998) An Americanized company in Germany. The Vereinigte Glanzstoff Fabriken AG in the 1950s. In: Kipping M, Bjarnar O (eds) The Americanization of European business. The Marshall plan and the transfer of US management models. Routledge, London, pp 171–189

Kleinschmidt C (2002) Der produktive Blick. Wahrnehmung amerikanischer und japanischer Management- und Produktionsmethoden durch deutsche Unternehmer 1950–1985. Akademie Verlag, Berlin

Kleinschmidt C (2004a) America and the resurgence of the German chemical and rubber industry after the Second World War. Hüls, Glanzstoff and Continental. In: Kudo A, Kipping M, Schröter HG (eds) German and Japanese business in the boom years. Transforming American management and technology models. Routledge, London, pp 161–174

Kleinschmidt C (2004b) Driving the West German consumer society: the introduction of US style production and marketing at Volkswagen, 1945–70. In: Kudo A, Kipping M, Schröter HG (eds) German and Japanese business in the boom year. Transforming American management and technology models. Routledge, London, pp 75–92
Kudo A (1999) 20 seiki Doitsu shihonshugi (20th-century German capitalism). Tokyo daigaku shuppankai, Tokyo
Kudo A, Kipping M, Schröter HG (2004) Americanization. Historical and conceptual issues. In: Kudo A, Kipping M, Schröter HG (eds) German and Japanese business in the boom years. Transforming American management and technology models. Routledge, London, pp 1–29
Lawrence P (1980) Managers and management in West Germany. Croom Helm, London
Lindler L, Holtfreich C-L (1997) Four decades of German export expansion—an enduring success story? In: Fischer W (ed) The economic development of Germany since 1870, vol II. Edward Elgar, Cheltenham, pp 402–435
Locke RR (1996) The collapse of the American management Mystique. Oxford University Press, New York
Lüdtke A, Marβolek I, Saldern AV (1997) Amerikanisierung: Traum und Alptraum im Deutschland des 20. Jahrhunderts. In: Jaraush K, Siegrist H (eds) Amerikanisierng und Sowjetisierung in Deutschland 1945–1970. Campus, Frankfurt am Main, pp 7–33
McCreary EA (1964) Die Dollar-Invasion. Amerikanische Firmen und Manager in Europa. Moderne, München
Miyajima H (1991) "Zaikai tsuiho" to shin keieisha no tojyo (Purge of managers from the economic world and emergence of new top managers). In: Will 10(7):136–144
Miyajima H (1992) Zaibatsu Kaitai (Dissolution of Zaibatsu). In: Hosei daigaku sangyo jyoho senta, Hashimoto J, Takeda H (eds) Nihon keizai no hatten to kigyou shudan (Development of Japanese economy and corporate groups). Tokyo daigaku shuppankai, Tokyo, pp 203–254
Miyazaki G (1966) Sengo Nihon no keizai kiko (Japanese economic system after World War II). Shin hyoron, Tokyo
Neebe R (1989) Technologietransfer und Auβenhandel in den Anfangsjahren der Bundesrepublik Deutschland. In: Vierteljahrschrift fur Sozial- und Wirtschaftsgeschichte 76:49–75
NHK Shuzaihan (1988) Nihon Nishi Doitsu (Japan West Germany). Nihon Hososhuppan Kyokai, Tokyo
Sato S, Hermann A (1997) Boeki shihontorihiki seisaku (Trade policy and capital transactions policy). In: Sakura Research Institute, Ifo Institut für Wirtschaftsforschung (eds) Nihon to Doitsu no keizai sangyo sisutemu no hikaku kenkyu (Comparative study of economic and industrial system in Japan and Germany). Springer, Tokyo, pp 199–218
Schröter HG (2005) Americanization of the European economy. A compact survey of American economic influence in Europe since the 1880s. Springer, Dordrecht
Siegel T, Freyberg TV (1991) Industrielle Rationalisierung unter dem Nationalsozialisumus. Campus, Frankfurt am Main
Soskice D (1999) Globalisierung und instutionelle Divergenz: Die USA und Deutschland im Vergleich. In: Geschichte und Gesellschaft 25(2):201–225
Stahlmann M (1993) Die Erste Revolution in der Autoindustrie. Management und Arbeitspolitik von 1900–1940. Campus, Frankfurt am Main
Statistisches Bundesamt (ed) (1956) Statistisches Jahrbuch für die Bundesrepublik Deutschland 1956. W. Kohlhammer, Stuttgart
Statistisches Bundesamt (ed) (1961) Statistisches Jahrbuch für die Bundesrepublik Deutschland 1961. W. Kohlhammer, Stuttgart
Statistisches Bundesamt (ed) (1971) Statistisches Jahrbuch für die Bundesrepublik Deutschland 1971. W. Kohlhammer, Stuttgart
Statistisches Bundesamt (ed) (1981) Statistisches Jahrbuch für die Bundesrepublik Deutschland 1981. W. Kohlhammer, Stuttgart

Streeck W (1997) German capitalism: do it exist? Can it survive? In: Crouch C, Streeck W (eds) Political economy of modern capitalism. Mapping convergence and diversity. Sage, London, pp 33–54

Thelen K (2003) How institutions evolve. In: Mathoney J, Rueschemeyer D (eds) Comparative historical analysis in the social sciences. Cambridge University Press, Cambridge, pp 208–240

von Freyberg T (1989) Industrielle Rationalisierung in der Weimarer Republik: Untersucht an Beispielen aus dem Maschinenbau und der Elektroindustrie. Campus, Frankfurt am Main

Vonyó T (2018) The Economic Consequences of the War. West Germany's Growth Miracle after 1945. Cambridge University Press, Cambridge

Wengenroth U (1997) Germany: competition abroad—cooperation at home, 1870–1990. In: Chandler AD Jr, Amatori F, Hikino T (eds) Big business and the wealth of nations. Cambridge University Press, Cambridge, pp 139–175

Yamazaki T (2013) German business management: A Japanese perspective on regional development factors. Moriyama shoten, Tokyo

Zeitlin J (2000) Introduction: Americanization and its limits: reworking US technology and management in post-war Europe and Japan. In: Zeitlin J, Herrigel G (eds) Americanization and its limits. Reworking US technology and management in post-war Europe and Japan. Oxford University Press, Oxford, pp 1–50

Part IV
Business Management in the Periods from the 1970s to the 1980s and After the 1990s

Chapter 13
Development of Mass Production Systems in Japan and Germany During the 1970–1980s and Its Significance

Abstract In the preceding chapters in Part II and III, changes of the system of industrial concentration and business management after the war were analyzed. In Part IV, as major management issues in the period from the 1970s to the present, reforms to mass production systems after the 1970s and transformations toward the American management model, represented by shareholder value-oriented management and capital market-oriented corporate governance system after the 1990s will be examined. This chapter discusses the reforms and developments of mass production systems from the 1970s to the 1980s. The American mass production system, represented by the Ford system, was deployed in major countries and greatly contributed to the development of the countries' enterprises and economies during the postwar period of high economic growth. However, the limitations of such a production system had become apparent with the shift toward low economic growth. As a result, reforms of the production system became an important issue in each country. In Japan and Germany, there were differences (as well as some commonalities) in the development of the production system. For example, the Japanese production system achieved high economic performance from the 1970s to the 1980s and its introduction was attempted in other countries, as seen in the phenomenon known as "Japanization." In contrast, in Germany, the reforms of the production system in the same period had certain limitations, which created difficulties for the country in its attempt to catch up to the Japanese system. Therefore, by analyzing these issues, this chapter clarifies the characteristics and significances of the developments of the production systems during this time period.

Keywords Flexibility · Japanese production system · Just-in-time production system · Labor formation · Microelectronics (ME) technology · Module production system · Subcontract system

Following the previous chapters' discussions in Part III, important issues of business management from the 1970s to the present are considered in Part IV. This chapter discusses the reforms and developments of mass production systems from the 1970s

T. Yamazaki, *Japanese and German Enterprises*,
https://doi.org/10.1007/978-981-97-4880-8_13

to the 1980s that were pursued as a countermeasure to the limitations of the American mass production system, represented by the Ford system. Chap. 14 examines the transformation toward shareholder value-oriented management and corporate governance after the 1990s, representing a resurgence of Americanized business management.

In the period after World War II, two factors that fostered economic growth were the development of a mass production system and the deployment of the American mass production method, known as the Ford system, in the process and assembly industries. As discussed in Chap. 9, in Japan and Germany, the American mass production system (i.e., the Ford system) was transformed/modified in accordance with country-specific conditions during periods of high economic growth. However, the limitations of this mass production system became prominent under the structural changes of capitalism after the 1970s, and reforms of the production system consequently became an important management problem.

Although reforms of the mass production system were attempted in many major capitalist countries from the 1970s to the 1980s, there are several questions regarding the processes. First, what problems occurred during the reforms in the 1970s? Second, how were the reforms specifically achieved in Japan and Germany? Third, what were the significances of such reforms?

This chapter answers these questions by analyzing the developments of the mass production system in both Japan and Germany during this period and by considering the subsequent outcomes.

Section 13.1 considers the social and economic backgrounds regarding the reforms of the mass production system. Sections 13.2 and 13.3 examine developments of the production system and their characteristics in Japan and Germany. Lastly, Section 13.4 clarifies the significances of the reforms of the mass production system in relation to the development of the module production system after the 1990s.

13.1 Socio-Economic Background Regarding the Reforms of the Mass Production System

The Ford system is a mass production method based on the principle of specialization and has greatly contributed to the realization of economies of scale. However, in cases wherein various products need to be manufactured in multiple production lines (which were organized on the basis of the principle of specialization), securing production flexibility in order to meet the changing demands of the market is impossible and such a rigid production method cannot adapt to the changes in the market. Therefore, it is necessary not only to establish mass markets for specific kinds of products but also to ensure the stability of the market. If such conditions cannot be secured, realizing economies of scale is very difficult.

Thus, reforms were necessary to allow the production process to cope with decreases in the average production lot per type of product and the change in demand among products with diverse types (intended to create new markets) led to the need for reforms of the production system in the period after the 1970s. In this regard, the increase in the types of products manufactured made it difficult to increase the demand of and expand each product in the market. As a result, the average production lot per type of product significantly decreased. For instance, the average production lot per type of automobile at Nissan in 1983 declined to 59.5% (in comparison with that in 1973) (Nissan jidosha kabushikigaisha shashi hensan iinkai 1975, pp. 606–607; Nissan jidosha kabushikigaisha soritsu gojyushunen kinen jigyo jikko iinkai 1985, pp. 48, 51–56), whereas the relevant numerical value at Toyota was 63.4% (Toyota jidosha kabushikigaisha 1987, pp. 97, 157, 201; Toyota jidosha hanbai kabushikigaisha shashi hensan iinkai 1980, pp. 48–50, 57–59; Doraiba 1973, pp. 180–187; Doraiba 1983, pp. 198–205). In Germany, Volkswagen had to produce approximately 14 product variants in 1982 in order to achieve the same number of sales as the Beetle ("Käfer"), which was previously a typical model of automobile produced by this company (Roth 1982, p. 130). The Volkswagen group began to transform their strategy drastically at the beginning of the 1970s. Although the ratio of the sales volume of the model (which was marketed after 1972) to the entire sales volume in the Volkswagen Group was only 14 in 1973, it increased to 70% in 1977 (*Volkswagen Archiv*, 119/447/1, Prospekt Volkswagenwerk Aktiengesellschaft Wolfsburg, Börseneinführung in Wien November 1978, S.12).

Under such situations, securing an operating rate that enabled companies to realize economies of scale with the American type of mass production system became extremely difficult. For example, the production of numerous types of products by the American mass production method was not easy given the problems regarding equipment investments and the amortization of fixed costs. Moreover, such efforts were not cost-effective and inflexible in the face of changing demands. As a result, achieving the mass production of various products while satisfying demand fluctuations between different types of products became an important issue for top management. One example can be seen in the automobile industry, wherein the pursuit of efficiency through flexibility became a new rationalization paradigm (Kern and Schumann 1990, p. 43; *Volkswagen Archiv*, 250/347/1, Protokoll der Vorstandssitzung Nr.10/78 vom 28.3.78, S. 1, S. 4–5; *Volkswagen Archiv*, 250/347/1, Protokoll der Vorstandssitzung Nr.12/77 vom 29.3.77, S. 4; *Volkswagen Archiv*, 119/447/2, Bericht über das Geschäftsjahr 1977 Volkswagenwerk Aktiengesellschaft Wolfsburg. Sperrfrist ! Veröffentlichung frei ab 27 April 1978, S. 15; *Volkswagen Archiv*, 119/441/1, Volkswagenwerk Aktiengesellschaft, Investitionen. Antrag auf Vorabgenehmigung zum Investitionsprogramm XXVIII, S. 2; *Volkswagen Archiv*, 119/441/1, Volkswagenwerk AG, Dokumentation zum Bericht des Vorstandes für die Hauptversammlung 1977, S. 26).

Even under such difficult conditions, the Japanese production system achieved high economic performance from the 1970s to the 1980s, which attracted worldwide attention. Referred to as "Japanization," the transfer of the Japanese production system to foreign countries became an important issue. Even in Germany, where high global competitiveness had been achieved in the automobile industry (which epitomized the efficient development of mass production systems till then), attempts to transform its production system were made to cope with the changes in the market and to match or exceed the performance of Japanese enterprises. However, such attempts greatly differed from those in Japan, after which the outcomes were limited.

On the basis of these findings, the following questions are raised. (1) What structure did the Japanese production system utilize to achieve high economic performance? (2) What mechanism allowed the Japanese system to overcome the limitations of the American production system? (3) How did the Japanese production model change the principle of the mass production system, and how did it affect the reproduction structure (accumulation structure) of capital? (4) What characteristics, meanings, significances, and limitations did the reforms of the production system in Germany have during this period? (5) How did the limitations determine the subsequent reforms and development of the production system? In summary, what kind of influence did the reform of the production system in the 1970s and the 1980s have on the development of the module production system after the 1990s? Accordingly, the reforms of the mass production system in Japan and Germany from the 1970s to the 1980s are examined in order to clarify the characteristics and significances of the new developments in the production systems of both countries. The findings in this chapter are important for considering such changes after the 1990s.

The development of the production system in Japan is examined in Sect. 13.2. Then, the reform of the production system in Germany is discussed in Sect. 13.3.

13.2 Production System Reforms in Japan and Their Characteristics

13.2.1 Characteristics of the Japanese Production System

The Japanese management system underwent general structural changes or "systematization" from the latter half of the 1970s to the 1980s, further continuing in the 1990s as well. During this period, the production system in Japan was established as the overall management system of companies, superseding any other method of the corporate management and production. In the 1980s, it became increasingly important for Japanese manufacturing industries to establish a flexible management and production system that could enable them to make cost reductions, increase profits, produce various products, and have the flexibility to shorten delivery dates and respond to various changes in the orders (Bato 1986, p. 76; Ono 1990, p. 130). Thus, in Japan, a "flexible management system" was established by integrating and systematizing major functions such as development, purchases, production, and sales in order to enable the effective production of many kinds of product with numerous variations. This system, unlike the American type of production system, was able to flexibly cope with the changes to the management environment.

During the latter half of the 1970s, the international competitiveness of Japanese enterprises became remarkable. The main industrial sectors that had such global competitiveness included the machines apparatus, capital goods, and durable consumer goods sectors in the processing and assembly industries. These were the very sectors that contributed to the decline in the international competitiveness of the United States and the increase in its dependence on imports. Three elements that determined the international competitiveness of Japanese companies can be identified: (1) high labor productivity, (2) high quality, and (3) product variety. Although it was generally difficult to realize all three elements simultaneously, Japanese enterprises built a new pattern of competitiveness by overcoming such difficulties (Suzuki 1994, introduction). Therefore, the next subsection examines the entire structure of the Japanese production system in the processing and assembly industries and the mechanism whereby this system functioned.

13.2.2 Structure and Function of the Japanese Production System

13.2.2.1 Mixed-Model Production and Its Characteristics

The mixed-model production is an important element of the Japanese production system. This method is not based on the principle of "specialization," as in the Ford system, but on "universalization" (generalization). The production volume of an entire facility and the efficiency of equipment operation can be increased by producing multiple products on the same production lines. Thus, in mixed-model production, production is not only efficient but also flexible enough to meet the changing demands between product types in the market. Overall, this method is important for several reasons. First, it allows production facilities to be cost-effective since they can produce multiple products on the same assembly lines. Second, it enables production facilities to achieve higher operating rates since the assembly lines are producing multiple products to meet demand fluctuations, thereby optimizing the utilization of the facilities. In this regard, when a facility only produces a single type of product, it increases the possibility that a part of the facility will be underutilized. In contrast, even if the demand of a product exceeds the production capacity, this product cannot be produced in other underutilized facilities. Thus, the mixed-model production method increases the operating rates of facilities close to the gross weight of the mass production, which is indispensable for optimal operation, by producing those products that are in demand.

In this way, the mass production of many kinds of products in the same line by the mixed-model production method was a countermeasure to the contradiction between production and consumption based on the market mechanisms under capitalistic production. The mixed-model production method showed the shift in realizing the economies of scale arising from mass production.

13.2.2.2 Use of Microelectronics Technology and Its Characteristics

In looking at technological change, an important basis of the flexible Japanese production system was microelectronics (ME) technology. This technology consisted of individual machines and equipment (e.g., numerous control [NC], machining center [MC], robots, automated guided vehicles [AGV]) that were based on the concept of flexible processing (i.e., stressing on product variety) and a flexible control system (programming and networking of the control system) (Sakamoto 1992, p. 50).

The most important aspect of ME technology was that such technology allowed enterprises to achieve generalization while maintaining the level of automation. Indeed, it was possible to realize automation by, for example, installing jigs in general-purpose machines while maintaining the necessary flexibility. However, such installations were not cost-effective, and there were limitations regarding their flexibility (Yuasa 1992, p. 161). Regardless of these issues, the ME equipment did increase the possibility of both various processing methods and a flexible response to non-normalcy. Overall, ME technology contributed to the automation of general-purpose machines, which, in turn, allowed a high level of efficiency (Shibui 1994, p. 99).

In the cases wherein only the same type of product is produced and the gross weight of the mass production that an individual machine assumes can be secured only through specific work or production, it is not necessary to utilize general-purpose machines; accordingly, single-purpose machines were developed. However, if the production capacity cannot be achieved through such specific work (rendering single-purpose machines ineffective), then it is important to increase production volumes by utilizing general-purpose machines (Ono 1994, p. 177). Just like in the cases wherein the production of multiple products in the same facilities can increase flexibility, the generalization of production equipment, especially those that include ME technology, can increase overall productivity.

13.2.2.3 Just-In-Time Production Method and Its Characteristics

The just-in-time production method is an important component of the Japanese production system. One of the most important aspects of this production system is its attempt to overcome the limitations of the Ford system. More specifically, one such limitation of the Ford system is visible in the production control: even though the synchronization of production within the process section where the flow production system is introduced can be achieved, the synchronization of production between the processes (e.g., the assembly process and the machining process) cannot be realized because of the use of the general-purpose transportation equipment. Therefore, the coordination of production between various sections became an important management issue (Yamazaki 2005, Chap. 6; Shiomi 1978, pp. 282, 286).

In the just-in-time production system, realizing the synchronization of production, especially between the parts and the assembly processes, becomes possible by combining the "withdrawal kanban" (a means of giving instructions for the conveyance of parts) with the "production-ordering kanban" (a means of giving instructions for the production of parts) in the pull-production method using the "kanban." For example, in the case wherein a line stop occurs in the assembly process (downstream process), the production order will not be given to the parts manufacturing process (upstream process) as receiving of the necessary parts from the assembly process will cease. As a result, production in the parts manufacturing process will also stop. Conversely, when production in the assembly process restarts, the production in the parts manufacturing process and the adjustment of both processes can be automatically performed by reinitiating production-ordering kanban. The overall significance of the just-in-time production lies in its ability to synchronize the main production processes at a high level.

In the pull-production method, wherein parts are received from the downstream process (e.g., the assembly process), each process only produces what is needed by the downstream process. In other words, each production process only produces the same quantity that the subsequent process receives and no more. The purpose of this method is to automatically secure the adjustment of production between processes by aligning the final production in accordance with the actual progress of the downstream process (Suzuki 1994, p. 50).

The kanban is an important information system for controlling the production volumes in all of the processes in order for such amounts to be harmonized. However, if various prerequisites for this method are not completely executed, then it becomes difficult to realize the just-in-time production method, even though the kanban system was introduced (Monden 1991b, p. 180). The just-in-time production method helps establish flow without stagnancy in the overall manufacturing process. Not only the pull-production method (wherein the parts are received by the downstream process) and the maintenance of quality and facility but also the production leveling and the shortening of the setup time for change of tool and die are necessary to achieve such flow.

Production leveling (*Heijyunka*) means that various types of products are produced in the same line so that the quantity and type of each part can be received with uniformity when the final assembly line receives parts from the upstream process (Monden 1991b, p. 183). In addition, production leveling entails that the production of the final products is directly related to the fluctuating demands of the market demand and the stock of finished goods is reduced by changing the item to be produced frequently according to the demand (Suzuki 1994, p. 52). "Heijunka is the leveling of production by both volume and product mix" and "does not build products according to the actual flow of customer orders, which can swing up and down wildly, but takes the total volume of orders in a period and levels them out so the same amount and mix are being made each day" (Liker 2004, p. 32, 116). As Liker points out, "a leveled schedule or *heijyunka* is necessary to keep the system and to allow for minimum inventory" (Liker 2004, p. 32). Although the idea of leveling of production was widely performed in the United States, Japanese enterprises expanded the application of this aspect from the assembly process to all production processes in the 1980s (Shimada 1988, p. 123). An important Japanese characteristic is evident in this general application by Japanese enterprises. For example, in the Toyota Production System, emphasis is placed on creating a smooth "flow" across all production processes, from the parts manufacturing process in an affiliated company to the final assembly process within the factory of the automobile company, including the production/purchase of materials and parts in/from other companies (Wada and Shiba 1995, pp. 126–127).

In addition, when looking at the shortening of the time required for changing the setup, frequent changes in the products become necessary in response to product leveling, especially in regard to producing multiple product types as well as single ones. For example, as seen in the exchange of the die as "a metal tool used for transferring a shape by pressurizing or casting a material" (Nichi-ei-chu jidosha yogo jiten henshu iinkai 2011, p. 254) in the press process, any change in the products requires adjustments in the setup of facility operations. However, if this change in setup takes too much time, then it becomes impossible to produce and provide parts immediately in response to changes of required parts in the downstream process. Thus, it becomes important to stock the necessary parts beforehand in response to production leveling, and the just-in-time production method, which views the reduction of stocks as an important objective, will face serious contradictions. It is necessary to shorten the time required for changing the setup as much as possible in order to avoid accumulating finished parts stocks. As a result of such shortening of setup times, Japanese companies realized the international competitive advantage regarding the costs of changing setups (setup time ÷ lot) even though such frequent changes led to a decrease in lot size. For instance, Toyota dramatically shortened its setup times (in comparison with that of its American counterparts) by shifting from the method in which setup was performed while stopping the production equipment to that where the setup was performed while the equipment was in operation. As a result of this shift, the efficiency of the flow of parts increased, even during the production of multiple products in small lots (Suzuki 1990, pp. 32–34; Suzuki 1994, pp. 53–56).

In order to apply the mixed-model production method in the same assembly line, it is necessary to replace "the internal setup" (wherein setup is performed when the equipment is stopped) with "the external setup" (wherein the setup is performed during the operation of the equipment). Such a transformation is an important premise of the production of small lots. In Japanese enterprises, significant knowledge regarding this measure has been accumulated through work experience and continuous improvements at the workplaces by workers. In contrast, neither the production of small lots of many types of products nor mixed-model production in the same lines progressed in European and American enterprises largely because of the insufficient accumulation of such knowledge (Komatsu 2009, pp. 100–101).

Furthermore, the concepts of "autonomation" and quality control are important in the discussion on the application of mixed-model production in the same assembly line. The interruption of production by the generation of dead stock and equipment problems can have a detrimental influence on the development of just-in-time production (Yuasa 1991, p. 43). This production system aims to reduce the amount of parts stock; moreover, it also reduces the number of defective articles in the upstream process, which can cause major problems in regard to quality control. Unlike the

American method of quality inspection, which involves removing defective articles in the final process, the Japanese method of quality control not only attempts to detect and remove the defective products in the process wherein the defective articles were produced but also determines their origin in order to improve future products. In addition, many technical devices are used in Japanese production facilities to decrease such incidences (Suzuki 1994, pp. 64–65; Suzuki 1990, pp. 30, 41). Technical processes are autonomation, which means automation with the "addition of an element of human intelligence to automated machinery," and a "poka-yoke," a mistake-proofing device that provides mechanisms that help equipment operators avoid mistakes and eliminate product defects (Matuzaki 2005, pp. 121–122, 169–170; Liker 2004, pp. 129–130).

13.2.2.4 Subcontract Division of Labor Production and Its Characteristics

An important characteristic of the just-in-time production system in the processing and assembly industries is that it is performed using the subcontracting system peculiar to Japan. The subcontract division of labor production is an important element that enables the timely supply of various parts (in the appropriate amounts) for flexible production in the Japanese system.

13.2.2.4.1 Fundamental Characteristics of the Subcontract Division of Labor Production

First, the fundamental characteristics of the Japanese subcontract division of labor production are examined in relation to the advantages and disadvantages of the social division of labor and vertical integration. In regard to the social division of labor, while it allows companies to flexibly perform in response to business fluctuations, it also includes significant limits when dealing with technological developments, quality improvements, and cost reductions given the uncertainty of information on trading partners. Conversely, in vertical integration, as seen in the internal production of parts, there are significant advantages regarding technological developments, quality improvements, and cost reductions since the close coordination between sections becomes possible through the easy assimilation of information and smooth internal communication between sections. However, since vertical integration refers to the fixation of capital, if production volume decreases with the declining economy, then the risk of unused production capacity accumulating increases.

Generally, in the case that incorrect information is obtained in market transactions, the appropriate information can be provided by internalization. However, since internalization can cause the immobilization of resources, it is difficult to ignore the merits of using transactions in the market to secure elasticity. Thus, if the information acquired without internalization is of the same quality, then companies tend to choose this form (Imai et al. 1982, pp. 38–40).

The use of the Japanese subcontracting system not only allows enterprises to take advantage of both the social division of labor and vertical integration but also enables them to eliminate some of the disadvantages to some degree. However, this system is not merely intended for making cost-effective purchases of necessary parts by utilizing the wage differences between big businesses and subcontracting companies. The essence of the subcontracting system lies in the close coordination between sections; this is achieved, as in the case of the complete vertical integration, through the easy assimilation of information and internal communication between both companies on the basis of the control by big business over subcontracting firms (Nakamura 1983, pp. 51–52).

In this regard, the Japanese subcontracting system serves as an "intermediate organization" that is situated between the social division of labor and vertical integration (Imai et al. 1982, Chaps. 2 and 7) or "quasi-vertical integration" (Nakamura 1983, p. 8). This system eventually becomes the indispensable condition for securing adjustments between sections (by vertical integration) as well as realizing the just-in-time production between the parts production process and the assembly process. The overall significance of the Japanese subcontract division of labor production is reflected in the fact that such a coordination can be achieved through outsourcing based on the use of a subcontracting firm without internalization.

13.2.2.4.2 **Hierarchical Subcontracting Structure and Its Significance**

Analyzing the subcontracting division of labor production in the Japanese processing and assembly industries, a prominent example employing this system is the automobile industry, wherein a hierarchical structure exists, comprising finished-vehicle producers at the top of the pyramid, followed by parts companies and then a significant number of smaller subcontracting companies that receive orders from these parts companies (Chusho kigyocho 1995, pp. 175–176). In this system, automobile companies are able to control subcontracting firms of all hierarchies, including enterprises below the second-tier level, by directly managing the first-tier parts suppliers in the top layer of the subcontracting system (Ikeda 1986, p. 81).

In the machine and metal industries, the first-tier subcontracting companies are usually in charge of assembling the finished parts and producing unit parts. The enterprises in this layer serve as "the bounds" (sub-assembly) between the companies on the order side and the second-tier subcontracting enterprises. The existence of the first-tier parts companies, which are in charge of this sub-assembly process, enables large companies to concentrate on the final assembly, the production of main parts, and the development of new products (Ueno and Kawasaki 1994, pp. 179–180; Ikeda 1986, p. 84).

Examining the first-tier subcontracting enterprises in which the majority were manufacturers of finished parts, cases wherein automobile manufacturers attempted to produce these parts themselves during the recession were rare because of the difficulties regarding technology, the assembly line, and facilities. Furthermore, as seen in "the methods based on approved drawings," "black box parts," or "design-in" (Asanuma 1997), in the first-tier parts makers that had a direct trading relationship with the automobile enterprise, there were many cases wherein such parts companies participated in the development of new models while closely cooperating with the finished-vehicle maker from the early stages of the development of the car. The finished-car manufacturer was able to develop the new models with a comparatively small number of technical experts (Asanuma 1997, Part III; Fujimoto 1997, pp. 170, 189–194; Fujimoto 1999, pp. 129–136). Thus, it can be said that the relationship between automobile companies and first-tier parts manufacturers was complementary.

However, the orders of many parts received by first-tier parts suppliers were actually subcontracted to second-tier parts suppliers. In addition, the production of parts performed by subcontracting enterprises below the second-tier level usually required special processing, such as cutting, press, surface treatment, casting, forging, and the production of metal mold or the component that was built into finished parts, in order to produce finished parts or unit parts. The second-tier and the third-tier subcontracting companies were generally in charge of processes that were labor-intensive, peripheral, and specialized (Ueno and Kawasaki 1994, p. 181; Chusho kigyocho 1995, pp. 176–177; Shimokawa 2004, pp. 51–52).

In addition, cases in which parts manufacturers designed the parts in their own way or were charged with designing the details of parts after an order had been placed were limited among the second-tier subcontracting firms when compared with the first-tier parts companies. Among the second-tier parts suppliers, there were many cases in which the design was made by the company that placed the order. In the third-tier parts suppliers, the ratio of the design by the customers was even higher. Hence, there were significant differences among the various layers of design power, production cooperation, and the development of new products (Fujimoto et al. 1994, pp. 16, 18, 21, 34; Chusho kigyocho 1995, p. 176).

Such conditions in which subcontracting companies participated in the design process determined the relationship between the companies that placed the orders and the subcontracting firms. Among companies below the second-tier level, it was relatively easy for them, as customers, to not only produce parts by themselves but also select the suppliers among the second-tier parts makers and third-tier parts suppliers, especially during the recession. Unlike the complementary relationship seen in the relation between automobile enterprises and first-tier parts suppliers, the relationship between first- and second-tier parts companies or between the second- and third-tier parts suppliers was interchangeable. The cost reductions made by decreasing parts stocks through just-in-time production and the overall flexibility were possible because of the hierarchical structure of the subcontracting division of labor production. Thus, it is important to examine the mechanism of such cost reductions and decreases in parts stocks.

Since the relationship between automobile companies and first-tier parts suppliers was a complementary relationship, maintaining a continuous long-term fixed relationship between both enterprises was important for finished-car manufacturers. Therefore, the compulsion of possessing finished parts stocks among first-tier parts suppliers was the cause of rising costs on the supplier's side. As a result, determining how the possession of finished parts stocks among first-tier parts suppliers can be avoided was an important issue for automobile manufacturers. Concerning this problem, companies have attempted to avoid overstocking finished parts by applying the just-in-time production method at the level of first-tier parts suppliers and the buffering function through stock possession among the subcontracting firms below the second-tier level.

Regarding the achievement of the just-in-time production for subcontracting companies, the introduction of such a production method among first-tier parts suppliers (and even in the largest second-tier parts suppliers, such as companies that belonged to cooperation organizations built by first-tier parts suppliers) advanced after the 1970s (Shiomi 1985, pp. 104–107). Among the largest second-tier parts suppliers, some produced components that were vital for the finished parts produced by the first-tier suppliers. Moreover, the enterprises with the latest technology had a significant influence on the quality of the finished parts. Thus, the realization of stable and efficient production by second-tier parts suppliers was important for automobile manufacturers in order to definitely achieve just-in-time production at the level of first-tier parts supplier.

In this regard, achieving the just-in-time production by automobile companies while avoiding stock possession among first-tier suppliers was based on the hierarchical subcontracting system unique to Japan.

However, the establishment of a system of management that enables automobile companies to almost completely control a significant number of subcontracting enterprises was also an important premise, as seen in the promotion of the just-in-time production method among the subcontracting firms of the upper layer to avoid stock of finished parts.

Concerning business fluctuations, the flexibility in the subcontracting system is evident in the fact that automobile companies do not require a full range of production equipment, which becomes a fixed cost through the subcontracting of parts. However, the issues of rising costs due to unutilized equipment of first-tier parts suppliers under the decline of the economy and of the rising prices of purchased parts have become important for effectively maintaining a stable long-term relationship between automobile manufacturers and first-tier subcontracting firms.

Actually, many orders for parts that first-tier parts suppliers receive are subcontracted to the suppliers below the second-tier level. Hence, the first-tier parts suppliers can overcome the issue of unutilized equipment. They can also restrain or cancel orders as per demand fluctuations while practically avoiding cost increases due to unused facilities. This is based on the interchangeable relationship between first- and second-tier subcontracting firms as well as the condition that the application of manufacturing techniques and production processes tends to increase as the hierarchical subcontracting system becomes less prominent. Thus, the problem of rigidity toward market fluctuations caused by the fixed and continuous long-term relationship between automobile enterprises and first-tier parts suppliers can be mitigated to a certain degree. Flexibility in response to changes in the market can also be secured to a certain degree. It is not possible to secure such flexibility in the case of internal production of parts.

As for the relationship between automobile companies and subcontracting firms, according to Asanuma (1997), the common idea is that since the use of subcontracting firms as buffers is unsuitable, the absorption of risk by finished-car manufacturers is more practical (Asanuma 1997, Chap. 8, p. 175). However, since such absorption of risk by finished-car manufacturers holds true for first-tier parts suppliers as well, this argument is somewhat limited (Yamazaki 2005, pp. 250–251; Ueda 2000, p. 20; Ueda 2001, p. 102; Watanabe 1997, pp. 29–30).

In Japan, the structure of the division of labor (based on the multilayered hierarchical subcontracting system) and the mechanism to impute the risk to subcontracting enterprises below the second-tier level depend on the interchangeable relationship between first- and second-tier subcontracting companies as well as between second- and third-tier parts suppliers. Actually, the evasion of risk arising from business fluctuations by automobile enterprises is enabled through the imputation of risks to the supplier below the second-tier level by first-tier parts suppliers. As for the issue of finished-car manufacturers using subcontracting as a buffer during business cycle fluctuations, an appropriate understanding of the mechanism that enables imputing and absorbing the risk through the hierarchical structure of the subcontracting system is important. The mechanism by which automobile firms can achieve such flexibility through the Japanese hierarchical subcontracting system cannot be grasped by analyses based on the transaction cost approach. Thus, the structural function of the Japanese hierarchical subcontracting system must be emphasized.

13.2.2.5 Labor Management and Its Characteristics

Another important element that supports flexible production in the Japanese production system is the "flexibilization" of personnel placement. Such flexibilization is enabled on the basis of the Japanese approach to labor formation, labor management, and labor practices. Whereas American labor formation includes three characteristics—(1) subdivision of duties, (2) exclusive use of workers (rigidity of workers), and (3) the principle of personnel responsibility—Japanese labor formation includes three different characteristics: (1) the comprehensiveness of labor; (2) the generality of workers (the flexibility of workers); and (3) the principle of collective responsibility (Suzuki 1994, pp. 72–77). The flexibilization of personnel placement is based on such Japanese comprehensiveness of labor. In addition, the teamwork based on this approach requires workers to have the ability to flexibly cope with the work of the entire team since it does not limit and/or specify the duties of the workers. Since the workers are multi-skilled, organizing teamwork becomes possible, and continuous improvement activities can also be achieved.

Thus, the workload is distributed within the team and easily completed (Maruyama 1995, p. 214). Such use of multi-skilled workers not only makes it easy to correspond with mass production of various types of products but also allows companies to optimize the number of team members as per market fluctuations (Maruyama 1995,

p. 181). Moreover, the multi-skilled workers must complete a series of different tasks within the cycle time as the time needed to produce one unit of product; this practice enabled achieving production in the method of one-piece flow production (Monden 1991b, pp. 183–184).

The existence of multi-skilled workers is a precondition for the "flexible manpower line" ("*Shojinka*"), which aimed at completing work with the minimum number of personnel (as per the market demand) by applying the just-in-time method (kanban method) to the placement of personnel (Maruyama 1995, p. 125, Monden 1991a, pp. 272, 281–282). Such use of multi-skilled workers is the rationale for reducing the necessary personnel for various projects (Aoyama 1991, pp. 62–63).

The worker is required to maintain constantly the gross weight of the work at a high level by the system in which workers help each other without strictly determining a fixed number of personnel. The true nature of the use of multi-skilled workers lies in the full utilization of their abilities; that is, the more flexible they are, the higher is the degree of freedom, which can increase their operating rates (Ono 1995, p. 665). In Japan, labor cost, which is originally a variable cost, has to have the characteristic of fixed cost under the lifetime employment system. In Japanese labor practices, the flexibility by generalization of labor use has an important meaning for fully utilizing the labor force. However, the extra working hours of full-time employees and peripheral workers (excluding permanent employees) are flexibly used in order to utilize fully the core workers as part of the fixed cost even when production volume decreases (Ono 1995, pp. 660–662).

Small group activities at the workplace, such as quality control (QC) circles and improvement suggestion activities, have made the flexible placement of personnel easy by facilitating the flexible designation of duties in order to reduce the number of required workers to the minimum extent, thereby creating the flexible manpower line. The kanban method includes two objectives. The first is to establish a flexible manpower line that eliminates surplus personnel by flexibly changing the composition of each line according to demand fluctuation. To this end, multi-skilled workers are developed by job rotation and the exchange of duties at the workplace. The second objective is autonomation for achieving quality control of the products. An example of such autonomation can be seen in the QC circles and suggestion system at Toyota (Maruyama 1989, p. 54). As J.L. Liker stresses, "flexibility required marshaling the ingenuity of the workers to continually improve processes" (Liker 2004, p. 22).

It is very important to understand the significances and limitations of flexible Japanese labor practices. Unlike in the American labor formation, based on the principle of specialization evident in the Taylor system, wherein job classifications are strictly decided and workers are only in charge of making specific parts, the Japanese labor formation allows job classifications to be decided by work teams led by a qualified manager (Maruyama 1995, p. 161). Such flexibility in the Japanese labor formation based on the autonomy of the work team has greatly contributed to securing an agreement and the accomplishment of responsibility among workers (Maruyama 1995, p. 217). In addition, as for the QC circles and improvement activities, workers also focus on improvements in their everyday tasks through the continuous improvement activities, which reflects in their performance. Given these findings, the integration of a plan and its execution can be realized, despite certain limitations, such as the fact that such activities should be performed according to the improvement objectives of the company and under the management of the company for continuous improvement while achieving the determined standard time (Maruyama 1995, p. 224). Moreover, such activities can improve the morale of the overworked workers under the Japanese production system by improving the "autonomy of the small group at the workplace." It is therefore important to grasp the dual character of Japanese labor flexibility, as seen in the autonomy of workers and the strict management by the company (Maruyama 1995, Chaps. 6 and 9; Kyotani 1993a, pp. 241–246, 271; Kyotani 1993b, pp. 39–41).

In this regard, it is possible to secure flexibility in the labor force in the Japanese production system by directly supporting the development of multi-skilled workers. In the American labor formation, the extreme subdivision and inflexibility of duties, based on the division of labor, has had a negative impact on morale, which, in turn, has increased the difficulty of implementing innovations such as ME technology (Aoyama 1991, p. 63). In sum, the Japanese labor formation and the use of its labor force have overcome such limitations.

13.3 Production System Reforms in Germany and Their Characteristics

13.3.1 Development of a Production System in German Enterprises

An important objective of the German automobile industry after the 1970s was to introduce a mass production model that could help them secure flexibility while utilizing ME technology. The industry sought new work organization such as group work, in which skilled workers formed the core given the emphasis on the product differentiation strategy and the high value-added strategy (rather than the competitive advantage of price). The German production model focused on deriving the advantages of flexible automation technologies, the utilization of specialized workers, the integration/synthesis of direct production functions, and the integration of indirect functions (i.e., maintenance, adjustment, and quality assurance) (Kazama 1997, pp. 287–288).

13.3.1.1 Flexibilization of a Production System Based on Microelectronics Technology

Regarding the use of ME technology, German automobile companies prioritized the introduction of industrial robots and numerical control (NC) machines in order to secure automation efficiency and technical flexibility (Volkswagen AG 1997, p. 15; Daimler-Benz AG 1982, p. 43; Daimler-Benz AG 1983, p. 39; Daimler-Benz AG 1985, p. 67). At Volkswagen, when the Beetle ("Käfer") was replaced by new models, such robot technology became even more important. In fact, by the end of fiscal year 1983, more than 1,200 industrial robots were in operation (Volkswagen AG 1983, p. 56). The goal of such new technologies was the extensive introduction of flexible, computer-based techniques, which not only included industrial robots but also computer numeric control (CNC) machines, instead of using single-purpose machines and manual forms of production (Jürgens et al. 1986, p. 259).

However, the situation of flexible automation greatly differed between process sections. Whereas such automation significantly advanced in the press and machining processes, there were fields such as welding (assembly of white body) and painting that used both high and low technology. In the unit and final assembly sections, although progressive automation of repetitive tasks was performed, even in the beginning of the 1990s, overall mechanization was not realized (Schumann et al. 1990, p. 49).

According to Schumann et al. (1990, p. 52), in the press process, the manual work to product as non-mechanized work performed by skilled workers did not already exist and the ratio of manual workers to highly automated machines was 86%. In the machining process, the ratio of manual workers to product was only 6% and that of manual workers to automated machines was 68%. Regarding the body manufacturing process, in fiscal year 1984, Opel (at its Bochum plant) replaced its welding equipment with flexible automatic welding equipment that could be freely programmed. As a result, 98% of the 4,200 welding points for the production of the Kadett was automatically performed (Adam Opel 1984, pp. 11–12). In the large-scale modernization of the Rüsselheim plant, which peaked around 1987, the transformation to flexible automation in the body assembly process played a significant role (Adam Opel AG 1987, p. 19). At the three plants of the Ford Motor Company in Germany, the automation rate of welding points increased from 82 to 92% within 1985 (Ford-Werke AG 1985, p. 39). In the new, flexible production of white body at the Emden plant of Volkswagen in 1987, the body parts were welded with a large number of automated welding machines (Volkswagen AG 1987, p. 34). However, whereas the ratio of the manual workers to production workers was 81% in the body manufacturing process, the ratio of manual workers to machines was only 14% (Schumann 1990, pp. 51–52).

In the assembly process, the overall change to flexible automation occurred in 1980s (Bispinck 1983, pp. 88–89, 94–95). However, the delay in the rationalization, in comparison with other processes, was largely due to various characteristics of the assembly process; consequently, overcoming this delay became an integral focus of the policy of modernization. Under such situations, assembly was the section in automobile production in which the largest profits were expected. In the 1980s, efforts to overcome the difficulties regarding the automation and mechanization of assembly work were made in two directions: through the "flexible assembly system" and through product technology, both of which could improve the assembly process (Kern and Schumann 1990, p. 60). As a result, the programmable automation system became the core system of the assembly process (Bispinck 1983, pp. 95, 97).

At Volkswagen, a representative example was the Halle 54, which signaled the introduction of the latest automation facilities in the assembly process in 1983. The Halle 54, as a symbol of the efforts to mechanize and automate the assembly process, integrated an automatic transportation system as well as a quality control system into the workplace (Volkswagen AG 1983, pp. 27, 48). In the design of the car, a design considering the use of a robot was required. As a result, the order of assembly process was altered according to the new technology and a change in design was performed for the purpose of effective use of robots in the Halle 54 (Volkswagen AG 1983, p. 57). Importantly, the new automatic system was adopted in the unit assembly plant and the Kassel transmission plant. In the Emden and the Braunchweig plants, large-scale projects for the Volkswagen group were promoted for automation (Volkswagen AG 1986, p. 33). By fiscal 1987, the automation system in the assembly process exemplified the flexibility of production (Volkswagen AG 1987, p. 34).

The reforms in which ME technology was a key factor were developed in connection with the humanization of labor and the use of skilled laborers (Volkswagen AG 1977, p. 15; Ford-Werke AG 1984, p. 47; Ford-Werke AG 1985, p. 39; BMW AG 1980, p. 11). At Volkswagen, investments for the humanization of labor at the workplace were made, along with investments toward rationalization and expansion (*Volkswagen Archiv*, 119/447/2; Beicht über das Geschäftsjahr 1977; Volkswagenwerk Aktiengesellschaft Wolfsburg. Sperrfrist; Veröffentlichung frei ab 27 April 1978, pp. 15, 17, 41; *Volkswage Archiv*, 119/447/1; Prospekt Volkswagenwerk Aktiengesellschaft Wolfsburg, Börseneinführung in Wien November 1978, pp. 17, 20). Furthermore, a new evaluation for the special qualities of human labor appeared in the paradigm switch of the labor policies and the fundamental changes in the strategies regarding the labor force (Schumann 2008, p. 380).

13.3.1.2 Introduction of Microelectronics Technology and New Role of Skilled Workers: Functional Integration of Direct and Indirect Labor

According to Kern and Schumann (1990), in the traditional production of white body, the complicated new technology was only able to be successfully introduced when special skills became available. On the one hand, personnel in charge of electronics and software also capable of programming the equipment were required. However, on the other hand, workers who were capable of diagnosing and repairing the equipment were still required during malfunctions and breakdowns of such equipment (Kern and Schumann 1990, pp. 76, 83). Thus, the integration of both aspects was necessary. This prominently occurred in the white body production process in which most of the maintenance was performed on-site, after which inspections were conducted by "line control workers" (Straßenführers), i.e., production workers with higher vocational value (Kern and Schumann 1990, p. 81). In the latter half of the 1980s, the segregation of such duties was abolished and the integration of indirect functions was advanced (Muster 1987, pp. 339, 341).

Flexible production and high technology, such as ME technology, required a more integrative approach (Jürgens et al. 1993, p. 372). That is, the skilled workers could avoid obstacles during breakdowns of the automated production facilities by participating in the maintenance of the equipment beforehand (Asendorf and Nuber 1988, pp. 271, 275). At Volkswagen, only skilled workers could utilize computer-aided design (CAD) technology, industrial robots, NC machines, and flexible manufacturing systems (FMSs) (Volkswagen AG 1982, p. 17). At BMW, programming of the welding robots was performed by specialists, beginning in the 1980s (BMW 1981, p. 33). In this way, the higher level of mechanization and automation based on ME technology increased the demand for skilled workers for the maintenance, adjustment, and programming of the equipment (Bispinck 1983, pp. 99–100). This created a new occupational category that added indirect functions such as maintenance and repair for workers. However, in the first half of the 1980s, the paradigm shift of labor formation through the functional integration of direct and indirect labor and the "re-professionalization" of workers on the basis of their skill were unable to be generalized (Kern and Schumann 1990, pp. 79, 98–99). In fact, under the condition that the conveyor work in the assembly process was maintained, there was only a slight possibility of such integration of duties (Kern and Schumann 1990, p. 54).

However, according to a study by Schumann et al. in 1994, system regulators in charge of addressing extremely simple disturbances and complicated mechanical engineering, electrical engineering, and electronic engineering repairs and conducting maintenance checks of ME equipment became extremely important. System regulators were one of the most important members in the high technology department as well as in the press and machining processes. For example, the ratio of workers as system regulators to production workers in the press and machining processes were 14 and 23%, respectively. In contrast, looking at the white body manufacturing process in which both high technology and low technology co-existed, the relevant numerical value in the latest welding robot line was 56%. However, the numerical value for this production process was only 5%. Despite differences between process sections and the various patterns of integration of duties, system regulators became the core personnel of the production workers (Schumann et al. 1994a, pp. 85–90; Schumann et al. 1990, pp. 51–53, 62, 68).

Thus, in the automobile industry, companies developed the integrated different strategies of work organization and labor input in order to secure and reinforce employee rights at the beginning of the 1990s. In the mechanized production section, the complete secession from the conventional work and management structures also occurred at an individual level. However, in the departments where manual work was still dominant, the combination of duties of the system regulators and the manual laborers was only seen in exceptional cases in which various activities were performed by different workers (Schumann et al. 1994a, pp. 165, 341).

Finally, although there were differences between process sections, the model of skilled workers was particularly important for modern technology management. Therefore, skilled workers and the understanding of their work (as a profession) were central to the German model (Jürgens et al. 1993, pp. 384–385).

13.3.1.3 Development of Group Work and Its Characteristics

In the reform of production system during this period, the team-work system was also introduced in relation with the humanization of labor. The formation of production teams represented an alternative to the development of a broader scope of work requirements (e.g., system regulation) for selected employees. The team-level concept for management was to integrate indirect specialists, such as maintenance and QC workers, into the teams of direct production workers (Jürgens et al. 1986, p. 269).

By the mid-1970s the dominant rationalization model in the German automobile industry was mainly oriented toward personnel placement through the division of labor and "labor formation based on the principle of the Taylor system." However, in the subsequent period, a new form of work organization aimed at securing flexibility of management was systematically tested, after which it was first implemented in the labor-intensive assembly section (Brumlop 1986, pp. 48–49).

At Volkswagen, partially autonomous group work was implemented in the latter half of the 1970s. The work was carried out in two assembly groups of which the members concurrently worked on four assembling islands. Large-scale skill training measures were developed so that the workers could successfully meet the demands for various works. However, job rotations were not possible because of the conflicts regarding grouping and also because united grouping was introduced very late (after the latter half of the 1970s) by the Works Council and IG Metall, the dominant metal-workers' union in Germany (Bispinck 1983, pp. 91; Volkswagen Ag 1980, pp. 23–36, 49–51). By the end of the 1980s, this new form of work organization was tested and introduced into all plants for enhancing productivity. A representative form of this organization was teamwork. Specifically, the teams comprised seven to 12 members who decided the work flow of the team and eventually assumed responsibility for production volume, quality, and facility maintenance. The overall goal of such a change of work organization was to transfer the important responsibilities to the workers and strengthen their cost awareness (Volkswagen AG 1989, p. 34).

At Opel, this form of group work, which was not a simple imitation of the Japanese model, was introduced in the Bochum plant. The concept of humanization of labor was integrated into the Japanese model of production. The group work at the Bochum plant aimed at more effectively using the knowledge of the group concerning production by having the members take charge of the indirect labor related to production (i.e., quality, repair, and maintenance) and by stronger participation of workers in the management's problem-solving decisions. The changes in the workplace were decided by each group, which formed an important part of the flexible autonomy. The introduction of the group work was related to a large-scale skill training program, which included 71 groups (with more than 800 workers). At the end of the 1990s, the first group project was organized in sections of the assembly plant and the press plant at Bohum, which comprised approximately 20,000 employees. However, the introduction of the group work into the flow of production still did not progress during this period (Minssen and Howaldt 1991, pp. 435–437, 441).

Despite these attempts, the concept of semi-autonomous teamwork was forced to temporarily retreat due to cost limitations. In the 1990s, the lean production (or lean manufacturing) system in Japan spread to Germany, after which the group work system was redeveloped (Watanabe 2003, pp. 110, 113–115). In Germany, the technical rationalization by ME technology was particularly emphasized as a measure to make the production system more flexible. However, the reforms in the field of organization were only complementary in character. In addition, during the introduction of the group work, supplementing and improving the production model on the basis of the Ford system, rather than overcoming the limitations of such a system, became a significant problem (Haipeter 2000, p. 312).

13.3.1.4 Small Group Activities at the Workplace and Their Characteristics

The introduction of small group activities at the workplace, such as QC circles and suggestion activities, was also an important part of the reforms of the production system. In the economic committee at Volkswagen on 25 November 1976, it was pointed out that the quality of products was well below the standards of other Japanese enterprises [*Volkswagen Archiv*, 119/911, Protokoll Nr.6/76 über die Sitzung des Wirtschaftsasschusses am 25.11.76 (14.12.1976), S. 3]. Under such conditions, the learning and adoption of Japanese management methods began in the 1980s, and the first QC Circle Council was held in November 1982. In the automobile industry, the Japanese model provided the stimulus for new methods of work organization. The early 1980s was the turning point in which German enterprises began accepting Japanese methods (Kleinschmidt 2002, pp. 369, 383).

In the Volkswagen group, QC circles and small group activities were introduced in 1982 in response to the "Japanese challenge," and 1,785 QC circles were organized at the Hannover plant by the end of the decade. However, these circles were not the result of simply transferring Japanese models; instead, they were developed on the basis of Germany's own experience as well, such as group work efforts (Kohlhoff 1992, p. 383).

One focal point regarding the expansion of workers' responsibilities was the transfer of quality control to direct production workers. For example, at the Ford Company in Germany, a newly created job classification called a "repair inspector" (through the integration of repair and quality control duties) was integrated into the production departments. In contrast, the functions of quality control were absorbed by the production departments and integrated into the standard job descriptions (without creating new job designations) at Volkswagen. In addition, quality control functions were decentralized by creating sub-systems comprising "pairs" of one quality control inspector and one worker. However, only a limited number of "action circles" existed in the mid-1980s, except at the Hannover plant, which included 120 quality circles. On the other hand, at Opel, although there were a limited number of quality control activities, the production-team concept was incorporated into the goals and functions of the quality circles in a more comprehensive manner. Thus, it can be stated that the development of quality circles was the most advanced at Ford and Opel in Germany. Meanwhile, the works councils of Daimler-Benz and Opel did not allow quality control to develop very far, owing to the belief that the union representatives could be overshadowed by the companies in which quality circles were prevalent (Jürgens et al. 1986, pp. 275–276).

Among the small group activities at the workplace, the suggestion system also had an important meaning. For example, at Volkswagen, the practical use of its suggestion system was regarded as an important issue in the latter half of the 1970s [*Volkswagen Archiv*, 119/218/1, Offene Fragen und Themen/Betriebsvereinbarungen (14.9.1979), S. 2; *Volkswagen Archiv*, 119/911, Protokoll Nr.2/77 über die Sitzung des Wirtschaftsasschusses am 22.02.1977, S. 2; *Volkswagen Archiv*, 119/911, Protokoll Nr.1/76 über die Sitzung des Wirtschaftsasschusses am 11.02.1976 (20.2.1976), S. 2; *Volkswagen Archiv*, 119/218/1, Kurzprotokoll.Besprechung zwischen Herrn Briam und dem Gesamtbetriebsausschuβ (18.5.1979); *Volkswagen Archiv*,119/218/1, Besprechungsunterlagen für die Gesamtbetriebsratssitzung in Braunschweig am Donnerstag, dem 1.Dezember 1977, 9.00 Uhr]. Meanwhile, at Opel, the suggestion system had been employed for approximately 25 years by fiscal year 1975. More specifically, approximately 280,000 suggestions had been collected and 18.4 million DM was paid as rewards in this period. In fiscal year 1975 alone, 37,339 suggestions were collected (Adam Opel AG 1975, p. 16). In fiscal year 1987, 29,235 suggestions for improvement were submitted, after which 9,438 cases were adopted and more than seven million DM was paid as bonuses (Adam Opel AG 1987, p. 24).

However, in Japan, the number of suggestions in 1978 reached 463,000 at Toyota. In addition, despite the development of small group activities, the defect rates in German companies were higher than those in Japanese enterprises. For instance, at Volkswagen, there were approximately 1,000 defects for every 4,000 automobiles produced. Looking at a comparable plant in a Japanese automobile company, there was no defect at all for 3,000 automobiles produced per day (Kleinschmidt 2002, pp. 379–380).

13.3.2 Limitations of the Reforms of the Production System in German Enterprises and Their Factors

13.3.2.1 Predominance of the Japanese Production System and Its Factors

The reforms of the production system emphasizing flexible mass production methods (based on ME technology and indirect and direct skilled workers) in Germany were related to the shift toward the product field and the market segment of high quality and high added value. In the upper segment in which price competition can be avoided/mitigated to some degree, the German production model was able to demonstrate some effectiveness. However, in the market segment with high demands and production volumes, the Japanese production system was more effective than the German system.

In Japan, establishing low defect rates and avoiding breakdowns in the production process were the subject of focus among the small group activities, the QC circles, and the suggestion systems. Multi-skilled workers also played significant roles in achieving such objectives. As a result, the Japanese model achieved high efficiency and adaptability, compared with its European and American counterparts. The Japanese production system also enabled small lot production of one type of product, which was not only seen in the automobile industry but also in the processing and assembly industries.

13.3.2.2 Limitations of the Reforms Based on the Microelectronics Technology-Dependent Production System

Despite the large-scale use of automation in the assembly process at Volkswagen, it was not possible to use ME equipment, such as robots, for various types of products flexibly. In contrast, the concept of module assembly at Opel enabled a very flexible production process without the use of such automation. Even in the 1990s, no unified strategy existed for introducing new technology in the automobile industry (Dolata 1990, pp. 40, 42). German enterprises regarded a strategy heavily based on ME technology as an effective means of achieving competitive advantages over their Japanese counterparts, which based their functioning on the effective management of personnel and labor formation (Jürgens 1990, p. 597).

However, technological advancement alone was not sufficient to catch up to the Japanese enterprises given the predominance of their labor formation and effective use of work force. Indeed, the German automobile industry was a pioneer in the use of industrial robots. However, the conditions in the use of such equipment greatly varied between production processes. For example, in the German automobile industry, the automation rates in 1983 and 1990 were 60 and 70% in the press process, respectively; 40–7% and 70% in the white body manufacturing process, respectively; 40 and 70% in the painting process, respectively; and 75 and 80% in the machining process, respectively. In contrast, the relevant numerical values in the unit assembly process for the same years were 25 and 45%, respectively and 10 and 20% in the final assembly process, respectively (Kern and Schumann 1990, p. 66). Moreover, despite the promotion of the strategy to increase flexibility in production, the production organizations at the core plants did not change. In fact, flexible production was only introduced with new car models at the branch plants (Schamp 1995, p. 103).

The rationalization of the assembly process was mainly achieved through the detour method, as seen in the designs that were more suitable for the assembly process (e.g., the Volkswagen Golf) and the exclusion of partial work from the main conveyor system (Dolata 1990, p. 40). In the automation of the assembly process, the technical difficulties were significant in comparison with other process sections, and there were numerous failures in the assembly work that was automated with an industrial robot. As a result, the skilled workers who were in charge of maintenance functions were required to cope with such situations. In this regard, attempts to automate the assembly process at Halle 54 of the Wolfsburg plant were ineffective (Keller 1993, pp. 173–175). In contrast to the automated production lines for the Volkswagen Beetle, the equipment and the process for the new Golf had a certain degree of flexibility. However, since this flexibility was limited to one model and its variations, the goals of cost-effectiveness and reducing manpower were not realized through assembly automation. Furthermore, building the Halle 54 helped Volkswagen reach its break-even point, which was crucial for the company in the 1990s (Jürgens 1998, pp. 292–293).

In this regard, competitive advantage was never secured, and the expected rapid improvement of productivity was not achieved in the 1980s despite capital investments in equipment and technology (Jürgens 1990, p. 598). After the financial crisis in the automobile industry in 1992/1993, since it was apparent that automation in the assembly process (particularly the final assembly process) was technically achievable but economically difficult, the push for automation declined (Schumann 1997, p. 223). By the 1990s, the use of non-automated systems in production facilities was promoted, especially in newly established production locations and former peripheral locations (Speidel 2005, p. 103). Thus, the automation that was strongly promoted in the 1980s was abandoned in the 1990s (Eckardt et al. 1999, p. 174).

13.3.2.3 Deployment of the Japanese Production System and Its Limitations

13.3.2.3.1 Deployment of the Japanese Labor Management Model and Its Limitations

Although the deployment of the Japanese model of mass production was attempted, such actions did not sufficiently advance. An important characteristic of the Japanese production system lies in the total systematization of processes. However, even from the end of the 1980s to the 1990s, the introduction of the Japanese system in German enterprises was limited to individual forms and systems such as the team-work system, QC circles, and the just-in-time production method (Jürgens 1990, p. 600).

Looking at the team-work system, in Germany, there were attempts to overcome the limitations regarding the "rigidity of the centralized corporate organization," as seen in the excessive specialization and bureaucratization based on the "separation of plan and execution" proposed by the Taylor system. However, as the limitations of automation became apparent, German enterprises introduced the team-work system in parallel with restructuring after the 1990s. After 1992/1993, especially when weak sales were significant, the team-work system emerged as an important means of improving labor policies and establishing lean production systems in the German automobile industry (Schumann 1997, p. 220).

In the 1990s, the principles of lean production were introduced in full scale at Opel's Eisenach plant, Volkswagen's Mosel plant, and Mercedes-Benz's Rastatt plant (Schamp 1995, pp. 103–104). By the mid-1990s, the concept of teamwork or group work had become central to German work organizations (Funder and Seitz 1997, p. 58). However, even at the end of the 1990s, the Salzgitter engine plant at Volkswagen was the only plant that included full-scale group work organization. Since there were various approaches toward group work between the plants, it was not considered as a strategic focal point in the restructuring of production organization in Germany (Jürgens 1998, p. 303).

In addition, regarding the QC circles, according to Schumann et al. (1994a, b), some companies utilized such activities, but there were more cases in which actual results were not achieved (Schumann et al. 1994a, p. 168; Schumann et al. 1994b, p. 408). Meanwhile, small group activities in Japanese companies were supported by the Japanese employment practices of lifetime employment and trade unions. This adoption of small group activities was impossible without such support, which was the main reason why the QC circles did not become widespread among American and German enterprises (Yasui 2003, p. 86).

Looking at the suggestion activities for improvement, in Japan, the recognition among employees that any reduction of personnel would not occur as a result of such activities was a key factor in receiving the approval of employees. In contrast, German enterprises strongly expected a reduction of personnel through the implementation of the suggestion activities for improvement. Thus, the practice of suggestion activities greatly differed between the two countries (Roth 1996b, p. 167). In addition, by the 1990s, quality assurance was regarded as a major problem outside of the direct production process and focus on quality control (emphasizing that each process should attempt to avoid producing any defective products) was lacking (Schumann et al 1994b, p. 69).

Furthermore, there were differences between the characteristics and the significances regarding skilled workers in Japan and Germany. In Germany, the pursuit of "horizontal flexibility" by taking charge of many production lines was performed as much as possible (Kern and Schumann 1990, p. 86). However, the skill of indirect function in German enterprises was different from that in Japanese enterprises, which, for example, had multi-skilled workers.

New production concepts in the German automobile industry were dominated by automation, even though manufacturing companies were cautious regarding the prospective gains of introducing Japanese organizational forms (Jürgens et al. 1986, pp. 273–274). Furthermore, in the German plants, change was not only seen in the integration of direct and indirect labor and arrangement of direct skilled workers but also in employee participation (Jürgens et al. 1993, p. 380). Hence, the differences between the small group activities in Japan and Germany were significant.

In the German automobile industry, the technology-oriented strategy was promoted in the 1980s; however, orientation toward Japanese methods became stronger in the 1990s. Accordingly, elements such as the suggestion system for improvement, total quality management (TQM), total productive maintenance (TPM), and teamwork were the main pillars of the production concepts (Roth 1996b, pp. 120, 135). However, labor unions in which the IG Metall occupied the core part supported the "flexibilization" of technical labor only if overcoming "non-human labor" under the traditional work organization (based on the Taylor system), realizing the "suitable labor for man," improving workers' professional qualifications, and increasing pay/rewards could be expected. Moreover, the desire for unrestricted flexibility (on the management side) was only pursued under the condition that social regulations were always exercised from the viewpoint of labor (Kazama 1997, p. 98).

Finally, works council members and union representatives could develop their own concepts and alternatives of the labor model on the basis of the principles of codetermination (Jürgens et al. 1993, p. 382). Such differences in the institutional conditions between Germany and Japan also influenced the introduction and development of the Japanese model of labor management.

13.3.2.3.2 Deployment of the Just-In-Time Production System and Its Limitations

In Germany, the integration of production processes, as seen in Japan, was not realized in the 1980s. At Volkswagen, the gradual achievement of the new logistics concept began in September 1983 in order to reduce stocks in all stages of procurement and production. The responsibility of management and the control of materials in the entire production process was single-handedly taken by the new logistics organization (Volkswagen AG 1983, p. 37). The integration of materials management and production control by computer was also promoted to combine all of the parts manufacturing processes into this logistics system. Similar actions were also performed at Daimler-Benz. However, this functional logistics system was only partly realized. The complicated structure of the network, ranging from the suppliers to the final product distributors, still faced numerous difficulties (Dolata 1990, S. 41). For example, at Daimler-Benz, the just-in-time method was strongly promoted in relation to the S-Class, which was sold in 1991. However, only eight parts groups, which had 1,760 of the 42,000 parts, were still purchased according to the just-in-time method. Although cooperative relationships with 16 parts suppliers that delivered parts in the just-in-time method were established after 1992, the ratio of the purchasing price of such parts to that of all parts was only 20% (Meiβner et al. 1994, p. 98). In addition, as seen in the relationship between Volkswagen and Freudenberg as a supplier, the symbiotic relationship seen between Japanese automobile companies and their parts manufacturers was not possible in their German counterparts (Kleinschmidt 2002, pp. 388–389).

It was not until the 1990s that the real introduction of the just-in-time method was promoted. At Volkswagen (except at the new Mosel plant where the just-in-time concept had already been developed), many projects based on this method were initiated from the end of the 1980s to the first half of the 1990s (Meiβner et al. 1994, p. 134). At Opel (excluding the Eisenach plant, where the buffer inventory was near zero), the just-in-time concept was limited to the suppliers within the production association of GM in Europe. In fact, one-third of the purchased parts from outside of the company utilized this method in the first half of the 1990s (Meiβner et al. 1994, pp. 112, 114, 116).

In Europe, including Germany, there was no structure regarding the division of labor according to the subcontracting system, as seen in Japan. In Germany, even in the mid-1990s, many parts enterprises dealt with the demand of just-in-time delivery by increasing their stocks. Indeed, the parts makers delivered their products with this method, but they did not produce the parts in the same manner (Meiβner et al. 1994, p. 25), which was a significant limitation.

13.4 Significances of the Reforms of the Mass Production System in Japan and Germany

Based on the foregoing discussions, this section clarifies significance of the production system reforms in Japan and Germany from the 1970s to the 1980s.

13.4.1 Significance of the Japanese Production System

In Sect. 13.2, the overall structure of the Japanese production system and the mechanism whereby such a system functions have been discussed. Accordingly, this section examines the significance of the Japanese production system.

In this production system, the principle of mass production did not change, even though the realization of the economies of scale did require some changes over time. The production of many types of products was achieved by organizing the overall production process according to the principle of generalization. The realization of economies of scale was supplemented by economies of scope arising from the principle of generalization. Meanwhile, the possibility of realizing the economic effect of mass production has been further improved by increasing the operating rates while remaining flexible to market changes. Securing flexibility played a significant role in the full operation of production facilities with fixed costs. In the Japanese production system, such flexibility can improve work flow and production (Ono 1995, pp. 655–666).

Flexibility in the mass production of many types of products, which is based on the principle of generalization, is also important, especially in response to the contradiction between production and consumption under capitalistic production. In this regard, the true nature of flexible production changed qualitatively, as seen in the realization of gross weight necessary for the full operation of the production capacity (Ono 1994, p. 181).

In the American type of mass production system based on the principle of the specialization, as seen in the Ford system, the costs must increase with the production of many types of products because of the decline in economic efficiency in adopting relatively small lots per type of product and the rigidity in adapting to changes in demand. In contrast, for the Japanese model of the flexible mass production of many types of products, the production costs are relatively low because of high adaptive capacity and improvements in operating rates. In other words, there is a higher ability to adjust between supply and demand given economies of scope.

Japanese enterprises in the processing and assembly industries were able to realize high international competitiveness through such a management and production system from the 1970s to the 1980s. As a result, in European and American enterprises, the deployment of the Japanese production system (or "Japanization") became an important issue in the 1980s, despite the fact that the production of multiple products in Europe and the United States was much less than that in Japan. According to a study on the automobile industry by Womack et al. (1990), many discussions and attempts were made to introduce the Japanese production system because of the structural advantages of such a system.

13.4.2 Development of the Module Production System after the 1990s as Countermeasure to Limitations of Production System Reforms in Germany

When looking at the factors that determined the aforementioned delays and limitations regarding the deployment of the Japanese production system in Germany, there are three points. First, German companies pursued a production method that matched the characteristics of the German domestic market and the European market, which generally emphasized the quality and functionality of the products. Second, despite the increase in the market shares of Japanese automobiles, their competitive advantage in the European market was not as decisive as that in the US market (Ward's automotive yearbook 1987, p. 72). Third, the full-scale development of the reforms of the production system using ME technology advanced in the 1980s; therefore, attempts to change the production system occurred during the middle of the progress.

However, flexible and quality production was extremely expensive under the German system. The product upgrading strategy also became a factor that raised production costs and product prices. These problems first became apparent in the American market (Jürgens et al. 1998, p. 296). Thus, in the 1990s, the transformation of the production system became an important issue given the aggravation of the profitability with the depression of sales.

Above all, the Eisenach plant, established by Opel in 1992, was regarded as the prototype for "lean" automobile plants with regard to logistics and model of production among the worldwide production unions of Opel and GM. At the Rüsselsheim plant, which opened in 2002, the logistics concept at the Eisenach plant was developed (Strinz 2000, p. 602). Such reforms were also emphasized by other enterprises (Schröder 2007, p. 600; Meise 2007, p. 601; Gebhardt 2007, p. 601). The core of the reforms in the automobile industry after the 1990s lay in the change from product orientation to process orientation among companies. Moreover, in the new production strategies of automobile companies, the priorities included establishing a just-in-time delivery system, transferring the responsibilities of development, production, and processing to the parts manufacturing companies and reorganizing the relationship between the parts companies (Kilper and Dilcher 1999, pp. 3, 7, 14).

Meanwhile, the building of new inter-firm structures of production networks had become a central management problem in Germany (Semlinger 1992a, pp. 98–99, 104–105; Semlinger 1992b, pp. 342, 350; Semlinger 1989, pp. 517, 524). However, the number of parts companies with which automobile enterprises had direct dealings ranged from 2,800 to 3,600 (Roth 1996a, p. 191), which was remarkable in comparison with Japan. In addition, the supplier system was not the multilayered and hierarchical structure that enabled high-level coordination between the assembly processes at automobile enterprises and the parts manufacturing processes at suppliers, as seen in Japan. In addition, cooperation and information exchange between automobile companies and part makers were required so that such production could function effectively. However, in Germany, the distribution of cooperation was often balanced in favor of the most powerful company (Semlinger 1992a, p. 110). According to a 1995 report by the European Commission, in Europe, there were traditionally adversarial relations between automotive companies and their suppliers, with the former continuously demanding lower prices and threatening to utilize their competition (European Commission 1995, Chap. 11, p. 20).

Not only the "Japanization" implying outside dependence in the supply of parts but also the "Japanization" concerning the development power of small- and medium-sized parts manufacturing firms had an important significance (Hiroe 1993, p. 41). However, German enterprises were generally reluctant in involving suppliers in the integrated systems of product development and began this practice quite late, i.e., after the 1990s (Jürgens 1998, p. 296).

In 1993, the shift toward "the design-in" method of development of automobiles began and the reorganization toward the Japanese subcontracting system, wherein major parts manufacturing companies called "system suppliers" formed the core, became strong (Ikeda 1995, p. 170; Ikeda 1998, p. 240). BMW's relationship with parts companies was newly established in the 1990s, with the parts companies even participating in the development process of automobile models from an early stage (Meißner et al. 1994, p. 69). At Volkswagen, the development of new parts by the design-in method and the global procurement of parts became a trend in the latter half of the 1990s (Volkswagen AG 1995, p. 36). At Daimler-Benz, parts manufacturers participated in the development of new models from the early stages of development. In addition, the responsibility of the development and production of the entire system was transferred in 1993 to parts companies, according to the new concept of cooperation, as seen in its relationship with TANDEM (Daimler-Benz AG 1993a, p. 21; Daimler-Benz AG 1993b, p. 21; Daimler-Benz AG 1996, p. 18). Overall, the supply and business relationships between automobile companies and parts manufacturers significantly improved through the implementation of purchases that were synchronized with the overall production process, securing of quality of parts, support to supplier, and more thorough cooperation with parts makers in the field of R&D (Reeg 1998, p. 244).

However, in Germany, this change was closely related to the introduction of the module production system. Even in reorganizing the division of labor with suppliers, cost reductions at parts manufacturing companies were insufficient, in comparison with those in Japan. Moreover, the guidance system established for the parts enterprises by the automobile manufacturer was weak. Under such conditions, German automobile companies focused on the introduction of the module production system and the support to the system module suppliers. In the German automotive industry, the "bidding" system—in which automobile manufacturers selected the parts manufacturers that offered the lowest prices from among several companies summoned as the trading partner for the next term—was introduced by the latter half of the 1990s. Thus, the cost reductions of parts were insufficient, which promoted the movement toward modularization (Ikeda 1998, pp. 219, 222, 239, 246). The development of the module production system, which included several advantages such as cost reductions in production and development by integrating individual components, was significant. Under such a situation, establishing a cooperative relationship with system suppliers for the module production system also became an important issue (Bauer 1993, pp. I–III; Lederer 1995, p. 69; Automobiltechnische Zeitschrift 1998, p. 271).

The first full-scale development of the module production system and the formation of the modular consortium based on the cooperative relationships with suppliers was seen in the new truck and bus plant in Resende, Brazil, by Volkswagen in the latter half of the 1990s. Subsequently, this production system was diffused in Europe (Lung et al. 1999; Fleury and Salerno 1998; Marx et al. 1997). As a result, the Volkswagen group became a driving force in the introduction of fractal production, as seen in the module production system in Europe (Lung et al. 1999, p. 239). In particular, whenever a new model was launched or a new assembly plant was built, modular orientation was increasingly integrated into the investments that the enterprises made in the industrialized countries (Lung et al. 1999, p. 254).

In addition, restricted conditions, as seen in the lack of the foundation for multi-skilled workers (as per Japanese labor practices and labor formation), were also important factors regarding the introduction of the module production system in

Germany. An important characteristic of the final assembly process is seen in many operating processes and a variety of types of work. That is, the flexible use of multi-skilled workers in the team-work system (supported by the flexible duties structure), the Japanese labor formation, and the labor management that promoted the QC circle and improvement activity had significant importance. An important means for "catching-up" to such predominance of Japanese enterprises was found in the module production system, which enabled companies to reduce the number of operating processes (labor hours) and simplify workloads by assembling key components beforehand, especially in the final assembly process.

For German enterprises, after the 1990s, the countermeasure to the Japanese production system's pursuit of efficiency and flexibility was found in the module production system under the aforementioned conditions. It was also based on the unit system and the principle of standardization of basic parts. The module production system was an attempt to make the final assembly process more flexible. It was also aimed to cope with the increasing complexities arising from the development of various products that were more "customer-specific" through the integration of parts companies into the assembly and distribution of unit parts divided by the interface to suppliers (Salgado 2008, p. 128). In addition, since each module was produced while maintaining an appropriate stock, the synchronization with the main line was no longer necessary and excessive workload disappeared in the main line. Meanwhile, the production line was shortened as the flexibility was increased (Otsuka 2010, pp. 315–316). In sum, the module production system was pursued as an important means of catching up to the production system in Japan since it enabled high synchronization between processes and flexible worker placement.

Thus, the reforms of the mass production system in the 1970s and the 1980s determined the development of the module production system in Germany after the 1990s as an alternative to the Japanese production system. Although the product concept with the module production system had been discussed for a long time, it was first introduced as a new production model in the German automobile industry (D'Alessio et al. 2000, p. 54). This movement differed from that in Japan; however, the reforms of the production system in Germany after the 1990s influenced other European countries under similar circumstances.

References

Adam Opel AG (1975) Geschäftsbericht 1975. Adam Opel AG, Rüsselsheim

Adam Opel AG (1984) Geschäftsbericht 1984. Adam Opel AG, Rüsselsheim

Adam Opel AG (1987) Geschäftsbericht 1987. Adam Opel AG, Rüsselsheim

Alessio ND', Oberbeck H, Seitz D (2000) 》Rationalisierung in Eigenenergie《. VSA-Verlag, Hamburg, Ansatzpunkte für den Bruch mit dem Taylorismus bei VW

Aoyama S (1991) Nihonteki keiei shisutemu no konnichiteki tokusitsu (The present characteristics of Japanese management system). In: Keizai (Economy) 326:59–72

Asanuma B (1997) Nihon no kigyo soshiki (Japanese corporate organization). Toyo keizai shinposha, Tokyo

Asendorf I, Nuber C (1988) Qualifizierte Produktionsarbeit——Die Renaissance des Facharbeiters in der industriellen Produktion?. In: Malsch T, Seltz R (eds) Die neuen Produktionskonzepte auf dem Prüfstand. Beiträge zur Entwicklung der Industriearbeit, 2nd ed. Edition Sigma, Berlin, pp 269–291

Automobiltechnische Zeitschrift (1998) Modultechnik bietet technische und wirtschaftliche Vorteile. In: Automobiltechnische Zeitschrift 100(4)

Bato T (1986) Wagakuni jidosha sangyo ni okeru ryosan taisei no kakuritsu to kigyo keiei (1) (Development of mass production system and business management in Japan, 1). In: Kagoshima keidai ronshu (The Kagoshima Keidai ronshu: the studies on the social and cultural sciences) 27(2):75-108

Bauer D (1993) Modultechnik in der Motorkühlung. In: Automobiltechnische Zeitschrift 95(9), ATZ-Supplement: I–III

Bispinck R (1983) Montagetätigkeit im Wandel—Arbeitsbedingungen zwischen Flieβband und Computer—. In: WSI Mitteilungen 36(2):88–101

BMW AG (1980) Bericht über das Geschäftsjahr 1980. BMW AG, München

BMW AG (1981) Bericht über das Geschäftsjahr 1981. BMW AG, München

Brumlop E (1986) Arbeitsbewertung bei flexiblem Personaleinsatz. Das Beispiel Volkswagen AG. Campus, Frankfurt am Main

Chusho kigyocho (ed) Heisei 7 nendoban chusho kigyo hakusho (White paper on small and medium firms. The fiscal year 1995). Okurasho insatsukyoku, Tokyo

Daimler-Benz AG (1982) Geschäftsbericht 1982. Daimler-Bnenz AG, Stuttgart

Daimler-Benz AG (1983) Geschäftsbericht 1983. Daimler-Bnenz AG, Stuttgart

Daimler-Benz AG (1985) Geschäftsbericht 1985. Daimler-Bnenz AG, Stuttgart

Daimler-Benz AG (1993a) Annual Report 1993. Daimler-Bnenz AG, Stuttgart

Daimler-Benz AG (1993b) Geschäftsbericht 1993. Daimler-Bnenz AG, Stuttgart

Daimler-Benz AG (1996) Annual Report 1996. Daimler-Bnenz AG, Stuttgart

Dolata U (1990) Modernisierung und Umprofilierung der Konzernstrukturen in der Automobilindustrie. In: WSI Mitteilungen 43(1):37–51

Doraiba (Driver) (1973) Doraiba (Driver). 20.11.1973

Doraiba (Driver) (1983) Doraiba (Driver). 20.11.1983

Eckardt A, Köhler H, Pries L (1999) Die Verschränkung von Globalisierung und Konzernmodernisierung oder: Der 'Elch-Test' für die deutsche Automobilindustrie. In: Schmidt G, Trinczek R (eds) Globalisierung. Ökonomische und soziale Herausforderungen am Ende des zwanzigsten Jahrhunderts, 1st ed. Nomos-Verlagsgesellschaft, Baden-Baden, pp 167–190

European Commission (1995) Panorama of EU industry 95/96. Office for Official Publications of the European Communities, Brussels

Fleury A, Salerno MS (1998) The transfer and hybridization of new models of production in the Brazilian automobile industry. In: Boyer R, Charron E, Jürgens U, Tolliday S (eds) Between imitation and innovation. The transfer and hybridization of productive models in the international automobile industry. Oxford University Press, Oxford, pp 278–294

Ford-Werke AG (1984) Geschäftsbericht 1984. Ford-Werke AG, Köln

Ford-Werke AG (1985) Geschäftsbericht 1985. Ford-Werke AG, Köln

Fujimoto T (1997) Seisan Sisutemu no Sinka Ron (Evolution of production system). Yuhikaku, Tokyo

Fujimoto T (1999) The evolution of a manufacturing system at Toyota. Oxford University Press, New York

Fujimoton T, Sei S, Takeishi A (1994) Nihon jidosha sangyo no sapuraiya shisutemu no zentaizo to sono tamensei (General view of the supplier system in the Japanese automobile industry and its diversity). In: Kikai keizai kenkyu (Bull Econ Res Inst Jpn Soc Promot Mach Ind) 24:11–36

Funder M, Seitz B (1997) Unternehemen (re)organisation und industrielle Beziehungen im Maschinenbau. Ergebnisse einer repräsentativen Studie. In: WSI Mitteilungen 50(1):57–64

Gebhardt J (2000) "Just-In-Time ist nicht mehr wegzudenken." In: Automobiltechnische Zeitschrift 102(78):601

Haipeter T (2000) Mitbestimmung bei VW. Neue Chancen für die betriebliche Interessenvertretung, 1st ed. Westfälisches Dampfboot, München

Hiroe A (1993) "Nihonka" susumeru Doitsu jidosha Sangyo (German automobile industry pursues "Japanization"). In: Chosa kiho (Res Q Rev) 25:25–42

Ikeda M (1986) Daikigyo to chusho kigyo (Large enterprises and small and medium enterprises). In: Kurumado M (ed) Chusho kigyo ron (Small and medium firms). Yachiyo shuppan, Tokyo, pp 74–107

Ikeda M (1995) Oshu jidosha sangyo no shitauke saihensei no doko (Trend of reorganization of the subcontracting system in the European automobile industry). In: Chuo daigaku keizai kenkyusho nenpo (Ann Inst Econ Res Chuo Univ) 25(II):147–172

Ikeda M (1998) Oshu jidosha meka no buhin chotatsu seisaku no daitenkan (Major changes in the parts purchasing policy of European automobile manufacturers). In: Chuo daigaku keizai kenkyusho nenpo (Ann Inst Econ Res Chuo Univ) 28:219–267

Imai K, Itami H, Koike K (1982) Naibu soshiki no keiziagaku (Economics of internal organization). Toyo keizai shinpohsa, Tokyo

Jürgens U (1990) Produkutionskonzepte und Standortstrategien in der Weltautomobilindustrie. In: WSI Mitteilungen 43(9):596–602

Jürgens U (1998) The development of Volkswagen's industrial model, 1967–1995. In: Freyssenet M, Mair A, Shimizu K, Volpato G (eds) One best way? Trajectories and industrial models of the world's automobile producers. Oxford University Press, Oxford, pp 273–310

Jürgens U, Dohse K, Malsch T (1986) New production concepts in West German car plants. In: Tolliday S, Zeitlin J (eds) The automobile industry and its works. Between Fordisum and flexibility. Berg, Cambridge, pp 258–281

Jürgens U, Malsch T, Dohse K (1993) Breaking from Taylorism. Changing forms of work in the automobile industry. Cambridge University Press, Cambridge

Kazama N (1997) Doitsuteki seisan moderu to furekishibiriti (German production model and flexibility). Chuo keizaisha, Tokyo

Keller M (1993) Collision. GM, Toyota, Volkswagen and the race to own the 21st century. Doubleday, New York

Kern H, Schumann M (1990) Das Ende der Arbeitsteilung? Rationalisierung in der industriellen Produktion, 2nd ed. C. H. Beck, München

Kilper H, Dilcher JS (1999) Auf dem Wege zum Ko-Produzenten. Über den Wandel der Produktions- und Lieferbeziehungen in der Automobilbranche. In: Pries L, Hertwig M (eds) Deutsche Autoproduktion im globalen Wandel. Gelsenkirchen, pp 1-16

Kleinschmidt C (2002) Der produktive Blick. Wahrnehmung amerikanischer und japanischer Management- und Produktionsmethoden durch deutsche Unternehmer 1950-1985. Akademie Verlag, Berlin

Kohlhoff AP- (1992) Das Fallbeispiel VW Hannover. In: Zeuner C (ed) Heidemann W, Kohlhoff AP-. Qualifizierung in der Autoproduktion. Europäische Automobilkonzern reagieren auf die japanische lean production. Schüren, Marburg, pp 105–112

Komatsu F (2009) Toyota seisan hoshiki ni okeru rodo to kanri (Labor and management in the Toyota production system). In: Suzuki Y, Nasuno K (eds) Nihon no monodukuri to keieigaku (Japanese manufacturing and business administration). Mineruva shobo, Kyoto, pp 95–119

Kyotani E (1993a) Furekishibiriti towa nanika. Gendai nihon no rodo katei (What is flexibility? Modern Japanese labor process). Madosha, Tokyo

Kyotani E (1993b) Posuto fodizumu dankai no rodo katei ronso (Labor process dispute in the post-Fordism stage). In: Nagano daigaku kiyo (Acad Bull Nagano Univ) 13(2 · 3):29-47

Lederer KG (1995) Neue Formen der Zusammenarbeit entwickeln. In: Automobitechnische Zeitschrift 97(2):69

Liker JL (2004) The Toyota way: 14 management principles from the world 's greatest manufacturer. McGraw-Hill, New York

Lung Y, Salerno MS, Zilbovicius M, Dias AVC (1999) Flexibility through modularity: experimentations with fractal production in Brazil and in Europe. In: Lung Y, Chanaron J-J, Fujimoto T, Raff D (eds) Coping with variety in the auto industry. Ashgate, Hampshire, pp 224–257

Maruyama Y (1989) Nihonteki keiei—Sono kozo to biheibia—(Japanese management—Its structure and behavior—). Nihon hyoronsha, Tokyo

Maruyama Y (1995) Nihonteki seisan shisutemu to furekisibiriti (Japanese production system and flexibility). Nihon Hyoronsha, Tokyo

Marx R, Zilbovicius M, Salerno M (1997) The Modular consortium in a new Volkswagen truck plant in Brazil: new forms of assembler and suppliers relationship. In: Integr Manuf Syst 8(5):292–298

Matsuzaki H (2005) Eigo de manabu Toyota seisan hosiki (Learning Toyota production system in English). Kenkyusha, Tokyo

Meise G (2000) "Auf Just-IN-Time folgt Order-to-Delivery" In: Automobiltechnische Zeitschrift 102(7–8):601

Meiβner H-R, Kisker KP, Bochum U, Aβmann J (1994) Die Teile und Die Herrschaft. Die Reorganisation der Automobilproduktion und der Zulieferbeziehungen. Edition Sigma, Berlin

Minssen H, Howaldt J (1991) Gruppenarbeit in der Automobilindustrie—Das Beispiel Opel Bochum—. In: WSI Mitteilungen 44(7):434–441

Monden Y (1991) Shin Toyota shisutemu (New Toyota system). Kodansha, Tokyo

Monden Y (1991b) Toyota no keiei shisutemu (Toyota management system). Daiyamondosha, Tokyo

Muster M (1987) Chancen und Schwierigkeiten arbeitspolitischer Interessenvertretung in der Autoindustrie. In: WSI Mitteilungen 40(6):337–345

Nakamura T (1983) Chusho kigyo to daikigyo (Small and medium firms and large firms). Toyo keizai shinposha, Tokyo

Nichi-ei-chu jidosha yogo jiten henshu iinkai (ed) (2011) Shin nichi-ei-chu jidosha yogo jiten (New Japanese-English-Chinese dictionary for automobiles). Jidosha gijutsukai, Tokyo

Nissan jidosha kabushikigaisha shashi hensan iinkai (ed) (1975) Nissan Jidosha shashi 1964–1973 (History of Nissan Motor Corpotration 1964–1973). Nissan jidosha kabushikigaisha, Tokyo

Nissan Jidosha kabushikingaisha soritsu gojushunen kinen jikko iinakai (ed) (1985) Nissan jidosha shashi 1974–1983 (History of Nissan Motor Corpotration 1974–1983). Nissan jidosha kabushikigaisha, Tokyo

Ono T (1990) Seisan no "jyunanka" ni tsuiteno kisoteki kosatsu (1) (A fundamental examination of the "flexibility" of production, 1). In: Meijyo shogaku (J Commer Econ) 40(1):129–165

Ono T (1994) Gendai nihon no seisan shisutemu no furekishibiriti (1) (Flexibility of the modern Japanese production system, 1). In: Shogaku ronsan (J Commer) 36(2):163–189

Ono T (1995) Gendai nihon no seisan shisutemu no furekishibiriti (2) (Flexibility of modern Japanese production system, 2). In: Shogaku ronsan (J Commer) 36(3 · 4):643–672. (Chapter 13)

Otsuka T (2010) Doitsu no shakai keiziateki sangyo kiban (Socio-economic industrial foundation in Germany). Kansai daigaku shuppanbu, Osaka

Reeg M (1998) Liefer- und Leistungsbeziehungen in der deutschen Automobilindustrie. Strukturelle Veränderungen aus unternehmerischer und wirtschaftspolitischer Sicht. Duncker und Humblot, Berlin

Roth S (1982) Rationalisierungsmaβnahmen der 80er Jahre und gewerkschaftliche Handlungsbedingungen. In: Gewerkschaftliche Monatshefte 33(3):129–143

Roth S (1996a) Automobilhersteller und ihre Zuliefer in Deutschland und Japan. In: Zwickel K (ed) Vorbild Japan? Stärken und schwächen der Industrieorte Deutschland und Japan. Bund-Verlag, Köln, pp 175–205

Roth S (1996b) Produktionskonzepte in Japan und Deutschland: Eine gewerkschaftliche Vergleichsstudie in der Automobilindustrie. In: Zwickel K (ed) Vorbild Japan? Stärken und schwächen der Industrieorte Deutschland und Japan. Bund-Verlag, Köln, pp 102–174

Sakamoto K (1992) Kokusai kyosoryoku to "Nihonteki seisan shisutemu" no tokushitsu (3) [International competitiveness and characteristic of "Japanese production system" (3)]. In: Keiei kenkyu (Bus Rev) 43(2):49–62
Salgado LGG (2008) Die Modulproduktion in der Automobilindustrie Brasiliens. Eine rechtliche und ökonomische Analyse. Duncker & Humblot, Berlin
Schamp EW (1995) The German automobile production system going European. In: Hudson R, Schamp EW (eds) Towards a new map of automobile manufacturing in Europe? New production concepts and spatial restructuring. Springer, Berlin, pp 93–116
Schröder B (2000) "Logistik im Zeichen des Wettbewerbs." In: Automobiltechnische Zeitschrift 102(7–8):600
Schumann M (1997) Die deutsche Automobilindustrie im Umbruch. In: WSI Mitteilungen 50(4):217–227
Schumann M (2008) Kampf um Rationalisierung-Suche nach neuer Übersichtlichkeit. In: WSI Mitteilungen 61(7):379–386
Schumann M, Kinsky VB-, Kuhlmann M, Kort C, Neumann U (1994a) Trendreport Rationalisierung. Automobilindustrie, Werkzeugmaschinenbau, Chemische Industrie, 2nd ed. Edition Sigma, Berlin
Schumann M, Kinsky VB-, Kuhlmann M, Kurz C, Neumann U (1994b) Rationalisierung im Übergang—Neue Befunde der Industriesoziologie zum Wandel der Produktionskonzepte und Arbeitsstrukturen—. In: WSI Mitteilungen 47(7):405–414
Schumann M, Kinsky V.B-, Neumann U, Springer R (1990) Breite Diffusion der Neuen Produktionskonzepte—zörgerlicher Wandel der Arbeitsstrukturen. Zwischenergebnisse aus dem "Trendreport—Rationalisierung in der Industrie". In: Soziale Welt 41(1):47–69
Semlinger K (1989) Fremdleistungsbezug als Flexibilitätsreservoir—Unternehmenspolitische und arbeitspolitische Risken in der Zulieferindustrie—. In: WSI Mitteilungen 42(9):517–525
Semlinger K (1992a) New developments in subcontracting: Mixing market and hierarchy. In: Amin A, Dietrich M (eds) Towards a new Europe? Structural change in the European economy. Edward Elgar, Aldershot, pp 96–115
Semlinger K (1992b) Small firms in big subcontracting. In: Altmann N, Köhler C, Meil P (eds) Technology and work in German industry. Routledge, London, pp 342–358
Shimada H (1988) Hyuman uea no keiziagaku (Economics of human ware). Iwanami shoten, Tokyo
Shimokawa K (2004) Gurobaru Jidosha Sangyo Keieishi (Global history of the automobile industry). Yuhikaku, Tokyo
Shiomi H (1978) Gendai tairyo seisan taiseiron (Modern mass production system). Moriyama shoten, Tokyo
Shiomi H (1985) Seisan rojisutikusu no kozo (Structure of production logistics). In Sakamoto K (ed) Gijyutsu kakushin to kigyo kozo (Technical innovation and enterprise structure). Mineruva shobo, Kyoto, pp 77–113
Suzuki Y (1990) Nihonteki kigyo shisutemu to kokusai kyosoryoku (Japanese corporate system and international competitiveness). In: Keizai to keiei (Econ Manag) 21(2):29–94
Suzuki Y (1994) Nihonteki seisan shisutemu to kigyo shakai (Japanese production system, management, and workers). Hokkaido daigaku tosho kankokai, Sapporo
Speidel F (2005) Mitbestimmte versus managementbestimmte Globalisierung in der Automobilindustrie. Ein Vergleich der Internationalisierungsstrategien und ihrer Verarbeitungen durch die Akteure der industriellen Beziehungen am Beispiel VWs und Renaults. R. Hampp, München
Strinz W (2000) "Der Lieferantenpark kommt ins Werk." In: Automobiltechnische Zeitschrift 102(7–8):602
Toyota jidosha hanbai kabushikigaisha shashi hensan iinkai (ed) (1980) Sekai no Ayumi (History of the world). Toyota jidosha hanbai kabushikigaisha, Nagoya
Toyota jidosha kabushikigaisha (ed) (1987) Sozo kagirinaku (Unlimited creation). Toyota jidosha kabushikigaisha, Toyota
Ueda H (2000) Sapuraiya ni kansuru ichi kosatsu (A study of suppliers). In: Kikan keizai kenkyu (Econ Study Q) 23(2):1–22

Ueda H (2001) Shitauke wa risuku shearingu ka (Is subcontracting system risk sharing?). In: Kamii Y, Nomura M (eds) Nihonkigyo. Riron to jissa (Japanese enterprises. Theory and practice). Mineruva shobo, Kyoto, pp 83–105

Ueno H, Kawasaki A (1994) Shitaukesei to kigyokan kankei (Subcontracting system and inter-firm relationship. In: Gendai kigyo kenkyukai (ed) Nihon no kigyokan kankei (Japanese inter-firm relationships). Chuo keizaisha, Tokyo, pp 175–203

Volkswagen AG (1977) Bericht über das Geschäftsjahr 1977. Volkswagen AG, Wolfsburg

Volkswagen AG (1980) Gruppenarbeit in der Motorenmontage. Ein Vergleich von Arbeitsstrukturen. Campus, Frankfurt am Main

Volkswagen AG (1982) Bericht über das Geschäftsjahr 1982. Volkswagen AG, Wolfsburg

Volkswagen AG (1983) Bericht über das Geschäftsjahr 1983. Volkswagen AG, Wolfsburg

Volkswagen AG (1986) Bericht über das Geschäftsjahr 1986. Volkswagen AG, Wolfsburg

Volkswagen AG (1987) Bericht über das Geschäftsjahr 1987. Volkswagen AG, Wolfsburg

Volkswagen AG (1989) Bericht über das Geschäftsjahr 1989. Volkswagen AG, Wolfsburg

Volkswagen AG (1995) Geschäftsbericht 1995. Volkswagen AG, Wolfsburg

Wada K, Shiba T (1995) Nihonteki seisan sisutemu no keisei (Formation of the Japanese production system). In: Yamazaki H, Kikkawa T (eds) "Nihonteki" keiei no renzoku to danzetsu (Continuity and discontinuity of "Japanese" management). Iwanami Shoten, Tokyo, pp 125–157

Ward's Automotive Yearbook (1987) Ward's Automotive Yearbook 1987, Ward's Communications, Detroit

Watanabe A (2003) Haiburido gata chimu kara jishu sekkeiteki chimu he (From hybrid type to self-organized team) —Doitsu ni okeru chimusei no hatten doko (Trend in team working system in Germany) —. In: Ohashi S, Takebayashi H (eds) Gendaino chimu sei (Modern team working system). Dobunkan shuppan, Tokyo, pp 109–126

Watanabe Y (1997) Nihon kikai kogyo no shakaiteki bungyo kozo (Structure of social division of labor in Japanese machine industry). Yuhikau, Tokyo

Womack JP, Jones DT, Roos D (1990) The machine that changed the world: How Japan's select weapon in the global auto wars will revolutionize Western industry. Harper Perennial, New York

Yamazaki T (2005) Gendai keieigaku no saikotiku (A study of the reconsttruction of business management study). Moriyama Shoten, Tokyo

Yasui T (2003) Sho shudan katsudo to chimu sagyo hoshiki (Small group activity and team working method). In: Ohashi S, Takebayashi H (eds) Gendai no chimu sei (Modern team working system). Dobunkan shuppan, Tokyo, pp 71-90

Yuasa Y (1991) Jidosha sangyo ni okeru gurobarizeshon to nihonteki seisan shisutemu (Ge) (Globalization and Japanese production system in the automobile industry, 2). In: Ehime keizai ronshu (Ehime Econ J) 11(2):41–68

Yuasa Y (1992) Furekisibiriti wo megutte (On flexibility). In: Keizai (Economy) 334:143–169

Chapter 14
Transformation Toward Shareholder Value-Oriented Management and Corporate Governance in Japan and Germany after the 1990s: Resurgence of the Americanization of Business Management

Abstract After the 1990s, influence and pressure on business management by the capital market became stronger under the United States-led "financialization" and the globalization of finance. Such changes can be seen in the transformation toward shareholder value-oriented management and capital market-oriented corporate governance. However, such a transformation toward the American management model greatly differs among nations with no tendency of convergence. Therefore, this chapter examines the transformation toward shareholder value-oriented management and corporate governance in both Japan and Germany in relation to the financing and ownership structures of companies, the changes in the managerial behaviors of banks, the values of management, and the organization of top management. Furthermore, it considers critical changes in the characteristic of the Americanization of business management after the 1990s compared with previous such phenomena and discusses the overall significance of these changes.

Keywords Americanization · Codetermination system · Corporate governance · Financialization · "Germany Inc." (die "Deutscheland AG") · Interlocking stockholding · Rhenish capitalism · Value management

After the 1990s, the "Americanization" of business management as well as the advancement of globalization emerged. The "American standard" was globally promoted and it strongly influenced business management as well as market economic models. Such American economic models were based on the neoliberalism ideology, which upholds that it is best to rely on the functions of market mechanisms in the commodity, financial, and labor markets. In regard to business management, the influences of Americanization can be seen in the transformation of management models and corporate governance of stockholder sovereignty aiming to maximize shareholder values under the increasing pressure of the capital market.

When considering the influence of the remarkable expansion of the finance economy and its subsequent effect on enterprises, also referred to as "financialization," it is distinguished as internal and external financialization. The former refers to "the strategist management's use of financial market-oriented performance

T. Yamazaki, *Japanese and German Enterprises*,
https://doi.org/10.1007/978-981-97-4880-8_14

standards and capital market-oriented systems of governing business processes and corporate restructuring initiatives." In contrast, the latter refers to "the influence which financial market, or the financial community and its opinion leaders respectively, wield over industrial enterprises and their management" (Kädtler and Sperling 2002b, p. 83; Kädtler and Sperling 2001, p. 40). The only interest to be considered in the concept of the shareholder value is the owner's financial profits (Baumüller 2010, p. 104). "Financialization" is the shift from a production-oriented strategy to a finance-oriented strategy, which is seen in "a change from campaigns of position and attrition in the product market, to those of movement with elements of surprise as concentrated forces" (Froud et al. 2000, pp. 103–104).

The spread of American corporate governance and shareholder value-oriented ideology have premised the worldwide diffusion of a unique system in the United States that has developed the stock market through "securitization" (Kudo 2011, p. 174). Reforms and the deregulation of the legal system along the US lines have been promoted in not only Japan but also both Germany and the European Union (EU). Moreover, the EU has pushed member countries toward financial market liberalization and considers the development of stock markets as a very important issue. As a result, it strengthened investor protection and accounting standards (Jackson 2005, p. 419; Schnitzler 2007, p. 229).

Corporate cultures in Japan and Germany have changed significantly after the 1990s. In Germany, from 1990 to approximately 1997, many companies that were on the principle of shareholder value were subsidiaries of large industrial groups that had headquarters in foreign countries. In contrast, the enterprises that were oriented toward worldwide development used such a principle from the 1990s to the beginning of the 2000s (Dörre and Holst 2009, p. 670; Dörre 2001). Thus, in the 1990s, the special condition of the financial services industries had been transformed to all the industrial enterprises and this spillover from the financial firms had caused "an inversion of the shareholder value principle from being the control principle to being the purpose of the firm" (Koslowski 2000, p. 140). However, the impact of the United States' influence and the actual transformation of the management model differed greatly among countries.

In Germany, the characteristic style of business management was built under a type of capitalism referred to as the "Rheinland Model" of capitalism ("Rhenish capitalism") (Albert 1991) or "the coordinated market economy" (Hall and Soskice 2001). The intertwining of industries and banks through the ownerships of capital and personnel interlocking, the cooperative relationships among banks, and the collaborative labor relations based on the codetermination system helped establish the German business enterprise and corporate governance system known as the "Deutschland AG" ("Germany Inc."). Such as system served as the foundation for maintaining the autonomy of business management, even under the strong pressures from the capital markets (Streeck and Höpner 2003; Zugehör 2003; Cromme 2005, p. 362; Beck et al. 2005a; Beck et al. 2005b, p. 228). In such cooperative inter-firm relationships based on stockholdings and personnel connections built through interlocking directorates, in addition to the large banks, the biggest insurance companies have also played significant roles (Eggenkämper et al. 2015, p. 248; Furch 2012, p. 67; Beyer 2006, p. 107).

In Japan, the defensive actions against external powers were demonstrated through interlocking stockholdings and the assignment of directors; the former action played a significant role in securing the autonomy of management. Regarding corporate governance, there is a distinction between the exit-based governance in the United States and the United Kingdom and the voice-based governance in Germany and Japan (Buck et al. 1998, p. 82).

The introduction of the American management model after the 1990s transformed the value standard of business management and company principles. Such transformation not only restricted the autonomy of management in enterprises but also had a considerable influence on both stakeholders and workers. As a result, the resistance to and conflicts with the American management model became stronger. Therefore, it is important to analyze the changes observed in business management in Japan and Germany under the pressure to transform to the American management model of stockholder sovereignty and capital market-oriented corporate governance. Along with commonalities with the United States, what types of unique developments emerged? How was US management model reformed to accommodate Japanese or German conditions? What was the significance of these developments? This chapter describes how American-style management model was implemented in both nations and the resulting changes in corporate management.

Section 14.1 considers the influences of the United States-led financialization in Japan and Germany. Sections 14.2 and 14.3 analyze the transformation toward shareholder value-oriented management in Japan and Germany, respectively. Based on these discussions, the "reframing" in the Americanization of business management in both countries is examined in Sect. 14.4. Section 14.5 elucidates the differences in the characteristics of the Americanization of business management after the 1990s compared with those in the previous periods.

14.1 Influence of United States-Led Financialization in Japan and Germany

This section considers the influences of the United States-led "financialization" in Japan and Germany in relation to changes in corporate financing, the ownership structure of companies, and the administrative behavior of banks.

14.1.1 *Influence of United States-led Financialization in Japan*

Changes in the Financing Conditions of Companies: In Japan, banks played a significant role in corporate financing, the structure of which greatly depended on indirect financing after World War II. Large banks that were designated as the main banks in each of the six industrial groups flexibly and resiliently provided payments and settlements for credit creation. These banks utilized the loans to affiliated companies (i.e., the *keiretsu* financing system) and capital procurement methods since Japanese corporations generally used indirect financing in the postwar era (Suzuki 1993, p. 140). The existence of main banks was important for companies until the beginning of the 1990s. According to a survey by the Fuji Institute in 1992, the ratio of companies that had main banks to 1,171 major companies was 94.9%, whereas the ratio of firms that had associate main banks to 1,094 major companies was 71.8% (Fuji sogo kenkyusho 1993, pp. 41, 44–45).

However, the financing conditions of companies changed because of the problems regarding the disposal of banks' bad loans and the influence of the protracted recession following the collapse of the bubble economy. In the first half of the 1990s, there were many cases in which the main banks decreased their financing to firms suffering from losses. This indicates that the main banks selected customers on the basis of their level of risk (Keizai kikakucho 1996, pp. 305–306). In addition, conditions of corporate financing through the capital market also changed under the liberalization of the capital market, the increasing international liquidity of capital, the development of information and communication technologies, and the globalization of finance. As a result, the tendencies shifted toward direct financing. However, in Japan, the slump of the stock market after the collapse of the bubble economy greatly influenced this shift.

Changes in the Ownership Structures of Companies: With regard to the changes in the ownership structures of companies, interlocking stockholdings were mainly performed between banks and industrial enterprises, among independent companies, or between the financial institutions within the same industrial groups (Matsumura 1997, pp. 69, 77, 82–83). The interlocking stockholdings between the enterprises of the same corporate groups were reinforced by the interlocking shareholdings with companies of other industrial groups. In addition, interlocking stockholdings with firms of other groups were based on the system of joint rule (Matsui 1979, pp. 33, 35), which played a significant role in securing the autonomy of management. Furthermore, agreements of interests established as mutual trust between the executives of the main banks and the managers of the industrial enterprises increased through the interlocking shareholdings (Matsumura 1997, pp. 24–25, 98). The tendencies of Japanese companies toward long-term orientation and their emphasis on sales amounts in management were also supported by the interlocking stockholdings (Keizai kikakucho 1998, p. 209).

However, the efficacy of interlocking shareholdings was reconsidered, and its influence decreased after the 1990s, with the emergence of challenges regarding the disposal of banks' bad loans and the shift to the practice of appraising financial assets based on fair market value. The overall changes of the stockholding structure in the Japanese market after the 1990s can be seen in three aspects: (1) the fluidity of the structure of interlocking stockholdings; (2) the increase in the presence of foreign investors and (3) the movement of financial assets from the stable form (e.g., bank deposits and postal savings) to risk preference investment (e.g., stock investments, investment trusts, foreign securities) (Matsuda 2009, pp. 113–114).

The ratios of stockholdings by financial institutions to all stockholdings in fiscal years 1990, 1998, 2007, 2013, and 2022 were 45.2%, 39.3%, 23.3%, 22.8%, and 25.5%, respectively. This ratio greatly declined after 1998. The groups including city banks and provincial banks, in particular, showed remarkable drops; their ratios of stockholdings in the same years were 16.4%, 14.0%, 3.5%, 2.8%, and 2.2%, respectively. Meanwhile, the holding rates of life insurance companies in the same years were 13.2%, 9.4%, 3.7%, 2.9%, and 2.8%, respectively. In contrast, the holding rates of industrial corporations in the same years were 25.2%, 24.1%, 24.8%, 23.3%, and 23.0%, respectively. In this regard, the decrease in the rates of the industrial corporations was not as large as that of the financial institutions. On the other hand, the possession rates of foreign corporations in the same years were 4.2%, 10.0%, 24.7%, 26.9%, and 25.6%, respectively, and rose significantly after the 1990s (Kabushiki-gaisha Tokyo shoken torihikisho et al. 2022, p. 12). Moreover, the presence of foreign investors increased as a substitute for the possessions of financial institutions (Tokyo shoken torihikisho 2015, p. 5; Zenkoku shoken torihikisho kyogikai 2005, p. 12).

The weakening of interlocking stockholding relations based on the stable shareholders and the fall of the possession ratio of the financial institutions after the 1990s also represented an increase in the possession rates of institutional investors. A remarkable increase in the shareholding ratios of foreign investors was also deeply related with these developments. The increase in the possession rates of institutional investors and foreign investors strengthened their activities as shareholders adopting voice-based governance (Hirschman 1970, pp. 30–36) and strongly prompted a transformation toward shareholder value management. For instance, the ratios of companies whose institutional investors and other shareholders voted "no" to the bill presented by the enterprises (overlapping answers) in fiscal years 2006, 2013, and 2015 were 63.5%, 62.7%, and 67.9%, respectively. In the same years, the relevant numerical values in companies having a capital of more than 100 billion yen were 89.2%, 87.1%, and 93.0%, respectively. The ratios of the bills that were rejected by such shareholders to the total number of bills in all the companies whose institutional investors voted "no" in fiscal year 2006 were 72.3% for a change in the article of association, 50.2% for the election of directors, and 40.3% for profit disposal. The relevant numerical values in fiscal year 2015 were 72.2% for the election of inside directors, 63.4% for the election of outside directors, 30.8% for the election of inside auditors, 44.3% for the election of outside auditors, and 34.3% for profit disposal (Shoji homu kenkyukai 2006, pp. 60–61; Shoji homu kenkyukai 2013, pp. 67; Shoji homu kenkyukai 2015, pp. 75–77).

Japanese corporations have been required to change to a type of management that emphasizes short-term capital efficiency. This management style focuses on increasing stock prices and dividends by increasing stockholdings by foreign investors, institutional investors, and investment funds. According to surveys conducted in 2005, 2012, and 2014 that focused on Japanese listed corporations in the Tokyo Stock Exchange (overlapping answers), the ratios of firms that regarded "maximization and appropriate levels of corporate value (shareholder value)" as the aims of corporate governance were 40.4%, 55.3%, and 52.8%, respectively (Tokyo shoken torihikisho 2005, exhibit, p. 1; Tokyo shoken torihikisho 2013, pp. 1–2; Tokyo shoke torihikisho 2015, p. 3).

Changes in the Administrative Behaviors of Banks: With regard to the changes in the administrative behaviors of banks, the roles and managerial behaviors of banks changed significantly, especially in regard to the assignment of directors following the decrease in interlocking stockholdings, for example, between banks and industrial corporations. Whereas general trading companies (rather than banks) generally combined many companies through the assignment of directors in the interlocking directorate, financial institutions represented by banks dispatched a significant number of directors (Nakata et al. 1997, pp. 141, 151; Iwanami 2005, pp. 178, 182–183).

Economic Policy of Japanese Government and Reforms of Corporate Governance: The Japanese economic policy on corporate governance reforms developed by the Abe cabinet that started its tenure at the end of 2012 had a significant influence. In addition to unprecedented monetary easing and flexible fiscal policy, growth strategy was regarded as one of the three pillars of this cabinet's economic policy, and corporate governance reform formed its core element. The fundamental direction of such reforms entailed reinforcing the involvement of shareholders, electing independent outside directors, and adopting a remuneration system linked with share price. These reforms led to the introduction of Japan's Stewardship Code and the Corporate Governance Code. While the former requires institutional investors to have active dialogue with the enterprises in which they invest, the latter demands improvement in corporate governance systems (Miyajima 2021, pp.6–7).

14.1.2 Influence of United States-led Financialization in Germany

This subsection considers the influence of United States-led financialization in Germany. There are three pillars of the traditional German system of corporate governance: (1) "the dominating role of the banks in company financing and supervisory boards," (2) "the system of industrial codetermination," and (3) "the productionalist, company-centered management system" (Jürgens et al. 2000, p. 59; Paetzmann 2008, p. 40). The US system of corporate governance relies on external participation, whereas German corporate governance is an insider-controlled system based on internal information (Mintz 2006, p. 31; Hackethal et al. 2005, p. 398; Weber 2011, p. 553). Banks also played a critical role in the German corporate governance system because of two reasons. The first is their direct ownership of shares and the system of proxy votes, and the second is that "industrial companies still finance themselves mostly via long- and short-term bank credits" (Jürgens et al. 2000, p. 62). Compared with other countries, the tendency of concentrating on stockholdings is strong in Germany, and the German model of finance is based on a bank-based finance system administered by universal banks. German banks have succeeded in preventing the proliferation of short-term investment funds through their disruptive influences on funding structures.

However, the increasing influence of money funds and their short-term investment strategies after the 1990s represented "a break with the financial practice of the past, where long-term orientation was one of the most important elements of the German model" (Oberbeck and D'Alessio 1997, pp. 86, 101–102). Thus, it is important to consider the influences of United States-led financialization in relation to the changes in the financing conditions, the ownership structure, and the administrative behaviors of banks.

Changes in the Financing Condition of Companies: Regarding the changes in corporate financing conditions, in Germany, the procurement of equity through the issuance of stocks only played a secondary role under the close relation between house banks and industrial enterprises. However, significant changes occurred after the 1990s, such as the liberalization of the domestic capital market, the surge of the international fluidity of capital, the intensification of international competition, and the rapid development of information and communication technologies. In addition, an increase in the capital needs of large multinational enterprises meant that capital could only be supplied by numerous individual and institutional investors (Beelitz 2002, pp. 577–578, 581). Moreover, innovation with large risks required sources of capital that would permit risk taking; thus, external financing was no longer suitable compared with financing through equity capital (Ifrim 2007, p.36).

In the mid-1990s, the liberalization of international capital markets enabled German firms (which had traditionally relied on bank financing) to consider alternative and cheaper methods to raise funds for growth. "Such changes meant that institutional investors, both local and foreign became active actors in corporate German firms, putting pressures on listed firms to restructure their operations and adopt management practices in line with their expectations" (Chizema 2010, p. 10).

The increase in the importance of owners such as investment and pension funds premised the decline of the role of banks as the supervisory organ of enterprises (Windolf 2005, pp. 9–10). However, there were many cases in which institutional investors served as the investment division of large financial institutions (Dörre 2009, p. 104); i.e., financial institutions still occupied an important position as institutional investors.

In addition to these changes in the financing condition of companies, new financial technologies enbaled banks to sell their credits to others through securitization and could use credit insurance. As a result, banks no longer need to assign director to the supervisory board of company in which they provide loan to defend risks bought about by an irrecoversable debt (Windolf 2014, p.80).

Change of the Ownership Structure of the Company: "Internationalization of capital markets went along with the emergence of institutional investors in Germany" (Fiss and Zajac 2004, p. 506). The shareholder orientation of companies was related to the increased presence of institutional investors, especially Anglo-American investors as shareholders of large German firms (Höpner 2001, pp. 13–14). British funds also played a significant role as institutional investors. For example, by 1999, British and American investment funds already owned the following percentages of stocks: 40% of Mannesmann, 31.3% of DaimlerChrysler, 27.5% of Deutsche Telekom, 22% of VEBA, and 20% of Bayer (Handelsblatt 1999, p. 22). The position of pension funds as institutional investors also became stronger (Jürgens et al. 2000, p. 71).

In addition, the changes in the law that abolished taxes for capital gains from sales of corporate assets in 2002 were important factors for reallocating corporate assets (Küke 2002, p. 136). As a result, the changes in the tax law promoted the sales of most of the large equity holdings by banks (Lane 2003, p. 88; Vitols 2005b, p. 362; Höpner 2000; Chizema and Buck 2006, p. 496; Matthes 2005, p. 231). Meanwhile, the stock corporation law that emphasized the protection of creditors was reformed to protect investors (Cromme 2005, p. 362). Moreover, the privatization of Deutsche Telekom promoted a shareholder culture, as seen in "the idea that ordinary citizens could own stock and buy stock from an initial public offering" (Ziegler 2000, p. 212, Gordon 1999, pp. 225, 227, 238).

Changes in the Administrative Behaviors of Banks: Overall, there were significant changes in the administrative behaviors of banks due to the various modifications in the ownership structure and the financing of companies. The global market, in line with prevailing Anglo-American practices, pressured the German model of corporate governance or the so-called "die Deutschland AG" to liberalize its corporate governance institutions in two ways. The first was the orientation of large private banks toward investment banking, which promoted a reduction in the ownership of industrial equity. The second was that "firms can increasingly raise money directly on capital markets and thus release themselves from credit-induced dependence on particular financial institutions" (Beck et al. 2005b, p. 228; Furch 2012, p. 155). The transformation of large banks in Germany according to the *Hausbank* paradigm, as the main bank for industrial enterprises, to the investment bank paradigm and the support of hostile takeovers by large banks promoted the shareholder-value orientation of enterprises. This was also related to the exposure of the market for corporate control (Höpner 2001, pp. 17–19). According to Höpner (2001), whereas until the beginning of the 1990s, banks generally opposed hostile takeovers, after the 1990s, the behavior of German banks changed substantially. Some banks were important actors in supporting hostile takeovers (Höpner and Jackson 2001, p. 18).

Under the concentration of ownership among a smaller number of banks and other financial institutions, managers in German firms enjoyed considerable insulation from the short-term pressures of an anonymous equity market (Ziegler 2000, p. 200). There was also an interest in the corporate strategy that all universal banks pursue through personnel connections and capital participation in order to decrease credit risks. However, if the external capital demand of large companies was largely met by stocks or bonds, risks were borne not by the banks but by the shareholders or owners who lost capital during the bankruptcy of the enterprise. As a result, the close uniting relations with industrial enterprises did not have a strategic meaning for pure investment banks. In addition, the type of risk changed with the increase in speculative trading. The advantages of internal monitoring systems reduced as higher transparency was achieved, as observed in Anglo-American systems. Conversely, the increase in the significance of mergers and acquisitions (M&As) for the development of companies made investment banking more attractive (Beyer 2001, pp. 6–7, 9–10; Beyer 2006, pp. 102–103, 105–106).

In addition, "financial internationalization weakens the hold that German banks have over the credit supply to German firms, which in turn weakens the bank's capacity and motivation to monitor company performance and promote prudent long-termism in company strategy" (Streeck 1997, p. 51). Thus, the role of German banks changed rapidly after the mid-1990s, and there was "a major shift from 'patient capital' to shareholder-value orientation in the German banking sector" (Jürgens et al. 2000, p. 69).

Banks not only reduced the mutual holding of stocks and reorganized relationships with industrial enterprises but also began to reduce the interlocking directorate. At the beginning of the 1990s, Deutsche Bank began to reduce its capital participation in the industrial company by more than 25% (Beyer 2001, p. 11; Furch 2012, p. 155). Deutsche Bank planned to reshuffle its holdings from top to bottom (Andrews 2000). In addition, the dispatch of the chairman of the supervisory board to industrial enterprises by financial institutions decreased after the mid-1990s when the shift to shareholder value-oriented management advanced and the banks' role in monitoring companies significantly decreased. For instance, "the chief financial executive officer of Deutsche Bank declared publicly that his bank had for some years not filled all the supervisory board positions which it was offered by other companies and would, in future, provide even fewer directors" (Jürgens et al 2000, p. 70; Monopolkommission 2008, p. 198). In fact, Deutsche Bank has been withdrawing its monitoring activities and has reduced the number of supervisory board chairs in German firms by approximately 50% (Höpner 2001, pp. 26, 50). As shown by J. Beyer, the change in business strategy was reflected in the attitude toward investment banking, which explained why Deutsche Bank was no longer considered "Germany Inc." ("die Deutschland AG") (Beyer 2006, p. 102).

14.2 Transformation Toward the Shareholder Value-Oriented Management Model and Its Characteristics in Japan

Following the discussion on the influence of United States-led financialization in Japan and Germany, Sect. 14.2 examines Japan's transformation toward the shareholder value-oriented management model.

14.2.1 *Transformation Toward the Shareholder Value-Oriented Management Model*

Regarding the general conditions in the transformation toward the shareholder value-oriented management model, this section considers the changes in the accounting standards, the introduction of stock options into management rewards, and the reforms in top management organization.

Change in the Accounting Standards: After the 1990s, a significant reform, known as the "Accounting Big Bang," was promoted, emphasizing convergence with the International Accounting Standards and the US GAAP. Subsequently, the movement toward the convergence of the Japanese standards and the International Accounting Standards and the examination of the adoption of such international standards advanced. Meanwhile, the influential revision of the International Accounting Standards to a set of standards different from those adopted during the Accounting Big Bang, also progressed (Fujii 2000, p. 109).

Such Americanization and internationalization of the accounting standard also had a significant meaning in investor relations. According to a 2005 study of Japanese listed companies in the Tokyo Stock Exchange, 59% of the enterprises that responded had a special section or a special person in charge of investor relations. The ratio of firms that did not have such a section or person was 33.5% (Tokyo shoken torihikisho 2005, exhibit, p. 10). The ratios of companies that included such a section or person in 2014 and 2022 were 80.4 and 93.7%, respectively. Whereas the ratios of firms that regularly held briefings for individual investors to all listed firms in the Tokyo Stock Exchange in 2014 and 2022 were 25.9 and 41.7%, respectively, the ratios of firms that held such briefings for foreign investors were only 10.8 and 25%, respectively. However, the ratios of firms that held briefings for analysts and institutional investors to all listed firms in the Tokyo Stock Exchange in the same years reached 67.2% and 78.1%, respectively (Tokyo shoken torihikisho 2015, pp. 73–75; Tokyo shoken torihikisho 2023, pp. 168–170). The behaviors of companies emphasizing institutional investors are evident in these findings.

Introduction of Stock Options into Management Rewards: This subsection considers the adoption of the stock option as the management rewards. In Japan, stock options were removed from general companies in 1997 (Segawa 2009, p. 117). According to a 2005 study of Japanese listed companies in the Tokyo Stock Exchange (overlapping answers), the ratio of firms that introduced stock options to all firms that responded was 31.3%, which greatly exceeded the usual rate for the performance-linked payment system (12.6%). The ratio of companies that introduced stock options for in-house directors and corporate officers to the firms that adopted this reward system reached 97% (Tokyo shoken torihikho 2005, p. 1, exhibit p. 22).

According to a similar survey in 2012, 87.2% of the listed companies in the Tokyo Stock Exchange implemented some measures in order to provide incentives. However, the similar numerical value in 2014 dropped to 53.7%. Moreover, the ratio of enterprises that adopted stock options to all listed enterprises in the Tokyo Stock Exchange in 2014 was 31.8%, which was slightly lower than the corresponding numerical value in 2008 (33.6%). The relevant numerical value of the listed corporations in the so-called "Mothers" (markets of high growth and emerging stocks) reached 77.8%, which greatly exceeded the ratio of the companies listed in the first (32.1%) and second sections of the Tokyo Stock Exchange (15.8%). In addition, the higher is the ratio of stockholdings by foreigners to all stockholdings, the higher the ratio of the adoption of stock options. This point is similar to the survey results of 2005 and 2012. The ratio of the introduction of this reward system in companies where the stockholding rates of foreigners were more than 30% reached 52.1% in 2014 (Tokyo shoken torihikisho 2013, pp. 58–81; Tokyo shoken torihikisho 2015, pp. 56–59). The ratio of enterprises that adopted stock options to listed enterprises in the "Mothers" listed enterprises in 2020 was 85.0%, which greatly exceeded the ratio of the companies listed in the first (28.6%) and second sections of the Tokyo Stock Exchange (18.3%) (Tokyo shoken torihikisho 2021, p. 87). The ratio of companies that adopted stock options to listed enterprises in the Growth Market listed enterprises in 2022 was 79.7%, which greatly exceeded the ratio of the companies listed in the Tokyo Stock Exchange (29.3%). Meanwhile, the ratio of companies that adopted performance-linked remuneration systems in the Prime Market listed enterprises was 66.1%, which exceeded the ratio of the companies listed in the Tokyo Stock Exchange (48.1%) (Tokyo shoken torihikisho 2023, p. 79–81). In this way, whereas the relevant numerical value in the "Mothers" listed enterprises is extremely high, the corresponding value of companies listed in the Tokyo Stock Exchange (first or second sections) is relatively low.

The ratios of firms that did not adopt stock options to the listed corporations in the Tokyo Stock Exchange in 2014 and 2022 were 68.2 and 70.7%, respectively (Tokyo shoken torihikisho 2015, pp. 57–58; Tokyo shoken torihikisho 2023, p. 80). Stock options were not adopted because this system was inappropriate as an incentive measure given the slump in stock prices and the differences in exercise prices. Some companies recognize that existing remuneration structures were sufficient and their doubts regarding reward payment from the short-term viewpoint and regarding the stock option system itself were important reasons. Another reason for the non-adoption of stock options is that "the stock option plan is a program to receive capital gains without downside risks and therefore is in conflict with shareholder interests" (Tokyo shoken torihikisho 2015, pp. 57–58). Furthermore, unlike Europe and the United States, Japan was experiencing an ongoing protracted slump in the stock market after the collapse of the bubble economy. There are cases in which stock option is not adopted "because the company aims to increase corporate value stably and over the mid- to long-term rather than aiming for short-term increases in profits or the stock price" (Tokyo shoken torihikisho 2023, p. 80).

Reforms in Top Management Organization: In Japan, an important characteristic of the transformation toward the shareholder value-oriented management model can be seen in the reforms of top management organization and the revisions of the legal system. Regarding the shift to committee-setting companies in line with the American corporate governance model, the ratio of firms that selected such reforms to all Japanese listed firms in the Tokyo Stock Exchange was only 1.7% in 2014. Of all the Japanese listed companies in the Tokyo Stock Exchange, 98.3% were companies with a corporate auditor system. However, the ratio of enterprises adopting the committee-style corporate governance system to enterprises in which foreigners' shareholding rates were more than 30%, from 20% to less than 30%, and from 10% to less than 20% were 7.3%, 3.6%, and 1.8%, respectively. In this way, the rate of companies that adopted such a system was generally high in companies where foreigners' stockholdings occupied a high ratio (Tokyo shoken torihikisho 2015, pp. 15–16).

In addition, regarding the outside directors who needed to occupy more than half the seats of each committee, which play important roles in supervising the executive officer, the ratio of firms that selected outside directors to Japanese listed firms in the Tokyo Stock Exchange was 54.7% in 2012 and increased to 64.4% in 2014. In 2006, this ratio was 42.3%. The same ratio for companies with a corporate audit system in 2014 was 63.8%, which was much higher than that in 2006 (40.8%). Thus, the shift toward electing outside directors proceeded remarkably. In addition, the rates of corporations in which the number of outside directors occupied more than one-third or the majority to the listed corporations in the Tokyo Stock Exchange were only 13.4% or 2.6%, respectively, in 2014. However, among the companies adopting the committee-style corporate governance system, the corresponding ratios were 93.9% and 51%, respectively, in 2012. In the companies with a corporate audit system in which foreigners' stockholding rate was 30% or more, 86.5% of such companies included outside directors, which was 1.86 times the average in 2014 (Tokyo shoken torihikisyo 2013, pp. 21, 23, 26; Tokyo shoken torihikisyo 2015, pp. 21, 24–26, 29).

The ratios of outside directors in the audit, reward, and nomination committees of the companies listed in the Tokyo Stock Exchange that adopted the committee-style corporate governance system were 82.8%, 74.1%, and 72.4%, respectively, in 2014. The rates of enterprises of which the chairmen of the audit, compensation, and nomination committees were outside directors were 68.4%, 61.4%, and 54.4%, respectively. The same values in 2010 were 54.9%, 51%, and 47.1%, respectively. Thus, the similar numerical values in 2014 increased in comparison with those in 2010 (Tokyo shoken torihikisho 2015, pp. 43–44).

Concerning appointment of independent directors, the ratio of companies that appointed independent directors to the listed corporations in the Tokyo Stock Exchange in 2020 reached 95.6%. The ratio of independent directors among outside directors was 89.5% (Tokyo shoken torihikisho 2021, pp. 92, 98). It increased to 92.5% in 2022 (Tokyo shoken torihikisho 2023, p. 38). In companies listed on the Prime Market, the ratio of enterprises that appointed two or more independent outside directors was 99.2% and that of enterprises that appointed at least one-third independent outside directors was 92.1%. The latter approach was particularly widespread among enterprises listed on the Prime Market because demand from institutional investors and proxy agencies increased following the revision of the Corporate Governance Code in 2021. Only 12.1% of the enterprises listed on the Prime Market appointed a majority of board members in 2022 (Tokyo shoken torihikisho 2023, pp. 35–36). In this way, the Corporate Governance Code has promoted the establishment of independent directors that did not progress languidly despite the movement to adopt them after the 2000s (Miyajima 2021, pp. 7, 15).

Furthermore, regarding outside auditors, in 2014, the number of auditors per company in firms with a corporate auditor system that were listed on the Tokyo Stock Exchange was 3.59. In these companies, the number of auditors was 2.47 persons on an average. However, unlike the cases of outside directors, there was no correlation between the stockholding rates of foreigners and the number of outside auditors (Tokyo shoken torihikisho 2015, pp. 37–39).

Looking at reasons for adoption of current corporate governance system on the basis of a survey regarding the companies listed in the Tokyo Stock Exchange in 2018, in Companies with *Kansayaku* Board, "there were many disclosures that described the roles and functions of outside directors as oversight of business execution by directors and the provision of advice to ensure the appropriateness of decision-making from a position independent from the management team." In Companies with Supervisory Committees, companies pointing out "the strengthening of the oversight function with outside directors" as a reason for adopting this form are many. In Companies with Three Committees, the percentage that mention "the separation of oversight and business execution" as a reason for adopting this form is higher compared with Companies with Supervisory Committees (Tokyo shoken torihikisho 2021, pp. 79–81).

The number of listed enterprises on the Prime Market that have established statutory and voluntary nomination and remuneration committees has tended to increase. The ratio of the number of enterprises that established a nomination committee or a remuneration committee to all listed enterprises in the Tokyo Stock Exchange was 56.3% or 60%, respectively, in 2022. These values for enterprises listed on the Prime Market were 83.6% or 85.5%, respectively. The ratios of outside directors, etc. to all members in nomination committees were 75.6% in Companies with Three Committees (nomination, remuneration, and audit committees), 67.1% in Companies with Supervisory Committee, and 58.8% in Companies with Board of Company Auditors. The percentages of outside directors, etc. to all members in remuneration committees were 76.8% in Companies with Three Committees, 67.1% in Companies with Supervisory Committee, and 57.4% in Companies with Board of Company Auditors (Tokyo shoken torihikisho 2023, pp. 52–55, 57–58).

Regarding the increase of dividends, the dividends in business corporations increased only slightly from 4,227,000 million yen in fiscal year 1990 to 4,831,600 million yen in fiscal year 2000. However, the dividends significantly increased after 2000 and peaked at 16,217,400 million yen in fiscal year 2006. Although the dividends later declined to 10,357,499 million yen in fiscal year 2010, it increased again to 13,957,400 million yen in fiscal year 2012, and to 16,888,300 million yen in fiscal year 2014. The dividend in fiscal year 2014 exceeded that in 2006. The dividends in fiscal years 2006 and 2014 reached 3.84 times and 4.0 times, respectively, of that in fiscal year 1990. The payout ratio in fiscal year 1990 was only 24.1%, while it increased to 100.7% in fiscal year 1993. It was in fiscal year 1999 that the payout ratio reached its peak of 194.7% in the period from 1990 to 2014 (Okurasho kinyu kenkyusho 1996, pp. 18–19; Zaimsho sogo kenkyusho 2003, pp. 18–19; Zaimusho zaise sogo kenkyusho 2013, pp. 24–25, Zaimusho zaisei sogo kenkyusho 2003, pp. 18–19; Zaimusho zaise sogo kenkyusho 2016, pp. 24–25). The dividend in fiscal year 2021 was 29,864,900 million yen and the ratio of the dividend to net profit was 47.4% (Zaimusho zaisei sogo kenkyusho 2022, pp. 9, 24–25).

Moreover, Japan's Stewardship Code promoted active involvement of institutional investors in corporate governance. It engendered important changes such as the positive participation of institutional investors entrusted by asset owners in governance activities, improved governance by traditional institutional investors, modified behavioral mode of life insurance companies that had been considered silent partners to long-term activist stockholders, and diversification and dynamization of activist funds (Miyajima 2021, p. 6).

14.2.2 Hybridization of the American Shareholder Value-Oriented Management Model and the Japanese Management Model

How is the transformation toward shareholder value-oriented management to be understood? Analyzing how companies considered corporate governance systems, according to a 2005 study of 1,379 Japanese listed corporations in the Tokyo Stock Exchange, the ratio of companies that stated that the American model or the European model was desirable for building an effective corporate governance system for investors was only 4.3% or 1.8%, respectively. In contrast, the rate of corporations that considered adopting an effective corporate governance model in a uniform manner without conforming to the overseas models was 41.9%, whereas the ratio of companies that considered building models suitable for each company on the basis of the corporate governance principle was 50% (Tokyo shoken torihikisho 2005, p. 1, exhibit, p. 4).

Indeed, the movement toward the American shareholder value-oriented management model progressed in response to the reforms of the legal system, the limitations and problems of the Japanese corporate governance system, and the increasing pressure by the capital market after the 1990s. However, in reality, the hybridization of the Japanese and American management models reflects the actual situation. Regarding this hybridization in relation to reforms of top management organization, there were many cases in which the parties involved, such as parent companies or business acquaintances, occupied the majority of the outside directors (Kataoka 2009, p. 96).

For instance, according to a 2005 study of the listed corporations in the Tokyo Stock Exchange (overlapping answers), the ratio of corporations that included officials in affiliates, including experienced individuals as outside directors, to corporations that elected outside directors was 37.5%. The ratio of companies that elected outside directors with whom these companies had interest relations to companies that had outside directors was 55.5% (Tokyo shoken torihikisho 2005, pp. 13–14). In

2014, the ratios of individuals who held additional posts, such as executive directors and officers, of other companies to the outside directors of the listed corporations in the Tokyo Stock Exchange were 38.6% for companies with a corporate auditor system and 31.0% for companies adopting a committee-style corporate governance system. The ratios of individuals who held additional posts, such as outside directors or outside auditors of other firms, were 38.0% in companies with a corporate auditor system and 57.1% in the committee-setting companies. The ratio of outside directors from parent companies or other affiliates to all outside directors was 7.2% or 9.8%, respectively. The ratio in which outside directors were the largest shareholders or worked for companies that were the largest stockholders was 11.7% (Tokyo shoken torihikisho 2013, pp. 29–31; Tokyo shoken torihikisho 2015, pp. 33–35).

In fact, the American model includes boards of directors and the Japanese model includes revision-type boards of directors. Revision of Japan's commercial law did not promote the selection of the American management model. Instead, the revision and the hybridization of the Japanese managing board model were promoted by combining the subsequent reforms of the legal systems. On the one hand, the "American type of hybridization" clearly separated the decision-making and supervision processes and business execution by enriching the committee system and the corporate officer system as well as strengthening the governance through outside directors. On the other hand, the "Japanese hybridization" aimed at evading complete separation between the decision-making processes and business execution while avoiding the introduction of outside directors, despite adopting systems such as the corporate officer system.

In particular, many companies that adopted the corporate officer system tended to adapt to changes in the outside environment, as seen in the "marketization" and the trend toward convergence, rather than shift toward the American model. The ratio of companies that shifted toward new management organization, such as the corporate officer system and the committee-setting system, was higher in competitive industries such as the pharmaceutical, precious instrument, and air transportation industries. In contrast, the same ratio was generally low in mature industries, such as the iron and steel, paper manufacturing, and mining industries as well as in monopolistic industries, such as the electric power and gas industries (Miyajima and Nitta 2007, pp. 29, 35–36, 48–49, 69).

Based on these findings, it is apparent that the hybridization of the Japanese and American types of management occurred. For example, Sony and Hoya transformed to committee-setting companies and Kirin Co. Ltd. adopted the corporate officer system similar to that in the American model. On the other hand, some companies adopted the revision-type board of directors of the Japanese model; the Hitachi Group transformed to a committee-setting company and Toyota and Panasonic introduced the corporate officer system (Miyajima and Nitta 2007, p. 37).

Overall, many corporations were generally passive toward including a board of directors, which gave independent outside directors significant authority (Segawa 2009, p. 122). Committee-setting companies were considered undesirable and generally rejected by many companies since the outside directors were strong authority figures in these companies (Sakuma 2009, p. 76). In addition, another Japanese characteristic of management was evident in cases in which responses to global competition through rapid decision-making became the subject of focus in top management organization. For example, Toyota attempted to systematically avoid the separation of strategic decision-making and business execution by assigning as a member of the managing board a managing director in charge of the generalization of the execution of duties and responsible for both functions. Such an approach aimed to make strategic decisions while grasping and understanding the true needs of each operational unit and workplace by combining these two functions. This approach was primarily pursued to reform the boards of directors, and accelerate the process of making management decisions, and immediately emphasize its apparent strengths (Inoue 2013, pp. 199–200).

14.2.3 Conflicts Between the American Shareholder Value-Oriented Management Model and the Japanese Management Model

The prevalence of the Japanese management model and the corporate governance system are still strong, despite the influence of the capital market and the considerable pressure to transform toward the American shareholder value-oriented management model and the capital market-oriented corporate governance system. Hence, this section considers factors that determine the conflicts between the American shareholder value-oriented management model and the Japanese management model.

First, the movement toward the dissolution of stable shareholders has not necessarily advanced in a uniform manner in all Japanese companies, including listed joint-stock corporations. In reality, as a result of the rational choices of financial institutions and industrial corporations, differentiation between the company groups that continued interlocking stockholdings and those that dissolved them emerged (Miyajima et al 2013, pp. 229–230; Segawa 2009, pp. 109–110). The movement toward the "dissolution" of interlocking shareholdings, which gathered pace after the 1990s, began with a view of improving financial constitutions that deteriorated under the long-term recession and not necessarily based on the aim to dissolve the interlocking shareholdings as the stable shareholder structure. The release of stocks that industrial enterprises, trading companies, and banks mutually held was performed among them, as long as it did not influence the stable shareholder structure. The ratio of possession stocks that increased during the bubble economy period (in the latter half of the 1980s) to the sales of stocks was large (Suzuki 1998, pp. 120, 129, 136; Suzuki 2008, pp. 227, 274). In the member companies that belonged to each of the six industrial groups, interlocking stockholdings were formed in response to the reciprocal trade between companies. The selling of possession stocks by industrial companies that occupied the most part of the "dissolution" of the interlocking stockholdings occurred between companies in which relations with other companies weakened and the strong "core" relationships tended to be maintained. Thus, such differentiation advanced (Suzuki 1998, p. 127; Suzuki 2008, pp. 216–217, 223–224).

Furthermore, around 2006, when interlocking stockholdings significantly decreased, the situations differed between industrial corporations. For example, the ratio of the industrial enterprises that were concerned with interlocking shareholdings to all enterprises declined from 91.3% in 1995 to 53.4% in 2006. In the same years, the relevant numerical values of the banks with interlocking stockholdings increased from 87.2 to 90.2%, respectively. Furthermore, the interlocking stockholdings between industrial corporations (based on the amount of money) increased from 1.57% in fiscal year 2001 to 2.97% in fiscal year 2006. In addition, new interlocking shareholdings occurred, especially in the iron and steel, electrical, and transportation equipment industries (Ito 2007).

Such a movement toward interlocking stockholdings was related to shareholder stabilization and played a significant role as the defensive measure to such purchases. One of the notable movements after 2000 was the increasing influence of investment funds in strategic purchases (Maeda 2010, p. 45). Many Japanese firms developed countermeasures to the marketization of M&As (the market for corporate control) to defend management rights, especially due to the appearance of stockholders whom corporations did not consider undesirable. One such measure was the concentration and control of voting rights by stable shareholders through the means of securing more stable shareholders based on strengthening cross-stockholdings. The reinforcement of interlocking stockholdings among the Nippon Steel Corporation, Sumitomo Metal Industries, Ltd., and Kobe Steel, Ltd. on March 29, 2006, was one of the most representative examples of such countermeasures (Maeda 2010, pp. 60–61).

Among the listed corporations, the number of companies that introduced defensive measures against takeovers increased. While only 29 companies introduced such measures at the end of 2005, this figure increased to 175 by the end of 2006, to 409 by the end of 2007, and to 569 by the end of 2008. By March 2014, 512 firms adopted such a measure, whereas 135 discontinued it (Recof 2014). Whereas the ratio of companies that adopted anti-takeover measures to the listed corporations in the Tokyo Stock Exchange in 2012 was 19.4%, the similar numerical figure in 2020 was 7.7% (Tokyo shoken torihikisho 2021, pp. 30–31). Among companies that did not adopt the defensive measure against such purchases, there were many cases in which the stable shareholders held the majority of issued stocks and, consequently, the need to respond to hostile takeovers was rather low. In addition, the financial crisis that emerged from the United States in the latter half of the 2000s led to a decrease in investment activities related to investment funds in Japan and such investment funds had not achieved their desired objectives (Maeda 2010, p. 63). A survey in 2020 pointed out whereas "the number of companies that put anti-takeover measures in place increased significantly around 2005 due to factors including changes in the management environment such as the unraveling of cross-shareholding and growing interest toward hostile takeover," "the number has gradually fallen recently as a result of the development of laws concerning abusive hostile acquisitions and the harsh view of investors toward anti-takeover measures" (Tokyo shoken torihikisho 2021, p. 30).

In addition, the depersonalization of stockholdings, as seen in the increase of institutional investors in Japan, differed from that in Great Britain and the United States. Stocks were widely used as securities for the instruments of control in Great Britain and the United States, whereas stocks were generally used as securities for income in Japan. Such a difference was also an important factor that was deeply related to the influence of stockholdings on business management and the problem of the transformation toward the shareholder value-oriented management model (Uetake 1999, p. 8).

Furthermore, the organization and the composition of the personnel on the boards in Japan, the hierarchy in the managing boards, the president's strong authority, and the overwhelming weight of the director in terms of inside promotion were not only factors that restrained the effectiveness of monitoring and checking management execution functions by the outside director but also eased the pressure from institutional investors, such as investment funds, in the capital market.

14.3 Transformation Toward the Shareholder Value-Oriented Management Model and Its Characteristics in Germany

Following the examination of Japan's transformation toward the American shareholder value-oriented management model, this section considers the issues of such a shift in Germany.

14.3.1 Transformation Toward the Shareholder Value-Oriented Management Model

14.3.1.1 General Conditions Regarding the Transformation Toward the Shareholder Value-Oriented Management

Martin Höpner pointed out that shareholder value policies can be viewed in three dimensions: (1) investor relations/accounting, (2) operational management, and (3) managerial compensation. He also emphasized four indicators as the degree of shareholder orientation in the 40 largest listed companies: (1) information quality of the annual report, (2) investor relations, (3) impact of business decisions on future cash flows, and (4) managerial compensation aspect of shareholder value (Höpner 2001, pp. 11–12). Thus, these issues will be considered.

Changes in the Accounting Standards: German accounting emphasizes extremely conservative prudence rules and creditor protection. In contrast, both the international accounting standards and the US GAAP are more investor-oriented and "are guided more exclusively by the notion of providing capital market participants with the necessary information to estimate true company value" (Höpner and Jackson 2001, p. 19; Bühner et al. 1997, p. 324). Accounting rules with higher transparency, such as the International Accounting Standards or the US GAAP, strongly influenced the German Commercial Code, especially after the increased significance of the capital market and the intensification of global competition (Rosen 2002, p. 603).

Germany adopted the liberalization of how corporate equity is used through various strategies such as stock swaps, stock options, and spin-offs and attempted to promote greater transparency and disclosure (Jackson and Moerke 2005, p. 354). Companies in continental Europe also began to adopt Anglo-American customs through the listings in the foreign stock market, in addition to the acceptance of the International Accounting Standards (Hassel et al. 2000, p. 507). Moreover, the Neuer Markt, created as a separate segment of the Frankfurt Stock Exchange in 1997, required all listed companies to provide information with greater transparency for investors through quarterly reports, minority-shareholder friendly accounting, and adherence to the International Accounting Standards or US GAAP (Sablowski and Ruppe 2001, p. 66; Vitols 2005a, p. 389). In fact, 43.3% of all DAX 30 companies adopted the International Accounting Standards in 1997 (Jürgens et al. 2000, p. 69) and by the 2000s, more than 400 public companies settled accounts on the basis of the standards (Beelitz 2002, p. 579).

Overall, any problems regarding the changes of accounting standards were related to the adoption of stock options. In this regard, a number of German firms that adopted stock options before 1999 had already shown value commitment by using more transparent accounting standards such as the US GAAP or the International Accounting Standards. By contrast, none of the firms that used the local German commercial law accounting standards had adopted stock options by 2004 (Chizema and Buck 2006, p. 500; Sanders and Tuschke 2007, pp. 49–50).

Given this background of changes in German accounting standards, the cases of individual companies are discussed next. In 1995, Deutsche Bank, as one of the strongest shareholder value-oriented companies, began publishing consolidated financial statements according to the International Accounting Standards. This was in light of the increasing globalization of capital markets (Deutsche Bank 1995, pp. 6, 39, 79). This bank also prepared consolidated financial statements for fiscal year 2001 in accordance with the US GAAP for the first time. The adoption of the US GAAP was a result of Deutsche Bank's listing on the New York Stock Exchange in the same year (Deutsche Bank 2001, p. 2). In 1998, Commerzbank disclosed its first consolidated financial statements based on the International Accounting Standards (Commerzbank 1998, p. 6), whereas the Allianz Group in the insurance sector also published financial statements in the same year under the same standards in order to enhance the transparency of figures for shareholders and strengthen its competitive position in the international capital market (Allianz Gruppe 1998, p. 23). Daimler-Benz obtained a New York Stock Exchange listing by switching to the US GAAP in 1993 (Vitols 2000, p. 7; Schlie and Warner 2000, p. 43), while Volkswagen published its consolidated financial statements for the fiscal year 2001 in accordance with the International Accounting Standards for the first time (Volkswagen 2001, pp. 28, 84). Beginning with fiscal year 2001, Siemens presented financial information according to the US GAAP (Siemens 2000, p. 54), and ThyssenKrupp brought its accounting standards in line with international standards through the US GAAP for the first time in 1998/99. Their objective was to meet stockholders' demands for greater transparency and international comparability, which gave this company direct access to the US capital market (ThyssenKrupp 1999, pp. 35–36).

Introduction of Stock Option into the Management Rewards: Regarding the adoption of stock options for top management, whereas stock options basically did not exist in Germany prior to 1996, the first stock option programs were on the agenda in the stockholder meetings of Deutsche Bank and Daimler-Benz in the same year (Wenger and Kaserer 1998, p. 513). More than 99% of the stockholders supported the stock option program of Deutsche Bank. In this case, proxy votes and cross holdings played an important role in easily overcoming any resistance by private shareholders (Wenger and Kaserer 1998, p. 517). Beginning in April 1999, BASF adopted its stock option program for approximately 1,200 top managers of its corporate group (BASF 2000, p. 9).

However, in general, the use of stock option programs was not widespread. They were only offered to top management in large German companies, especially those that were oriented toward the shareholder value principle. In some cases, high-tech firms in the Neuer Markt used them as management rewards. In addition, stock options were generally only supplements to normal salaries (Jürgens et al. 2000, p. 74). Hartmut Berghoff points out "in terms of compensation, German corporations did not fully adopt American practices" (Berghoff 2016, p. 98).

Approximately 60% of all DAX 30 companies adopted stock options for managers in 1997 (Jürgens et al. 2000, p. 69), and in 2000, more than half of the top 30 German firms introduced American-style stock options as an incentive for senior managers (Williams 2000, p. 5). By 2004, all DAX 30 companies adopted stock options (Chizema and Buck 2006, p. 499), and according to Chizema (2010), out of the 125 big firms, 65 adopted stock options in 2006 while 22 had already introduced this scheme by 1998 (Chizema 2010, p. 13).

Several factors influenced companies to adopt stock options. More specifically, exogenous factors such as US investor and foreign ownership, value commitment (shareholder-value orientation), and power dependence (dispersed shareholdings or blockholdings) were positively related to the adoption of stock options. Above all, the extent of German companies' dependence on American investors influenced the introduction of such programs (Buck and Chizema 2008, pp. 256, 258).

Ownership structure was a key factor in the early adoption of this scheme. In fact, the adoption of stock options tends to be greatest in companies with moderate levels of ownership concentration (Tuschuke and Sanders 2003, pp. 634, 645). Family ownership generally opposes the adoption of stock options. Since stock options focus on share prices rather than employment stability, employers resisted the stock options scheme, especially between 1992 and 1998. Chizema (2010) pointed out that although such resistance is weak and waning with time, potential resistance to shareholder-oriented reforms should not be underestimated in an economy such as Germany, which includes institutions founded on a national culture of high collectivism and uncertainty avoidance. Hence, the adoption of stock options that have the potential to widen the compensation gap between management and employees could be seen as illegitimate by some stakeholders (such as employees) (Chizema 2010, pp. 16–17).

In Germany, this adoption implies "an important litmus test in relation to the Americanization of related governance" and should be seen as "the most important explanatory factor for the transformation of US corporate governance" (Chizema and Buck 2006, p. 490; Börsch 2004, p. 377). Most large German firms have established stock option plans since 1997. However, German firms tend to use stock options to a much lesser degree than Anglo-American firms (Vitols 2004b, p. 371). According to Sanders and Tuschke (2007), "a boost in compensation through company stock and stock options was not met in line with the egalitarian, stakeholder-oriented governance system in Germany" (Sanders and Tuschuke 2007, p. 40).

Thus, stock option schemes in German firms have some different characteristics from those in American firms. For example, German companies adopted stock option schemes that are more egalitarian in the sense of covering a smaller proportion of the company's share capital and a larger number of senior managers. Bruce et al. (2005) point out that "German schemes embody a greater number of performance conditions and qualitatively tougher performance conditions" (Bruce et al. 2005, p. 1503).

In addition, the incentive of stock options for executives in German firms is not as great as those for executives in American firms, given their low rates. Moreover, stock options are only one element in the compensation packages of executives. Thus, stock options in German companies have some distinctively un-American features (Buck and Shahrim 2005, p. 58; Siemans 2000, pp. 51–52). As seen in the cases of Siemens, Daimler-Benz, and Thyssen, the incentive scheme of stock options in German enterprises generally stressed long-term performance (Börsch 2004, pp. 377, 381; DaimlerChrysler 2005, p. 110; ThyssenKrupp 1999, p. 37; ThyssenKrupp 2002, p. 190). In this regard, German firms attempted to adopt the American compensation scheme to the German environment. Furthermore, as Schlie and Warner point out that "stakeholder interests are more diffuse in the traditional German approach, thus making it difficult to set up straightforward incentive schemes" (Schlie and Waner 2000, p. 43). The internal voices of shareholders committed to companies in the long term and employee representation on supervisory boards greatly influenced executive pay. Employees, as important stakeholders, are generally in much stronger positions to participate in company decisions. Furthermore, the stable, relational shareholdings of banks and networked companies are institutional characteristics that influence executive compensation (Bruce et al. 2005, pp. 1501–1503).

Cultural factors in German firms have also strongly influenced the adoption of stock options. German managers apparently focus on long-term performance and the importance of planning and warning against the dangers of manipulation. German society is also a consensus-oriented one; therefore, stock options are widely regarded as risk incentive instruments. The difference in the willingness to accept risk could be regarded as one major reason why German managers accept less stock options than their American counterparts. In addition, the capital market in Germany is less developed than that in the Anglo-Saxon, and the capital market does not play an influential role in the German economy. German managers tend to compromise to avert risk and also place less importance on shareholder value than American managers do (Scott 2008, pp. 18, 20–26, 29–34).

Indeed, Anglo-American cross-listing places additional pressure on companies to perform well. As a result, part of the higher compensation may represent a risk premium (Oxelheim and Randøy 2005, p. 481). However, management value and cultural characteristics, such as the attitudes toward the acceptance of risk, are important factors that constrain the introduction of the American stock options scheme in Germany.

Thus, the introduction of stock options in Germany witnessed numerous cases with modifications and adaptations to German environment. Goutas and Lane point out that "the adoption of international accounting standards, the compliance with the German Code of Corporate Governance, the use of certain performance measurement tools, and the implementation of certain practices pertaining toward an active investor relations department were all adopted at Daimler-Benz and Volkswagen with minimal modification." In contrast, the conditions were different in the adoption of stock options (Goutas and Lane 2009, p. 341).

In addition, as seen in both companies, stock options were introduced not only to higher management, such as company managers and the board of management, but also to shop floor employees (Goutas and Lane 2009, pp. 335–337, 340; Bayer 2000, p. 6). However, such introduction of stock options in Germany served as a form of cooperation between labor and management, rather than a more thorough form of American shareholder value management.

Development of Shareholder Value-Oriented Restructuring: In the 1980s, German institutional contexts placed greater emphasis on the competing claims of multiple stakeholder groups. The incentives for and scope of efforts of restructuring that primarily benefit shareholders were limited under such circumstances (Bühner et al. 1997, p. 334). However, such situations have significantly changed. The increasing influences of the capital market have placed pressure on companies to strengthen their core businesses through means such as centralization on the core business and M&As (Herden and Reinhard 1999, p. 526; Völcker 2009, p. 18). Representative cases of such pressure can be seen in the sales of non-core and underperforming business units in VEBA, the return to and concentration on automobile manufacturing as the core business field in Daimler-Benz, the withdrawal from low-profit, low-growth industrial chemical businesses, and the abandonment of German identity in the merger of Hoechst with Rhone-Poulenc to form Aventis, a new France-based company (Vitols 2000, p. 7).

In addition, German financial services companies, particularly banks, have faced increasing criticism from institutional investors because of their low profitability in comparison with Anglo-American banks. One of the demands of institutional investors was the implementation of mergers for achieving economies of scale and reducing the degree of "overbanking" (Vitols 2004b, p. 369). Dore (2000) points out that "it is the M&A bit of restructuring, the preoccupation with buying and selling chunks of productive capacity—and indeed the tendency to make this the core element of the enterprise strategy which top executives define as their role — which is a major factor in making a high share price a dominant managerial objective, at the expense, inevitably, of a concern for employee welfare" (Dore 2000, p. 194).

However, even when restructuring was strengthened under the pressures of the capital market, there were cases in which such measurement was not always developed according to shareholder value orientation. For instance, at Siemens, the semiconductor division was spun-off and listed on the New York and Frankfurt Stock Exchanges as a separate firm on the assumption that Siemens would have shareholdings enabling it to secure control as a new company and also because the works councils of business establishments in Germany supported the spin-off. From the shareholder value perspective, this spin-off was not a far-reaching movement (Börsch 2004, pp. 380–381). Zugehör pointed out that the codetermination in this company was too weak to protect workers sufficiently in the process of business reorganization (Zugehör 2003, p. 166). However, as Börsch indicated, Zugehör only focused on the influences of the unions and the workers' representatives on the supervisory boards (Börsch 2004, p. 387), rendering Zugehör's argument inadequate. It should be stressed that cooperative relationships with works councils generally restrained shareholder value-oriented restructuring.

14.3.1.2 Transformation Toward the Shareholder Value-Oriented Management Model in Major Industries

This section considers some representative industries in which the pressure to transform toward the shareholder value-oriented management model appeared most strongly. More specifically, it focuses on the automobile industry and the chemical industry as representative examples in the non-financial sector.

14.3.1.2.1 Transformation Toward the Shareholder Value-Oriented Management Model in the Automobile Industry

While the power of financing and the requirements of financial investors have increased, automobile companies have had to deal with persistent or even increased production requirements. Thus, a new balance between financial and production logics was required. The mass production of standard and specialty products is both strategies that require long-term access to resources and broad internal competence. The automobile industry has been largely based on industrial mass production. The conditions of the product market also conform to the generalized demands of the financial market, albeit to a limited degree. In addition, actors at the operative level have considerable power and are thus able to constitute a balance to top management's primary orientation toward financial parameters.

Although automobile companies adhere to the general norms of the financial community by concentrating on the firm's core competencies, by reducing the degree of vertical integration and decentralizing the corporate structures into profit centers, the norms and requirements of the production economy have consistently provided a potent counterweight to financial parameters. In reality, widespread agreement is evident regarding the necessity for corporate strategies in the financial market. Thus, the automobile industry is a representative example of the conflict between the industrial real economy and the new requirement regarding the control of financial markets while acknowledging the limits of financialization (Kädtler and Sperling 2002b, pp. 81, 84–86, 91–93; Kädtler and Sperling 2001, pp. 32–33).

Thus, "the increasing imperatives of financialization and the options of globalization are at least partly counter-balanced by bargaining in complex relations of production." Such conditions can be seen in the "decisions concerning the location or relocation of plants," which are not made by simply applying financial parameters (Kädtler and Sperling 2002a, pp. 164–165). Thus, the logic of production is not always completely substituted by that of the financial market. For instance, in DaimlerChrysler and Volkswagen, the concept of shareholder value was adopted at both the ideological and organizational practice levels and in the communicative, operational, and compensation-related dimensions for managers. However, as L. Gotus and C. Lane point out, "this does not mean that shareholder value was adopted in its entirety." DaimlerChrysler adopted a long-term shareholder value orientation, instead of short-term value maximization (Goutas and Lane 2009, pp. 338–340, 342).

Although Volkswagen has accepted shareholder value as a company goal, it continues its policy of being cautious of the capital market's expectations. This policy was carried out jointly by the management and the works council. In this case, shareholder value has not become the dominant goal and has been balanced with other goals, as is evident in the balance between shareholder and workholder values. Thus, this enterprise has followed a general stakeholder approach (Jürgens et al. 2002, pp. 69–73). The growing role of financial criteria is not an indication of a full shareholder-value policy. Volkswagen has followed "a deal strategy of trying to enhance their stock market valuation on the one hand and of erecting protective barriers against hostile takeovers on the other" (Jürgens et al. 2002, p. 78). The strategic interests of this company are not based on the short-term maximization of shareholder value but the long-term growth of the company. Volkswagen has attempted to harmonize long-term profit orientation with the idea of shareholder value as well as reconcile the interests of shareholders and those of other stakeholders, particularly the workers (Goutas and Lane 2009, pp. 333–336, 339, 341).

The merger of DaimlerChrysler is generally regarded as a financial market-oriented merger. However, Kädtler and Sperling stated that "the merger of DaimlerChrysler, undertaken with strong reference to the logic of financial markets, has to be seen, at least for a large part, as a strategy to prevent the companies from being too strictly subordinated to the short-term interests of shareholders or financial actors." In addition, Daimler-Benz's management aimed at driving up market capitalization to reduce the risks of hostile takeovers. This means that DaimlerChrysler's merger was not always strongly oriented toward shareholders (Kädtler and Sperling 2002a, pp. 161, 164). Therefore, such defensive motives were also strong.

14.3.1.2.2 Transformation Toward the Shareholder Value-Oriented Management Model in the Chemical Industry

Analyzing the chemical industry, the diversification has been questioned on the basis of the shareholder value concept and by players in the capital market. In addition, the pressure to transform to the shareholder value-oriented management model has promoted the development of restructuring in this industry. However, there are significant differences among companies in response to the pressure on shareholder value-oriented management and its strategy. An important reason for this is the difference in the company's business portfolios and economic positions, and the administration's consideration of the interests of important investors in the financial market (Becker 2003, pp. 235–236).

Hoechst, which adopted a pure "life science" strategy and pursued mergers, was a typical shareholder value-oriented company. Its top management was committed to a radical version of shareholder value under the leadership of J. Dormann, who was a senior manager from the field of finance and was promoted to chief executive officer (CEO) in 1994. Hoechst presents a case of the most radical departure from the postwar model among the so-called "Big 3" in the German chemical industry (i.e., BASF, Bayer, and Hoechst) (Hoechst AG, Bericht des Vorsitzenden des Vorstands Jürgen Dormann. Ordentlche Hauptversammlung am 25. April 1995, p.6, *Hoechst Archiv*, Hauptversammlung 1995, Hoechst AG, Bericht des Vorsitzenden des Vorstands Jürgen Dormann. Ordentlche Hauptversammlung am 5. Mai 1998, p. 7, *Hoechst Archiv*, Hauptversammlung 12/1998; Vitols 2002, pp. 310–311, 315; Vitols 2003, pp. 199, 211).

In contrast, Bayer committed to an integrated chemical/pharmaceutical strategy and maintained the "Rheinland" model of capitalism, despite the appointment of Manfred Schneider, also a senior manager from the finance field, as CEO. The top management at Bayer deemed it to be the best approach to implement moderate change within the framework of the company's traditional culture and diversified its product portfolio. This was seen in the maintaining of the four core business areas (i.e., polymers, chemicals, health care, and agro). Bayer also resisted the initiatives of US investors and the advice of analysts to split up the company and has pursued an integration strategy ("Verbund" strategy) (Vitols 2002, pp. 310–311, 318–319; Vitols 2003, pp. 199, 211–213). At Bayer, even at the 2001 general meeting when Hoechst merged with Rhone-Poulenc with the support of more than 90% of the stockholders and was given a high level of cash flow, many institutional investors and financial intermediaries did not intend to dismantle the structure of the corporate group (Becker 2003, p. 238).

Furthermore, BASF's top management also believed that maintaining the traditional integration strategy ("Verbund" strategy), which emphasized the economies of scale and transactions through vertical integration at a small number of production sites, was the best way to ensure the company's survival. BASF also developed a competitive strategy that combined innovation and high-quality products with cost leadership in the core market. In addition, the company pursued an explicit stakeholder approach in the principle of corporate governance (Vitols 2002, pp. 310–311,

320–321; Vitols 2003, pp. 213–215). BASF is a prominent case in which the administration resisted the demand for reorganizing the structure of the corporate group by important players in the capital market (Becker 2003, pp. 238–239); this scenario greatly differs from that of Heochst.

14.3.2 Limitations in the Transformation Toward the Shareholder Value-Oriented Management Model

Although the transformation toward the shareholder value-oriented management model advanced after the 1990s, the influence of the principle of shareholder value was not strong. Even in comparison with other countries in continental Europe, Germany moved rather slowly toward a shareholder value economy. Changes in the latter half of 1990s primarily affected a handful of large firms such as DaimlerChrysler and Siemens. Moreover, in Germany, the economic base for a shareholder value economy was extremely narrow in the 1990s (Jürgens et al. 2000, pp. 74–75). Despite the various minor changes toward shareholder value-oriented management, the pillars of the German corporate governance system were maintained. Meanwhile, bank-based financing, the codetermination system, and production management orientation hindered the growth of shareholder value through the 1990s (Williams 2000, p. 5). As a result of the collapse of the high-tech boom and share prices in the beginning of the 2000s, stock market capitalism was no longer as popular as it was during the 1990s (Lane 2003, p. 99). In addition, as seen in the Bayer case, some companies delisted from the New York Stock Exchange and terminated their registration with the US Securities and Exchange Commission (Bayer 2007, p. 19).

When considering the limits of transforming toward the shareholder value-oriented management model in relation to corporate governance, a strong convergence toward the US exit-based governance system has not occurred in Germany (Chizema 2010, p. 9; Jackson and Moerke 2005, p. 358; Gerum 2007, pp. 114, 418, 431, 434–435). Generally, despite the important reforms of the German corporate governance system's individual elements, the main characteristics of the traditional German system as a whole have been maintained. In other words, the insider-control system has not given way to a market-based system. Since then, the changes have not been challenged and no fundamental changes have occurred (Hackethal et al. 2005, pp. 397–398, 401, 404–405; Gerum 2007, pp. 434–435; Matthes 2005, pp. 239–240; Weber 2011, p. 554).

For instance, in 2010, Metten pointed out that there was a clear shift from the shareholder value concept to the company interests over the previous five years. Whereas many of the DAX companies were still forced to emphasize shareholder value in fiscal year 2002, approximately half pursued company interests and emphasized this approach as their core strategy. In addition, one-third of the DAX enterprises pursued a hybrid strategy that stressed company interests rather than those of shareholders, especially from the perspective of pluralistic interests (Metten 2010, pp. 256–257).

The movement toward the shareholder value-oriented management model and capital market-oriented corporate governance greatly differed among companies. For example, Siemens and DaimlerChrysler both had a strong orientation toward the shareholder value management model; however, DaimlerChrysler's model included some measure of cross-continental integration, whereas Siemens's model allowed limited changes under similar pressures (Carr 2005, p. 1158). Although Siemens introduced several elements of the shareholder value approach, it imported neither all features nor the characteristics equivalent to the Anglo-Saxon standards. Even in information policy and transparency, both of which represented the greatest changes, the greater capital market orientation did not influence other main features of financial policies such as financing and dividend policies (Börsch 2004, p. 381).

In addition, the manner in which companies were exposed to international competition was also an important factor that affected the transformation toward the shareholder value management model. Companies in sheltered sectors were generally less shareholder-oriented than those in internationally competing sectors (Höpner 2001, pp. 15–16; Höpner 2003, p. 204). The companies that introduced the American corporate governance system, as observed through their establishment of audit committees with supervisory functions, were firms with high ratios of sale in the international market. In this case, the differences between companies that pursued a large ratio of sales in the international market and those that did not were substantial (Knapp 2009, pp. 73, 185, 188).

Furthermore, the difference in the ownership structure was also a factor that affected various companies. Whereas there was a consistent adoption of the Anglo-American management style and a strong orientation toward shareholder value in public companies, the conditions greatly differed in family-owned companies (Carr 2005, pp. 1171, 1174). Moreover, there were divergences in corporate governance between larger companies (in which ownership and control were shared between smaller blockholders and dispersed institutional investors) and small- and medium-sized listed companies, most of which had a controlling owner. The changes in corporate governance for the former group have been more extensive, whereas the latter group has experienced limited changes (Vitols 2005b, p. 358).

In this regard, the model in opposition to the coordinated market economy has spread neither in a pure form nor over the entire German economy. An important reason for this was the fact that the segment of listed corporations was limited, and there were large non-listed enterprises and large firms (other than joint-stock companies) with legal and ownership forms (Faust et al. 2011, pp. 397–399). Considering such conditions, it can be stated that the explanation concerning corporate governance mainly from the perspective of the capital market does not hold true for many German enterprises, including family-owned companies (Paetzmann 2008, p. 43).

14.3.3 Hybridization of the American Shareholder Value-Oriented Management Model and the German Management Model

As seen in our previous discussions, although some elements of the shareholder value-oriented management model were introduced in German enterprises, the hybridization of the American shareholder value-oriented management model and the German management model occurred. According to S. Vitols, "corporate change in Germany is characterized by considerable heterogeneity, covering the whole spectrum from radical acceptance of shareholder value to stubborn resistance to change. The path of least resistance however appears not to be any generalized convergence to the Anglo-American model, but rather the adoption of 'hybrid' models of corporate organization combing a partial upgrading of the status of minority shareholders (mainly through increased financial transparency and a nominal commitment to increasing share price) with traditional stakeholders practices such as concensus bargaining among management and between management and labor" (Vitols 2000, p. 1).

German firms have adopted a more "moderate" form of shareholder value than that adopted by companies in the United States and the United Kingdom. This behavior of German companies reflects the continuing influence of traditional stakeholders, despite the increased pressures from institutional investors (Vitols 2004a, p. 334). In reality, the typical goals of German firms, such as sales growth, employment stability, and product quality, have been enhanced, rather than replaced, by shareholder value. Therefore, the German variant of shareholder value can be characterized as "negotiated shareholder value." In this regard, the interests of institutional investors must first be negotiated with other members of the stakeholder coalition such as large shareholders and employee representatives. In addition, compromises that typically alter the nature of the demands made by institutional investors need to be identified because of the different interests of the members of the stakeholder coalition. Reflecting the balance of power among stakeholder representatives, many shareholder value measures are modified during negotiations and assume significantly different forms in Germany, compared with those in the United States and the United Kingdom (Vitols 2004b, pp. 358, 368, 372).

Reiner Zugehör also pointed out that there were situations in which the capital market and codetermination in enterprises congruently coexist, as seen in "the adaptation of German corporate governance to an Anglo-Saxon shareholder action" on the one hand and "the stability of the codetermination" on the other (Zugehör 2003, p. 186). Furthermore, the difference in the ownership structure is also a factor that influences various companies. Goutas and Lane indicated that although DaimlerCrysler and Volkswagen introduced elements of shareholder value to different degrees and in different ways, "both created 'hybrid' forms of corporate governance through the adoption of certain elements of shareholder value." They also stress that "the introduction of shareholder value and its related practices was 'blended' in with the institutional practices and ideas that already existed in the two companies" (Goutas and Lane 2009, pp. 340, 342).

14.3.4 Conflicts Between the American Shareholder Value-Oriented Management Model and the German Management Model

The foregoing discussions considered the transformation toward the American shareholder value-oriented management model as well as its characteristics. Thus, this section examines the conflicts between this model and the German management model and the factors in the German characteristics that determine the movement toward the American management model.

14.3.4.1 Conflicts Between the American Shareholder Value-Oriented Management Model and the German Management Model with Relation to Inter-Firm Relationships Based on Capital and Personnel Networks

According to Onetti and Pisoni (2009), although the proportion of stocks owned by financial institutions declined, there were the only weak relations between stock ownership and supervisory mandates. In addition, changes in the "German model" of business management and corporate governance were relatively small. The total number of stockholdings held by the "Big Four" banks (i.e., Deutsche Bank, Dresdner Bank, Commerzbank, and Bayerische Hypo- und Vereinsbank) and the two large insurance companies (Allianz and Münchener Rückversicherungsgesellschaft) among the 100 largest German non-financial firms decreased by almost half in 2005, in comparison with the total stockholdings held from 1998 to 2001. On the other hand, the number of mandates among the six financial institutions in 1998, 2001, and 2005 were 118, 189, and 130, respectively. Although the number in 2005 was lower than that in 2001, it was still higher than that in 1998 (Onetti and Pisoni 2009, pp. 61, 64, 66–67, 72).

Since the early 1990s, insurance companies, particularly Allianz (the largest life insurance company in Germany), have significantly increased their stockholdings, thus filling the gap created by the partial withdrawal of banks from the ownership of other companies' stocks. Insurance companies tend to take a more patient, long-term view of investment, compared with other institutional investors, such as hedge funds and mutual funds (Vitols 2005a, pp. 387, 391, 395). Thus, large shareholders (other than banks) continue to remain committed to the strong corporate governance system. Vitols points out that "on the institutional level, the major modification of the postwar stakeholder model has been integrated of institutional investors into an augmented stakeholder coalition" (Vitols 2004b, pp. 368, 372).

According to research conducted by the monopoly commission, German large financial enterprises had decreased their capital participation in the largest 100 enterprises to approximately two-thirds between 1996 and 2008. For instance, Deutsche Bank implemented capital participation in 15 companies; this number decreased to nine. Similarly, this number decreased from six to three for Commerzbank, from 28 to 11 for Allianz, and from 13 to two for Münchener Rückversicherungsgesellschaft (Monopolkommission 2010, p. 149).

"The German bank-firm relationship is based on a network of tightly joined financial institutions, which together exert a considerable influence on industrial companies." Onetti and Pisoni also indicated that the rates of stocks owned by financial institutions can only partially explain the percentage of mandates of financial institutions as shareholders to the total number of members on the supervisory boards that are representatives of the shareholders (Onetti and Pisoni 2009, p. 70).

The majority of bankers were represented on the supervisory boards of the top 10 German firms. Moreover, the proportion of voting rights, which the six financial institutions could exert in the supervisory boards of the industrial companies, was clearly higher for the three considered years. Furthermore, the control exerted by the main financial institutions was based on a network of relationships rather than the position of a single financial institution (Onetti and Pisoni 2009, pp. 61, 64, 66–67, 71–72).

It has been highlighted that personal connections did not necessarily decrease overall, and the changes observed were smaller than those seen in the aspect of capital. The sales of stocks by banks and the decreased dispatches of supervisory board members to other companies did not represent the decisive decrease in the roles of banks in corporate governance (Jansen 2008, p. 31; Vitols 2005a, p. 395). Furthermore, the significance of the deposited stocks combined with the shareholdings by banks was still high. Overall, the main outcome of the withdrawal of bank managers from supervisory boards was the large increase in the number of former full-time executive members who were moving up to the supervisory boards upon retirement. This process occurred instead of recruiting "independent directors," as in the Anglo-Saxon model (Vitols 2005b, pp. 358, 363–366, Höpner 2003, 206).

Indeed, personnel connections have greatly decreased since 2000. For example, Deutsche Bank assigned its directors to 35 of the largest 100 companies in Germany; however, this number declined to 17 in 1998 and only five in 2002 (Beyer 2006, p. 106). In the case of Deutsche Bank, four members of the managing board held a total of six mandates on the supervisory boards of other enterprises in the fiscal year 2022 (Deutsche Bank 2023, pp. 475–480). In the case of Commerzbank, six members of the managing board held seven mandates on the supervisory boards of other enterprises in the fiscal year 2022; among these interlocking posts, three were in Commerz Real AG and one was in CommerzVentures GmbH, a subsidiary of Commerzbank (Commerzbank 2022, p. 310). This dissolution of personnel connections occurred in the core enterprises of "Germany Inc." and not in peripheral ones (Beyer 2006, p. 130). However, in general, antinomy could be observed. While banks and insurance companies have decreased both their capital participation and personnel connections, in non-financial enterprises, the dissolution of capital participation and particularly personnel connections can be regarded as more modest. Regarding personnel ties, financial companies invite fewer members outside the company and assign fewer of their managing board members, thus strengthening the function of market mechanism; in contrast, non-financial companies promote close personnel networks that greatly contribute to restricting competition or inter-company coordination (Furch

2012, pp. 164, 175, 230–232, 235). With regard to personnel connections among the largest 100 companies, the numbers of mandates held by directors of financial (banks and insurance) companies were 76 in 1996, 20 in 2008, and seven in 2020; thus, the value held in 2020 was only 9.2% of that in 1996. Meanwhile, these values for directors in non-financial sectors were 76 in 1996, 42 in 2008, and 25 in 2020; the 2020 value was 32.9% of the 1996 value (Monopolkommision 2022, p. 35). In addition, the supervisory board in which codetermination system is applied encounters no radical changes (Furch 2012, p. 175). Furthermore, interlocking directorates built through the assignment of directors on the managing board of a company to the supervisory board of another company tended to decrease more rapidly than those established through supervisory board members' holding of supervisory board mandates of other enterprises (Heinz 2002, p. 403; Heinz 2004, p. 230).

Institutional changes in the German system of corporate governance had a partial influence on the network of interlocking directorates. However, these influences were quantitative rather than structural in nature (Heinze 2004, p. 232). S. Vitols emphasized that the impact of the changes in the role of banks on the German corporate governance system was much less dramatic than what had been discussed in many studies (Vitols 2005b, p. 358). In fact, German banks still exert a certain level of control over some supervisory boards, given their ability to appoint the "right" persons in the right positions. The banks' control is further enhanced in cases wherein the chairmen of the supervisory boards are also the bank representatives (Plessis et al. 2012, p. 357).

Regarding changes in the capital market, the brief flirtation with market-based equity financing immediately ended with the collapse of the bubble economy in 2000/2001. The ambitions of the largest banks to transform the financial system in Germany into a more market-based one failed. However, the banks continued to serve as key actors in the German financial system (Vitols 2005a, p. 387). In addition, the business relations between banks and companies and the German corporate governance system showed both continuity and change. Indeed, the erosion of the relations was substantial among the largest blue-chip companies; however, at the same time, other segments of companies continued to have strong relations with banks. Overall, the close relationship between banks and companies, which was based on bank loans, did not completely diminish. Instead, it shifted toward different groups of companies (Jackson and Moerke 2005, p. 356; Klages 2006, pp. 37–38). P. Klages stressed that despite using the Anglo-American approach in the German corporate governance system, the consistency of the ownership structure, strengthening of the supervisory board, and reproduction of codetermination indicate possibly rigid internal governance mechanisms and partial continuity of strategic coordination mechanisms (Klages 2006, p. 51).

Even around the mid-2000s, bank loans were still, by far, the most important financial resource. Meanwhile, capital markets still did not play an important role in corporate governance, because of the high concentration of ownership in German business enterprises, the increasing role of managers of other firms and former managers of the same firms, and the governing coalition by players such as larger shareholders, employees, and banks that supported the insider-control system (Hackethal et al.

2005, pp. 401, 404–405). In addition, companies' orientation being dependent on banks and corporate financing through the capital market offered German joint-stock companies more choices (Gerum 2007, pp. 114, 418–419). German companies have maintained their existing long-term financing patterns and continue to have access to long-term, patient capital. Thus, the core of the German system of financing and corporate governance largely continued to be maintained (Goutas and Lane 2009, p. 342). Christian Marx and Morten Leitmeyer also stress that despite the great change witnessed in the dissolution of the corporate network, "many traditional features of the corporate governance regime were preserved" (Marx and Morten 2022, p. 25).

In general, banks have the strongest influence among outside associations, and their interests are still considered by the management on the basis of the universal banking system (Beisel 2002, p. 22). In addition, equity-oriented performance goals tend to create conflicts between bank stakeholders and institutional investors regarding performance criteria (Wu and Delios 2009, p. 333).

Notably, only Deutsch Bank has successfully developed its strategy and been able to establish itself on firm ground as an international investment bank. David Furch highlighted in 2012 that Commerzbank and Dresdner Bank had strongly pursued the concentration of their traditional businesses again, which could be interpreted as a step toward increased monitoring by banks (Furch 2012, p. 231). According to Ralf Ahrens, despite prominent transitions of some banks toward international investment banking and loosening of their networks, most banks continued to engage in relationship banking (Ahrens 2022, p. 130). Stephanie Gross points out that the case of Deutsche Bank indicates the significance of creating share-holder value as well as the resistance to this management concept observed within the German banking sector (Gross 2006, p. 1). Hartmut Berghoff also stresses that "with the exception of Deutsche Bank, no German bank made it into the top tier of international investment banks." He provides two reasons: "the weak tradition of international finance and the loss of expertise through the persecution of Jewish bankers" over a long period (Berghoff 2016, p. 91).

14.3.4.2 Conflicts Between the American Shareholder Value-Oriented Management Model and the German Management Model with Relation to the Influences of Institutional Investors

As J. Hendry points out, whereas in the United States, "the shareholdings of listed companies are arguably too diversified for any voice to be felt," in European countries other than the UK, "most companies are effectively controlled by a single block-holder, so that an institutional investor has little to gain from activism" (Hendry et al 2007, p. 237). Vitols also stresses that "even for companies where banks have exited and no other investors have in quiet a few cases stepped in and acquired blockholdings" (Vitols 2005b, pp. 363–364). Overall, large insurance companies and specific types of funds that differ from typical mutual funds tend to be oriented toward concentrated, long-term investments (Vitols 2005b, p. 364). Leo McCann stressed in 2014 that ownership of the largest publicly listed firms in Germany remained much more concentrated than in the United States, with large blockholdings that made it extremely hard to develop a US-style market for corporate control (McCann 2014, p. 166; also see Furch 2012, S. 65). In the smaller listed companies, the concentration of ownership tends to remain relatively high compared with the Anglo-American economy (Ringe 2015, p. 516). According to Evgeni Peev, in 2018–2019, "the nontraditional owners of 'Deutschland AG' such as foreign blockholders and widely held companies together account for 25% of the top 20 firms, 36% of the top 100 and 36% of listed German companies," whereas "German individuals, families and other German companies still appear to be the key blockholders in the top 20 (65% of firms), top 100 (54%) and listed German companies (53%)" (Peev 2023, pp. 106–107).

In addition, regarding the nature of the institutional investors, there are differences between a delegate management fund or an investment company and a directly managed pension funds. The former tends to be subject to much greater short-term financial profitability pressures, whereas the latter emphasizes the durable commitment of assets and pursues long-term investment strategies. In general, delegate management funds or investment companies tend to pursue an "exit" strategy, whereas directly managed pension funds have the tendency to emphasize a "voice" strategy. However, in Germany, even delegate management funds do not always lead to significant changes in the strategic decision-making process, particularly regarding reorientation toward shareholder value predominance. According to Dupuy and Lung, the influence of delegate management funds on German automakers' strategic choices remains limited (Dupuy and Lung 2002, pp. 52–53, 56–57). After the corporate governance crisis in the early 2000s, new trends are emerging that are oriented toward the predominance of long-term institutional investors in corporate governance, including criticism against shareholder value (Aglietta 2009, pp. 203, 220).

14.3.4.3 Conflicts Between the American Shareholder Value-Oriented Management Model and the German Management Model with Relation to Management Values Emphasizing Production, Organization of Top Management, and Personnel Structure of Managers

Management value emphasizing on production (Yamazaki 2009, 2013), organization of top management, and personnel structure of managers influence the conflicts between the shareholder value-oriented management model and the German management model. In line with this fact, the following statistics and cases are considered. Engineers generally have greater representation in the top management of German companies than in companies based in other countries. According to a 2004 survey by Gerum, regarding directors of companies, the ratio of individuals from the fields of engineering and natural science to university graduates was 32% and the ratio of individuals from the field of science, including information science, mathematics, and mental science, to university graduates was approximately 40% (Gerum 2007,

p. 143). An investigation in 2003 further clarified that 32.6% of chairmen on the executive board were persons from the field of finance and control, 27.4% were from marketing and sale, and 26.3% were from production and technology (Beyer 2006, p. 131). Indeed, the managing board members in large German corporations became less oriented toward technology in the ten years from 2000 onward. However, their orientation was stronger compared with that of directors in the United States (Furch 2012, p. 172). This orientation of German directors on executive boards toward production and technology contradicted the performance paradigm based on the share market orientation of Anglo-Saxon executives (Heinz 2002, pp. 394–395).

The concept of regarding a company not as a "money-making machine" but as a place where products are designed, produced, and eventually sold has been connected with a greater emphasis on production objectives over financial ones. This is a crucial factor that makes shareholder value maximization less important for top managers (Fiss and Zajac 2004, p. 505). In addition, regarding management value emphasizing technology, production, and the personnel composition of managers in Germany, the high rate of internal promotions of managers is also an important factor that created a conflict between the American shareholder value-oriented management model and the German management model.

The role of the external labor market (for both managers and financial experts) has been clearly rising since the 1990s. According to Höpner (2001), regarding the careers of all 90 top managers who were chief executives in the 40 largest listed industrial corporations in Germany, the proportion of top managers who were recruited from outside the company increased from 17% in 1990 to more than 35% in 1999. In addition, the percentage of chief executives classified as financial experts increased from approximately 25% in 1990 to 35% in 1996. There is "a trend toward professionalization, a greater importance of economic and financial issues, recruitment from the external labor market for managers, and shorter times in office." M. Höpner points out "these data suggests that the changing social world' of top managers helps explain why shareholder value strategies enjoy the high reputation among managers" (Höpner 2001, pp. 21–24, 49). In reality, the proportion of top managers recruited from the inside of companies is still high. Moreover, a strong culture of independent directors in the Anglo-Saxon sense has not emerged in Germany (Vitols 2005b, pp. 358, 365). The liquidity of German top managers in labor markets tends to be lower than generally considered, and they remain in one company for very long terms (Furch 2012, p. 172).

There were numerous cases in which the orientation toward shareholder value management was related to top management personalities; executives such as Jürgen Schrempp (CEO of DaimlerChrysler) and Heinrich von Pierer (CEO of Siemens) are the most typical examples. As Jürgens et al. (2000) point out, "shareholder valve in Germany stands for the programs of radical corporate change which have been introduced by these active, celebrity chief executives" (Jürgens et al. 2000, p. 68). Hartmut Berghoff provides certain examples of the changing management elite. For instance, Ron Sommer, who took over as CEO of Deutsche Telekom in 1995; Thomas Middelhoff, who was the CEO of Bartelsmann from 1998 to 2002; and Klaus Esser, who joined the Mannesmann board in 1994 and was promoted to CEO in 1998.

However, Berghoff stresses these three persons are not regarded as typical of the German management elite (Berghoff 2016, pp. 95–97).

In addition, regarding the organization of the top management and the role of CEOs, German law regards the board of directors to be "a collegial entity with collective responsibility for corporate decisions" (Höpner and Jackson 2001, p. 21). The strong orientation toward consensus decision-making within a board of directors itself is an important characteristic (Höpner and Jackson 2001, p. 21; Gerum 2007, pp. 419, 432–433; Mänyysaari 2005, p. 398; Dyas and Thanheiser 1976, pp. 129, 137). As S M. Mintz points out, "in the U.S., while the role of top manager typically is vested by the board in the CEO, the principles permit that function to be vested in a group of senior executives" (Mintz 2006, p. 28). Conversely, in Germany, this is not intended to place the chairmen of boards of directors in charge of functions that are similar to those of CEOs; in fact, the chairmen of the boards of directors do not assume the role of the CEO (Gerum 2007, pp. 419, 421, 432–433).

The dual-board system in Germany, which consists of supervisory boards and boards of directors, supports a consensus approach to corporate governance. In such a system, the head of the managing board typically plays a role as the "speaker" rather than the "chairman." Individual members of the management boards, who are equally responsible for decision-making, are responsible to the supervisory boards rather than to the chairmen or speakers (Vitols 2005b, pp. 360–361). Since there is no hierarchical difference among members of the boards of directors and given that chief executives or chairmen of the boards do not receive any direct orders, the American hierarchical model, such as that for CEOs, is incompatible with the German corporate governance system (Witt 2009, p. 306).

In this way, each member of the boards of directors in German companies enjoys great autonomy in decision-making. Furthermore, each member can obtain political support from his/her own constituency, which also contributes to the securing of such autonomy. Decisions in the managing boards are typically made on a consensus basis. Such a system of decision-making is an important factor that makes it quite difficult to reach an agreement on radical changes at the board level (Vitols 2000, p. 6). In addition, an important outcome of the consensus management approach (e.g., collegial management) can be seen in the fact that the "turnover of managers in Germany is relatively low in comparison with Anglo-Saxon nations" (Vitols 2005b, p. 361). The personnel structure of top managers, based on the internal labor market, is also a factor that restricts the increase in the proportion of executives recruited from outside of companies and their influence. Finally, the term in office for directors in German companies is longer than that for directors in American companies. This is another important factor that enables them to be liberated from the pressures of short-term management objectives (Witt 2009, p. 306).

14.3.4.4 Conflicts Between the American Shareholder Value-Oriented Management Model and the German Management Model with Relation to the Codetermination System

This subsection analyzes the influence of the codetermination system. Labor unions tend to fight against "excessive externalization"—i.e., against the infringement of their own interests due to shareholders' requirements, such as maximization of shareholder values in the supervisory board through cooperation with the top management. Such a cooperative system has formed an important basis that has restricted the strong influence of American financialization in the management process of companies in Germany (Schwarz 2003, p. 78). The interests of labor under the codetermination system and the interests of securing the autonomy of management on the management side are in accordance.

Labor participation on supervisory boards, half of which comprised labor representatives as mandated by the Codetermination Act for the Coal, Iron and Steel Industries and the 1976 Law on Codetermination indicated a relative decrease in the composition of external members on the supervisory board, such as banks and corporate shareholders or even general investors. Accordingly, to corporations and internal supervisory board members as well as directors responsible for business execution, this was an opportunity for less external influence and involvement. Corporations used this as an opportunity to reduce potential external influence and involvement. From the objectives of labor, the codetermination system secured soundness and security in employment and corporate management. This feature further strengthened collaboration between corporations and labor. In particular, a majority of supervisory board seats were seized by obtaining the approval of labor representatives through prior internal discussion with the supervisory board and between its employee members and directors (Mitbestimmungskommission 1970, p. 63); this made it possible to greatly mitigate or even circumvent external influence, resulting in a chance to increase autonomous execution of business functions for both the supervisory board and the board of directors. This is noteworthy especially when considering the characteristics and nature of German corporate governance.

Moreover, when the composition of investor representatives on the supervisory board was limited to half, strengthening defensive functions by cooperating with banks became possible. In these cases, even if external influences planned to take control of management authority by gaining majority voting rights in general meetings, in reality, it was difficult to grasp the reins of business management. A fundamental point in the "Rheinland Model of capitalism" ("Rhenish capitalism") can be seen here.

When examining defensive functions against the pressures of capital market and autonomy of business management from a contemporary viewpoint, the codetermination at the level of supervisory boards creates the possibility for the management to restrict and moderate the influences of short-term capital owners, such as foreign investors and investment funds, through the participation of half of the workers' representatives in the supervisory board. In companies where the 1976 Law on Codetermination was applied, if the management cooperates with the supervisory members from the workers' perspectives, then it becomes difficult for outside powers to realize their interests, unless they are able to secure all the members of the supervisory boards who are stockholders.

As seen in the share buyback movement of recent years, that is, with corporations wanting to regain ownership of their stocks, securing even one investor representative on their supervisory board makes control for external forces possible by cooperation with labor representatives on the supervisory board. To secure and stabilize employment, the interest in maintaining and improving labor conditions and developing and strengthening of labor relations based on the codetermination system built a foundation for a partnership between labor and management.

A characteristic of decision-making in German companies can be seen in their need to reach agreements regarding key policy changes with work councils as the codetermination organs. Although the key demands of institutional investors are the adoption of remuneration (which is closely tied to performance) for employees and managers, the closing/selling of underperforming business units, changes in the compensation system for employees, and the plans for closures and large-scale layoffs or drastic job cuts must be negotiated with the company's works council. In the process of negotiations regarding changes in remuneration systems, the works council generally requires elements of collective regulation and limits on the extent of pay linked to performance. The involvement of the works council can make it more difficult and expensive to execute closures, given its right to negotiate social plans for large-scale layoffs; this means that the way in which the problem of underperforming business units is dealt with could be altered. This right to negotiate includes negotiating with potential buyers and influencing the decision in favor of buyers who will take better consideration of employees' interests. These are typical examples of the involvement of works councils in negotiations over the introduction of shareholder value (Vitols 2004b, pp. 370–371). In addition, "labor solidarity" is a crucial variable that affects the ability of works councils to resist management demands for shareholder value (Vitols 2000, p. 7).

Indeed, shareholder value has strengthened the general trend toward the efficiency orientation of codetermination. However, as M. Höpner points out, "codetermination and central collective agreements are not jeopardized by shareholder value, and at this point shareholder value and codetermination are getting along better than one might have expected" (Höpner 2001, pp. 35–36). Such conditions have not fundamentally changed even in the present day. Actually, even investors in the Anglo-Saxon market have acknowledged the economic advantages of codetermination (Faust and Kädtler 2009, p. 24; Zugehör 2003, p. 182).

Although they attempted to maximize short-term shareholder value in German corporations, such behavior was not necessarily effective given the German system of management and the mechanism of corporate governance. Thus, for investors in the Anglo-Saxon market, it can be effective to pursue increases in mid- and long-term shareholder value rather than the maximization of short-term shareholder value. This can also be achieved while utilizing the characteristics and effectiveness of German business management and investing in the US and UK capital markets more emphatically, which are more suitable for securing higher investment efficiency.

In this way, "the legal model of codetermination and strong welfare state has allowed German firms to more rapidly adapt their stakeholder model toward greater shareholder value than in Japan" (Jackson 2005, p. 426). Clark indicated that, for instance, in Volkswagen, "the emergence of shareholder value strategies for capital and management has not undermined codetermination and collective bargaining as core institutions in the German business system" (Clark 2006, pp. 599, 604).

The influence of shareholders can be controlled and the room for decision-making on the management side has an inclination to be narrowed under the strong consideration of stockholders' interests. However, essential factors, such as supervisory boards and the codetermination system, have only slightly changed (Matthes 2005, p. 239; Furch 2012, p. 175), and the effectiveness of combining banks and industrial enterprises has not decreased (Matthes 2005, p. 239). In Germany, deviations from financialization could be observed owing to the greater influence of various stakeholders other than stockholders and managers compared with their counterparts in the United States. Hermut Berghoff stresses the following: "financialization changed German capitalism but not enough to dissolve Germany Inc." and "despite dramatic changes in some of its parts, the most important pillars of Germany Inc. remained intact" (Berghoff 2016, p. 106). In addition, given the worldwide financial crisis and the economic crisis tied to the Lehman Brothers shock, criticism and reflection of the American shareholder value-oriented management model and the capital market-oriented corporate governance system has further strengthened (Kazama 2012).

14.4 Reframing in the "Americanization" of Business Management in Japan and Germany

Based on the preceding discussions, this subsection captures the movement toward American shareholder-value-oriented management model after the 1990s from "reframing" angle outlined in Chap. 1 as author's own framework of analyzing the international transfer of business management.

In Japan, an important characteristic of the transformation toward the shareholder value-oriented management model and the corporate governance system emphasizing capital market can be seen in the reforms of top management organization and the revisions of the legal system. Such trends are indicated in the shift to committee-setting companies in line with the American corporate governance model. As clarified in Sect. 14.2, for instance, of all the Japanese listed companies in the Tokyo Stock Exchange, many companies have done such reforms.

However, in reality, the hybridization of the Japanese and American management models reflects the actual situation. In the American system, the decision-making and supervision processes and business execution are clearly separated by enriching the committee system and the corporate officer system as well as strengthening the governance through outside directors. Meanwhile, the "Japanese hybridization" aimed at evading complete separation between the decision-making processes and business execution while avoiding the introduction of outside directors, despite adopting systems such as the corporate officer system.

Considering some factors determining reframing in the Americanization of business management, institutional factors have strongly influenced the transformation toward American management model. The organization and the composition of the personnel on the boards in Japan, the hierarchy in the managing boards, the president's strong authority, and the overwhelming weight of the director in terms of inside promotion tended to restrain the effectiveness of monitoring and checking management execution functions by the outside director. They may enable executives to moderate the pressure from institutional investors, such as investment funds, in the capital market.

Management traditions in Japan also effects on reforms of management model and corporate governance system. Management tradition such as seen in the longer term in office for directors in Japan than that for directors in American companies may be an important factor that decreases the pressure of short-term management from the capital market. It has also been a foundation for management emphasizing sales volume and market share.

American ideology that regards companies as a "nexus of contracts" and considers them the objective of buying or selling reflected social structure in the United States based on the thought of the contracting society is not compatible for Japanese social background. Such difference between the United States and Japan has also impacted Japanese corporations' management values and the transformation toward shareholder value-oriented management model and the corporate governance system focusing on the interests of capital market players.

Regarding the influence of market structure, the personnel structure of top managers, based on the internal labor market, is a factor that restricts the increase in the proportion of executives recruited from outside of companies and their influence.

Meanwhile in Germany, American shareholder value-oriented management model was not appropriate for German business conditions and conflicts between American shareholder value-oriented management model and German management model were great due to the changes of characteristics in the "Americanization" of business management after the 1990s (transformation from the production-based approach to the finance-based approach).

When examining the amalgamation of German and American elements, German corporate governance system aiming at increasing values of enterprise as social community has been fused with American corporate governance system stressing short-term results and interests of shareholder. Hybridization of German-style management model emphasizing stakeholder value and American-style management models focusing on maximization of shareholder value can be observed.

Institutional factors are deeply concerned with reframing in the deployment of American management model and corporate governance system. Inter-firm relationships, in particular industry–bank relationships, codetermination system, and industrial relations based on such worker participation system in management greatly influenced and restricted the transformation toward shareholder value management. Labor relations represented by the codetermination system determined German corporations' pursuit of shareholder value based on the negotiation with the worker side. German specific board-majority system in the board of directors and differences in the roles and positions of chief executive officer (CEO) as top person in the top management team between Germany and the United States also became factor restraining finance-oriented management model and corporate governance system and promoted orientation toward more moderate shareholder value than the countermeasure in the United States.

Considering the influence of management values and tradition, enterprise is not regarded as a "nexus of contract" and tended to be considered the place in which workers corporate and socially useful products are manufactured and distributed. Such management values are different from those in the United States, which heavily emphasize the interest of stockholders. This emphasis on stakeholder interests and management values has significantly affected German-style management. Management tradition and management values emphasizing technology, quality, and production and relatively high proportion of executive from technical background in top management are also one of the important factors determining reframing of American management model. Although the ratio of top managers from financial field has increased after the 1990s, German management values emphasizing technical worth has not decisively changed, which promoted reframing in the Americanization process. In addition, management tradition such as seen in the trend of longer term in office for directors in Germany than that for directors in American companies is also an important factor that decreases the pressure of short-term management from capital market.

Such adaptation process in the Americanization of business management is also deeply connected with characteristics of German capitalism. Regarding characteristics of market structure, based on competitiveness in market emphasizing quality, high share of exports to the EU area in all Germany's exports and complementary relationships in the European markets with other countries in this region have had great meaning for maintaining of long-term oriented management instead orientation toward short-term management. Such characteristics of market structure are an important background of the pursuit of increasing of shareholder value emphasizing competitive advantage of German enterprise in European markets.

Regarding the conditions surrounding the transformation toward shareholder-value-oriented management model and corporate governance system in Japan and Germany during the period after the 1990s as well as "reframing" and the factors defining, Table 14.1 shows an inline comparison of the respective countries, based on the discussion so far in this chapter.

Table 14.1 Comparison of conditions surrounding the transformation toward shareholder value management model in Japan and Germany

Deployment and factors affecting them	Management methods	
	Shareholder value management model and corporate governance system	
	Japanese management methods	German management methods
Overall conditions in the deployment of American management methods	• Trend of convergence in the adoption of International Accounting Standards and US GAAP in listed corporations • Diffusion and strengthening of investor relations measures • Trends in which the higher the ratio of stockholdings by foreigners to total stockholdings, the higher the ratio of stock option adoption • A higher proportion of enterprises that adopted stock options to listed enterprises in the "Mothers" or "Prime" category • Trend toward adopting the committee-style corporate governance system in the listed corporations • A higher proportion of companies adopted a committee-style corporate governance system in companies with a high proportion of foreign stockholders	• Convergence trend in the adoption of International Accounting Standards and US GAAP in DAX companies and New York Stock Exchange-listed corporations • Diffusion of investor relations measures • The implementation and diffusion of stock options as an incentive system for executives to promote shareholder value-oriented management and corporate governance • Implementation of shareholder value-oriented restructuring

(continued)

Table 14.1 (continued)

Deployment and factors affecting them	Management methods	
	Shareholder value management model and corporate governance system	
	Japanese management methods	German management methods
Deployment characteristics of American management methods	• Changes in top management organization reforms and legal system revisions • The inclusion of a board of directors was generally regarded as passive, with independent outside directors wielding significant power • Through the strengthening of interlocking stockholdings, a defensive measure movement toward shareholder stabilization is being undertaken • Cases in which top management organizations focused on responding to global competition through rapid decision-making • In competitive industries, there is a higher proportion of enterprises that have shifted toward new management structures, such as the corporate officer system and the committee-setting system	• Case of transformational management emphasizing shareholder value by pursuing a balance of financial and production logics • Orientation toward moderate shareholder value via bargaining between management and labor, as well as among stakeholders • Management changes based on a shareholder approach that considers shareholder interests • Use of various forms of stock options system such as a relatively low weight of stock option remuneration for top managers • Differences in the conditions for transitioning to a shareholder-value-oriented management model among enterprises and industrial sectors • The impact of ownership structure on the shift toward shareholder value management

(continued)

Table 14.1 (continued)

Deployment and factors affecting them	Management methods	
	Shareholder value management model and corporate governance system	
	Japanese management methods	German management methods
Modifications in American management methods	• Revision and hybridization of the Japanese management board model encouraged by combining subsequent legal system reforms • Japanese approaches to modifying the American committee-style management model by enriching the committee system and corporate officer systems, as well as strengthening the governance through outside directors	• Implementation of a moderate stock option system based on long-term oriented management and a management culture emphasizing equality rather than an American-style strong incentive system for executives • German approaches to modifying the capital market-oriented management model and corporate governance system while taking stakeholders' interest into account
Amalgamation of American and Japanese elements	• Combination of Japanese-style and American-style management board systems via "hybridization of American-type" features such as clear separation of decision-making, supervision processes, and business execution • Despite the adoption of systems such as the corporate officer system, "Japanese hybridization" aims to avoid complete separation between decision-making processes and business execution while avoiding the introduction of outside directors	• Combination of German-style management models emphasizing stakeholder value and American-style management models emphasizing shareholder value maximization • Hybridization of the German corporate governance system aimed at increasing enterprise values as a social community with the American corporate governance system focusing on short-term results and shareholder interests

(continued)

Table 14.1 (continued)

Deployment and factors affecting them		Management methods	
		Shareholder value management model and corporate governance system	
		Japanese management methods	German management methods
Factors of modification of American management method	Influence of traditions, cultural factors, and management values	• Reduces the pressure from the capital market on short-term management due to management tradition, such as the longer term in office for directors in Japan than for directors in American companies (a foundation for management emphasizing sales volume and market share) • Conflicts between Japanese management culture and American ideology which sees companies as a "nexus of contracts" with the goal of buying or selling	• Reduction of the pressure on short-term management from the capital market as a result of management tradition, as evidenced by directors in Germany serving longer terms in office than directors in American companies • Conflicts between German management value, which sees companies as a place for producing and distributing socially useful products, and American ideology, which sees businesses as a "nexus of contracts" with the goal of buying or selling • Management tradition and values centered on technology, quality, and production • A relatively high proportion of top management executives come from a technical background, and management values emphasize technical worth, products quality, and production

(continued)

Table 14.1 (continued)

Deployment and factors affecting them		Management methods	
		Shareholder value management model and corporate governance system	
		Japanese management methods	German management methods
	Influence of institutional factors	• The president wields considerable power within the management boards • The director who is promoted within the company carries a disproportionate amount of weight on top management members	• Inter-firm relationships, in a specific industry–bank relationships • The labor relations framework is represented by a codetermination system, which necessitates negotiations with the worker side • The board of directors in Germany uses a board-majority system • The roles and position of the chief executive officer (CEO) as the top person in the top management team differ between Germany and the United States • Equality in social structure and mutual agreement
	Influencing factors of the productive forces	–	–

(continued)

Table 14.1 (continued)

Deployment and factors affecting them		Management methods	
		Shareholder value management model and corporate governance system	
		Japanese management methods	German management methods
	Influence of industrial structure factors	–	–
	Influence of market structure factors	• Top management personnel structure based on the internal labor market	• High share of all Germany exports to the EU area, as well as complementary relationships in European markets with other countries in this region based on market competitiveness emphasizing quality • The pursuit of increasing shareholder value by emphasizing German enterprise's competitive advantage in European markets

Source This table was compiled by the author, based on discussions in this chapter

14.5 Changes of Characteristic in the "Americanization" of Business Management After the 1990s and Their Significance

When in looking at the Americanization of business management after the 1990s, one of the most important points can be seen in the changes of its characteristic Therefore, this section considers the changes in the characteristics of the Americanization of business management after the 1990s in comparison with those in the previous periods.

The movement toward shareholder value-oriented management and capital market-oriented corporate governance in Japan and Germany after the 1990s can be understood as the Americanization of business management. However, concerning this point, it is important to note that the characteristics of this Americanization have changed in comparison with three waves of the Americanization of business management, as seen in the aforementioned periods.

Historically, four waves of Americanization are evident in business management: (1) the period from the beginning of the Twentieth century to the outbreak of World War I; (2) the period after World War I, especially the 1920s; (3) the period after World War II to the 1970s; and (4) the period after the 1990s (Yamazaki 2013a, b). Most of the American management methods and techniques that were deployed in the first, second, and third waves reflected the management principles and behavioral mechanisms of companies, as seen in the "improvement of efficiency" and the pragmatic management climate of the United States.

Furthermore, the principle of efficiency improvement became an important behavioral mechanism for companies in both Japan and Germany. However, the part that reflected such American conditions was based on the pragmatic sense of value, which was not necessarily compatible with Japanese and German circumstances. Although American methods were deployed by modifying their individual elements, American management methods and techniques based on the principle of efficiency improvement were driving forces in not only the expansion of enterprises but also the economic development in both nations. Hence, the Americanization of business management in these three waves had significant meaning for both countries as well as other European countries.

In contrast, the introduction and transfer of the American conception of companies and the ideology that regards companies as a "nexus of contracts" (with the objective of buying/selling and increasing the American management value) became an important problem in the fourth wave regarding the Americanization of business management after the 1990s. Such American management systems and the standard of value emphasizing the company's short-term interests and investors' returns in the capital market, such as increases in shareholder value, differ from the system and the standards of the real economy. They can oppose corporate behavior such as efficiency improvement and strategic development in market competition.

Therefore, the American management model and system can have a negative impact on business management and capital accumulation in companies. This indicates an important change of characteristic in the Americanization of business management after the 1990s. The worldwide strategic shifts from the production-based approach of "retain and reinvest" to finance-based policies of "downsize and distribute" for shareholder value became more disconnected with the real economy, especially in the beginning of the 2000s. According to Kädtler and Sperling (2002a, p. 152), this trend has continued. Overall, the conflicts between the American shareholder value-oriented management model and the Japanese or German management model have been significant because of the changes in the Americanization of business management.

References

Aglietta M (2009) New trends in corporate governance: the prominent role of the long run investor. In: Compet Change 12(2):203–222

Ahrens R (2022) Financing Rhenish capitalism: 'Bank Power' and the business of crisis management in the 1960s and 1970s. In: Marx C, Leitmeyer M (eds) Rhenish capitalism. New insights from a business history perspective. Routledge, London, New York, pp 119–13

Albert M (1991) Capitalisme contre capitalisme. Ed.du Seuil, Paris

Allianz Gruppe (1998) *Geschäftsbericht 1998*. Allianz, München

Andrews EL (2000) The metamorphosis of Germany Inc. In: The New York Times, 12.3.2000

BASF AG (2000) *Jahresbericht 2000*. BASF AG, Ludwichshafen

Baumüller JFH (2010) Post Shareholder Value. Zukünftige Unternehmensführungskonzepte nach dem Shareholder Konzept. VDM Verlag Dr, Müller, Saarbrücken

Bayer AG (2000) Geschäftsbericht 2000. Bayer AG, Leverkusen

Bayer AG (2007) Geschäftsbericht 2007. Bayer AG, Leverkusen

Beck S, Klobes F, Scherrer C (2005a) Introduction. In: Beck S., Klobes F, Scherrer C (eds) Surviving globalization? Perspectives for the German economic model. Springer, Dordrecht, pp 1–14

Beck S, Klobes F, Scherrer C (2005b) Conclusion. In: Beck S., Klobes F, Scherrer C (eds) Surviving globalization? Perspectives for the German economic model. Springer, Dordrecht, pp 225–235

Becker S (2003) Der Einfluss des Kapitalmarkts und seine Grenzen: Die Chemie- und Pharmaindustrie. In: Streeck W, Höpner M (eds) Alle Macht dem Markt? Fallstudien zur Abwicklung der Deutchland AG. Campus, Berlin, New York, pp 222–248

Beelitz FF (2002) Shareholder Value und Kapitalmarktorientierung im bundesdeutschen Umfeld im Umbruch. In: Siegwart H, Mahari J (Hrsg), Ruffner M (Gasthrsg) Corporate Governance, Shareholder Value & Finanz. Helbing & Lichtenhahn, Basel, pp 575–587

Beisel K (2002) Deutsche Corporate Governance-Identifikation und Interessenanlage der relevanten Akteure, 1st edn. GRIN Verlag, München

Berghoff H (2016) Varieties of Financialization? Evidence from German Industry in the 1990s. In: Bus Hist Rev 90(1) 81–108

Beyer J (2001) Deutschland AG a.D.: Deutsche Bank, Allianz und das Verflechtungszentrum groβer deutscher Unternehmen. In: MPIfG (MaxPlank-Institut für Gesellschaftsforschung) Working Paper 02/4, pp 1–26

Beyer J (2006) Pfadabhängigkeit. Über institutionelle Kontinuität, anfällige Stabiltät und fundamentalen Wandel. Campus, Frankfurt am Main

Börsch A (2004) Globalisation, shareholder value, restructuring: the (non)-transformation of Siemens. In: New Polit Econ 9(3):365–387

Bruce A, Buck T, Main BGM (2005) Top executive remuneration: a view from Europe. In: J Manag Stud 42(7):1493–1506
Buck T, Chizema A (2008) The adoption of an American executive pay practice in Germany. In: Strange R, Jackson G (eds) Corporate governance and international business. Strategy, performance and instituitional change, Palgrave Macmillan, Basingstoke, pp 242–265
Buck T, Filatotchev I, Wright M (1998) Agents, stakeholders and corporate governance in Russian firms. In: *Journal of Management Studies*. 35 (1): 81–104
Buck T, Shahrim A (2005) The translation of corporate governance changes across national cultures: the case of Germany. In: J Int Bus Stud 36(1):42–61
Bühner R, Raheed A, Rosenstein J (1997) Corporate restructuring patterns in the US and Germany: a comparative empirical investigation. In: Manag Int Rev 37(4):319–338
Carr C (2005) Are German, Japanese and Anglo-Saxin strategic decision styles still divergent in the context of globalization? In: J Manag Stud 42(6):1155–1188
Chizema A (2010) Early and late adoption of American-style executive pay in Germany: governance and institutions. In: J World Bus 45(1):9–18
Chizema A, Buck T (2006) Neoinstitutional theory and institutional change: towards empirical test on the "Americanaization" of German executive pay. In: Int Bus Rev 25(5):488–504
Clark I (2006) Another third way? VW and the trials of stakeholder capitalism. In: Ind Relat J 37(6):593–606
Commerzbank AG (1998) Geschäftsbericht 1998. Commerzbank AG, Frankfurt am Main
Commerzbank AG (2022) Geschäftsbericht 2022. Commerzbank AG, Frankfurt am Main
Cromme G (2005) Corporate governance in Germany and the German Corporate Code. Corp Gov Int Rev 13(3):362–367
DaimlerChrysler AG (2005) Geschäftsbericht 2005. DaimlerChrysler AG, Stuttgart
Deutsche Bank AG (1995) Geschäftsbericht 1995. Deutsche Bank AG, Frankfurt am Main
Deutsche Bank AG (2001) Geschäftsbericht 2001. Deutsche Bank AG, Frankfurt am Main
Deutsche Bank AG (2023) Geschäftsbericht 2022. Deutsche Bank AG, Frankfurt am Main
Dore R (2000) Stock market capitalism. Japan and Germany versus the Anglo-Saxons. Oxford University Press, Oxford, Tokyo
Dörre K (2009) Finanzmarktkapitalismus contra Mitbestimmung? Kapitalmarkt- orientierte Steuerungsformen und organisierte Arbeitsbeziehungen. In: Huffschmid J, Köppen M, Rhode W (eds) Finanzinvestoren: Retter oder Raubritte? VSA-Verlag, Hamburg, Neue Herausforderungen durch die internationalen Kapitalmärkte, pp 104–123
Dörre K, Holst H (2009) Nach dem Shareholder Value? Kapitalmarktorientierte Unternehmenssteuerung in der Krise. In: WSI Mitteilungen 62(12):667–674
Dörre K (2001) Kampf um Beteiligung, Arbeit, Partizipation und industrielle Beziehungen im flexiblen Kapitalismus. Eine Studie aus dem Soziologischen Forschungsinstitut Göttingen (SOFI), 1st edn. Westdeutscher Verlag, Wiesbaden
du Plessis JJ, Groβfeld B, Luttermann C et al (2012) German corporate governance in international and European context, 2nd edn. Springer, Heidelberg
Dupuy C, Lung Y (2002) Institutional investors and the car industry geographic focalisation and industrial strategies. In: Compet Change 6(1):43–60
Dyas GP, Thanheiser HT (1976) The emerging European enterprise. Strategy and structure in French and German industry. The Macmillan Press, London
Eggenkämper B, Modert G and Pretzlik S (2015) Die Allianz. Geschichte des Unternehmens 1890–2015. Verlag C. H. Beck, München
Faust M, Bahnmüller R, Fisecker C (2011) Das kapitalmarktorientierte Unternehemen. Externe Erwartungen, Unternehmenspolitik, Personalwesen und Mitbestimmung, Edition Sigma, Berlin
Faust M, Kädtler J (2009) Nach Dem Shareholder-value. In: Die Mitbestimmung 55(6):22–25
Fiss PC, Zajac EJ (2004) The diffusion of ideas over contested terrain: The (Non) adoption of a shareholder value orientation among German firms. In: Adm Sci Q 49(4):501–534
Froud F, Haslam C, Johal S et al (2000) Shareholder value and financialization: Consultancy promises, management moves. In: Econ Soc 29(1):80–110

Fuji Sogo kenkyusho (1993) "Mein bank shisutemu oyobi kabushiki mochiai" ni tsuiteno chosa. Hokokusho (Investigation regarding "main banking system and cross-shareholding." Report). Fuji sogo kenkyusho, Tokyo

Fujii Y (2000) Kinyu kiki to jika kaikei (Financial institution and market price accounting). In: Shirota J (ed) Kinyu kiki to shoken sijyo no saisei (Financial crisis and resuscitation of the stock market). Dobunkan, Tokyo, pp 105–124

Furch D (2012) Marktwirtschaften unter dem Druck globalisierter Finanzmärkte, Finanzsysteme und Corporate-Governance-Strukturen in Deutschland und Italien. Springer NV, Wiesbaden

Gerum E (2007) Das Corporate Governance-System. Ein empirische Untersuchung. Schäffer-Poeschel, Stuttgart

Gordon JN (1999) Pathways to corporate convergence? Two steps on the road to shareholder capitalism in Germany. In: Columbia J Econ Law 5(219):219–241

Goutas L, Lane C (2009) The translation of shareholder value in the German business system: a comparative study of DaimlerChrysler and Volkswagen AG. In: Compet Change 13(4):327–346

Gross S (2006) Bank und Shareholder value. An overview of bank valuation und empirical evidence on shareholder value for banks, Der Deutsche Universitäts-Verlag, Wiesbaden

Hackethal A, Schmidt RH, Tyrell M (2005) Banks and German corporate governance: on the way to a capital market based system? In: Corp Gov Int Rev 13(3):397–407

Hall PA, Soskice D (eds) (2001) Varieties of capitalism: the institutional foundations of comparative advantage. Oxford University Press, Oxford

Handelsblatt (1999) Fonds kapitalisieren Europas Firmenelite. In: Handelsblatt 216: 22

Hassel A, Höpner M, Kurdelbusch A et al (2000) Zwei Dimension der Internationalisierung: Eine empirische Analyse deutscher Grossunternehmen. In: Kölner Zeitschrift für Soziologie und Sozialpsychologie 52(3):500–519

Heinz H (2002) Die Struktur der Personalverflechtung großer deutscher Aktiengesellschaften zwischen 1989 und 2001/The Structure of the network of interlocking directorates of large German enterprises between 1989 und 2001. In: Zeitschrift für Soziologie 31(5):391–410

Heinze T (2004) Dynamics in the German system of corporate governance? Empirical findings regarding interlocking directors. In: Econ Soc 33(2):218–238

Hendry J, Sanderson P, Baker R et al (2007) Resoponsible ownership, shareholder value and the new shareholder activism. In: Compet Change 11(3):223–240

Herden RW, Reinhard H (1999) M & A-Volumen in Europa setzt neue Maβstäbe. In: M&A Rev 12:525–529

Hirschman AO (1970) Exit, voice, and loyalty responses to decline in firms, organizations, and state. Harvard University Press, Cambridge, Massachusetts

Höpner M (2000) Unternehmensverflechtung im Zwielicht. Hans Eichels Plan zur Auflösung der Deutschland AG. In: WSI Mitteilungen 53(10):655–663

Höpner M (2001) Corporate governance in transition: Ten empirical findings on shareholder value and industrial relations in Germany. In: MPIfG (MaxPlanck- Institut für Gesellschaftsforschung) Discussion Paper 01/5: 1–61

Höpner M (2003) Wer beherrscht die Unternehmen? Shareholder Value, Managerschaft und Mitbestimmung in Deutschland. Campus, Frankfurt am Main

Höpner M, Jackson G (2001) An emerging market for corporate control? The Mannesmann takeover and German corporate governance. In: MPIfG (MaxPlanck-Institut für Gesellschaftsforschung) Discussion Paper 01/4: 1–53

Ifrim S (2007) Erosion der Deutschland AG-Ursachen und konsequenzen veränderter Personal- und Kapitalverflechtungen aud dem deutschen Kapitalmarkt. Examicus Verlag, Frankfurt am Main

Inoue T (2013) Toyota jidosha no koporeto・gabanansu ni kansuru ichi kosatsu (A study of corporate governance in Toyota Motor Corporation). In: Financ Rev 68:194–202

Ito M (2007) Kyoka ga tsuzuku jigyo gaisha no kabushiki mochiai (Trend of increasing cross-stockholding of industrial company). Daiwa soken. http://www.dir.co.jp/research/esg/esg-report/07112701viewpoint.html. Accessed 15 Apr 2014

Iwanami F (2005) Torishimari yakukai kaikaku to shagai torishimariyaku, shagai kansayaku no kino (Reform of the managing board and functions of outside directors and auditors). In: Nakata M (ed) Hikaku koporeto gabanansu kenkyu (Comparative study of corporate governance). Chuo keizaisha, Tokyo, pp 170–185
Jackson G (2005) Stakeholders under pressure: corporate governance and labour management in Germany and Japan. In: Corp Gov Int Rev 13(3):419–428
Jackson G, Moerke A (2005) Continuity and change in corporate governance: Comparing Germany and Japan. In: Corp Gov Int Rev 13(3):351–361
Jansen SA (2008) Mergers & Acquisitions. Unternehmensakquisition und -Kooperation. Eine strategische, organisatorische und kapitalmarkttheoretische Einführung. 5th edn. Gabler, Wiesbaden
Jürgens U, Lung Y, Volpato G et al (2002) The arrival of shareholder value in the European auto industry. A case study comparison of four car makers. In: Compet Change 6(1):61–80
Jürgens U, Naumann K, Rupp J (2000) Shareholder value in an adverse environment: the German case. In: Econ Soc 29(1):54–79
Kabushikigaisha Tokyo shoken torihikisho, Kabushikigaisha Nagoya shoken torihikisho, Shoken kaiinsei hojin Fukuoka shoken torihikisho (2022) 2022 nendo no kabushiki bunpu jyokyo chosa kekka no gaiyo (Summary of survey results of Stock distribution in the fiscal year 2022). Kabushikigaisha Tokyo shoken torihikisho, Kabushikigaisha Nagoya shoken torihikisho, Shoken kaiinsei hojin Fukuoka shoken torihikisho and Shoken kaiinsei hojin Sapporo shoken torihikisho
Kazama N (2012) Kinyu · keizai kiki to Doitsu no kigyo touchi (Financial and economic crisis and German corporate governance system). In: Shogaku ronsan (The journal of commerce) 53(5–6):185–221
Kädtler J, Sperling HJ (2001) Worauf beruht und wie wirkt die Herrschaft der Finanzmärkte auf der Ebene von Unternehemen? Order: Taugt Finanzialisierung als neue Software für die Automobilindustrie? In: SOFI-Mitteilungen 29:23–43
Kädtler J, Sperling HJ (2002a) After globalisation and financialisation: logics of bargaining in the German automotive industry. In: Compet Change 6(2):149–168
Kädtler J, Sperling HJ (2002b) The power of financial markets and the resilience of operations: argument and evidence from the German car industry. In: Compet Change 6(1):81–94
Kataoka S (2009) Torishimariyakukai no kaikaku to kaisha keieisha (Reform of the managing board and executive). In: Hosokawa T, Sakurai T (eds) Tenkanki no kabushikigaisha (Joint stock company in a transition period). Mineruva shobo, Kyoto, pp 78–97
Keizai kikakucho (ed) (1996) Heisei hachinendo ban keizai hakusho (Economic white paper for the financial year 1996). Okurasho insatsukyoku. Tokyo
Keizai kikakucho (ed) (1998) Heisei junendo ban keizai hakusho (Economic white paper for the financial year 1998). Okurasho insatsukyoku, Tokyo
Klages P (2006) Zwischen instutiotioneller Innovation und Reprodokution. Zum Wandel des deutschen Corporate Governance-Systems in den 1990ern. In: Berliner Journal für Soziologie 16(1):37–54
Knapp E (2009) Interne Revision und Corporate Governance. Aufgaben und Entwicklungen für die Überwachung, 2nd edn. E. Schmidt, Berlin
Koslowski P (2000) The limits of shareholder value. In: J Bus Ethics 27(1/2):137–148
Kudo A (2011) Nichidoku keizai kankeishi jyosetsu (Introduction to the history of Japanese-German economic relations). Sakurai shoten, Tokyo
Küke J (2002) Corporate governance in Germany: an empirical investigation. Physica-Verlag, Heidelberg
Lane C (2003) Changes in corporate governance of German corporations: convergence to the Anglo-American model? In: Compet Change 7(2–3):79–100
Maeda M (2010) Kinyu kiki to kigyo baishu (Financial crisis and corporate purchase). In: Shirota J (ed) Kinyu kiki to shoken sijyo no saisei (Financial crisis and resuscitation of the stock market). Dobunkan shuppan, Tokyo, pp 43–66
McCann L (2014) International and comparative foundations of political economies. SAGE, London

Mäntysaari P (2005) Comparative corporate governance. Shareholders as a rulemaker. Springer, Heidelberg

Marxs C, Morten L (2022) Introduction: Rhenish capitalism and business history. In: Marx C, Morten L (eds) Rhenish capitalism. New insights from a business history perspective. Routledge, London, New York, pp 1–40

Matshui K (1979) Nichibei kigyo no kabushiki shoyu kozo to kabuka keisei (jyo) (Stockholding structure of Japanese and US enterprises and formation of share price). In: Shoken keizai (JSIR J Financ Secur Mark) 128:18–63

Matsuda T (2009) Nihon no koporeto・gabanansu no tokucho to kadai (Characteristics and tasks of Japanese corporate governance). In: Kaido N, Kazama N (eds) Koporeto・gabanasu to keiiegaku. Mineruva shobo (Corporate governance and business administration), Kyoto, pp 105–132

Matsumura K (1997) Nihonteki keiei zaimu to koporeto・gabanansu (Japanese corporate finance and corporate governance). Chuo keizaisha, Tokyo

Matthes J (2005) Das deutsche Corporate-Governance-System im Wandel. Übergang zum angelsächsischen System oder nur leichte Annährung? In: Storz C, Lageman B (eds) Konvergenz oder Divergenz? Der Wandel der Unternehemensstrukturen in Japan und Deutschland. Metropolis-Verlag, Marburg, pp 201–247

Metten M (2010) Corporate governance. Eine aktienrechtliche und institutionen ökonomische Analyse der Leistungsmaxime von Aktiengesellschaften, 1st edn. Gabler, Wiesbaden

Mintz SM (2006) A comparison of corporate governance systems in the U.S., UK and Germany. In: Corp Ownersh Control 3(4):24–34

Mitbestimmungskommission (1970) Mitbestimmung im Unternehmen.Bericht der Sachverständigenkommission zur Auswertung der bisherigen Erfahrung bei der Mitbestimmung. Stuttgart, Berlin, Köln, Mainz

Miyajima H (2021) Nihongata moderu Ver2.0 ni mukete: Kabushikigaisha no mokuteki, torishimariyaku no yakuwari, shoyu kozo (Toward Japanese corporate governance model Ver2.0: Purpose of joint stock company, role of directors, and ownership structure). In: RIETI Policy Discussion Paper Series 21-p-020: 1–32

Miyajima H, Nitta K (2007) Nihongata torishimariyakukai no tagenteki sinka (Multifaceted evolution of Japanese type of managing board). In: Kanda H, Zaimusho zaimu sogo seisaku kenkyusho (eds) Kigyo touchi no tayosei to tenbo (Diversity and view of corporate governance). Kinzai, Tokyo, pp 27–77

Miyajima H, Haramura K, Enami Y (2013) Sengo nihon kigyo no kabushiki shoyu kozo (Stockholding structure of postwar Japanese enterprises). In: Financ Rev 68:203–236

Monopolkommission (2008) Hauptgutachten 2006/2007. Weniger Staat, mehr Wettbewerb. Gesundheitsmärkte und staatliche Beihilfen in der Wettbewerbsordnung (Hauptgutachten der Monopolkommission, XVII), 1st edn. Nomos-Verlagsgesellschaft, Baden-Baden

Monopolkommission (2010) Hauptgutachten 2008/2009. Mehr Wettbewerb, wenig Ausnahemn (Hauptgutachten der Monopolkommission,18), 1st edn. Nomos-Verlagsgesellschaft, Baden-Baden

Monopolkommission (2022) Hauptgutachten 2022. Wettbewerb 2022 (XXIV.Hauptgutachten der Monopolkommission), Nomos-Verlagsgesellschaft, Baden-Baden

Nakata N, Hosoi K, Iwanami F (1997) Kigyokan no jinteki nettowaku—torishimariyaku kenninsei no nichibei hikaku—(Personnel networks between enterprises—Comparison of interlocking directorships in Japan and the United States—). Dobunkan, Tokyo

Oberbeck H, D'Alessio N (1997) The end of the German model? Developmental tendencies in the German banking industry. In: Morgan G, Knights D (eds) Regulation and deregulation in European financial services. Macmillan, Basingstoke, pp 86–89

Okurasho zaisei kinyu kenkyusho (1996) Hojin kigyo tokei nenpo tokushu (Heisei 7 nendo) [Special edition of the yearbook of statistics on financial statements of incorporated businesses]. In: Zaisei kinyu tokei geppo (Fiscal Monet Stat Monthly Rep) 532:1–137

Onetti A, Pisoni A (2009) Ownership and control in Germany: Do Cross-shareholdings reflect bank control on large companies? In: Corp Ownersh Control 6(4):54–77

Oxelheim L, Randøy T (2005) The Anglo-American financial influence on CEO compensation in non-Anglo-American firms. In: J Int Bus Stud 36(4):470–483

Paetzmann K (2008) Corporate governance. Strategische Marktrisken, Controlling, Überwachung. Springer, Berlin, Heidelberg

Peev E (2023) Germany. In: Gugler K, Peev E (eds) The European corporation. Ownership and control after 25 years of corporate governance reforms. Cambridge University Press, Cambridge, pp 84–107

Recof (2014) Baishu boeisaku no donyu jyokyo (Conditons of the protective measures against merger). https://www.marr.jp/mainfo/entry/4317;jsessionid=78C00399E7577EEE24A09Fo7302C969.ap. Accessed 9 May 2014

Ringe W-G (2015) Changing law and ownership patterns in Germany: corporate governance and the Erosion of Deutschland AG. In: Am J Comp Law 63(2):493–538

Rosen RV (2002) Corporate Governance—Neue Denkansätze in Deutschland. In: Siegwart H, Mahari J (Hrsg), Ruffner M (Gasthrsg) Corporate Governance, Shareholder Value & Finanz. Helbing und Lichtenhahn, Basel, pp 589–609

Sablowski T, Ruppe J (2001) Die neue Ökonomie des Shareholder Value Corporate Governance im Wandel. In: PROKLA 31(1):47–78

Sakuma N (2009) Kabushikigaisha no kikan sekkei to koporeto・gabanansu (Institutional design of joint-stock company and corporate governance). In: Hosokawa T, Sakurai T (eds) Tenkanki no kabushikigaisha. Mineruva shobo, Kyoto, pp 57–77

Sanders WMG, Tuschke A (2007) The adoption of institutionally contested organizational practices: the emergence of stock option pay in Germany. In: Acad Manag J 50(1):33–56

Schlie EH, Warner M (2000) The 'Americanization' of German management. In: J General Manag 25(3):33–49

Schnitzler W (2007) Implementierung der Anforderungen des Sarbanes-Oxley Acts in einem deutschen Groβunternehmen. In: Freidank C-C, Altes P (eds) Rechnungslegung und Corporate Governance. Reporting, Steuerung und Überwachung der Unternehmen im Umbruch. Erich Schmidt, Berlin, pp 225–246

Schwarz F (2003) Die Deutsche Bank. Riese auf tönernen Füβen. Campus, Frankfurt am Main

Scott C (2008) The influence of national culture on stock-option-programms as motivatiors. The case of managers in Germany. In: Int German Manag Assoc Rev 2:2–36

Segawa S (2009) Kabushiki shoyu kozo to kabunushi kodo no henka (Changes in stockholding structure and behavior of shareholders). In: Hosokawa T, Sakurai T (eds) Tenkanki no kabushikigaisha (Joint-stock company in a transition period). Mineruva shobo, Kyoto, pp 98–125

Shoji homu kenkyukai (ed) (2006) Kabunushi sokai hakusho 2006 nenban (General meeting white paper. 2006 edition). In: Jyunkan shoji homu (Ten-day judicial affairs) 1784:3–128

Shoji homu kenkyukai (ed) (2013) Kabunushi sokai hakusho 2013 nenban (General meeting white paper. 2013 edition). In: Jyunkan shoji homu (Ten-day judicial affairs) 2016:3–156

Shoji homu kenkyukai (ed) (2015) Kabunushi sokai hakusho 2015 nenban (General meeting white paper. 2015 edition). In: Jyunkan shoji homu (Ten-day judicial affairs) 2085:3–157

Siemens AG (2000) Geschäftsbericht 2000. Siemens AG, München

Streeck W (1997) German capitalism: Does it exist? Can it survive? In: Crouch C, Streeck W (eds) Political economy of modern capitalism. Mapping convergence and diversity. SAGE, London, pp 33–54

Streeck W, Höpner M (eds.) (2003) Alle Macht dem Markt? Fallstudien zur Abwicklung der Deutchland AG. Campus, Berlin, New York

Suzuki K (1993) Nihon no kigyo shudan—Sengo nihon no kigyo to ginko—(Japanese corporate groups—Enterprise and bank in postwar Japan—). Otsuki shoten, Tokyo

Suzuki K (1998) Mein banku to kigyo shudan—Sengo nihon no kigyokan shisutemu—(Main bank and corporate group—Corporate system in postwar Japan—). Mineruva shobo, Kyoto

Suzuki K (2008) Rokudai kigyo shudan no hokai (Collapse of six large corporate groups). Shinnihon shuppansha, Tokyo
ThyssenKrupp AG (1999) Geschäftsbericht 1998/99. ThyssenKrupp AG, Essen
ThyssenKrupp AG (2002) Geschäftsbericht 2001/2002. ThyssenKrupp AG, Essen
Tokyo shoken torihikisho (2005) Koporeto · gabanansu ni kansuru anketo chosa kekka ni tsuite (Results of questionnaire on corporate governance). Tokyo shoken torihikisho, Tokyo
Tokyo shoken torihikisho (2013) Tosho jyojyo gaisha koporeto · gabanansu hakusho (Tokyo Stock Exchange-listed companies: white paper on corporate governance 2013). Tokyo shoken torihikisho jyojyobu, Tokyo
Tokyo shoken torihikisho (2015) Tosho jyojyo gaisha koporeto · gabanansu hakusho 2015 (Tokyo Stock Exchange-listed companies white paper on corporate governance 2015). Tokyo shoken torihikisho jyojyobu, Tokyo
Tokyo shoken torihikisho (2021) Tosho jyojyo gaisha koporeto · gabanansuhakusho 2021 (Tokyo Stock Exchange-listed companies white paper on corporate governance 2021). Tokyo shoken torihikisho jyojyobu, Tokyo
Tokyo shoken torihikisho (2023) Tosho jyojyo gaisha koporeto · gabanansuhakusho 2023 (Tokyo Stock Exchange-listed companies white paper on corporate governance 2023). Tokyo shoken torihikisho jyojyobu, Tokyo
Tuschuke A, Sanders WG (2003) Antecedents and consequences of corporate governance reform: the case of Germany. In: Strateg Manag J 23(7):631–649
Uetaka A (1999) Gendai kigyo no gabanansu kozo to keiei kodo (Governance structure and administrative behavior of modern enterprises). In: Uetake A,Nakata M (eds) Gendai kigyo no shoyu · sihai · kanri (Ownership, control, and management of modern enterprises). Mineruva shobo, Kyoto, pp 1–20
Vitols S (2000) The reconstruction of German corporate governance: reassessing the role of capital market pressures. Wissenschaftszentrum Berlin für Sozialforschung
Vitols S (2002) Shareholder value, management culture and production regimes in the transformation of the German Chemical-Pharmaceutical industry. In: Compet Change 6(3):309–325
Vitols S (2003) Viele Wege nach Rom? BASF, Bayer und Hoechst. In: Streeck W, Höpner M (eds) Alle Macht dem Markt? Fallstudien zur Abwicklung der Deutchland AG. Campus, Berlin, New York, pp 197–221
Vitols S (2004a) Continuity and change: making sence of the German model. In: Compet Change 8(4):331–337
Vitols S (2004b) Negotiated shareholder value: the German variant of an Anglo-American practice. In: Compet Change 8(4):357–374
Vitols S (2005a) Changes in Germany's bank-based financial system: implication for corporate governance. In: Corp Gov Int Rev 13(3):386–396
Vitols S (2005b) German corporate governance in transition: Implications of bank exit from monitoring and control. In: *International Journal of Disclosure and Governance* 2 (4): 357–367
Völcker M (2009) 'Das Wars mit der Deutschland AG'—Der Schareholder-Value-Kapitalismus und dessen (soziale) Folgen, 1st edn. GRIN Verlag, München
Volkswagen AG (2001) Geschäftsbericht 2001. Volkswagen AG, Wolfsburg
Weber SC (2011) Externes Corporate Governance Reporting börsennotierter Publikumsgesellschaften. Konzeptionelle Vorschläge zur Weiterentwicklung der Unternehmerischen Berichterstattung, 1st edn. Gabler, Wiesbaden
Wenger E, Kaserer C (1998) German banks and corprate governance: a critical view. In: Hopt KJ, Kanda H, Roe MJ et al (eds) Comparative corporate governance—The state of the art and emerging research. Oxford University Press, Oxford, New York, pp 499–536
Williams K (2000) From shareholder value to presentday capitalism. In: *Economy and Society* 29 (1): 1–12
Windolf P (2005) Die neuen Eigentümer. In: Windolf P (ed) Finazmarkt-Kapitalismus. Analysen zum Wandel von Produktionsregimen. VS Verlag für Sozialwissenschaften, Wiesbaden, pp 8–19

Windolf P (2014) The corporate networks in Germany, 1896–2010. In: David T, Weserhuis F (eds) The power of corporate networks. A comparative and historical perspective. Routledge, New York, pp 66–85

Witt P (2009) Vorstand, Aufsichtsrat und ihr Zusammenwirken aus betriebswirtschaftlicher Sicht. In: Hommelhoff P, Hopt KJ, Werder Av (eds) Handbuch Corporate Governance. Leitung und Überwachung börsennotierter Unternehmen in der Rechts und Wirtschaftspraxis, 2nd edn. Schäffer-Poeschel, Stuttgart, pp 303–319

Wu Z, Delios A (2009) The emergence of portfolio restructuring in Japan. In: Manag Int Rev 49(3):313–335

Yamazaki T (2009) Sengo Doitsu shihonsyugi to kigyo keiei (German capitalism and business managemet after World War II). Moriyama shoten, Tokyo

Yamazaki T (2013a) Gendai no Doitsu kigyo—Sono gurobaru chiikika to keiei tokushitsu—(Contemporary German enterprises—their global-regionalization and characteristics of business management—). Moriyama shoten, Tokyo

Yamazaki T (2013b) German buisness management: A Japanese perspective on regional development factors. Springer, Tokyo

Zaimusho zaisei sogo kenkyusho (2003) Hojin kigyo tokei nenpo tokushu (Heisei juyonendo) (Annual report on statistics of financial statements of incorporated businesses in fiscal year 2002). In: Zaisei Kinyu Tokei Geppo (Minist Financ Stat Monthly) 616:1–139

Zaimusho zaisei sogo kenkyusho (2013) Hojin kigyo tokei nenpo tokushu (Heisei nijuyonendo) (Annual report on statistics of financial statements of incorporated businesses in fiscal year 2012). In: Zaisei Kinyu Tokei Geppo (Minist Financ Stat Monthly) 738:1–225

Zaimusho zaisei sogo kenkyusho (2022) Hojin kigyo tokei nenpo tokushu (Reiwa sannendo) (Annual report on statistics of financial statements of incorporated businesses in fiscal year 2021). In: Zaisei kinyu tokei geppo (Ministry of Finance statistics monthly) 846: 1–238

Zenkoku shoken torihikisho kyogikai (2005) Heisei junananendo kabushiki bunpu chosa no chosa kekka ni tsuite (Investigation results of the distribution of shares in the fiscal year 2005). Zenkoku shoken torihikisho kyogikai, Tokyo

Ziegler JN (2000) Corporate governance and the politics of property rights in Germany. In: Polit Soc 28(2):195–221

Zugehör R (2003) Die Zukunft des rheinischen Kapitalismus: Unternehmen zwischen Kapitalmarkt und Mitbestimmung. Leske+Burdich, Opladen

Chapter 15
Conclusion: Significance of Comparative Study of Business Management in Japan and Germany

Abstract Following the preceding chapters' topics, this chapter clarifies the implications of the comparative study of business management in Japan and Germany through re-examining the changes in management and corporate expansion after World War II. First, it investigates the pursuit of economic rationality, which is emphasized in business management in each country and is deeply concerned with the characteristics of a country's capitalism. Following that, changes in business management and corporate expansion in both countries are investigated about some important enterprise-related factors. How differences of the postwar reforms, industrial development and industrial structure, inter-firm relationships system, and regional environment in Japan and Germany influenced each country's specific development of business management and how Japanese-style management and German-style management determined corporate expansion is analyzed. The significance of the German business management model that evolved in the European environment is examined by contrasting Germany's situation in Europe with Japan's situation in Asia. The origins of differences in contemporary economic and business conditions in relation to economic relations with the United States, as well as how corporate expansion in Japan and Germany following World War II determined each country's path toward global-regionalization, will be clarified.

Keywords Americanization · Asianization · Corporate expansion · Economic rationality · Europeanization · Global regionalization · Industrial structure · Inter-firm relationships · Postwar reform

Based on the foregoing discussions, this chapter reevaluates the changes in business management in postwar Japan and Germany in relation to corporate expansion. Business management and enterprise development are inextricably linked to each country's pursuit of economic rationality, which is emphasized in the market economy. There are differences in the methods used to achieve economic rationality among the three major countries of the United States, Japan, and Germany. As a

T. Yamazaki, *Japanese and German Enterprises*,
https://doi.org/10.1007/978-981-97-4880-8_15

result, first, this chapter explains the pursuit of economic rationality as an important ideological foundation for business management and economic growth through comparison among these three nations.

Furthermore, this chapter examines business management and corporate expansion in Japan and Germany following WWII, with a focus on some critical conditions surrounding enterprises, such as postwar reforms and democratization of the economy, characteristics of industrial development and industrial structure, inter-firm relationships system, and regional situation. How did these environmental factors influence differences in business management in postwar Japan and Germany? And how did Japanese-style management and German-style management determine corporate expansion in each country? Influences of regional environment are examined by comparing the Japanese business management model that developed based on the US market as well as the domestic market with the German business management model that developed in the European environment; and comparing Germany's situation in Europe with that of Japan's in Asia. This chapter explains how the transformation of German business management in the 1950s and 1960s laid the groundwork for the formation of today's European Union, whereas the transformation of Japanese business management during this period did not result in an independent development path from the United States. Through these analyses, the significance of the comparative study of business management in Japan and Germany after the war is clarified.

In Sect. 15.1, first, the pursuit of economic rationality that is deeply concerned with business management in each country is considered. Following that, in Sects. 15.2, 15.3, 15.4 and 15.5, business management and corporate expansion in postwar Japan and Germany are clarified by analyzing some of the aforementioned company-related factors.

15.1 Pursuit of Economic Rationality in Each Country: Comparison of the United States, Germany, and Japan

Business management and enterprise development in Japan and Germany are inextricably linked to the characteristics of each nation's emphasis on economic rationality. As a result, this issue is first addressed in this section by comparing it to the United States, a significant nation that has exemplified the postwar management model.

In the United States, the pursuit and realization of economic rationality through the improvement of efficiency under the free competition has been emphasized as the basic principle of business management. Such thinking is based on a belief in market functions such as market mechanisms and emphasizes the benefits of creativity and merit brought about by competition. In this country, the market should be the sole judge, and whether a company succeeds or fails in acquiring a market is the sole basis for a high position (Hampden-Turner and Trompenaars 1993, p. 169). Pragmatism as a social ideology is an important background of the priority of such rationality. In the American-type of the pursuit of economic rationality, "rationality for capital" is emphasized in business and management as an important element of management value for enterprises, which is deeply concerned with the profit orientation of the US enterprises. According to this way of thinking, a company is regarded as "the nexus of contract" and is thus regarded as an objective to be sold and purchased as a means of improving economic efficiency regardless of the interests of labor forces and society. The freedom of companies to engage in merger-acquisition-takeover business maneuvers is fundamental in such a scheme of thinking, which is entirely consistent with the dominance of equity financing, short-termism, and the priority given to shareholder value (Barsoux and Lawrence 1991, p. 199). Thus, "US companies are managed toward the maximization of profits and the short-term satisfaction of shareholders: managers are rewarded mainly on profitability targets and strategies are designed to improve return on investments" (Calori 1994, p. 13).

Meanwhile, in Germany, managers, industrialists, and workers tended to not believe the effectiveness of market mechanism as those in the United States and the UK did (Locke 1996, p. 57). Under such circumstances, "social rationality" rather than "rationality for capital" has been emphasized. It is economic prudence centered on the coordination of the interests of various stakeholders, including workers. In such ideologies, the importance of long-term profit rather than short-term profit in business, as well as the nature of enterprise as a "social community," is emphasized. While being labor relations such as the codetermination system as regal labor participation at the plant and corporate levels and the collective agreement system, German-style management has been established, emphasizing the company as a social community. The transformation of "rationality for capital" to "social rationality" in pursuit of economic rationality has been highlighted in German management. The stress of such rationality has not only been an important determining characteristic of business management in Germany, but also an ideological foundation for an economic system known as "coordinated market economy."

Compared with an emphasis of economic rationality in management in these two countries, Japanese conditions are different. In comparison with the United States, securing and pursuit of long-term profit has tended to be stressed and this point is similar to the German trend. However, in Japan, reliance on dense human relationships tends to lead to cooperation between company and workers, as well as among workers and between enterprises, which has been regarded as an important contributing factor to increased performance. The pursuit of such economic rationality is deeply concerned with the stakeholder orientation and Japanese collectivism trends. In Japan, the importance of how a company has contributed to society and the community is emphasized as the essence of the cooperative society principle (Hampden-Turner and Trompenaars 1993, p. 182). However, compared with the emphasis on economic rationality in Germany, the perspective of the emphasis of rationality for capital is stronger emphasized, and the economic rationality stressed in Japan is more resemble that in the US reflecting the difference of institutional factors such as industrial relations between Japan and Germany.

Perspectives emphasized in the pursuit of economic rationality are an important background of business management in each country by reflecting in management value as business management standards. The characteristics of enterprise and business management in the United States, Japan, and Germany are inextricably linked to differences in stressed business values. The importance of American economic rationality based on the neoliberalism ideology, in which complete reliance on market mechanisms is regarded as the optimal and best measure in all commodities, financial, and labor markets, has grown since the 1990s as a result of the globalization process and the Americanization of business management. However, the integration of American-style management—with an ideology that stresses the pursuit of economic rationality and management values based on this ideology—cannot always be observed. Despite the stronger influence of American ideology, each country's management style has been modified while retaining a country-specific management style through the reproduction of management values and business culture. Nonetheless, it can be stated that the transformation of "rationality for capital" to "social rationality" is becoming an increasingly important issue as the contradictions of the capitalistic market economy become more visible.

In Sect. 15.1, characteristics of economic rationality emphasized in each country that is intensely connected with not only characteristic of capitalism but also management style peculiar to a specific nation are examined. Based on these discussions, the following sections examine business management and corporate expansion in Japan and Germany after WWII in relation to some critical conditions surrounding enterprises. These sections clarify their characteristics by focusing on four key factors: (1) postwar reforms and economic democratization, (2) industrial development and industrial structure characteristics, (3) inter-firm relationships, and (4) regional environmental situation.

15.2 The Postwar Reforms and Democratization of Economy and Their Influences on Business Management and Corporate Expansion in Japan and Germany

The postwar reforms and democratization of the economy greatly influenced patterns of business management in Japan and Germany. Because both countries were defeated in World War II, they were forced to be heavily influenced by the occupation policies of the victorious nations. One of the most significant influences is the de-concentration of monopolies.

In Japan, however, economic democratization such as the dissolution of the *zaibatsu* became an important foundation for management based on an inter-firm corporation that belonged to the same industrial group through business relations, which promoted the business emphasizing the long-term perspective and sales volume rather than short-term profitability while maintaining the autonomy of management supported by mutual trust of member enterprises in each industrial group. The legal recognition of workers' rights, including labor unions, as well as the growing labor movement, exacerbated the conflict between labor and management. However, in Japan's postwar corporate modernization efforts, democratization of labor promoted management styles emphasizing mutual trust relationships between enterprise and worker as well as among labor forces. Such labor relations promoted management methods emphasizing roles and autonomy in the production spot based on cooperative collectivism, which enabled the flexible formation of work organization, the elastic personnel arrangement, and the small group activities such as the QC circle and the suggestion system. This could be a critical factor in a company's ability to respond to changes in demand in a flexible manner. The labor-relations system based on lifetime employment, the seniority wage system, and the company union was an important foundation for such Japanese business management patterns.

Compared with the influences of the postwar reform and the democratization of the economy in Japan, their effects of them were smaller in Germany. The need to modernize and democratize management was not as strong as it was in Japan. However, the legal establishment of systems for employee participation in management, such as codetermination, established the postwar framework for labor relations, determining the deep differences between Japan and Germany. The complementary labor agreement with codetermination at the plant and top management levels formed the framework of industrial relations during the postWorld War II period. Thus, labor relations in Germany arose from legal systems. Such labor-relations reforms encouraged collaboration between management and labor as well as investments in vocational education for corporate workers, which became an important factor in increasing German enterprises' international competitiveness by emphasizing product technique, quality, and functionality.

Even under the strong influence of occupation policy, in Germany, impacts on the restructuring of monopolies were different from those in Japan. Although large banks were dissolved, the universal banking system was maintained as a core system for industrial development, which became an important foundation for the close inter-firm relationships between bank and industrial enterprise through various mechanisms such as financing, shareholdings, deposited stock system, and personnel connection through the interlocking directorate. This was an important premise of the cooperative inter-firm relationships and corporate expansion peculiar to Germany. The emphasis of the de-concentration of large enterprises lay in the dissolution of the corporate group under the same capital in a specific industrial sector. This was different from the dissolution of the *Zaibatsu* as an industrial complex in Japan, which determined different patterns of reconcentration of dissolved enterprises and the building of corporate groups from that in Japan.

15.3 Industrial Development and Industrial Structure and Their Influences on Business Management and Corporate Expansion in Japan and Germany

In considering influences of industrial development and industrial structure determined by the process of the former, an important commonality between Japan and Germany can be observed in the rapid development of the durable consumer goods industries after the war. However, in Japan, the delay in the development of the heavy and chemical industries prior to World War II, as well as the rapid progress of these industrial sectors and the durable consumer goods industries, influenced the structure of industry that could build international competitiveness. In particular, the iron and steel industry became one of the industrial sectors with competitive power in the 1960s, and later, in the 1970s and 1980s, process and assembly industries such as automobile and electrical became representative sectors that established international competitiveness through the Japanese mass production system. Furthermore, the semiconductor industry developed significant international competitive power in a specific product field.

In Germany, on the other hand, though the dominance of the producer goods industries already established before World War II tended to continue after the war as well, the development of the durable consumer goods industries such as the automobile and the home appliance sectors also progressed rapidly. The following were included like industrial structures, the makeup of internationally competitive industrial sectors, and the characteristics of these industries: the interconnectedness of key industrial sectors and international competition; industrial characteristics (technological, market, and product characteristics); and each company's position within the national economy, as evidenced by their interconnectedness within industrial sectors and international competition. Among these, the changes in German business management were related to the level of transformation; for instance, the transition from an industrial structure based on producer goods to one developing the durable consumer goods sector.

Aside from these differences in industrial development and structure between Japan and Germany, the difference in industrial structure between countries that were the heart of the export market was also essential for business management and corporate expansion. Because of the differences in industrial structure across countries in this region, Germany has been able to develop a complementary relationship with other European countries as a core market, allowing German businesses to boost exports while avoiding trade frictions. German management system emphasizing values of technique, quality, and functionality of products could play an important role in building and maintaining international competitive power in Europe. In contrast, Japanese industrial sectors with international competitiveness were US key industries, preventing Japanese firms from establishing complementary relationships with US enterprises producers in the American market and forcing them to become an important factor in serious trade frictions. As a result, the conditions under which a specific management style and system developed during the postwar period could be effective differed greatly between Germany and Japan.

15.4 Inter-Firm Relationships and Their Influences on Business Management and Corporate Expansion in Japan and Germany

Inter-firm relationships were also an important factor that determined business management and the development of enterprise in Japan and Germany. In terms of inter-firm relationships, various measures such as corporate group, business alliance, personnel connection through the interlocking directorate, and subcontracting system between large company and part producing company are important.

In Japan, the large corporate groups formed after the war spanned several industries, with industrial corporations, banks, and trading companies at its core. The industrial groups comprised a full set of industries and conducted financing, interlocking stockholding, mutual business transactions, and joint investments internally. Six industrial groups coordinated among themselves through an organization, the Network of Presidents, with decisions primarily made by those in a certain position, such as presidents of group companies. Japanese industrial groups created more advantageous conditions of accumulation and maintained constant relationships by forming a system of stable shareholders through interlocking stockholdings (Suzuki 1998, p. 238).

The existence of the six industrial groups built the foundation for Japanese management style which prioritized profits by securing management autonomy from the threats and pressures of the stock market, developing management from a long-term perspective, and promoting distribution policies that prioritized the industrial groups. Corporate groups of this kind also functioned as a system of mutual insurance concerning corporate performance by banks' help in case of emergency as well as poorly performing companies. The system of mutual insurance became the mechanism that supported the stable growth of member companies in the groups (Nakatani 1983, pp. 80–84). In Japan, banks assumed the core positions in each industrial group and the major banks served as the main banks in the industrial groups to which they belonged. However, large banks that composed of industrial groups did not establish combination relations with many corporate groups, including other industrial groups. As a result, Japanese banks were unable to perform functions beyond the sphere of the industrial group to which they belonged, such as information exchanges and the adjustment of interests.

Thus, industrial groups shaped the characteristics of Japanese business management and contributed to the creation of more advantageous accumulation conditions. They imported raw materials at the lowest possible cost, which benefited member businesses. Member enterprises in each group were aware of the price and quality of concerning products outside the group on the basis of market information, as well as mutually demanded products among member enterprises at better or the same terms as those obtained from the market (Hampden-Turner and Trompenaars 1993, pp. 190–191).

However, the existence of large companies in the same industry that belonged to each industrial group had to bring about strong competition among these companies, which determined the difference of competition structure between Japan and Germany. This greatly influenced Japanese enterprises' behavior mode emphasizing an increase in sales volume and market share.

In contrast, corporate groups in postwar Germany were not fully set types that encompassed a broad range of industries. They were essentially corporate groups with a single industry structure. This type of concentration aided in the creation of a system that exhibited economies of scale due to the advantages of specialization and division of labor, and such industry-specific groups were adaptable to postwar oligopolistic competition. The functional aspects based on the corporate division of labor were highlighted. This type of development enhanced the inter-firm relationship systems. These relationships formed an important foundation for the expansion of corporate activities that emphasized market segments in the form of "division of labor complementary to each product." Relationships of "complementary product-based divisions of labor" can also be seen between large corporate groups, which has important implications for the restriction of competition among firms in the same industry.

Under the specific systems such as the two-layer top management organs composed of the supervisory board and the board of directors, the universal banking system, and the deposited stock system, relationships between the bank and industrial enterprise peculiar to Germany have been also built. Compared with Japanese banks, banks in Germany are broadly associated with large corporate groups rather than with a specific corporate group (Maekawa 1997, p. 58). German banks widely developed combination relations with many groups in the competitive market and the companies that belonged to such groups, which was significant in the adjustment of interests between competing enterprises. This was critical for competition avoidance or mitigation.

Such cooperative inter-firm relationships, as well as large corporate group systems, contributed to the establishment of an important foundation for corporate behavioral modes emphasizing nonprice competition based on product quality, technical superiority, and functionality while avoiding strict price competition. These ties were important for the mechanisms and functions of information sharing and coordinating various conflicts and interests between enterprises through discussions rather than as a result of market competition. A system of this kind was deeply related to the competitive structure and the function of industrial concentration that avoided competition, particularly price competition. The system of industrial concentration based on inter-firm relationships and industry–bank relationships supported the cooperative characteristic of German capitalism, as seen in the restraint of competition through complementary division of labor in product fields between companies or large corporate groups.

Regarding the driving forces determining the reconcentration of monopolistic enterprises and the development of the postwar industrial concentration system, in both Japan and Germany, influences of the path dependency strongly appeared. The postwar concentration process was influenced by characteristics of industrial development and structure, anti-monopoly regulation, and the development of production technology. When compared to Germany, the establishment of industrial complexes including wide sectors such as the *zaibatsu* and their economic domination established a distinct path toward monopoly breakdown, reconcentration, and the restructuring of major corporate groups in Japan. In Japan, however, the delay of the development of capital markets, the financial policy of Japanese government promoting indirect financing under such conditions, and necessity of stabilization of shareholders brought about by the dissolution of the *zaibatsu* and the release of shares of *zaibatsu* enterprises made it important and effective to concentrate many enterprises in various industrial sectors into each corporate group. This sort of reconcentration was undertaken to supplement accumulation circumstances by ensuring mutual demand through industrial links. The slow expansion of the heavy and chemical industries before the war, the quick expansion of those industries after the war, and the insufficient development of the home market were all major factors in this shift. Such a system had greatly contributed to corporate expansion and industrial development till the late 1980s. However, it has been considerably modified as a result of the reconstruction of six former industrial groupings in conjunction with structural changes in financial sectors following the 1990s, implying a significant shift in the foundation for firm development.

In contrast to Japan, in Germany, the anti-monopoly policy fundamentally permitting cartel from the perspectives of industrial policy and trade policy before World War II (Yamazaki 2015, Chap. 1; Yanagisawa 1991, p. 74), industrial concentration system based on giant trusts and the broad existence of cartels before the war, and the prohibition of cartel agreement after the war effected on the concentration of enterprises. The limitations of an industrial concentration system dominated by the excessive trust before World War II determined the reconstruction of monopolies that enabled the corporate group to cope with oligopolistic market conditions after the war by building "the product complementary division of labor" within the corporate group. As a result, resilient trust structures were created that were not present in large enterprises before the war. Not only was the reconstruction of the market through the dissolution of monopolies and the removal of cartels emphasized in such a transformation process, but so was the pursuit of economies of scale. America's policy also aided such movements. Thus, in Germany, influences of the path dependency were stronger than in Japan.

The positions that the banks hold in German companies had provided wide opportunities to influence industrial decision making and banks can give a common effect on industries and monitor the broad policy that their competitive companies are pursuing (Smyser 1992, p. 85). Before World War II, personnel connections in Germany were established through interlocking directorates of members of the supervisory board and the board of directors, and they played an important role as a system of cooperative inter-firm relationships. Interlocking directorates were also established in key manufacturing industries such as mining, iron and steel, chemical, electrical, and automobile, as well as other sectors such as other producing industries, distribution, financial, and service industries. Personnel links formed by large banks with multiple firms, on the other hand, are stronger than those formed by industrial enterprises (Yamazaki 2019, 2024).

There are several cases in which personnel connections are established through interlocking directorates with a mandate of an important position such as chairman or vice-chairman of the supervisory board (Yamazaki 2024, Part I; Yamazaki 2019, Part II). For example, in the late 1960s, following the passage of the 1965 Corporations Law, which limited the number of supervisory board mandates that one person could hold, and when a basic system of interlocking directorates was established in postwar Germany, the numbers of companies and mandates in which members of the supervisory board and the board of directors of Deutsche Bank built interlocking directorates on the supervisory boards were 167 and 201, respectively, as illustrated by the increased members. The numbers of interlocking chairman and vice-chairman positions were 84 and 43, respectively. When considering cases, where members of the supervisory board and board of directors of Deutsche Bank had more than two mandates on the supervisory boards of other companies, the numbers of enterprises and mandates, were 25 and 59, respectively (Yamazaki 2024, 6.1.1 and 17.1.1). Representatives from banks as the house bankers not only attend meetings of the supervisory board of companies but also one or plural representatives would be expected to grasp affairs of the enterprise concerned closely between board meetings and provide appropriate or needed services and financing (Smyser 1992, p. 88).

In this way, an individual enterprise, as an independent behavioral agent, does not always make decisions on its own, but rather develops businesses through interactions and interdependence among companies, including competing enterprises. When considering a system of inter-firm relationships from the international perspective, in Germany, the interactive relationships between enterprises differ from those in other countries. In Germany, such a system is an important factor in determining the characteristics of not only corporate behavior but also the social-economic system known as "cooperative capitalism." Such interactive and interdependent relationships are typically formed through various contacts and information exchanges based on personnel connections via interlocking directorates between enterprises. In such a system of inter-firm relationships, various conflicts and interests between companies, including those of a bank and a manufacturing firm, can be coordinated through discussion based on personnel connections in the form of interlocking directorates rather than market competition. Large banks had played a significant role in such inter-firm relationships (Yamazaki 2019).

Of German big banks, Deutsche Bank played prominent roles as a first-class center in examining and deciding policy regarding industries (Eglau 1990, p. 125) and many cases in which this bank decisively influenced the business policy of enterprises that trusted control of chairman of the supervisory board from this bank can be observed (Eglau 1990, p. 178). Unlike Japan in which industrial policies had been taken charge of by the Ministry of International Trade and Industry after World War II, it is even pointed out that such functions had been in charge of by Deutsche Bank (Aizawa

1994, p. 145). As a result, banks in Germany can develop policy at the mesoeconomic or industrial levels. Such policy is a type of non-state-led policy for each industry (Hampden-Turner and Trompenaars 1993, p. 204).

In Japan, in addition to corporate group and industry–bank relationships, an important characteristic of inter-firm relationships can be also seen in the subcontracting system. Since the 1970s, the Japanese subcontracting system, which is a multi-tier hierarchical structure, and the mechanism of business relations based on such a multi-tier system, have contributed to establishing international competitiveness in the process and assembly industries, particularly the automobile industry. It enabled automobile enterprises to realize the synchronization between production processes including part producing companies through the just-in-time production system and played a significant role in flexible adaptation to demand change, which was an important factor of the high international competitive power of Japanese enterprises. The Japanese subcontracting system was based on mutual trust between enterprises and was a system of insurance in which subcontracting companies can receive orders, which contributed to stable corporate expansion for suppliers. In contrast, there is no subcontracting system in Germany based on a multi-tier hierarchical structure, as seen in Japanese process and assembly industries, which became an important factor determining reforms of the mass production system after the 1970s and the pursuit of the module production system after the 1990s as an important countermeasure to overcome the Japanese production system's competitive disadvantage.

15.5 Regional Conditions and Their Influences on Business Management and Corporate Expansion: Different Paths Toward Global Regionalization in Japan and Germany

This section illustrates how the development of Japanese and German firms after World War II, particularly in the 1960s and 1970s, influenced later periods, based on the preceding debates. By highlighting Germany's situation in Europe with that of Japan in Asia and economic relations with the United States during the postwar boom years, this issue explains the root of current-day circumstances in Germany and its corporations as they Europeanize, even amid Americanization and globalization.

Although both Germany and Japan were defeated in World War II, these countries realized rapid economic restoration and development through US assistance and the deployment of US technology and management methods in the postwar period. Consequently, they became major trading countries. However, the process of enterprise development and economic growth greatly differs between Japan and Germany.

Shortly after the war, Japan could not have markets nearby as did Germany in Europe; this is primarily because many Asian countries had been colonies. As a result, Japan's development of productive forces could be sufficient only if it expanded its domestic markets and exports to the United States, imposing a deeper reliance on the United States. Furthermore, massive productive forces in the material industrial sectors, such as the heavy and chemical industries, were confronted with major structural issues, with excess production capacity becoming apparent in the event of economic stagnation (Murakami 2013, p. 58). Under such circumstances, even if Japan attempted to expand by restructuring the system of large corporate groups and deploying American management methods, Japanese companies could establish accumulation structures in the form of heavy reliance on the United States for exports.

Later, in the 1970s and 1980s, Japanese companies bolstered their competitiveness in the processing and assembly industries, particularly the car industry, by obtaining low costs and high quality, as measured by few faults, as a weapon to enhance the Japanese manufacturing system. However, this technique was pushed to result in significantly higher shipments to the United States. Furthermore, because of the reduction and saving of labor forces, rationalization based on ME technology and downsizing strategy had to result in a decline in domestic demand. As a result, international demand particularly increased exports to the United States, had to fill the gap between production and consumption (Murakami 2013, pp. 94–95; 247–248). However, as Japanese industrial sectors that had international competitive power and expanded export were US key industries, it could not establish complementary relationships with US producers and industries in the American market and were compelled to maintain a competitive relationship with the United States. Because of its reliance on exports to the United States, Japan's independent development became somewhat problematic under these circumstances, leaving it vulnerable to yen versus dollar exchange rate changes for a long period. As a result, industries have been hollowed down, placing firms in a precarious position.

Under such conditions, Japanese enterprises have tended to pursue "Asianization" through establishing production, sales, and development bases after the 1990s. The proportion of the number of Japanese companies' foreign subsidiaries in Asia to that of the world reached 67.8% in the fiscal year 2021 (Keizaisangyosho daijin kanbo chosatoukei gurupu kozo・kigyotoukeisitsu 2022, p. 8). Considering the condition in the automobile industry, for example, in Toyota Motor Corporation, the rate of production in foreign countries to that in the world increased from 60.17% in 2011 to 70.58% in 2022. Toyota Motor Corporation's production volume of the automobile in Asia in 2022 (3,239,744) is 2.87 times that in the United States (1,129,988) and even that in China (1,839,772) is about 1.63 times that in the United States. Sales volume in Asia (3,324,735) in the same year is approximately 1.58 times that in the United States (2,108,460) and that in China (1,940,590) reaches 92% of that in the United States (Toyota jidosha kabusikigaisya 2023). Such a shift to Asia is critical for Japanese businesses and economies to break free from reliance on the United States. As a result, since the 1990s, Japanese firms have prioritized regions other than the former core export market in order to advance.

However, even today, a common market structure like the European Union that should enable Japanese companies to develop business more advantageously in both export and production does not exist in Asia. The fact that the Japanese government is compelled to pursue the formation of economic agreements in the Asian region based on free trade agreements (FTA) and economic partnership agreements (EPA) is determined by such circumstances. Indeed, in recent years, while economic agreements with EU and the United States such as the Japan-EU Economic Partnership Agreement and the Trade Agreement between the United States and Japan have been formed, the frameworks of economic cooperation in Asian region such as the Regional Comprehensive Economic Partnership (RCEP) Agreement including China and the Republic of Korea and the Trans-Pacific Partnership (TPP) Agreement as well as the economic agreement with the individual country have been also advanced by the Japanese government. Nonetheless, despite Japan's efforts, Asia has formed no regional economic integration comparable to that of the EU, which unifies market and currency, both of which have a significant impact on the accumulation conditions for Japanese firms.

In addition to such problems of market structure, the growth of China has greatly influenced the presence and behaviors of Japanese enterprises. Between 2000 and 2017, China emerged as an important hub in traditional trade and simple global value chain networks (Li et al 2019, pp. 9, 40; Dollar 2019, p. 1). Li et al (2019) have stressed that China's rise has dramatically affected the whole topology of global value chains from the demand and supply sides (Li et al 2019, pp. 35, 40–41). Thus, China's influence has greatly increased. China surpassed Japan's role and position, becoming "a regional supply hub with an important inflow linkage from the United States and outflow linkages to other Asian economies" and "a global supply hub of value-added export through final products trade" (Li et al 2019, pp. 26, 31). China had important linkages with its Asian neighbors as well as emerging countries such as Russia and Brazil and other hubs such as the United States and Germany. Meanwhile, between 2000 and 2014, "a dramatical change from a smile curve to an inverted slime curve-frown" was observed in Japan's final automobile products export-related value chain. Japan's automobile sector has since strengthened its comparative advantage by further outsourcing upstream and downstream tasks formerly done by Japanese employees to China through global value chains (Li et al. 2019, pp. 25–26). The expansive and rapid growth of China in the global value chain has substantially influenced Japanese industries.

For Japanese automobile firms, the primary factors of competitive advantage have changed. In the period from the 1970s to the end of the 1980s, a production system peculiar to Japan—known as the "Japanese production system" or "Toyota production system"—was foundational for competitiveness. After the 1990s, establishing the global supply chain through the most suitable allocation and distribution of productive forces within the primary region and outsourcing became significant for building and maintaining competitive power, particularly for Asian countries and especially for China. However, in the period after the 2010s, the transition to electric vehicles; reorganization of production networks, including the global supply chain, based on technological developments such as Internet of Things, big data, and artificial intelligence; and continued development of auto driving technology has contributed significantly to developing and reinforcing competitive advantage. Such changes in the business circumstances have greatly influenced the competitiveness of Japanese automobile enterprises.

From Japan's viewpoint, Germany can develop independently. Although German enterprises went through an Americanization of business, they could grow by reframing the structure of productive forces and industrial structures following European market structures and competition. Furthermore, they have been able to develop diverse quality production, relying on skilled workers, market structures, and product characteristics centered on quality and functionality. Furthermore, German corporate management values reflect these market characteristics both within Germany and in Europe's core export regions. The promotion of investments in vocational education for company workers and the employment security and wage guarantee systems based on the codetermination system were also of significance. German firms have grown in line with European market conditions. Instead of US-style mass production based on the principles of thorough standardization or Japanese workers' multi-process skills, they have developed a production system that enables product differentiation in quality and functionality by relying on the specialized skill and experience of their workers. German product quality emphasizes on functionality and durability and the German production system attempts to differentiate on quality, not price. German enterprises have grown on the back of a German strategy that emphasizes quality differentiation as a means of gaining a competitive advantage. As a result, Germany has become internationally competitive in industrial sectors such as investment goods, capital goods, and durable consumer goods, and has established foreign trade patterns that complement products in the European region, aided by differences in industrial structures among other European countries. As a result, Germany has developed corporate and economic independence without having to adhere to the global strategy of the United States.

However, this type of development which focuses on the quality and functionality of products was particularly effective due to European market conditions. As a result, Germany sought to build and strengthen a European reproduction structure (accumulation structures) and advanced with European integration, leading to today's EU, to lay a foundation compatible with that strategy. Although isolated within Europe, this movement toward European integration that enabled development rooted in the well-integrated region of Europe was created at the business management level. The development of German companies during the 1950s and 1960s set the direction toward European integration and laid the foundation for today's EU. German enterprises have pursued regionalization emphasizing Europe as the core market for exports and the core of production networks more strongly since the 1990s while the world faced the advance of globalization. The fact that Germany supported the EU during the European debt crisis in the first half of the 2010s was deeply concerned with German capitalism's European-style accumulation, as well as financial system stabilization issues and Germany's large economic strength.

In this way, one of the prominent characteristics of Germany's economic development after the war can be seen in the "Europeanization" in dual meaning: (1) business management and corporate expansion heavily relying on the European region and (2) pursuit of endeavor to advance European integration including the unification of market and currency. Of these two the former became an important factor determining the movement toward the latter.

After the 2000s, changes could be observed in business management that relied heavily on European production networks and value chains. Intra-European global value chain activities declined compared with inter-regional transactions owing to the increasing prevalence of the Factory Asia phenomenon. However, value chains continued to depend on Europe and remained largely regional. While intra-regional global value chain linkages in West Europe showed a relative decline, these linkages increased in Eastern Europe (Li et al. 2019, pp. 9, 20–21). Although "China has emerged as a new hub through rapid industrial upgrading, represented by its more high-tech intermediate exports and imports," Germany has remained the most important hub in complex global value chain networks representing "the breadth of regional production linkages" (Li et al. 2019, pp. 20, 40–41). According to Li et al. (2019), "Germany is the largest supply hub in the European area, because the majority of value-added imports in final products by almost all European countries is from Germany" (Li et al. 2019, p. 26).

Considering the higher labor compensation in the German car industry and lower labor compensation in upstream and downstream industries, the entire global value chain indicates "an inverted smile curve." Degain et al. (2017) have highlighted that "to some entent, this may reflect the successful transition of the German car industry from traditional mass producer to mass customizer and to individual design based on digital technology and artificial intelligence." They have stressed that "the mass customized and individual design manufacturing stage accounts for a relatively large portion of the total value gain, while the traditional high-end design and sales functions account for only a small portion of total value gain and mostly in foreign countries" (Degain et al. 2017, p. 56). This trend is also evident across Europe, including in the central and eastern regions, with the EU providing a more advantageous framework for international division of labor in this domain.

Thus, although both Japan and Germany are world leaders in manufacturing and trade, Germany has regionalized its industrial production and established complementary relationships with other European countries in this field. Conversely, Japan continues to lack a common Asian market and no complementary relationships with the United States. These differences were caused by the process of corporate expansion during the postwar boom years' economic growth, which was shaped by regional characteristics. These regional differences in markets and cultures explain capitalism and business management in Japan and Germany after the war, as well as the Americanization of business management.

References

Aizawa K (1994) Oshu saikyo no kinyu teikoku (The strongest financial empire in Europe). Nihon keizai shinbunsha, Tokyo

Barsoux J-L, Lawrence P (1991) Countries, cultures and constraints. In: Calori R, Lawrence P (eds) The business of Europe. Managing change. SAGE, London, pp 198–217

Calori R (1994) The diversity of management systems. In: Calori R, Woot P de (eds) A European management model. Beyond diversity, Prentice Hall, New York, Tokyo, pp 11–30

Degain C, Meng B, Wang Z (2017) Recent trends in global trade and global value chains. The World Bank, Global Value Chain Development Report 2017. Measuring and analysing the impact of GVCs on Economic development. The World Bank, Washington DC, pp 37–68
Dollar D (2019) Executive summary. In: World trade organization, global value chain development report 2019. Technological innovation, supply chain trade, and workers in a globalized world. World Trade Organization, Geneva, pp 1–7
Eglau HO (1990) Wie Gott in Frankfurt: Die Deutsche Bank und die deutsche Industrie, 3rd edn. Econ Verlag, Dusseldorf
Hampden-Turner C, Trompenaars A (1993) The seven cultures of capitalism: value systems for creating wealth in the United States, Japan, Germany, France, Britain, Sweden, and the Netherlands. Currency and Doubleday, New York
Keizaisangyosho daijin kanbo chosatoukei gurupu kozu・kigyotoukeisitsu (2022) Dai 52 kai Kaigai jigyo katudo kihon chosa gaiyo (Summary of the 52nd fundamental investigation of overseas business activities). C:/temp/r4_gaiyo_52.pdf. Accessed 3 Nov 2023
Li X, Meng B, Wang Z (2019) Recent patterns of global production and GVC participation. In: World trade organization, global value chain development report 2019. Technological innovation, supply chain trade, and workers in a globalized world. World Trade Organization, Geneva, pp 9–43
Locke RR (1996) The collapse of the American management mystique. Oxford University Press, Oxford
Maekawa K (1997) Nichidoku hikaku kigyoron eno michi (Comparative study of Japanese and German enterprise). Moriyama Shoten, Tokyo
Murakami K (2013) Gendai Nihon saiseisan kozo bunseki (Analysis of modern Japanese reproduction structure). Nihon keizai hyoronsha, Tokyo
Nakatani I (1983) Nihon keizai no "himitsu" wo toku kagi. Kigyo shudan to nihonteki keiei (Key to clarifying the "secret" of the Japanese economy. Corporate groups and Japanese management). In: Ekonomisuto (Economist) 2500:78–85
Smyser WR (1992) The economy of United Germany: colossus at crossroads. St. Martin's Press, New York
Suzuki K (1998) Mein banku to kigyo shudan—Sengo nihon no kigyokan shisutemu— (Main bank and corporate group—Inter-firm system in postwar Japan). Mineruva shobo, Kyoto
Toyota jidosha kabusikigaisya (2023) Kaisya gaiyo Hanbai・seisan・yusyutsu jisseki (Synopnis of company. sales, production, and export results). https://view.officeapps.live.com/op/view.aspx?src=https%3A%2F%2Fglobal.toyota%2Fpages%2Fglobal_toyota%2Fcompany%2Fprofile%2Fproduction-sales-gures%2Fproduction_sales_figures_jp.xls&wdOrigin=BROWSELINK. Accessed 3 Nov 2023
Yamazaki T (2015) Doitsu senzenki keieishi kenkyu (German business history until the end of World War II). Moriyama Shoten, Tokyo
Yamazaki T (2019) Doitsu no kigyokan kankei—Kigyokan jinteki ketugo no kozo to kino (German inter-firm relationships—Structute and functions of personnel connections). Moriyama Shoten, Tokyo
Yamazaki T (2024) Relationships between Industry and Bank in Germany: A historical analysis of personnel connections built through interlocking directorate and bank's advisory council system. Springer Nature, Singapore
Yanagisawa O (1991) Doitsu ni okeru sengo kaikaku to shihonshugi no tenkan (Postwar reform and conversion of capitalism in Germany). In: Tanaka T, Yanagisawa O, Ono J et al (eds) Kindai sekai no henyo (Transformation of the modern world). Ribro Port, Tokyo, pp 65–87

Archival Sources

1. Historisches Archiv Krupp, Essen

WA70/1.

2. thyssenkrupp Corporate Archives, Duisburg

A/1207, A/30778, A/30819, A/31870, A/31927B, A/32196, A/33073, A/34272, WVS/148, NST/82

3. Konzernarchiv der Henkel AG & CO. KGAA, Düsseldorf

153/9, 153/20, 153/42, 251/1, 251/2, 251/9, 251/10, 314/96, 314/133, 451/55, K160.

4. Bayer Archiv, Leverkusen

001-004-001, 001-004-002, 001-004-003, 010-004-005,210-001, 221/6, 329/737.

5. BASF Archiv, Ludwigshafen

C0, C19/13, C19/14, C19/15, BASF Information

6. Hoechst Archiv, Frankfurt am Main

H0028468, H0136339, H0136347, H0136364, Hauptversammlung 1995, Hauptversammlung 12/1998

7. Hüls Archiv, Marl

I-5-8, VII-7, VII-7-1/1, VI-8-3/1, ohne Signatur

8. Siemens Archiv, Berlin

4/Lr302-20, 33/Ld603, 37/Lk975, 49/Lb457, 64/Lt350, 68/Li137, 7882, 8679, 9871, 12799, 16020

T. Yamazaki, *Japanese and German Enterprises*,
https://doi.org/10.1007/978-981-97-4880-8

9. Volkswagen Archiv, Wolfsburg

61/2036, 119/218/1, 119/441/1, 119/447/1, 119/447/2, 119/911, 174/742, 174/1033, 174/1035, 174/1039, 174/1043, 174/1588, 250/347/1, Z174/Nr.2037, Z174/Nr.2366, Volkswagen Informationsdienst

10. Mercedes-Benz Classic Archiv, Stuttgart

Konecke 122, Jahresbericht 1959 des Werkes Stuttgart-Untertürkheim, Jahresbericht 1961 des Werkes Stuttgart-Untertürkheim, Jahresbericht 1962 des Werkes Stuttgart-Untertürkheim, Jahresbericht 1963 des Werkes Stuttgart-Untertürkheim, Jahresbericht 1965 des Werkes Stuttgart-Untertürkheim, Jahresbericht 1966 des Werkes Stuttgart-Untertürkheim, Jahresbericht 1967 des Werkes Stuttgart-Untertürkheim, Jahresbericht 1970 des Werkes Stuttgart-Untertürkheim

11. National Archives, Washington D.C.

RG59, 862A.054, RG59, 862A.14, RG59, 862A.33, RG59, 862A.331, RG469

12. Bundesarchiv Koblenz, Koblenz

B102/37023, B102/37261, B149/5697, B393/17, B393/27

13. Historisches Archiv des Deutschen Technikmuseum, Berlin

GS839, GS2052, GS3501, U0438, Ü-V0438

14. Rheinisch-Westfälisches Wirtschaftsarchiv zu Köln, Köln

Abt 195, F5-5, Abt 195, F7-4, Abt 195, F7-5, Abt 1,517.6

15. Mitsubishi Historical Archives (Mitsubishi Shiryokan), Tokyo

MEL-00156

Index

T. Yamazaki, *Japanese and German Enterprises*,
https://doi.org/10.1007/978-981-97-4880-8

T

MIX
Papier aus verantwortungsvollen Quellen
Paper from responsible sources
FSC® C105338
FSC
www.fsc.org

If you have any concerns about our products,
you can contact us on
ProductSafety@springernature.com

In case Publisher is established outside the EU,
the EU authorized representative is:
Springer Nature Customer Service Center GmbH
Europaplatz 3, 69115 Heidelberg, Germany

Printed by Libri Plureos GmbH
in Hamburg, Germany